INTRODUCTION TO QUALITATIVE METHODS IN PSYCHOLOGY

Dennis Howitt

Loughborough University

Prentice Hall
is an imprint of

Harlow, England • London • New York • Boston • San Francisco • Toronto • Sydney • Singapore • Hong Kong
Tokyo • Seoul • Taipei • New Delhi • Cape Town • Madrid • Mexico City • Amsterdam • Munich • Paris • Milan

Pearson Education Limited
Edinburgh Gate
Harlow
Essex CM20 2JE
England

and Associated Companies throughout the world

Visit us on the World Wide Web at:
www.pearsoned.co.uk

First published 2010

© Pearson Education Limited 2010

ISBN: 978-0-13-206874-1

British Library Cataloguing-in-Publication Data
A catalogue record for this book is available from the British Library

Library of Congress Cataloging-in-Publication Data
Howitt, Dennis.
    Introduction to qualitative methods in psychology / Dennis Howitt.
        p. cm.
    Includes bibliographical references and index.
    ISBN 978-0-13-206874-1 (pbk.)
1. Psychology-Research.   2. Psychology-Research-Methodology.   I. Title.
    BF76.5.H694   2010
    150.72'1-dc22   2009053356

10 9 8 7 6 5 4 3 2
14 13 12 11

Typeset in 10/12.5pt Sabon by 35
Printed by Ashford Colour Press Ltd, Gosport, UK

The publisher's policy is to use paper manufactured from sustainable forests.

BRIEF CONTENTS

Supporting resources

Visit www.pearsoned.co.uk/howitt to find valuable online resources

Companion Website for students

- Multiple choice questions to test your learning
- Flashcards to test your understanding of key terms
- Annotated links to relevant sites on the web
- Essay questions to check your understanding at a deeper level

For instructors

- Downloadable Powerpoint slides of figures and tables from the book

Also: The Companion Website provides the following features:

- Search tool to help locate specific items of content
- E-mail results and profile tools to send results of quizzes to instructors
- Online help and support to assist with website usage and troubleshooting

For more information please contact your local Pearson Education sales representative or visit www.pearsoned.co.uk/howitt

CONTENTS

GUIDED TOUR OF THE BOOK

PART 1

Background to qualitative methods in psychology

Qualitative methods may seem to be relatively new in psychology but they have a deep, complex history both in psychology and, importantly, in other disciplines. While it is possible to claim that the growth spurt of the embryo qualitative psychology can be clearly seen to have its origins in the 1980s, a qualitative tradition can be identified which harks back to the beginnings of modern psychology in the late nineteenth century and no doubt earlier. The scope of qualitative methods in psychology is quite broad and a range of intellectual traditions in psychology and other disciplines have made substantial contribution to the field. Thus there is a richness in the history of qualitative methods in psychology which belies many accounts of the history of psychology and which should be appreciated by any researcher wishing to understand this expanding field. Of course, qualitative psychology is different from quantitative psychology in endless ways and any researcher trained on a purely quantitative diet typical of many psychologists may experience something of a culture shock. This does not mean that they will hate and loathe qualitative psychology – merely that it may appear alien and different, though perhaps whetting the appetite for new challenges. After all, the philosophical foundations of qualitative psychology are very different from those of quantitative psychology, and its methodological foundations are in many ways the reverse of the dominant approaches of mainstream psychology. The procedures for data analysis in qualitative psychology involve an intimacy of working with the data which those used to conventional quantitative analysis involving statistical methods may find disconcerting.

CHAPTER 11

Interpretative phenomenological analysis (IPA)

Overview

- Interpretative phenomenological analysis (IPA) was primarily developed within health psychology in the 1990s as a way of understanding the experience of health issues such as pain. It has also grown in social psychology and clinical psychology.
- The primary concern of IPA is with how individuals experience phenomena and the psychological interpretations of these experiences.
- Like social interactionism and other perspectives, IPA assumes that people attempt to make sense of (give meaning to) their experiences.
- IPA has its roots in phenomenology together with hermeneutics and symbolic interactionism. It emphasises the ideographic as well as the nomothetic. Case studies or small samples characterise the IPA approach.
- Semi-structured interviews tend to be the preferred data for IPA analyses. In these interviews, people are encouraged to freely recall their experiences. The questioning style is designed to encourage richly detailed descriptions of experiences of phenomena. Alternative sources of data may be used if they meet the method's requirements.
- The recording of the interview is usually transcribed using a literal, verbatim approach.
- The account of one participant is usually analysed in depth before the researcher moves on to compare this with accounts from other participants. Themes developed in the initial analysis may be used or added to for the later analyses. Similarities and differences between accounts are important aspects of the analysis.
- Following a period of data familiarisation, the researcher notes impressions and ideas in the left-hand margin of the transcript.

Part introduction

The book is divided into four parts addressing:

1) Background to qualitative methods in psychology;
2) Qualitative data collection;
3) Qualitative data analysis;
4) Planning and writing up qualitative research.

Each part of the book opens with an overview of that part and details of the chapters covered.

Chapter overview

Clearly introduces the chapter to give a feel for the topics covered, enabling students to map their learning.

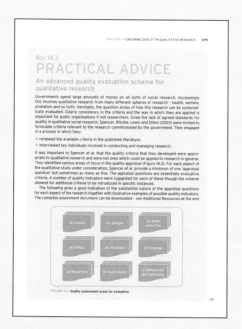

Practical advice

Especially prominent in Part 4, this feature gives handy tips for *doing* qualitative research.

Key concepts

Gives a clear and succinct overview of the major ideas in qualitative research.

Illustrative research study

Identifies and explores key studies which have used qualitative research methods, detailing their findings and impact.

Step-by-step instructions

Guides the new researcher though the stages of the research process in an easy to follow, step-by-step format.

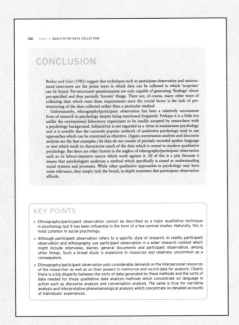

Conclusion

Briefly summarises the lessons from the chapter, helping the student researcher to critically weigh up the pros and cons of a particular type or aspect of qualitative research.

Key points

A handy recap tool, this draws together the key points covered for quick reference.

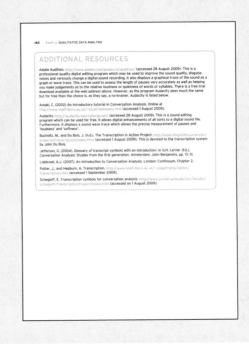

Additional resources

Each chapter ends with a useful list of extra books, journals, websites and more to help students to further their understanding of the theories and practicalities of qualitative research.

Companion Website

The student companion website is a great resource for students to test their understanding, using features such as interactive *flashcards*, *essay questions*, and *multiple choice questions*. Useful *weblinks* are also included to other resources which can help further students' understanding of the topics in each chapter.

CUSTOM PUBLISHING

Custom publishing allows academics to pick and choose content from one or more texts for their course and combine it into a definitive course text.

Here are some examples of the types of custom publishing solutions we offer:

- Combine different chapters from across our publishing imprints into one book
- Combine Lecturer's own material with textbook chapters or publish it in a separate booklet
- Add any third party cases and articles you are keen for your students to read as part of the course
- Apply any combination of the above

The Pearson Education Custom text published for your course is professionally produced and bound - just as you would expect from a normal Pearson Education text. You can even choose your own cover design and add your university logo. Since many of our titles have online resources accompanying them we can even build a Custom website that matches your course text.

Whatever your choice, our dedicated Editorial and Production teams will work with you throughout the process, right until you receive a copy of your Custom text.

To browse material from across our entire portfolio, please visit: www.pearsoned.co.uk

If, once you have had time to review this title, you feel Custom publishing might benefit you and your course, please do get in contact. However minor, or major the change - we can help you out.

You can contact us at: www.pearsoncustom.co.uk or via your local representative at: www.pearsoned.co.uk/replocator

PREFACE

In psychology, the received understanding holds that qualitative methods have emerged in force during the last three decades. Before this time, mainstream psychology was a quantitative monolith smothering any other perspective on what psychology should be. This is not entirely a fiction but it is a creation myth rather than a precise and historically accurate account of the dark days before qualitative psychology. Probably my experience is a little different from that of most psychologists. At the end of my first year as a psychology student I was sent for six months to the factory floor (and eventually the personnel offices) of Morganite Carbon which was then in Battersea, London. The reason? Essentially to experience life as a factory worker and to write a project on my experiences. In other words, *participant observation* or *ethnography* – and the experience of real life. At the end of every couple of terms we were sent to other locations. I spent six months at the prison in Wakefield and another six months at St George's Hospital, London. At Wakefield, I did my first study of sex offenders (possibly the first ever study by a psychologist of sex offenders in the United Kingdom). This was an interest which was to resurface years later with my studies of sexual abuse and paedophiles. At St George's Hospital my colleagues included Fay Fransella, an important figure in the field of George Kelly's *personal construct theory* – an early precursor of social constructionist approaches in qualitative psychology. Indeed, I attended the first conference on personal construct theory while at Brunel University and, I am assured though cannot vouchsafe it, was in the presence of George Kelly himself. Actually we got rather a lot of personal construct theory.

At Brunel, I remember being fascinated by the sessions on psychoanalysis given to us by Professor Elliot Jacques. Not only was Jacques famous at the time as an organisational psychologist bringing psychoanalytic ideas to industry but he was the originator of the concept of the midlife crisis! However, the key influence on any psychology student who studied at Brunel University at that time was Marie Jahoda. Ideas and questions were what counted for Marie Jahoda. She had worked with or knew anyone who was important in the social sciences at large. Sigmund Freud was a friend of her family. She would speak of 'Robert' in lectures – this was Robert Merton, the great theorist of sociology. She had worked with and had been married to Paul Lazarsfeld, the great methodologist of sociology. And she had been involved in some of the most innovatory research in psychology – the Marienthal unemployment study. The 'problem' – meaning the intellectual task – was key to doing research. The ways of collecting data merely followed, they did not lead; analysis was a way of life.

I have never worked in an environment with just a single academic discipline – always there have been sociologists, psychologists and a smattering of others. My first academic job ever was at the Centre for Mass Communications Research at the University of Leicester. Now it is remarkable just how important the field of mass communications research has been in the development of qualitative research methods. For example, the focus group, participant observation, audience studies, narrative/life histories and so forth either began in that field or were substantially advanced by it. More than anything, it was a field where psychologists and sociologists collectively contributed. Of course, the styles of research varied from the deeply quantitative to the equally deeply qualitative. Different problems called for different methods. I also remember some radical figures visiting, such as Aaron Cicourel, a cognitive sociologist influenced by Erving Goffman and Harold Garfinkel. Cicourel was a pioneer in the use of video in his research. During a seminar in which he agonised over the issues of coding and categorisation I remember asking Cicourel why he did not simply publish his videotapes. There was a several seconds delay but eventually the reply came. But it still seems to me an interesting issue – that ethnographic methods are the methods of ordinary people so why bother with the researcher?

Paradoxically, I have always been involved in teaching quantitative methods – I was paid to do so as a postgraduate and from then on. Nevertheless, in academic life you are what you teach for some curious reason. The opposition of qualitative and quantative is not inevitable; many researchers do both. Aaron Cicourel went along a similar route:

> I am NOT opposed to quantification or formalization or modeling, but do not want to pursue quantitative methods that are not commensurate with the research phenomena addressed. (Cicourel interviewed by Andreas Witzel and Günter Mey, 2004, p. 1)

He spent a lot of time as a postgraduate student learning mathematics and quantitative methods:

> . . . if I criticized such methods, I would have to show that my concern about their use was not based on an inability to know and use them, but was due to a genuine interest in finding methods that were congruent or in correspondence with the phenomena we call social interaction and the ethnographic conditions associated with routine language use in informal and formal everyday life settings. (Witzel and Mey, 2004, p. 1)

There is another reason which Cicourel overlooks. Quantitative methods can have a compelling effect on government and general social policy. Being able to speak and write on equal terms with quantitative researchers is important in the type of policy areas upon which my research was based.

By concentrating on the problem, rather than the method, a researcher makes choices which are more to do with getting the best possible answer to the question than getting a particular sort of answer to the question. For that reason, qualitative approaches are just part of my research. However, where the question demands contextualised, detailed data then the method became little more than me, my participants and my recording machine. Some of my favourites among my own research involved just these.

Qualitative methods in psychology are becoming diverse. Nevertheless, there is not quite the spread of different styles of research or *epistemologies* for research that one finds in other disciplines. Ethnographic methods, for example, have not been common in the history of psychology – a situation which persists to date. But discourse analytic approaches, in contrast, have become relatively common. This is not to encourage the adoption of either of these methods (or any other for that matter) unless they help address one's research question. This may not please all qualitative researchers but any *hegemony* in terms of method in psychology to my mind has to be a retrograde step. So this book takes a broad-brush approach to qualitative methods in psychology. First of all, it invites readers to understand better how to gather qualitative data. These are seriously difficult ways of collecting data if properly considered and there is little excuse ever for sloppy and inappropriate data collection methods. They are simply counterproductive. It is all too easy to take the view that an in-depth interview or a focus group is an easy approach to data collection simply because they might appear to involve little other than conversational skills. But one has only to look at some of the transcripts of such data published in journal articles to realise that the researcher has not put on a skilled performance. It needs time, practice, discussion and training to do qualitative data collection well. Secondly, I have covered some very different forms of qualitative data analysis methods in this book. These are not all mutually compatible approaches in every respect. Their roots lie in very different spheres. *Grounded theory* derives from the sociology of the 1960s as does *conversation analysis*. *Discourse analysis* not only has its roots in the ideas of the French philosopher Michel Foucault but also in the sociology of science of the 1970s. *Interpretative phenomenological analysis* is dependent on phenomenology with its roots in philosophy and psychology. *Narrative analysis* has a multitude of roots but primarily in the *narrative psychology* of the 1990s. And *thematic analysis*? Well – it all depends what you mean by thematic analysis as we shall see.

There is an important issue to raise. Perhaps it is best raised by quoting from Kenneth J. Gergen, one of the key, original figures in the move towards qualitative methods in psychology. In the following he describes his early experience as a psychological researcher:

> My early training was in scientific psychology, that is, a psychology based on the promise that through the application of empirical methods, sound measures, and statistical analysis we would begin to approach the truth of mental functioning . . . I learned my lessons well, how to produce from the messy confines of laboratory life the kinds of clear and compelling 'facts' acceptable to the professional journals. A few tricks of the trade: pre-test the experimental manipulations so to ensure that the desired effects are obtained; use multiple measures so to ensure that at least one will demonstrate the effects; if the first statistical test doesn't yield a reliable difference, try others that will; if there are subjects who dramatically contradict the desired effect, even the smallest effect can reach significance; be sure to cite early research to express historical depth; cite recent research to demonstrate 'up-to-date' knowledge; do not cite Freud, Jung or any other 'pre-scientific' psychologist; cite the research of scientists who are supported by the findings as they are likely to be asked for evaluations by the journal. Nor was it simply that mastering the craft of research management allowed me to 'generate facts' in the scientific journals; success also meant research grants, reputation, and higher status jobs. (Gergen, 1999, p. 58)

Quite what Gergen hoped to achieve by this 'confession' is difficult to fathom. As a joking pastiche of mainstream psychology it fails to amuse. In writing this book, I hope to share some of the very positive things that qualitative psychologists can achieve and important ideas which can inform the research of all psychologists irrespective of their point of balance on the qualitative–quantitative dimension. Making research better, then, is an important objective of this book – deriding the work of researchers struggling, as we all do, to understand the world they live in is not on my agenda. Research is about knowing in the best way possible – which is not an issue of the general superiority of one method over others.

This book has a modular structure. It is not designed to be read cover to cover but, instead, it can be used as a resource and read in any order as need demands. To this end, the following pedagogic features should be noted:

- There is a glossary covering both the key terms in qualitative analysis in this book and the field of qualitative research in general.

- Most of the chapters have a common structure wherever possible. So the chapters on data collection methods have a common structure and the data analysis chapters have a common structure.

- Material is carefully organised in sections permitting unwanted sections to be ignored, perhaps to be read some time later.

- Each chapter includes a variety of boxes in which key concepts are discussed, examples of relevant studies described, and special topics introduced.

- Each chapter begins with a summary of the major points in the chapter.

- Each chapter ends with recommended resources for further study including books, journal articles and web pages as appropriate.

Dennis Howitt
April 2010

ACKNOWLEDGEMENTS

Author's acknowledgements

A book like this involved the talents of numerous people whose energies not only turned the manuscript into a book but contributed to its contents in endless ways. So I would like to thank them all and sorry to anyone inadvertently omitted.

This book was not my idea but that of Janey Webb, the psychology editor at Pearson Education. She was a powerhouse at every stage. I have learned a lot about the importance of pedagogics (what a dreadful word for learning aids) from Janey. Hopefully you will find them of use. In particular, the glossary is a novel inclusion in books on qualitative psychology – it would not have happened but for Janey's persuasive powers. She found academics willing to comment positively about the manuscript at every stage and was more than willing to read chapters and ask some of the most incisive questions imaginable. Ouch! A big thank you. Janey was more than ably assisted by Catherine Morrissey who did excellent work on keeping things organised and providing summaries of feedback from academics – welcome even when it arrived at the very moment that it wasn't!

The production guru, Anita Atkinson, is a mixture of Superwoman, Wonderwoman and lots more like that. Things happen exactly when Anita says they will happen and one simply falls into line no question. More than that, no detail is too small to escape her. She can do things during a book's production that are impossible – but she can do the impossible when it is far too late and the car has gone over the cliff! Don't get the wrong idea, these are all really nice people.

Kevin Ancient is the token male but his contribution was a vitally important one. He designed the text of the book so that its complex structure actually works extremely well in practice but looked dreadful in my manuscript. This is really very clever, subtle work. I have worked with Ros Woodward on a number of books and she never fails to amaze me. She worked as copy editor on this book and turned my manuscript into Kevin's design. This book is big and complex for a first edition so Ros's work is even more important. The proof reader was Sue Gard. If she hadn't before, she must now have learned the patience of a saint coping with everything that I wanted to change at the proof stage while at the same time searching for everything that I should have spotted but didn't.

Academic reviewers have contributed greatly to this book. At many points their ideas have been taken on board if not downright stolen. While their criticisms were not always welcome, they were always apposite and positively made. They were responded to by me in the same spirit. My apologies if one or two things have to wait until a later edition but they should rest assured that their points have all sunk in. So my thanks to the following reviewers for everything that they contributed:

Sonja Ellis – Sheffield Hallam University, UK
Anita Gärling – Luleå University of Technology, Sweden
Susan Hansen – Nottingham Trent University, UK
Abigail Locke – University of Huddersfield, UK
Peter Musaeus – Aarhus University, Denmark

Finally, one or two people usually get overlooked because they are involved in the book's companion website. One is John Matthews, the 'boffin' who makes the website move in mysterious ways and work so well. But also I should thank Alex Craven of Loughborough University's Department of Social Sciences. The website benefits from the multiple choice questions and Alex is responsible for these. Ten out of ten.

Publisher's acknowledgements

The publishers would like to express their thanks and appreciation to the reviewers who have provided invaluable advice and support throughout the development of this book.

We are grateful to the following for permission to reproduce copyright material:

Figures

Figure 8.3 from Being rejected and expelled from the workplace: experiences of bullying in the public service sector, *Qualitative Research in Psychology*, 4(1), pp. 1–14 (Strandmark, M. and Hallberg, L. R. -M. 2007), Taylor & Francis, reprinted by permission of the publisher (Taylor & Francis Group, http://www.informaworld.com)

In some instances we have been unable to trace the owners of copyright material, and we would appreciate any information that would enable us to do so.

PART 1

Background to qualitative methods in psychology

Qualitative methods may seem to be relatively new in psychology but they have a deep, complex history both in psychology and, importantly, in other disciplines. While it is possible to claim that the growth spurt of the embryo qualitative psychology can be clearly seen to have its origins in the 1980s, a qualitative tradition can be identified which harks back to the beginnings of modern psychology in the late nineteenth century and no doubt earlier. The scope of qualitative methods in psychology is quite broad and a range of intellectual traditions in psychology and other disciplines have made substantial contribution to the field. Thus there is a richness in the history of qualitative methods in psychology which belies many accounts of the history of psychology and which should be appreciated by any researcher wishing to understand this expanding field. Of course, qualitative psychology is different from quantitative psychology in endless ways and any researcher trained on a purely quantitative diet typical of many psychologists may experience something of a culture shock. This does not mean that they will hate and loathe qualitative psychology – merely that it may appear alien and different, though perhaps whetting the appetite for new challenges. After all, the philosophical foundations of qualitative psychology are very different from those of quantitative psychology, and its methodological foundations are in many ways the reverse of the dominant approaches of mainstream psychology. The procedures for data analysis in qualitative psychology involve an intimacy of working with the data which those used to conventional quantitative analysis involving statistical methods may find disconcerting.

The two chapters which constitute Part 1 of this book involve some embedded objectives:

- To provide a broad understanding of how qualitative psychology differs from quantitative psychology.
- To provide a review of the history of psychology which explains just why qualitative methods were so slow in emerging in psychology compared to related disciplines.
- To provide a picture of the development of qualitative psychology from within the discipline, under the influence of related disciplines such as sociology and, as a consequence, of some of the disillusionment with the methods of mainstream psychology.

There is no comprehensive history of qualitative research in psychology. The references to the history of qualitative psychology tend to be brief and, if not mistaken, suggest that mainstream psychology essentially smothered qualitative psychology in the antagonist philosophy of *positivism*. Positivism is essentially a description of the assumptions and characteristics of sciences such as physics and chemistry. For example, they are characterised by the search for universal laws, quantification and empirical investigation. It is claimed by qualitative researchers and others that psychology adopted this approach to its detriment. There are doubts that qualitative psychology was anathema to positivism though claims which are made frequently tend eventually to be believed. What seems clear is that the majority of psychologists in the early history of modern psychology adopted working practices which were not conducive to the ideas of qualitative psychology. Where did these research practices come from? They seem to have originated in attempts by psychologists to emulate the working practices of the natural sciences. Amongst these, especially physics had had spectacular successes in the nineteenth century. Practices such as experimentation, measurement, *reductionist* thinking and so forth are all fundamental influences of the natural sciences on early psychological researchers. The problem was not just solely for psychology and one should remember qualitative methods were also fairly poorly developed in related disciplines such as sociology in the nineteenth and early twentieth centuries. It was not until the 1950s and 1960s that qualitative methods began to develop as an effective challenge to quantitative methods and *grand theory* in sociology. Thus it is not absolutely correct to suggest that distinctive features of the discipline of psychology were responsible for the late emergence of qualitative psychology. For some reason, though, qualitative psychology emerged two or three decades later than did the qualitative tradition in sociology, though both disciplines were, of course, subject to many of the same influences.

The idea of qualitative psychology eventually defeating the dragon of positivism is a heroic view on the history of qualitative psychology but essentially a false one. We shall see that positivism did dominate the early period of modern psychology but not to the exclusion of quite different approaches. Positivism and qualitative psychology are not entirely incompatible – if one understands quite what positivism assumes and something about what qualitative methods involve. Pinning the blame for the late emergence of qualitative psychology on positivism amounts to a 'creation myth' rather than an explanation. Positivism was not seen as applying to every academic discipline or aspects thereof. The ideas of positivism really only apply to the physical sciences though there is plenty of evidence that psychologists thought that it applied to psychology itself. This is, then, not attributable to positivism but to practitioners' erroneous ideas about positivism. It would be something of a shame if qualitative researchers – who arguably have and need a relatively subtle understanding of the philosophical under-pinnings of their chosen approach – propagate erroneous versions of the history of psychology themselves. It is probable that the 'received' vision of the nature of psychological research was responsible for the relative neglect of qualitative methods in psychology. Furthermore, the success of the quantitative version of psychology should not be overlooked. To be sure, qualitative researchers have numerous cogent criticisms of main-stream psychology. But these do not take away the influential position, if not power, achieved by psychology during the twentieth century and still today compared with many other disciplines. Thus psychology is a profession in the fullest meaning of the word whereas this is nowhere near so clear for related disciplines such as sociology and social anthropology. This is a plea for clarity about the history of psychology as well as one for understanding of the influence of other social scientific disciplines on the development of qualitative psychology. Quantitative research provided an effective and rewarding model for psychologists during the twentieth century which was not emulated in the same way or to anywhere near the same degree of success in other disciplines.

Finally, we read history with hindsight and from a current perspective. It is impossible – albeit desirable – to understand history as it was experienced. One can't, and to attempt to do so is a fruitless endeavour. But simple things might help provide a more acceptable rounded understanding of the development of qualitative methods. The numbers of psychology students graduating today are massive compared with the early days of the discipline. This means that part of the reason for the late development of qualitative psychology may be due to the limited numbers of personnel. Other fields of psychology, besides qualitative methods, began to flourish in the 1980s and 1990s – these include decidedly non-qualitative sub-fields of psychology such as forensic, health and counselling psychology. Forensic psychology had lain largely dormant from the early 1900s only to begin to prosper in the 1980s – just when qualitative psychology emerged. The point is, of course, that as psychology approached a critical mass it achieved more potential to embrace a wider variety of interests. Indeed, some might say that the critical mass encouraged these changes. For much of its history, as embraced in the first two chapters of this book, psychology as a discipline would only have been able to muster in total the numbers who devoted themselves to these recent specialised interests in psychology.

Chapter 1 concentrates on two things:

- Describing the essential characteristics of qualitative methods in psychology.
- Discussing the origins of quantification in psychology, including statistical thinking.

The chapter demonstrates something of the subtlety of the philosophical underpinnings of the quantitative-qualitative debate.

Chapter 2 looks at the varied contributions that psychologists have made throughout the history of psychology which are essentially qualitative in nature and tries to explain the roots of these approaches in psychology and related disciplines. The following seem clear:

- Qualitative approaches have been part of psychology throughout its modern history.
- Many of the early examples of qualitative research in psychology have become 'classics' but it is hard to find a clear legacy of them in the history of modern psychology.
- Most of the early examples of qualitative research in psychology involve distinctly qualitative data collection methods although distinct and frequently used methods of qualitative data analysis did not really emerge until the 1950s and 1960s in related disciplines and, probably, not until the 1980s in psychology.
- Qualitative psychology has developed a basis in the institutions of psychology (learned societies, conferences, specialised journals, etc.) which largely eluded it in its early history.

CHAPTER 1

What is qualitative research in psychology and was it really hidden?

Overview

- Qualitative research in psychology is rapidly emerging as an important focus for psychological research and theory. Although there is a long history of qualitative methods in psychology, it is only since the 1980s that qualitative methods have made significant inroads. Among the distinguishing features of qualitative research are its preference for data rich in description, the belief that reality is constructed socially, and that research is about interpretation and not about hypothesis testing, for example.

- Psychology has historically constructed itself as being a science but, then, largely identified the characteristics of science in terms of numbers and quantification which are not essential features of science.

- Positivism has frequently been blamed for the distorted nature of psychology's conception of science. This, however, tends to overlook that both Comte's positivism and logical positivism were more conducive to qualitative methods than mainstream practitioners of psychology ever permitted.

- The dominant psychologies since the 'birth' of psychology in the 1870s have been introspectionism, behaviourism and cognitivism.

- The 'quantitative imperative' in psychology has ancient roots in psychology and first emerges in the work of Pythagoras. The imperative involves the belief that science is about quantification. Early psychology, with its eyes cast firmly in the direction of physics as the best model to follow, was imbued with the spirit of quantification from the start.
- Statistical methods, although part of the ethos of quantification, were largely fairly late introductions into psychology.
- Quantification in psychology, including statistical methods, provided part of a highly successful 'shop front' for psychology which served it particularly well in the market for research monies that developed in the United States in the second half of the twentieth century.

What is qualitative research?

According to Smith (2008), 'We are witnessing an explosion of interest in qualitative psychology. This is a significant shift in a discipline which has hitherto emphasized the importance of quantitative psychology' (p. 1). The history of qualitative research in psychology has been somewhat enigmatic but there is a history nonetheless. It would be impossible to ignore the new focus on qualitative psychology in psychology though it is doubtful whether this is indicative of a demise of mainstream psychology, many parts of which are untouched by the new qualitative methods. It seems certain that psychologists in the future will be much better versed in qualitative as well as quantitative methods. Psychological research continues to expand exponentially and the sophistication of researchers also increases as new demands are made on the discipline. Qualitative methods are decidedly part of the future of psychology and they are more likely to be better integrated into the mainstream of psychology than at any time previously. Inevitably, then, qualitative psychology will be a feature of every psychologist's training.

It is surprisingly difficult to define what qualitative psychology is. For one thing, it has many different constituent parts. Probably many students see in qualitative methods freedom from the tyranny of numbers and statistics which mars their training in psychology. To equate qualitative with the absence of numerical methods has the advantage of mapping closely onto the experiences of many students of psychology. But it is not quite so simple. It is not the case that psychology breaks down into research in which numbers and statistics are used and research where they are not. There are many research reports which lack numbers and statistics yet are nevertheless decidedly quantitative overall rather than qualitative in their tone. Similarly, you will find numbers and statistics in research reports which are decidedly qualitative in their approach but for which some quantitative information is helpful. So the idea of qualitative research being entirely in a statistics-free zone fails to effectively distinguish qualitative from quantitative research.

It is impossible to suggest one characteristic which invariably, unassailably and essentially distinguishes qualitative from quantitative methods. Consequently, it is preferable to identify the range of features which typify qualitative research methods though by no means are all of them characteristic of all types of qualitative research methods. The following are the five features which Denzin and Lincoln (2000) list as major defining characteristics of qualitative research:

- *Concern with the richness of description*   Qualitative researchers value data which is rich in its descriptive attributes. So they tend to favour data collection methods which obtain detailed, descriptive data such as that produced by using in-depth interviewing methods, focus groups and the taking of detailed field notes. In contrast, perhaps a little stereotypically, quantitative researchers obtain much more restricted and structured information from their research participants. This is inevitably the case when simple rating scales or multiple choice questionnaire methods are used.

- *Capturing the individual's perspective*   Qualitative methods emphasise the perspective of the individual and their individuality. The use of rich data-gathering methods such as the in-depth interview and focus groups encourage this emphasis on the individual's perspective. Quantitative researchers, to the extent that they deal with individuals, will tend to focus on comparisons of people on some sort of abstract dimension such as a personality dimension.

- *The rejection of positivism and the use of post-modern perspectives*   Qualitative researchers tend to reject *positivist* approaches (i.e. those based on a conventional view of what science is – or *scientism*) though qualitative and quantitative researchers both rely on gathering empirical evidence which is an important aspect of positivism. Quantitative researchers tend to retain the view that reality can be known despite the problems involved in knowing it. For example, the quantitative researcher mostly uses language data as if such data directly represent reality (i.e. the data refer to some sort of reality) whereas most modern qualitative researchers take the view that language may be a window onto reality but cannot represent reality. The post-positivist view argues that, irrespective of whether or not there is truly a real world, a researcher's knowledge of that reality can only be approximate and that there are multiple versions of reality. In qualitative research, relatively few researchers believe that the purpose of research is the creation of generalisable knowledge. This is a major objective of quantitative research, of course, and quantitative researchers are inclined to make generalisations on the basis of limited data – sometimes as if universally applicable principles have been identified. Positivism is discussed in detail in Box 1.1 and pages 15–18 of this chapter.

- *Adherence to the postmodern sensibility*   The *postmodern* sensibility, for example, reveals itself in the way that qualitative researchers are much more likely to use methods which get them close to the real-life experiences of people (in-depth interviews, for example) than quantitative researchers who are often content with a degree of artificiality such as that arising from the use of laboratory studies. Verisimilitude seems much more important to qualitative researchers as a whole and less so to many quantitative researchers in psychology. Qualitative researchers are often portrayed as having a caring ethic in their research and they may undertake 'political' action conjointly with their participants as well as engaging in extensive dialogue with them. The sense of personal responsibility in their interactions with their research participants is often promoted as a feature of qualitative research. Some of these features are particularly evident in feminist (action) research where the

Box 1.1
KEY CONCEPT
Auguste Comte's positivism

Perhaps more important than the notion of science in critiques of mainstream psychology are the numerous references to 'positivism'. Indeed, the terms positivism and positivist take on the aspect of pejorative terms when used by researchers. Better to use a four-letter word than either of these. Given that positivism is not easily defined and that it is used as an 'emotive term' (Silverman, 1997, p. 12), its popularity as an abusive epithet may reveal a lack of understanding rather than an insightful analysis. Nevertheless, the term positivism refers to a major epistemological position in psychology and other related disciplines. Epistemology means the study of knowledge and is concerned with (a) how we can go about knowing things and (b) the validation of knowledge (the value of what we know). Positivism is a philosophy of science which had its historical beginnings in the Enlightenment. This is the important historical period which dominated the eighteenth century. The idea of positivism was systematised in the work of Auguste Comte (1798–1857) in France – he is also credited with coining the term *sociologie* or sociology (it was previously social physics!). In his writings, Comte proposed a social progression which he referred to as the *law of three phases* to describe the process of social evolution.

The phases are the theological, the metaphysical and the scientific (Figure 1.1). Importantly, the scientific phase was also named by Comte the positive phase – hence the close link to this day between the terms science and positivism. The theological phase is the earliest and in which, essentially, knowledge about society was through reference to God and religion. Religion is a major factor in the continuity of people's beliefs so that people's beliefs in the theological phase are the ones that their ancestors previously held. The metaphysical phase is also known as the stage of investigation as it involved reasoning and the asking of questions rather than the reference to established theological given-knowledge. This phase is

FIGURE 1.1 **Comte's stages of social evolution**

based on the idea that there are human rights beyond ones which could be countermanded by any human. The scientific phase involved ways of bringing change to society which are not based on theological arguments or human rights. Science was capable of answering the questions which society needed the answer to. Historically, it is easy to see theism (belief in God as a source of knowledge in this context) as characterising Western societies such as France for most of their existence and the metaphysical stage as reflecting the period of the Enlightenment. Since then, society has been in the scientific period.

In Auguste Comte's writings, observable and observed facts had an important role in the accumulation of valid knowledge. So it is easy to see how 'positivistic' describes the mainstream of psychological research. However, this is a position shared by qualitative researchers for the most part. On the other hand, Comte did not believe that quantification, if by quantification we mean mathematical analysis, was a realistic possibility beyond the physical sciences. We should be 'abstaining from introducing considerations of quantities, and mathematical laws, which is beyond our power to apply' (Comte, 1975, p. 112). So there is nothing in Comte's positivism which is alien to qualitative research. Of course, that is somewhat different from what some commentators have written.

objectives of the researcher, for example, is not merely to identify women's experiences but to change the way things are done on the basis of this research. For instance, in feminist research on pornography (e.g. Itzin, 1993) researchers and activists have often been indistinguishable (i.e. they are one and the same person). Other good examples of this in feminist research are child abuse, rape, domestic violence and so forth.

- *Examination of the constraints of everyday life* Some argue that quantitative researchers overlook characteristics of the everyday social world which may have an important bearing on the experiences of their research participants. Qualitative researchers tend to have their feet more firmly planted in this social world, it is argued. So, for instance, in qualitative research reports much greater detail is found about the lives of individual research participants than would be characteristic of quantitative research reports.

Based even on these criteria, it should be readily seen why it is easier to come to an overall judgement that a particular study is qualitative or quantitative than to come up with a simple acid test to say which is which. So we should not be surprised to find that other authorities list different but overlapping characteristics which they believe capture the broad flavour of the difference between qualitative and quantitative research. Consequently, it is intriguing to note that Denzin and Lincoln's (2000) list given above of the characteristics of qualitative research has very little in common with those of Bryman (1988). Nevertheless, most researchers would feel that the following list from Bryman also does a lot to capture this essential difference between qualitative and quantitative research:

- Quantitative data is regarded as hard and reliable whereas qualitative data is regarded as rich and deep. Traditionally, mainstream psychologists often spoke of hard data as opposed to the more subjective soft data.

- Research strategies in quantitative research tend to be highly structured whereas those of qualitative research are relatively unstructured.

FIGURE 1.2 **The major characteristics of qualitative research**

- The social relationship between the researcher and participant is distant in quantitative research but close in qualitative research.
- Quantitative researchers tend to see themselves as outsiders whereas qualitative researchers tend to see themselves as insiders. That is, there is relatively little 'distance' between researcher and participant in qualitative research.
- Quantitative research tends to be about the confirmation of theoretical notions and concepts (as in hypothesis testing) whereas qualitative research is about emerging theory and concepts.
- Research findings in quantitative research tend to be *nomothetic* whereas they tend to be *idiographic* in qualitative research. Nomothetic refers to studying groups or classes of individuals, which leads to generalised explanations, whereas idiographic refers to the study of an individual as an individual.
- In quantitative research, social reality is seen as static and external to the individual whereas in qualitative research social reality is constructed by the individual.

Some approaches to qualitative psychology, however, lack some of these 'defining' characteristics. That is, researchers sometimes mix-and-match the different features of qualitative and quantitative research. Figure 1.2 summarises the major characteristics of qualitative research.

Science as normal practice in qualitative and quantitative research

Mainstream psychology usually defines itself as being scientific. The word science has its roots in the Latin *scire* which means 'to know'. However, science has come to mean a particular way of knowing – what we call the scientific approach. Psychology textbooks are replete with claims about psychology as a science. The professional bodies controlling psychology seem to have no qualms about identifying psychology as a science. For example, the British

Psychological Society, on its website, announces that 'Psychology is the scientific study of people, the mind and behaviour. It is both a thriving academic discipline and a vital professional practice' (http://www.bps.org.uk/, retrieved 25 August 2009). Similarly the American Psychological Association claims, 'The objects of the American Psychological Association shall be to advance psychology as a science and profession and as a means of promoting health, education, and human welfare . . .' (http://www.apa.org/about/, retrieved 15 July 2008). Precisely what this means, in practice, is far harder to pin down. Just how do psychologists construe science? Come what may, precisely what psychologists take to be science is not clarified anywhere on these websites. One accusation regularly made against psychology is that in actuality it employs a somewhat idiosyncratic (if not peculiar) 'received view' of what science is.

This received view of science can more or less be effectively summarised as follows (Woolgar, 1996, p. 13):

- Objects in the natural world are objective and real, and they enjoy an existence independent of human beings. Human agency is basically incidental to the objective character of the world 'out there'.
- It follows from this that scientific knowledge is determined by the actual character of the physical world.
- Science comprises a unitary set of methods and procedures, concerning which there is, by and large, a consensus.
- Science is an activity that is individualistic and mentalistic. The latter is sometimes expressed as 'cognitive'.

Woolgar argues that none of the above has survived critical examination by researchers studying the scientific process. That is, psychology's conception of science is flawed – a point which has been echoed repeatedly by qualitative researchers. Each has been overturned and appear in reverse form as principles in qualitative psychology. The alternative argument is that science is *socially constructed* by human beings:

- who can never directly observe the 'real' world;
- who impose a view of the nature of the world through science;
- who show relatively little consensus as to the appropriate methods and procedures; and
- who act collectively and socially as part of the enterprise of science.

Qualitative researchers commonly refer to the constructivist nature of science as if it is a justification for the qualitative approach to psychological research. Maybe so, but it is questionable whether quantitative researchers, in general, would disagree with them. Hammersley (1996) paints a picture of the typical researcher as being involved to a degree in both qualitative and quantitative research. They make a rational choice between them in the light of the research task in hand. There is a lot of research which refuses to be easily classified as either qualitative or quantitative. According to Hammersley:

> It is certainly not the case that there are just two kinds of researcher, one who uses only numbers and another who uses only words. It *is* true that there are research reports that provide only numerical data and others that provide only verbal data, but there is a large proportion of studies that use both. (Hammersley, 1996, p. 161)

Possibly a picture of multitasking qualitative and quantitative researchers is not so true of psychology as other disciplines.

Nevertheless, the image of researchers able to flit between qualitative and quantitative research methods is a reassuring one. However, one should be careful about the implication of the claim. It is quite common that researchers collect both qualitative and quantitative data within the same study. For example, they might use both questionnaires and in-depth interviews in a study. In other words, the mixture is in terms of data collection methods. It is probably not so true that researchers commonly flit between quantitative and qualitative data analysis methods of the sort dealt with later in this book. Qualitative methods in psychology include a substantial range of different research activities. This range includes focus groups, in-depth interviewing, discourse analysis, conversation analysis, narrative psychology, grounded theory, phenomenology, interpretative phenomenological analysis, participant observation, ethnographic studies, narrative analysis and so forth. Importantly, this list includes both qualitative data collection methods (e.g. focus groups) and qualitative data analysis methods (e.g. grounded theory). It is important to distinguish between the two since qualitative data collection methods do not necessarily mean a qualitative data analysis method will be used. This is a really important matter since what distinguishes current qualitative research from that which occurred in psychology's historic past is its interest in qualitative analysis procedures. Qualitative data collection methods such as in-depth interviewing have a long history in psychology; in contrast, qualitative data analysis methods are a comparatively recent feature (see Figure 1.3).

According to Hammersley (1996), there is a view among qualitative researchers that qualitative and quantitative research can be regarded as two separate and distinct paradigms for research. The idea of scientific paradigms originated in Thomas Kuhn's (1922–1996) book *The Structure of Scientific Revolutions* (1962). Kuhn's argument was that science does not progress gradually through a steady accumulation of knowledge. Instead, the process involves revolutionary shifts in the way science looks at its subject matter. A paradigm shift describes

Qualitative data collection (e.g. participant observation) began early in psychology

Qualitative data analysis methods (e.g. grounded theory) began in sociology and related disciplines from the 1960s onwards

Qualitative data analysis methods increasingly common in psychology from the 1980s onwards (e.g. discourse analysis)

FIGURE 1.3 The relation between the origins of qualitative data collection methods and qualitative data analysis methods when one view becomes untenable and is replaced by something radically different. A paradigm is a sort of worldview – a comprehensive way of looking at things which is more extensive than, say, a theory is. So a paradigm shift is a fundamental change in the ways in which scientists view the world. As scientists become aware of anomalies thrown up by the current paradigm then this eventually leads to a crisis in the discipline which encourages new ideas to be tried. Perhaps the move from behaviourism to cognitivism in psychology can be regarded as an example of a paradigm shift. Kuhn's book was a milestone and particularly notable for promoting the idea that science is socially constructed. Again this is an important view of science for qualitative researchers. However, be very careful as Kuhn does not write about the social sciences in the book.

It seems unlikely that we are on the cusp of a paradigm shift in psychology in which a failing quantitative paradigm is being replaced by a newer qualitative one. For one thing, mainstream psychology is a demonstrably successful enterprise in all sorts of walks of life and in a whole variety of research areas. Psychology has never at any point in its modern history been monolithically quantitative in nature – alternative voices have regularly been heard both criticising and offering alternatives to quantification. While qualitative research was never dominant in the history of psychology, nevertheless qualitative and quantitative research have coexisted and this can be illustrated in various significant research studies throughout psychology's history. Whether this coexistence has always been one of happy bedfellows is quite a different question.

The beginnings of modern psychology: introspectionism

It is a matter of choice whether one chooses 1876 or 1879 as the symbolic origin of modern psychology. If one opts for 1876 then this is the date when William James (1842–1910) set up a small laboratory at Harvard University for *teaching* physiological psychology. Opt for 1879 then this is the date when the first psychology laboratory for *research* purposes was established by Wilhelm Wundt (1832–1920) in Leipzig, Germany. Of course, one can find much psychology written before this time but either 1876 or 1879 can be regarded as a particularly iconic moment in the history of psychology. The history of modern psychology pans out fairly smoothly from that time on and, more importantly, either date entwines the origins of psychology as lying in the psychology laboratory. Jones and Elcock (2001) describe this as an origin myth (i.e. creation myth) which involves a self-serving element whereby the beginnings of modern psychology are identified as being in the psychology laboratory. For much of the twentieth century the laboratory experiment was the mainstay of psychology and one of its most characteristic features. This probably gives the impression that psychology and statistical quantification went hand-in-hand from that time onwards. Not quite so.

To put this in quite another way, what sort of psychology would have been taught at the time of the founding of these two laboratories? According to Adams (2000) and others, introspectionism was a major force in German and then American psychology around the time when modern psychology 'was born'. Introspectionism is the doctrine that valid psychological knowledge should be best on the researcher 'looking inward' at their own conscious sensations, perceptions, thoughts and so forth. The purpose of introspection was the identification of the elements of the mind – much as chemists produced tables of the elements of the physical world. The interrelationships between the different elements were also an aspect of the study. They had few philosophical concerns and were essentially empiricists cataloguing their observations. The method of introspection was to turn thinking 'inwards' in order to scrutinise the researcher's own experiences. In other words, introspection is internal self-observation. As a research methodology, introspection is a distinctly first-person approach and very different from the third-person study which characterises the vast outpourings of psychological research over the last 150 years or so. It is interesting then that not only has Wilhelm Wundt been lofted on high as the founding father of psychology because he set up the first psychology research laboratory but he has also been dubbed the founder of introspectionism. In other words, the first scientific psychology was introspectionism which held sway between 1860 and 1927, by which time behaviourism was beginning to dominate the discipline. However, it is wrong to characterise Wundt as an introspectionist if this term is intended to imply an exclusive commitment to introspectionist methods.

According to Baars (1986), the typical account of Wundt in modern psychology is a caricature of the man himself originally misformulated by introspectionism's leading American advocate Edward Titchener (1867–1927), who had been a student of Wundt's. The term structuralism was used in place of introspectionism by Titchener since introspectionists studied the structure of human thought. The truth is that Wundt did see a place for the systematic self-observation of introspectionism but felt that it was useless for more complex mental processes such as the higher mental functions and emotions. Equally he did not feel that social and cultural psychology could be advanced using the experimental methods of the introspectionists. Wundt, nevertheless, did produce a popular account of self-observation in 1912/1973. This provides a good illustration of how the introspectionist would go about research. Basically the research is carried out on oneself and, in the following, one is being directed to listen to a series of beats of a metronome:

> Now let us proceed in the opposite direction by making the metronome beats follow each other after intervals of ½ to ¼ of a second, and we notice that the feelings of strain and relaxation disappear. In their place appears excitement that increases with the rapidity of the impressions, and along with this we have generally a more or less lively feeling of displeasure . . . (Wundt, 1912/1973, p. 51)

Titchener and another of Wundt's students, Oswald Külpe (1862–1915), were responsible for the method of trained observation which characterised introspectionism. The behaviourist psychology which displaced introspectionism was fiercely critical of the product of these trained observations.

Control and replicability were part of the intellectual armoury of introspectionism. It should be added that among the general principles of introspection, according to Titchener (1898), was one of impartiality, which meant that the researcher should not approach the investigation with preconceived ideas or expectations of what they are likely to find. Another principle was that of attentiveness, which meant that the researcher should not speculate about the research activity and why the research is being done during the introspection phase. The study is to be taken seriously in its own right. These principles resonate with some of the principles of modern qualitative research – for example, bracketing (or epoché) in interpretative phenomenological analysis (Chapter 11) calls for the analyst to abandon outside influences. However, this concept came into interpretative phenomenological analysis from phenomenology not directly from introspectionism. After Titchener's death, few psychologists practised internal observation of the sort employed by introspectionism. Instead, the observations turned to third parties such as rats.

It is important also to distinguish between introspectionism and phenomenology which has had an important influence on qualitative psychology through interpretative phenomenological analysis. Phenomenology is not a subfield of introspectionism but a reaction against introspectionism. The important name in phenomenology was the Austrian-born philosopher Edmund Husserl (1859–1938). In the following, Husserl's name and phenomenology are used interchangeably but the message is clear – introspectionism and phenomenology are distinct and incompatible intellectual traditions:

> Husserl's tendency is in a different direction. If anything, his philosophy is 'extrospective,' moving toward phenomena as objects, in the broadest sense, of perceptual acts. The 'glance' – to use Husserl's language – of the phenomenologist is directed toward what is represented in experience, not toward a repository of mixed sensations within the psyche. The only way to account for the persistence of the accusation of introspectionism in connection with phenomenology is that the term itself has been abused, turned first into an epithet and then into an anachronism. (Natanson, 1973, p. 43)

Husserl's phenomenology went on to have a major influence on philosophy in continental Europe. However, the real battle against introspectionism was won by behaviourism which dominated the psychology of the United States and much of the rest of the world for the greater part of the twentieth century. The behaviourist's fight was led by ideas drawn from logical positivism. So behaviourism replaced introspectionism as the dominant form of psychology early in the twentieth century.

The logical positivists, behaviourism and psychology

The word positivism has its origins in the work of Auguste Comte (Box 1.1). Positivism is another of those concepts which is used somewhat imprecisely but also can be used as an epithet with pejorative connotations to describe mainstream, non-qualitative, psychology. Positivism became the dominant view in the philosophy of science during the first part of the twentieth century – especially *logical positivism* which had a profound impact on behaviourism in terms of what science was seen as being. The defining features of logical positivism were its dependency on empiricism together with the use of logical deductions from mathematics and other concepts. The logical positivist movement began to emerge in Vienna prior to the First World War though only became widely established in the rest of Europe and America in the 1920s and 1930s. Migration of important members of the movement was largely responsible for its spread and leading figures in logical positivism moved to the United States. Nevertheless, it was not until 1931 that the American philosopher A.E. Blumberg (1906–1997) first used the term logical positivism to describe the philosophy of the Vienna School. The Austrian philosopher Herbert Feigl (1902–1988) and the German philosopher Rudolf Carnap (1891–1970), important members of the school, moved to the United States and were highly influential on a key player in the methodology of behaviourist psychology, S.S. Stevens (1906–1973). One might be forgiven for not knowing who Feigl or Carnap were; however, Stevens's legacy impacts to this day on every student who has struggled with the concepts of nominal, ordinal, interval and ratio levels of measurement in statistics classes. He was also primarily responsible for the idea of operational definitions entering psychology in the mid-1930s – which he got from the logical positivists although it was the physicist Percy Bridgeman's (1882–1961) idea. Operationism is the idea that concepts in science (including psychology) are defined by the processes used to measure them.

Logical positivism was a philosophy of science and also selectively defined what science was for *behaviourism*'s adherents. Behaviourism developed in the United States under the influence of the psychologist John Watson (1878–1958) though behaviourism in psychology took a number of directions. Watson's behaviourism saw psychology as (a) part of natural science and (b) an objective experimental approach to the prediction and control of behaviour – following Comte's view that the purpose of science lay in prediction. The behaviourist school of psychology embodied key positivist principles in a search for the laws of human behaviour. Sometimes these laws were formulated in mathematical terms, as in the work of Clark Hull (1884–1952).

Logical positivism argued that, scientifically, knowledge came from one's direct observations based on experience and from the application of tight logical reasoning (i.e. logical tautologies – the operational definition is a good example of a logical tautology since it has to be true no matter what). Among the characteristics of science according to the positivist view and hence behaviourism were the following:

- Science is a cumulative process.
- Sciences are reducible ultimately to a single science of the real world.
- Science is independent of the characteristics of the investigator.

Most qualitative researchers would reject most of this.

Watson saw that replacing introspectionism by his vision of a behaviourist psychology brought with it the possibility of making psychology like other sciences:

> This suggested elimination of states of consciousness as proper objects of investigation in themselves will remove the barrier from psychology which exists between it and the other sciences. The findings of psychology become the functional correlates of structure and lend themselves to explanation in physico-chemical terms. (Watson, 1913, p. 175)

In other words, psychology would be reducible to physiology in keeping with the reductionist principle in logical positivism. For Watson, psychology was a natural science which would eventually be reducible to a science like physics and chemistry. The influence and dominance of behaviourism on psychology was most apparent between the 1920s and 1960s after which it was in decline and cognitive psychology was in its ascendency. Important behaviourist psychologists included Edward Thorndike (1874–1949), Edward Tolman (1886–1959) and, for the very early part of his career, Albert Bandura (1925–) who later had a major impact on cognitive psychology. Particular mention should be made of the radical behaviourism of B.F. Skinner (1904–1990). Perhaps because of its tight logical foundation, which is a characteristic inherited from the logical positivists, radical behaviourism can be seen as the epitome of logical positivism in psychology.

Logical positivism, it should be noted, gave to psychology through its influence on behaviourism the principle of verification. This means that ideas (maybe theories or hypotheses) are only meaningful to the extent that empirical research allows them to be tested to see whether they remain true or whether they should be rejected. This principle is shared by quantitative as well as some qualitative psychology though in a slightly modified form.

The Australian philosopher John Passmore (1914–2004) famously signalled the ultimate demise of logical positivism in the following words:

> Logical positivism, then, is dead, or as dead as a philosophical movement ever becomes. But it has left a legacy behind. In the German-speaking countries, indeed, it wholly failed; German philosophy, as exhibited in the works of Heidegger and his disciples, represents everything to which the positivists were most bitterly opposed . . . But insofar as it is widely agreed that . . . philosophers ought to set an example of precision and clarity, that philosophy should make use of technical devices, derived from logic, in order to solve problems relating to the philosophy of science, that philosophy is not about 'the world' but about the language through which men speak about the world, we can detect in contemporary philosophy, at least, the persistence of the spirit which inspired the Vienna circle. (Passmore, 1967, p. 55)

Once again, in this we can see in logical positivism traces of ideas which are endemic in qualitative psychology. For example, the phrase 'the language through which men speak about the world' is almost a sentiment straight from discourse analysis (Chapter 9). Nevertheless, as Passmore explains in his reference to Martin Heidegger (1889–1976), logical positivism lost the intellectual battle to philosophies which played a central role in the development of postmodernism, deconstruction and hermeneutics, all of which are key aspects of some forms of qualitative psychology.

Given the response of psychology to logical positivism, it is noteworthy that the logical positivists in general did not write about the possibility of a qualitative psychology (Michell, 2003). However, an exception to this was Rudolf Carnap who was mentioned earlier. Michell summarises the relationship between positivism and qualitative psychology based on Carnap's writings as follows:

> Positivism does not dismiss the possibility of non-quantitative methods in psychology. It was actually a much more subtle, complex and tolerant philosophical position than many detractors now recognize. At heart, it involved a romantic view of science, and it anticipated post-positivist relativism, but the fact that positivists valued science meant that they were sensitive to the dangers of applying quantitative methods in inappropriate contexts. (Michell, 2003, pp. 24–5)

Unfortunately, even if logical positivism was not entirely antagonistic to qualitative psychology, this was probably lost to the mainstream behaviourist psychologist. A careful reading of logical positivist writings might have served the working psychologist well but, if we accept Michell's analysis, the signs are that few went back to logical positivist philosophers in order to understand what they actually wrote.

Possibly the reasons underlying the model of science used by behaviourist psychologists may not reside primarily in positivism. For example, Noam Chomsky (1928–), a linguist and philosopher but highly influential on the demise of behaviourism and the rise of cognitive science, raised a quite distinct level of explanation when asked about behaviourist psychology's impact:

> Well, now you've raised the question of why behaviorist psychology has such an enormous vogue, particularly in the United States. And I'm not sure what the answer to that is. I think, in part, it had to do with the very erroneous idea that by keeping close to observation of data, to manipulation, it was somehow being scientific. That belief is a grotesque caricature and distortion of science but there's no doubt that many people did have that belief. I suppose, if you want to go deeper into the question, one would have to give a sociological analysis of the use of American psychology for manipulation, for advertising, for control. A large part of the vogue for behaviorist psychology has to do with its ideological role. (Chomsky, quoted in Cohen, 1977).

One way of interpreting Chomsky's comments is to suggest that there was big money for universities selling the technology of behavioural control. Whatever the accoutrements of such a discipline then they would be reinforced by this economic success.

The quantitative dominance of mainstream psychology

A full understanding of the position of qualitative methods in psychology requires an appreciation of the nature and extent of the ethos of quantification which has pervaded psychology for much of its history. Histories of psychology, almost without exception, simply do not include qualitative approaches. Try as one may, it seems impossible to identify precisely when the distinction between quantitative and qualitative research emerged in psychology (or other disciplines for that matter). Maybe this is because different words such as objective–subjective or hard–soft research were used for essentially the same distinction though with their own particular (unacceptable) overtones. Whatever the words used, quantification has long been a source of criticism from within psychology. The earliest psychological writing contrasting quantitative and qualitative that I have found is by Gordon Allport:

> If we rejoice, for example, that present-day psychology is . . . increasingly *empirical, mechanistic, quantitative, nomothetic, analytic,* and *operational,* we should also beware of demanding slavish subservience to these presuppositions. Why not allow psychology as a science – for science is a broad and beneficent term – to be also *rational, teleological, qualitative, idiographic, synoptic,* and even *non-operational*? I mention these antitheses of virtue with deliberation, for the simple reason that great insights of psychology in the past – for example, those of Aristotle, Locke, Fechner, James, Freud – have stemmed from one or more of these unfashionable presuppositions. (Allport, 1940, p. 25)

A later but perhaps more thorough critique of quantitative methods is to be found in Brower (1949). Reading his criticism, it is evident that a vision of what quantification's alternative might be is missing. Furthermore, no mention of the word qualitative is to be found in Brower's paper – he merely writes about 'non-quantitative' as if the alternative was the absence of quantification. It is interesting to read Brower's account of quantification in psychology as being 'insistently demanded', a 'natural accompaniment' of an age of engineering and physical science, and emulating physics as the prototypical science:

> Quantitative methods have found an extraordinary degree of application in psychology and have been insistently demanded on the American scene for a number of reasons. First of all, they represent a natural accompaniment of our mechanical age and the emphasis on engineering and physical science. Secondly, we have unwittingly attempted to emulate physics as the prototype of science without elaborating the intrinsic differences between psychology and physics. The methodology of physics makes possible a degree of detachment of subject-matter from observer which can, thus far, be obtained in psychology only by doing damage to the phenomenon through artificialization. In the history of modern physics, astronomy, chemistry, etc., the recognition of the 'personal equation' certainly was a boon to the development of those fields. While the facts of individual differences in perception were derived from psychology, physical scientists did not find it necessary to incorporate psychological methods, e.g. introspection, along with their factual data. As psychology grew on the substrate of natural science, however, not only were the facts of physics incorporated into psychology but the principal method as well: quantification. (Brower, 1949, pp. 325–326)

In other words, one does not need to dig too deeply into the philosophical basis of psychology in order to understand why quantification is so deeply embedded in its collective psyche. The way in which psychologists go about the practice of psychological research is the consequence of their understanding of what that practice consists of. There is no doubt, and examples will be provided later, that there has been a qualitative ethos in psychology which has manifested itself in some classic studies. Nevertheless, it is clear that quantitative approaches have tended to dominate the ways that psychologists believed that psychology should be carried out. Box 1.2 discusses a radically different conceptualisation of the nature of science.

If positivism does not account for the dominance of quantitative methods in psychology, then what does? Michell (2003) argues that the 'quantitative imperative' best describes psychology's orientation rather than any philosophical considerations. The quantitative imperative is the idea that the scientific study of anything involves measuring that thing. Science and measurement go together and, as a consequence, non-quantitative methods are held to be pre-scientific. But where does this 'quantitative imperative' originate? According to Michell, it is an ancient, still deeply ingrained idea. The notion that quantification and science are inseparable has it roots in the Ancient Greek pre-Socratic Pythagoreans (some 500 years BC). Of course, Pythagoras was an important figure in mathematics who believed that mathematics underlay the principles governing phenomena observed in the world. Such a belief is understandable given some of Pythagoras's achievements. For instance, Pythagoras discovered mathematical ratios in things so apparently different as geometry, astronomy and music. For example, in music, a note an octave above another in pitch has twice

Box 1.2

KEY CONCEPT

Social constructionism

Social constructionism is a broad church and the beliefs of social constructionist thinkers difficult to define. That is, there are a range of intellectual foundations of social constructionism and none are shared by every social constructionist thinker. Burr (2003) suggests that to be described as a social constructionist, one of the following assumptions derived from Gergen (1985a) have to be met at a minimum (see Figure 1.4):

- *Knowledge sustained by social processes*   Social constructionists argue that knowledge is constructed by people through their interactions. Our version of knowledge is therefore substantially the product of language in the form of conversation, etc. in our everyday lives.

- *Historical and cultural specificity of language*   The way that we think about any aspect of the world will vary in different cultures and in the same culture at different time periods. For example, once suicide was regarded as a crime and the body of a person committing suicide punished as if they were alive (Ssasz, 1986). Within living memory, attempted suicide was a crime in the United Kingdom.

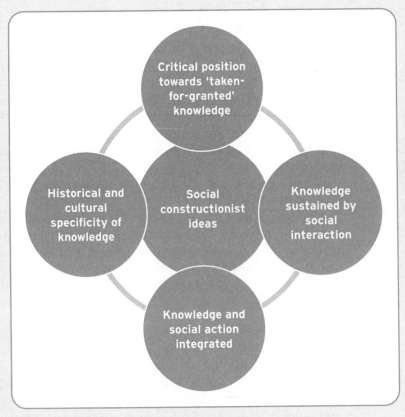

FIGURE 1.4 Characteristics of social constructionist thought

- *Critical position on 'taken-for-granted' knowledge*   The usual view of mainstream psychology, it is argued, is that the researcher can observe the world objectively. This sort of assumption as well as other assumptions of mainstream psychology would be questioned from the social constructionist perspective which holds that the ways in which people perceive the world do not correspond to a reality.

- *Knowledge and social action are integrated*   The different constructions that we have about the world each have their implications for different sorts of social action. So the idea that illegal drug users are 'medically sick' has implications for their treatment which are different from the implications of regarding them as criminals.

The origins of social constructionist thinking dig deep into the history of postmodernism itself which has its background in the arts such as cultural studies and literature. Postmodernism rejects modernistic ideas which even in art included basic rules such as the 'rule of thirds' putatively underlying good composition. The postmodern position is one of a multiplicity of different perspectives on the world which are incompatible with the idea that there can be grand theories which explain what underlie the world and existence. Berger and Luckmann (1966) produced a crucial book *The Social Construction of Reality* (discussed in Chapter 2) which was a decisive moment in sociology as well as establishing the constructionist perspective in the social sciences as a whole – and eventually psychology. In general, in psychology the constructionist position served as a radical critique of the work of mainstream psychologists. However, more importantly, it became a focus of styles of research – many of them discussed in this text – which can broadly be divided into two sorts:

- *Interactionally focused*   This is what Burr (2003) calls micro-social constructionism and Danziger (1997) called light social constructionism. This is essentially the idea that the world as experienced by people is created or constructed through the regular everyday social interactions such as conversations between people (one aspect of discourse). This is a continual, regular process of everyday life. Although this is part of the work of discourse analysts and, to a lesser extent, conversation analysts, this approach can be attributed to the work of Kenneth Gergen (e.g. 1999) and John Shotter (e.g. 1995).

- *Societally focused*   Burr (2003) calls this macro-social constructionism and Danziger (1997) calls this dark social constructionism. This form of social constructionist thinking regards social power as being central and a crucial aspect of what is constructed through discourse. Michel Foucault was particularly influential on this particular form of social constructionism. So it concentrates on such things as institutional practices and social structures.

The distinction between these two types of social construction is more or less in terms of the idea of agency (Burr, 2003). The type of social interaction which is involved in the interactionally focused form of social constructionism involves an active participant in a conversation contributing to the process of construction. In the societally focused form of social constructionism the idea is created that the participant in conversation is relatively powerless to produce social change – that is, change in the power structure of society.

The differences between social constructionist approaches to psychology and the quantitative approaches which tend to dominate the field are clearly major. They are not entirely incompatible but they are opposites on a major continuum. Related, but not identical, dimensions of the differences between social constructionist and quantitative approaches include the following:

→

- *Realism-relativism*: That is the difference between the quantitative assumption that there is a physical reality which can be assessed through research and the social constructionist view that there are a multitude of different perspectives or views on reality none of which corresponds to reality.
- *Agency-determinism*: This is the difference between the quantitative assumption that human behaviour is determined by external forces and the social constructionist view that people determine their own actions.

Most of the characteristics of qualitative research are related to this basic assumption of the social construction of knowledge. Of course, it is a powerful idea but it does have a number of limitations. One of the most important of these is that it can appear a relatively weak theory in that researchers often fail to specify just exactly what is being socially constructed and just where a particular social construction will prevail and why.

the frequency of vibration. Nevertheless, Aristotle (384–322 BC) questioned how attributes such as colours and tastes could be numbers.

The idea that mathematics underlies all that we experience has had an unchequered presence in ideas about science from Pythagorian times until the present. A closely linked idea is that mathematics would replace other sciences. Physics, especially, among the sciences has had spectacular success in terms of expressing its findings mathematically from Isaac Newton's (1643–1727) discoveries onward and this accelerated in the light of scientific successes in the first part of the twentieth century. Consequently:

> It dominated scientific thinking in the physical sciences, and this meant that it cast an irresistible shadow over aspiring sciences, such as psychology, that were modeled upon quantitative natural science. (Michell, 2003, p. 12)

The belief in the success of the science of physics buttressed the quantitative imperative in psychology which, as a developing discipline, sought to emulate the science of physics (Michell, 2003, p. 12). Not surprisingly, early experimental work in psychology could be distinctly quantitative in nature. A good illustration lies in psychophysics which involved studying things such as the way in which we perceive loudness or brightness or weight. Important researchers including Gustav Fechner (1801–1887) developed mathematical models to link experience with the physical reality underlying such sensations.

Statistics and the quantitative ethos in psychology

In the 1930s and then following the Second World War, there was a growing methodological consensus in psychology which involved various elements thought to be necessary for scientific rigour. These include null hypothesis testing and Fisher's work on experimental design which gave rise to the analysis of variance. For Michell (2003), as with Chomsky (1973), this methodological consensus 'owed more to the values of window-dressing than to any values implicit in logical positivism' (p. 16). Michell shares the view of others that the methodological consensus served psychology well in terms of the economics of research funding and was responsible for the resistance to qualitative methods. That is to say, the sophisticated quantitative methodologies used by psychologists resulted in high status for their research and, hence, attracted funding. Current dominant psychological research has remained substantially determinedly quantitative in style.

Although statistical techniques were first developed in late Victorian times, they were not generally and routinely incorporated into psychological research until just before the mid-twentieth century. While it is important to differentiate between quantification in psychology and the use of statistics in psychology (i.e. it is possible to have a quantitative psychology without statistics), there is little doubt that statistics played a powerful role in shaping much of modern psychology.

Concepts which seem to be fundamentally psychological in nature frequently have their origins in statistics. In particular, the concept of the variable is so wedded to psychological thinking that it vies to be one of the discipline's core concepts. But variables did not enter psychological thinking until towards the middle of the twentieth century – long after the first psychology laboratory. We will return to this later. Statistical methods have influenced many aspects of psychological theory. For example, statistical techniques such as factor analysis have had important impacts on the study of personality and intelligence. In modern times, to give a rather different example, smallest space analysis has had a major impact on quantitative approaches to profiling crime from the characteristics of the crime scene. In brief, smallest space analysis allows a researcher to find the underlying dimensions along which different crime scenes differ. This simplifies the way in which different crime scenes may be compared. Without dwelling on the point too long, the intimate relationship between psychological research and statistics verges on the indecent. That is, the influence of statistics on psychology has sometimes left the discipline exposed as concentrating on trivial matters such as significance testing and neglecting substantial questions about the nature of psychology itself. Nevertheless, it is impossible to know how differently psychology would have developed without the influence of statistics. As we have seen, psychology has had a powerful impetus towards quantification for all of its modern history.

The relationship between statistical thinking and mainstream psychology is, historically, a fairly confusing one. There have always been a small number of psychologists who have contributed to the development of statistical techniques which are now part of psychology but also other disciplines. Good examples of these are Charles Spearman (1863–1945) who is known for a version of the correlation coefficient known as the Spearman rank correlation coefficient but, more importantly, developed the earliest most basic form of factor analysis as part of his studies of the structure of intelligence; Louis Thurstone (1887–1955) who extended this work in ways that led to one of the most useful, early techniques of factor analysis, which played an enormous role in the development of psychological tests and measurements; and Louis Guttman (1916–1987) who could be described as much as being a sociologist as a psychologist, contributed statistical methods such as multidimensional scaling to the statistical repertoire. No doubt there are others but the point remains that typically psychologists are not the innovators in the field of statistics but its users.

So like their philosophy, psychologists often borrow their statistical techniques. The typical psychologist just uses statistics. Many of the statistical innovations which have been utilised by psychologists were imported from other fields. The origins of regression and the correlation coefficient, for example, were outside psychology. Regression is a biological concept and the statistical analysis of regression was introduced by Francis Galton (1822–1911). Galton was interested in the inheritance of characteristics. His ideas eventually led to what we now know as the correlation coefficient – the standard deviation came from Galton's ideas too. The form of the correlation coefficient which is known to all psychologists worldwide was developed by Karl Pearson (1857–1936) – the Pearson (product–moment) correlation coefficient. Pearson was not a psychologist and is probably best described as a mathematical statistician. He eventually became a professor of eugenics. His son, Egon Pearson (1895–1980), was also a statistician and he, along with Jerzy Neyman (1894–1981), was responsible for one of the most important statistical influences on psychology which also vies for the title of the most destructive – hypothesis testing and statistical significance. This process of testing the null hypothesis to see whether it can be rejected has almost been drummed into every psychology student since the middle of the twentieth century. Worse still, it is presented as the process by which good research proceeds! That is, statistical significance becomes the primary criterion of worthwhile research to the exclusion of every other indicator of quality in research. Finally, one should not overlook the dominance of the ideas of Ronald Fisher (1890–1962) on the design of experiments and the all-important statistical method of analysis of variance. Virtually all of these statistical techniques will be familiar in name if not in more detail to practically any psychologist, no matter where in the world. They have grown to be the common currency of the discipline.

However, statistical techniques were not integral to psychology during the 50 years after the first psychological laboratory had been set up. According to Danziger and Dzinas (1997), psychologists, in general, were becoming familiar with statistical ideas from about the 1930s onwards. As previously noted, the 1930s marked the introduction of the term 'variable' into psychology. While the 'variable' is embedded in psychology talk nowadays (it was another concept originating in the work of Karl Pearson), its absorption into psychology was initially fairly slow. However, it was the cognitive-behavioural psychologist Edward Tolman (1886–1959) who actually made significant impact on psychology when he introduced the terms independent and dependent variables. Whether or not we regard the term variable as a piece of jargon, its use in psychology has resulted in a view of the world as being made up of variables. Seen as conceptual conveniences, variables constitute a way in which psychologists tend to distance themselves from what they study. The attraction of using the terms independent and dependent variables, according to Danziger and Dzinas (1997) was that they effectively replace the terms stimulus and response which were the legacy of behaviourism. The growth in the use of the term variables cannot be accounted for by the growth in the use of statistics in research. The increased use of statistics in the 1940s and 1950s followed after the term variable had been virtually universally adopted by psychologists. Robert Woodworth's (1869–1962) highly influential psychology textbook of that time incorporated the independent–dependent variable terminology so this may have been a major influence. Whatever the reason, with a few rare exceptions such as Guttman's facet theory (Canter, 1983; Shye and Elizur, 1994), mainstream psychologists have lived comfortably in a world constructed from variables. Variable, despite being a common term throughout psychology, is rarely found in qualitative research reports and stands out like a sore thumb when it occurs in that context.

It is worth noting that there have been claims that the quantitative psychologist is a disappearing breed with few keen to take their place (Clay, 2005). This is not a suggestion that mainstream quantitative psychology is declining but signals a shortage of psychologists with specialist training in statistics, measurement and methodology rather than those who routinely use quantification in their research work:

> Psychologists of the 1960s . . . saw themselves as leaders in statistical, measurement and design issues. Psychology departments often had quantitative specialists, and graduate students were well equipped to handle the quantitative aspects of their research. By 1990, that legacy had faded along with the number of students aware of, interested in and able to enter the field. (Clay, 2005, p. 26 print version)

This could be another way of saying that the forces which shaped behaviourist psychology are no longer so potent. Nevertheless, there are still a lot of psychologists with more than a passing interest in quantitative research.

The trouble with history is that the imagination includes the now. So, without really ever thinking it, our picture of the psychology of the past is seen through the psychology of today. And it is difficult to imagine this earlier psychology free from the methodological and statistical baggage that has dominated psychology for more than half a century. But such a psychology can be found in some of the classic papers in psychology. A good example comes from the work of Edward Tolman who was responsible for the introduction of the concept of cognitive maps – which is still a current concept in research. The most sophisticated 'statistical' method in his *Cognitive Maps in Rats and Men* (Tolman, 1948) is graphs. This is readily available on the Web at Classics in the History of Psychology (http://psychclassics.yorku.ca/Tolman/Maps/maps.htm). Other papers in this archive will give you a feel of the nature of early psychological writings.

CONCLUSION

The story so far has taken us through the philosophical changes in psychology that shaped the discipline since Victorian times until the 1960s. Our quest was to find just why psychology as a whole took a quantitative route over this period. Although positivism is often held to be responsible for this, this philosophy either in Comte's version or as logical positivism does not reject qualitative methods in psychology. However, perhaps it is wrong to assume that psychologists' philosophical knowledge was typically sophisticated enough to appreciate this. The great emphasis of psychology on experimentation for much of its history is very evident and the best model for how to do experiments was the highly successful and quantitative, science of physics. Of course, historically psychology as a discipline was closer to the sciences in terms of what it studied and consequently how it should be studied than were the social sciences in general. In other words, the bias to quantification was a matter of psychological practices rather than philosophy. There is a clear bias towards quantification. However, quite why psychology took its quantitative route is difficult to explain in terms of those philosophies.

The dominance of behaviourist psychology in the first half of the twentieth century brought with it the stimulus and response taken from the physiological work of Ivan Pavlov (1849–1936) on the conditioned reflex. Psychology was reduced to seeking the stimulus which led to the response which, in itself, pushes the researcher towards quantification – there is not a lot more to do but count. All of this happened long before psychologists in general included statistics into the psychology toolkit. Indeed, it is important to distinguish between quantification in psychology and statistical applications in psychology. They are very different. Quantification in psychology is about the idea that psychological systems are fundamentally mathematical in nature. Statistics is built on top of this principle; nevertheless statistics is not the reason for the principle. Of course, statistics is the most obvious interface for most psychologists with quantification in psychology so inevitably the ideas of quantification and statistics tend to meld together. Statistical thinking had not fully integrated into the work of psychologists until the 1950s. It can be seen as the consequence of the quantitative imperative in psychology rather than its cause. In a phrase, psychology was a quantitative discipline long before it was a statistical one.

There had been many voices of dissent against positivism in psychology. As we will see in Chapter 2, the vocal tide for change strengthened throughout the twentieth century. However, Henwood and Pidgeon (1994) identify Wilhelm Dilthey (1833–1911) as possibly the earliest proponent of the view that psychology should seek understanding rather than causal mechanisms. Prus commented:

> Dilthey clearly articulated his disenchantments not only with the positivistic notions of determinism, causation, and reductionism that were already rampant in psychology at the time, but also with what he felt was the misplaced irrelevancy of their inquiry to human lived experience . . . He was particularly troubled by the failure of psychology to recognize the culturally mediated (intersubjective) nature of human experience. (Prus, 1996, p. 38)

Although still a major force, the behaviourism project was on the brink of its decline in the 1950s. Withering criticisms were part of it but it increasingly could not deliver what psychologists needed it to deliver. The emergence of behaviourism caused psychology 'to lose its mind'. Its predecessor introspection was all in the researcher's mind. Psychologists were becoming dissatisfied with the hard-science project of behaviourism but researchers in fields such as sociology were also examining their disciplines critically. In sociology, wanton empiricism and theory so grand that it did not join up with research data brought about a major reorientation to qualitative research which, generally, had had poor esteem up to this point. A general shift to qualitative research was underway in the discipline at this time – a shift which was to have its impact on qualitative psychology some years later (and other disciplines on the way). In psychology, the shift was in a different direction and towards cognition or cognitivism in which psychology got back its senses. Cognitive science began to be a big player in the 1960s. It was interdisciplinary in scope and cognition in various guises has dominated psychology ever since.

In the next chapter, we will unpick the story of qualitative methods in psychology and the influence of the broader social sciences on this process.

KEY POINTS

- Many characteristic features have been suggested to differentiate qualitative research from quantitative research. While none of these definitely separates the two in every circumstance, it is clear that the ethos of qualitative psychology is different from the ethos of quantitative research in psychology. Qualitative and quantitative psychology often appear to have very different conceptions of the nature of science.

- Positivism has been argued to have been the philosophical force behind behaviourism which dominated academic psychology for much of the first half of the twentieth century. There is some question about this since logical positivism and Comte's positivism do not, in themselves, dismiss the possibility of a qualitative approach to psychology.

- The quantitative ethos in psychology is part of the long-term view that the world, ultimately, can be reduced to mathematical relationships. This view emerged from the work of Pythagoras and was reinforced by the mathematical successes of physics as the dominant discipline in science.

- Statistics was a relatively late introduction to psychology and so is best seen as the product of the quantitative imperative in psychology rather than its cause.

ADDITIONAL RESOURCES

Brown, S.D., & Lock, A. (2008). Social psychology. In C. Willig and W. Stainton-Rogers (Eds.), *The SAGE Handbook of Qualitative Research in Psychology*. London: Sage, pp. 373-389.

Burr, V. (2003). *Social Constructionism*, 2nd Edition. London: Routledge.

Michell, J. (2003). The quantitative imperative: positivism, naïve realism and the place of qualitative methods in psychology. *Theory & Psychology 13* (1), 5-31.

Parker, I. (2005). *Qualitative Psychology: Introducing radical research*. Buckingham: Open University Press.

Potter, J. (1996). *Representing Reality: Discourse, rhetoric and social construction*. London: Sage.

Vidich, A.J., and Lyman, S.M. (2000). Qualitative methods: their history in sociology and anthropology. In N.L. Denzin and Y.S. Lincoln (Eds.), *Handbook of Qualitative Research*, 2nd Edition. Thousand Oaks, CA: Sage, pp. 37-84.

CHAPTER 2

How qualitative methods developed in psychology

Overview

- The most significant period of growth in qualitative methods in psychology occurred from the 1990s onward. This has been demonstrated by studies of the major database in psychology, PsycINFO, which provides a historical record of virtually all of psychology's output. Much of the growth in research output has been in the least central journals and in books. Cross-disciplinary journals have a more impressive record of publishing qualitative research.

- The publication of new journals devoted to qualitative psychology and the creation of professional organisations devoted to qualitative psychology are evidence of the recognition and newfound status of qualitative psychology (e.g. *Qualitative Research in Psychology*).

- Case studies might be considered one of the earliest qualitative methods in psychology though there are problems with this. Originally case studies were for the purposes of education and training. They illustrated what was known through other research methods. It is also questionable the extent to which Freud's case studies can be regarded as qualitative in nature. There are many recent examples of case studies in qualitative research. Case studies can be qualitative or quantitative in nature.

- Participant observation studies in psychology followed on the heels of their introduction into social anthropology and sociology of the Chicago School where the term ethnology was used. The motivation of the researchers involved was essentially a profound concern with particular social problems (such as unemployment or racism) with which they were faced and the inadequacy of mainstream psychological methods at tackling the issue appropriately.

- The period 1950-1970 saw the demise of behaviourism, the rise of cognitivism in mainstream psychology, and a number of innovations which led to the important new approaches such as social constructionism, grounded theory and conversation analysis. Linguistics and philosophy had their role in developing key ideas basic to discourse analysis.

- For the most part, the innovations of the 1950s and 1960s took place within sociology rather than psychology.

- Changes in society contributed to the incorporation of qualitative ideas into psychology. In particular, feminism required a constructivist approach and one which was capable of giving women a voice through feminist psychology research.

Documenting the growth of qualitative methods in psychology

The challenge of documenting the growth of qualitative methods in psychology

While it is hard to explain, quantitative methods dominated psychology for most of its history. This generally has the status of a self-evident truth. It would take a remarkable revisionist historian of psychology to argue otherwise – and there is no sign of contenders for that particular role. On the other hand, recently there have been claims that qualitative methods have made a breakthrough in psychology and provide a viable and visible alternative to quantitative methods. A complete history of the development of qualitative methods in psychology waits to be written. What is available tends to be, at best, sketchy and, at worst, inaccurate. While it transpires that there has been a steady stream of non-quantitative research in psychology for most of its history, the general consensus would seem to be that the rise of qualitative methods has become substantially more dramatic since the 1980s. Of course, problems of definition make the writing of worthwhile history of qualitative psychology a very difficult task. Do we count as qualitative anything which is non-quantitative, for example? The problem with doing so is that there are many studies which do not involve quantification but are imbued with the quantitative rather than the qualitative ethos. Should we confine our search to research which involves a clear, qualitative data analysis method or do we include any research which involves qualitative data collection methods? Some terms such as discourse analysis, which is one of the archetypal qualitative methods in psychology and emerged in the 1980s, actually cover both quantitative and qualitative research. So one cannot rely on the label 'discourse analysis' to guarantee a qualitative approach. Since the concept of qualitative research was not around when modern psychology began and for many years afterward, the search for qualitative methods in the history of psychology is not a simple matter. Of course, it would be nigh on impossible to review the vast output of psychology in the last hundred years or so in the hope of identifying just what is qualitative in nature – we are fast approaching the time when the three millionth psychology paper will come into print!

Tracking qualitative methods using PsycINFO

The most effective way of documenting the rise of qualitative psychology is to use the massive digital databases available to psychologists. Superficially, the task of doing research using these is simple:

- Make a list of key words or search terms which are likely to find qualitative research.
- Use the appropriate research database to search for publications which use any of these search terms.
- Examine these publications (e.g. using the summary provided by the database) to make sure that they are truly qualitative in nature.

There are two studies which have attempted to track the emergence of qualitative methods in psychology in this way – both used the American Psychological Association's PsycINFO database. This consists of abstracts (short summaries) of published works, bibliographic citations and so forth. By June 2009, 2 700 000 records of publications had been listed. The current rate of expansion is 130 000 additional publications each year. Over 2000 journals are reviewed, of which the vast majority are peer reviewed – that is, assessed for satisfactory quality by two or three eminent researchers in that field. Some 300 of the journals are automatically included in their entirety and the rest are surveyed for articles which are relevant to psychology. PsycINFO includes a vast range of scholarly journal publications in the behavioural and social sciences starting as early as 1894 and books go back to 1840. Books' chapters are also included, as are PhD dissertations. It is a truly international compendium and the items included involve almost 30 different languages and 50 different countries (American Psychological Association, 2009). In other words, PsycINFO is the result of a massive cataloguing operation and provides the best source of what has been published for most of the history of modern psychology. While it would be foolish to regard PsycINFO as the perfect tool for historical research in psychology, it has great potential as part of a broadbrush research approach.

So what are the general trends in qualitative research for the twentieth century? Rennie, Watson and Monteiro (2002) used PsycINFO to identify the qualitative research publications for each decade between 1900 and 1999. They tried various possible search terms and came up with the following as their final list: qualitative research, grounded theory, empirical phenomenological, phenomenological psychology and discourse analy* (the wild card format of this meant that discourse analysis, discourse analytic and other similar terms would be found). Of course, it could be debated whether additional search terms should have been used – for example, there is no mention of thematic analysis or conversation analysis or narrative analysis. Over 3000 records were identified as potential instances of a qualitative study. However, the sifting or weeding-out process eliminated some false hits, leaving about 2500 records dealing with qualitative research. Phenomenological psychology was the only search term which appeared in the database fairly commonly prior to 1970. The remaining terms really only appeared from the 1980s onwards. So qualitative research, grounded theory, and discourse analysis and related terms began to appear much more frequently in the 1990s.

Qualitative publications tended not to be located in mainstream or prime psychology journals but more likely in non-psychology publications. This perhaps indicates a greater interest in qualitative methods outside of mainstream psychology. Rennie *et al.* conclude:

> Overall, the rise in qualitative research as reflected by three of our search terms, at least, has been dramatic, especially in the last 10 years or so . . . the growth of publications has been heavily swayed by the production of just a few journals that were created for qualitative research . . . (Rennie *et al.*, 2002, p. 188)

This study provides evidence for what might have been suspected for other reasons – the growth of qualitative methods started in psychology in or about the 1980s but more emphatically so from the 1990s onwards.

Another study using PsycINFO used a shorter historical period but perhaps a slightly more sophisticated analysis. Marchel and Owens (2007) chose to classify each journal as one of three tiers in the following way:

- Tier 1: Journals owned by the American Psychological Association.
- Tier 2: Journals published by but not owned by the American Psychological Association.
- Tier 3: Journals associated with particular divisions of the American Psychological Association.

In other words, an additional criterion was involved in this study – not only had the publications to be in PsycINFO but they had to be associated with the American Psychological Association in some way. This is a much more stringent criterion than that used by Rennie *et al.* (2002) and likely to produce fewer 'hits'. The study covered each of the decades from the 1950s onwards until the 1990s. They also brought the study more up to date by including later years up until 2002 since the researchers had noted that the rate of increase in numbers of qualitative publications seemed to be accelerating. In this study, the following key words or search terms were chosen: *action research, autoethnology, case study, discourse analysis, ethnography, ethnomethodology, grounded theory, life history, participant observation, phenomenology* and *qualitative*. The list then overlaps but does not replicate that used by Rennie *et al.* (2002). For each of the publications found using any of these key words, two raters were used to check the content in more detail. About half of the articles generated by the computer search could not be meaningfully described as qualitative in nature – many more than in Rennie *et al.*'s study. This left about 600 abstracts containing qualitative research from the 33 American Psychological Association journals studied.

This clearly suggests that the amount of qualitative research in American Psychological Association journals is small. The journal with the largest percentage of qualitative studies was *Humanistic Psychologist* which had 22 per cent of qualitative research followed by *The Journal of Theoretical and Philosophical Psychology* which contained about 7 per cent of qualitative research. Overall, the American Psychological Association journals included very little qualitative research relative to the number of articles published in total. This proportion is probably in the region of 1 per cent of all articles published.

According to Marchel and Owens (2007), a qualitative researcher would be well advised to bear in mind the following:

- The most acclaimed or top journals (Tier 1) tend to publish very little qualitative research. Assuming that this is the result of selection preferences, these journals should be avoided by qualitative researchers. There is an exception to this in that theoretical articles seem to be well received by these top journals. This is possibly because the most prestigious journals hold theory at a premium.

● Some newly established journals and those affiliated to specific divisions of the American Psychological Association are more likely to publish qualitative research. This may reflect a gradual process by which qualitative research is entering psychology through more peripheral journals where there is greater variety and flexibility of approaches.

● Cross-disciplinary journals (that is, those not publishing psychological research exclusively) have the best record of publishing qualitative research. Thus the qualitative researcher might well consider publishing in such journals if the subject matter of the research falls into the ambit of a particular journal. For example, if the article is in the field of education then a cross-disciplinary education journal is a good choice for publishing a qualitative research paper.

These points present a somewhat negative picture of the penetration of qualitative research into the mainstream of psychology. The overall picture is one of some inroads but qualitative research seems marginal to mainstream psychology. Of course, this rather negative view might partly be a function of the choice made by Marchel and Owens to concentrate solely on American Psychological Association related publications. Mainstream psychology journals tend to cater for the needs of long-term specialisms within psychology. It is not surprising that such journals are not particularly conducive environments for qualitative research. In this context, it is worthwhile noting that the American Psychological Association rejected establishing a Division of Qualitative Inquiry in 2008. Given that the qualitative movement in psychology is much more European in its origins and in its nature, to search American psychology journals for qualitative research might be seen as a biased starting point, unlikely to generate much qualitative research.

One of the reasons why these data show only a low representation of qualitative research in psychology might be because journals are not the most prolific publishers of qualitative research. Rennie *et al.* (2002) themselves point out that their hit rate for qualitative research is less than 0.5 per cent of PsycINFO records. However, this ignores the superior hit rates found for books and book chapters. Books and chapters in books were as responsible for the increase in qualitative research as were journal articles. These authors identify Sage books as a key player in this expansion; they point out that these alternative forms of publication are a good way of sidestepping the prejudices against qualitative research which might be found in the journal publication system. This sort of reliance on a single publisher is not entirely unprecedented in qualitative research. For example, the Sociology Press has as its objective the keeping of important grounded theory publications in print.

Other factors which can be indicative of the successful development of a branch of an academic discipline are to do with whether its institutional foundations are in place. So it is then important to note where learned and professional associations have actively incorporated the new area of research into their professional structures. The best news on this front is that the British Psychological Society established a section devoted to Qualitative Methods in Psychology in 2006. This claims to be the 'newest and largest' section of the Society with over 1000 members, though it should be quickly added that the major parts of the Society are called Divisions, several of which are larger than the Qualitative Methods section. Unfortunately, as previously noted, attempts in the United States to launch a Division for Qualitative Inquiry failed in 2008. Similarly, there seems to be a steady growth in the number of journals devoted to qualitative methods in psychology (e.g. *Qualitative Research in Psychology*). However, the list of journals specialising in or prepared to accept qualitative research is well in excess of one hundred (St Louis University, 2009) though relatively few of these are exclusively aimed at psychology.

Although the historical dominance of quantitative methods in psychology is obvious, the emergence of qualitative methods still needs documenting. The emergence of truly qualitative methods and especially qualitative analysis methods has characterised only the last three decades. Systematic histories of qualitative methods in psychology are more conspicuous by their absence than anything else. What histories are available tend to confirm this impression that the development of qualitative psychology has largely been since the 1980s. This is defensible up to a point but, as we shall see, qualitative methods have a much longer history in psychology than that. Whether the rise in qualitative methods reflects a decline in quantitative methods is a moot point. For one thing, the growth in numbers of psychologists could easily accommodate a proportion of them diverting their energies into qualitative psychology. One key aspect of this is the dramatic growth in the number of psychologists in employment over the last hundred years or so. For example, the British Psychological Society had 1900 members in 1950, 2700 members in 1960, 10 000 members in the 1980s, and 33 000 members currently. Given what we have learnt about the numbers of qualitative publications compared with the total number of publications, it seems difficult to argue that, as yet, qualitative methods are replacing quantitative ones – both seem to be growing. Things might change, of course, especially at a time when training in qualitative methods is increasingly featuring in the education of psychologists in many countries. Testament to this is provided by the growing number of textbooks devoted to qualitative research methods in psychology.

Box 2.1 discusses critical realism – a key concept in qualitative research.

Box 2.1
KEY CONCEPT
Critical realism

One of the critiques of quantitative research is that it adopts a realist position. The term *realism* is applicable to positivism and psychology in general. Unlike the broadly constructivist approaches to qualitative research, realism assumes that there is a reality - a physical world - which science can get to understand. Subjectivism, on the other hand, is the view that there is no reality that the researcher can actually directly research. This is the general stance of qualitative researchers who recognise that there are many views of reality but these always are views through a lens and that lenses will, to greater or lesser extents, ensure that reality cannot be directly observed. Qualitative researchers stress that the scientific search for a constant and knowable reality is a pointless task because of this. A faith that we live in a quantifiable world encourages the belief that there are laws of science and to the extent that physical sciences such as physics have succeeded in the quest for quantification then the realist position becomes more tenable. However, this was shattered when modern physics found that even the act of measurement had a reactive effect on whatever is being measured. So if the science of physics does not have an unfettered view of reality then what chance psychology?

One important philosophical position having a relevance to qualitative research in psychology is known as *critical realism*. This is a philosophical position which does not deny that there is a real world – but it questions whether a researcher's observations can fully reflect the real world. The typical qualitative researcher appreciates that reality is viewed through numerous windows or lenses used by the researcher (e.g. different informants or different data collection methods) which means that reality cannot be precisely glimpsed. Each window or lens distorts reality in its own way. This means that there will be different perspectives of reality depending on what window it is being studied through. There is no way of knowing just what degree of distortion there is. Furthermore, research in psychology, as much as that in the other social sciences, greatly depends on linguistic data. Language can never be reality, merely a window on reality. Hence, qualitative researchers value the diversity of researchers' views of reality. One cannot combine these different views to know what the nature of reality is – they are merely different views of that reality. The most extreme anti-realist in qualitative psychology is likely to ignore a warning not to step onto the road because a car is coming! What varies is the assumption of what exactly can be known from words.

There is a view that every method of measuring reality is fundamentally flawed but if different views of reality tend to concur then maybe this takes us somewhere towards understanding what the reality is. In other words, all observers bring to research expectations and other 'baggage' which influence the outcome of the research. This baggage includes our culture, our particular interests and our personal perspectives on life. Furthermore, qualitative researchers tend to recognise that the instrumentation (techniques of psychological measurement) have their own built-in theories and assumptions which also affect how reality is viewed. Given this, and it is likely that all psychologists accept it, then how can it be dealt with? One approach taken by qualitative researchers is to provide our observations to others in order to obtain their critical responses as part of the analysis of our data. Critical realism is an approach to the philosophy of science associated importantly with the work of Roy Bhaskar (1944-). It is at odds with the positivist view that the social world can be understood using a natural science approach but, equally, it rejects the view that the purpose of social research is to elucidate the meanings imposed on the world by people and society (which is broadly the position of some qualitative researchers but by no means all). At its centre it defines something as real if it has a causal effect. It does not matter if this is an aspect of the natural or physical world (electricity – which, say, can drive a motor) or the social world. Thus unemployment is real because it can be established that it has effects. Scientific investigation involves the requirement that what is being studied has mechanisms which can lead to outcomes. This is different from the positivist notion of cause and effect in which a constant relationship is expected between events. This does not mean that social scientific methods are identical to those of the natural sciences since social structures are in a more constant state of change than are physical structures. Social structures come before individuals historically yet the state of flux of social structures is a result of the actions of individuals. So, in this sense, human activity is transformational.

The main qualitative methods in psychology up to the 1950s

Just where does one look for examples of qualitative research methods in the early history of psychology? In the argot of psychologists the distinction between soft and hard data/science is an important one though somewhat passé in recent psychology, where quantitative–qualitative seems to be the preferred choice. The hard–soft distinction would lead us to look for early examples of qualitative work in psychology in the 'soft' types of research. Paramount among these would be Freudian psychoanalysis and its commonest method – the case study. Another place to look are the points where psychology might be or has been influenced by developments in research disciplines related to psychology. An excellent example of this would be participant observation which had its origins in social anthropology and has sometimes been adopted by psychologists. However, the question is whether either of these is genuinely a precursor of recent qualitative methods in psychology.

Case studies

There is little doubt that case studies have been a regular feature of psychology almost since the beginning of modern psychology in the late nineteenth century. The real question is whether it is correct to characterise all case studies as qualitative in nature. Superficially, at least, the case study seems to have some qualitative characteristics in that frequently it consists of verbal descriptions. Hence, case studies are mentioned as early forms of qualitative approaches in psychology. Nevertheless, it is questionable the extent to which all case studies represent a research method. Case studies were adopted into psychology from medicine where they are common. Their original function was to illustrate, pedagogically, what was known about a particular medical condition through an example. It is, therefore, fairly evident that this form of case study does not really amount to research. Substantial numbers of case studies can be found in PsycINFO. From its beginnings in the nineteenth century until 2009, about 21 000 entries refer to case studies (i.e. case study is mentioned in the abstract) but the vast majority of these are after 1960.

A case study is an intensive investigation of a single case – this may be a person, an organisation, a community, an event and so forth and it may feature an extreme case, a typical case, or a deviant case. Usually, in psychology, case studies have usually involved individuals in keeping with the discipline's largely individualistic nature. There are advocates of the use of the case study as a research method (e.g. Yin, 2003) though their research use is seen as very different from their use in illustrative and teaching settings. The phrase 'case study' in the literature covers the difficult circumstance for the quantitative researcher where there is no sample or, in other words, where the sample size equals one (see Barlow & Hersen, 1984, for a discussion of experimental research where the sample size is one). Modern qualitative research has quite a different view of sampling from that endemic in quantitative research as we shall see elsewhere in this book (e.g. Chapter 8 on grounded theory). There are many examples of case study approaches in modern qualitative research. Good examples of this sort of approach include the following but there are many more also: MacMillan and Edwards (1999), Potter and Edwards (1990) and Locke and Edwards (2003). These examples do not focus on individuals but events which have been extensively covered in the media. And they are not identified as case studies. The big problem, if we change our gaze from that of a quantitative researcher to that of a qualitative approach, is that routinely qualitative researchers are happy to work with just a single instance rather than multiple instances of that which they are studying. Quite often, for example, a qualitative research study will focus on just a small amount of data taken from, say, a single conversation. This is not regarded as in some way different from what qualitative researchers normally do – it is very typical of some qualitative analysis procedures. Neither would there be a feeling that such an analysis necessarily warrants supplementing with further instances. In contrast, the quantitative researcher would be uneasy if a single case study was all that there was.

Cowles (1888) reported a very early psychological case study. He describes a 28-year-old woman who had extreme fixed ideas as a consequence of a paranoid mental condition. Cowles wrote:

> The problem of this case was to discover the genesis, the growth and the fixation of the central idea, which in this instance had the peculiarity of being unusually complicated. In the first place, there was probably no special hereditary influence in its origin; the paranoic element is excluded; certainly the right to infer it must be questioned. If it be said to have been 'acquired' because of the typhoid fever at the pubertic period, etc., a neurasthenia must be admitted. But if acquired organic defect be admitted also – while inquiry is excited as to the consistency of this inference – it remains that the 'fixed idea' was conceived some years before, disappeared, and was revived and developed when the supposable new factor of paranoiac defect came in. (Cowles, 1888, p. 262)

Quite clearly, Cowles's study does not involve a qualitative approach. Instead it draws a comparison between this woman's case and what happened with other people. Furthermore, the reference to the 'laws of habit' reveals, perhaps, the writer's positivistic stance. It seems very close to the original meaning of case study in medicine.

Of course, the reason why case studies are sometimes suggested to be early forms of qualitative research in psychology is that often they lack any manifest quantification. Often they include extensive amounts of descriptive material which is lacking from conventional quantitative studies based on substantial numbers of participants. So, in the sense that they lack numbers and contain fairly rich descriptive material, the temptation is to regard some case studies as qualitative in nature. On the other hand, it is very difficult to recognise any elements in recent qualitative analysis methods of the sort discussed later in this book. These typically involve analyses which are led by the data and not by what is already known. Qualitative methods characteristically are exploratory and theory generating – the very reverse of what happens in many case studies.

So it is an open question whether the classic case studies in the history of psychology can truly be described as early forms of qualitative study as opposed to a variant of quantitative research. Probably different answers will be given depending on what features of the case study in question are concentrated on. The psychoanalytic case studies of Sigmund Freud (1856–1939) are a case in point. Freud brought a different sort of intellectual tradition from that of psychology's mainstream though one which was positivist in nature rather than qualitative. He had been, after all, a doctor and a physiological researcher. Several of his case studies are extremely well known even beyond psychology. However, Freud actually wrote very few of them in total. Among the most famous case studies in the history of psychology is that of Little Hans (Freud, 1909) which involved the analysis of a phobia in a 5-year-old boy. The Little Hans study came about when Freud asked people he knew to supply him with observations about the sexual life of children in an attempt to understand infantile sexuality. As a 4-year-old, Little Hans had been a witness to awful events in which a horse pulled its cart over during a fit. A passer-by was killed in the incident. The boy became scared of leaving home and was particularly afraid of horses and over-laden transport. Little Hans's parents were among these informants and, eventually, at the age of 5 Little Hans became a patient of Freud. The fact is that Freud only saw Little Hans once as the boy's father actually carried out the boy's psychoanalysis under Freud's supervision. Despite the obvious source of the fear, Freud and the father chose to explain the fear in psychosexual terms, though Freud much more subtly than the father. One could describe the data as rich, detailed and complex since accounts of the boy's dreams, behaviour and answers to various questions were included. Such richness and depth of data are characteristic of the work of current qualitative researchers. But, unlike many recent qualitative psychologists, Freud was some-what detached from the process of data collection (as it was largely collected by the boy's father). The Little Hans case study did not primarily serve to generate ideas but, instead, it was primarily a vehicle to enable Freud to illustrate his theories of infantile sexuality. Furthermore, many of the psychological concepts used by Freud (e.g. id, ego and superego) refer to internal mental processes which qualitative psychologists tend to reject. Freud's ideas, themselves, are alien in many ways to those of present-day qualitative researchers. Thus, Freud's case studies neglect crucial aspects of qualitative research methodology.

There are other classic examples of case studies in the history of psychology. One particularly important one was Luria and Bruner's (1987) *The Mind of a Mnemonist: A little book about a vast memory*. This concerned the real-life problems of a man with a prodigious memory capacity. In this book, the reader is provided with a detailed account of how a man with neurological problems dealt with his profound memory and perceptual difficulties. The *Mind of a Mnemonist* is clearly essentially quantitative in nature and contains relatively little purely descriptive material about the man's everyday experience of memory. In fact, the book includes descriptions of many little experiments carried out on the man's memory. At the other end of what would seem to be a continuum, *The Man Who Mistook His Wife for a Hat* by Oliver W. Sacks (1985) ought to be mentioned as it concerns a man with no proper memory. *The Man Who Mistook His Wife for a Hat* is much more descriptive and might, in its own way, be said to be a qualitative study.

Despite its relatively early appearance in the psychological literature, the case study in psychology is not readily classified as an early form of qualitative research. This is despite the fact that they are frequently descriptive in nature and often contain no obvious characteristics of quantitative research such as numbers and statistics. But this lack of obvious quantification should not be taken to indicate that most case studies are qualitative in nature. What other of the characteristics of qualitative methods do case studies incorporate? Look back at Figure 1.2 which describes many of the features of qualitative research and then ask yourself the question of just how many of these actually describe the case studies of early psychologists. Some do, some do not. There is clearly a problem with the qualitative–quantitative divide since case studies are difficult to locate on either side. There seems to be a case for arguing that we need a third category – non-quantitative – to cover the situation where a study seems to have emerged from a quantitative orientation but does not involve quantification as such. A good discussion of case studies in their many guises and how they should be conceptualised can be found in Flyvbjerg (2006).

Participant observation and ethnography

Participant observation is part of ethnography and is rarely discussed separately from it nowadays. It would seldom be carried out without other ethnographic methods. So we can speak of participant observation and ethnography as one although ethnography is the more up-to-date term. Participant observation and ethnography are unquestionably qualitative in nature. Some such studies may include some elements of quantification but this is not a defining feature and generally they don't. They also happen to be the longest-established qualitative data collecting method with the possible exception of in-depth interviewing. So the history of participant observation/ethnography in psychology is particularly important in terms of qualitative research in psychology. Ethnography is the discipline which generates descriptive studies of different human societies through the use of fieldwork (as opposed to, say, secondary sources). It involves a holistic methodology in which all aspects of a social system are viewed as interacting rather than acting independently. It remains at the core of cultural anthropology and is an important aspect of modern sociology. Interestingly, ethnography is the most important method in Vidich and Lyman's (2000) history of qualitative methods in sociology and anthropology. However, this dominance is not repeated in the history of qualitative methods in psychology at all forcefully. In participant observation, the researcher is, to varying degrees, immersed in the activities of a community over an extended period of time, collecting extensive and valuable information. The methods employed for obtaining data within this broad approach include active participation in the activities of the group, collecting life histories from members of the group, direct observation, group discussions and self-analysis by the researcher. The descriptive data collected in an ethnographic study are rich and detailed, as demanded by qualitative researchers.

The earliest ethnographers, who were largely missionaries and travellers, saw 'primitive peoples' as constituting part of a chain of development which had led to Western culture. Thus by studying other cultures, the early stages of the development of Western cultures could be better understood. However, the sheer diversity of societies throughout the world, according to Vidich and Lyman (2000), made it very difficult to explain the very different moral values of these societies compared with modern Western values. This revelation sat very uncomfortably with the view that Christianity had a monopoly on legitimacy and truth. Furthermore, the work of early ethnographers often provided justifications for the extremes of colonialism and imperialism.

In the late nineteenth century, the cultural diversity of immigrants and others in American cities drew attention to the need to find out more within the Western world. W.E.B. Du Bois (1868–1963), an African-American himself, carried out the first study of an American community which was published in 1899 as *The Philadelphia Negro*. This included 5000 interviews and simply described the Black population of Philadelphia. It also was intended by the local Quaker community, which financed it, as a way of uplifting the Black community. But really this is the start of qualitative research in American sociology and influenced the Chicago School of Sociology in the 1920s and 1930s. The first professor of sociology at Chicago was Robert Park (1864–1944) who, significantly, had been a journalist, but also trained in psychology. He saw in sociology a means to social reform. He famously told his students in 1927 'gentlemen, go get the seat of your pants dirty in real research' (cited in Bulmer, 1984, p. 97). Members of the Chicago School in the 1920s and 1930s employed participant observation in very much the anthropological style. The big development was that the Chicago School applied the method to then contemporary Western communities under the name of ethnography. The church sponsored a good proportion of these early investigations. Robert Lynd (1892–1970) and Helen Lynd (1896–1982) wrote the book *Middletown: A study in contemporary American culture* (Lynd & Lynd, 1929) which was another example of this influence on qualitative research. Their later *Middletown in Transition: A study in cultural conflicts* (Lynd & Lynd, 1937) shed the church influence in favour of a much more Marxist stance.

In early but crucial anthropological research, Bronislaw Malinowski (1884–1942) travelled to the Trobriand Islands in Papua New Guinea in 1914. His intention was to carry out the fieldwork for his PhD at the London School of Economics. Stranded there by the advent of the First World War, he eventually overcame his initial reluctance and began to live life much more as one of the Trobriand Islanders – that is, as a participant observer. There is an interesting link to early psychology as Malinowski had previously spent time at the University of Leipzig where he came under the influence of the psychologist Wilhelm Wundt. Despite being often seen as the founding figure of experimental psychology as we saw in Chapter 1, Wundt actually saw limitations in this approach (which he called *Physiologischen* – psychology) and argued for a different form of psychology (*Volkerpsychologie* – sometimes translated as folk-psychology) to deal with the role which social and community living had on the human mind. Malinowski laid down the principles of participant observation though the influence of Wundt on him has largely been overlooked by psychologists. Later, Frank Boas (1858–1942) and his student Margaret Mead (1901–1978) promoted similar approaches to fieldwork in American cultural anthropology.

Participant observation is common in the PsycINFO records from the 1930s on and the abstracts of nearly 3000 records include the phrase up to 2009. One very early mention of participant observation to be found in psychology journals lies in a book review by Dearborn (1920) of an anthropological study in Northern Rhodesia (now Zambia). An excerpt in which Dearborn comments is illustrative:

> To them, the union of the sexes is on the same plane as eating and drinking, to be indulged in without stint on every possible occasion. One would like to know as to the relative number of neurones in their (inhibitory) neopalliuni compared with those in a restrained man cultured and virile with habitual self control; would Sigmund Freud expect to find the number equal? (Dearborn, 1920, p. 284)

So in addition to the routine scientific racism of the first sentence (Howitt and Owusu-Bempah, 1994), Dearborn's consideration of the anthropological study basically becomes translated as a matter of physiology – that is, essentially a quantitative approach to what he actually regards as a rich anthropological study! Dearborn is wondering whether the brain structures of civilised people are different from those of what he regarded as primitive people. Dearborn, thus, offers a somewhat racist biological reductionist perspective from psychology about the complex social system of the people of Northern Rhodesia. In the reference to Freud, there is a reminder that Freud made extensive use of anthropology in some of his writings – especially in his book *Totem and Taboo* (1918; published in Germany in 1913 *Totem und Tabu: Einige Übereinstimmungen im Seelenleben der Wilden und der Neurotiker*). Freud, of course, like others at this time, did not carry out original anthropological research himself and his work based on anthropological studies is probably best described by the phrase non-quantitative rather than qualitative. Freud had trained in medicine and his psychoanalytic work was essentially a version of positivism highly influenced by the physiological research of the time. However, the inference of internal mental states such as the id, ego and superego not only was alien to behaviourism but, interestingly, alien also to most current qualitative approaches which reject the search for internal mental states. Discourse analysis and conversation analysis are examples of this position.

We have noted already that the coverage of the PsycINFO database goes beyond quintessentially psychological publications to include those which, although coming from other disciplines, are of psychological interest. So to some extent, the first appearance of particular qualitative methods in the major psychological research database may merely signal the possible interest of psychologists in the method rather than their actual adoption of the method. Nevertheless, there is clear evidence that some psychologists adopted participant observation for their research in the 1930s and 1940s.

One of the earliest and most significant examples of participant observation studies in psychology was the Marienthal study by the psychologist Marie Jahoda (1907–2001) and the sociologists Paul Lazarsfeld (1901–1976) and Hans Zeisel (1905–1992). This was the first study of unemployment and was first published in Austria in the 1930s (Jahoda, Lazarsfeld & Zeisel, 1933) and reprinted most recently nearly 70 years later (Jahoda, Lazarsfeld & Zeisel, 2002). Marienthal, itself, was an Austrian town devastated when dreadful economic circumstances led to the closure of the local factory which had been the major source of jobs. High levels of unemployment were the result of this. The details of the study are given in Chapter 5 (Box 5.1). Jahoda *et al.* describe their study in the following terms:

> It was the aim of the study to draw an image of the psychological situation of a community suffering from unemployment, using cutting edge methods of research. From the outset we focused our attention on two objectives. One with regard to substance: contributing material concerning the problem of unemployment – and a methodological one: trying to give a comprehensive and objective account of the socio-psychological facts. (Jahoda *et al.*, 2002, p. v)

In other words, the Marienthal study was essentially ethnographic in nature using participant observation and interviews, for example, together with some quantification too. Furthermore, the cross-disciplinary nature of the study was unusual at this time.

So different is the Marienthal study from the typical behaviourist laboratory experiment of the period that it is worthwhile noting that the ethos (and ethic) underlying Marienthal was more concerned with 'the problem' which motivated the research than any abstract philosophical notion:

> In a speech in 1994, Marie Jahoda announced her 'testament': a relevant social psychology draws its themes from the problems of the social present, not from abstract theories; does not look for answers independent of their time, but recognises that social events and human behaviour take place in a context; does not want to prove but to discover . . . Because things count which cannot be counted, qualitative methods have their place in it as well as quantitative ones. And with all the difficulties that this brings, the unfashionableness and the lack, in some scientific circles, of prestige, it also brings the deep satisfaction of making it possible to master the problems of the day. (Klein, 2001)

There were elements of action research in the study but more so the concern that the researchers had for the participants in their study is refreshingly modern and a typical sentiment of recent qualitative researchers. The Marienthal study married together both qualitative and quantitative data in addressing the researchers' research question.

A few years after Jahoda *et al.*'s study, John Dollard (1900–1980) travelled from Yale University to the deep south American town he called Southerntown. Racial segregation was endemic at the time. The original intention was to study the personality of Black people using interviews, but he rapidly realised that whiteness and White people were an essential part of their personality. So the study changed to that of the study of the community. Kidder and Fine (1997) discuss Dollard's study in terms of what they call the 'qualitative stance' which 'enables researchers to carve open territory about which they have vague hunches rather than clear predictions' (p. 37). What Dollard has to say about his own research makes fascinating reading:

> Many times during the conduct of the research and the arrangement of the materials I have had a bad conscience on the score of method. Should the researcher expect to be believed if he cannot lock his findings into the number system and present them in the manner conventional in the physical sciences? So far I have managed to stave off this pressure by such consolations as these: the first loyalty of a scientist is to his material; he must seek where it can be found and grasp it as it permits. (Dollard, 1937, pp. 16–17)

Dollard's methods in Southerntown were purely participant observation. He spent months as a member of a community just knowing and interacting with different people. He rejected the idea of interviewing members of the community since that would have been problematic in this intensely racial context.

The book *When Prophecy Fails: a social and psychological study of a modern group that predicted the destruction of the world* (Festinger, Riecken & Schachter, 1956) was a novel participant observation study which led to a great deal of experimentation on the topic of cognitive dissonance – one of the most famous concepts in the history of psychology and which is primarily associated with the name of Leon Festinger (1919–1989). The researchers were intrigued by a prophecy reported in the local newspaper that there would be a great flood which would bring about the end of the world. Marion Keech, through automatic-writing in which the movements of one's hand seem to be under external and not personal control, had received messages from a planet known as Clarion to that effect. The flood would occur on 21 December.

A group of believers led by Mrs Keech had given up the jobs and studies, given away their money and possessions, and left their families. They believed that a flying saucer would rescue 'believers'. Festinger and his co-workers decided to infiltrate this group in order to understand what would happen when the world did not come to an end at the appointed time. In the hours prior to the time of the predicted cataclysm, the group actively avoided publicity and only true believers had access. However, on the 20 December no flying saucer arrived to rescue the true believers. A few hours later Mrs Keech, through automatic-writing, received a message that the God of the Earth had stopped the cataclysm. Finally, in the afternoon of the day of the predicted cataclysm the group sought the attention of the news media, thus reversing its previous shunning of publicity, and the group urgently campaigned to broadcast its message to a wide audience. In other words, when the belief about doomsday was threatened, cognitions changed in ways which allowed the belief to survive. The impact of this essentially qualitative study was in terms of the generation of numerous studies using laboratory methods – the typical psychology of the time – rather than a rush to using participant observation in psychology.

While both participant observation and case studies have been seen by modern qualitative researchers as early examples of qualitative research in psychology, they do not seem to typify current qualitative psychology. Recent textbooks on qualitative methods in psychology do not cover case studies in any significant detail compared with other data collection methods. Similarly, participant observation or ethnology is sometimes covered but it is not at the core of qualitative methods as it would be in other disciplines. Case studies can be presented from a range of perspectives – the quantitative, the qualitative, the psychoanalytic, the pedagogic and so forth. Participant observation/ethnographic studies may also straddle the quantitative and the qualitative. Generally speaking, the impact of case studies and participant observation/ethnology on the substance of psychology has been very modest indeed. They appear more to be admired as novelties rather than the core of psychological knowledge. Few appear in psychology textbooks, for example. Related social sciences disciplines have embraced these methods and the comparison between psychology and these disciplines is quite dramatic.

The radical innovations of 1950–1970

Historically, qualitative psychology has been fed by other disciplines – principally sociology and philosophy, both of which relate to sociolinguistics, which is a third major input. Sociology was changing in the 1950s and 1960s and these changes had a big impact on qualitative psychology, albeit after a rather substantial delay. Changes within psychology also played a role in paving the way for recent qualitative psychology. We have seen that positivism and behaviourism did not completely monopolise psychology in the first half of the twentieth century. It is probably true to suggest that clinical and similar areas of psychology were less enamoured with behaviourist approaches than much of the rest of psychology. Not surprisingly then, these fields also generated fresh ways of looking at their subject matter. So, in the next section, we shall describe important developments which moved psychology towards qualitative methods in the 1950s and 1960s.

The constructed nature of reality

The work of the clinician Carl Rogers (1902–1987) was both based on humanism and phenomenology – probably the idea of client-centred therapy is the key enduring Rogerian innovation. But more important in this context was the work of George Kelly (1905–1967) who published in 1955 the two-volume book *The Psychology of Personal Constructs* (Kelly, 1955a, b). Personal construct theory involves the fundamental view that an individual constructs their own world and the job of psychology is to understand this constructed version of reality. Underlying personal construct psychology are the processes by which individuals construct a meaningful understanding of their lives and change these understandings in the light of experience. His influence is probably greatest on psychotherapy, clinical psychology and counselling psychology, though this does not represent the full breadth of his influence. One of his important metaphors was that of individuals as (incipient) scientists who created, tested and recreated their self and the world. Among the consequences of this is that people's theories allowed them to deal with future events. Psychological problems occur when a person's personal constructions of the world did not effectively incorporate new events or did not articulate with those of people around them. This process of construct formation and change is clearly ongoing and lacks fixedness – which fits well with postmodern conceptualisations in qualitative psychology. The therapist (or researcher) may identify an individual's personal constructions using the repertory grid methods. In the repertory grid method, the individual is asked to differentiate between three important persons in their lives by saying which two are similar (and how) and which one is different (and how). They then apply this similarity–difference 'dimension' to other people in their world. This process is repeated for different sets of three individuals. By comparing the patterns of descriptions across different people the psychologist begins to see beyond the descriptions used into the nature of the underlying constructs used by the individual.

Personal construct theory is seen as an early precursor to more recent social constructionist approaches. It should not be regarded as an example of social constructionism, however (Ashworth, 2008). Personal constructs are cognitive in nature and, as a consequence, not entirely compatible with some recent approaches to qualitative psychology (e.g. discourse analysis) which have theoretical disagreements with cognitivism (see Chapter 9 on discourse analysis). Nevertheless, in some ways Kelly came frustratingly close to an even more profound breakthrough which occurred in the work of two European sociologists, Peter L. Berger (1929–) and Thomas Luckmann (1927–). They were the first to use the term social construction although their basic idea did have earlier roots. Their book *The Social Construction of Reality* (1966) is a major classic in the social sciences and is best regarded as a theory of knowledge. Their idea was that people and groups of people interact together as a social system. Within this system, they begin to generate ways of understanding the actions of members of the system. These ways of understanding (or concepts or representations) become consolidated in the relationships within the system. Eventually conceptions of reality become institutionalised into social structures and become, in this sense, the reality. In other words, although ideas and activities can appear to have a natural or built-in character, they are best considered to be created by members of that society. So ideas which seem to be common sense are the product of social interactions in which the actors believe that they share an understanding of the world and this understanding comes to be regarded as reality as a consequence. The process of social construction is a continuous one and the product of the dynamics of interaction. A major figure in the promotion of social constructionist ideas in psychology is Kenneth J. Gergen (1935–). On the way to this, Gergen wrote in the 1970s an article conceptualising social psychology as history (Gergen, 1973). The underlying argument of this was that psychological truths are transient and changing partly because of the interaction between the institution of psychology and the people that it studies. Psychological knowledge is therefore subject to revision in the process of interaction. For example, he points out that certain generally accepted concepts in psychology may be affected:

> . . . psychological principles pose a potential threat to all those for whom they are germane. Investments in freedom may thus potentiate behavior designed to invalidate the theory. We are satisfied with principles of attitude change until we find them being used in information campaigns dedicated to changing our behavior. At this point, we may feel resentful and react recalcitrantly. The more potent the theory is in predicting behavior, the broader its public dissemination and the more prevalent and resounding the reaction. Thus, strong theories may be subject to more rapid invalidation than weak ones. (Gergen, 1973, p. 314)

Essentially this reflects one version of the key assumptions of social constructionist psychology (Gergen, 1985b) – that knowledge is historically and culturally specific. Another is that social constructionist psychology is critical of 'taken-for-granted' and common-sense assumptions about the way we explain and describe people. But, ultimately, this leads to a more critical and complex understanding which includes the political:

> Social constructionists are concerned with examining the words that people use and the ways in which people understand the world, the social and political processes that influence how people define words and explain events, and the implications of these definitions and explanations – who benefits and who loses because of how we describe and understand the world . . . From this perspective, a single, uncontested, universal, or true definition of any concept does not exist. Definitions of terms depend on who gets to define them; thus, definitions reflect the interests of people with power. (Muehlenhard & Kimes, 1999, p. 234)

According to Potter (1996), there is a wide variety of qualitative methods which are essentially constructionist. These include conversation analysis, discourse analysis, ethnomethodology and rhetoric.

The need for the discovery of grounded theory

As crucial as any other event in the development of qualitative methods in psychology was the introduction of grounded theory by Barney Glaser (1930–) and Anselm Strauss (1916–1996). This is probably still the commonest method of qualitative data analysis and several qualitative data analysis methods in psychology use some of its principles. The name 'grounded theory' is indicative of the close relationship between the data being used and the theoretical ideas derived from the data. So there is a sense in which the theory is closely tied to the data. This is a better way of putting it than suggesting that grounded theory is embedded or emerges out of the data. It is not – it is created by the hard work of the researcher. Grounded theory stands in distinct contrast to the idea common in mainstream psychology that the data are there to test a pre-established theory. The ideas were published in Glaser and Strauss's (1967) book *The Discovery of Grounded Theory*. Grounded theory does not allow the use of hypotheses derived prior to the analysis of the data. So a grounded theory analyst may choose to avoid the adverse influences of things such as literature reviews in order to escape predetermining their ideas. Basic to the approach is that the researcher should be generating new categories based on the data with the proviso that these categories should demonstrate a good fit with the data. Grounded theory involves constant repetition of aspects of the analysis in order to obtain ultimately the best possible fit of the analysis with the data.

Famously, Glaser and Strauss later went in different directions in terms of grounded theory. Glaser continued with the general tack of *The Discovery of Grounded Theory* with the publication of his book *Theoretical Sensitivity* in 1978. Strauss and Corbin (1990) presented a version of grounded theory which left Glaser so unhappy that he wrote a book-length refutation of their work (Glaser, 1992). The core issue between them was the extent to which the theory should be left to emerge out of the data rather than forcing the data into a partially preconceived structure or framework. Glaser took the view that theory should emerge out of the data, Strauss preferred preconceived frameworks. Despite the influence of grounded theory on many modern qualitative methods, there is a degree of selectivity concerning what aspects (and versions) of grounded theory are used. For example, grounded theory according to Glaser eschews recording and transcribing interviews as essentially counterproductive with no benefits. This is because the grounded theory analysis can be much speedier when the researcher produces field notes (a written account) which are completed as soon as possible after the interview and begins to identify concepts which have a good fit with the field note data shortly after that. In other words, the detailed transcription of recorded data which characterises conversation analysis and some forms of discourse analysis is not central in Glaser's version of grounded theory. The links of grounded theory to ethnology which relied on field notes rather than recordings are evident in this. However, Glaser's view is very much a minority one and researchers adopting Strauss's perspective typically make use of recordings. Of course, that methods change in detail over time is not at all surprising whether they are quantitative or qualitative in nature.

Phenomenology in sociology

Phenomenology has a long history in psychology as we saw in Chapter 1. Its influence can also be seen in the writings of George Kelly discussed earlier in this chapter. However, the more direct route of phenomenology into recent qualitative psychology was through sociology and the ethnomethological approach developed by the sociologist Harold Garfinkel (1917–) in the 1950s and 1960s. The term ethnomethodology literally refers to the methods or ways that people use to understand their day-to-day worlds. It does not simply apply to individuals but also to groups of individuals such as in the case of organisations. Ethnomethodology's basic idea is that the way in which a person understands their everyday world constitutes a social fact. Individuals and groups in society create these social facts. Understanding these social facts is the role of the researcher. The nature of individual's accounts of social situations and how they make sense of the world are important aspects of the theory. Thus explaining to one's boss why one has to have the next day off is an account. But the methods by which these accounts are made meaningful to another person is more important. Many accounts used in explaining one's behaviour or understanding social behaviour do not normally have to be given in any detail because of their taken-for-granted character. In order to elucidate such 'taken-for-granted' accounts, ethnomethodologists have sometimes employed procedures which violate the expectations based on these. For example, imagine a scenario in which guests were invited to dinner but no food was provided. One likelihood is that the guests would formulate accounts for the host's behaviour. People have good ability to account for social order where it fails and, in so doing, maintain that social order.

The influence of ethnomethodology on conversation analysis (Chapter 10) is readily seen. Conversation analysis essentially deals with what superficially may seem like a disorganised aspect of social interaction – conversation – but shows that it has an underlying order and that those who take part in a conversation are aware of the 'rules' which govern conversation. It was developed in the 1960s by Harvey Sacks (1935–1975), though his early death in a motor accident led to Gail Jefferson (1938–2008) and Emanuel Schegloff (1937–) promoting and developing his ideas subsequently. For example, recordings of lectures by Sacks had been transcribed by Jefferson and eventually published as a book after his death as he was not a prolific publisher of academic papers. Many aspects of conversation came within his purview – the selection of the next speaker in conversation, conversational turn-taking, the openings of conversations, and the repairs of 'errors' made during conversation.

Radical linguistics

In the 1950s, it was the general view in linguistics that speech and language are representational – a way of communicating what is inside the mind to the outside world. The word was an essential unit in understanding speech. Ludwig Wittgenstein's (1889–1951) idea that language is essentially a toolkit to do things was reflected in developments in linguistic theory in the 1950s and 1960s. John Austin (1911–1960) importantly contributed speech act theory which essentially involved the idea that speech is social action and does things rather than represents things. Paul Grice (1913–1988) with his maxims of good conversation established the rule-driven nature of conversation. These, and many others, were important in revising the subject matter of linguistics and the eventual development of discourse analysis. In passing, it might be noted that Wittgenstein was influential on the logical positivists though they may not always have interpreted him in the way he would have preferred. Table 2.1 presents a timeline of qualitative methods in psychology.

TABLE 2.1 Timeline of qualitative methods in psychology

Decade	Key events	Impact
Eighteenth century	The Age of Enlightenment in Western Europe.	Led to the ideas of positivism which dominated much of the early history of modern psychology.
1860s	Introspectionism or structuralism began to emerge out of the early work of Fechner.	Introspectionism was the first major school of scientific psychology and lasted until the 1920s. It aimed to quantify and is not generally regarded as a qualitative approach. It should not be confused with phenomenology which is a qualitative method.
1870s	William James founded the first laboratory to teach physiological psychology in 1876.	Both of these have been seen as seminal moments in the development of modern psychology.
	Wilhelm Wundt founded the first psychological research laboratory at the University of Leipzig in 1879.	Symbolically they mark the beginning of the dominance of laboratory research in psychology which lasted throughout most of the twentieth century.
1880s	First published psychology case study by Edward Cowles.	This method is imported from medicine. It tends to be illustrative rather than analytic and thus is *not* an early qualitative method. Famous examples by Sigmund Freud came later. Similar questions can be asked about these.
1890s	About this time and later some of the most well-known statistical techniques, common today, were developed.	Statistics has been a major force in psychology since the 1930s onward and, in many ways, has very much defined the discipline.
1900s	The American Psychological Association was founded in 1892 and the British Psychological Society in 1901.	The importance of professional bodies in the development of psychology cannot be stressed too much. The APA has about 150000 members. The growth of trained psychologists has increased dramatically since the Second World War. The dominance of quantitative approaches in these organisations probably held back the development of qualitative research in psychology.
1910s	Logical positivism developed by the Vienna School but not so-named until 1930s.	Highly influential on behaviourism as it developed in the first half of the twentieth century.
	The anthropologist Malinowski began studying other cultures through a process of immersion and involvement.	This was the beginnings of participant observation which is now commonly described as ethnography. Participant observation common in psychological publications from 1930s onwards. Earlier writers on anthropology often took the observations of others such as missionaries as the source of their data.
1920s	The Chicago School of Ethnography.	Brought anthropological methods to studying American city life.
1930s	In this decade, most psychologists had knowledge of statistical techniques though these started to be developed in the late nineteenth century.	Statistics generally is seen as a prime feature of quantification and partly responsible for the inadequacies of quantitative research.
	Jahoda, Lazarsfeld and Zeisel (1933) conducted the Marienthal study of the experience of unemployment in Austria. It was essentially a psychological ethnographic study and included participant observation among a mixture of innovative qualitative and quantitative data collection methods.	This study would have been impossible had a pure behavioural psychological approach been taken. It is a still-relevant, major exposition of qualitative psychology with its emphasis on the context of experience and radically different research ethic.

TABLE 2.1 (*continued*)

Decade	Key events	Impact
1940s	Content analysis was developed during this period by media researchers such as Paul Lazarsfeld. However, this work was essentially quantitative in nature although more qualitative approaches emerged later.	Content analysis was an early method of dealing with textual material such as media content. It tended to be quantitative in nature.
	The first publications of research involving focus groups was conducted by Paul Lazarsfeld.	Slowly developed through marketing research to blossom in the social sciences in the 1990s.
1950s	The emergence of cognitive psychology.	Cognitive psychology and its derivatives now dominates psychology.
	George Kelly publishes *The Psychology of Personal Constructs* in 1955.	Personal construct psychology was widely influential in the 1960s as an alternative to mainstream behaviourist psychology. It is regarded by some as a precursor to social constructionist approaches.
	Harold Garfinkel begins to establish ethnomethodology as an approach in sociology.	Probably most important as an influence on conversation analysis.
1960s	Berger and Luckman publish *The Social Construction of Reality* in 1966.	Led to social constructionist ideas which began to enter psychology in the 1970s and 1980s.
	Glaser and Strauss publish *The Discovery of Grounded Theory* in 1967.	Provided the archetypal analytic method in qualitative research – grounded theory – which underpins much qualitative analysis.
	Harvey Sacks establishes basic concepts of conversation analysis and Schegloff publishes the first conversation analysis paper in 1968.	Conversation analysis has some adherents in psychological qualitative methods. Increasingly allied with discourse analysis.
1970s	Feminism begins to emerge as a significant force in psychology.	Feminist psychology needed constructionist explanations of gender as a way of countering the dominant, negative view of women promoted by mainstream quantitative psychology and the opportunity to give women a voice.
	Gilbert and Mulkay's studies of the way in which scientists write in journals about science and the way it is presented, for example, in conversation.	This was an important step in the development of discourse analysis as it demonstrated the way in which accounts vary in different contexts.
1980s	Julian Henriques, Wendy Hollway, Cathy Urwin, Couze Venn and Valerie Walkerdine publish *Changing the Subject: Psychology, social regulation, and subjectivity* (1984).	This book marks a major, early attempt to introduce Foucauldian ideas into psychology.
	Jonathan Potter and Margaret Wetherell publish *Discourse and Social Psychology* in 1987.	This book had a big impact and has since been cited by over 800 publications in PsycINFO.
1990s	Ian Parker and coworkers publish important work on Foucauldian discourse analysis and major fields of psychology in *Deconstructing Psychopathology* (Parker et al., 1995) and *Deconstructing Psychotherapy* (Parker, 1999).	Parker established a research focus for Foucauldian discourse analysis.
	Jonathan Smith publishes first paper on interpersonal phenomenological analysis (IPA) in 1996.	IPA has had an important influence on the way in which health psychology, in particular, approaches qualitative research. This is the first attempt at a systematic qualitative method with its roots based almost exclusively in psychology.

TABLE 2.1 (*continued*)

Decade	Key events	Impact
2000s	The Qualitative Methods Section of the British Psychological Society established in 2006 and has about 1000 members. An attempt to establish a Division for Qualitative Inquiry for the American Psychological Association failed in 2008.	The progress of new areas of psychology is substantially determined by building a professional infrastructure. To have a section of a professional society devoted to an area of interest is part of the way that this can be achieved.
	Funding bodies such as the ESRC require that doctoral students in psychology (and other disciplines) are trained in both quantitative and qualitative methods.	Increasingly, academically trained psychologists are aware of qualitative methods.
	Specialist qualitative methods-based journals such as *Qualitative Research in Psychology* established.	A similar outcome is achieved by the setting up of specialised publications in particular areas of research. By having a qualitative research journal for psychological publications it may be possible to encourage distinctly psychological approaches to qualitative methods.
2010s?		

The recent history of qualitative psychology

The rise in qualitative methods in psychology has been to some degree accompanied by a reduced allegiance among quantitative researchers for many of the trappings of science and positivism. It is like two graphs going in opposite directions. For example, few psychologists, if any, today would take the view that the aim of their research is to develop universal scientific laws applying to their subject matter. Although psychology, as a whole, remains resolutely empirical, just what characterises the research mindset of the typical psychologist currently? Silverman (1997) argues that the quest of the typical modern researcher is to achieve 'cumulative, theoretically defined generalisations deriving from the critical sifting of data' (p. 12). To call this positivism would be to wring most of the meaning out of the term. Nevertheless, mainstream psychologists are still prone to prefer decontextualised understanding in which generalisations are made from data but with little or no attention to culture or other contextual matters. However, some believe that psychology is rendered virtually useless beyond the Western population on which it was based as a consequence (Owusu-Bempah & Howitt, 2000).

Willig and Stainton-Rogers (2008) argue that 'qualitative approaches have been part and parcel of psychology from its very beginnings. While marginalized and muted for about the first 80 years of the 20th century, they never completely went away,' (p. 3). However, Billig (2008) claims that the reaction against modernism in psychology is much older than this. He suggests qualitative psychologists '. . . have tended to accept somewhat shallow histories of their own ideas' (p. 186) while claiming that the Earl of Shaftesbury (1671–1713) was 'almost a pre-post-modern figure' (p. 123)! Nevertheless, a psychologist time-warped from any point in the history of psychology (whenever we want that to begin) would be utterly confused by the array of different approaches to qualitative research in current psychology. It, then, would also to be true to say that over the past 30 years much of the resistance to qualitative methods has melted away – especially those parts of the world where the grip of behaviourism and positivism was not so tight. It is tempting but misleading to suggest that the epicentre of research has shifted in the sense that qualitative research is much more in the European intellectual tradition than the American. Evidence of this is in the backgrounds of the key figures discussed throughout this book. Nevertheless, we should not overlook the fact that origins of statistics and positivism were also in Europe.

The recent history of qualitative methods in psychology has been less about new data collection methods and more about new methods of data analysis. This is a key distinction but largely overlooked. Recent textbooks on qualitative methods in psychology tend to dwell on data analysis methods but neglect data collection. This trend precisely identifies what has been happening in qualitative methods for the most part in the past 20 or 30 years.

One can explain recent developments in many different ways but understanding something of the origins of different aspects of qualitative psychology is important. So in later chapters you will find an account of how each of the approaches originated – so the origins of qualitative data collection methods (e.g. focus groups and in-depth interviews) as well as qualitative data analysis methods (e.g. conversation analysis and interpretative phenomenological analysis) are presented in detail in later chapters. Table 2.2 indicates where the origins of individual methods are discussed. Of course, this does not account for why some approaches begin to be adopted more widely whereas other contenders for glory are stillborn and largely forgotten. Broad changes within a discipline are helpful when trying to unravel this puzzle but broader changes beyond the discipline can also be crucial. Political changes and other social forces may be involved. A good instance of this is the development of feminist psychology which has had enormous impact on qualitative methods in psychology. Feminism has been a major impetus to qualitative research in psychology since the 'second wave of feminism' started in the 1960s but showed substantial expansion in the 1980s and onwards. The politics of feminism had a great deal to say about how research was typically conducted in psychology at the time. The available research tended to be advantageous to male power and disadvantageous to women. Wilkinson (1997) is just one psychologist who has provided an account of what she calls the 'patriarchal control of women' (p. 253) that is aided by mainstream psychology. But, perhaps more importantly, the relationship between

TABLE 2.2 Where the detailed development of qualitative methods in psychology can be found in this book

Qualitative data collection methods	Qualitative data analysis methods
• Interviewing, Chapter 3 • Focus groups, Chapter 4 • Ethnography, Chapter 5	• Thematic analysis, Chapter 7 • Grounded theory, Chapter 8 • Discourse analysis, Chapter 9 • Conversation analysis, Chapter 10 • IPA, Chapter 11 • Narrative analysis, Chapter 12

the researcher and his/her subject matter – women – was different in feminist research. Instead of being neutral, feminist researchers were political and involved professionally with the women they studied. The mainstream psychology of 30 or 40 years ago would tend to regard itself as value neutral and objective about issues which feminists felt passionately about. Also feminists saw that part of their task was 'giving voice' to women in all sorts of contexts. So giving a voice to victims of sexual violence and domestic violence was an important aim and the very sort of topic at which qualitative research excels. Similarly, women's bodies became a major area for study in relation to pornography, objectification of the body, eating disorders, menopause and so forth.

Of course, mainstream positivist psychology in the 1960s and 1970s was the place where feminist psychology of that time had to begin and some, at least, chose quantitative research as their basic research orientation (Gergen, 2008). However, at a time when definitions of gender and related matters were in a state of flux, something different was needed – something which did not regard matters as fixed and determined but something which allowed for change. Inevitably, constructionist approaches provided part of the answer to this. And, since Berger and Luckmann's (1966) *The Social Construction of Reality* such an alternative was available. Many of the current qualitative psychology research methods which are at their roots constructionist in nature have increasingly been recruited by feminist researchers for their research. These would include conversation analysis and discourse analysis, of course. Equally, qualitative data collection methods have the potential for giving the voice to women of all sorts. Research methods such as focus groups have a particular role here since they do not cut off a woman from other women in the same way as in-depth interviews can do.

Furthermore, feminist psychology was one of the first areas of psychology to involve specialist journals more than amenable to publishing qualitative research in psychology. *Feminism & Psychology*, founded in 1991, had a major impact and, while not totally excluding quantification, has an agenda which is archetypically qualitative in ethos.

CONCLUSION

We have seen that even during the years when positivism and behaviourism were at their most potent and powerful, psychologists were sometimes drawn to qualitative investigations. Generally this was because their interest in a topic could not be addressed effectively through laboratory experiments or even questionnaires. These psychologists cannot be described as isolated renegades since they were usually more than capable of operating both within and outside of the psychological mainstream. Several ways of linking qualitative and quantitative research exist. There is the classic view that the qualitative approach provides information to the researcher who then verifies ideas quantitatively. In many respects, this describes the study by Festinger *et al.* (1956) into the failed doomsday prophecy. The number of laboratory and related studies which stemmed from this was countless. There is a second view that the qualitative and the quantitative can both usefully inform the same research question. Jahoda *et al.*'s (1933) study of unemployment is a good example of this. As will be seen in later chapters, Paul Lazarsfeld, who also worked on this project, made various important contributions to methodology in sociology (and related disciplines) including both qualitative and quantitative ones. And there is the third view which was inherent in Dollard's (1937) study in Southerntown where he abandoned his original research plan when he realised that it failed to deal with the compelling nature of the situation. Despite his quantitative socialisation, he saw that his intellectual needs in terms of his research could not be fulfilled without putting quantification on hold.

There is another example of the lost opportunities of psychology which perhaps helps to explain the slow emergence of qualitative methods in psychology. Roger Barker (1903–1990) and Herbert Wright (1907–1990) were innovatory ecological psychologists. For example, they published a book in which they observed and described the activities of a particular boy over a particular day (Barker and Wright, 1951). Unusually, the famous sociologist Aaron Cicourel when interviewed suggested that this book was influential on his own ethnographic style of research (Witzel & Mey, 2004). In 1947, the same authors set up the Midwest Field Station at a town they called 'Midwest' in Kansas. This operated for 25 years studying people in their ecological setting and gave rise to one form of ecological psychology:

> Psychology knows how people behave under the conditions of experiments and clinical procedures, but it knows little about the distribution of these and other conditions, and of their behavior resultants, outside of laboratories and clinics. (Barker, 1968, p. 2)

This does not apply to scientific disciplines such as chemistry (e.g. chemists know the distribution of oxgygen, hydrogen and other elements in nature) and entomology (e.g. entomologists know about, say, how malaria is distributed in the real world). Psychologists know no more than ordinary people, in general, about the real-world occurrence of their concepts such as punishment, fear and social pressure. In this book, Barker puts forward an important statement of his behavioural settings theory. A behavioural setting is a substantial and natural environmental unit which normal people recognise as a part of their everyday lives. A behavioural setting has specific time, place and object features but, more importantly, it has a shared expectation about behaviour within that setting. The environmental setting is a powerful determinant of what people do. Despite some enthusiasm for the theory, it has not grown to be a significant part of modern psychology. In part, Scott (2005) asks the question why this innovatory approach faded rather than prospered. Among his reasons are:

- Psychology was (is) dominated by individualistic approaches which made it difficult for a form of psychology based largely on non-individualistic concepts to prosper.
- The practice of psychology was generally the laboratory experiment which has core assumptions which are not favourable to naturalistic methods of data collection.
- Field methods are frequently extremely labour intensive.
- Those who succeeded Barker in the field did not find themselves working in institutions and funding environments as those which allowed the Midwest Field Station to be set up.
- Scott believes that there is a 'critical' mass in terms of doctoral students in a particular field which helps to spread the field more widely. For example, training programmes in ecological psychology had not been created. Other fields of psychology have suffered similarly – i.e. in the case of Gestalt psychology because its advocates were migrants from Europe who had to work in smaller departments with less chance of developing this critical mass.

- Ecological psychology was not about psychology as most psychologists considered it to be. How, then, could ecological psychology attach itself to mainstream psychology at the time?

We have to remember that Barker's ecological psychology was an active field at much the same time as psychology was resisting a qualitative turn – and at precisely the same period in the 1950s and 1960s when other disciplines including sociology took that turn. What is interesting is that we know that in some ways psychology began to be responsive to a wider variety of approaches from the 1970s onwards. Some of these changes probably made it much easier for certain sorts of qualitative methods to emerge. Most of the qualitative analysis methods in this book do not rely on any of the large-scale ecological methods advocated by Barker. Indeed, it is clear that ethnographic methods have not been attractive to many psychologists and few truly ethnographic studies have been carried out in psychology. The data for modern qualitative analyses are relatively straightforward to collect and can be carried out with relatively small amounts of data if those data are sufficiently analytically rich.

Gilbert and Mulkay (1984, p. iii) reproduce the following at the start of their important book on the discourse of scientists. There might be a more general lesson to be learnt from it – no matter what, it is a fitting end to this chapter as it says so much about qualitative methods:

The physicist Leo Szilard once announced to his friend Hans Bethe that he was thinking of keeping a diary: 'I don't intend to publish it; I am merely going to record the facts for the information of God.' 'Don't you think God knows the facts?' Bethe asked. 'Yes', said Szilard. 'He knows the facts, but he does not know *this version of the facts*.' Freeman Dyson, *Disturbing the Universe* (Preface)

KEY POINTS

- The evidence, based on publications' databases, is clear that qualitative methods began to grow in psychology in the 1980s and have generally expanded fairly quickly since the 1990s. However, in real terms, qualitative research publications are a small percentage of the total numbers of publications.

- There are fascinating examples of qualitative research in the history of psychology. In some cases, these are seminal studies in psychology which have been reprinted on several occasions. Nevertheless, caution is in order when evaluating the credibility of some of these methods as exemplars of qualitative methods in psychology. For example, case studies are not intrinsically quantitative or qualitative in nature. Indeed, the original function of case studies was for educational/illustrative purposes rather than research purposes.

- Qualitative data collection methods have a far longer history in psychology than qualitative analysis methods which are much more recent.

- Psychology lagged behind other disciplines in the turn to qualitative methods which first started in sociology, for example, in the 1950s and 1960s. Many of the most important qualitative analysis methods had their origins at this time. Grounded theory and conversation analysis are cases in point.

ADDITIONAL RESOURCES

Ashworth, P. (2008). Conceptual foundations of qualitative psychology. In J.A. Smith (Ed.), *Qualitative Psychology: A Practical Guide to Research Methods*. London: Sage, pp. 4-25.

Vidich, A.J., and Lyman, S.M. (2000). Qualitative methods: their history in sociology and anthropology. In N.L. Denzin and Y.S. Lincoln (Eds.), *Handbook of Qualitative Research*, 2nd Edition. Thousand Oaks, CA: Sage, pp. 37-84.

Willig, C. (2008). *Introducing Qualitative Research in Psychology*. Maidenhead: Open University Press, pp. 1-14.

PART 2

Qualitative data collection

Qualitative data vary enormously in terms of their sources. Qualitative data include new data collected using qualitative research methods such as interviewing, focus groups and participant observation (ethnography) and already existing data obtained from other sources such as the Internet, the media or recordings of therapeutic interviews. Thus there are few formal limits to the types and origins of data which are suitable for qualitative data analysis. Most of the media of mass communications can be sources of material relevant to qualitative analysis – reports in newspapers, interviews in magazines and newspapers, recordings of interviews broadcast on television or radio and so forth are all potentially rich data sources for the qualitative researcher. So some researchers might find autobiographical material from books, magazines, newspapers, diaries and the like relevant to their research interest in identity. For researchers interested in conversation, the Internet is a rewarding source in the form of e-mails, for example, which despite being written down have many conversation-like features. Chatrooms and the like are also potential sources of conversation-like data. Text messaging on mobile telephones similarly has its own conversational aspect which might be utilised in qualitative research. The following may be helpful to anyone wishing to use Internet-based data in their research:

Evans, A., Elford, J., and Wiggins, D. (2008). Using the Internet for qualitative research. In C. Willig & W. Stainton-Rogers (Eds.), *The SAGE Handbook of Qualitative Research in Psychology*. London: Sage, pp. 315–333.

Mann, C., and Stewart, F. (2000). *Internet Communication and Qualitative Research: A handbook for researching online*. London: Sage Publications.

In the next three chapters we deal with what are probably the most demanding data collection methods for qualitative research. These are qualitative interviewing (Chapter 3), focus group interviewing (Chapter 4) and participant observation/ethnography (Chapter 5). These are somewhat traditional data collection techniques in the social sciences in general including psychology. Each requires considerable interpersonal skills, which some people have in copious quantities but others struggle to muster, as well as the professional skills of the well-rounded qualitative researcher. Appropriate training in interviewing is often in short supply in the education of psychologists. Becoming a highly skilled interviewer is not the simplest of matters since interviewing is rarely dealt with in sufficient depth as part of psychology methods training. The apparent conversational nature of interviews is somewhat misleading as they do not merely involve good conversational skills, for example, but a great deal more besides. It should be mentioned, however, that some researchers deliberately adopt a conversational style in interviews which allows them to be analysed as conversation. While this may be all-well-and-good for the conversation analyst, it is not so good for narrative analysis where the important thing is not how people talk about things together but how people experience and describe significant episodes in their lives. This requires a more reflective stance. In these circumstances, a rapid exchange of speech turns between the interviewer and interviewee, for example, would most likely be counterproductive. Like most matters in research, these are issues of both judgement and clarity about the purpose of one's research.

There is another matter which is addressed in the next three chapters. It is no good merely learning the skills of interviewing, focus group moderation and participant observation narrowly defined. A few tips on how to conduct face-to-face interviews do not constitute the skills of a qualitative researcher. Data collection needs to be treated as a process involving a range of activities before and after data collection. For example, where can the researcher go for help with their ideas, how can the researcher go about recruiting volunteers to take part in their study, and how does one go about making sure that those who agree to take part in research actually do so? These aspects of managing research effectively make all of the difference but are rarely taught to students. So for this reason you will find in Chapters 3 to 5 a lot of advice on all aspects of data collection including the sort of stuff that research methodology textbooks frequently overlook:

- Chapter 3 deals with qualitative research interviewing.
- Chapter 4 explains what a focus group is and how they should be conducted.
- Chapter 5 introduces participant observation (ethnography) – an important qualitative method but one which is too frequently neglected in modern qualitative research in psychology.

Qualitative interviewing

Overview

- Interviews of all sorts are ubiquitous in all aspects of modern society.

- The qualitative interview is a common tool in psychology and social sciences research. It has potential for most forms of qualitative data analysis though it may not yield the natural conversation that researchers in some fields of qualitative research would seek.

- Typically a distinction is drawn between the open and the closed interview or the structured and the semi-/unstructured interview or the quantitative and the qualitative interview. Open-ended, semi-structured interviewing characterises qualitative data collection.

- Early examples of interviewing can be seen in Thucydides' history of the Peloponnesian War (about 400 BC). However, interviewing as a social sciences research tool emerged with the work of the Victorian philanthropist Charles Booth in the late 1800s, when he began his research on poverty amongst Londoners. Freud, Piaget and Dichter are among the influential psychologists whose work was founded on interviewing.

- The use of sound recordings of interviews was accepted and fairly common by the mid-1950s.

- During qualitative interviewing the researcher needs to take the stance of an active listener, aware of the detail of what is said while steering the research along the pathways demanded by the research question.

- An interview guide is prepared to provide clarity as to the areas or questions to be covered. The 'guide' is an aid rather than something to be read out verbatim during the interview.

- It is important to consider the qualitative interview as a process which begins prior to the interviews and continues into the interview and beyond. A great deal of preparation goes into planning an interview and a great deal of skill goes into the successful execution of an interview. Aspects of the research need active management by the researcher if the interview is to proceed to its maximum effect.

● It is possible to discern the use of more conversational styles of interviewing in some forms of qualitative research where the interactional nature of the interview is evident. This may be appropriate where the interview is to be analysed more or less as if it is conversation but less appropriate where, for example, the researcher is seeking to obtain a narrative life history. Views differ as to the suitability of interviews as the preferred kind of data as opposed to recordings of real-life conversation – discourse analysts have debated this issue, for example.

● Qualitative interviewing is a key aspect of interpretative phenomenological analysis. However, other analysis methods such as thematic analysis, grounded theory and discourse analysis may be used to effectively analyse qualitative interview data.

● Narrative analysis has its own preferred protocol (see Chapter 12) for interviewing so general advice about interviewing applies here too.

What is qualitative interviewing?

Interviews feature in many parts of our lives. Job interviews, psychiatric interviews, university application interviews, market research interviews, magazine and television interviews, and police interviews are just a few examples. No unitary set of principles cover how to conduct all of these since each differs in its context, purpose, objectives, format and structure. Qualitative research interviews may superficially have much in common with these other forms of interview but they have their own distinctive features and their own requirements. Qualitative interviewing is a common qualitative data collection method though it is not a completely standardised approach. It characteristically involves questions and probes by the interviewer designed to encourage the interviewee to talk freely and extensively about the topic(s) defined by the researcher. Success is not guaranteed as factors such as the skills of the interviewer, the topic and interviewee's potential to provide good qualitative data have a part to play. The objectives of the research interview are not the same as, say, those of a journalistic interview and the contexts are very different. For example, (a) the qualitative researcher is bound to adhere to the values and ethics of research and (b) the researcher has a responsibility to help develop theory out of the interview data – things which other forms of interviewing lack. Of course, it is perfectly possible to carry out qualitative analyses of journalistic interviews if the research question allows this. Qualitative research is very flexible in terms of the data it uses.

Interviews are often described as varying between the structured and the unstructured. Most of us have, at some stage, taken part in a market research interview in the street or over the telephone. Such interviews typify structured interviews. The questions asked are often simply read from a list and the interviewee chooses from another list of possible answers for each question. There is little opportunity for the interviewer to depart from the prepared 'script'. In other words, as much as possible is planned and predetermined. Almost always the market research interviewer is a casual 'employee' rather than the researcher. In general, structured interviewing achieves the following:

- The interviewer ensures that participants are chosen for the study who have the required characteristics to fulfil sampling requirements (i.e. a quota sampling procedure is being employed). Furthermore, since the interviewer actively recruits research participants at the time of the interview, reasonably large samples can be obtained and speedily. Such interviews can be fairly alienating for the participants who may feel it impossible to effectively communicate their position. Equally, such methods effectively distance the researchers from the subject matter of their research. The use of a list of a limited number of reply alternatives (i.e. the multiple choice pre-coded answer format) allows for the data to be quickly transferred to a computer for analysis.

- Provided that the necessary infrastructure is in place, the structured interview may be implemented as soon as the questionnaire design and general research plan are completed. The infrastructure would include a team of interviewers and data entry assistants as well as responsible researchers. A research report can be delivered to commissioning clients in a matter of a few weeks or even days.

Academic quantitative researchers use variations on the theme of structured interviewing in their research. The strengths and weaknesses of the approach remain much the same. If structured interviewing meets the needs of one's research, then data can be collected fairly economically in terms of both time and financial costs. (Another version of the structured approach is the self-completion (tick-box) questionnaire.)

In contrast, few of us are likely to have been participants in qualitative interviewing. Qualitative interviews are time consuming for everyone involved and are more complex in terms of planning and recruiting suitable participants than structured interviews. Often qualitative interviews are referred to as semi-structured. In theory there is also the unstructured interview which lacks any preplanned structure. It is not usual for qualitative researchers to choose to collect their data using unstructured interviews as they are something of an oxymoron. Is it really possible to conduct an interviewing with no preplanning? However, the semi-structured interview can vary enormously in terms of the amount of pre-structuring. The whole point of the qualitative interview is that it generally generates extensive and rich data from participants in the study. Such reasons for using qualitative interviewing touch on the ethos of qualitative research just as much as structured interviewing reflects the quantitative ethos. Unlike everyday conversation, the qualitative interview is built on the principle that the interviewee does most of the talking – the researcher merely steers and guides the interviewee, probes for more information and interjects in other ways when necessary. It is not generally expected that the interviewer will answer questions – that is the role of the interviewee. Equally, the interviewee does not ask the interviewer personal questions of the sort that the interviewer is free to pose. That is not in the 'rules' of the interview. The interviewee can be asked to talk at some length about matters that are difficult for them – perhaps because they have not thought about the issue, perhaps because the topic of the interview is embarrassing, and so forth. The task of the interviewer is also a demanding one. The interviewer has to conduct the business of the interview while at the same time absorbing a great deal of information that bombards them during the interview. This information has to be absorbed and retained so that probes using this new information can be inserted wherever necessary. Although a sound recorder is important to most qualitative interviewers, this does not lighten the burden of absorbing, understanding and reflecting upon what the interviewee has to say during the course of the interview.

The contrast between the highly structured quantitative interview and the qualitative interview is mostly to do with the amount of freedom available to the researcher and interviewee in the qualitative interview compared with the structured interview. In this chapter, we refer to qualitative interviews rather than unstructured or semi-structured interviews since it is a misconception to think that qualitative interviews lack structure – they simply do not follow a prescribed structure. This freedom is not achieved with a haphazard approach to the interview since the successful interview requires preparation of both the interview content and setting. A good qualitative interviewer needs highly developed listening skills, on-the-spot analytic skills, satisfactory interpersonal skills and experience. Qualitative interviewing skills take time to develop.

It is useful to contrast qualitative interviews with structured interviews and, consequently, the similar but self-completed (tick-box) questionnaires. Table 3.1 provides an extended comparison of structured interviewing and qualitative interviewing (drawing partially on Bryman & Bell, 2003; Howitt & Cramer, 2008).

Structured questionnaires (and their frustrations and inadequacies) are familiar to everyone – it is difficult to be in a job without having to complete them at some stage, for example. Structured interviews and questionnaires have the enormous advantage of being quick and easy to process – which is their *raison d'être*. Both involve a list of pre-specified questions which are administered in a standard form with as little variation as possible. In other words, the questions and answers are determined by the researcher in the planning stage of the research. Of course, structured interviews (and questionnaires) are strongly associated with quantification in psychology and, hence, clash with the general qualitative research ethos. But the emphasis of quantitative questionnaires on 'identifying' dimensions of differences between people (as in psychological scales) rather than understanding individuals as individuals is another bone of contention. The qualitative researcher rejects all of this and the accompanying ease of data analysis by adopting an approach to interviewing which allows interviewees far greater opportunity to control and structure the data provided by them. Thus, in contrast to structured interviewing, qualitative interviewers hand a great deal of control, albeit temporarily, to the interviewee.

The ubiquity of the interview in qualitative research might encourage the idea that qualitative interviewing is easy. However, their relative lack of pre-determined structure should not be taken to indicate that they are casual ways of collecting data. The qualitative interview, like all forms of research methods, requires the researcher to develop understanding of the method, experience of using the method, and familiarity with analysing the data gathered using the method. Some researchers have remarked on the conversational nature of the qualitative interview. Burgess (1984, p. 102) referred to them as 'conversations with a purpose'. This, although a common view, is questionable. It is wrong to imagine that qualitative interviewing is easy in the sense that conversation is easy.

TABLE 3.1 A comparison of structured versus qualitative interviewing

Structured interview	Qualitative interview
1. The interview uses a pre-written list of 'closed' questions which is not usually departed from and the questions are asked in a standard fashion.	1. Although the researcher usually has a list of 'areas' to explore through questioning, there is no rigid structure and flexibility is vital.
2. Answers are usually selected from a pre-specified list given to the participant or, alternatively, the interviewer classifies the answer according to a pre-specified scheme.	2. The researcher wishes to encourage 'open' answers in which the interviewee provides elaborate and detailed answers.
3. The structured interview facilitates a quantitative analysis.	3. The qualitative interview normally does not lend itself to quantitative analysis methods.
4. Structured interviews are relatively short as well as being fairly predictable in duration.	4. Qualitative interviewers encourage 'rich' detailed replies leading to lengthy interviews of a somewhat unpredictable duration.
5. Structured interviews are not normally recorded.	5. Some form of tape or digital recording is virtually essential for most qualitative interviews.
6. The high degree of structuring facilitates reliability, validity and similar assessments.	6. The assessment of the reliability and validity of a qualitative interview is a complex issue and not easily addressed. However, see Box 3.1.
7. The interviewer in the structured interview is basically a question asker and answer recorder.	7. The qualitative interview requires the interviewer to be an active listener concentrating on what the interviewee says while formulating questions to help the interviewee expand on and clarify what has already been said.
8. The structured interview is driven by the researcher's agenda and is based on prior knowledge and theory. That is, the structured interview is not generally exploratory.	8. The qualitative interview is largely steered by the responses of the interviewee which the interviewer may explore further with the use of careful questioning. The qualitative interview seeks to explore the thinking of the interviewee.
9. Interviewees have little choice other than to keep to the agenda as set by the researcher. There is limited or no scope for idiosyncratic responses to be made. There may be a somewhat token opportunity for the interviewee to ask the interviewer questions or to express additional thoughts.	9. Sometimes it is suggested that qualitative interviewing encourages 'rambling' answers which may provide a wider perspective on the subject matter of the interview.
10. Standardisation of the questions asked and the possible answers is a characteristic of structured interviewing.	10. A lack of standardisation is inevitable in qualitative interviews and the interviewer expects to rephrase questions, generate new questions in response to the interviewee's answers, probe the meaning of what the interviewee says, and so forth.
11. Inflexible.	11. Flexible.
12. The interviewer is often a 'hired assistant' rather than someone involved in the planning of the research.	12. In many cases it is ideal if the qualitative interview is conducted by the researcher. This allows the researcher to respond quickly to matters emerging in the interviews and make changes if necessary.
13. Some would suggest that structured interviews can best be used for hypothesis testing purposes.	13. Some would suggest that qualitative interviews are exploratory and more to do with hypothesis generation than hypothesis testing.
14. Repeat interviewing is uncommon in structured interviews except for longitudinal studies.	14. Additional or repeat interviewing is appropriate in qualitative interviewing as it provides the researcher with an opportunity to reformulate their ideas or 'regroup'. Repeat interviewing allows the researcher to check their analysis against the perceptions of the participants in their research.

Furthermore, qualitative interviews are not subject to the same conversational principles as a typical everyday conversation. There are many differences between an interview and what modern research has taught us about conversation. Conversations do not normally consist of one person asking another a series of questions, for example. So what is the advantage of conceiving qualitative interviews as conversations? There is a debate in discourse analysis about the usefulness of qualitative interviews for discourse analytic purposes. Research interviews simply are not natural conversation and are less informative about the social use of language than more naturalistic conversation would be. Nevertheless, some discourse analysts are happy to use qualitative interviews on the grounds that interviews are a form of conversation which occurs in everyday life, albeit a highly specialised form of conversation in the case of the research interview. Quite often, discourse analysis researchers who wish to use interviews in discourse analysis carry out a very conversational form of interaction which is very interactive in character compared with the usual qualitative interview. However, this conversational style often produces data which are as revealing about the interviewer as they are about the interviewee. For an interpretive phenomenological analysis or a narrative analysis this 'conversational' style of interviewing might be too glib to produce the needed sort of data for these approaches. Qualitative interviewing calls on many skills which are not those involved in ordinary conversation. In addition, the effective use of qualitative interviewing involves much more than the interaction between researcher and participant during data collection.

The development of qualitative interviewing

The interview has a long history (Kvale, 2007). Among early examples was Thucydides (460–395 BC) who wrote an eight-volume history of the 27-year Peloponnesian War between Athens and Sparta based on interviews with those involved. It is known that the ancient Egyptians carried out population censuses (Fontana and Frey, 2000) and, of course, Jesus Christ was born in Bethlehem where Joseph and Mary had travelled for the Roman tax census. Perhaps more importantly in terms of qualitative interviewing, the earliest journalistic interview was with Brigham Young, the leader of the Mormon religion, which appeared in the *New York Herald Tribune*. The interview had been conducted by the newspaper editor and politician Horace Greeley in Salt Lake City, Utah, on 13 July 1859. Among other things, the Mormon leader described slavery as 'of Divine institution'!

More directly, the use of interviewing in the social sciences was a development out of the work of Charles Booth, a Victorian philanthropist, who in 1886 surveyed the social and economic circumstances of Londoners (Fontana and Frey, 2000). This was eventually published as *Life and Labour of the People of London* in various editions from 1889 onwards. Interestingly, Booth was dismissive of the quality of the information gathered in census returns which led to his studies of poverty (pauperism) among London's East Enders. The findings from these interviews led Booth to argue in favour of the introduction of pensions for the elderly. Methodologically it was an early instance of triangulation (see Chapter 14) since Booth used the data from both interviews and from ethnographic observations in reaching his conclusions.

Kvale (2007) claims that there have been instances of qualitative interviews 'throughout the history of psychology' which were 'a key method' in the creation of 'scientific and professional knowledge' (p. 5). He associates qualitative interviews with some of the most significant contributions to psychology:

● Sigmund Freud (1856–1939) is discussed because of his extensive therapeutic interviews – including the client's free associations during the interview. The method of free association encourages the client to talk about things as they come to their mind without restraint. Free association requires the avoidance of self-censorship which, in its turn, requires the interviewer to be accepting of what is said and to avoid exhibiting any signs of being judgemental. There is no orderly basis to the free association and the therapist interviewer does not know in advance just where the interview will lead. In this sense, the Freudian interview is clearly one of the more unstructured forms of qualitative interviewing. Of course, generally the objective of this sort of interviewing is to unveil new personal insights and understandings rather than, say, to collect information for future analysis.

● The work of Jean Piaget (1896–1980) was based on interviewing children, at length, in a natural setting. He commonly introduced tasks for the child to carry out as part of the interview. Because Piaget had trained in psychoanalysis, his approach to interviewing had parallels with those of Freud. Through the use of these methods, Piaget began to understand the meaning of ideas such as number, size and weight which were central aspects of his work.

● Another important use of qualitative interviews was developed by Ernest Dichter (1907–1991), a market research psychologist who founded motivational research. Dichter described the influence of psychoanalytic methods on his use of qualitative interviewing in his studies of consumer motivation. His whole approach to marketing was based on ideas about motivation stemming from psychoanalytic principles.

It is of some interest that all of the psychologists identified by Kvale as central to the history of qualitative interviewing in psychology were of European origin, though Dichter spent most of his working life in the United States. In this context, it is also worth mentioning that Kvale describes how the famous, although largely discredited, Hawthorne Study was seminal research involving qualitative interviews (Mayo, 1949). In this, thousands of employees working at the Hawthorne Electrical Plant were interviewed in depth as well as being studied in other ways. Although Kvale attributes this work to Fritz Jules Roethlisberger (1898–1974) and William J. Dixon, the prime mover in these studies was a European psychologist and sociologist Elton Mayo (1880–1949). Quite clearly, the influence of European researchers, philosophers and social thinkers on the use of qualitative interviewing as a 'qualitative' research method is noteworthy. However, these historically important users of qualitative interviewing would employ other data collection methods in addition to the interview – this is evident in the work of Piaget and Mayo in particular.

Seemingly simple factors have encouraged the development of qualitative interviewing in psychology as well as other disciplines. It is too easy to ignore the role of technological advances in enabling and simplifying qualitative data collection methods. One important factor was the increasing availability of accessible methods of recording long interviews in their totality. Sound recording only became generally available in the period after the Second World

War with the introduction of magnetic tape sound recording. This meant that an hour or two of interview could be recorded without interruption, thus eliminating the need for note-taking during and after interviews. Of course, note-taking during the course of an interview can interfere with the smooth flow of the interview and detract the interviewer. McBain (1956) published an early paper on the use of tape recorders in psychological laboratories in which he mentions that their use was common by that time in communication, personality and clinical research and that it had advantages in terms of transcription. However, even earlier, Bevis (1949) was recommending the use of recording as a method of reducing 'bias' in interview research. The ability to record interviews was a major contribution in that it provides far greater opportunities for both checking and transcribing the contents of interviews. Transcription recorders can speed up the process of transcribing by allowing re-tracking back to a particular point in the recording. The advent of computers and high quality digital recording equipment was a further impetus to qualitative interviewing. Not only is it now possible to study the sound patterns in detail but word processing allows the rapid cutting and pasting of data files. Furthermore, computer programs allow the easy movement back and forwards in a digital sound file in order to facilitate editing its contents.

By the 1970s and 1980s, the interview had become a common research tool in other disciplines, especially sociology, thus further encouraging its use among the somewhat more reluctant psychology community. References to semi-structured interviewing in psychological journals are fairly rare up to 1980 at about 100 and structured interviews are referred to about 400 times during the same period. However, there was a massive increase between 1980 and 2010 when the figures were approximately 6000 publications using semi-structured interviews and 11 000 using structured interviews. The main point of these figures is that they reveal a major increase in the use of interview methods of all sorts and, especially important here, clear evidence of the growing role of qualitative interviewing in psychological research.

How to conduct qualitative interviews

Generally speaking, it is regarded as important that researchers carry out their own qualitative interviews since it promotes familiarity with the detail of one's data. Fundamentally, the qualitative interview needs to be understood as a product of a special social situation with its own very distinctive characteristics which make it different from other social situations. There has been a lot of research into interviewing in various branches of psychology and it is worthwhile bearing in mind findings from this research in connection with qualitative interviewing – for example, obtaining good rapport with participants in one's research. The need to avoid leading the interviewee is a feature of most forms of interviewing. So by studying interviewing in general it is possible to avoid many of the basic errors that novices make. Good interviewing skills together with careful preparation are the major aspects of success in qualitative interviewing. It is one of the crucial features of qualitative research that the researcher uses extensive, rich, dense and detailed data no matter its source. Consequently, the efforts of the interviewer have to focus on encouraging this descriptive richness. While training and experience are needed in order to carry out an interview well, success involves many different features of the data collection process other than just the interview itself. The researcher needs to be in command of all stages of the research process which include recruitment and retaining of participants.

The qualitative interview is very flexible and it can be carried out in a variety of ways to meet the demands of a particular research study. The following indicate some of the dimensions on which qualitative interviews vary:

- Traditionally interviews are seen as a dyad – the interviewee plus the interviewer. Qualitative researchers are much more flexible than this in terms of the format of interviews. For example, the focus group is a sort of group interview which may involve more than one interviewer and two or more interviewees (see Chapter 4 which discusses focus groups in detail). Equally, qualitative interviews may be carried out with more than one interviewee at the same time such as when partners (e.g. married couples) are the subject of the research. The interviewer–interviewee dyad may not always be the best in all circumstances. Indeed, it may not be possible always to adopt the traditional structure – for example, other family members may wish to join in.

- Interviews do not have to be carried out on a face-to-face basis. The telephone interview is a feasible substitute in some circumstances. It has the big advantage of being economical in terms of time and money. There is no travelling between interviews, for example, which can be very time consuming and not every person who agrees to be interviewed can be relied on to make the appointment. Some researchers claim that the telephone interview may be useful where a highly sensitive topic is being discussed but, equally, it may be the case that the telephone interview seems a little casual and superficial when very sensitive topics are being raised. So, for example, the telephone interview may be appropriate when sexual matters are being discussed but inappropriate, say, where a recent bereavement is the focus of the discussion. Each circumstance is different and the researcher needs to consider many factors when reaching a decision about the style of interviewing to employ. One important and major criticism of telephone interviews – poor response rates – actually has little or no relevance to qualitative research since sampling in qualitative research is usually for theoretical purposes rather than in order to represent the characteristics of the population from which a sample is taken. Of course, the other major drawback of the telephone interview is the loss of non-verbal features of communication which, in some circumstances, can be informative. There are also possibilities for carrying out qualitative interviews over the Internet. The likelihood is that these are written text not involving the spoken word.

- For some researchers, especially those who approach research from a mixed method strategy (i.e. being willing to combine qualitative and quantitative methods in a creative fusion), there may be advantages in using both fairly structured questions in combination with relatively unstructured ones. In this way, fairly simple data (e.g. demographic and other background details) may be quickly collected while at the same time providing the opportunity to allow the participant to discuss their feelings, experiences, life histories and so forth in detail.

The qualitative interview, as we have seen, falls more towards the unstructured than the structured end of the dimension. But this can be misleading since structure here refers largely to the pre-planning of the interview. It should not be taken to imply that qualitative interviews are somewhat haphazard or shambolic events. The fact that the questions asked during the course of a qualitative interview cannot be entirely known prior to that interview does not mean that the interview is chaotic. It merely means that the interviewer has to work hard all through the interview to make the interview as structurally coherent as possible. As we have seen, the difference between the quantitative and the qualitative interview is largely to do with the lack of constraints placed on the replies of the participants and the freedom of the researcher to create appropriate questions within the qualitative interview. The totally unstructured interview is rarely if ever found in qualitative research and it is wrong to imagine there are successful interviews where the researcher has no particular agenda in mind. The qualitative or semi-structured interview, because of its very nature, demands that the researcher has good question-asking skills together with well-developed listening skills. Asking good questions is impossible without having absorbed and understood what has gone before in the interview.

Preparatory stage for the qualitative interview

The qualitative interview requires careful planning if it is to be fully effective. Although the constraints on student work may be somewhat different from those on professional research, the newcomer needs to be familiar with all of these preparatory stages. Since the qualitative interview is *not* normally a free-wheeling conversation but a planned process, a number of factors have to be taken into account early on. In some cases, some of the preparatory stages will involve relatively little work as they are fairly straightforward but these same stages can be exacting in other circumstances. For example, participants may be difficult to obtain if they are a highly specialised sample but, if just members of the public or fellow-students will suffice, then there may be little difficulty in obtaining suitable people for interview.

Like all research, qualitative interviewing needs to be focused. It is rare for qualitative interviews to be carried out over a lengthy period of time with limitless opportunities to ask further questions. (Such research would only be practicable with just a single participant or a small number of participants.) Just what length of time then is available for a typical qualitative interview? Normally, qualitative interviews should take no longer than about two hours or so. Within this constraint, it is obvious that there must be considerable selectivity in the coverage of most qualitative interviews. Indeed, without some focus to the interview, participants might find the range of questions asked somewhat perplexing and, possibly, intrusive. Participants need to understand the interview's purpose not least because they have an important part to play in ensuring that the interview meets its objectives. Without the cooperation of the participants then qualitative interviews are destined to fail.

The following are the major stages in preparation for the qualitative interview – see Table 3.2 for an overview:

Step 1   **Research conceptualisation and development**   It is difficult to generalise about how research ideas develop. However, it is always important to develop clarity about the objectives and purposes of one's research as soon as possible in the research process. Now this is not to suggest that the researcher has to

→

TABLE 3.2 **Stages in the qualitative interview process**

Prior to the interview	During the interview	What happens after the interview?
1 Research conceptualisation and development	1 Recording the interview	1 Support for the interviewer
2 Preparation of the interview guide (interview schedule)	2 Orientation stage of the interview	2 Data protection and management
3 Suitability of the sample for in-depth interviewing	3 What qualitative interviewers 'do' when interviewing	3 Data transcription
4 Interview trialling (piloting)	4 Bringing the interview to a conclusion	
5 Inter-interview comparison		
6 Communication between interviewers		
7 Sample recruitment and selection		
8 Participant management		
9 The preparation/selection of the interview location		

 have complete clarity about the research topic under consideration. There are many circumstances in which the researcher needs to gather data simply to understand a phenomenon better: that is, the extant research in the field may be poorly developed and the interviews are needed to shed light on the topic in question. The qualitative researcher needs, at this stage, to develop a clear understanding of why qualitative interviews are required to meet the objectives of the study. Now this justification does not need to be elaborate but a choice has been made and the researcher should be able to articulate the basis their decision.

Step 2   **Preparation of the interview guide**   Standard practice in the use of qualitative interviewing dictates that a skeletal outline of the interview should be prepared prior to beginning the main data collection phase. Such an outline structure is referred to as the *interview guide*. This may be as simple as a list of areas or topics to be covered or it may list the questions. Of course, topics may be covered and questions answered during the course of the interview without any direct prompt from the researcher which means that the interviewer needs to be flexible as to whether each question on the interview guide needs to be asked directly. Asking a question when the participant has already answered it in response to earlier questioning can be perceived by the interviewee as lack of interest on the part of the interviewer rather than their inexperience. The guide may be adapted in the light of experience – perhaps an important but unanticipated issue seems to be emerging in the interviews which is felt should be systematically included in subsequent interviews. While this is a reparative action, it is characteristic of the flexibility of qualitative research interviewing. Structured interviews, in contrast, cannot be responsive in this way. The interview guide is not the focus of the interview in the same way as the questionnaire is in the structured interview. It is not necessarily consulted throughout the interview but the interviewer may take time-out towards the end of the interview to check that everything has been covered. Don't worry, the interviewee will understand why this is necessary. The guide is usually quite short and so easily memorised. After a few interviews, the interviewer may only make cursory reference to it.

For inexperienced interviewers, there is a danger that the interview guide becomes overly the focus of the researcher's attention to the detriment of the interview's quality. The interview guide is employed in the background of the interview rather than being the lynchpin of the interaction as the structured interview questionnaire is. The primary focus of the qualitative interview is on what the interviewee has to say and ensuring that sufficient supplementary questions/probes are introduced to fully explore the issue from the participant's perspective. In other words, the qualitative interviewer is an *active listener*. The active listener needs to (a) absorb as much of what is being said as possible and (b) formulate further questions to 'fill the gaps' in the interviewee's replies where their account is unclear, contradictory or too short, for example. The interview guide provides the structure through which the richness of the participant's replies is maximised. The purpose of the qualitative interview and its success lie in the richness of the data which emerges. In summary:

- The interview guide should structure the questions or topics to be covered in a natural, sensible and helpful sequence. This, of course, may need to be varied in each interview as, for example, it is pointless and counterproductive to ask a question when the required information has already been mentioned by the participant. Furthermore, a disorganised sequence of questioning makes the interview difficult for both the interviewer and interviewee. There is a considerable amount of memory work during an interview and a logical and natural structure can help both parties in an interview.

- Even if one is conducting a qualitative interview it may be desirable to collect simple basic and routine information using direct and structured questioning. Basic demographic information such as age, gender, educational qualifications, occupation and so forth may be effectively collected using such structured methods. This is not a recommendation but merely a possible resource for the researcher. There are dangers in that it may set up an atmosphere of short questions and answers. Furthermore, in some contexts, the researcher might wish to explore in depth matters such as education which, in other contexts, would be regarded as relatively unimportant.

- The interview guide is not a list of all of the obvious questions or topics which might be of interest. Research is carried out for a purpose and the interview needs to be informed by the questions and ideas guiding the research. It is simply impossible to include every question that might be thought up about a topic. There are practical limits to the length of any interview and two hours or so is the likely maximum length tolerable. Much longer than that and considerable strain is placed on both interviewer and interviewee.

Step 3   **Suitability of the sample for qualitative interviewing**   It is difficult, but not impossible, to carry out an effective qualitative interview with certain types of individuals – for example, young children – but the use of language appropriate for the group in question can certainly help. However, the richness of response required in the qualitative interview may simply not emerge with such groups no matter what adjustments the researcher makes. The qualitative

→ approach, in this case, may not be appropriate. The advice of knowledgeable informants about such groups together with pilot interviews may be helpful in planning such difficult research.

Step 4   Interview trialling (piloting)   One cannot guarantee that the early interviews in a series will produce data of the quality expected. There are many reasons for this, including the skill of the interviewer as well as the adequacy of the interview guide. For this reason, it is a wise step to try out one's interviewing style and procedures in advance of the main data collection phase. This is the pilot study stage. Such an early trial can involve either:

- a number of practice interviews as part of gaining experience and identifying problems; or
- beginning the main data collection but recognising that the early interviews may have problems which may need to be addressed by modifying one's procedures.

The choice between these two depends very much on the scarcity of suitable participants. Where participants of the right type are hard to obtain then even inadequate interviews might be of value. Of course, trialling interviews is best done by obtaining the comments of both the interviewees and others such as members of the research team or a research supervisor.

Step 5   Inter-interview comparison   Interviews are usually part of a series of interviews rather than one-off events in research. As a consequence, the interviewer will have completed other interviews or be aware of interviews that colleagues have done. Issues which have emerged in these earlier interviews must impinge on the current interview. The interviewer may have already incorporated these topics into the new interview but sometimes things which have emerged before may not emerge in the current interview. The researcher needs to consider this and possibly seek the reasons why this is the case by carefully questioning. This across-the-board view of a series of interviews adds to the complexity of the interviewer's task.

Step 6   Communication between interviewers   Just how many differen researchers will be conducting the interviews? Using two or more different interviewers produces problems in terms of ensuring similarity and evenness of coverage across interviews. How are developments to be communicated between the interviewers? It is possibly worth considering the use of much more structured interviews if the logistics of using several interviewers become too complex. However, this may well be problematic and there may not be any enthusiasm for, or advantage in, a structured approach.

Step 7   Sample recruitment and selection   Although conventional random sampling is very unusual in qualitative research, nevertheless the researcher needs to employ a strategy to recruit appropriate sorts of participants. Sometimes this strategy may be relatively simple where selection is not restricted to a special group of participants. Where a specialised group of individuals is required then more care and ingenuity have to be exercised. For example, a health psychologist may be interested in people with a particular type of medical condition (cancer, chronic pain, carers of persons with dementia and so forth)

→

for which no publicly available list of names exists. That is, in conventional research terms, there is no accessible sampling frame such as the electoral list from which participants may be selected. Of course, it would be a long, difficult and, ultimately, pointless task to contact people from the electoral list to find out whether they fit the required characteristics for inclusion in the study. The alternative approach involves drawing up a list of individuals or organisations who may be able to help recruit suitable people for the study. For example, if the researcher wishes to interview chronic pain sufferers then among the possible 'contacts' are:

- hospital departments dealing with chronic pain sufferers – perhaps a 'flyer' may be left around to publicise the research and obtain recruits though they may have suitable contact lists;
- GPs who may be able to identify a number of their patients who fall into this category;
- self-help groups for chronic pain sufferers;
- a snowball sample in which a few known sufferers are identified and asked to nominate others that they know in the same circumstances;
- advertising in a local newspaper.

The researcher should ask themselves why a particular individual or organisation should be prepared to help in this way. There are many reasons why individuals and organisations will not cooperate with researchers and, of course, the researcher may need to work hard in order to prevent these reasons from prevailing. Generally, researchers need to try to establish a good relationship with key members of organisations with the aim of securing their trust and eventually cooperation. Interpersonal contacts (e.g. who do you know who might be helpful?), in these circumstances, are more likely to be fruitful than formal letters requesting cooperation. Once cooperation has been obtained, the organisation may still impose conditions and requirements. It might be insisted, for example, that the initial contacts with potential research participants are made by a member of the organisation rather than the researcher.

Establishing credibility and cooperation can be a time-consuming process – and it may, of course, end in failure. A contact may appear enthusiastic to help but turn out to be in no position to ensure the organisation's cooperation. Organisations are unlikely to cooperate with researchers who are not broadly sympathetic with the aims of that organisation. All of this might be seen as risking compromising the research. Sometimes one's primary sample recruitment method may fail. It would appear to be difficult, for example, to do research on burglars if one fails to obtain the cooperation of prisons or the probation service. In these circumstances, alternative methods of sample recruitment may have to be resorted to. For example, organisations dealing with ex-offenders might be a source of recruits or, conceivably, a snowball sample of burglars might be obtained if one could make initial contacts with a few members of the burglar fraternity.

Step 8   **Participant management**   One of the frustrating aspects of qualitative interviewing is the extent to which the researcher is dependent on the participant being at a certain place at a certain time and happy to be interviewed. It is very easy to waste time and effort setting up interview appointments only to find that the interviewee fails to turn up. Now this may be because of all sorts of reasons. It is not appropriate to assume that such no-shows indicate that the would-be participant is not really interested in taking part. Sometimes they may simply forget. So it is important to 'keep the participant on-board' during the period before the appointment for the interview. This involves such things as:

- writing letters thanking the participant for agreeing to take part while at the same time reminding them of the date, time and place of the interview;

- using courtesy telephone calls the day before or the morning of the interview to remind the participant of the interview and to check whether any problems or issues have arisen;

- providing the participants with some background details about the research and its purpose together with a description of the ethical arrangements involved in the research. Participants who lack such information may get the wrong idea about the nature of the research and back-out for the wrong reasons.

Step 9   **The preparation/selection of the interview location**   There are many potential locations for research interviews, each with its advantages and risks. Precisely what the possibilities are depends somewhat on the individuals being studied and judgements as to what is appropriate. The lengthy nature of the qualitative interview means that one would rarely interview participants in the street or on the doorstep as commonly occurs in market research interviews. One obvious choice is for the interviewee to travel to the researcher's workplace. Among the problems with this is that the researcher is relying on the participant to do all of the work in meeting the appointment. There may be some complex logistics involved which result in the loss of some interviews. There are other difficulties such as:

- the need to find a suitable uninterrupted, quiet place;

- the communication problems which might be involved in ensuring that all relevant colleagues are informed that the interview is taking place – they need to know where to direct the interviewee when they arrive, for example;

- some offices may appear to be cold and sterile places in which to conduct interviews on sensitive topics;

- offices tend to be available during the working day which may be when the interviewee is not available because of their job.

An obvious alternative is to visit the interviewee at home. An advantage is that interviewees may be more relaxed on home ground. However, the home may not be a suitable location for a number of reasons:

- There may be too many distractions from children, animals, etc. There may be other people around in front of whom the interviewee might not wish to discuss certain problems – or, alternatively, the other people might want to contribute to the interview.

- It is more difficult to set up recording equipment in someone's home since setting up has to be done on the spot – or there may be a canary singing in the background, making it harder to transcribe the recording.

→ Of course, there are many other locations which may be considered. The main point is that location needs to be actively considered in order to serve the interests of the research best. Also remember that there may not be a single best interview location for all research participants.

There may be safety issues involved in the use of certain locations. Visiting interviewees at home is not without its dangers and arrangements may need to be made concerning the interviewer's safety. Similarly, some research locations may be intrinsically more dangerous than others (e.g. prison) and again appropriate consideration may need to be given to interviewer safety. Boxes 3.1 and 3.2 give details of two studies in which qualitative interviewing was involved.

Box 3.1
ILLUSTRATIVE RESEARCH STUDY

Interviewing sex offenders about pornography

One of the notable features about a lot of psychological research is that it concentrates on relationships among aspects of the data rather than describing the psychological phenomenon being researched. But there are times in research when the topic that the researcher is studying is little known about. In these circumstances, it would seem important that the researcher seeks to familiarise themselves in whatever way they can. If there is no substantial research literature then interviews and other methods might be called upon to fill in the picture. When Howitt (1995) began work interviewing paedophiles he was motivated by a desire to explore the topic of fantasy. Now fantasy is a word which means something to most of us but usually not quite the same thing. For some of us it may be a 'pipe dream' like winning the National Lottery, for others it may be unrealistic ideas about what is going on around us. From trying to interview ordinary people about their fantasies it was clear that what they had to say did not stimulate the researchers in their understanding of fantasy.

As happens in research, serendipity then took a hand. Howitt and Cumberbatch (1990) had published a detailed review of the research literature on pornography for a government department. As you can imagine, this sort of task is a political hot-potato. Everyone, including politicians, has their own views on such a topic. Happenchance, Howitt heard Ray Wyre (1951-2008), an expert on counselling sex offending, criticise Howitt and Cumberbatch's report in a radio interview. It then dawned on him that this was the context in which to begin to study fantasy – that is, fantasy and sex offenders. Fortunately, Ray Wyre was more than helpful in providing Howitt with access to sex offenders at the then famous Gracewell Institute. It also became rapidly apparent that relatively little published research was available on paedophiles at that time. There has been a massive escalation since then but things can move very fast in new research fields.

In the previous few sentences is hidden a lot that is relevant to this chapter. In particular, virtually all of the preliminary requirements for planning the research were dealt with or defined by the choice to base the research on sex offenders at a sex offender treatment clinic. The sample was clearly defined by this, the location was determined by this, managing the participants was essentially done by the clinic, and so forth. Even issues such as the suitability of the men for qualitative interviewing was also predetermined since the men had been selected for therapy based on cognitive methods in which they needed to be able to reflect but also discuss their offending with others. Similarly, the clinical environment was not a distraction for the simple reason that the men's days were spent in this environment.

Of course, the researcher needed to plan the interviews. The interview guide was simply a list of the areas which the researcher wanted to explore in the interview – things like the men's childhoods, their offending behaviour in detail, pornography, fantasy, parents, adult relationships and so forth. No true piloting was carried out. The first interview or two were somewhat tentative and explorative of the methodology but it rapidly became apparent that the interviews worked in the sense that they produced copious in-depth data. The men seemed to benefit from the process – perhaps as a way of trying to make-good for the harm that they had caused, perhaps because they were receiving relatively benign contact compared with the somewhat hostile and challenging group therapy work that they were engaged in, or perhaps because they began to understand themselves better. Of course, there was the occasional minor crisis to deal with – the man might become emotional or cry, areas of the interview might result in the man refusing to give information (e.g. it was too emotional to discuss their mother or their violent crimes). These were not predictable. No notes were taken during the interviews but the material committed itself readily to memory because of its emotive nature. The recording was made on professional quality equipment and monitored during the interview for quality.

Interviews with such men which included graphic detail are a challenge to the interviewer. Not only are they physically and mentally tiring but they are emotionally draining. This is partly because of the nature of the interviews' contents but also because these men often had fairly distressing childhoods and sad lives in general. This meant that the interviewer needed to find the opportunity to talk with sympathetic others in order to share the experiences which, in a way, was a contribution to formulating an analysis of the data. The interviews were transcribed in a verbatim form. However, what was apparent quite early on in the interview series was that analytic ideas came to the researcher out of those interviews. In other words, not only was the analysis beginning to be formulated during the interviews but this analysis could feed back into the later interviews in terms of ensuring relevant areas were covered. For example, it became clear very early in the interview series that there was a connection between abuse experienced by the man in his own childhood and early sexual experiences with other children with the abuse that he perpetrated on children in his adult years. Howitt describes this as homology. So, for example, the offender tended to offend against a child of a similar age to his own when he had the sexual experience in childhood. In all of this is a hint that the more vivid interview material is, the easier it is for this detailed familiarity with the data to translate into analytic ideas. At the more descriptive level, it became clear that pornography in relation to paedophiles can be a rather complex thing. The research was conducted before the widespread use of the Internet so the use of Internet child pornography was not an issue. However, what was significant was that the offenders tended to use otherwise innocuous films and television programmes as part of their sexual fantasy about children. So a Walt Disney film featuring children could be used to feed fantasy without any need for the material to be sexually explicit.

Ultimately, there is no other way than the qualitative interview of collecting data for research such as this. With care, a detailed narrative can be collected which not only explores the research issue in detail but allows the researcher to contextualise this in the lives of the interviewees.

Box 3.2

ILLUSTRATIVE RESEARCH STUDY

Distressing 'unfeminine' medical symptoms

Polycystic ovarian syndrome (PCOS) is a medical condition in which both ovaries are impaired by cysts. The condition results in dysfunction in the reproductive system together with physically more apparent characteristics such as obesity and excessive hair growth as well as hair loss which follows the characteristic pattern of men. Since its identification in the 1930s, polycystic ovarian syndrome has been covered in the medical literature from a medical perspective. Kitzinger and Willmott (2002) suggest that the condition has received little general discussion, apart from this, and what references there are to it tend to be to 'bearded ladies' and other 'deviations' from 'true' femininity. Women with PCOS, according to research, experience stress associated with the symptoms of their condition and the attendant distress though probably not psychopathology. Quite obviously, PCOS can cause identity problems in women and Kitzinger and Willmott adopted a feminist perspective towards trying to understand how sufferers manage their female identities. The researchers describe their key finding being the way in which such women experience themselves as 'freaks' (a term used by many of the women) who fail to conform to 'the norms of "proper" womanhood'. Body and facial hair were the most disturbing symptoms that the women experienced in relation to the condition. Proper women, in the women's view, are free from hair on their bodies and faces, have regular menstrual periods, and are capable of childbearing.

In this context, we are more interested in the method of interviewing adopted by Kitzinger and Willmott (2002) who describe their methodology in some detail. They interviewed 32 women of whom nearly all were volunteers recruited through a 'flyer' distributed by a PCOS self-help group. Although more women volunteered, the researchers restricted their interviews to those volunteers who were geographically convenient, relatively inexpensive to visit at home for the purposes of the study, and could be seen within the timescale of the study. The typical volunteer to the study was white, heterosexual and aged between 25 and 34 years. Interviews lasted between 45 and 90 minutes and were based on a broad and wide-ranging interview guide (schedule). The intention of the guide was for the women to tell their stories rather than provide a fixed structure. Open-ended questions were used together with prompts, if necessary, and follow-up questions. According to Kitzinger and Willmott, the final interview structure explored the following areas:

- how the woman came to be diagnosed with PCOS;
- the symptoms that they personally experienced;
- what their personal symptoms were and how they dealt with these symptoms;
- how the woman felt about suffering PCOS.

All of the interviews were transcribed using an orthographic procedure and the analysis was based on organising the data into 'recurrent themes'. Kitzinger and Willmott describe this as 'thematic analysis' though it is unclear whether they involved all of the procedures described in Chapter 7 on thematic analysis. The authors felt that it was inappropriate to use any form of quantification because the interviews were 'loosely structured'. They suggest that a checklist of symptoms might be appropriate if it was desired to quantify just how many women experienced each symptom. They illustrate each theme in their analysis in their research report by verbatim quotations from the interviews. They clearly locate their analysis of the data closer to the 'realist' approach rather than to relativist positions:

> We differ in our analysis from some discourse analysts in that we take what women say as evidence for what they experience, i.e. we treat their talk as 'interpretative autobiography' rather than as locally specific 'action'. (p. 351)

So Kitzinger and Willmott describe a number of decisions that they took as researchers which reflect some of the points made in this chapter. In particular, the use of a self-help group greatly facilitates this sort of sample gathering. Some of the women involved did not know other women with the same complaint so methods such as snowball sampling simply would not work as a consequence. The choice to interview the women in their homes was a sensitive one given that the condition discourages the women from venturing into some contexts. Given that so little is known about the experience of the syndrome, the need to explore using open-ended interview methods is virtually self-evident. Most importantly of all, the researchers precisely define how they intend to analyse the data as textual evidence about the experiences of the women in their sample. Kitzinger and Willmott were well aware of the debate in qualitative research about qualitative interview data so theirs was a thought-out decision and not evidence of any naivety about the qualitative ethos.

The qualitative interview stage

While a good interview involves the interviewee seemingly doing most of the work, in reality the interviewer has to maintain a great deal of involvement in what is happening during the interview. In particular, the qualitative interview is highly dependent on the researcher's quick absorption of the detail of what is being said. Kvale describes the good interviewer in the following terms:

> The interviewer must continually make quick choices about what to ask and how; which aspects of a subject's answer to follow up – and which not; which answers to interpret – and which not. Interviewers should be knowledgeable in the topics investigated, master conversational skills, and be proficient in language with an ear for their subject's linguistic style. The interviewer should have a sense for good stories and be able to assist the subjects in the unfolding of their narratives. (Kvale, 1996, p. 147)

The following are some important considerations for the interview stage:

Step 1   Recording the interview   Few authorities dispute that qualitative interviews should be recorded in their entirety. Recordings of interviews are critical to producing good quality transcriptions. The following are key considerations:

- Do *not* assume that it is sufficient to speak into a voice recorder to check the quality of the recorder. A recorder which is adequate for individuals to use to make memos, etc. may not be suitable to record an interview which is a much more complex recording situation. Always try out the equipment in a situation as close as possible to the research setting.

- Use the best quality recorder available since high quality recordings both save time in the long run and help maximise transcript quality.

- If one is transcribing large amounts of interview material, then a recorder which facilitates back-and-forward movement through the recording is a big advantage. However, there are computer programs which can help with this when used with a foot control.

- It is useful to be able to monitor the sound quality during the course of the interview which means that a recorder capable of simultaneous recording and playback through headphones/earphones is a boon. It also means that the risk of nothing being recorded because of operator error is minimal.

- Digital recordings are generally to be preferred.

- Take precautions to make sure that you have the capacity to record a lengthy interview on your recorder.

- The quality of the microphone used will affect the quality of the recording. The use of an external microphone is usually to be preferred as it ensures a better quality recording of conversation. There are some microphones which are particular good at recording more than one individual.

- The quality of the recording will be affected by how close participants are to the microphone so try to ensure that all participants are seated near to it. Generally, faced with a choice, it is better to maximise the quality of the recording of the interviewee than the interviewer.

- Extraneous noise in the environment affects the clarity of the recording. Directional microphones may help if this is a problem.

- Try to avoid setting up the microphone in such a way that it picks up sounds caused by the movements of the interviewer or interviewee. Moving papers on the desk on which the microphone is placed may result in parts of the recording being impossible to transcribe.

- Stereo recordings are usually easier to transcribe.

- Video recording is more difficult and also more intrusive on the interview situation than sound recording. The interviewee may be reluctant to be recorded on video because they feel uncomfortable or embarrassed. This suggests that you should think very carefully before using video (and perhaps try out video as a preliminary before carrying out the research) when investigating highly sensitive research topics since videoing may exacerbate the situation. If your research does not really require video, it is probably best avoided. However, if your analysis is to involve the transcription of gesture and gaze then the use of video is essential.

Step 2   **Orientation stage of the interview**   The major spoken contribution of the researcher in a qualitative interview is the introductory stage of the interview. In this, the interviewer begins the process of engaging with the interviewee by:

→ • introducing themselves;

• explaining the purpose of the interview and what it is hoped to achieve during the session;

• indicating the typical amount of time the interview will take;

• explaining the ethical basis of the research in general and in particular explaining that they, the interviewee, is free to withdraw at any stage and ask for their data to be destroyed;

• allowing an opportunity to the interviewee to ask any questions before the interview starts;

• throughout this process encouraging the interviewee to speak and respond extensively;

• explaining that it is the interviewee's views, perceptions, responses, etc. that the researcher is interested in and that time is not constrained in terms of giving answers.

Step 3   **What qualitative researchers 'do' when interviewing**   The role of the interviewer in qualitative research can be best understood by considering what the researcher does and does not do during an interview:

• The interviewer does *not* normally take detailed notes. The detail often required for many types of qualitative analysis can only be achieved using a sound recording together with careful transcription. Generally speaking, the most detailed notes are inadequate for this purpose. Some researchers may prefer to take notes as an aid to their memory but this is not a requisite. Some, however, would question whether note-taking is appropriate during the qualitative interview. The case against note-taking is that it takes up some of the interviewer's attention during the interview and that for the interviewee it may be distracting. For example, it may appear to signal that the interviewee has just said something particularly 'noteworthy'. In contrast, it might be thought that note-taking is part of the interviewer's active synthesis of what is being said during the interview. For the novice researcher, taking notes complicates an already difficult task and, perhaps, should be avoided until the other skills involved in qualitative interviewing have been mastered. If notes are to be taken, the question arises about what these should consist of. If the notes are seen as purely an aide memoire then it becomes obvious that things such as names and dates should be noted down as one may refer to particular family members by name or sort out the chronological order of events.

• The qualitative interviewer normally does *not* do a lot of talking during the course of the interview itself. It can be a sign of problems in the interview or inexperience.

• The qualitative interviewer does not interrupt the interviewee's replies. Of course, accidental interruptions can happen but generally the interviewer should defer to the interviewee in these circumstances.

• During a qualitative interview, once the scene has been set and the arrangements clarified, the researcher is largely listening to the replies to the questions and issues raised by the interviewer. The direction of the interview is largely in the control of the interviewee though the interviewer may have to intervene

→

→   when there is too much drift – the researcher's primary role is to steer the interview when it needs to be focused or expanded.

● During the qualitative interview, the researcher is actively building a mental picture and understanding of what the interviewee is saying. It is essential that the researcher engages with the replies of the interviewee as it may be necessary to consider extending the questioning, insert probes, seek clarification or identify problems in the account. Sometimes this may involve very minor but crucial points of clarification (for example, just who is the participant talking about at this time?). Sometimes the structure of the narrative might be questioned (e.g. 'So just when did this happen? Was it before you left the children's home?'). The researcher needs to ask themselves questions about whether what is being said by the interviewee makes sense in terms of what has been said before. The interviewer's objective is to ensure that the detail in the participant's answers is sufficient and to interrogate the information as it is being collected if necessary. This is very much in keeping with the view that qualitative data analysis starts at the stage of data collection. It also reflects the qualitative ideal that progress in research depends on the early and repeated processing of the data. The qualitative interview, because it requires active listening, absorption of what is being said and asking appropriate supplementary questions, places considerable demands on the interviewer. Consider the structured interview in contrast where recording the interviewee's answers precisely is the most important task. There is no need in the structured interview to do much more than get brief answers from the respondent in order to 'tick the right boxes'. This can be achieved without the level of involvement required by the qualitative interviewer whose work is likely to be ineffective without their full engagement with what is being said.

● The qualitative interviewer needs to be able to use silence effectively. One of the biggest faults of novice interviewers is not allowing the interviewee the necessary 'space' in which to both think and talk. A gap of silence does not indicate that a qualitative interview is going badly. Neither does it indicate a lack of skill on the part of the interviewer. Quite the contrary: being comfortable with silences is indicative of a good interviewer. This is quite different from normal conversation in which gaps in conversation tend to be avoided. By using silences effectively, not only does the researcher avoid shutting up the interviewee prematurely but the interviewee is encouraged into a more thoughtful and considered way of responding. From the viewpoint of the interviewee, if the researcher quickly fills silences then the impression may be created that the interviewer wants to proceed more quickly and that the interviewee is giving answers that are too long. Clearly this is an undesirable situation in the light of the objectives of some qualitative interviews.

● Question asking: Unlike the structured interview, question asking in the qualitative interview should not be regarded as primarily for the purpose of presenting a standardised stimulus for the interviewee to respond to. Generally, in structured interviewing, the interviewer is encouraged to ask exactly the same question in exactly same way. Only where it is apparent that the interviewee does not understand or asks is the standard interview 'script' departed from. In qualitative interviewing, the objective is to get the interviewee talking freely and extensively about the topic of the questioning.

→

→   This means that the way questions are put will vary from interview to interview since the needs of the interviewees will vary. Furthermore, because it is vitally important in the qualitative interview that the interviewer understands what is being said then the questioning needs to reflect this. Thus reading the question out word-for-word may be inappropriate since it may be better to engage the eye of the interviewee to establish the person-to-person nature of the interview than to keep one's head down in the list of questions. Questions in the qualitative interview are structured in ways which encourage extensive responses and inhibit simple yes or no replies. So, for example, a question such as 'Do you have a good relationship with your parents?' may be an excellent question for a structured interview but inadequate for a qualitative interview, where a question like 'Can you describe to me your relationship with your parents?' may be more productive.

Step 4   **Bringing the interview to a conclusion**   The end of a qualitative interview is not signalled simply by the final topic on the interview guide being reached. The satisfaction of the researcher and the interviewee is an additional important criterion. So there needs to be some consideration of the interview experience as part of the process of concluding the interview. It is always wise, at this stage, to leave the voice recorder running given that important information often emerges at this stage. The following are some of the steps which may be associated with the finishing of the interview:

- The interviewer may wish to take a short 'time-out' break to review the interview guide in the light of how the interview proceeded. Topics not adequately covered may be returned to at this stage.

- The interviewee may be given the opportunity to discuss things that they think are of some relevance but which have not emerged thus far in the interview.

- The interviewer should thank the interviewee formally.

- The interviewer should enter a debriefing stage in which the interviewee's experience of the interview is discussed. This may involve (a) allowing the interviewee to answer any questions they wish about the research; (b) checking that the interviewee remains happy that the recording can be part of the research; (c) providing names and contact details of organisations, etc. which might be able to deal with issues of a counselling or therapeutic nature arising from the interview (a psychologist must be qualified in order to offer such support and researchers are not in that position); and (d) obtaining feedback about the interview content and interviewing methods employed.

Box 3.3 explains how quality can be achieved in qualitative interviews.

What happens following the qualitative interview?

There are a number of post-interview considerations to bear in mind:

- *Support for the interviewer*   While not all qualitative interviews involve sensitive and perhaps distressing material, some of them do. Interviews with victims of sexual abuse, sexual abusers, domestic abusers, those suffering bereavements and so forth all have potential for distressing the interviewer as well as the interviewee. Of course, during the interview,

Box 3.3

KEY CONCEPT

Ensuring quality in qualitative interviewing

Just how does a researcher know whether their qualitative interviews have achieved a satis-factory quality? Of course, not all interviews with all participants have a potential to achieve the highest standards. Some interviewees will provide less than optimum data no matter who the interviewer is. This is a built-in inevitability with qualitative interviewing. But the participant is not the only source of variability in interview quality. The approach of the inter-viewer has a lot to contribute. However, it is important for the interviewer to get a feeling for how well the interview process is going. If things appear to be less than optimal then there may be an opportunity to revise one's approach. Kvale (1996) has a number of criteria which may be indicative of the interview quality:

- Are the interviewer's questions comparatively much shorter than the replies of the interviewee?
- Are the interviewee's replies to the point of the interview and extensive? Kvale (1996) uses the terms spontaneous, rich, specific and relevant (p. 145) to describe good quality answers.
- Does the interviewer follow up the relevant parts of the interview and seek clarification of what is being said?
- Is the interview complete in itself? That is, is the story that it contains self-contained and requires little by way of extra explanation or description for it to make sense?
- Are important features of the interviewee's answers summarised and/or interpreted by the interviewer during the course of the interview?
- Does the interviewer validate or verify their interpretations of the answers during the interview itself?
- Is the interviewer knowledgeable about the topic of the interview? The more generally informed the interviewer is concerning the research topic the easier the interview will be. Of course, this also allows the interviewer to be frank about aspects of the interview that they do not understand.
- Does the interviewer ask questions in a straightforward, clear and simple fashion? Is the interviewer easily understood and do they avoid the use of jargon which might not be shared by the interviewee?
- Does the interviewer impose a clear structure to the interview and provide useful summaries at appropriate points of the interview?
- Is the interviewer sensitive to what the interviewee is saying? Does the interviewer seek to clarify any nuances of meaning that a reply may have? Is the interviewer sensitive to emotionality in replies and does he or she deal with this effectively?
- Does the interviewer have a gentle approach to the interview which allows the interviewee to respond at their own pace and in their own time? This includes being accepting of pauses and thinking time by not interrupting these. Does the interviewer avoid interrupting what the participant is saying?

- Does the interviewer exhibit openness to what the interviewee is saying? For example, does he or she allow the introduction of new aspects of the topic by the interviewee?
- Does the interviewer appear to remember what the interviewee has said previously? A poor interviewer may appear not to have registered what the interviewee has already said and so, for example, may pose questions which the interviewee has essentially already answered.
- Is the interviewer prepared to be critical or questioning of what has been said? Does he or she question the interviewee in ways which might help establish the validity of what has been said? Matters of logical consistency might be raised.
- Does the interviewer show evidence that they are steering the interview in ways which are relevant to the purpose of the research? That is, does the interviewer seem to have a firm grasp on what the research is about? For example, the interviewer may need to ensure that the interviewee does not digress too much from the topic of the interview.

Obviously, the more of the indicators met by the interviewer the better, in general, the interview will be.

the interviewer avoids demonstrating their feelings and emotions. However, these will remain as baggage after the interview is over. How are they best dealt with? One approach is for the interviewer to have a confidant with which he/she may work through the interview experience. This may be little other than just someone to talk to. Having 'buddies' who have experience of similar interviews or are currently involved in the same sort of interview has its advantages. These are not therapeutic sessions in any formal sense but involve social and emotional support where necessary. This said, such discussions are not necessarily emotionally heavy but may, instead, be emotionally relieving in other ways. For example, while outsiders might think that discussions of interviews with child molesters induce strong negative emotions, post-interview sessions of this sort may be riddled with laughter. This is common in any work group dealing with distressing situations.

- *Data protection and management*   Usually as part of the ethical considerations for qualitative research, plans are presented or requirements imposed about matters such as the safe storage of the interview recording and its eventual disposal. These should be followed at the appropriate time.
- *Data transcription*   Issues surrounding the transcription of recorded data and methods of transcription are discussed in Chapter 6.

How to analyse a qualitative interview

There are circumstances in which qualitative interviews conducted by, for example, therapists and counsellors can be regarded as 'natural' for the purposes of research. This is standard practice, for example, in conversation analysis. Numerous examples of qualitative researchers using interviews in this way exist. For example, the interviews conducted by police officers with suspects (e.g. Benneworth, 2006) and the interviews of therapists with their clients (e.g. Antaki, 2007). In these cases, the interviews were initially for professional purposes and their eventual research use secondary and even fortuitous. The ethics of using such resources in research needs to be considered (Chapter 15). Participants, for example, may not know or expect that the recordings would be used for research purposes. Is it appropriate, then, to use their data?

The choice of analysis methods for qualitative interview data is constrained by whether such data are natural conversation or not. If it can be regarded as natural conversation then qualitative analysis methods such as conversation analysis and discourse analysis are not ruled out. That is why therapeutic interviews are regarded as suitable for analysis – they are not produced for research purposes. Opinions seem to vary considerably on this issue of whether research interviews can be regarded as natural conversational data. One example of where research interviews have been used in this way is Rapley (2001). In this he raises the question of the role of the interviewer as a key player in the production of interview talk. The argument is that since interviews can be conceived of as being social interactions, then potentially they may be analysed in ways appropriate to any other social interactions. In Rapley's paper, he explains how both the interviewer and the interviewee construct themselves through talk as particular types of people. The local detail of the production of interview data within a particular interview is important in analysing interview data irrespective of the analytic method adopted, he argues. Whether one would wish to carry out research interviews solely for such analyses to take place is somewhat unlikely – Rapley uses published interviews to make his points, for instance. Furthermore, judging from the extracts he reports, these interviews were very conversational in nature since the contributions or turns of the interviewer and the interviewee were relatively short. It might be much more difficult to apply such an analysis to more typical qualitative interviewing.

This reflects the distinction that Seale (1998) makes between (a) using interview data as a research topic and (b) using interview data as a resource for obtaining information which has some bearing on the reality of the interviewee's life outside of the interview context. If one wishes to use research interviews as the object of study as Rapley (2001) does then this is a clear focus, but one which is very different from using the research interview as a means of gaining a perspective on the life and experiences of the interviewee. Although these constitute clear choices for the researcher, they are both appropriate methods of qualitative data analysis using research interview data. Box 3.2 describes an interview study in which a perspective very different from that of Rapley's is represented.

According to Potter (2003) among the disadvantages of the research interview for discourse analysis is that interviewees tend to take the role of theorists and experts since they are abstracted from the social context they normally inhabit. Furthermore, the relative value of an interview about a particular topic may be low compared with naturalistic talk if this can be obtained. One strategy that can be adopted is to base the interview on a more everyday conversation style in which the interviewer is a more active participant than in the more formal qualitative interview. Of course, this cannot be regarded as exactly the same as everyday conversation, though published excerpts from such studies tend to appear very conversational in nature.

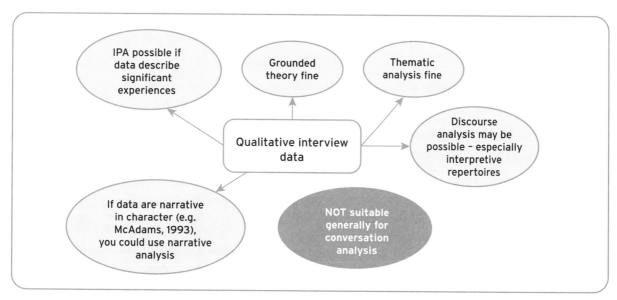

FIGURE 3.1 How to analyse qualitative interview data

Irrespective of all this, there are a number of analytic procedures which could be used, appropriately, in order to analyse the data from qualitative interviews (Figure 3.1):

- Grounded theory (Chapter 8) can be construed as a somewhat generic approach to qualitative data analysis which is not constrained by a particular interest in language in action, for example, unlike conversation analysis and certain forms of discourse analysis.

- Thematic analysis (Chapter 7) could be used since this merely seeks the dominant themes which underlie the content of the conversation.

- Interpretative phenomenological analysis (Chapter 11) might be an appropriate approach if the interviews concentrate on how individuals experience phenomena such as health matters.

- Narrative analysis might be appropriate if the interviews took a substantial life-history/narrative form. However, some narrative analysts prefer to construct their qualitative interviews following McAdams's (1993) scheme and those of others (see Chapter 12).

Finally, in some circumstances a formal method of data analysis may not be necessary. This is most clearly the case where the researcher is using interviews as a way of obtaining basic knowledge and understanding before planning, say, a more focused research study.

When to use qualitative interviews

Qualitative interviewing is a potential data collection method for a range of styles of qualitative research. It is probably least useful to the researcher whose primary objective is the study of naturally occurring conversation. Despite numerous advantages, there is no sense in which the research interview can be construed as naturally occurring conversation though it may share some features with it. We have seen that it is important to distinguish between the research interview and other forms of interviews by professionals and their clients which are commonplace. The job selection interview, interviews between doctors and patients and police interviews can be conceived as naturally occurring conversation and, as such, analysed using methods designed for application to everyday conversations. Against the general rule, narrative analysis (Chapter 12) tends to use McAdams's (1993) approach to qualitative interviews. However, this does not prevent the use of any other form of qualitative interview for narrative analysis if it elicits appropriate narrative material from the interviewee.

A researcher's position in the realism–relativism debate also has a bearing on appropriate methods of data analysis. Researchers who adopt, say, a realist approach may find in the qualitative interview content which provides them with a viable perspective on a person's life. That is, if the researcher accepts that what people say maps onto social reality though, perhaps, not with complete fidelity then the qualitative interview can provide narrative information which contributes substantially to a particular field of research. At the same time, it is obvious that the qualitative interview sheds no light into how groups of individuals talk together about a particular topic. Focus groups (Chapter 4), because of their interactive nature, are much better at doing this.

Careful thought must go into the decision to prefer to use qualitative interviews in a particular study. While, in some cases, it is difficult to conceive of any other method, there are frequently alternatives to be debated. There is no question that such interviews are expensive in terms of time and resources. Consequently, they may be out of the question if, for whatever reason, the researcher needs a large sample. Now large samples are not typical of qualitative research, anyway, since the purpose of qualitative research is interpretation and not estimates of population characteristics. So the need for a large sample should set warning bells ringing questioning the status of the research as qualitative research. Of course, the general question of whether the research is truly qualitative in nature should always be asked. For example, if a relatively simple research question is involved then a quantitative approach might be more appropriate given that structured questionnaires are cost minimal compared with qualitative interviews. This may appear to be a little patronising but experience indicates that sometimes student researchers, especially, reject a quantitative approach simply because they wish to avoid the problems associated with using statistics. However, if their research question is one which implies quantification or is expressed in quantitative terms, then a detour through qualitative methods is not only wasteful but it is also unproductive. So once the research question has been clarified (usually it helps to write this down) then its position on the quantitative–qualitative dimension needs to be assessed. As a simple example, how many women have depression after childbirth is clearly a quantitative question but how do women experience depression after childbirth is most probably qualitative.

The qualitative interview can take a variety of forms, of course. Normally, we think of it as a one-on-one, face-to-face situation in which there is an interviewer and an interviewee. But this is far from the only possibility. There may be two or more interviewers and two or more interviewees. These have their own dynamics and their own requirements in terms of ethics (see Chapter 15) among other things. The reasons for these variations are numerous. For example, an interview at home with a sex offender may require more than one interviewer for safety reasons. A researcher may arrive at someone's home expecting to interview one person but the entire family wants to be involved. Furthermore, the face-to-face situation may be replaced with telephone interviews or lengthy exchanges over the Internet. These, for some research, may have advantages though their impersonal nature may impact on the research in a variety of ways.

Evaluation of qualitative interviewing

The ideal circumstances in which to use a qualitative interview are where the experiences, thoughts, life histories and feelings of an individual (as opposed to individuals as part of a group) are the researcher's primary focus. The interview may, of course, be part of a series of interviews with different people allowing for comparisons between different participants or different types of participants. The qualitative interview might be regarded as one of the archetypal data collection methods in qualitative research in general. Nevertheless, the qualitative interview is not always the preferred source of qualitative data for all qualitative analyses. So, although the qualitative interview would be the data collection method of preference for interpretative phenomenological analysis because of its capacity to provide detailed accounts of experiences, it would not normally be the preferred method for conversation analysis given that research interviews are not the ordinary conversations of ordinary people. There is no set way of analysing the qualitative interview, which makes a simple evaluation of such interviews impossible and one is almost always faced with a choice of qualitative analysis methods. The method chosen will depend partly on what research questions the researcher is addressing. Of course, the actual quality of the interview is determined by rather different factors from the ones which determine that it is relevant and appropriate for a particular research study. The qualitative interview requires careful preparation if it is to achieve its full potential as a way of collecting pertinent data.

The following may be helpful in putting the method into context:

● The apparent subjectivity of the qualitative interview is not a particular problem in qualitative research terms – indeed it is an advantage. The ethos of quantitative research may be to seek to capture an objective reality but this is not the case for qualitative research. The qualitative researcher may, instead, wish to explore the different viewpoints of participants in the research or the ways in which participants talk about the research topic. Subjectivity issues, of course, do arise where the researcher seeks to regard interview data as representing reality rather than different viewpoints on reality. In a sentence, ultimately interviews are about what the participants say about what they think and do rather than about what they actually think and do. Participant observation/ethnography (Chapter 5) might be more appropriate where it is important to document what people do rather than what they say about what they do.

- The qualitative interview has advantages over focus groups (Chapter 4) in that it allows the researcher substantial control over the data collected. In contrast, the focus group hands even more control to the group under the researcher's guidance. A group of individuals may develop an agenda for discussion which is quite distinct from those of the individual members. This does not make it invalid, it merely is different. Focus group researchers have far less time to devote to the individual than do individual interviews. But, then, the focus group is not intended to serve the same purpose as the individual qualitative interview.

- Like most other qualitative data collection methods, the qualitative interview is extremely flexible and is not necessarily constrained by a conventional structure. For example, the researcher might wish to use family photographs and get the participant to talk about these as part of a study of families.

- In qualitative research, qualitative interviews may be combined with other data collection methods. An obvious example of this is their use in the context of ethnographic or participant observation approaches (Chapter 5).

- The qualitative interview can be used in a variety of ways in relation to research. For instance, many researchers have used the interview as part of a preliminary, exploratory, stage for their research especially when the topic is a relatively new one and the researcher cannot rely on the inspiration of the previous research literature on which to build their ideas. Quite simply, there may be a lack of knowledge on a particular topic and the obvious initial stage of research would be to talk to those people who may have experiences, thoughts and ideas which are relevant to the research topic. Out of these interviews, the researcher hopes to generate ideas for research which are grounded in people's experiences.

- However, it is wrong to think of the qualitative interview as merely an idea-generating technique. It may be useful used in this way but this use tends to undermine the qualitative interview since it implies that there are better methods of doing the 'real' research. The qualitative interview can provide data which is, in itself, sufficient for the purposes of the research.

- The resource-intensive nature of qualitative interviewing should always be a consideration. This, in the end, may lead to the view that the qualitative interview is the only practicable choice to achieve the researcher's aims. On the other hand, the researcher should question why it is that they need to use the qualitative interview. What is it about the research question which cannot be addressed in different ways? Indeed, has the researcher done sufficient preparatory work (e.g. the literature review) to be sure that the research question could not be addressed in other ways more effectively?

- There are many circumstances in which there are no feasible alternative ways of data collection. For example, it is not possible to do observation-based studies of contraception use.

CONCLUSION

The qualitative interview has enormous attractions as a qualitative data collection method. Indeed, it is difficult to imagine research questions which could not be, in part, informed by interviews with relevant participants. A great deal of research would benefit from giving a 'voice' to the participants in the research. The qualitative interview is an excellent way of doing this. As a stand-alone data collection method it has few challengers. Properly carried out, it supplies rich data that other methods can only serve to supplement. Nevertheless, the limitations of qualitative interviewing especially in terms of the heavy drain on resources are important. Furthermore, the practicalities of research ensure that most interviews are carried out on a one-to-one basis.

The qualitative interview is an archetypal approach to data collection both in qualitative research and research in general. For the qualitative researcher, though, it may not be appropriate for every research purpose. For example, it is a somewhat 'unnatural' form of conversation and, consequently, may not be ideal when the researcher wishes to study natural, real-life conversation. Like all data collection methods, its value depends on how precisely it maps to the researcher's purpose.

This chapter has stressed that qualitative interviewing is quite a sophisticated research skill despite its apparently, but superficially, conversational nature. Doing a good qualitative interview draws on all aspects of a researcher's skills – including analytic and theoretical ones. Of course, there are everyday conversational skills which are helpful in developing good qualitative interviewing ability – for example, they may help develop a good rapport. Nevertheless, the qualitative interviewer is carrying out a particular sort of performance which is different from those normally involved in being a good conversationalist. For example, the listening skills of the researcher are essential to a good interview as is their ability to remember what has been said so far in the interview. Normal conversation may be effective without this. A transcript of an interview is very one-sided compared with everyday conversation – typically the researcher says little at most stages of an interview and the interviewee appears to be contributing disproportionately.

KEY POINTS

- The qualitative interview in its various forms is the bedrock of qualitative research. It supplies a means of gathering extensive and detailed data on virtually any topic. Of course, the focus group is a variant of this. Nevertheless, it does not always supply appropriate data for every research purpose and so is the data collection method of choice for only some qualitative research.

- A researcher planning to use qualitative interviews needs to appreciate that they involve a planning/preparatory stage, the interview itself and post-interview considerations. A researcher who fails to plan properly for the interview may waste their time in any number of ways. For example, the interviewee may fail to make the appointment, the researcher may badly structure the interview and dominate the exchanges through lack of planning, or the interview is inaudible on the recording and so cannot be used. These are just some of the possible problems.

- A distinction should be made between the quality of an interview and its suitability for particular research purposes. Ideally, the researcher should be technically proficient in interviewing but also clear in terms of the overall strategy of the research.

- There is potential to analyse qualitative interview data using a variety of different analysis methods. Of course, it is better where the researcher matches the content of the interview to the requirements of the method. Each of the different methods of analysis will provide a different form of analysis according to the theoretical basis of the method.

ADDITIONAL RESOURCES

Arksey, H., and Knight, P.T. (1999). *Interviewing for Social Scientists: An introductory resource with examples*. London: Sage.

Busher, H., and James, N. (2009). *Online Interviewing*. London: Sage.

Fontana, A., and Frey, J.H. (2000). The interview: from structured questions to negotiated text. In N.K. Denzin and Y.S. Lincoln (Eds.), *Handbook of Qualitative Research*, 2nd Edition. Thousand Oaks, CA: Sage Publications, pp. 645–672.

Kvale, S. (1996). *Interviews*. Thousand Oaks, CA: Sage.

Kvale, S. (2007). *Doing Interviews*. Los Angeles, CA: Sage.

Opdenakker, R. (2006). Advantages and disadvantages of four interview techniques in qualitative research. *Forum Qualitative Social Research*, 7 (4), Article 11. http://www.qualitative-research.net/index.php/fqs/article/viewArticle/175/391 (accessed 13 August 2009).

TRQMUL (n.d.). Data Set Teaching Resources Files. http://www.psychology.heacademy.ac.uk/Webdocs_not_nof/tqrmul/dataset/ (accessed 17 August 2009). This is a very useful resource containing a number of video interviews together with Jefferson and playscript transcriptions.

Truesdell, B. (n.d.). Oral History Techniques: How to organize and conduct oral history interviews. http://www.indiana.edu/~cshm/oral_history_techniques.pdf (accessed 13 August 2009).

CHAPTER 4

Focus groups

Overview

- A focus group is a sort of collective interview, directed by the researcher (moderator), which exploits the interactive potential of the situation in order to generate rich data.

- There is no single use for focus groups since they can be used as a preliminary exploration of a topic for the guidance of the research or a way of evaluating a project when it is completed, for example.

- Although currently a somewhat ubiquitous data-gathering approach, its origins were in the work of Robert Merton on the focused interview in the 1940s. The approach was fairly rapidly adopted by market researchers but relatively ignored by academic researchers until the 1970s and afterwards when it became increasingly accepted in academic research.

- Focus groups basically consist of a moderator plus six to ten group members. It is usual to have about four separate focus groups for every category of group being studied.

- The planning stage is crucial if the best quality data are to be obtained. In particular, a plan needs to be drawn up specifying the sorts of participants that each group should contain. Groups should be chosen with the quality of discussion in mind. For example, one should avoid groups in which status differentials might encourage some members to defer to their formal superiors. Planning can also include decisions about what sorts of people would provide the richest data on the topic in question.

- Focus groups have a structure and unfold in an orderly questioning sequence in order to facilitate the quality of the discussion.

- Moderators (group leaders) need to be socially skilled in order to ensure that the focus groups are not dominated by a few individuals.

- The analysis of focus group data is a matter of choice but several qualitative data analysis methods can be used. It has recently been proposed that the discussions of focus groups can be analysed using discourse analysis approaches.

What are focus groups?

Like many other qualitative data collection methods, it is difficult to say precisely what a focus group is. Gibbs (1997) summarises the variety of available definitions by identifying what appear to be the key features of a focus group. These, she suggests, are:

- organised discussion;
- collective activity;
- social events;
- interaction.

From these, it is clear that a focus group involves interaction. But so do other research methodologies. So, for example, how does a focus group differ from a normal interview? Well, a focus group does involve a researcher asking questions – though the interviewer is called a 'moderator' in focus group research. There can be more than one moderator – one an expert in focus group methodology and the other an expert in the subject matter of the research, for instance. However, a focus group involves not a single interviewee but typically six to ten 'members' (the recommended range varies). But even these two features do not fully define a focus group since the key to focus groups is the opportunities for interaction between members of the group when responding to the questions posed by the moderator. This dynamic interaction between people in the focus group is the remaining major distinctive feature of focus groups though could be claimed to characterise participant observation and ethnography too. So, obviously, focus groups have some of the elements of an interview – that is, the researcher guides the discussion by posing questions. Nevertheless, it would be incorrect to describe focus groups as multi-respondent interviews because this fails to recognise the centrality of group interaction in focus groups. Furthermore, it cannot be described as a group discussion because the focus group discussion is planned, steered and controlled by the group moderator rather than members of the group.

Figure 4.1 illustrates this schematically. In the interview, the interviewer has the strongest control on events with, normally, the interviewee being less influential. Typically in a focus group, the moderator has considerable control but this is impacted by the relatively greater influence of the group and the interaction between group members. The point of a focus group is to take advantage of the interaction between group members which may produce information different in certain respects from that produced by a separate interview with each group member. Considerable effort is taken when planning a focus group study to optimise the contribution of these group dynamics. This is why, for example, the size of a focus group is usually stipulated to be in the six to ten range. This is not so big that members feel swamped by the number of other people trying to have their say and not so small that the group dynamic fails to generate good discussion. Similarly, focus groups try to avoid other features which might adversely affect interaction. So, for example, the members of any particular focus group are chosen so that they are similar in status. Sitting in a focus group with, say, your line manager and the top boss would not only inhibit most of us from participating but would also influence what we have to say. This is one reason why members of focus groups are often (but not always) chosen because they are strangers and unlikely to be in contact with

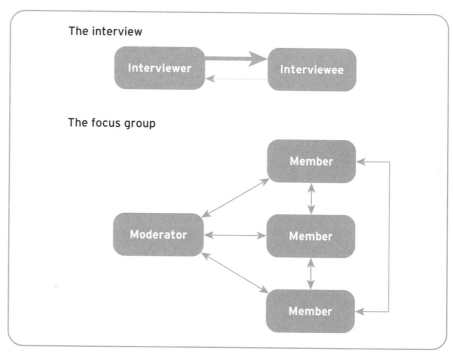

FIGURE 4.1 Relationships in interviews and focus groups

each other in the future. Just a caution – focus group practice is extremely varied and there are always exceptions to every rule, seemingly. The advice given in this chapter does not constitute a set of rules but some rules of thumb plus a little insight which will help you plan a focus group.

So focus groups have their dynamic quality as a defining feature. It should be pointed out that other data-gathering methods have their own dynamics. However, the focus group relies on the self-stimulating power of the group to generate data which might not be available through other means. It has to be remembered that focus groups generate data which are partly a product of the focus group dynamic. Consequently it may be a mistake to think that what is said in a focus group reflects motivating factors in other situations. This ability to generate ideas through discussion is one of the advantages of the focus group method promoted by its advocates. In effect, the members of the focus group are given the task of making sense of the issue. This is achieved through group dynamics – that is, through the relatively normal processes of discussion and debate among ordinary people. This is very hard to emulate using conventional interviewing techniques with a single interviewee.

Focus groups may be used in at least three different ways:

- As an early stage of research in order to explore and identify what the significant issues are.

- To generate broadly conversational data on a topic to be analysed in its own right.

- To evaluate the findings of research in the eyes of the people that the research is about. That is, in discussions of research conclusions.

For the researcher, the focus group has other advantages; that is, most of the resources come from the participants. The researcher generally 'facilitates' the group processes in order to ensure that a pre-planned range of issues is covered but, at the same time, allowing unexpected material to enter the discussion. So, ideally, the researcher does not dominate the proceedings. If necessary, the researcher steers the discussion along more productive lines if the group seems to be 'running out of steam'. For this reason, the researcher running the focus group is known as the moderator or the facilitator.

It is probably misleading, if not wrong, to regard focus groups as an alternative to ordinary interviews. They simply are not the same thing and cannot meet the same functions. In much the same way, it is clear that focus groups do not aspire to the same representative sampling that surveys do. Indeed focus group methodology adopts a radically different approach to participant selection and recruitment. The focus group method needs to be understood in its own right and not regarded as a 'cheap and cheerful' substitute for 'better' ways of conducting research.

The development of focus groups

Many of the early developments in social psychology (and the social sciences in general) were the consequence of considerable research interest in the new mass media of radio, cinema and eventually television in the 1920s, 1930s and 1940s. More than any other research at the time, research into the mass media demanded approaches which were grounded in social reality and, consequently, research methods capable of tapping into real life. The funding of the research was often from commercial organisations – not the usual source of academic funding (Morrison, 1998). Paul Lazarsfeld (1901–1976) and Robert Merton (1910–2003) were two major figures in this field who made significant methodological innovations in a number of areas. For example, the panel study was developed to study how voting intentions changed during the course of an American election campaign. This needed samples of people to be assessed at several different stages in the election campaign. In other words, the panel study was developed to study the effects of the election campaign.

Much the same sort of background was responsible for the development of focus group methodology. It had become clear from research in the early part of the twentieth century that the mass media were not as powerful at changing the behaviour and attitudes of the audience as many had feared. Out of this realisation came a new emphasis in mass media research, known as 'uses and gratifications', which stressed the importance of understanding how the audience made use of the media and what, psychologically and sociologically, the media provided. This clearly demanded new research methods. Even more pressing was the Second World War and its need to mobilise all resources including social sciences research. Merton developed the focused interview (the focus group) as a method of understanding audience responses to wartime propaganda (Merton and Kendall, 1946). Merton and others:

> . . . were assigned by several war agencies to study the social and psychological effects of specific efforts to build morale (Merton, Fiske & Kendall, 1956, p. 5).

In these early days, the members of the focus group often 'focused' on pamphlets, radio programmes, films and the like. In other words, the early focus group was more than a guided group discussion and had specific materials to focus on. Certainly it is the general consensus that Robert Merton was the direct originator of the focus group. It has to be said that others had previously carried out group interviews, notably Emory Bogardus (1882–1973) (Bogardus, 1926) but these were dominated by the researcher posing questions to individuals in the group – that is, the key dynamic aspect of the focus group was missing. While Merton was to argue that the focus group was in some ways different from the focused interview (Merton, 1987), there is sufficient overlap for the focused interview to be generally regarded as the precursor of the focus group. Among Merton's complaints was that the modern use of focus groups is in the absence of related quantitative studies. Reading early accounts of the method (Merton *et al.*, 1956), it is clear how early some features of the focus group were established as issues. For example, the optimum size of a group was held to be about 10 to 12 people (which is slightly higher than the modern recommended range), homogeneity (similarity) of group membership was considered important to ensuring a good group dynamic, and attention was paid to the spatial arrangements whereby classroom-style seating was replaced by a circular pattern. Of course, modern focus group practice sometimes ignores these basic requirements – especially homogeneity.

So in the academic field of mass communications research, the divide between the commercial interests of market researchers and the academic interests of university people was blurred. Some academics such as Paul Lazarsfeld would cross-fund their academic work by taking on market research projects with little academic potential. It was in advertising and marketing that the focus group first took a fresh hold. Academic researchers were slow to adopt it. According to Morrison (1998), following the early promise of focus groups in the 1940s, focus groups were 'lost sight of' by academic researchers until the 1970s when they were rediscovered as an 'exploratory tool' and eventually gained respectability in the 1980s – and this process of adoption occurred later in psychology. So for the three decades from 1950 onwards, focus groups were largely in the domain of the market researchers. Academics were keener to use large sample surveys to collect data on public opinion and the focus group is the antithesis of these. In the minds of academics, focus groups were 'tainted' by their association with commercial interests – and commerce was anathema and a distortion of academic values to them. The term focus group only begins to make the occasional appearance in the psychological databases in the 1970s and then in connection with marketing-focused research. Calder (1977), whose background is in social psychology, discusses focus groups with reference to qualitative marketing research. As if to illustrate the gradual emergence of focus groups out of marketing, Festervand (1984–85) discussed the potential application of focus group research to the healthcare services. Suddenly interest in focus groups grew markedly in psychology in the 1990s over a range of psychological research areas. Now the method is common, with scores of studies using the method in psychology being published every year. Puchta and Potter (2004) point out the focus group research of Lunt and Livingstone (1996) as being among the earliest in psychology. In this, Lunt and Livingstone examine how the audience understands political messages – thus essentially bringing focus groups back firmly to their origins in mass communication research.

Ultimately, like some other methods in the social sciences, focus groups are now highly familiar to members of the public. We are all well aware of their ubiquity in modern politics, for example their use by modern political parties. There are claims that it is the most commonly used research methodology on Earth. Such familiarity should not, however, lead to the view that focus groups are easy data-gathering methods or that they can be conducted with very little training or skill. Like other qualitative methods, focus groups may appear easy but this is illusory. Of course, it takes little effort to gather together a group of people to discuss a topic but it is another thing to ensure that the best quality, focused discussion results.

How to conduct focus groups

One could typify the focus group as a group interview with about six to ten similar people, conducted by a skilled moderator, and lasting up to about one and a half to two hours. The focus group is dynamic in the sense that the moderator encourages interaction between participants but controls the situation so that all participants get an opportunity to contribute. A lot of hard work goes into the planning, organisation and analysis of focus groups in order to produce good quality data. For example, the size of a focus group – usually, but not invariably, between six and ten people – is important. As has been mentioned, the consequence of having too many group members is that it is harder to get a turn at speaking and some may not like speaking to a large group of people. If there are too few members in a group then the focus group may lack stimulation, thus stultifying proceedings.

The work of the researcher can be divided into a number of components:

- planning;
- recruitment of participants;
- running the focus group;
- analysis of the focus group data.

One must appreciate that focus group methodology has no single purpose and that focus groups can be used for several, quite distinct purposes. According to Calder (1977), there are three different approaches to the use of focus groups:

- The *exploratory*   This describes attempts to generate information and know-ledge in a field which has previously been largely under-researched. So it is a trawling approach which seeks basic knowledge and ideas in a new field.
- The *clinical*   This describes attempts to understand why people do what they do which are accessible to a trained analyst or expert.
- The *phenomenological*   This is the use of focus groups by researchers to understand things from the point of view of other groups in society. The researcher will learn how different sorts of people feel about something.

This list is, perhaps, less than complete since the focus group can be used for purposes which are not listed. So the trialling of new consumer products in focus groups in order to consider improvements prior to production would, at best, only loosely fit into the first category. But we can see something of the flexibility of the focus group in Calder's scheme.

FIGURE 4.2 **The steps in a focus group study**

Although it is usual to speak of focus group methodology, it would be only in exceptional cases that a researcher conducts just one focus group. Normally, the researcher plans to compare several focus groups on a topic using different categories of members for different focus groups. However, advice on how to conduct a focus group can vary. The following summarises the broad strategy (Figure 4.2):

Step 1   **Planning the study**   The origins of a study may be at the initiative of the researcher or may be instigated by other people such as organisations commissioning research. In either case, it is important to develop a (shared) understanding of what the study is about. So there should be clarity about the following (according to Krueger & Casey, 2000):

- The research problem that the study will attempt to illuminate.
- The factors which led to the study being commissioned. Often, for student work, these factors will be a class exercise, a dissertation or research project as part of one's degree, or similar. Each of these will place different demands on the study planned.
- The specific purpose of the study.
- The types of information which it is hoped the study will obtain.
- What types of information are the priority for the data collection.
- The person or persons who want the information that the study will collect.
- What will be done with the information.

Each of these is relevant to the planning of the research in detail. Of course, some may seem irrelevant to student research. But that may be illusory. For a student, their supervisor is an important 'client'. Has a clear understanding been reached between you and your supervisor on these matters? Even if there is no obvious 'client' for your research, can you address these questions?

Also remember to have an appropriate degree of humility as a researcher and do not be afraid to seek the help and advice of other people. The job of the researcher is to find out, not to know. So you may wish to talk over issues to do with the research with key informants.

→   **Step 2**   Optimising the choice of group participants   Just what are the important characteristics of the participants in your focus groups? This is a matter not of defining sampling characteristics but of maximising the richness of the data. What sorts of participants will yield the most satisfactory information relevant to your research question? These, of course, may not be the most readily available potential participants since we are not talking 'convenience sampling' here but purposive sampling aimed at optimising data quality and relevance. A good example of this is the customers who send for a holiday brochure but never purchase any of the holidays. This would be a particularly good group of participants for a focus group study trying to understand the factors which are influential on holiday purchases. One approach is to provide such non-buyers with a free holiday with the only cost being taking part in a focus group for a couple of hours.

Of course, without having details of a proposed study it is difficult to suggest groups of potentially data-rich participants. The only rule-of-thumb would be that there is likely to be a variety of particularly significant types of group members and that the more effort put into their inclusion the better.

One consequence of such a strategy is that people in the optimum categories are likely to be at a premium since they have particular characteristics. So it is important to do as much as possible to ensure that those approached actually turn up to the focus group:

- Ask yourself why people would be prepared to take part in your study. What is the best way of making your request to ensure that they will take part? What are the gains for them as individuals or as members of society?

- Consider appropriate inducements though in the light of ethical considerations (see Chapter 15).

- Contact potential group members at least two weeks before the intended date of the focus group. This gives them time to plan their attendance by putting it in their diary and rescheduling their activities if necessary. The closer to the day of the focus group the more likely that you find that participants have other things scheduled.

- Follow up an agreement to participate with a 'courtesy' thank you letter.

- Remember to give participants a 'courtesy' telephone call on the day of the group meeting (or the day before perhaps) to check whether any problems have arisen. The main point of this is as a reminder.

- Consider the convenience of your study for potential participants rather than yourself. Make it easy for people to take part. There is little point in scheduling your focus groups at times which make it difficult for your ideal participants to attend because, say, they have to be at work. Similarly, where would it be most convenient to hold the focus groups from the point of view of the participants? They may be deterred by lengthy journeys to the research site and so forth.

- Choose the best person to make the invitations. Although it may feel natural that the researcher should invite people to participate, there are circumstances in which someone else might do a better job at recruitment. Personal contacts are often the most effective. So if you can persuade the organiser of a cancer support group to help you, they may be more successful in persuading people than you would be. For one reason, they help establish your bona fides as a researcher.

→

→ You will also need to put thought into the question of how you are going to recruit people with the characteristics you desire in your study. So you may wish to consider the following possibilities:

- Are there any key individuals who may have access to the sorts of people that you need? For example, if you wish to study people who have survived cancer are there organisations to support cancer survivors?
- Can the organisation commissioning the research help provide access to suitable groups of participants?
- Would it be possible to contact a few suitable group members and then ask them to nominate others similar to themselves – as in snowball sampling?

Focus groups do not include representative samples and the choice of participants is largely to optimise the productivity of the discussion. At best participants in a focus group typify the sort of person with the characteristics specified by the researcher. If a variety of different sorts of participant is selected for a particular focus group, they should be chosen in a way which would be expected to maximise the productivity of the group discussion – some mixes of participants could inhibit discussion or make the focus group unmanageable. Of course, experience in running focus groups will lead to better and more refined judgements about group membership.

Finally, in this step, you need to think carefully about what you tell your recruits concerning the focus group before the group meets. Gibbs (1997) offers the following practical advice. Only provide focus group members with sufficient detail to allow them to decide whether or not to participate. They should not be given any indications of the questions that will be asked in advance of the meeting otherwise they may work out their own views which may be fixed and not responsive to group processes at the meeting.

Step 3   **Optimising the group structures**   The point of a focus group lies in the directed discussion produced by the focus group members. It follows from this that a focus group should involve all of the group members reasonably equally. If one or two members dominate the focus group then this defeats the purpose. Although it is the responsibility of the moderator to prevent individuals from dominating the proceedings, problems may be built into a focus group if the choice of members was not optimal. In particular, it is generally the case that a focus group with similar people of equivalent status is conducive to quality data in focus group research. On the other hand, a focus group consisting of people of different social statuses or superiors and subordinates have a built-in imbalance which may result in some people dominating the group. The moderator can limit this to a certain extent by inviting individuals to talk in various ways or limiting the length of contributions to a minute or two. However, groups whose dynamics are likely to inhibit some members from full participation are to be avoided. As already hinted, two obvious factors can contribute to this:

- If the group is too homogeneous so that everyone shares much the same perspective on the subject matter then discussion is likely to be curtailed. For that reason, it is sometimes suggested that focus groups should be heterogeneous in terms of their membership, though there are limits to this.
- If the group contains people of an apparently superior status then the group may defer to them. This may simply be that certain group members appear to be more knowledgeable than the others who 'defer' to their superior knowledge.

→

→   Ultimately, experience is the basis for anticipating such problems. A focus group which fails to generate discussion warrants careful attention in order to assess why this was the case. Plans may have to be revised.

It is not a part of focus group methodology to simply use a single focus group. No matter how productive a single group may be in terms of ideas and interesting responses, the researcher needs to plan to run several different groups. At a minimum, three or four groups should be run when there is no attempt to use a variety of different categories of groups. Krueger and Casey (2000) refer to this as a single-category design. It is the simplest structure for focus group research. In addition to single-category designs, they list the following designs:

- *Multiple-category design*   This is where the focus groups are organised into several particular types of respondents. For example, in a study of the experience of cancer the multiple-categories might be (a) cancer patients, (b) cancer survivors and (c) carers of cancer patients.

- *Double-layered design*   This is where the groups employed are distinguishable on two dimensions. These dimensions might be age (young and old) and cancer sufferer versus cancer survivor. This would give us four groups: (1) young cancer sufferers, (2) old cancer sufferers, (3) young cancer survivors and (4) old cancer survivors. The researcher would probably study three or four groups in each of these four categories.

- *Broad-involvement design*   This acknowledges that there are some areas of research in which a broad range of groups might feel they have a relevant voice. As a consequence, a spread of groups are identified to represent this range of interest groups. For example, the researcher may be studying neighbour disputes. Groups which might have an interest in taking part in focus groups might include: (a) mediators employed by local authorities, (b) the police, (c) people with difficult neighbours, (c) neighbours who have been taken to court by the authorities, (d) officers of the local authority and (e) the police. Of course, by including such a wide range of groups, the research adopts a broader perspective which, in some circumstances, may be beneficial.

Step 4   **Planning how many focus groups**   Although one rule of thumb would be to have three or four groups for every category of group studied, this is not a definitive statement of numbers of groups. There are problems in stipulating the number of focus groups to run even with some knowledge about the purpose of the study in question. The 'saturation' criterion might be appropriate. This suggests that the researcher collects data until it appears that no new things are emerging out of the study. It could be argued that this is a subjective criterion. Nevertheless, it is one which is of some practical value within the ethos of qualitative research. It is a concept from grounded theory (see Chapter 8).

Step 5   **Planning what questions to ask and when**   It is generally accepted that relatively few questions are required for a focus group compared with the equivalent structured interview. A researcher who finds that they have to ask a great many questions to keep the discussion going might suspect that the focus group is not going particularly well. Possibly it implies that the group dynamic is just not working or, equally, it could be a sign that the questions are in some way faulty.

→

→   There are two main issues with questions for focus groups: (1) 'what are the characteristics of a good question?' and (2) 'ideally how should questions be organised or sequenced during the course of the focus group?' The first is the easiest to address. A good question is posed in a way which communicates well and avoids causing confusion – so the basic question-framing skills that you may have from in-depth interviewing would be appropriate here. Among other things, the questions should be phrased in a style suitable for a conversation rather than writing-down. The acid test is whether the question slips off the tongue readily without clumsiness, errors or stumbling over one's words. The questions should be pitched at a level using appropriate language for the sorts of people participating in your focus group; long questions are to be avoided as should complex ones (i.e. compound questions). Complex questions really contain more than one question. This can be inadvertently the outcome of using two words instead of one. So asking whether the participants had found the focus group 'interesting and useful' is really to ask two separate questions and the hearer may be confused as to how to answer the question. They may have found the group interesting but not very useful. As a consequence, they may find it hard to answer a question which the researcher believes to be simple and straightforward.

The sequencing of questions is not so easily dealt with. Krueger and Casey (2000) present a model of the sequencing of questions for focus groups which can be summarised as shown in Figure 4.3. It is a useful way of illustrating the flow of a focus group session. Without appropriate sequencing of questions, the focus group can become problematic. According to Krueger and Casey, the sequence consists of (1) opening questions, (2) introductory questions, (3) transition questions, (4) key questions and (5) ending questions. Jump in too soon with a key question, for example, and the participants may be inhibited by the complexity of giving an adequate response. Shy group members will not have been eased into the group dynamic and the focus group may fail to provide the quality of evidence that the researcher is seeking. The flow of the questions in Figure 4.3 can readily be seen as facilitating group processes. There are other helpful sequencing rules which can be incorporated. Krueger and Casey argue that (a) general questions should come before specific questions; (b) questions asking about positive features of something should precede questions soliciting the negative aspects; and (c) uncued questions should precede cued questions – that is, one would ask the group about their experiences of hospital before asking for their experiences of specific aspects of the hospital such as food, information, medical care and so forth. This describes one version of the process of funnelling questions.

Step 6   **Things that the moderator does**   There are a number of characteristics which researchers see as important in a moderator (Gibbs, 1997):

- avoids expressing personal opinions;
- avoids appearing judgemental.

The moderator is responsible for the efficient and successful running of each focus group whether or not they are the main investigator. It is clearly a skilled and complex role which places considerable demands on the moderator in terms of interpersonal skills but also the discipline of remaining essentially detached from the discussion. Moderators, for example, do not involve themselves in the debates. Among the many tasks of the focus group moderator are the following

→

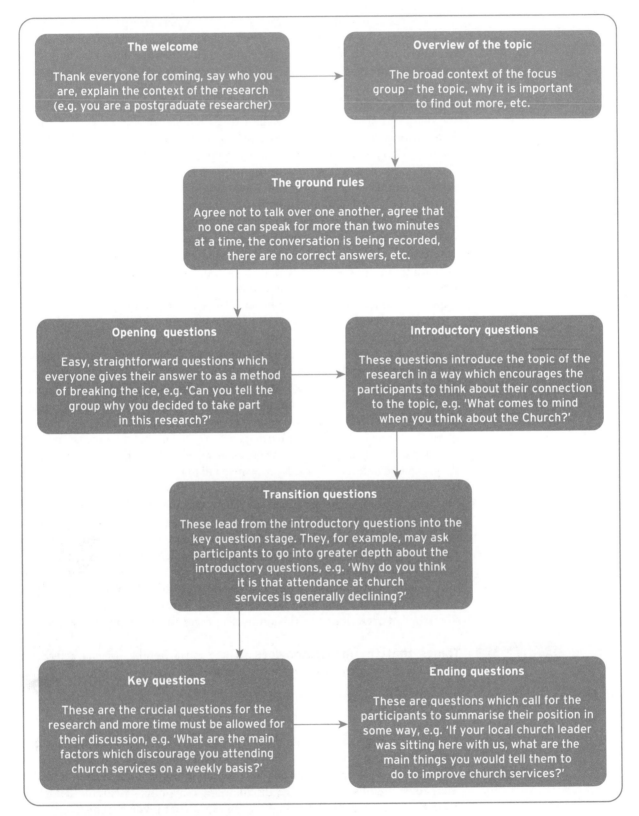

FIGURE 4.3 The flow of a focus group

→ (Gibbs, 1997), though it should be appreciated that things vary more in practice. For example, there are circumstances in which the moderator allows much freer debate and does little steering (Flick, 2002). This would depend very much on the purpose of the research. The moderator's tasks include:

- At the start of the meeting, describing and explaining the purpose and objectives of the session.
- Ensuring that members of the focus group feel relaxed and comfortable in the situation and feel, ultimately, that this was a positive experience.
- Posing clear questions for discussion.
- Controlling the discussion by asking supplementary questions designed to open up the debate or to encourage the participants to focus more precisely on the issues which are fundamental to the research.
- Ensuring that all members of the group participate and preventing the dominance of a small number of individuals. There are various ways to achieve this, including targeting some individuals with questions aimed at encouraging them to participate.
- Highlighting differences in perspectives which emerge in the focus group discussion in order that the group might engage with the nature of the differences.
- Stopping conversational drifts which steer the conversation away from the topic of the focus group.
- The moderator is responsible for recording the focus group session (either just the conversation or video) but it is usually the case that the moderator also takes notes during the course of the session.
- In circumstances where the moderator has an assistant then that assistant might take much more comprehensive notes than the moderator is in a position to, take responsibility for recording the session, and deal with logistic issues such as refreshments. The assistant can be involved more actively such as asking supplementary questions (Krueger & Casey, 2000).

Boxes 4.1 and 4.2 describe studies relying on focus groups for the collection of data.

Box 4.1

ILLUSTRATIVE RESEARCH STUDY

The experience of womanhood

How do Black women and White women perceive womanhood? What are the similarities and what are the differences? Settles, Pratt-Hyatt and Buchanan (2008) expected that, on the basis of the existing research literature, both to be concerned about their roles as (a) mothers, (b) partners and (c) workers. The groups were likely to differ in terms of (d) the amount of role

→

flexibility they had in terms of managing work-family responsibilities, (e) the types of sexism and sexual harassment they experienced and (f) the sexual mistreatment they report may differ along the lines of different stereotypes of the groups. According to the researchers, 'there is little or no empirical research that focuses simultaneously on Black and White women's thoughts and feelings about their experiences as women and how those perceptions shape their sense of self and the world' (p. 456). This led them to the view that the best way to examine their research question was to use qualitative focus groups in which women were encouraged to discuss their 'lived experiences' rather than adopt a methodology which essentially imposed the researchers' preconceptions onto the research and data collection.

The researchers used a total of 14 Black women and 17 White women as participants of one or other of the six focus groups that they ran. For four of the focus groups, newspaper advertisements and flyers were used to recruit the participants together with suggestions about other possible participants from the women (i.e. snowball sampling). For the remaining two focus groups, the participants were recruited from the 'subject pool' of psychology under-graduates at an American university. For what it is worth, there were no significant differences between the Black and White groups of participants in terms of socio-demographic factors such as age (which spread from 18 years to 84 years), education, being parents, number of offspring and sexual orientation though, as the researchers suggest, the sample sizes may have been too small to show differences. On the other hand, Black women were significantly more likely to be single whereas White women had greater likelihood of being unemployed.

The focus groups were limited to a maximum of ten participants though the maximum in practice of seven participants. The size of groups varied according to the availability of suit-able participants. Although the groups were designed to be heterogeneous in terms of factors such as age, each group was homogeneous in terms of race. So there were three Black focus groups and three White focus groups in total. In their groups, the women were asked about 'their positive and negative gender- and race-related experiences' (p. 456). Interestingly, their participants were deliberately selected to be varied in terms of their ages and socio-economic backgrounds in order to maximise the diversity of the women's 'experiences and responses' (p. 456). The facilitator and her assistant were of the same race (and gender) as the members of the group in question. This was done, according to the researchers, to 'increase group com-fort and cohesion' (p. 457). Before each focus group began, the women participating in the research signed consent forms agreeing to participate and that the session could be recorded and completed a short demographic questionnaire. The focus group facilitator had the task of asking the group the questions for discussion whereas her assistant was responsible for man-aging the audio-visual equipment and taking notes about the interaction. The focus groups lasted for about two hours each.

At the start of the session, the facilitator outlined the general purpose of the focus group and informed the participants of their (ethical) rights. She also listed the ground rules governing discussions within the focus group which included the idea that there were no right or wrong answers to the questions, that participants should regard themselves as free to speak, and that all participants should be respectful of any differences in terms of points of view that manifested themselves. As an 'icebreaker' to the group discussion, each session began with an opportunity for each participant to talk about something important relevant to their sense of self. This, for example, might be their role as a mother or partner. The focus group interview was carefully structured and followed a guide or protocol in order to 'ensure consistency across groups' (p. 457). The initial questions were very open ended or broad such as:

- 'How has being a woman positively (negatively) influenced your life?'
- 'What are some of the advantages (disadvantages) of being a woman?'
- 'Does being a woman help you to know more about who you are or give your life a sense of purpose?'
- 'Are there things that you find special or valuable about being a woman, even if they make your life harder?'

Questions about positive aspects of womanhood were posed before those about the negative aspects. Rather more specific questions were used as the follow-up questions in order to stimulate the group discussion or to encourage participants to elaborate what they have already said. Examples of such questions included:

- 'Do you have home or care-giving responsibilities? If so, what types?'
- 'Are there unique, different or special things about being a woman? If so, what are they?'

The focus group ended with the participants being debriefed, compensated for their time and thanked. The women recruited from the community received a small cash payment plus a meal whereas the university students were rewarded by being given course credit. Of course, there may be ethical concerns about the involvement of students in research by their professors for credits of this sort (see Chapter 15).

The researchers argue that the appropriate method of analysing their data was grounded theory since no convincing existing theory was available to guide the analysis. (See Chapter 8 for a detailed discussion of grounded theory.) The analysis was carried out using eight trained coders who were either university students or faculty. The analysis proceeded on a line-by-line analysis of verbatim transcripts of the recordings of the focus group sessions. The analysts were seeking 'salient' categories in the data. They applied 'conceptual ordering analysis' which involves ordering the categories developed from the most concrete to the most abstract (Strauss & Corbin, 1998). The analysts met on a weekly basis to reach a consensus about the themes generated during the analysis. A simple quantitative analysis was then applied to the data in order to identify the group participants who mentioned each of the themes developed during the analysis. This had nearly 90 per cent inter-rater agreement.

The researchers identified a number of primary themes during the analysis which represented the views of women of both races. They are as follows together with the component subthemes:

- Theme 1: Gender-based mistreatment
  - Gender discrimination
  - Sexual harassment
  - Concerns for safety
  - Sexism
- Theme 2: Perceived advantages
  - Ability to express emotions
  - Leniency from men in power
  - Equality with men
- Theme 3: Friendships and community
  - Women value and form deep friendships
  - Friendships offer social support

- Difficulty forming friendships with women
- Negative aspects of friendships with women
- Theme 4: Caretaking
  - Positive aspects of caretaking
  - Caretaker role is meaningful
  - Mother role is important to future self
  - Difficulties associated with caretaking, overall
- Theme 5: Work and family options
  - Value having options/have more options than men
  - Difficulty making work-family balance choices
  - Challenges integrating work and family

A secondary theme, which applied only to Black women, was:

- Theme 6: Inner strength
  - Strength learned from other Black women
  - Characteristics of inner strength

Each of the themes is carefully discussed with illustrative quotations. The researchers indicate that these have minor edits such as the removal of material which detracts from clarity in their view.

Box 4.2
ILLUSTRATIVE RESEARCH STUDY
The practice of focus groups

While researchers have typically concentrated on the content of the group interaction in focus groups, other approaches are possible. In their book *Focus Group Practice*, Puchta and Potter (2004) explore another aspect of the focus group - the interaction between the group moderator and the group members. They concentrate on such things as how opinions are produced in the group and how the moderator encourages informality in the group. We will concentrate on the latter. Informality does not just happen - it has to be worked on if it is to be achieved. Putting people 'at their ease' is an important skill in focus group moderation. Puchta and Potter (2004) point out that research with nominal groups and Delphi groups may be different from their focus groups since in these group members are asked to contribute in turn thus the group dynamic is reduced.

Puchta and Potter give detailed examples of how interaction is generated so as to maintain informality while at the same time managing things in order to achieve the researcher's ends. Their main findings can be summarised as follows:

- The moderator construes the interaction as talking and chatting rather than something more formal such as a classroom.
- The moderator's talk does not appear as if it were scripted or highly planned. Instead, pauses and hesitancies help reinforce the impression of informality while the use of idiomatic language works to the same end.
- The physical environment of the focus group is more suggestive of a domestic rather than an office setting.
- The moderator claims to be seeking 'gut feelings' which suggests that contributions can be thrown in spontaneously without the need for rational explanations.

Thus the moderator may work to reduce any perceptions of him- or herself as being aloof in the eyes of the group members. Another way in which this is achieved is by using language devices which characterise everyday language but are rarely to be found in formal situations. They describe how in a focus group on hair shampoo one participant mistakes a reference to roots (as in hair roots) for roots as a reference to roots music (i.e. world music, African music, etc.). The moderator uses the word 'oh' when she finally realises the speaker's mistake. Oh is commonly used in everyday language to indicate a revision of understanding or a 'change in knowledge state' (Puchta and Potter, 2004, p. 43). Puchta and Potter argue that the focus group moderator will only use 'oh' when to do so has no potential impact on the moderator's perceived neutrality as in this case. Had the participant said something like 'this shampoo is aimed at selling to pensioners' then to respond to this with 'oh' would imply that the moderator does not share the same view as the speaker. In the same 'roots' episode, the moderator laughs about the speaker's misunderstanding when it becomes apparent. To laugh in the focus group context may risk creating the impression of the moderator's aloofness if it in some way signals the assumed superiority of the moderator because it is essentially judgemental. However, in the 'roots' exchange, Puchta and Potter suggest that the laughter is akin to the laughter of friends when there is a similar misunderstanding. In other words, in very precise circumstances 'oh' and laughter can be used non-judgementally to produce the informality which otherwise would be seen as aloofness and counter to the informality that the focus group moderator is there to achieve.

How to analyse data from focus groups

There are numerous approaches to the analysis of focus group data. However, it needs to be appreciated that focus groups have a long history and that modern qualitative research is just a small fraction of their use. The role of focus groups in marketing has meant that the analysis of focus group data has been built on rather different intellectual traditions from those which form the basis of modern qualitative psychology. In particular, market researchers tended to regard their subject matter from the point of view of Freudian psychoanalysis with its emphasis on hidden motivations. So many focus group researchers have looked to focus groups as a way of revealing why people make the choices that they do. In

FIGURE 4.4 Ways of analysing focus group data

other words, beware of the fact that focus groups have been analysed from a range of perspectives which may not share the approaches favoured in qualitative psychology. At the most basic level, some merely present their impressions of what the groups had to say, perhaps picking out particular quotations to illustrate a point. This, of course, hardly warrants the description 'analysis' though it may be sufficient for the sponsors of the research. Remember that much focus group research is carried out for market research purposes and the sponsor's needs in terms of analysis may not be very sophisticated. Ultimately, the chosen analysis route for focus group data will largely be dependent on the particular reasons why a focus group was the preferred method to collect data (see Figure 4.4):

- Perhaps the focus group study was carried out to generate research ideas to be pursued in some depth at a later stage in the research. In these circumstances, the needs of the researcher may be met by listing the major and most significant themes emerging out of the focus groups and identifying any research questions that these might suggest.

- On the other hand, the researcher may have collected the focus group data to better understand how people experience the topic being discussed by the focus group. So, the researcher may wish to understand people's experience of chronic pain. The content of what is said in the focus groups on this forms the basis of the analysis. In these circumstances, the researcher may wish to conduct a thematic analysis (Chapter 7) on a transcript of the data.

- Another researcher may be interested in the focus group discussion as conversation and may study the way in which conversation is governed during the course of focus groups. The data, in this case, may need to be transcribed using the Jefferson transcription system (Chapter 6).

- Transcribed focus group data usually will be suitable for grounded theory analysis (Chapter 8) but its use in discourse analysis (Chapter 9) would depend very much on the researcher's purpose and, perhaps, whether focus group data are sufficiently conversational.

Puchta and Potter (2004) adopt an approach in which the interaction in a focus group is regarded as data for understanding the discursive processes involved in the running of a focus group. This is described in Box 4.2.

When to use focus groups

Focus groups are a means of obtaining data which would be difficult to obtain using other forms of data collection method. People's opinions, beliefs, feelings and experiences are highlighted in focus groups in a way which other forms of interviewing simply cannot match. Furthermore, the focus group allows the researcher to capture responses of the group to the expressed opinions, beliefs, feelings and experiences of other group members. Other data collection methods such as observation and interviewing simply cannot capture such things. Because the participants have an active role in the focus group, it becomes apparent what they regard as the priorities in relation to a particular topic. Other data collection methods tend to impose the researcher's priorities onto the situation. The focus group is seen to be particularly good at eliciting clear understandings of the members' feelings, attitudes and beliefs. Of course, we need to be careful when suggesting that focus groups can identify people's attitudes. As Puchta and Potter (2004) argue, there are two conceptions of attitudes. One regards attitudes as preformed – already built into the individual before the research. The other conception regards attitudes as performed – meaning that the attitude emerges from the research situation. There is probably examples of both of these things to be found in most focus groups. However, performed attitudes are of very limited use if one wishes to use attitudes to understand why people do things.

Focus groups can be used in a variety of ways. Especially for multi-method studies, they can be exploratory in the sense that they stimulate discussion on a topic and ideas are thrown up by the group. If the researcher has no knowledge base on which to build then this is a vital function. For example, it may help the researcher plan questions for a survey or even suggest hypotheses to quantitative researchers. On the other hand, a focus group can be used to evaluate people's reactions to a study just completed by the researcher. It can be a way of providing feedback on the main research's findings.

In contrast to other data collection methods, focus groups have a rationale which is not always shared with other data collection methods, especially in terms of sampling. They do not attempt to estimate the distribution of characteristics in the population which is possible, to some extent, using interviews with formal sampling methods. Populations are not sampled in focus group methodology which, instead, selects group members intentionally in order to gain the maximum richness in the data. It thus employs a purposeful selection strategy rather than a random procedure. Focus groups, nevertheless, do allow contrasts and comparisons to be drawn in terms of different categories of group members. It is nonsensical to evaluate focus group methodology as an alternative to the individual interview since a focus group is not a cheap alternative to the individual interview and the two are not in competition essentially. It is unlikely that focus groups can be used successfully to gather extensive life-history or narrative accounts from individuals (Barbour, 2007). The interview may be a better approach. Consequently, focus groups may not be useful, in general, to interpretive phenomenological analysis or narrative analysis.

There is a sense in which participation in focus groups can be empowering. They provide a collective means of addressing issues which are otherwise the province of decision makers. The participant takes part in a decision-making process in which their voice is important. Partly as a consequence of this, focus groups have been popular in feminist research.

Evaluation of focus groups

A focus group provides a dynamic way of researching the beliefs, ideas, opinions and experiences of group participants engaged interactively. Because of the researcher's degree of control through the moderator of the broad discussion, it can be an effective and efficient way of obtaining a variety of perspectives. Out of the data is likely to emerge some understanding of why participants think in particular ways. No other data collection method achieves this degree of control with a dynamic and interactive approach. Interviews allow greater control but involve no group processes; participant observation allows group processes but leaves the researcher with little control over the moment-to-moment interaction. So focus group methodology stands as a distinct data-gathering resource for researchers. Consequently, one should be cautious about regarding focus groups as a way of understanding 'social reality' or even real-life social interaction because of their degree of artificiality. The discussions that are held in a focus group may have little bearing on what happens in everyday conversations.

Of course, focus group methodology should not be judged against criteria that it is not designed to meet. In particular, focus groups are not miniature sample surveys which allow one to estimate distributions of ideas, opinions, beliefs and so forth in the general population – or any other population for that matter. One would not expect to be able to map the results of a focus group-based investigation onto the results of a sample survey. The focus group cannot achieve representativeness in the same sense and the sample survey cannot provide the dynamic account that focus group data can.

Sloppy focus group research may not be very demanding but good quality, well-prepared focus group studies place a big drain on a researcher's resources. They take time, are not easy to organise and produce data which, often, cannot be effectively dealt with in a routine fashion. To run a focus group requires good interpersonal skills, a well-honed understanding of the research question, and an ability to focus on the needs of the research within the focus group context. While just about anyone could run a focus group of sorts, it requires great skill to generate data which is relevant to the research question. One has only to look at television discussions to understand something of the things that can go wrong – people merely expressing entrenched positions, people talking over each other, people not addressing the issue at hand and so forth are common.

The focus group presents particular ethical issues which are not characteristic of other data collection methods. In particular, it is not possible to ensure anonymity and confidentiality for things said in an open setting. The researcher may be in a position to guarantee anonymity and confidentiality in publications but the data have been collected in a public setting. It is worthwhile discussing this problem with the group in order to solicit an agreement of confidentiality concerning the group discussion but this cannot be policed and, as a consequence, may not be regarded as perfectly satisfactory.

Finally, focus group methodology is an approach to qualitative data collection. In itself, the methodology does not have specific analytical procedures associated with it. As a result, one should not judge the method on the basis of what may appear to be examples of poor data analysis. Sometimes a report of a focus group study may simply highlight a few somewhat unexpected things for discussion. Such selected highlights may not be regarded as a careful and thorough analysis of the data. But this is not to be blamed on the data collection method since it is a consequence of the lack of rigour in the analysis applied.

CONCLUSION

The focus group is a commonplace data collection method in the modern world. It would, therefore, seem almost inevitable that its use in academic psychological research will also expand further. No doubt distinctive academic styles of focus group will emerge to meet the specific requirements of qualitative psychology. This is certainly the case with the analysis of focus group data but it also may apply to the conduct of the focus group. We have seen that mainstream market research focus groups may be built on theoretical (interpretative) frameworks which are not shared by academic qualitative researchers. In particular, the rise of focus group methodology in market research paralleled the rise in psychodynamic (psychoanalytic) theories about consumer motivation in commerce. Rarely does academic qualitative research show any theoretical allegiance to psychoanalysis – quite the reverse. This means that the caucus of market research focus group studies may have very little to say of relevance to the analysis of this form of qualitative data. Thus, qualitative researchers may feel that qualitative data analysis methods such as grounded theory, thematic analysis, conversation analysis and discourse analysis are the preferred approaches. Of course, this opens up a whole variety of research questions which market research focus groups simply are not intended to address. For example, the focus group could be modified to enhance its potential to generate naturalistic conversation. In academic focus groups some of the conventions of the market research focus group could be eschewed. In particular, the role of the moderator in controlling the focus of the group discussion might be lessened in favour of letting the conversation take a more 'natural course'.

KEY POINTS

- A focus group usually consists of a group of six to ten dynamically interacting individuals discussing a topic in response to questioning by the researcher (moderator). In order to facilitate discussion, the focus group is relatively informal and the researcher plans the groups in a way which will maximise the interactive nature of the discussion. For this reason, focus group members are often selected to be strangers to each other and obvious status differentials which might inhibit some group members from participation or encourage others to dominate the situation are avoided. There are normally at least three or four groups in a study for each type of group included in the researcher's design.

- The organisation of a focus group can be a complex matter since it is the researcher's responsibility to select groups in a way which will ensure effective collection of data relevant to the research question. A strategy for obtaining appropriate participants by using, say, existing interest groups or key informants is important. There is no attempt in focus group methodology to draw statistically representative samples. The organisation of the focus group meeting should be cognisant of the needs of the group members in order to maximise their likelihood of participation. The moderator of the focus group needs considerable social and research skills to ensure good quality data are collected.

- The analysis of focus group data can employ a variety of methods. Traditionally, the analysis of market research focus groups has tended to be guided by a psychodynamic theory of consumer motivation. This is inappropriate for the work of most qualitative researchers, for example. But, of course, the appropriate form of qualitative analysis for focus group data depends on the research purposes of the researcher. Some of the common qualitative data analysis methods discussed in this book – grounded theory, discourse analysis, etc. – could be used if they match the purposes of the researcher.

ADDITIONAL RESOURCES

Barbour, R. (2007). *Doing Focus Groups*. Los Angeles: Sage.

Dawson, S., and Manderson, L. (n.d.) A Manual for the Use of Focus Groups. http://www.unu.edu/unupress/food2/UIN03E/UIN03E00.HTM (accessed 27 August 2009).

Krueger, R.A., and Casey, M.A. (2009). *Focus Groups*, 4th Edition. Thousand Oaks, CA: Sage.

Morrison, D.E. (1998). *The Search for a Method: Focus groups and the development of mass communication research*. Luton: University of Luton Press.

Stewart, D.W., Shamdasani, P.N., and Rook, D. (2007). *Focus Groups: Theory and practice*. Thousand Oaks, CA: Sage.

Wilkinson, S. (2008). Focus groups. In J.A. Smith (Ed.), *Qualitative Psychology: A practical guide to research methods*, 2nd Edition. London: Sage, pp. 186-206.

CHAPTER 5

Ethnography/ participant observation

Overview

- Participant observation refers specifically to observational techniques in which researchers involve themselves extensively and in depth with a group or community.

- More generally, participant observation refers to a wider set of methods including intensive observation which are also known as ethnographic methods. Ethnography is the better term to use as it is in keeping with other disciplines.

- There are different forms of participant observation which vary in terms of how much the researcher is integrated into the group concerned and how apparent the researcher's actual role is.

- Field notes are the basis of ethnography/participant observation and are made after the observation has been completed. They are detailed and may be structured in terms of separate observations and interpretations sections.

- Ethnography/participant observation is one of the most complex research methods and places both intellectual and interpersonal demands on the researcher. The intellectual demands include formulating the research questions, questioning whether the particular research question can benefit from participant observation, deciding what issues to address in the observation process, and writing effective field notes. Among the interpersonal demands are defining the researcher's role, gaining and maintaining entry to the research context, and effectively using key informants.

- Ethnography/participant observation is primarily a data collection method. It, in itself, is not a method of analysis. Given the age of the method, there are a variety of ways of analysing the data but the grounded theory approach (Chapter 8) is typically used in recent research.

● From the point of view of a researcher, there are a number of problems in using ethnography/participant observation. These include the labour- and time-intensive nature of the process, the complexity of the data collected and the need to integrate different aspects of the data, the possibility of subjectivity in the procedure and accusations of subjectivity.

● Although ethnography/participant observation has been uncommon in psychology, the potential of the method warrants its consideration by qualitative researchers.

What is ethnography/participant observation?

Participant observation is best regarded as a data collection method rather than a data analysis method. There is no standard way of carrying out the analysis of field notes, etc. though grounded theory (Chapter 8) does offer a commonly used systematic approach. Participant observation has its origins in the work of anthropologists working in non-Western cultures. But it has many other applications in modern research. Confusingly, participant observation refers to two distinct things:

● A very specific methodology, named participant observation, which involves the researcher's observations when closely immersed in a group or culture which are recorded and analysed. Its most significant feature is the close involvement of the researcher in the research setting through participation or engaging with a group or community over a protracted period of time.

● A general methodology or broad strategy for collecting data in a field setting. This sometimes is called participant observation and it includes the more specific approach described above. So a formal definition of participant observation would also identify it as a broad strategy for collecting data in a field setting. It involves collecting a variety of different sorts of data pertinent to answering the research question.

There is another concept, ethnography, which is essentially the study of cultures. For the purposes of this chapter, it is possible to regard both ethnography and participant observation as similar where we are referring to a complex simultaneous method of data collection in field settings. The overlap is considerable as rarely is participant observation (the specific technique) used on its own without the involvement of other methods. Ethnography seems to have emerged as the preferred term in the 1970s (Bryman, 2004). Furthermore, it should be noted that the term ethnography also refers to the product of ethnographic research – the published account based on the research.

Ethnography/participant observation can be seen as a blanket term covering a range of related methods. It can also be suggested that participant observation studies vary along a number of dimensions. The following are some of the more important of these (Dereshiwsky, 1999; also based on Patton, 1986):

- *The observer's role in the setting*   The observer's involvement may vary from that of a complete outsider uninvolved in the group dynamics to full membership of the group.

- *The group's knowledge of observation process*   If the participants know that they are being studied then this is known as overt observation. Covert observation involves the participants not knowing that they are part of a study.

- *Explication of the study's purpose*   This can range from full explication to even misleading explanations.

- *Length*   The observation may be a relatively short single session of just one hour or there may be multiple observations which continue for weeks or even years.

- *Focus*   The focus of the researcher may be on a relatively narrow aspect of the situation or it may be more holistic in which rich data are collected through the observation of a number of aspects of the situation in depth.

Participant observation literally implies that the researcher is not simply an observer of events in a social or cultural context but also has 'hands on' experience. The participant observer may take part in the activities of members of the community involved. While the extent to which the participant observer is a full participant in the community (living life completely as a member of the community) rather than as a guest in the community varies, the expectation is of a substantial term of engagement with the community. (There are other methods of observation which do not require such involvement. For example, a study of whether drivers of new cars jump traffic lights more frequently than drivers of older cars could probably be carried out using a simple checklist identifying the age of the car – e.g. from its number plate – and ratings of whether the driver crosses the lights legally or illegally.) Part of the ethos of participant observation is that the perspective of members of the group or community studied is a major focus. Diversity, of course, would be a feature expected of the different members of the group or community in terms of their roles, their activities, and so forth. Thus participant observation can be seen as diametrically opposite to *surveillance* which demands no participation and might be possible through purely technological resources such as CCTV cameras.

There are, of course, also instances of researchers observing communities without those who are being observed being aware of the fact. This would be rare in modern research for ethical reasons. The term 'immersion' is frequently used to describe this process. The 'immersion' can involve living with the group being studied (as in the early anthropological studies of other cultures) but, equally, the immersion may be confined to the working day or some other more limited arrangement. The latter is more typical of participant observation in one's own culture as practised by sociologists and other modern users of ethnographic approaches. A participant observer cannot be expected to be equivalent to any other member of that community since he or she often comes from a very different social background. However, the expectation is that participant observers come closer to the experiences of regular members of the community than is typical in research. In this way, hopefully, the careful and conscientious observer obtains a reasonably full understanding of the way that the society functions.

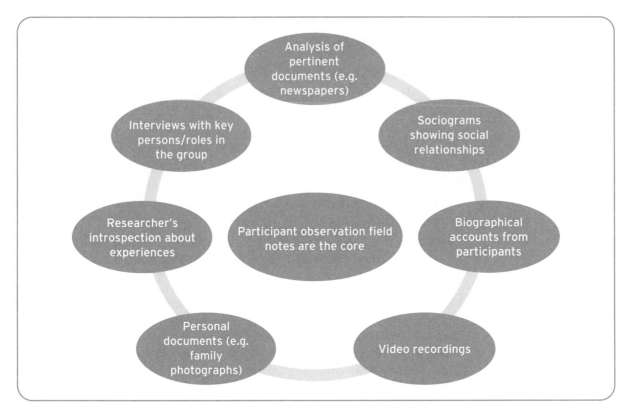

FIGURE 5.1 **Possible elements of a participant observation/ethnographic study**

Traditionally, data are collected primarily in the form of field notes written-up by the observer as soon after the events as possible. This would normally take place in 'private time' away from the community. There is no reason why, in appropriate circumstances, the data collection should not use technological aids such as voice recordings of field observations, computers, or even video though these can be intrusive. Using computers for writing field notes is advantageous as these can be fed directly into computer-aided qualitative data analysis programs such as NVivo. As we have seen, there is every reason why the researcher should be confined solely to the observations recorded in the field notes as sources of data. It is possible to incorporate the following and more (see Figure 5.1):

- semi-structured interviews;
- group discussions;
- life histories of members of the community;
- personal documents including photographs;
- relevant media coverage;
- other documentation.

These are familiar methods in their own right but in the context of ethnography/ participant observation they can be seen as a resource which can be compared with the researcher's direct experiences. There is a sense in which participant observation can be regarded as too narrow a phrase to capture what is actually done in such studies and ethnography might be seen as the more appropriate broader term. Even quantification is not unknown in participant observation-based studies. The field notes which are made should be recorded in a relatively pure form – that is, the observations and the interpretations of the observations kept separate. In other words, the 'experiences' of the observer are the primary form of data in participant observation but these 'experiences' should be distinguished from more analytic statements in the field notes. This is a common requirement in qualitative research of all sorts. One way of doing this is to keep the 'pure' observations on one side of a notebook and analytic comments relevant to them on the other side – the two separated by a margin, for example.

Participant observation can provide the researcher with an initial relatively full picture on which to base a major research initiative. Although there are other ways of doing this, the knowledge of situations based on participant observation may provide the researcher with a better understanding of what to include in their questionnaires and so forth. Thus participant observation can be seen as a way of ensuring the researcher is able to ask the right questions pertinent to the participants in the research.

The role of the observer in this sort of field research varies in terms of the extent to which the observation and participation are manifest:

- *Total or complete participation* The researcher assumes entirely the role of a member of the group or organisation being studied without revealing their additional role as researcher to the other group members. For example, the researcher obtains work in a factory in order to understand aspects of the experience of work.

- *Total or complete observation* In this, personal involvement in the community is minimised and the researcher remains detached. There is no doubt as to the observer's role. So, for example, the researcher may spend time on a factory floor making observations or taking notes while at the same time making no efforts to engage with the workers there.

- *Participant as an observer* The researcher's identity as a researcher is made known to the group being studied. For example, the researcher spends time in a youth club and may engage in the activities of the club members who are aware of the observer's status as both a club member and a researcher. Of course with this status, the observer need not necessarily fully participate in the group's activities.

- *Observer as non-participant* This is not a form of participant observation since there is no direct engagement with the group in its day-to-day activities. Sometimes the term ethology is used in psychology, for this, but this really refers to the study of animal behaviour.

Of course, it is not entirely in the researcher's hands which variant of participant observation is used. Some may be excluded by the particular circumstances or the particular research question which the researcher is pursuing. Some of the dimensions along which participant observation/ethnographic studies differ are illustrated in Figure 5.2.

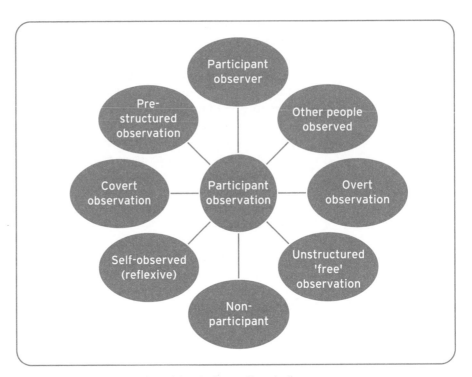

FIGURE 5.2 Dimensions of participant observation studies

The development of ethnography/participant observation

The origins of participant observation lie in anthropology initially and then in the Chicago School of Sociology. Of course, the roots of anthropology in history are very long since a traveller to another culture who wrote an account of their experiences could be regarded as an anthropologist of sorts. The era of Western colonisation starting in the fifteenth century provided an impetus to anthropology and scholars during the Age of Enlightenment (eighteenth century) began to approach the study of other cultures more analytically though drawing heavily on the information provided by colonisers and travellers. This is not the place to provide a complete history of anthropology, of course, but it is important to realise that even until the beginning of the twentieth century, cultural anthropologists tended to rely on secondary sources such as travellers' writings as the bases of their analyses and data were collected through informants rather than observation. The first identifiable user of participant observation was the American researcher Frank Hamilton Cushing (1857–1900) who joined an anthropological expedition to New Mexico where he lived with native American people (Zuni Pueblo) for five years beginning in 1879. Cushing eventually became accepted into the Zuni community and took part in their activities.

More influential though, were the crucial changes which occurred as a result of Bronislaw Malinowski (1884–1942) being stranded in the Trobriand Islands in the area we now refer to as New Guinea. Malinowski was born in Krakow, Poland, where he studied for a doctorate in philosophy. He became interested in anthropology and studied at Leipzig University (he was somewhat influenced by Wilhelm Wundt there) but then moved to the London School of Economics since many of the most eminent anthropologists at the time were British. In 1914, while studying for his doctorate in anthropology, Malinowski travelled to Papua and then to the Trobriand Islands. The First World War broke out, but he was a citizen in the Austrian-Hungarian Empire in a British-protected region of the world. He chose to be exiled in the Trobriand Islands as an alternative to being interned for the rest of the war. Malinowski initially played the part of the aloof colonial anthropologist relying on formal interviews with informants and avoiding direct contact with the indigenous Trobriand people who he initially construed as 'savages'. The long months of exile and the concomitant boredom and loneliness led him to interact with them and, in so doing, he learnt the language and made friends. During this period of exile, he developed his ideas about participant observation and the importance of day-to-day experience of the community in developing a finely tuned understanding of how the community works.

A second important stream in the development of participant observation was the urban sociology of the first Chicago School. This approach to sociology was concerned with understanding urban environments and the earliest of this research was carried out in Chicago itself, though urban sociology became a general approach in American sociology. However, in addition to this, the anthropologist Lloyd Warner (1898–1970) was also a graduate student there between 1929 and 1935 and taught there between 1935 and 1959. William Foote Whyte (1914–2000) explained how he went to the University of Chicago specifically to study with Lloyd Warner (Whyte, 1984). This is important because William Foote Whyte was the author of probably the best known example of participant observation research in American sociology – *Street Corner Society* (Whyte, 1943). This study was of an Italian immigrant community in Boston where Whyte lived for 18 months.

Lloyd Warner was involved in one of the most famous studies in the history of psychology – the Hawthorne Experiments, which gave birth to the phrase 'the Hawthorne effect'. He began working with the psychologist Elton Mayo (1880–1949) on a series of integrated studies of factory life and the effect of introduction of various sorts of changes on the dynamics of the work groups within those factories; for example, changes in the lighting conditions and payment levels within the factory. Warner's influence was principally on the 'Bank Wiring Room' experiment in which he recommended the use of anthropological methods to observe the natural work-group behaviours of workers. The researchers made records of all that they could observe of the behaviour of the groups just as an anthropologist would a different culture. This led to the construction of 'sociograms' which are diagrams indicating the levels of interpersonal involvement of members of the work group based on these observations.

Despite a number of notable exceptions, such as those described in Boxes 5.1 and 5.2, participant observation/ethnography has not been a major data collection method in psychology and has not featured greatly in the recent rise of interest in qualitative methods despite numerous references to it in the writings of qualitative researchers. Miller, Hengst and Wang (2003) explain that Wilhelm Wundt (1832–1920), the parent of modern psychology, wrote extensively in the field of cultural psychology and pursued his interest in ethnographic material determinedly. Nevertheless, ethnographic methods have generally been marginalised in psychology. However, a recent upsurge of interest in cultural psychology and especially cultural child development has stimulated more interest in ethnographic methods.

Box 5.1

ILLUSTRATIVE
RESEARCH STUDY

A crucial participant observation study: Mariethal

Otto Bauer (1991–1938), who was a leading figure of the left-wing Social Democrat party in Austria in the late 1920s, suggested to the Austrian research community that it would be an important venture to study unemployment. Researchers from the Austrian Research Unit for Economic Psychology worked under the direction of the famous sociologist Paul Lazarsfeld (1901–1976). The research planning began in 1930 at exactly the time Marienthal's textile factory closed down. Marienthal is a town close to Vienna. The field work for the research was carried out largely by a researcher Lotte Schenk-Danzinger (1905–1992) who was working as the supervisor of a relief group which distributed second-hand clothing. Apparently a total of 24 working weeks were spent on the fieldwork and the weight of the research materials collected was about 30 kilograms (An Unemployed Community: Marienthal. http://agso.uni-graz.at/ marienthal/english/english.htm, accessed 17 July 2008).

A book based on the study, mostly written by Marie Jahoda, was published in 1933 although the authors' obviously Jewish names did not appear on the front of the book as a concession to the National Socialist government at the time. The authors, Jahoda, Lazarsfeld and Zeisel, wrote:

> It was the aim of the study to draw an image of the psychological situation of a community suffering from unemployment, using cutting-edge methods of research. From the outset we focused our attention on two objectives. One with regard to substance: contributing material concerning the problem of unemployment – and a methodological one: trying to give a comprehensive and objective account of the socio-psychological facts. (Jahoda *et al.*, 2002, p. v)

Not only was this the first psychological study of unemployment, but it was also notable for its varied approach to methodology and data collection. These included the analysis of documents, observation techniques, participant observation, surveys and so forth. The book is exceptionally vivid in terms of its descriptive material. The scientifically dry material is presented using verbal portraits of unemployed individuals and even materials taken from children's school essays. The involvement of researchers in Marienthal was also guided by the principle that they should fit naturally into the community by participating in activities of use to the community. The flavour of relationship between the researchers and the unemployed families can be assessed from the following:

> Our investigations in Marienthal began with visits to the homes of about one hundred families. The ostensible occasion was to ask them about their particular needs in connection with our proposed distribution of clothing. The observations and interviews recorded during these visits taught us much about the basic posture of the families. Whichever member of the family eventually came to collect the clothes was asked to tell us his life history which was usually done willingly. These people were then observed in a variety of surroundings: at our courses and at political meetings we talked about them and with them, taking notes of everything as we went along. From these notes and from the special information obtained from meal records, time sheets, etc., detailed descriptions of each family emerged. (Jahoda *et al.*, 2002, p. 45)

Of course, such an approach would be familiar to cultural anthropologists of the time as well as sociologists of the Chicago School. The extent of the involvement and interaction between researchers and participants is not surprising in this context. Some modern qualitative research exhibits similar features but, of course, this extensive interaction would equally not characterise recent developments in qualitative psychology analysis.

At the end of the book, biographies of some of the unemployed in Marienthal were presented though many more were collected which could not be included. This would not be unusual in some reports of modern qualitative research. What might surprise modern qualitative researchers is the extent to which the researchers systematically incorporated quantitative data with the qualitative. This included data on the diet of the families and data on the walking speed of those living in this community dominated by unemployment. Such diverse information allowed the researchers to study the experience and structure of time for the unemployed. Paul Lazarsfeld, who became a highly influential sociologist in the United States, is probably mainly regarded for his quantitative methodological work. Rigid separation between qualitative and quantitative research may not always be desirable. Quite the reverse is probably closer to the truth.

Box 5.2

ILLUSTRATIVE RESEARCH STUDY

Ethnography: violent football supporters

Suggestions that ethnographic approaches and participant observation hold promise in psychology are far more common than studies actually using them. One exceptionally import- ant ethnographic study was Marsh, Rosser and Harré's (1978) study of a football crowd. One could say that the book was an investigation of football hooliganism – it was in a sense but it also totally reformulated ideas about how to understand such behaviour. Football violence is presented in the book as a social construction by 'moral entrepreneurs' (such as media and politicians) rather than representing an accurate picture about what happens at matches:

Vandalism, for example, might be thought of as a collection of clearly identifiable acts requiring sanctions for the simple reason that they offend against the property, both individual and collective, of members of society. But contrast the reaction to football fans who run through a town creating damage as they go with the reaction to university students during rag week creating similar damage. The former damage will be viewed as the result of 'destructive hooliganism' and dealt with accordingly, whilst the latter will be seen as arising from an excess of good-natured high spirits and over-enthusiasm. Although the damaging acts are very similar, football fans are 'deviants' whilst students, for reasons not made explicit, are somehow excused. (Marsh et al., 1978, p. 10)

The research is described by its authors as being ethogenic in nature which means that it is essentially about the speech which makes intelligible the action which accompanies that speech. That is, ethogenic is about the speech which accounts for one's actions. Nevertheless, the methodology employed by Marsh *et al.* is decidedly ethnographic in nature. (At the time of the research the idea of ethnography was the conceptual new kid on the block.) The research involved a mixture of data collection methods including observation, interviewing, descriptions of incidents and the collection of cultural artefacts such as threatening and offensive chants against the opposing team and its fans. The observation utilised existing surveillance cameras which were spread liberally around the football ground. The participants in the study were a relatively small number of the local fans of the football club in question. What this means is that the observation part of the ethnographic study was covert and, therefore, cannot be described as participant observation.

At the time when the study was carried out, football grounds had a mixture of seating and standing places which allowed more movement than the all-seater stadiums which characterise modern football. Special areas were fenced in typically where the young visiting team fans would congregate. The police would send fans as appropriate to these fenced areas – a process known to all concerned as 'penning'. Thus the police essentially separated different groups of fans in the most effective way possible. This segregation was a cooperative activity between the police and the fans – both of which repulsed or ejected marauding fans from the 'other side' when they entered the 'wrong' area. When the videos of the 'standing' fans were analysed it emerged that there was an essentially stable pattern of groups which the fans themselves recognised when they were interviewed. Not only that, the different groups had important behavioural and social characteristics which could be attributed to them.

For example, Group A consisted essentially of young males in the 12–17-year-old age group. They had a pattern of dress which could be described as the 'aggro outfit' together with 'emblems of allegiance' such as flags and banners. They are the most noisy group of fans. This group had several different social roles including a system of chant leaders who were responsible for organising the chanting as well as writing some chants when needed; aggro leaders who were always at the forefront of hostilities with the opposition team's fans; nutters who engaged in some of the more outrageous incidents; heavy drinkers with a reputation for excessive drunkenness who were regularly ejected from the ground; the fighters who were a small group renowned for being violent (they are different from the aggro leaders who only engage in ritual conflict with the other team supporters); and the organiser who would organise the coaches to transport the fans to other football grounds for away matches. In contrast, Group C exhibited no particular style of dress from that worn by young men of their age group in general. They were older and up to the age of 25 years. Distinguishing clothing, flags and banners were not part of the make-up of this group and they would not have been identifiable as football fans outside of the football ground. Generally speaking, membership of Group C was of higher status than membership of other groups and it was an aspiration to join Group C from other groups.

The organised nature of the football crowd even extended to the coaches taking the fans to and from the match. There was a natural order of who was allowed to sit where on the coach. Failure to comply with the 'natural' order would result in the offender being told to move and where. The researchers carried out extensive qualitative interviews with members of the various groups of fans. Interestingly, the fans were generally well aware of the various groups in this football ground culture. The researchers had videotapes of various incidents which had happened at football matches. The important thing was how the fans accounted for these events irrespective of whether these accounts reflected the contents of the tapes precisely. For example, there was a basic observation on the part of the researchers that fans talk about fights being extremely violent while injury was fairly uncommon. The researchers would stop their tape-recorded interviews and play them back to the fans for their comments.

This often brought about some reflection on the part of the fans about what they had said. So Wayne, a fan, in the first part of the interview expressed the following view:

> Kids go charging in – there's boots flying all over – real mad sometimes. With teams like Sunderland – they're mad – just lash out. So now we try to get the boot in first – as they arrive and before they can get together. You can get the boot in first and maybe scare them off a bit. We got a couple as they were coming up from their coach and they didn't know what hit them. It makes them think, don't it? (pp. 93–94)

After hearing the tape played back, he said:

> You goes in there – sort of going in to nut people, or give them a kicking or something like that. But, normally, anyway, the kids don't all get beaten up. You can tell when somebody's had enough – really you're trying to stop them giving you a lot of mouth. You get mad at them but you know when to stop. (p. 95)

These may be seen as two somewhat contradictory accounts – the first very violent whereas the second seemingly describing rule-bound activities. It is a picture of conflict but control is an important element of it. The violent view is very much the dominant view of the football fan which could be found in newspapers, etc. as out of control and extreme. The evidence from this ethnographic study was that where a fight actually occurred then the fans could provide justifications for this happening as opposed to the usual situation where the 'aggro' between groups of fans was largely ritualistic in nature – that is, threatening displays in the form of offensive and threatening chants but no real threat of violence for the most part because 'aggro' is governed by rules which usually prevent extreme violence taking place.

According to Marsh *et al.*, the rules can be seen in the accounts that the fans gave in explanation of their actions and the justifications they see for some acts. This does not mean that the fans had a comprehensive understanding of the 'rules' which governed their actions at football matches. The researchers tried a simple device of changing aspects of real events on the basis that this might help them understand better the rule-driven nature of the activities of the fans. The fans realised that there were things wrong with these 'incorrect' sequences of events and suggested what 'should' have happened in reality. Similarly, they were given examples of events which 'went wrong' because someone was hurt and the fans could explain the reasons for this. In other words, the rule-driven nature of the behaviour of fans at football matches could be identified from circumstances in which the 'rules' had failed. Ethnomethodologists have taken similar approaches when they immersed people in essentially chaotic situations and found that people treated the chaotic situation as meaningful (see Chapter 10 on conversation analysis for a discussion of this type of research). These studies are known as *breaching* studies.

This study by Marsh *et al.* (1978) demonstrates the potential of ethnographic style research in psychology. They essentially took a notorious problem – violence at football matches – and generated an analysis which substantially revised many of the 'common-sense' views of the problem which could be found throughout the media and among the general public at large. None of this would have been possible simply by interviewing the football fans since many of their initial comments seemed to reflect the views of people on the outside. It was only when the fans were asked to account for actual events at matches that a new picture emerged of the rule-driven nature of the interactions among different groups of fans. One might suggest that because the researchers were outsiders to the fans' culture then they saw events and heard discussions through new eyes and ears. Without the careful observation of the crowds at the football ground, they may have been left with the impression of the violence of an undifferentiated mass of people. Instead they were able to see the intricate structure which helped them identify very different patterns of conduct associated with these various groups within the crowd of fans.

FIGURE 5.3 Important aspects of a participant observation study

How to conduct ethnography/participant observation

We have already seen how, typically, participant observation is part of a web of various methods, several of which are used in any one study. Thus it is hard to describe how to carry out a participant observation without reference to the other methods of data collection used at the same time. Nevertheless, the core of the method and the thing which makes it different is the use of an observer to collect data. So this needs to be the focus of our description of participant observation though it should be patently obvious that participant observation requires researchers with a very broad range of skills both in terms of experience of research methods as well as the interpersonal skills to function effectively in the field context as an observer and a participant.

The following are some of the important stages in participant observation – see Figure 5.3 for an overview.

Step 1 **Formulating the research question** Participant observation will be employed where the researcher has a broad area of study to address though it is unlikely that at the initial stages they will have a focused research question in mind. The normal expectation is that the researcher will begin to understand the specific aspects that need to be focused on. In other words, the researcher will start to re-formulate or otherwise develop their ideas during the course of the participant observation. This sort of process is not unusual in qualitative research and is not especially problematic in terms of participant observation. This does not give the researcher a *carte blanche* since it is essential that if participant observation is to be used that the research question is one which can be effectively addressed by participant observation. Whyte put it this way:

→ The planning process is begun but not completed before the researcher enters the field. I am not proposing that we enter with blank minds, leaving it to subsequent observations and experience to shape research plans. Striving for such a state of unconsciousness would be folly, but it is important to avoid the other extreme of becoming so fixated on a previously prepared and detailed research design as to miss opportunities to gather data about problems that may turn out to be more important. (Whyte, 1984, p. 35)

One of the important skills which any researcher has to learn is the selection of appropriate research methods to address particular issues. This needs knowledge and experience to do well.

Step 2   **Question whether a particular area of interest lends itself to participant observation**   There are many activities which are regarded as essentially private and these are unlikely to be amenable to investigation using participant observation or any other sort of observation. Obvious examples of this are the activities which we regard as private – sexual activity, toileting and consultations with a doctor, for example. There may be areas of these activities where the researcher might gain access but generally these are things which one would need to consider alternative data collection methods for. Or, of course, where the ethical risks of covert observation are substantial despite its feasibility then a rethink of approach will be necessary.

Step 3   **Define what is to be addressed in the observation process**   The clear definition of the research question will be of use here since it will help identify the aspects of the situation that the researcher will study. There will be a degree of selectivity in what is observed purposefully though, of course, one cannot be totally sure just what will be relevant especially in types of situations with which one has little or no familiarity.

Step 4   **Defining the researcher's role**   A major consideration in participant observation/ethnography is for the researcher to define a viable role which permits the researcher to participate in a setting or to be sufficiently at its periphery to enable the observation to take place. There is no single approach to this which will work for all circumstances. There are many reasons for this, including the characteristics of the researcher – adult researchers cannot be full participant observers in a class of schoolchildren for obvious physical reasons. On the other hand, they might be able to function as an adult assistant in the classroom. Social characteristics may also hinder entry into a research setting. Public field settings with a lack of structure are probably the easiest to participate in. So it is easy to be a participant observer of music concerts as a member of the audience.

Step 5   **Entry to the research location/entry to the community**   The research locations for participant observation/ethnography vary in the extent to which they are formal settings such as a factory or informal settings in the community such as, say, a football match. The means of entry will differ between the two. The formal organisation usually requires a formal request for entry to carry out research – so, for example, the researcher may need to approach senior managers. The informal organisation, however, is not one without a

→

social structure. There may be key individuals – often called gatekeepers – who may facilitate the entry of the participant observer into the group. Of course, somewhat informal ways will be needed to contact such individuals. Care is needed to match the entry method to the community in question. For example, in his classic study of the Italian-American slum district in the North End of Boston, Whyte (1943) initially attempted to gain entry to this working-class community by approaching social workers in a settlement house. Whyte identifies himself as middle class and eventually realised that it was incongruous to approach middle-class gatekeepers in trying to achieve his ends. He likens this to trying to gain entry to, say, Ghanaian communities by contacting the American Embassy for help! So what would be a more appropriate means of entry? Well, Whyte heard from a social worker about a particular member of the community, Doc, who was eventually contacted. Doc helped Whyte's passage into the community. Of course, this is a complex matter and one which is difficult to discuss without reference to a particular example. It is also important to remember that modern researchers are likely to require permission from research committees in order to enter organisations for research purposes. For example, research in hospitals will require such ethical clearance. This adds stages of complexity to the process of gaining entry to research sites. There is a distinction to be made between overt and covert observation. Covert observation occurs when the researcher does not identify herself or himself to the community as a researcher making observations. The researcher does not need to contact others for help and there is no process by which the researcher needs to explain or justify their activities to those about to be observed. But, then, of course, considerable ethical problems may arise (Chapter 15).

Step 6   **Continuing access**   Participant observation/ethnography involves maintaining relations with the group studied and not just the entry process to the research location. Considerable thought and skill are needed in terms of interpersonal relations since those being studied may have concerns about the nature of the researcher's activity. The completely covert research study does not entirely avoid this risk as there may be difficulties over matters such as credibility. For example, a researcher who gains access to a factory floor by obtaining employment there may, nevertheless, appear different from others working there. For example, their accent may not match that of the group members and so might arouse interest or they may not be able to engage in simple conversations such as 'What did you do at the weekend?' or 'Where do you live?' without risking revealing their identity. Researchers who have indicated their status as a researcher may come under suspicion as to their 'true' identity – the researcher may be seen as being from social security, a management spy and so forth. The outcome of all of this is unlikely to be a direct confrontation such as a demand that the researcher stops his or her activities or some form of abuse. Instead, the resistance may take the form of providing misinformation deliberately to sabotage the research. Of course, the extent of these suspicions may vary according to the individuals involved – some of those being observed may be relaxed about it whereas others may be more inherently suspicious. The researcher has to be sensitive to such issues and deal with them to the best of their ability. This will vary according to circumstances but it would generally be wise to avoid situations which are likely to promote suspicion. For example, a

→ researcher who seems unnecessarily friendly to members of management is more likely to come under suspicion since they may be seen as more likely to, say, inadvertently let slip information to them. Equally important is the possibility of providing written information about issues such as data confidentiality, data security, anonymity of individuals in any reports and so forth. This would need to be specifically tailored to the particular research situation. But there is a further aspect to this. The preceding comments perhaps imply that any hostility or suspicions of the researcher reflect on the competence of the researcher. This may be the case but, equally, it may reflect pre-existing tensions or relationships in the group into which the researcher inadvertently stumbles. In this sense, the response of those being observed constitutes valuable data which provides insight into the group. No matter what, this should be recorded in the field notes. It is not something to be quietly ignored.

Step 7 **The use of key informants** In any social environment, some individuals take on more important roles in our lives than others. Similarly, in ethnography/participant observation, some individuals tend to have a more important role in relation to the researcher. There can be several reasons for this. In particular, the key informant (a) may play a more central role in most aspects of the group's activities than others, (b) may have an interest in the research which is greater than that of the others, or (c) may have a special rapport with the researcher and so forth. Key informants can play a role in smoothing out the research process and may act as a source of social support at difficult times. In some contexts, the key informants may choose to provide information of what the group is planning to do in the future – for example, it might be helpful for the researcher who is studying a delinquent gang to know that they are planning a seaside trip at the weekend.

Step 8 **Field notes/data logging** The making of field notes is probably the only defining characteristic of the data for participant observation. The objective of taking field notes is to have a comprehensive database of one's observations in the field setting. Thus, the more complete the notes the better. But this is an unrealistic requirement in many ways since it begs the question just how much detail is enough? Furthermore, are there no restrictions on the observations which are recorded? This is not to imply that the participant observer should record everything since this would be a limitless and impossible task. Completeness in terms of the field notes is relative to the particular study in question and the theoretical and conceptual issues that the researcher brings to the field. Also, since these theoretical and conceptual issues will be modified in the light of experience, then what is a sufficiently complete set of field notes will also change. These are difficult matters to address in the abstract but the following ought to be taken into account:

● One important function of field notes is to help the research familiarise themselves with the social context of the research setting including the people within that setting and the interrelations between the two. Good field notes will contain such information in order to build up a picture of these important social relationships as well as helping to identify key figures in understanding what happens in the group.

→

- Memory will adversely affect the quality of the field notes if there is too much delay between the observation and the making of the field notes. It will also be affected by the nature of the intervening events, so the general advice is to make the field notes as soon as possible after the observation. The normal advice is to do it the same day without fail. Of course, in some circumstances, it would be helpful to make some brief notes immediately after the observation if it is not possible to do the full version until later. This can be done in a number of ways such as using a voice recorder but this may increase the labour rather than ease it. Handwritten or computer written notes are probably better in most circumstances.

- It may be helpful to carefully plan the periods of observation in a way which allows the making of notes easier. For example, one can plan the observation periods so as to give sufficient time for lengthy field note-making periods immediately afterwards. This could be something as simple as using lunch breaks for field note-making rather than more observation. The longer the periods of observation the more difficult it is to make field notes effectively.

- Note-making must not be rushed since these are the records that you will use for your analysis later on and if you don't understand what you wrote then the notes are not useful. So you need to write with a high degree of clarity and to make the notes as detailed and graphic as possible in order to achieve this.

It is incorrect to assume that the observations will be at the same level throughout the period of the study. Spradley (1980) suggests three distinct phases: (a) descriptive observation – the initial stage where the researcher is struggling to understand the complexity of the research situation; (b) focused observation which is narrower and focuses on aspects which are most relevant to the research question; and (c) selective observation which occurs near the end of the study when the researcher is seeking further evidence about something that has emerged in the focused observation stage.

Some pointers to the adequacy of one's field notes lie in: (a) greater variety in terms of the researcher being able to interact and relate to the group being studied will improve field notes, e.g. by involving people of a wide variety of different roles and statuses as well as a wide variety of group activities; (b) the greater the involvement of the observer with the group the more likely they are to understand the meanings of what is said and the nature of what is done; and (c) the more that the observer and those they are researching understand each other then the better the interpretation of events as included in the field notes.

What should be observed? This is another matter which is very difficult to address in general terms without specifying more precisely the purpose or research aims of the project. Few psychologists are likely to be in the open-ended situation of travelling to a totally different culture to try to understand that culture. Instead, they will be working in a specific location to understand a particular issue. For example, they may wish to understand the activities of work-groups within a hospital context. In these circumstances, the research will be rather more focused and precise. While participant observation studies usually progress from rather general to rather more specific observations on

→ the basis of the experiences of the researchers, the starting points for different studies can vary widely. Ethnography/participant observation is very flexible – one of the strengths of the method. Flexibility does not indicate vacillation but a process of reflection throughout the timescale of the research project. By thinking about what has been observed, the key features of the situation will begin to be more apparent. Once this is achieved, then alteration is appropriate and not to accommodate to developing ideas in the research would be to miss the point of ethnography/participant observation.

Step 9   **How to sample**   In participant observation, the objective of the researcher is to understand better the community or group under observation. Rarely, if ever, is the task to obtain estimates of the rates of occurrence of different sorts of characteristic such as the average age of the members of the community, for example. Consequently, the probability sampling used by some quantitative researchers is simply inappropriate for participant observation which endeavours to find explanations of key aspects of the workings of the group or community. To achieve this aim, it is clearly more important to seek out situations and individuals who have the most to contribute in order to develop this understanding. By way of illustration, imagine research taking place on the factory floor. Random sampling of informants has a good chance of omitting the one or two individuals who are the most crucial in the activities of the factory floor. The participant observer would be looking for these individuals actively by obtaining information, for example, from key providers of information as to whom they may be.

Step 10   **When to stop fieldwork**   Most research is constrained by resources. This applies as much to research by students as research financed by, say, the Government. These constraints may determine how much fieldwork can be done. However, sometimes another strategy is used. The term theoretical saturation is used to describe the situation where additional data collection produces nothing additional relevant to the concepts, ideas and theories which are guiding the research. When this occurs, the researcher has established a pattern of strong relationships between his or her analytic categories. Furthermore, the categories developing in the analysis will be well understood when the point of saturation is reached. That is, the researcher is clear about the properties or characteristics of the category and additional data collection is doing nothing to encourage a reassessment of the characteristics of that analytic category (Strauss & Corbin, 1998). Or, another way of conceiving this is to simply discontinue the observation when it is clear that new entries in one's field notes seem very familiar in terms of what was written in earlier field notes.

How to analyse ethnography/participant observation

Burgess points out that it is a common comment by researchers that participant observation and ethnographic data simply fail to 'speak for itself' (Burgess, 1982, p. 236). Furthermore, field research does not neatly divide into the stages which usually are claimed to typify quantitative research – literature review, research question formulation, data collection, data analysis, etc. The analysis of

FIGURE 5.4 How to analyse participant observation data

a participant observation/ethnography study must start with the realisation that it is primarily part of understanding culture, social structures and organisations by immersion of the researcher in relevant contexts (Figure 5.4). A number of things follow from this, the most important of which is the broad nature of the data collection methods that may be involved. This means that the researcher's skills are at a premium simply because so many different types of data have been employed. Of course, the task is less complex if the study involves only participation observation, though this would rarely be the case.

Reading this chapter, the following should be clear:

- There is no 'cookbook' approach to the analysis of participant observation/ ethnography taken in its widest sense. While this may feel like a deterrent against such studies, it should be seen as a positive aspect rather than a negative one. There are many forms of research which are easier than participant observation/ethnography.

- There may be very different approaches to data collection involved in participant observation/ethnography so the linking of different analyses is an inevitable component of the process. That is, just how do you link the outcomes of a participant observation study with the outcomes of the related in-depth interviewing study?

- Participant observation/ethnography is typical of qualitative research, in general, since its objective is the collection of extended in-depth or rich data. Thus, it would be expected that such data may be amenable to certain forms of qualitative analysis – grounded theory being the obvious example. Equally clearly, some forms of qualitative analysis are ruled out – discourse analysis and conversation analysis, for example – since they are dependent on an exact and detailed transcription of texts. The field notes for participant observation/ethnography simply do not attempt to record conversation in this form.

The analysis of participant observation/ethnography has largely been in ways which are highly redolent of 'grounded theory' (see Chapter 8). This is not to say that grounded theory has always been formally involved in the analysis – however, there are distinct similarities:

- The analysis is seen as starting with the initial data-gathering phase rather than being a distinct and separate processing.
- The analysis works by a process of formulating largely descriptive field notes to which the researcher adds interpretative (or analytic notes). This is not dissimilar to the process of coding data in thematic analysis, grounded theory, discourse analysis and so forth.
- The analytic process proceeds by a process of data examination, tentative analytic ideas, re-examination of the data in the light of this tentative analysis, the reformation of the analytic ideas and so forth.

Burgess (1982) describes one approach to the analysis of fieldwork which translates into the process presented in Figure 5.5. The similarities to grounded theory are clear.

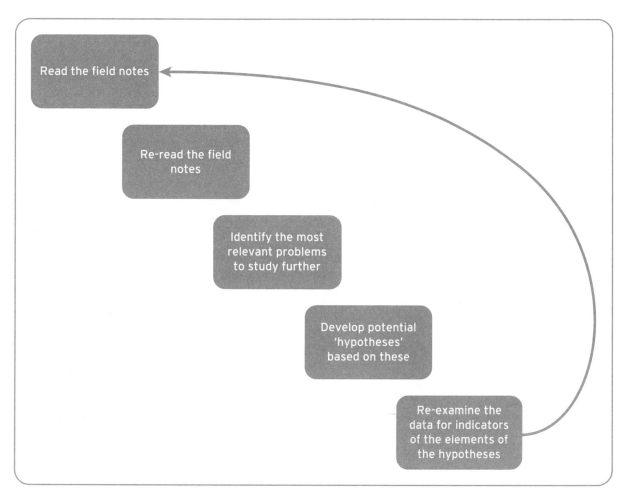

FIGURE 5.5 One approach to fieldwork analysis

When to use ethnography/participant observation

Ethnography/participant observation is at its most useful:

- When one wishes to understand the operation of a naturally occurring group, community or culture. The assumption is that if the researcher engages with the group skilfully and at length, they will see the group acting in a natural way without being affected significantly by being involved in a research study.

- When broad observations are appropriate rather than narrowly focused ones. Thus, ethnography/participant observation is quite different from the fine-grained approaches which, for example, conversation analysis and discourse analysis deal with. It does not operate at the same level of detail. Ethnography/participant observation is about studying social interaction and cultures in as full and natural a way as possible.

Ethnography/participant observation can be regarded as a method in its own right capable of generating a rich variety of data which are unobtainable in any other way. However, it is a resource-hungry approach compared with most other methods of qualitative research. As a method, it has a lot to commend it to qualitative psychologists though the concentration of much qualitative psychology almost purely on language is probably a limitation on its usefulness. However, what else can compete with it as a way of studying groups in their social environment?

While it is reasonable to suggest that participant observation/ethnology is not a frequently used method in psychological research, it has a somewhat wider role in psychology than research. You will find that observation is used in a variety of professional contexts in psychology such as in business, counselling and education. So taking the method seriously as a research tool would add to the general practical skills of any psychologist.

Evaluation of ethnography/participant observation

Any evaluation of ethnography/participant observation needs to take into account the range of things which can be included in such a study. Observation, alone, would be rare and this is not the place to evaluate every method used. This said, among the criticisms that may be attached to participant observation are the following:

- Participant observation, being primarily a qualitative data *collection* method, is not clearly associated with particular methods of data analysis. This means that once having collected the data, the researcher may be left with important questions about how to analyse the data. To some extent, this is always the case in research.

- Participant observation is resource-intensive. It takes a lot of time and consequently money to do properly. The traditional anthropologist or ethnographer had the luxury of time. Of course, not every researcher has a year or two to devote to fieldwork but, then, not every piece of research involving participant observation needs that much time. Early anthropologists, for example, might familiarise themselves with the local language and engage with the culture before beginning their main fieldwork. Furthermore, they may have seen their work as much more exploratory and less built on previous research and theory than modern researchers. Researchers with a predefined or more limited focus than traditional anthropologists may require substantially less time in the field.

- Mainstream psychologists may question the objectivity of participant observation methods. Consequently the first task of the participant observer is to make notes about what was actually seen and heard. It is incumbent on the participant observer that they try to keep description separate from interpretation. Keeping these separate when writing up field notes is inevitably difficult at times but nevertheless essential. Of course, some styles of recording events are intrinsically better than others. For example, it may be objective to write that 'when Debby approached she was not smiling' than to write 'Debby approached hostilely'. Although she might have been hostile, this cannot be assessed from the fact that she was not smiling.

- Field note-taking can be problematic. While the methodology of participant observation may appear simple, practically things are rather more complex since the researcher is often unable to make field notes immediately after observing the group, though this would, perhaps, be the ideal. Given the nature of participant observation, it is not so easy to use technological help such as digital recordings as it would be, say, for an interview. Not only do delays in writing-down fieldwork observations risk producing distortions due to memory, they mean that the participant observer needs to be extremely well disciplined about making the notes each day on a regular basis.

- Participant observation, because of its very nature and its resource intensiveness, realistically cannot be employed for representative work on major organisations or even national issues – that is to say, participant observation might not be feasible when representative samples of a large organisation are to be studied. Other methods would be more appropriate such as surveys, although participant observation might be employed as a means of exploring issues prior to the full-scale study.

- Often participant observation is used in conjunction with other methods. This means that analytic methods have to be developed which integrate the several different aspects of the research.

- Pole and Lampard write of participant observation:

  Observation is a research method which perhaps more than any other relies on the capacity of the researcher to interpret a situation as it unfolds around him/her . . . Moreover, where participation is emphasised, the researcher may also be directly responsible for some of the social action which he/she is observing. Taking all of this into account, observation is perhaps the most demanding of research methods, necessitating a great deal of thought and practice. The problem here, of course, is that practice can only effectively occur in real research situations. (Pole and Lampard, 2003, p. 71).

If we add to this other demands on the participant observer, such as the additional range of research and interpersonal skills required by the method, then it is evident that participant observation is a demanding form of research, probably unsuited to the complete novice other than as a training exercise.

CONCLUSION

Becker and Geer (1982) suggest that techniques such as participant observation and unstructured interviews are the prime ways in which data can be collected in which 'surprises' can be found. Pre-structured questionnaires are only capable of generating 'findings' about pre-specified and thus partially 'known' things. There are, of course, many other ways of collecting data which meet these requirements since the crucial factor is the lack of pre-structuring of the data collected rather than a particular method.

Unfortunately, ethnography/participant observation has been a relatively uncommon form of research in psychology despite being mentioned frequently. Perhaps it is a little too unlike the conventional laboratory experiment to be readily accepted by researchers with a psychology background. Subjectivity is not regarded as a virtue in mainstream psychology and it is notable that the currently popular methods of qualitative psychology tend to use approaches which can be construed as objective. (Again conversation analysis and discourse analysis are the best examples.) Its data do not consist of precisely recorded spoken language or text which tends to characterise much of the data which is central to modern qualitative psychology. But there are other factors in the neglect of ethnography/participant observation such as its labour-intensive nature which work against it. All of this is a pity because it means that psychologists underuse a method which specifically is aimed at understanding social systems and processes. While other qualitative approaches in psychology may have some relevance, they simply lack the broad, in-depth treatment that participant observation affords.

KEY POINTS

- Ethnography/participant observation cannot be described as a major qualitative technique in psychology but it has been influential in the form of a few seminal studies. Naturally, this is most common in social psychology.

- Although participant observation refers to a specific style of research, in reality participant observation and ethnography use participant observation in a wider research context which might include interviews, diaries, general documents and participant observation, among other things. Such a broad study is expensive in resources and relatively uncommon as a consequence.

- Ethnography/participant observation puts considerable demands on the interpersonal resources of the researcher as well as on their powers to memorise and record data for analysis. Clearly there is a big disparity between the sorts of data generated by these methods and the sorts of data needed for those qualitative data analysis methods which concentrate on language in action such as discourse analysis and conversation analysis. The same is true for narrative analysis and interpretative phenomenological analysis which concentrate on detailed accounts of individuals' experiences.

ADDITIONAL RESOURCES

Genzuk, M. (2003). A Synthesis of Ethnographic Research. http://www-rcf.usc.edu/~genzuk/Ethnographic_Research.pdf (accessed 27 August 2009).

Miller, P.J., Hengst, J.A., and Wang, S.-H. (2003). Ethnographic methods: applications from developmental cultural psychology. In P.M. Camic, J.E. Rhodes and L. Yardley (Eds.), *Qualitative Research in Psychology: Expanding methods in methodology and design*. Washington, DC: American Psychological Association, 219-233.

O'Reilly, K. (2009). *Key Concepts in Ethnography*. London: Sage.

Penn Anthropology (n.d.). How to Do Ethnographic Research: A Simplified Guide. http://www.sas.upenn.edu/anthro/anthro/cpiamethods (accessed 18 August 2009).

PART 3

Qualitative data analysis

Mostly qualitative methods produce data in the form of words. There are qualitative analyses carried out on visual data but this is relatively uncommon. So when we think of qualitative psychology we are largely thinking words. There are numerous different ways of conceptualising language and, characteristically, there are different methods of analysis in qualitative psychology depending on how the researcher wishes to use these words. Of course, a newcomer to qualitative psychology may experience difficulty getting a sufficient overview of the various methods of analysis in order to understand what each achieves. So in this Introduction to Part 3 the focus will be on how to select an appropriate analytic method for your data. The six different analytic methods discussed in the next few chapters are based on very different epistemological and historical roots – something which is not usually an issue when choosing different quantitative methods but is important in relation to qualitative research. These different epistemological roots are summarised in Table P3.1. Furthermore, the different names given to the different methods can cover quite a range of different forms of analysis. So, for example, there is a great variety of different techniques which use the same overall title of discourse analysis. Within psychology, the range is slightly smaller yet ranges from social constructionist discourse analysis to Foucauldian discourse analysis. A reader unaware of this might struggle to understand exactly what the nature of discourse analysis is. These are not fully compatible approaches and they can have very different concerns. This is a problem built into the field and newcomers to discourse analysis cannot be blamed for the confusion that this may cause. So it is perhaps a case of being forewarned is forearmed. It does raise the question of whether to deal with the methods separately. This has its drawbacks since it fails to recognise how they overlap quite substantially. Consequently,

TABLE P3.1 Backgrounds and epistemological basis of qualitative analysis methods

Thematic analysis	• The epistemological basis of thematic analysis is relatively unspecific other than it follows the broad general features of qualitative approaches.
Grounded theory	• Grounded theory is a reaction to the large-scale social theory of sociology prior to 1960s. It provided rigorous methodological procedures for theory building.
Discourse analysis	• The roots of discourse analysis are in the idea of speech as action as well as Foucault's approach to social systems.
Conversation analysis	• Conversation analysis adopts a strongly ethnomethodological approach to language in its attempt to understand conversation as a skilled performance.
Interpretative phenomenological analysis	• Interpretative phenomenological analysis is strongly based on phenomenology and a number of related approaches. It concentrates on experiences as experienced by the individual.
Narrative psychology	• Narrative psychology concentrates on life-story data which it interprets from a critical realist perspective. In many respects it shares many of the perspectives of interpretative phenomenological analysis.

they are discussed together in Chapter 9 but put into the context of various related approaches.

In this book, six different approaches to qualitative data analysis in psychology are discussed in detail. It so happens that they fall fairly naturally into three major groupings. This is not to suggest that they are treated this way in the research literature but that understanding what these three groupings are helps unravel what the field of qualitative data analysis involves. Of course, judgements of similarity are bound to be contentious so this scheme may not be accepted by all. Researchers sometimes claim to be using a variety of analytic methods – which may be from more than one grouping. This is probably because many of the analytic methods have overlapping procedures. Indeed, despite the different epistemologies, often very similar processes are involved. So where a researcher claims to be carrying out a discourse analysis and grounded theory analysis they are probably indicating that their method of discourse analysis has many overlapping features with grounded theory. Nevertheless, Figure P3.1 should be useful. It is important to note the following:

- Most qualitative analytic methods tend to be dependent on transcribing the data from, usually, an aural to a written form. Thus the figure starts with transcription. This is dealt with in Chapter 6. Of course, if the data are already in written form, it will not be necessary to involve transcription. For the most part, just a word-by-word transcript is sufficient but for conversation analysis and some aspects of discourse analysis it is important to use the Jefferson transcription system. This includes more additional features of language such as overlapping speakers and gaps in the conversation.

- Thematic analysis and grounded theory are fairly generic qualitative data analysis methods. Thematic analysis is basically various methods for categorising the data into a number of major themes or descriptive categories. Grounded theory does this and more, and is better conceived

FIGURE P3.1 Pathways through Part 3 of the book

as a strategy for data collection and data analysis since it has procedures for sampling to maximise the relevance of the data to theory as well as ways of coding the data to produce themes. But then it goes further and involves ways of generating more general theories. Both of these approaches are less constrained by epistemological factors than any of the other methods described in the next few chapters.

- Conversation analysis is a coherent approach to the structure of conversation as an orderly aspect of social interaction. In contrast, the term discourse analysis is far wider and includes activities, at one pole, very similar to those of conversation analysis but, then, involves aspects of the work of the French academic Michel Foucault who provided a critical approach to social institutions at the other pole. Both of these can legitimately be called discourse analysis but to assume that they overlap greatly can lead to confusion.

- Narrative analysis and Interpretative phenomenological analysis are in many ways similar. They both rely strongly on qualitative data and, usually, in-depth interview data. They both can be seen as versions of critical realism since although they are sensitive to the qualitative idea of relativism (i.e. we can never know reality exactly – it is always perceived through a mirror), they both essentially take the view that there is something 'real' which is central to the experiences of individuals. Both concentrate on describing what this reality is. Nevertheless, interpretative phenomenological analysis has strong roots in phenomenology whereas narrative analysis is dependent on the developments in personality theory known as narrative psychology.

To what extent can these different analytic procedures be regarded as fundamentally incompatible? In some ways they are but researchers often have careers in which they use a variety of fundamentally irreconcilable methods in their research. For example, questionnaire studies and experiments have very different epistemological foundations. With exceptions, this happens unproblematically. Difficulties and issues can occur between researchers using nominally the same method. This can be seen in the case of discourse analysis between the social constructionist and the Foucauldian poles. Such disagreements are the meat of academic life no matter the field and should be regarded as broadly positive aspects of qualitative psychology rather than damaging schisms.

Another way of looking at all of this involves understanding that the different approaches to qualitative analysis tend to be associated with different subdivisions of psychology. So, for example, a qualitative researcher in the field of health psychology would naturally be more likely to turn to interpretative phenomenological analysis since it originated in that field and is more tailored to the needs of researchers in that field. Similarly, narrative analysis is more tailored to personality and clinical psychology. Social psychologists have tended to be the most involved with conversation analysis and discourse analysis to the extent that these deal with social interaction through language. Other fields of psychology tend to pick and choose their approach. For example, educational psychology has used interpretative phenomenological analysis approaches. Doubtless other subfields of psychology will generate their own chosen qualitative analysis methods.

CHAPTER 6

Data transcription methods

Overview

- Transcription is the process of turning sound (and video) recordings into written text prior to the further analysis of the material. Orthographic (or secretarial or playscript) transcription simply attempts to note down the words spoken. Other forms of transcription do more to describe more precisely the way that the words are said etc.

- There are a number of transcription systems but largely they have made no inroads into psychology. The exception is the Jefferson transcription system which is important in conversation analysis (Chapter 10) and the social constructionist version of discourse analysis (Chapter 9).

- The Jefferson transcription system was devised by Gail Jefferson, an important figure in the development of conversation analysis. It tries to give a clearer indication of how words are said but it does not include all relevant features such as the facial expression or gestures accompanying the words. That is, transcription inevitably loses information from the original speech though precisely what is lost depends on the method used.

- There is no requirement that Jefferson transcription is used for all qualitative data analysis though it is especially important when one is treating language as an activity which does things rather than simply communicating information. Transcription techniques are much better developed for auditory than for visual recordings.

- Transcription is a time-consuming process which is prone to errors. A researcher should always choose a method of transcription which matches the purpose of their research. The transcriber should avoid putting more into the transcription than their analysis calls for though this is not adhered to in many published studies.

- Jefferson transcription uses keyboard strokes which are universal on modern keyboards but uses them to symbolise different aspects of the way in which the words spoken are said.

- Jefferson transcription can be seen as a low-level coding system since it high-lights certain aspects of the data, so deeming them important, but ignores others. This is easily seen as the original conversation is richer than the recording of that event which is richer than the transcription of the event.

- It is anticipated that digital files of transcripts, recordings and mixed audio-transcript material will be made available by researchers via the Internet more frequently than at the present.

What is transcription?

Data for qualitative researchers take many different forms. However, among the commonest forms of data is the spoken word. Transcription is the process by which a sound (or video) recording of the spoken word is turned into written language for subsequent analysis. It is important to note that the spoken word and the written word are not the same thing since the spoken word has features which normally the written word lacks. Simple examples of the difference are pitch, volume and pace characteristics, along with other variations which the spoken word exhibits in profusion but which the same words written down usually lack. Although it is perfectly possible for summaries of language data to be used for some research purposes, it is virtually universal in modern qualitative research that one works with a written transcript which is a *verbatim* (word-for-word) record of the spoken word or, in some cases, sections of spoken word particularly relevant to the research question. The basic choices of transcription methods which are commonly used in qualitative psychology are:

- The orthographic/secretarial/playscript transcription which concentrates solely on the words which are said, not how they are said. This is the form of transcription that most types of qualitative research use.

- Jefferson transcription which uses common symbols to provide additional information over and above what is available in the secretarial transcription. The additions are things like the way in which the words are said, where speakers overlap, and so forth. This system of transcription is used mainly in conversation analysis (Chapter 10) and in the type of social constructionist discourse analysis associated with Potter and Wetherell (1987) (Chapter 9).

Research imposes limitations on the data which are collected. For example, the decision to audio-record a focus group discussion imposes its own para-meters and a decision to video-record changes the situation too. Should the researcher choose to take notes during an interview then this also has its influence. For example, the note-taking researcher might appear to be rather more formal. Whatever choices are made in research, they will have a bearing on the nature of the data and, as a consequence, what can be done with the data. Much the same is true of transcription: once a choice is made about who transcribes, what is transcribed and how it is transcribed then these choices have consequences. For example, Potter and Hepburn (2009) suggest:

Crucially, advocates of a straightforward orthographic or 'play-script' version of transcript . . . often fail to appreciate that they are not a more neutral or simple record. Rather they are highly consequential transformations. For example, orthographic transcript imposes the conventions of written language which are designed to be broadly independent of specific readers. Such a transformation systematically wipes out evidence of intricate coordination and recipient design. It encourages the analyst to interpret talk by reference to an individual speaker or focus on abstract relations between word and world.

The point is that by *not* indicating how words are being said, the analysis is steered to interpreting the words just in the way they would be in formal written language. In consequence, many of the features of language as it is used in interaction to achieve certain ends are lost. So if the researcher's emphasis is on what language does then the secretarial, orthographic or playscript transcription is inappropriate. Ultimately, however, no transcription is the same as the original spoken words on which it is based.

In just what ways do transcriptions differ in terms of spoken words being written down? These differences should identify some of the limitations of the orthographic/secretarial/playscript transcription. Among the additional non-verbal communications that occur during an interview or focus group are the following:

- *Proxemic communication*   The use of the physical space between persons in a conversation. For example, think of the way in which ordinary women on television reality shows will physically move their chairs apart to indicate their loathing for an ex-partner who refuses to believe that her baby is his.
- *Kinesic communication*   The range of body movements and postures which may reveal more than the spoken word does. For example, the individual who folds their arms during a conversation might be perceived and interpreted in a particular way.
- *Paralinguistic communication*   This includes the changes in volume, pitch and other characteristics of the voice. For example, it is known from research that many people's voices rise in pitch when they lie.
- *Chronemic communication*   The variations in the pace of speech and the silences which are introduced into speech. For example, people may speak faster when they are in an emotional state.

None of these appears in a word-for-word orthographic/secretarial/playscript transcription but some transcription methods do allow for their partial inclusion. Other methods of transcription, such as the Jefferson transcription method, partly include these 'missing' elements. However, no transcription method is available which includes all of the above. There are some aspects of human interaction for which transcription procedures are just beginning to be developed. For example, Hepburn (2004) seeks to provide methods by which crying during the course of interaction may be described and transcribed by the researcher.

O'Connell and Kowal (1995) carried out a systematic evaluation of a variety of different transcription methods including that of Jefferson. They found that all of the methods did a good job of simply recording the actual words said. Where they differed was in the other aspects of speech which were captured. Some transcription systems were good at indicating paralinguistic features (such as when words are accompanied by laughter, sighs or even groans; the Jefferson system does this to some extent), others were good at including prosodic features such as how loud or soft some words were and which parts of words were emphasised (the Jefferson system is also a good example of this), and others were good at recording extra-linguistic features such as accompanying facial expressions or hand gestures (the Jefferson system is poor at this). No single system was good at doing all of these things. Ultimately, in O'Connell and Kowal's (1995) phrase, there is no sense in which a transcription can be regarded as 'a genuine photograph of the spoken word' (p. 105).

In much the same vein, Coates and Thornborrow argue that there is no such thing:

> . . . as the perfect transcript, the 'true' version of a recording (audio or video) of spoken interaction. A transcript of the speech recorded on audio- or videotape is always a partial affair. Different researchers focus on different aspects of language: a phonetician will make a fine-grained phonetic transcript; a linguist interested in collaborative talk will use a stave to capture the inter- action of different voices; a narrative analyst may transcribe stories in 'idea units' . . . the decision about how to transcribe is always a theoretical one. In other words, the same chunk of data can be transcribed in many different ways: each method of transcription will represent the data in a particular way and will illuminate certain features of talk but will almost certainly obscure others. (Coates & Thornborrow, 1999, pp. 595–596)

So it has to be recognised that the notion of complete fidelity between a recorded source and a transcript is unrealistic and misleading. But even more mundane considerations come into play. Nikander suggests that:

> Practical compromises are typically made between the ideals of faithfulness to the original, the readability and accessibility of the final transcript, as well as time and space issues. (Nikander, 2008, p. 226)

Such compromises are a matter of judgement which will be easier for the seasoned qualitative researcher than the newcomer to qualitative research.

Ashmore and Reed (2000) systematically address the issue of the differences between, among other things, the event which occurred, the recording of the event, and the transcription of the event. Each of these is different in sub- stantial ways. One of the crucial things they point out is that transcriptions of different recordings of otherwise exactly the same event can differ. That is, a recording with the microphone nearer the first speaker produces a different transcript from a recording made with the microphone nearer another speaker. This is not a matter of transcriber errors but reflects that different things can be heard at different locations. So even the recording is something of a reconstruc- tion imposed on the original event just as the transcription is a reconstruction built on the recording.

Despite its initially appearing somewhat daunting, the Jefferson transcription system uses many symbols and conventions which make intuitive sense. For example, the use of underlining in this system denotes emphasis and capitals are used to indicate that some words are being said LOUDLY. There is noth- ing complicated in any of this – the difficulty is more to do with the number of conventions in the Jefferson system rather than any of the individual elements each of which is simple in itself. Furthermore, the Jefferson transcription system is built up, almost exclusively, from characters universally available on standard computer and typewriter keyboards. This means that Jefferson transcription is readily implemented by any researcher prepared to spend some time learning its basics. Of course, the keystrokes used in the Jefferson system do not have the same meaning as they would normally. Actually, it would be more correct to say that some symbols have both their normal and an additional meaning in the Jefferson system. Thus capital letters have their conventional meaning but, as we have already mentioned, words in capitals are spoken louder than the other words around them. The use of (brackets) is indicative of a word not identified with complete certainty from the recording. Overall, these additional keystroke symbols basically tell the reader how the words in the transcript are actually being said. The Jefferson system includes methods of indicating pitch, speech volume, speech speed, emphasis within words, pauses or their lack of, over-lapping speaking, laughter and other non-words, and extra information from the transcriber. The main Jefferson conventions are given in Table 6.1. Refer back to this table whenever necessary to understand what is happening in a transcript. You may also spot that there are slight differences between transcribers on certain matters of detail. The Jefferson system evolved as part of a gradual process and will probably continue to do so. Not surprisingly then, new symbols were added at different stages in the development of this method of transcription. In addition, sometimes transcription symbols were replaced by others. This occasionally adds somewhat to the problems involved in using Jefferson transcriptions. In particular, it may be a problem when it comes to studying research which used slightly earlier versions of the Jefferson transcription method. Hutchby and Wooffitt (1998) also go into more detail about Jefferson transcription.

Reading a Jefferson transcription is not too difficult, especially if you use Table 6.1 to check the meaning of the transcription symbols. For illustration, consider the following study of neighbour dispute mediation. The transcript is of a section of a recording of a meeting between two couples and a dispute mediator. The couples are Graham and Louise (G and L) and Bob and Ellen (B and E). Bob does not appear in this segment of transcript. In case you have any difficulties, you can find an annotated version of the transcript on p. 148. This contains examples of each of the different features in the transcript. The transcript is not as complex as some and it does not include every transcription notation symbol but it makes a very clear starting point.

TABLE 6.1 **The Jefferson transcription system (as described in Jefferson, 2004)**

Jefferson symbol	Example	Usage
Pitch indicators		
↑	absol↑utely	Pitch rise symbol. Bearing in mind that there are continuous variations in the pitch of speech, ↑ indicates that the following has an 'unexpectedly' markedly higher pitch than the previous speech. Multiple arrows may be used to indicate greater extents of this.
↓	absolutel↓y	Again considering the normal variations in the pitch of speech, ↓ indicates that the following is spoken at a markedly lower pitch than the previous speech.
*	I'm sor*ry	What follows the asterisk is spoken in a squeaky or creaky voice.
.	sure.	The word before is spoken with a falling intonation possibly indicative of stopping though it does not have to be followed by a pause.

TABLE 6.1 (*continued*)

Jefferson symbol	Example	Usage
Speech volume indicators		
CAPITALS	for GOODNESS sake	CAPITALS mark speech that is noticeably spoken at a louder volume than the speech around it. This is assessed in terms of that speaker's general volume. It is incorrect to put a loud speaker's talk in capitals throughout.
underlining	For goodness sake	This indicates speech spoken louder than the surrounding text though underlining does not indicate things are quite so loud as the use of capitals does.
° °	And when I discovered that she had °died°	The superscript ° or degree sign is used to mark the start and end of noticeably quieter speech.
Speech speed indicators		
><	Then I said >we'd better hurry home<	The speech between these signs is faster than surrounding speech.
<>	On reflection, I think things are <best left alone>	The speech between these signs is slower than surrounding words.
Emphasis indicators within words		
:	de::licious	The colons show the elongation of the previous sound. Multiple colons can be used to indicate the extent of the elongation.
?	right?	The ? indicates that there is a questioning (rising) tone whether or not the speaker is grammatically asking a question.
underlining	kerumbs	The use of underlining shows emphasis made in a word. It indicates both where the emphasis is and the strength of the emphasis. The emphasis can be in pitch or loudness.
Pauses or lack of		
(0.1)	Let me think (3.1) no I don't remember	The numbers enclosed by round brackets (3.1) indicate the length of a pause in speech expressed in tenths of a second. So (3.1) indicates a pause of three and three tenths of a second. This is a long pause and they are more typically 0.3, 0.5 and so forth. If they are clearly a part of a particular speaker's speaking then they are included in their speech. If they do not involve a particular speaker then they are put on another line of transcript. A new line is used where there is any uncertainty about this.
(.)	I was thinking (.) would you like a break	The stop in brackets (.) can be described as a micropause which is apparent but too brief to measure precisely.
-	r-r-really	The preceding sound is cut off by the hyphen.
[ ]	I [think the] job [No if you]	The square brackets [ ] show where one section of talk is immediately followed by successive talk with no interval between. It can happen when the speaker changes but also within the talk of a single individual.

TABLE 6.1 (*continued*)

Jefferson symbol	Example	Usage
Overlapping speaking		
= =	I =think the= job =No if you =	Sometimes equals = signs are used instead of square brackets to indicate the same thing.*
Laughter and other non-words		
hhh	hhh I'm sorry that it has come to this	The h indicates an audible breathing out – several can be used to indicate its length.
.hhh	so to recapitulate .hhh the committee has voted against	The .h indicates audible breathing in. The h gives an indication of the length of the breath.
heh heh	heh heh HEH	This is voiced laughter much as in ha ha ha. Since it is equivalent to a word one can add other symbols.
h	Do(h)n't tick(h)le m(h)e	The (h) indicates that laughter is occurring within speech.
Extra information from the researcher		
((note))	((Clare speaks in a mock Scottish accent))	Double round brackets enclose comments made by the transcriber which indicate things such as the characteristics of the delivery or something to do with the context of the speech, for example.
( )	the treasure is buried under the ( ) and it is all mine	Round brackets with just space inside indicate that something has been said which the transcriber cannot recognise. The amount of space indicates the approximate length of the 'missing' word.
(word)	she had a (bunion) operation	Round brackets with a word inside mean that the subscriber is not absolutely certain what word has been said but believes that it is the word in brackets.
(word)/(word)	(nights)/(likes)	Indicates two equally possible hearings of what was said.
→	John: →	The use of the side arrow indicates that a particular line of transcript is of special importance in terms of the analytic points being made by the analyst.
Gaze (for video transcription)		
_____......	62 _____...... 62 if you would just	Some transcribers use an unbroken line to indicate that a person is gazing directly at another person while speaking and then a dotted line to indicate the gaze has broken. Essentially it involves adding an extra line (with the same number as the text) to indicate gaze.

*See the text of this chapter for details of how overlaps appear in transcriptions.

1 G: y'know it's getting – it's getting real serious this is (.) ↑but the

2   lad keeps getting away with it (.) unfortunately (.) his mother hasn't

3   got a bloke there (.) so she is talking in [front of the children

4 L: [she's not living there half

5   the time is she=

6 G: =no she's out at night and they are using it as a- a rendezvous for the

7   gang

[. . .]

8 G: that's the whole top [and bottom of it

9 L: [it's like the dustbin left out for a week (?) on

10   [the pavement

11 G: [IT'S ALL TO DO with this one lad (.) right (.) we've had report- we've

12   got connections at the school (.) they said 'what's the point of him

13   coming to school he knows nothing (.) he only causes trouble' (0.5) so

14   [they never bothered about him

15 L: [it's like they've had words with this woman and can't get through to

16   her from school you know [course (.) he's left now so

17 G: [(?)

[. . .]

18 G: (?) °no no° I mean the funny thing about this is that (.) in actual

19   fact (.) I mean the lady's got to be responsible (.) she's got to

20   be responsible [at the end of the day because [she's never there [she

21 E: [well she's never there is she

22 L: [( ) she's effing and

23 G: can't control him

24 E: yeah

(from Stokoe, 2003, p. 326)

It is important to understand the intellectual origins of Jefferson's approach to transcription. In terms of research, her focus was on the fine detail of interaction between people. In particular, she was not so much interested in the broad patterns of conversation but on the ways that aspects of conversation are shaped in a continuous fashion by what has happened earlier in the conversation. In other words, speech is endlessly contingent on itself. Just as a flavour, on one famous occasion the British Prime Minister, Gordon Brown, performed a slip of the tongue in which instead of saying that he 'saved the banks' he actually came out with the words 'saved the world' when answering questions in Parliament. Of course, one way of looking at this is to suggest that it was a Freudian slip which revealed truly what the Prime Minister was thinking. However, Atkinson (2008) was reminded of Gail Jefferson's paper 'On the poetics of ordinary talk' in which she discusses how the choice of a wrong word was the consequence of the words which immediately preceded it. So Atkinson checked what the Prime Minister had actually said:

> GORDON BROWN: 'The first point of recapitalisation was to save banks that would otherwise have collapsed and we've not only saved the world – erh – saved the banks.'

Notice that the extract contains a sequence of 'w' sounds – _w_as, _w_ould, other_w_ise, and _w_e've. Thus Gordon Brown's error can be seen as an unfortunate recapitulation of the 'w' sound rather than any manifestation of his personal psychology. Jefferson was adamant that such speech-induced errors are not the consequence of hidden psychological motivations as is the case with Freudian slips.

Potter (2003) makes the point of Jefferson transcription clear using the following excerpt from a telephone call inviting someone over (Davidson, 1984, p. 105):

> A: C'mon down _he_:re, = it's oka:y,
>
> (0.2 sec)
>
> A: I got lotta stuff, = _I_ got be:er en stuff

Potter writes:

> Note the way the speaker upgrades the invitation. Why might this be? The likely reason is that the pause of 0.2 of a second is a cue to an impending refusal. Conversational actions such as invitation refusals are typically prefaced by some delay, and research has shown that speakers modify their actions on the basis of such predictions . . . (Potter, 2003, p. 82)

In other words, without the indication of a delay the interpretation of this short snippet is less clear. The situation would not be rectified by later refusals or acceptances from the other person since the upgraded invitation may or may not be effective.

Remarkably, there appear to be no 'rules' governing the orthographic/secretarial/playscript approaches to transcription. Just what should go into the transcript and just what can be left out? For example, does the transcriber identify things which cannot be heard clearly or do they insert their best attempt, when is it appropriate to transcribe the accent of the speaker, and what does one do about overlaps in speaking? For this reason, it would be appropriate to use Jefferson transcription conventions about these basic matters even when the additional linguistic codings which Jefferson transcription adds are not used.

What the transcription symbols mean

Graham is the speaker for the first three lines

There is a brief, unmeasured, pause in the speech

Graham says 'but' at a markedly higher pitch

```
 1 G:   y'know it's getting – it's getting real serious this is (.) ↑but the

 2      lad keeps getting away with it (.) unfortunately (.) his mother hasn't

 3      got a bloke there (.) so she is talking in [front of the children

 4 L:                                              [she's not living there half

 5      the time is she=

 6 G:   =no she's out at night and they are using it as a- a rendezvous for the

 7      gang

[ ... ]

 8 G:   that's the whole top [and bottom of it

 9 L:                        [it's like the dustbin left out for a week (?) on

10      [the pavement

11 G:   [IT'S ALL TO DO with this one lad (.) right (.) we've had report- we've

12      got connections at the school (.) they said 'what's the point of him

13      coming to school he knows nothing (.) he only causes trouble' (0.5) so

14      [they never bothered about him

15 L:   [it's like they've had words with this woman and can't get through to

16      her from school you know [course (.) he's left now so

17 G:                            [(?)

[ ... ]

18 G:   (?) ºno noº I mean the funny thing about this is that (.) in actual

19      fact (.) I mean the lady's got to be responsible (.) she's got to

20      be responsible [at the end of the day because [she's never there [she

21 E:                  [well she's never there is she

22 L:                                                 [( ) she's effing and

23 G:   can't control him

24 E:   yeah
```

Graham and Louise are speaking together

Graham takes over conversation from Louise without pause

Graham talks loudly

A pause timed at half a second

Transcriber cannot hear

Some text omitted

no no is spoken noticeably quietly

Ellen begins talking at the same time as Graham then Louise overlaps with Graham

The development of transcription

Just who the first person was to instigate an orthographic/secretarial/playscript transcription of social scientific data is unknown. Perhaps it is not such a big step from having a typist transcribe from the boss's Dictaphone tape to having another typist transcribe research interviews and other data. Phonetic transcriptions of language began in the twentieth century with systems such as the *International Phonetic Alphabet*.

Gail Jefferson (1938–2008) has been an influential figure in many disciplines including sociology and anthropology – and more recently psychology. The questions which guided her research cross the boundaries of different disciplines. Fortune led her to conversation analysis (Chapter 10) as it was being developed by Harvey Sacks (1935–1975). She took one of his courses to complete a requirement of the degree in dancing that she was taking (see the Jefferson tribute website 'Born to Transcribe Watergate', http://www.gailjefferson.com/index.html). It so happened that Jefferson had previous experience of doing orthographic/secretarial/playscript transcriptions from when she had been a typist. Jefferson began transcribing some of the lectures by Sacks that had been recorded. Sacks was not the most prolific of writers and Jefferson's transcriptions of his recorded lectures are an important part of his legacy (e.g. Sacks, 1992). Eventually Jefferson began her PhD under the supervision of Sacks. It was at this time that her methods of tracing the really fine detail of interaction began to develop and evolve. Her method was an attempt to combine both a precise record of what was said with the way in which it was said. As a consequence, rather than simply note that the speaker laughs she tried to indicate more of the detail of how that person's laughter was combined into the speech. Jefferson's is not the only language transcription system, of course. One which competes in many respects was developed by the linguist John Du Bois (Du Bois, Schuetze-Coburn, Cumming & Paolino, 1993). This does much the same as the Jefferson system. Indeed his system shares a lot of notation conventions with the Jefferson system but differs in detail. But there are others such as HIAT or Heuristic Interpretative Auditory Transcriptions (Ehlich, 1993), John Gumperz's Transcription Notation (Gumperz & Berenz, 1993) and CHAT (Codes for the Human Analysis of Transcripts) (MacWhinney, 1995). These seldom, if ever, appear in qualitative psychology.

As in so many areas of research, the advent of the personal computer has eased the task of transcribing interactions considerably. The Jefferson system, for example, involves the transcription of silences, gaps and pauses in speech fairly accurately. Computer programs such as Audacity and Adobe Audition (formerly Cool Edit) allow the transcriber to assess these with a greater degree of accuracy by allowing the measurements to be made against a wave trace of the sounds. See Additional Resources at the end of this chapter for more details.

Transcription in the future may be affected by the availability of digital voice recognition software. If a computer can turn digital recordings into words then this might facilitate the making of the verbatim transcription. There is software that can do this though it is not readily available. However, the big problem is that the software needs to be able to distinguish between two or more speakers given the nature of much qualitative data. Matheson (2008) discusses her system for doing so and the general problems of voice recognition software in qualitative research. Of course, this is a long way away from software that can transcribe using the Jefferson system.

Gail Jefferson's story is closely connected to conversation analysis and much more detail about the background to this can be found in Chapter 10.

How to do Jefferson transcription

Jefferson transcription was initially developed using manual typewriters before technological advances in the form of computers made transcription much easier (Potter, 2004). This is important since anywhere from 10 to 24 hours of work may be required to transcribe 1 hour of recording. (The figure varies according to who is making the estimate.) It also means that one should be careful to match one's transcription needs to the purpose for which the data are being transcribed. Thus the essential and central assumption is that the choice of transcription methods should match the needs of your particular analysis. This is no time to routinely devote so much labour to an unnecessary task. For example, you may decide that Jefferson transcription suits your purposes because of its fine-grained perspective on language data but feel that the bulk of what is on the recording is irrelevant for your purposes. So long as you have a basic set of principles to help you determine what is relevant and what is irrelevant and these principles are consistently applied then there is nothing against such a partial analysis. Almost certainly, the use of the Jefferson transcription system is *de rigueur* for conversation analysis of one's data though researchers have questioned its ubiquity in all forms of qualitative research including discourse analysis.

Given that there are so many different varieties of qualitative research, a one-size-fits-all approach to transcription may not be adequate. One suggestion is that novices use the Jefferson system in order to establish whether or not it works for their style of analysis. There is little point in using the elaborate system if just a transcript of the words said would suffice. One might initially be guided by the approach taken by other researchers who study in areas similar to yours. They, after all, may have had more experience in the use of transcription and probably have a more considered approach to what is essential for a particular type of research. The researcher who is interested in the processes which occur in conversation may well need an elaborate transcription procedure compared with a researcher who is more interested in the substance of what is said rather than how it is said. For the researcher interested in conversation, the literal words used may be inadequate for understanding the processes of conversation. A researcher who is interested in regional accents in conversation may find both the literal transcription and the Jefferson transcription inadequate because neither adequately deals with this aspect of how words sound. Phonetic transcription would be more appropriate in this case though this is virtually unknown in psychological research. A transcription method needs to be carefully considered to see whether what it does would meet the purposes of your research (Potter, 1997).

Irrespective of the transcription method chosen, there are some basic principles which constitute valuable advice for those planning the transcription of spoken language (O'Connell & Kowal, 1995):

- *The principle of parsimony*   This suggests that a researcher should not transcribe features of speech which are not intended to be part of the analysis. In other words, only do in transcription that which will be helpful.

- *Keep transcriptions in reports as simple as possible*   This means that transcriptions provided in reports of your research should only include features which are important in making your analysis intelligible to the reader. Thus, a Jefferson transcript may not be appropriate even though it has been carried out by the researcher.

- *Avoid creating a spurious impression of accuracy in your report*   O'Connell and Kowal (1995) found that transcribers working on radio interviews actually ignored the vast majority of short pauses when transcribing the interviews. About a fifth of short pauses were included but the basis for their inclusion was not at all clear. Similarly, if the researcher assesses the lengths of pauses subjectively then it is misleading to use the convention (0.9) which implies a greater degree of accuracy in measurement than was the case. This does not apply to all research, of course, and computer-assisted methods employed by transcribers may increase the accuracy of such judgements.

- *Checking transcriptions*   One would not expect transcriptions to be error-free and transcriber errors are common. Things such as verbal omissions and additions, translocations and word substitutions may all occur in transcriptions. Consequently there is a case for using an independent checker to look for such errors.

Like most aspects of research methods, transcription is best learnt if one has a basic understanding of how it is used and presented in research publications. So general reading of qualitative papers featuring transcription is recommended as a preliminary stage before beginning transcription yourself. You have already had the opportunity of using the neighbour disputes transcript presented earlier. But transcripts can be rather more detailed than that one, especially where the transcript contains a lot of laughter or where the speaker breaks up a lot of words as they speak. By reading papers using transcription you will encounter the work of different transcribers, which can look extremely complicated at first. Experience with a variety of transcripts will help you better understand what is expected. When reading transcripts, pay attention to (a) understanding what has been said and (b) understanding how it is said. Right from the start, you will probably find that parts of many transcriptions are meaningful since some of the transcription symbols are, to a degree, self-evident: for example, capital letters for loudly spoken words, up and down arrows for rising or falling pitch respectively, a ? for a questioning tone, and so forth. In context, you might be able to have a stab at some of the less obvious conventions such as °to indicate a quietly spoken passage°. You can check the main conventions by consulting Table 6.1 which lists Jefferson transcription methods, explains them and provides illustrations. They have been organised into different aspects of spoken language for convenience. Of course, to begin with you will consult this table regularly but gradually it will become second nature to use the notation method.

It is not recommended that you attempt any major transcription of data until you have practised on a manageable segment of your recording and begun to gain confidence. Of course, you will also have queries which you may need to resolve by checking Table 6.1 for details of the Jefferson system or by consulting with people more experienced in transcription than yourself if necessary. There are a number of websites which help with learning transcription, some of which provide recordings to transcribe.

TABLE 6.2 **Steps in transcription**

Step 1: tuning into the recorded interaction	Step 2: rough transcription	Step 3: adding Jefferson symbols and transcribing sequencing accurately
• Listen to the recording several times • Decide whether all of the material needs transcribing • If not, decide what parts need to be transcribed	• Names of speakers for each segment of conversation • The words said written down as pronounced typically • Put any non-transcribable features in brackets, e.g. ((gun fired)) • Only use continuous capitals for loud passages and nowhere else • Indicate pauses, etc. for later more precise measurement	• Add the fine detail of the transcription symbols taking special care with overlaps, etc. • Make sure that the transcription is in its clearest form for readers

The following are the main stages in carrying out a Jefferson transcription, based on the approaches of Atkinson and Heritage (1984), Gumperz and Berenz (1993), Langford (1994) and Roberts (2007). The procedures described are not absolutely fixed and eventually you will develop your own working methods. However, the following may be reassuring to a novice transcriber (see also Table 6.2):

Step 1 **Tuning into the recorded interaction** Transcription is a focused activity rather than a completely routinised process. For this reason, you need to listen a number of times to the recorded interaction that you are to transcribe. By listening to the recording repeatedly you should be able to reach the following decisions:

- Am I going to transcribe all of the recording? While this seems to be an obvious choice to make, it does have its consequences. In particular, transcription takes a considerable amount of time, effort and similar resources. Consequently, complete transcription risks being a little rough or inaccurate. If a section of the recording is unlikely to be analysed then what is the point in straining resources by transcribing it?

- If not, what aspects of the recording am I going to transcribe? In this case you need to have a means of identifying the parts of the recordings you will transcribe. So, for example, you may be studying how children of migrants construe their national identity. In this case, you are looking for material on the recording which refers to this topic. The boundaries may be determined, for example, by a relevant question from an interviewer or a focus group leader. But content is not the only possible criterion. For example, the researcher may be interested in how adult family members bring children into family conversations, in which case, the boundaries will be around the entry of a child into the family conversation. Boundaries may sometimes be very clear but sometimes not so.

The segment of recording should be listened to several times in order to reach a general understanding of what is going on in that sequence of interaction.

→ Effort should be made to identify each of the speakers. This may not be easy, especially in circumstances in which the transcriber was not the data collector. Also, the number of overlapping sequences has a considerable bearing on speaker identification. This process can be difficult so it should be carried out independently of or separately from capturing the words said and the way they are said. This is also where the value of a stereo recording becomes most self-evident.

Step 2   **Rough transcription**   Take a look at Box 6.1 which gives some advice on how a transcription should be laid out and also at the transcription provided on page 146. The important thing to remember is that these are guides as to style and that some things are probably better left until last. Inserting line numbers is one such late job to be done. This is because the precise layout of a transcription is a matter of judgement, not simply the application of rules. Line length in transcription is affected by the need to be able to insert overlapping speech clearly. This may involve trial-and-error until the ideal is achieved. Although in some transcription systems the line number refers to an individual speaker's turn, in Jefferson transcription the line lengths are arbitrary. As a rule they are kept to a moderate number of words. One way of doing this is to use the natural groupings that occur in speech such as the words which are said before a breath is taken or the words which amount to one or two specific information inputs into the interaction. But, clearly, there is room for variation in terms of how things appear on the transcript. This, normally, is of little or no consequence.

At the end of the rough transcription then the transcriber should have recorded the following:

- The names of the speakers for each turn in the conversation or interaction.
- All of the words spoken usually attempting to use the word sounds as spoken by the speaker rather than how they would appear in standard English. For example, 'summat' for 'something' or 'yer' for 'you' or 'your'. But this is not an area where standardisation among transcribers is apparent. Of course, a great many features of accents can be represented reasonably accurately using conventional orthography (methods of writing down words). One could, also, use phonetic spelling systems but this requires a degree of sophistication on the part of the reader which may not be met. Alternatively, some transcribers use 'pseudo-phonetic' forms as used in comic books (e.g. b'cuz I luv ya). In the end, all of these things make a transcription more difficult to read and, as such, may be not be desirable. On the other hand, there are circumstances where the precise pronunciation of words may be very important. For example, where a speaker mocks another speaker by speaking in an exaggerated version of their accent.
- Any non-transcribable features such as when the speaker coughs or clears their throat. These will be put in double brackets ((clears throat)).
- Remember that capitals are not used in Jefferson transcription other than for proper names which will start with a capital letter. Capitals are used in the system to indicate things spoken distinctly loudly.
- Points where there are any pauses. You will probably find it easier to mark these with brackets enclosing x's (e.g. (xx)) as an indication that the fine timing should be entered in the next phase.

→

Box 6.1
PRACTICAL ADVICE
How to lay out a transcription

According to Potter and Hepburn (2009), the following is the best way of laying out a Jefferson transcription:

- *Font* It is important to use a proportional font otherwise the spacing of overlapping conversation, for example, is very difficult. Their recommended font is Courier in 10pt size.

- *Line numbers* Each line of a Jefferson transcription includes a line number. Although these can be typed in manually, they can be inserted automatically by Word. The important steps are (a) end each line of transcript by pressing the Enter key to force a line break; (b) select all of the lines which you want numbered using your mouse; and (c) right click with your mouse and select number (or numbering in some versions). Remember that line lengths are arbitrary so you can force line breaks where you feel that it is convenient. The line numbering convention helps you identify an excerpt from a transcript since the line numbers will be part way through the sequence. The line numbering is fairly arbitrary and the same recording transcribed by a different researcher may have lines of different length and perhaps more or fewer lines for the same amount of the original recording. This arbitrariness is important in that it gives the flexibility needed to be able to indicate overlapping speech.

- *Layout* (a) Use 25 mm (1 inch) margins at top, bottom, left and right of the page and (b) use a code number for the extract and ideally include some indicator of the source of the extract.

- *Speaker's/contributor's name* Have the speaker's/contributor's name in bold and try to clearly separate this from what they say with some space.

- *Blank space* Because you may wish to make notes on the transcript, it is important to include a copious amount of blank space to the right of the text. Judicious use of the Enter key will help you with that.

→ It has to be remembered that this is the rough transcription phase and the rough transcription may not meet all of these criteria. This is not particularly important since the final phase of transcription provides plenty of opportunity to correct any inadequacies left over. Two important things to consider throughout this stage are issues concerning effective communications with the reader and how the transcript contributes to this.

Technology for transcription has improved rapidly since the era of the typewriter and the reel-to-reel magnetic tape recorder. Digital recording equipment (and videorecorders) means that digital files are readily available for computer processing. These, generally, are of a very high quality. Computer software is available which make for easy copying and editing of these files together with easy search facilities. Faces and voices may be disguised and names edited out of the recording for ethical reasons. According to Potter:

→ The simplest way to transcribe is to work with two windows on a computer screen, one running the audio file, the other running the word processor. Audio programs are available that allow a stepwise movement through the file using a physical representation of the wave form that is ideal for timing pauses and noting overlaps. (Potter, 2003, p. 82)

Step 3   Adding Jefferson symbols and accurately transcribing sequencing   This final stage is the one in which the transcript is finally transformed by adding the detailed Jefferson transcription symbols where they apply. Up to this point you have done most of the straightforward work including adding some of the Jefferson notation. But that is not necessarily the fine detail or the best arrangement for the reader to understand. This stage concentrates on the detailed sequencing of the conversation and not merely the words said. These symbols are the square brackets to indicate overlapping or simultaneous utterances by two or more people. Examples are to be found in the Stokoe (2003) excerpt on page 146 but they are so important in Jefferson transcription that they bear repeating. So look at the following, which uses double square brackets [ ]:

11 Gary: where do you think that we ought to [go out tonight?]

12 Sarah: [is there anything] on the
             television?

The square brackets ([) above each other simply indicate the point at which Sarah starts to speak at the same time as Gary is speaking and the closing square brackets (]) above each other indicate when Sarah and Gary stop speaking together. Single brackets are used to indicate when two people start talking at the same time:

17 Sarah: i wouldn't mind watching something

18 Gary   [well

19 Sarah: [like a documentary

Equals signs (=) are used to indicate latching, which is where another speaker takes over the conversation from another speaker without a pause:

28 Sarah: you always want what you want on=

29 Gary   =what m↑e?

Things can be more complex in conversation and more than one speaker can latch at the same time in which case square brackets ([) might be needed to indicate this. For example:

→

→

```
28 Sarah:  you always want what you want on=
29 Gary:   =[what m↑e?]
30 Shane  =[too right]
```

Of course, there are other speech characteristics which could be included – those which indicate how individual words are said in the recording. These are common in Jefferson transcriptions and explained in Table 6.1. Refer to this for clarification whenever necessary but it can also serve as a memory aid to ensure that you have considered all of the different transcription possibilities. As with most things, experience is essential in order to ensure quality transcriptions which are useful both to the researcher but also to the reader.

Pauses in conversation are common. Largely in Jefferson transcription they are signalled using (.) or (0.5) to indicate different lengths of pause (see Table 6.1). However, look at the following:

```
38 Sarah:  you choose
39         (.)
40 Gary:   i'm not bothered
41         (.)
42 Sarah:  are you sulking?
```

In this exchange the pauses are not attributed to either Sarah or Gary since they are given a separate line. They are pauses in the conversation and *not* pauses in what either Sarah or Gary are saying individually. If the pause was clearly attributable to, say, Sarah, then it would appear in a line indicated to be said by Sarah.

Remember that there are limitations to any transcribing system and the features of speech that you wish to include are not part of the system. If you need to add additional transcription features, which may not be part of the Jefferson system, then this is a choice open to you. Of course, you need to carefully describe and explain any such additional coding.

Certain computer programs are often recommended to students to help them with the process of analysis. A complete novice to transcription may prefer to leave this aside until they have built up basic transcription skills. It also has to be said that many transcriptions are made without their benefits and that they are not adopted by all qualitative researchers. They do have various advantages such as enabling a degree of 'noise reduction' to improve the sound quality of the digital recording. They also permit other forms of editing of sound excerpts. Perhaps more importantly, they also display the waveforms of the sound in the recording. In this way it is possible to measure very precisely pauses in conversation and to note where sounds are exceptionally loud or exceptionally soft. The main programs to consider are Audacity and Adobe Audition. The former is a free download and the latter has a free trial download option. See the Additional Resources section at the end of this chapter for more details.

When to use Jefferson transcription

The decision to use Jefferson transcription rather than an orthographic, secretarial or playscript word-for-word record should be a serious consideration (Table 6.3). If the research takes a conversation analysis perspective then it would not be credible not to use the Jefferson transcription system – this is true also for some forms of discourse analysis. This might be expected because of the intimate association of Gail Jefferson's work with the development of conversation analysis. But not all researchers, by any means, are interested in the approach to conversation taken by Jefferson and her colleagues. Some qualitative researchers may be interested in other aspects of the contents of conversations, interviews and the like, not because they are interested in the way participants structure these things but because of what the participants in the conversations have to say about topics relevant to their research question. For example, if the researcher is interested in the life histories of sex offenders it is the substantive material about each offender's life history which can be found on the recording which is important to that researcher. Issues such as how the offender 'recovers' from errors made in telling his life history are not likely to be a particular interest of the researcher in this case. So it is questionable whether there would be any benefit to using Jefferson transcription in this instance. It is clear that there would be considerable resource costs accruing from choosing to do Jefferson transcriptions, the question is whether there would be any research gains from doing so. The resources spent on the Jefferson transcriptions could be used for other things.

It is mainly where speech is being researched as social action that Jefferson transcription comes into its own. Clearly, researchers employing conversation analysis and discourse analytic perspectives view research in these terms and it would benefit from the use of Jefferson transcription in many cases. This does not mean that such a researcher would *always* gain from using such a fine-grained transcription method as Jefferson's. There is, in research, always a question of the level of analysis which needs to be employed. For example, in general, it is very difficult to see the advantages of using Jefferson transcription when the likely sort of data analysis method to be employed is a thematic analysis. Such an analysis is based on developing relatively broad categories which describe the contents of interviews, focus groups and so forth. This does not require the fine-grained transcription method provided by Jefferson. A secretarial or playscript transcription will be almost certainly all that is required in these circumstances. Similarly, it should be noted that some analytic methods tend not to employ the Jefferson transcription system. For example, research

TABLE 6.3 **When to use Jefferson transcription**

Definitely use Jefferson transcription	**Possibly use Jefferson transcription**	**No advantage in using Jefferson transcription so use orthographic transcription**
● Conversation analysis	● Discourse analysis (especially Potter and Wetherell version)	● Narrative analysis ● Interpretative phenomenological analysis ● Thematic analysis ● Grounded theory

in the interpretative phenomenological analysis tradition (see Chapter 11) typically does not use the Jefferson system. This is true for narrative analysis (Chapter 12), grounded theory (Chapter 8) and thematic analysis (Chapter 7).

Given that transcriptions are often available for further analysis by other qualitative researchers, there is a case for fully transcribing the data using the Jefferson system. This is simply because the Jefferson transcription maximises the additional information available to the secondary analyst. Without it, the value of the transcript is reduced. It is also an argument against using 'stripped down' (less complex) versions of Jefferson transcription such as Jefferson 'Lite' which is recommended by some (e.g. Parker, 2005). But these are issues of some controversy in qualitative psychology for which no definitive answer is available.

Evaluation of Jefferson transcription

It needs to be remembered what the Jefferson system does. The words said are recorded in ways which suggest something of the way that they sound though this does not amount to a fully phonetic rendition. So you will see some words written down as they sound in dialect, for example. This, of course, adds to the difficulty of reading some transcripts. Table 6.4 provides an evaluation of the advantages and disadvantages of the Jefferson transcription system.

O'Connell and Kowal (1999) are somewhat critical of some aspects of transcription that appear in the psychological literature. They go so far as referring to some of the 'standardisation practices' in transcriptions as pseudo-scientific:

TABLE 6.4 Advantages and disadvantages of the Jefferson transcription system

Advantages of Jefferson system	Problems with the Jefferson system
1. It records talk as experienced by participants in the conversation and so keeps the analysis focused on this rather than merely the words used.	1. While the Jefferson symbols can sometimes be used very precisely such as times in tenths of a second, other symbols such as : are less carefully defined.
2. Analysis of conversational interaction is facilitated by the system compared with a secretarial transcript.	2. It is restricted in terms of what aspects of interaction it deals with. For example, it is not good for coding emotion.
3. Even if the words are the focus of their analysis, it allows other researchers to more adequately check the original analysis as the transcript is closer to what is on the recording.	3. Although the system may be modified, it tends to set the format of and the parameters for what is transcribed.
4. It has gained dominance over other methods so can be regarded as the standard system of notation.	4. Its origins in the days of typewriters means that it does not capitalise on the potential of computers to use colour and a range of characters, fonts and sizes.
5. By forcing the researcher to spend time in transcribing, it encourages a more thorough approach to analysis.	5. It is very time consuming for the researcher to use.
6. It requires skilled transcribers and cannot be carried out by, say, secretarial assistants.	6. There is disagreement about the value of Jefferson transcription even among discourse analysts.
7. One can use the line numbers to rapidly refer to a particular part of the transcript.	

- They point to instances of elaborate Jefferson transcriptions which contribute nothing to the author's interpretation of their data and which, often, are not referred to in the publication. The question then becomes one of why include something that seems to add no value.

- They question the breaking up of words when the transcript is intended to be read by others. Thus indications of the prolongation (e.g. wa::s), pitch movement and so forth which occur within words or within syllables interfere greatly with the lexical integrity of the transcript. This occurs frequently in transcriptions using the Jefferson method and its value is difficult to appreciate in circumstances in which these things are not referred to in the analysis of the discourse. They may be useful for the researcher but are they useful to the reader?

- They dislike the use of the same notation symbol to mean different things. For example, this has occurred in the Jefferson system during its evolution when a – is used to indicate a cut-off word but also a brief, unmeasured pause.

- Measurement of such things as variations in pitch are not objective in general.

CONCLUSION

The process of transcribing recorded speech is regarded by many qualitative researchers has having beneficial spin-off effects. The close familiarity with the data which many forms of qualitative analysis require means that transcription is necessary to help achieve this intimate knowledge. For this reason, transcription is not something that the analyst should generally delegate to assistants. Transcription is:

> an integral part of the analytic process. This, then, precludes 'farming out' the transcription (i.e., having it done by a professional transcriber or clerical help). Time-consuming and tedious, it nonetheless provides the analyst with an intimate acquaintance with his/her data. (Psathas & Anderson, 1990, p. 77)

Of course, this applies to the novice qualitative researcher even more strongly since they will learn little by getting a friend or partner to do their data transcription for them. So there is little choice but for most qualitative researchers to spend considerable numbers of hours on the, at times, rather mundane task of transcription. But, in qualitative research terms, this is good for the soul.

The use of a speech transcription system is more or less essential in research using language data. Methods of using recordings in an untranscribed form are not really available although it has been controversially suggested that the analysis of the data does not necessarily require the transcription stage (see Chapter 8 on grounded theory). It is self-evident that the transcription is a very resource-intensive process. Jefferson's system of transcription operates at a finer level of detail than literal transcriptions of the same recording and so is even more time consuming. As a consequence, a researcher needs to question just what they are trying to achieve by using transcription. Simple questions such as why an orthographic/ secretarial/playscript transcription will not suffice need to be addressed. Even if a method of transcription such as Jefferson's is used it is appropriate to ask whether there are additional aspects of interaction which should be used in the transcript. The Jefferson transcription system evolved largely to serve the requirements of conversation analysis which imposes its own intellectual ethos on its subject matter, so why is the system needed for research which does not share this ethos?

Researchers need to appreciate that their data are not actually speech as such but transcriptions based on recordings (or video) of speech. The recording is less than or a reduction of the original interaction and the transcription is less than that recording. Although the Jefferson system is correctly described as a system of spoken language transcription, this tends to hide the fact that it can also be regarded as a low-level coding or categorisation system. By this is meant that the use of the Jefferson system imposes a degree of structuring on the data in terms of what is included and what is not included. While researchers tend to focus primarily on the things which the system includes it is evident that what it excludes is also important. For example, in the Jefferson system there is scant attention given to things such as regional accents which we know from research can have a bearing on how speech is received. Similarly, the emotional aspects of speech are not systematically included in the Jefferson transcript – things such as anger or irritation might be heard in the recording but are not transcribed. Of course, if a researcher wants a complete transcription of the recorded speech then it is difficult to better the sound recording itself. What the transcription supplies (Jefferson or otherwise) is a somewhat simplified version of events which omits systematically certain aspects of the original. Unfortunately, the original recording is not particularly conducive to analysis using any of the major qualitative analysis methods. It is almost inevitable that coded or categorised material (including transcriptions which can be seen as a low level of coding) misses out whatever the coding system is not designed to address and highlights those features which the system is designed to address. So conversational difficulties, for example, become very clear from a transcription using the Jefferson system since these are part of conversation analysis which sired the Jefferson system. On the other hand, interpersonal difficulties which may be apparent to members of the conversation are not fully highlighted in the Jefferson system. This is not surprising when one considers that the Jefferson system does little to include such revealing factors as the facial expressions, sidelong glances and the like through which interpersonal factors may be expressed in a group of people conversing. In defence of Jefferson transcription, if one is needed, things can appear on the transcript which indicate bad relations between people. For example, lengthy and awkward pauses (silences), interrupting another person consistently and rudely, and not allowing a person to speak when it is their turn to talk are all indicative of animosity. Furthermore, further details such as the emotional tone of the speaker (e.g. sarcasm) may be given in brackets if the transcriber considers this pertinent.

A researcher may feel that it is important to include additional features into the transcription system that they use. If the system does not address the aspects of interaction which the researcher believes to be important than there is every reason to develop or modify an existing system if not create one anew. For example, Butler (2008), while sticking with conventional conversation analysis transcription symbols adds / to indicate syllables spoken in the same staccato voice as in Good mor:ning ev'/ry/o:ne/ (p. 202).

The transcript is a very portable form of data and easily handled in a research context. It provides a primary focus for the analysis, a means of communicating with other researchers about your data, and a means of including the data in publications. It does have the drawback, however, that it is lengthy compared with a typical publication in a psychological journal. Partly for that reason, it might be anticipated that the Internet will be increasingly used because of the ease and cheapness of circulating substantial amounts of transcript data, its potential for circulating audio and video files within ethical constraints, and its potential for combining audio and transcript material together. All of this will mean that more substantial data extracts can be circulated among researchers than is possible within the confines of a journal article.

KEY POINTS

- Transcription is not a neutral activity but one in which the transcriber makes numerous choices. While this may be a subtle process, different transcribers transcribing the same segment of a recording may not completely agree in terms of what is in the transcription. This, generally, is not a question of one transcription being better than the other but simply reflects the nature of communication between people and the difficulty of defining transcription systems with perfect accuracy.

- While for some purposes a straightforward literal transcription of the words which are spoken in conversation may be sufficient, some analyses need to pay attention to how things are said and not to what things are said. Conversation analysis is exacting in terms of its transcription requirements and uses the Jefferson transcription system to indicate how words are being spoken. Discourse analysts also tend to use this system. However, it is pointless doing all of the work involved in a Jefferson transcription where the analysis does not call for it.

- Transcription should never be regarded as a tedious but necessary chore. It is hard work but the point of this hard work is that not only does the transcription get done but the transcriber (usually the researcher) begins to be increasingly familiar with the data. As a data familiarisation process, transcription generates the intimate knowledge of the data which begins to stimulate the researcher into generating ideas about what is going on in the data. Without this familiarity, analysis is impossible.

- Since transcription will lose aspects of the original recording, it is always important to check the transcript against the recording. This, of course, can be done by the researcher themselves. Nevertheless, there are advantages in seeking the opinion of experienced colleagues about the veracity of the transcript to the recording. This is especially important with novice researchers.

ADDITIONAL RESOURCES

Adobe Audition. http://www.adobe.com/products/audition/ (accessed 28 August 2009). This is a professional quality digital editing program which may be used to improve the sound quality, disguise voices and variously change a digital sound recording. It also displays a graphical trace of the sound as a graph or wave trace. This can be used to assess the length of pauses very accurately as well as helping you make judgements as to the relative loudness or quietness of words or syllables. There is a free trial download available at the web address above. However, as the program Audacity does much the same but for free then the choice is, as they say, a no-brainer. Audacity is listed below.

Antaki, C. (2002) An introductory tutorial in Conversation Analysis. Online at http://www-staff.lboro.ac.uk/~sscal/sitemenu.htm (accessed 1 August 2009).

Audacity. http://audacity.sourceforge.net/ (accessed 28 August 2009). This is a sound editing program which can be used for free. It allows digital enhancements of all sorts to a digital sound file. Furthermore, it displays a sound wave trace which allows the precise measurement of pauses and 'loudness' and 'softness'.

Bucholtz, M., and Du Bois, J. (n.d.). The Transcription in Action Project. http://www.linguistics.ucsb.edu/projects/transcription/index.html (accessed 1 August 2009). This is devoted to the transcription system by John Du Bois.

Jefferson, G. (2004). Glossary of transcript symbols with an introduction. In G.H. Lerner (Ed.), *Conversation Analysis: Studies from the first generation*. Amsterdam: John Benjamins, pp. 13–31.

Liddicoat, A.J. (2007). *An Introduction to Conversation Analysis*. London: Continuum, Chapter 2.

Potter, J., and Hepburn, A. Transcription. http://www-staff.lboro.ac.uk/~ssjap/transcription/transcription.htm (accessed 1 September 2009).

Schegloff, E. Transcription symbols for conversation analysis. http://www.sscnet.ucla.edu/soc/faculty/schegloff/TranscriptionProject/index.html (accessed on 1 August 2009).

CHAPTER 7

Thematic analysis

Overview

- Thematic analysis is an important and relatively straightforward form of qualitative analysis. It is an excellent starting point to begin qualitative research as it is conceptually only moderately demanding.

- Thematic analysis is a commonly referred to qualitative data analysis method. However, it has been criticised in terms of lacking a consistent and transparent formulation. This chapter seeks to rectify this by outlining a more rigorous approach to thematic analysis. Studies using thematic analysis should always include detailed information about how the analysis was carried out. Accounts of how to do thematic analysis were scarce until recently.

- Thematic analysis is just what it says – an analysis of the major themes to be found in interview and other qualitative data. It is much less dependent on theory than are, say, discourse analysis (Chapter 9), conversation analysis (Chapter 10) and narrative analysis (Chapter 12). This makes thematic analysis a more accessible introduction to qualitative data analysis for students and other newcomers to qualitative methods.

- The history of thematic analysis goes back to the 1950s and the development of quantitative content analysis. Calls for a qualitative approach to content analysis emerged at that time. Thematic analysis shares a lot in common with qualitative content analysis though the latter has been more systematically developed especially in Europe.

- Thematic analysis requires the researcher to identify a limited number of themes to adequately describe what is happening in textual data such as interviews. This is easy to do superficially but a set of themes which describe in depth what is going on in the data is more demanding to achieve.

- Thematic analysis requires that the analyst has an intimate knowledge of their data which can be achieved by collecting the data oneself, transcribing the data oneself, and reading and re-reading the data a number of times. Then the researcher begins to code the data – perhaps line by line or every two or three lines – to indicate the contents of small quantities of the data. Codings are brief descriptions of small chunks of data. There are no 'rules' to say precisely how this is done but the more 'conceptual' the codings are the better.

- The codings are a level of abstraction away from the data. From these codings the researcher tries to develop or identify the themes which describe the major features of the data. This process can involve the sorting of cards each bearing the name of a coding or a theme on a table. In this way, it may become more evident just which codings go closely together and, consequently, what the themes might be. Each theme needs to be carefully defined and differentiated from other themes.

- As the analytic ideas develop, the researcher may re-check the data or the codings in order to maximise the fit between the data, the codings and the themes.

- Thematic analysis is a descriptive method rather than a theory building approach to qualitative research (in contrast to grounded theory). Among its advantages is that it tends to generate research findings which are readily understood by the general public and policy makers.

What is thematic analysis?

Thematic analysis is the analysis of what is said rather than how it is said. Generally it can be recommended as an introduction to qualitative research because of its relative lack of complexity. Quite simply, one's data are examined in order to identify relatively broad themes which summarise the content of the data, hopefully, fairly completely. Recently there have been attempts to provide systematic guidelines about how to do thematic analysis in order to correct some of the perceived weaknesses of the method. Braun and Clarke (2006) proposed a more stringent version of thematic analysis though they do write a little disparagingly about the previous state of affairs with thematic analysis. They state: 'Thematic analysis is a poorly demarcated, rarely acknowledged, yet widely used qualitative analytic method within psychology' (Braun and Clarke, 2006, p. 77). One has to have some sympathy with this since it is relatively easy to find thematic analysis studies which appear to have adopted a somewhat basic and unsystematic approach to analysis. Accounts of the detail of how a particular thematic analysis was carried out have been traditionally missing from reports though, of course, this is a situation which is easily rectified once researchers become aware of the problem: 'It can be seen as a very poorly "branded" method, in that it does not appear to exist as a "named" analysis in the same way that other methods do . . .' (Braun and Clarke, 2006, pp. 79–80).

The analysis which is presented in thematic analysis consists of categories or themes. Thematic analyses often refer to the themes 'emerging' from the data as if it were something that themes did on their own without the active involvement of the researcher. Generally, the impression is created that the researcher simply reads through transcripts of interviews or some other form of data a few times and then 'sees' five or six (or even fewer) themes which reoccur commonly in the transcripts. These themes are laced together in a report with illustrative quotes or excerpts from the transcripts for each theme. One major problem with this is that the researcher appears not to be doing a great deal of analytic work in order to develop the themes. The task seems too easy – so long as a few themes are suggested and a few illustrative quotes found, then the job of analysis is done. What this means is that the researcher fails to present the argument justifying their particular analysis. The intellectual demands on the researcher seem to be minimal but, more importantly, the fit of the themes with the bulk of the data is unknown. In Potter's (1998) terms, this is little different from a researcher thinking up a few plausible themes and then trawling through the transcripts to find extracts that illustrate these themes. The problem is that this gross disrespect for and injustice to the data does not constitute a qualitative analysis. Basically it is little different from the way in which quantitative data collection forces data into predetermined categories. Since there are no criteria to decide on the themes, who can say that there is anything wrong with this analysis? So there is a basic, underlying lack of transparency in many thematic analyses. Just what did the researcher do with their data in order to develop the themes? To what extent do the themes encompass all of the data? It may be that key features of the data are ignored along with key analytical insights. The lack of clear, consistent and extensive effort going into the analysis means that the reader may lack confidence in the value of the analysis. This is hardly a satisfactory situation. Hence the need for a more systematic and transparent approach to thematic analysis. Such approaches have been formulated recently (Braun & Clarke, 2006; Howitt & Cramer, 2008). Thematic analysis as discussed in this chapter is based on these.

Thematic analysis, even in its recent more structured forms, is a useful technique which is fairly accessible to novice researchers. As a form of qualitative data analysis it is less demanding than the other methods of qualitative analysis discussed in the next few chapters. The main reason for this is that the process of data analysis is not intimately linked to particular areas of theory as it is with other methods. In some respects, thematic analysis is most similar to grounded theory, though it does not involve the same level of sophistication in data collection and theory building. However, properly done, thematic analysis has quite a lot in common with these other analytic methods. Certainly, the practical skills of data analysis learnt through thematic analysis will help a researcher when they move on to these other approaches. None of this is a criticism of thematic analysis – merely a recognition of its more limited horizons.

Bringing these and other points together, thematic analysis is a useful analytic approach in circumstances in which:

- the data collection is complete;
- there are no strong theoretical perspectives to drive the analysis – though Braun and Clarke (2006) suggest that there are two forms of thematic analysis whereby some are driven by pre-existing theoretical concerns and others are driven by the data;
- the data consist of detailed textual material such as interviews, focus groups, newspaper articles and the like;
- the data are rich in the sense of being full of detail and information such as will occur in in-depth interviews and materials taken from the media, etc.

Quite clearly these are fairly minimal demands for a qualitative study. Since no particular theoretical orientation is associated with thematic analysis and it is flexible in terms of how and why it is carried out, as a qualitative analysis method it is probably the one most available to anyone lacking previous experience of qualitative research methods. So it may be useful to any researcher who wishes to include detailed interviews as part of their research in a systematic way. Even laboratory researchers, the archetypal quantitative demon for qualitative researchers, may wish to extensively interview participants in their research. Thematic analysis may provide a way of organising and analysing these data. Similarly, researchers planning to develop a structured questionnaire may wish to explore the topic first of all by interviewing informants about the research topic. Thematic analysis may provide them with a suitable way of dealing with these data.

In some ways, thematic analysis occupies the middle ground between quantitative and qualitative analysis. Basically, thematic analysis does not carry the theoretical 'baggage' that many qualitative analysis methods do (and quantitative ones too for that matter). For example, the researcher may have a realist position in relation to what the participants say in their interviews. (Generally such a position is problematic in qualitative data analysis where a subjectivist or relativist position is often regarded as *de rigueur*.) This is not to say that anything goes in thematic analysis.

Thematic analysis, despite its currency in research publications, rarely gains more than a perfunctory mention in psychological research textbooks. There are exceptions to this and Howitt and Cramer (2008) cover thematic analysis at some length in their general research methods text. As we have seen, there have been other signs of a revival of interest in thematic analysis where a systematic approach is involved. While it is not possible to provide a completely standard or universal set of guidelines on how to do thematic analysis, it is important to establish it as a method and not just a loose label to attach to simple studies involving codifying data.

According to Howitt and Cramer (2008), the central processes involved in thematic analysis are transcription, analytic effort and theme identification. While conceptually these are three separate processes, in reality they do not follow this rigid order and the processes overlap considerably. Just as in grounded theory (Chapter 8) and many other forms of qualitative analysis, the researcher may feel it necessary to go back-and-forward between stages in order to check and refine the themes that are being developed (see Figure 7.1):

● *Transcribing textual material* Any form of textual material can be used ranging from, say, material from the Internet to transcriptions of in-depth interviews or focus groups. The transcription method used in most published thematic analyses is a secretarial/playscript one (see Chapter 6) and, in general, there is no reason to use a more detailed Jefferson transcription. Of course, if you can think of a reason for doing Jefferson transcription for a thematic analysis then there is no reason not to do so, though who can say what these circumstances might be? Transcription, in qualitative research, is not to be seen as a tedious chore since, in the hands of a good researcher, transcription familiarises the researcher with the data and is an early push or stimulus towards trying to understand and, hence, analyse the data. The familiarity that transcription brings with the data is very closely focused and systematic because of the nature of transcription. The analysis might begin

FIGURE 7.1 Basic thematic analysis

much earlier during the data collection phase for the in-depth interview or focus group, for example.

● *Analytic effort* This is crucial in all forms of qualitative analysis and short cuts to a successful analysis are rarely to be found. Analytic effort is the work or processing that the researcher does on the text in order to generate the final themes – that is the thematic analysis. The analytic effort includes the following components: (a) familiarisation with the data so that it is known in detail to the researcher; (b) the detailed codings and conceptualisations which the researcher applies to their data such as line-by-line coding or much broader-brush approaches to identifying the overall themes; (c) the extent to which the researcher is prepared to process and reprocess the data analysis to ensure that the analysis fits the data as closely as possible; (d) the extent to which the researcher is presented with difficulties during the course of the analysis and what effort is put into resolving these difficulties; and (e) the frequency and thoroughness of the researcher's checks between the analysis of the data and the data.

● *Identifying themes and sub-themes* While the naming of themes and sub-themes is the end point of thematic analysis, there is considerable variation in the extent to which researchers refine the themes for presentation in reports, etc. A researcher might decide that five or six themes effectively describe what they have identified as the key features of the data. Other researchers might well be dissatisfied with the same themes since they feel that they less than completely describe what is happening in the data. All of this continues with the analytic work through to the end product of the total thematic analysis. Since the identification of themes is partly dependent on the amount and quality of analytic effort the researcher has put into their analysis, it is likely that different researchers looking at the same data will end up with rather more or rather less sophisticated findings from their analyses. This underlines the importance of understanding precisely what the researcher has done to generate the themes which are discussed in the report. Of course, in qualitative research it is accepted that different researchers will have different readings of the same data. These can be equally meretricious. This is not at all the same as different analysts producing different analyses simply because they differ in terms of how diligent their analyses have been or how closely they have stuck to the principles of good thematic analysis.

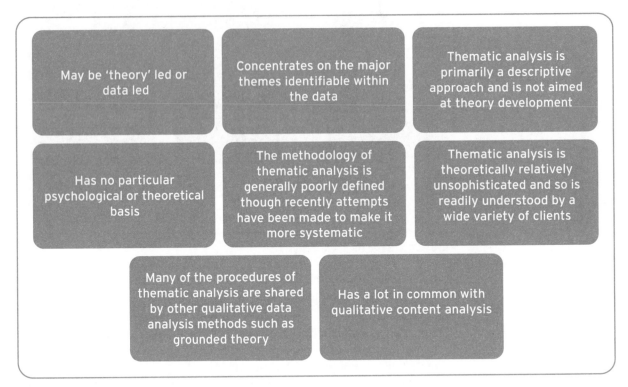

FIGURE 7.2 The key elements of thematic analysis

Figure 7.2 presents some of the key elements of thematic analysis which help to differentiate it from other forms of qualitative data analysis.

The development of thematic analysis

The phrase thematic analysis first appeared in psychological journals in 1943 though it is substantially more common now. For instance, in the years between 1998 and 2008 there were nearly 1000 publications which included thematic analysis in their summaries. Despite this, one has to accept the 'poor relative' status of thematic analysis in the field of qualitative research (Howitt & Cramer, 2008). Hopefully this is changing. Interestingly, thematic analysis has lacked the high profile advocates that characterise some other forms of qualitative analysis. Researchers who used thematic analysis typically provided little or no detail about how they carried out their analyses other than a phrase such as 'we conducted a thematic analysis of . . .'. Some researchers, although they essentially identify themes, made no reference to thematic analysis as their method. For example, Gee, Ward and Eccleston (2003) suggested different types of cognitive distortions among sex offenders by using what they describe as a 'Data-driven approach to model development (grounded theory) . . . to analyse the interview transcripts' (p. 44) though their research appears to be thematic analysis since it lacks crucial features of grounded theory.

Is thematic analysis just a simple version of grounded theory? While anyone carrying out a thematic analysis may learn a lot from considering the grounded theory approach, there is no indication that thematic analysis is in any sense a derivative of grounded theory. Indeed, thematic analysis seems to pre-date grounded theory very substantially. And why should this not be the case? The basic idea of thematic analysis is a simple one – that complex qualitative data might be effectively summarised by identifying the major themes which re-occur within it. This is hardly a rocket-science breakthrough given that themes are little other than categories and that the process of categorisation is a basic attribute of human thinking. It also has to be acknowledged that thematic analysis is a relatively common form of qualitative data analysis in psychology so it must resonate with the needs of substantial numbers of researchers more than some other qualitative analysis methods.

While the full history of thematic analysis will probably never be written, it is possible that thematic analysis did not emerge initially out of qualitative research but out of quantitative research. Content analysis is the generic name given to various approaches to the analysis of the media such as news articles, television programmes and so forth which had its origins in mass communications research in the first half of the twentieth century. The first book on content analysis was Bernard Berelson's (1912–1979) *Content Analysis in Communication Research* published in 1952. However, content analysis had been developing in mass communications research during the 1920s and onwards. Important figures in this early history were Paul Lazarsfeld (1901–1976) and Harold Lasswell (1902–1978). Content analysis was central to the analysis of propaganda demanded by the US Government during the Second World War. Basically this form of content analysis sought to find coding categories which effectively described substantial aspects of the data – once these had been developed then the frequencies of occurrence of each of these categories could be quantified. It would also be possible to cross-tabulate one category against another in a typical, quantitative manner. There is a famous sentence in mass communications research which goes 'Who says what to whom in what channel with what effect'. In the form of who, what, whom, what channel and to what effect, this phrase appears as the nub of many content analyses.

However, the publication of Berelson's book in 1952 led to the immediate demand that a qualitative form of content analysis was also needed. Siegfried Kracauer (1889–1966) responded to its publication with the claim that qualitative aspects of the text were being ignored in favour of counting and measuring (Kracauer, 1952) which must count as a fairly early rehearsal of the qualitative/quantitative debate. The response to this was far from swift, though Kohlbacher (2006) sees the legacy of this early debate in the work of Altheide (1996) and others. There is also the possibility that qualitative content analysis had a major emergence in continental Europe with the work of Philip Mayring in the 1980s and beyond though the impact elsewhere was not great. However, the methodologies employed are more than a little redolent of major principles of qualitative analysis. Bryman suggests that qualitative content analysis 'comprises a searching-out of underlying themes in the materials being analysed' (Bryman, 2004, p. 392). This seems very close to being a definition of thematic analysis.

The interplay between qualitative content analysis and thematic analysis, however, is not really evident in the literature in general, so all of this is speculative. One lesson from all of this may be that qualitative researchers sometimes need broader-brush approaches to qualitative analysis than methods such as discourse and conversation analysis achieve in general.

How to do thematic analysis

If one is looking for an up-to-date account of thematic analysis methodology written by psychologists then the guidelines that Braun and Clarke (2006) provide are the best available systematic approach to thematic analysis. Theirs is a toughened-up description of how to do thematic analysis which draws heavily on their familiarity and involvement with other forms of qualitative analysis. Their approach imposes high standards on thematic analysis and the work of the analyst with the aim of improving the end product of thematic analysis. According to Braun and Clarke (2006), the process of carrying out a thematic analysis may be broken down into six separate stages though, as with most qualitative analysis, there is a great deal of unbridled going backwards and forwards between the different stages of the analysis. The process of thematic analysis may be visualised as being much as in Figure 7.3. The six steps of the analysis are clearly listed in sequential order but the overlap of the stages is patently obvious. While doing a thematic analysis the researcher may move backwards and forwards between stages with the purposes of checking one aspect of the analysis against one or more of the other steps in the analysis. Obviously checking is more frequent between steps which are close together but this does not preclude checking, say, what is written in the report against the original data. The distinction between different stages of the analysis is conceptual for the most part since the different stages may not be totally distinct

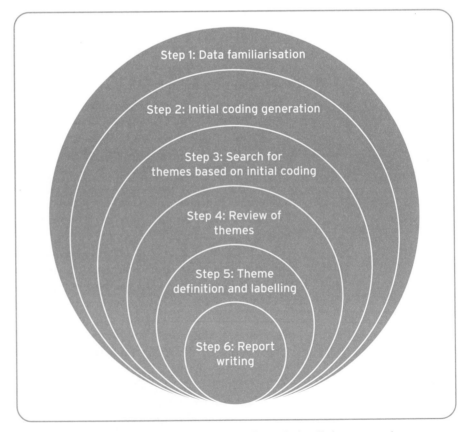

FIGURE 7.3 Braun and Clarke's model of thematic analysis: all steps may refer backwards and forwards to other steps

in practice and are often concurrent. Looping backwards and forwards are ways of improving the analysis – they are not signs that the analysis is proceeding badly. Without this looping backwards and forwards, the analytic effort going into the process is probably insufficient. You might wish to read Box 7.1 next as it describes the practical process of carrying out a thematic analysis.

Box 7.1

ILLUSTRATIVE RESEARCH STUDY

Thematic analysis: Functions of pornography

Just what does a researcher do when faced with a substantial number of transcripts of interviews which need analysing? Thematic analysis is an obvious choice. Internet sex offenders – basically men who use and download child pornography in this case – are a key group to understand if sex offending research itself is to develop (Sheldon and Howitt, 2007). Just how are these men different from traditional contact paedophiles? Just what does the Internet offender get out of using child pornography on the Internet? The primary source of information about Internet sex offenders, given the relative paucity of previous research in this area, has to be interviews with the offenders themselves. What are the functions of Internet child abuse images in the lives of such offenders? The answer to this question, of course, lies in the 51 interviews conducted with Internet sex offenders and contact offenders that the authors carried out. The transcripts of such a large number of in-depth interviews produce a great deal of information which needs to be effectively summarised. The analysis by Sheldon and Howitt (2007) produced perhaps some predictable outcomes but, also, some 'surprises'. Internet sex offenders clearly have a strong sexual proclivity towards children since, for example, they are sexually aroused by children. So it might be expected that sexual arousal might be the main function that child pornography serves for these men. The research confirmed this expectation but added other functions which were not so predictable.

During the course of lengthy interviews, the Internet sex offenders were asked about their use of child pornography images. All of the interviews for this study were conducted by Kerry Sheldon who carried out the analysis. In terms of the data analysis, she had (a) interviewed all of the participants in the study and (b) transcribed in full all of the interviews using direct literal (secretarial) methods. There was no reason to carry out a Jefferson-style transcription (Chapter 6) since the objective was to understand how the offenders accounted for their offending. Because of the close involvement of one researcher with the interviewing and transcriptions, the data were very familiar before the analysis stage of the research began.

Of course, the interviews and transcripts contained much data irrelevant to the question of the functions of Internet child pornography, consequently relevant material to this topic needed to be identified. Since only certain aspects of the questioning were pertinent to this, it is relatively easy to identify the relevant material. This was done by cutting-and-pasting the relevant material from the computer files of the transcripts into a new file. However, an equally viable approach would be to highlight the relevant text on the transcript with a highlighter pen or change the font colour on the computer. In this case, the substantial

→

quantities of data meant that it was best to use a computer to store the relevant material ready for perusal when coding the data.

The phases of the thematic analysis employed were similar to those used in other forms of qualitative analysis. The coding process began with a descriptive level of coding which involved the minimum of interpretation or abstraction. The codings were applied, as was appropriate, to 'chunks' of data or transcript. So it could be just a word, a phrase, a sentence or a paragraph. For example, the avoidance of negative feelings/moods was described by some offenders as their reason for using child pornography and so the code 'negavoidance' was given each time this occurred in the transcripts. Coding was a complex, interconnected process so the initial codings would be revised in the light of things which appeared later in the transcript and so forth. Some codes would be subdivided or revised if the initial codes seemed to be an inadequate fit to the data or codes would be combined if they overlapped too much in terms of meaning. Writing and jotting down of ideas and codes was an integral part of this early stage – somewhat similar to the 'memo' in grounded theory (see Chapter 8).

The next stage of data analysis (theme development) involved more interpretation and inductive reasoning. That is to say, constructs which embraced a number of the initial codes were identified. These captured the overall meaning of some of the initial descriptive coding. Throughout the analysis, the analyst would move backwards and forwards between the data (interview extracts) and the codes as well as between the developing themes and the codes. In order to facilitate theme development, the individual codings were written onto different postcards together with a brief clarifying description. These cards could then be moved and shuffled around and organised into 'theme piles' where they seemed to have a great deal in common. This allowed the analyst to establish whether the themes 'worked' in relation to the codings (and the extracts).

Although the initial stages of this particular thematic analysis were led by the data, in the final stage the researcher drew from psychological theory and research as an aid to interpreting the codings into overarching themes. Engagement with the literature was considered very important in that it led to better understanding of the meaning and implications of the patterns in the codings (i.e. the themes). The researcher simultaneously sought to generate clear definitions of each theme and a clear name. Overall, only a few themes were created during this thematic analysis but these themes were general concepts which subsumed the lower levels of coding.

Of course, if themes are very clearly defined it becomes possible to quantify their occurrence in the data. There are different ways in which this could be done:

- How prevalent is a theme? That is, how many (or what percentage) of interviews included each theme.

- What is the incidence of a particular theme? That is, how often a particular theme occurs throughout the data or how often it is mentioned by each participant. The former is generally the easier.

After the thematic analysis was completed, the interviews were scrutinised again and the number of interviews which mentioned a particular theme was counted. The importance of a theme is not a function of the number of times it appears. There will be certain themes which are more important than others because they are particularly pertinent to the research question.

There were four themes identified in what the offenders told the researchers about the functions of child pornography in their lives. These were: (a) Sexual arousal, (b) Emotional avoidance, (c) Collecting and (d) Facilitating social relationships. These are very different themes and they could not have been anticipated in their entirety prior to the data collection and analysis. The themes identified through the thematic analysis were illustrated by excerpts, examples of which are given below:

- Theme 1: Sexual arousal. 'Girls got dressed up in school uniforms at University [disco revivals] which was a turn-on so I started to look for school uniforms, school girls on the Internet.' This was the overwhelming theme in terms of frequency of occurrence.

- Theme 2: Emotional avoidance. 'But when I was online it was a completely discreet and isolated world.'

- Theme 3: Collecting. 'Particularly when the images were getting younger and I noticed . . . you would get sets of images as well and that played quite a big part as well . . . to get complete sets of things.'

- Theme 4: Facilitating social relationships. 'I was more interested in the conversations I was getting, the friendship I was getting . . . the images . . . provided me with a form of communication . . . that was my pleasure . . . I was very lonely . . . to prove that they were genuine they sent me the indecent stuff . . . I had to prove myself that I were genuine by doing the same to them.'

Of course, this amounts to a classification system for men's reasons for using child pornography. Although the sexual arousal function was extremely common (75 per cent of Internet-only sex offenders), there is clearly potential to use the system in order to further develop research and theory in this field. For example, could it be that certain types of use are more associated with eventual contact offences against children than others? The fit of the excerpts to the names of the themes seems good. Also, certainly in terms of the examples cited though this is more generally true, the themes are conceptually very different. Of course, there are some offenders who mentioned things which corresponded to more than one theme but these different themes were clearly distinguishable from each other. If the illustrative excerpts do not fit the themes very well then this may be a signal that the analysis is not complete and more work needs to be done. It is a common error in student work and the mismatch of excerpt to theme is a sign that all is not well with the analysis process.

Step 1   **Data familiarisation**   In this early stage, the researcher becomes familiar with the close detail of the transcript or whatever other text is to be used. Quite when data familiarisation occurs will differ according to the details of the study concerned. If the researcher had conducted interviews and focus groups then they are likely to be actively processing these while the data are being collected. Data familiarisation will also take place during the process of transcription – if the researcher is transcribing their own data. Otherwise and additionally, playing a recording through repeatedly or reading a transcript through several times are important steps in data familiarisation. Although someone else may do the interviews or make the transcripts, no one but the researcher can do data familiarisation since this is a key stage in developing the analysis. During the data familiarisation stage, the researcher will begin to think about what is happening in the data – this is inevitable but the qualitative researcher should plan to put substantial time into doing this. The more data from the more participants there are, the easier it is to begin to formulate patterns which cohere. These early thoughts about what is happening in the data may suggest ways in which the data might be coded or, indeed, ideas about the themes apparent in the data.

Thematic analysis normally uses a literal transcription after the style of a secretary. While it is not impossible to use the Jefferson transcription (Chapter 6), it is difficult to see what function Jefferson transcription will achieve in thematic analysis since it is largely about expressing how things are said rather than what is said. Thematic analysis concentrates on what is being said and so has no way of coping with this additional detail. Transcription is not a mindless chore in qualitative research but a positive and important aspect of data analysis. It is, therefore, sound advice to a novice researcher that they should do all of the data collection and transcription themselves. Many professional researchers would not want to do any different.

Step 2   **Initial coding generation**   On the principle that higher levels of analytic effort lead to better research, the initial, formal analysis step in thematic analysis is the line-by-line coding of the data. These codings are not the themes that the research will generate, but a stage in the process of working towards those themes. By coding each line, the researcher is working with the detail of the data rather than the broad sweep of the data. A coding is little other than a label to describe the contents of a line (or two) of transcript or textual data. The lines are basically arbitrary as the text or transcript is usually surrounded by white space on the paper on which the researcher makes his or her notes. Since the themes are abstractions from the data, the initial codings are usually best if they are based on an abstraction rather than something more concrete. In other words, the more conceptual the researcher's codings the better the final themes are likely to be. The researcher's coding should indicate something that is interesting or important about that snippet of the data. Initial codings involve the researcher systematically working through the entirety of the data – or a subset of the data selected because it deals with a particular topic or matter of interest to the researcher. Coding does not have to be done line-by-line – if every line is not possible then every two or three lines would probably be all right. It really does depend on circumstances. There is no requirement even that the numbers of lines to be coded have to be equal every time. Furthermore, the researcher may choose a unit of analysis other than the line of text. There is nothing wrong with coding sentences in their entirety if the researcher feels that this might be advantageous. Initial codings seek to capture a segment of text's essence; it is not the intention at this stage to identify broader themes though, of course, ideas as to what the themes might be may and will occur at any stage in the analysis. Initial codings are not sophisticated analyses of the data – sometimes they may appear to be nothing other than jottings or notes which summarise bits of the text.

Do not forget that the researcher, at this stage, already has a broad picture of the data rather than simply the brief initial codings. This means that the initial codings are likely to be guided by this fuller picture and not simply a line or two of text. Initial coding development (and the later development of themes) is not something that simply happens when a researcher looks at their data. Coding do *not* emerge from the data according to Braun and Clarke (2006) but are actively created by the researcher trying out ideas in relation to their data. Codings and themes are not located in the data as such but created in the interplay between the data and the work that the researcher is investing in the data analysis.

There may be two different approaches depending on whether the data are data led or theory led according to Braun and Clarke (2006):

- *The data-led approach*   This is dominated by the characteristics of the data and the codings are primarily guided by a careful analysis of what is in the data. This is the approach taken in the example in Box 7.1.
- *The theory-led approach*   The structure for the initial codings is suggested by the key elements of the theory being applied by the researcher. Feminist theory, for example, stresses that relationships between men and women are dominated by the power and dominance of the male gender over the female gender in a wide variety of aspects of the social world including employment, domestic life and the law. Thus a thematic analysis based on feminist theory would be orientated to the expression of power relationships in any textual material.

Of course, there is something of a dilemma here since it is unclear just how a researcher can avoid applying elements of a theoretical perspective during the analysis process. Just how would it be possible to differentiate between a theory-led coding and a data-led coding unless the researcher makes this explicit in their writings?

Initial codings are not usually reported by researchers using thematic analysis but Clarke, Burns and Burgoyne *et al.* (2008) do describe some of their initial codings for a number of lines of text. It is useful to look at these since they show that initial codings are often nothing particularly sophisticated and that there is nothing magical in them given that they are quite mundane. The codings are for the piece of text on the left as a whole, not line by line:

it's too much like hard work I mean how much paper have you got to sign	1. Talked about with partner
to change a flippin' name no I I mean no I no we we have thought about it	2. Too much hassle to change name
((inaudible)) half heartedly and thought no no I jus- I can't be bothered,	
it's too much like hard work.	

It would be difficult to argue that these codings required a great deal of insight, creativity or any sort of special powers to create. They are little other than a succinct way of putting things in this example. It is not difficult to see that hard work is a dominant aspect of this snippet and that the discussion ('we have thought about it') is the second aspect. Of course, the researchers might equally have coded the contents as 'paperwork is a deterrent' and 'partners have considered name change'. Notice that there are other aspects of the excerpt that different researchers with different research aims might have coded if they wished. For example, the codings might be 1. Rhetorical question ('it's too much like hard work I mean how much paper have you got to sign to change a flippin 'name') and 2. Change of personal pronoun from 'I' to 'we' and back. In other words, the codings are partially guided by the researcher's perspective on the research and not just the contents of the interview.

Of course, the researcher will notice that they have initial codings which are very similar to each other despite differences in wording. So it may be appropriate to re-name these with the same coding – provided, of course, that the researcher is convinced that the different codings mean the same thing. Otherwise, things may be left alone until the following has been done.

At the point at which the initial-coding stage has been completed, the researcher will naturally need to understand better the material which Coding A includes compared with, say, the material which Coding C includes. In other words, the researcher should put together all of the transcript or text which has received Coding A, likewise for Coding B, Coding C and so forth. One way of doing this is simply to copy-and-paste the material from a word processor file under these different headings. On examining the material which has received Coding C, for example, it may become clear to the researcher that:

- The coding's label is not quite accurate or precise enough and needs to be changed.
- Some of the material which has received that coding is different in important ways and so a new coding may be identified for the parts of the data which do not really match with the other material.
- That the material which has received Coding C is not really different from the material which has received Coding F, for example. So the researcher may decide to combine these codings.

Obviously it is far better that you practise the process of coding on a small piece of text rather than for the first time once your data has been collected. You may find it helpful to copy some text from the Internet, say Chatrooms, etc. which have a lot of potentially usable material. Try coding some of this.

Step 3   **Searching for themes based on the initial coding**   The sequence is close reading of text, producing codings for each line or group of lines of text, and then turning these codings into themes. The question is just how codings can be turned into themes. The answer is more hard work: more analytic effort on the part of the researcher. At this point the researcher will probably notice that although the list of initial codings that has been developed seems to be useful in that the data and the codings given to the data make sense and distinguish one sort of material from another sort of material, nevertheless some of the codings on the list have more to do with each other than they do to other codings on the list. In other words, what are the patterns among the codings? To take a silly example, if the codings were dog, lettuce, cat, carrot, apple, rabbit, aardvark then one might be inclined to suggest that these different codings are related to two categories – (1) animals and (2) vegetables. Actually, one might suggest that the second group is fruit and vegetables – or a group and a subgroup perhaps. These groups are pretty much what a theme is. So themes are basically the result of categorising the codings into meaningful groups of codings. Of course,

→ it is possible to develop themes which are relatively mundane if the analysis is somewhat concrete. The researcher needs to use their powers of abstract thought if the analysis is to be of a good quality, but that is what research is all about anyway. Themes identify major patterns in the initial codings and so can be thought of as a secondary level of interpreting the text. Of course, it may be that the initial coding process has identified aspects of the data of considerable importance which warrant that coding itself being described as a theme. Like all aspects of qualitative data analysis, it is practically impossible to completely separate the coding phase from the theme-generation phase. There is an interplay which no description of the process can quite capture.

What can be done to encourage the researcher to conceptualise themes from the codings? Well, in many ways this is to ask how one can encourage the processes of categorisation and reasoning which characterise human thinking in general. That is, anything which facilitates or encourages abstract thinking is to be recommended. In some circumstances the themes may well be fairly obvious from the codings which have been developed. But there may be a need to work harder and more effectively to develop themes. For example, simple methods of sorting might help. Each coding might be written on a small card or slip of paper. This allows the codings to be sorted and resorted into piles on the basis of similarity. Placing the piles in approximate relative positions is a good idea as this tentatively indicates the relationships between the different themes. In the course of this, the researcher may decide that there are some piles of codings which do not constitute a single theme but are close together. These may be thought of as sub-themes within a more general theme.

In some analyses, it may become obvious that certain codings are the reverse of other codings. This is quite a different situation from codings being thematically different. In this case, the codings belong to the same theme but indicate opposing aspects of the same theme. It would be quite wrong and misleading to treat these 'polar opposites' as if they were different themes.

'No pain no gain' is not quite the way to describe the process of theme development but it does get close. While pain is not essential, hard work is key to ensuring that themes are as well developed and useful in the data interpretation as possible. Computers may help with the data management for a thematic analysis and ease the pressures due to large amounts of material to analyse. Word processing programs have the facility to allow limitless cutting-and-pasting. However, there are some specialist computer programs (especially NVivo) which can help achieve the same ends and more but in a different way.

Step 4   **Review of the themes**   So far we have gone through the process of developing a set of tentative themes which help to understand the data. Depending on circumstances, it is possible that these themes are not fully defined or even particularly refined at this stage. It is essential, then, to examine these themes against the original data. Once again, the researcher needs to organise the data around the themes just as previously the data have been organised around the codings. This is simply a matter of cutting-and-pasting the material which had previously been organised around the different codings so that it is now organised around the different themes. In other words, all of the evidence in support of a particular theme has been drawn together. Like all qualitative analyses, any analysis can be regarded as tentative and so the researcher may decide to review the themes

→

→ or even the codings in the light of what is to be found associated with these developing themes. The more systematic the analysis is the greater becomes the task of data management during this process of theme development. With larger data sets, the researcher might prefer to analyse half of the data first then refine this analysis on the basis of how well it deals with the second half of the data set.

There are a number of possibilities:

- you may find that there is very little in the data to support a theme that you have identified, so the theme may have to be abandoned or modified in the light of this;

- you may find that a theme needs to be divided or subdivided since the data which are supposed to link together into the one theme imply two different themes or sub-themes; and

- you may feel that the theme works by and large but does not fit some of the data which initially you believed were part of that theme so you may have to find a new theme to deal with the non-fitting data. You may need to check the applicability of your themes to selected extracts as well as to the entire data set.

Step 5   **Theme definition and labelling**   Accuracy and precision are the watchwords of any academic research. It is unlikely that a researcher can define and label the themes emerging in their research without being prepared to reconsider and refine the analysis at all stages. While it may appear easy to give a label to a theme, it may prove more troublesome to define precisely what the theme is. Most important is the extent to which a particular theme that has been identified by the researcher can be distinguished conceptually from all of the other themes. That is, for each theme, can the researcher say just what it is and just what it is not? Of course, an analysis which attempts to deal with all of the data will be more exacting than one which deals only with particular aspects of the data. The process of developing sub-themes is likely to continue at this stage. As the themes become clearer, data which previously were hard to code just might become understandable in the light of conceptual developments during the analysis.

Up to this point, thematic analysis has been described in ways which suggest that it is all in the head (and on the desk) of the researcher. This is a somewhat solitary process. Going 'public' with your analysis is probably a good idea at any stage but, especially, in the step in which the analysis is being refined. Simply talking with other people about your ideas, in itself, will help you to identify problems in your ideas or your own understanding of your ideas. It helps you see the wood for the trees but also continues the process of clarification in a different modality. But, additionally, talking with others may allow them to question you about your ideas and, possibly, throw in analytic ideas of their own.

Step 6   **Report writing**   The report – which might be a student dissertation or an article for a prestigious research journal – is a sufficiently detailed description of the stages of the research (see Chapter 13). It tends not to be a 'warts and all' account in the sense that the write-up is usually more orderly than the research had actually ever been. Qualitative writing tends to include more description of the problems of analysis than other forms of research report. It is notable that many if not most reports involving thematic analysis fail to include much detail

→

about the analytic process. It is almost as if the analysis emerges fully from the data with little happening in the middle. This is an erroneous picture of qualitative analysis and good practice would insist on some detail of the process of analysis being included. Difficulties in the analysis should be highlighted – it is no use to other researchers if problems are swept under the carpet.

Report writing can be construed as the final stage of data analysis – that is, it is the stage at which the researcher may have to refine and alter the analysis in the light of problems which emerge when the analysis is put together completely during the process of writing-up. All stages of the analysis process relate back to each other and the strength of the research question which initiated the research study is part of the success of the study. Indeed, the research question may well be reformulated a number of times during the course of the analysis – even at the stage of writing the report. So report writing is not merely telling the essence of the 'mechanics' of the research project – the steps in the research – but a further opportunity to reflect on one's data, one's analysis and the adequacy of the data in relation to the analysis and vice versa. The story told in the report reflects the researcher's final thinking. Report writing is not to be regarded as a chore but part of the data analysis process which involves the final synthesis. Nevertheless, it is understandable why report writing can feel something of an uphill struggle.

The explanation and description of the themes in the final report involve, in thematic analysis, appropriate illustrations taken from the material which is associated with the theme. Among the criteria that might be applied to this selection are the following:

- How typical the material is of the data which 'belong' to a particular theme.

- How apposite the material is in relation to the theme. Some excerpts might illustrate particular features of the theme better than others.

- How 'eye-catching' the excerpt is. Some data may be rather more vivid than other data and so may be chosen in preference to other excerpts.

- You may prefer to illustrate the various themes using excerpts from, say, just one of the participants in the research. In this way it may be possible to get into a little more depth about a particular case – to put the analysis in the context of an individual's life.

Each of the above implies a somewhat different selection strategy. It is clearly helpful to indicate in your report the basis for your excerpt selection.

The final report will provide a discussion of the relevant research literature. Typically in thematic analysis the researcher will have little, if any, reluctance about informing the developing analysis using previous research findings though this is a choice that the researcher always has to make. This may be either (a) the previous research literature that helps justify why you have posed your particular research question or (b) the research literature which relates to your analysis once it has been formulated – that is, how does your analysis relate to other analyses of similar material? Of course, it could be both. It might be pointed out that the previous research may primarily be quantitative in nature. In which case, it might be appropriate to review this literature as part of the explanation why a qualitative approach is needed in addition. Since there are no previous qualitative analyses, the new qualitative analysis will not be so

→   affected by these findings. The study reported in Box 7.2 is one in which the literature review is largely quantitative and so has reduced relevance to the development of themes. Whatever the approach taken to the literature review in relation to the data analysis, the final report must include your attempt at synthesis and integration of the previous research literature with your new analysis. The development of this synthesis is part of understanding the nature of the themes that you have identified.

Irrespective of the steps described above, at its heart thematic analysis involves the data, the coding of data and the identification of themes. This is not a linear process in the sense that the researcher may frequently go backwards and forwards between all three, creating extra loops in the analysis process. This helps check and also refine the analysis which is being carried out. The data and the analysis of the data are constantly juxtaposed to both check the adequacy of the analysis but also to encourage its refinement.

Box 7.2

ILLUSTRATIVE RESEARCH STUDY

Thematic analysis: a website for women paedophiles

Female sex offenders have only the sparsest of coverage in the psychological literature (Howitt, 1995) for any number of reasons – that they are rare in the criminal justice system being the most important one. Lambert and O'Halloran (2008) carried out a deductive thematic analysis, which they attributed to Braun and Clarke (2006), concerning female sex offenders. My overall impression is that Lambert and O'Halloran's paper is more quantitative than qualitative in ethos. In their paper, Lambert and O'Halloran describe their analysis of the 'personal stories' of six women and the 'frequently asked questions' (FAQs) that they found on a website for women with a sexual interest in children. They describe the data as being written by women with a sexual interest in children for other women with a similar sexual interest. There are claims that in terms of the Internet perhaps up to one-third of 'offenders' are female (Finkelhor, Mitchell, & Wolak, 2000).

Lambert and O'Halloran give no indication of the amount of material involved but describe the stages of the analysis in some detail:

- Stage 1: The material on the website was read several times and the material for the analysis identified and copied onto a document. A more detailed examination of this data set was initiated and any thoughts about the data were put inside the left-hand margin. 'These notes related to concepts and phrases that the researcher considered interesting or significant.' (p. 287).

- Stage 2: The data set was re-read a number of times more and the notes made at Stage 1 were converted into themes. They define a theme as 'something important that relates to the research interest, and represents some level of patterned response or meaning within the data set' (p. 287).

Interestingly, and in keeping with the general 'quantitative' aura of this 'qualitative' report, a second researcher also carried out an analysis of the data set and developed her own set of themes. The final set of themes was a result of a negotiation between the two researchers 'until agreement was reached as to the validity and appropriateness of each theme' (p. 288).

- Stage 3: The data were re-read and the themes formed into 'specific clusters' of themes by drawing on known psychological concepts. Nine themes (e.g. 'child as seducer', 'sex with children is natural' and 'child sexuality oppressed in society') which relate to the concept of cognitive distortions were categorised into the broad theme of cognitive distortions.

- Stage 4: 'The clusters were categorized based on their relationships to a specific psycho-logical concept' (p. 288). In addition to cognitive distortions, the themes of sexual motivation, recognition barriers, personal factors and role of the Internet were also created.

- Stage 5: The researchers identified statements from the data to illustrate each of the themes in each of the categories. Actually, the researchers say that they were to 'provide evidence of the existence of each theme within the various categories' (p. 288). These illustrative extracts were further examined in order to relate them back to the research question ('to investigate how women with a sexual interest in children engage with the Internet', p. 284) and the relevant research literature in order to produce a 'scholarly report'.

An example of a text excerpt used to support a theme is the following which is used to clarify the theme 'child as seducer':

B: 'an hour later I had really had my first lesbian experience with a 10 yr old and I was truly ashamed of myself as I had let her do what she wanted with me and I had responded to her requests and I had become a victim. I hadn't touched her but she had done things to me like I could not believe, even down to a very good session of oral sex and I was 12 years older than her.' (p. 291)

Despite the researchers identifying this theme and despite their penchant for quantifica-tion, there are no indications in the report of how common the theme of 'child as seducer' was identified in the data.

It is very clear from the report that this thematic analysis was guided not particularly by the data but by existing psychological theories and concepts related to male sex offenders – but applied to women with a sexual interest in children. In other words, this analysis was led by the literature review rather than by the data. Now this may be a useful way of analysing data but it is questionable whether it constitutes a qualitative data analysis in the fullest meaning of the phrase. Indeed, it might be regarded by some qualitative researchers as an elaborate way of trawling for examples to illustrate well-known themes. In other words, this thematic analysis seems largely to confirm what we know already from research on male sex offenders. Quite clearly it is useful to know that there is such a correspondence but whether one should regard this as thematic analysis is open to debate. Interestingly, since the themes were ostensibly developed from the data, rarely does the analysis question what has previously emerged from studies of male offenders. There are occasions when the researchers raise some slight criticisms of what is already known and its relevance to female offenders: 'Maternal incest is seen as particularly rare but the stories posted on the website show this to be untrue and it is argued that this form of abuse is much more prevalent than many assume . . .' (p. 293).

When to use thematic analysis

Thematic analysis is what it is and probably has little to offer the researcher whose perspective is in, say, conversation analysis and discourse analysis. It does not have the level of sophisticated theory associated with it that these do. On the other hand, this 'theory' may not really be the researcher's interest and it may not be found helpful. The following points may be helpful in helping determine whether thematic analysis is appropriate:

● Thematic analysis is best seen as a descriptive method in that it attempts to come up with a limited number of themes or categories to describe what is going on in the data.

● Thematic analysis, unlike grounded theory, is not aimed at theory generation although it may be helpful in this regard. For example, the themes developed in thematic analysis are not expected to be related or interconnected in some way, whereas the categories identified from a grounded theory analysis do need to be explored in terms of their relationships with each other.

● Similarly, thematic analysis is not primarily aimed at providing a detailed interpretation of the data as opposed to describing its broad features. While interpretation and description do overlap, thematic analysis can serve its purpose by simply describing what is going on in the data.

● Thematic analysis provides a rather broad-brush approach to data analysis as opposed to the fine-grained approaches which characterise some qualitative research methods.

● Thematic analysis does not have a strong voice on the data which are collected and the process by which they are collected. So, unlike grounded theory, thematic analysis may be used on a completed data set and there is no requirement that the data being collected are reviewed part-way through the analysis and new approaches to sampling, etc. instigated if necessary.

● Thematic analysis, generally, is not steeped in the intriguing but sometimes frustrating epistemological debates that other qualitative methods are. Indeed, thematic analysis fits comfortably with some of the assumptions of quantitative research. Hence it may be a way for quantitative researchers to feel comfortable with qualitative data.

● Thematic analysis may, in some cases, be amenable to simple quantification since a theme may be coded as present or absent in, say, a percentage of the interviews.

Quite clearly, the closest method to thematic analysis is grounded theory. However, despite the fact that many of the stages in thematic analysis have their parallels in grounded theory, the two approaches are substantially different as can be seen from the above bullet points. So it would not be fair to suggest that thematic analysis is a simplified or 'lite' version of grounded theory. However, it is probably true to suggest that there are some grounded theory analyses which produce outcomes which are indistinguishable from those of thematic analysis.

Evaluation of thematic analysis

When evaluating thematic analysis, it is important to remember that the Braun and Clarke (2006) version of the procedure may be substantially better than those adopted by other researchers claiming to use thematic analysis. That is, thematic analysis covers a range of procedures and not all of them would meet Braun and Clarke's ideals. So what may be true of their approach may not always apply to what has happened in practice. The following are some of the positive things which Braun and Clarke say can be claimed about thematic analysis:

- Compared with other forms of qualitative analysis, thematic analysis makes fewer demands in terms of data collection and fewer constraints in terms of data analysis.
- Thematic analysis is relatively easy to learn and understand compared with other qualitative methods. Consequently it may be used by a novice researcher with little difficulty.
- Thematic analysis findings are easily understood by intelligent and educated members of the community.
- Its accessibility to the general public means that it can be used for participatory studies involving particular groups and the researcher. For example, it is unlikely that a thematic analysis of interviews with staff in a casualty unit will produce findings which they will fail to understand.
- Thematic analysis summarises large amounts of data by offering descriptive themes which can be rich in information.
- Thematic analysis can be useful in qualitative research which may inform policy development because of its accessibility and use of data produced by involved individuals.

Braun and Clarke also suggest, though without any systematic evidence, that:

- 'unanticipated insights' may be gained through thematic analysis – this, however, is only likely if the procedures adopted are centred on the data and the researcher revises their analysis in the light of the data;
- it 'allows for social as well as psychological interpretations of data' (p. 97) – while this is true, it suggests that the purpose of thematic analysis is to provide interpretations of this sort rather than descriptions.

On the other hand, experience suggests that thematic analysis is such a catch-all term that some research described as thematic analysis fails to live up to Braun and Clarke's expectation or the expectations of qualitative researchers in general. In my experience, there are any number of student dissertations, for example, which seem to pluck a few quotations out of the data, label them with a theme, and basically fail to meet the ideals of a thematic analysis or qualitative analysis in general. But, as we have seen, it is easy to do far better than this. Figure 7.4 summarises some of the quality criteria which can be applied to a thematic analysis.

Transcription/ textual material	Coding	Analysis	Overall	Written report
Transcription is at appropriate level of detail for this particular analysis.	All parts of the data have been subject to equal analytic scrutiny.	The data are analysed – interpreted and made sense of. Paraphrasing and description are *not* analysis.	All steps in the process should have received adequate time and attention with nothing rushed.	The conceptualisation matched the epistemological assumptions of the analysis.
Transcription checked for fit with original recorded interview, etc.	Themes are dependent on *all* data, not just a few striking excerpts.	There is a strong relationship between the analysis and the data – the excerpts used to support the analytic claim.		The researcher is an active component of the research. The analysis does not 'emerge' but is constructed.
	All excerpts indicative of a theme have been brought together for scrutiny.	There is a strong story being told about the data in relation to the chosen topic for discussion.		A careful account is given of the assumptions of thematic analysis and the specific form of thematic analysis carried out.
	Cross-checking of each theme against other themes and the data has been carried out.	The analysis is not dominated by the illustrative excerpts rather than the actual analysis.		There is a consistency between the excerpts and the analysis presented.
	'Themes are internally coherent, consistent, and distinctive.' p. 96			

FIGURE 7.4 The quality criteria for a thematic analysis (after Braun & Clarke, 2006)

CONCLUSION

The label thematic analysis says more or less what is involved in this sort of analysis. Thematic analysis is a research procedure in which textual material (newspapers, interviews and so forth) is analysed in order to indicate the major themes to be found in that text. *The Concise Oxford Dictionary* defines a theme as 'a subject or topic on which a person speaks, writes, or thinks'. While this is not quite the sense of the word 'theme' as used in thematic analysis, it is a common-sense meaning which gets sufficiently close. Those new to qualitative analysis are probably right to be considering thematic analysis as their first steps in qualitative research. Its lack of a theoretical infrastructure as well as the limited demands it places on the researcher are good enough reasons in themselves to try out thematic analysis. Its user-friendly reputation is a boon but it is capable of generating useful, if limited, summary descriptions of the data in the form of themes. Adopting a superficial approach to thematic analysis will show in the very limited scope of the analysis generated. Ideally the researcher will not be satisfied with the mundane and superficial. The approach described in this chapter should allow researchers to avoid the trap. The simplicity of thematic analysis disguises the fact that it is the hard work of the analyst which is decisive in generating the themes. The more the researcher is prepared to challenge the analysis at each stage the better the final outcome is likely to be. No matter how tempting it is to suggest a few themes which then become 'the analysis', this does disservice to the idea of thematic analysis.

KEY POINTS

- Historically, thematic analysis has existed as a method virtually without any well-known advocates. As a consequence, its development as a methodology has been delayed until very recently. It is notable, then, how readily the method can be brought into line with the major objectives of most qualitative analysis. Ultimately, because it is a descriptive method rather than a theory-directed approach, thematic analysis cannot substitute effectively for the theoretically stronger methods discussed in the next few chapters.

- A good thematic analysis is built on a great deal of analytic work on the part of the researcher. The processes involved are generally very familiar to qualitative researchers and are based on the intense, detailed and hard work of the analyst. The major processes are data familiarisation, data coding, date recoding and theme development. A researcher unwilling to devote the required amount of intense effort will tend to produce weaker and less-convincing analyses. They only have superficially analysed their data so produce less insightful and comprehensive themes.

- In order to ensure the future development of thematic analysis as a sophisticated procedure, researchers should report in some great detail the way in which they went about the thematic analysis. The analysis does not simply 'emerge' from the data but is the consequence of a lot of good practices and a lot of hard work employed by the researcher which should be described in the report.

- Almost without exception, a good thematic analysis may be amenable to quantification. If themes can be properly defined then it should be unproblematic to count, for example, the number of times a particular theme emerges in different interviews. Prevalence is the number of participants who say things relevant to a particular theme and incidence is the frequency of occurrence of the theme throughout the data set or the average number of times it occurs in each participant's data.

ADDITIONAL RESOURCES

Aronson, J. (1994). A pragmatic view of thematic analysis. *The Qualitative Report, 2* (1) http://www.nova.edu/ssss/QR/BackIssues/QR2-1/aronson.html) (accessed 19 August 2009).

Boyatzis, R.E. (1998). *Transforming Qualitative Information*. Thousand Oaks, CA: Sage.

Braun, V., and Clarke, V. (2006). Using thematic analysis in psychology. *Qualitative Research in Psychology, 3*, 77-101.

Howitt, D., and Cramer, D. (2008). *Introduction to Research Methods in Psychology*. Harlow: Pearson. (This also contains a simpler approach to thematic analysis.)

Miles, M., and Huberman, M. (1994). *Qualitative Data Analysis: An expanded sourcebook*. London: Sage.

CHAPTER 8

Qualitative data analysis: Grounded theory development

Overview

- Grounded theory was seminal in defining qualitative research as a systematic form of research. It grew out of the work of Barney Glaser and Anselm Strauss in the 1960s although subsequently Glaser and Strauss developed somewhat different emphases in terms of how grounded theory research is carried out.

- Grounded theory is theory which develops out of a close interaction between the data and the developing understanding of the data. The fit between the theory and the data should be close in grounded theory. The process of theory building involves constant checking backwards and forwards between different aspects of the analysis process.

- Typically grounded theory proceeds from the initial data collection and analysis stage to the collection of further new data guided by the initial analysis (theoretical sampling). The process is typically one of line-by-coding of transcribed texts such as interviews or focus groups. These codings are then sorted into categories from which the basic theoretical ideas and relationships can be identified. The process may proceed to other stages including the collection of fresh data to help 'validate' the study's emerging theoretical ideas and to also examine whether the theory is more generally applicable.

- The researcher writes ideas, concepts and other analytic notions in a memo as an aid to theory development.

- Grounded theory probably works best where people's common-sense understandings of the world provide appropriate data to help answer the research question.

- There are a number of criticisms of grounded theory. Some question the nature of the 'theory' which emerges, the delay it imposes on the use of theory may be counterproductive where there is relevant theory already available, and its frequent lack of clarity, for example.

- It is notable that a good proportion of grounded theory studies concentrate solely on the initial theory building stages. These generate the categories which largely constitute the theory in many studies. Some researchers are reluctant to go beyond this stage to test out the theory and hypotheses derived from the theory in order to broaden its applicability.

What is grounded theory?

According to Bryman (2004), grounded theory is the most widely used way of analysing qualitative data. Grounded theory was groundbreaking in the sense of providing a relatively formal but vigorous approach to the analysis of qualitative data. It was a development of the 1960s when among the discontent of academics was the gulf between *empirical* research and theory building as well as the general feeling that *qualitative* research lacked the rigour that academic disciplines require. It grew from the work of the sociologists Barney Glaser (1930–) and Anselm Strauss (1916–1996). While nowadays it is commonplace for qualitative researchers to take great pains to establish the validity of their analyses, such concerns were really the contribution of Glaser, Strauss and grounded theory. (See Chapter 15 for a discussion of some of the many quality criteria that have been proposed by qualitative researchers.)

The first major publication detailing grounded theory was Glaser and Strauss's (1967) *The Discovery of Grounded Theory*. It can be regarded as both innovative and radical as well as being decisive in undermining the dominant sociology of the time. The book determinedly argued for a close relation between empirical research data and theory to replace the highly speculative grand sociological theories of the time which had little grounding in research data and, equally, the barren wastes of atheoretical empiricism which gave much research a bad name then. Grounded theory essentially assumed that there must be a close link between empirical data and theory building and required that the data analyses which led to the theory and the theory itself were thoroughly tested and convincingly questioned and challenged. Grounded theory provided a way forward in the development of qualitative research – though it never was intended exclusively for qualitative data. There are clearly potential credibility issues in qualitative research methods. A stereotype of qualitative research around the 1950s/1960s would highlight the apparent subjectivity of the analysis process. None of the usual quality checks which pervade quantitative research – issues such as reliability and validity – typified qualitative research at the time. Not that Glaser and Strauss were advocates of reliability and validity in the form that they take in quantitative research. They were uncertain as to whether traditional concepts of reliability and validity were appropriate to grounded theory and felt that they stultify the process of discovery through research.

Instead, for example, their approach to validity would include respondent validation – the idea that the theory developed out of research should make sense to those participating in the research. But, of course, there is much more to validation in qualitative research than that (see Chapter 14).

Glaser and Strauss's early work on grounded theory was written at a time when positivism and quantification had the upper hand. Perhaps it then should come as no surprise that Glaser and Strauss wrote of the 'discovery' of theory much as positivist psychologists had sought to 'discover' the laws of psychology. A few years later, the growing idea that scientific knowledge is constructed by researchers rather than discovered by them (Gergen & Graumann, 1996) probably made this view contested in grounded theory. This is one example of how grounded theory has changed over time and is part of the explanation why apparently different factions of grounded theory researchers have emerged. Indeed, Glaser and Strauss parted academic company in the 1990s over the matter of how grounded theory should be done. (Remember, grounded theory incorporates quantitative research although it is regarded primarily as a qualitative analysis method.)

The grounded in grounded theory is fairly straightforward since theory in grounded theory is situated in the empirical work involved in data collection. However, the nature of theory in grounded theory might cause some problems. This is not a problem per se for newcomers to grounded theory alone. The word 'theory' itself is hardly the most consistently applied term in psychology and its meaning just about embraces anything which is not just an empirical relationship. Theory can be a very loosely defined phrase referring to things such as broad principles or personal reflections but it can also involve relatively 'hard' definitions. So theory can also include things such as 'a well-developed system of ideas which integrate considerable amounts of knowledge' and, maybe, 'has the potential for allowing prediction'. Fish (1989) rejects the value of the notion of theory since, in his view, it really refers to 'theory talk' which is a way of thinking about things in research which has acquired 'cachet and prestige'. This can be seen quite often in fashionable conceptualisations in psychology which are major talking points but then fade from researchers' radar screen. So don't worry too much if discussions of 'theory' seem to be beyond your grasp.

One frequently reads the phrase 'middle range' theories to describe grounded theories but this is not a self-evident term either. There is a problem in that many grounded theory analyses do not push the method or its use of data to its limits. Consequently, some of the theory generated by grounded theory analyses fails to represent grounded theory in its fullest meaning as intended in some of the original publications of Glaser and Strauss. It is important to remember that much of the data used in grounded theory analyses consist of 'rich' data from individuals in the form of interviews, focus groups, diaries and so forth. This, then, implies that grounded theory is theory for which these forms of data are pertinent. However the term middle-range theory was put forward by the distinguished American sociologist Robert Merton in his book *Social Theory and Social Structure* in 1949. The middle-range theory occupies the space between the sort of simple, everyday hypotheses or explanations that researchers use when describing their empirical observations and the relationships in their empirical data and the much more complex, all-inclusive grand theories which are drawn up to explain major areas of life. Actually, it is harder to come up with examples of grand theories in recent psychology than it is to think of middle-ground theories. Most of the best examples of grand theories come from classic fields of psychology such as Freud's psychoanalytic theory, Piaget's theory of cognitive development, symbolic interactionism, Eysenck's personality theory, Cattell's personality theory, Vygotsky's cultural historical school of psychology and so forth. According to Merton, grand theories do little to guide researchers directly in terms of how to collect pertinent empirical evidence. They tend to be rather abstract and, consequently, somewhat difficult to apply directly in empirical research. For one reason, they were major integrations of many aspects of a particular field of psychology and, therefore, fail to meet the highly specific needs of researchers planning research.

Middle ground is a description which applies to many theories in psychology which are based in data but synthesise a range of studies and findings. Psychology is replete with examples of simple, empirical generalisations which do little than attempt to explain the relationship between a pair of variables. So middle-ground theory goes beyond the requirements of a highly particular piece of empirical research but falls well short of being all-embracing, all-encompassing theory. Examples of middle-ground theory in psychology are then numerous. Theories such as the just-world theory, cognitive dissonance, the pathways model of sexual offending, relative judgement theory might all be considered psychological, middle-range theories. These are examples of middle-ground theory in mainstream psychology *not* middle-ground theory developed from grounded theory. It is not being suggested that middle-range theories in psychology are developed using grounded theory – very few have gained currency to date.

Grounded theory is grounded in particular sorts of data pertinent to the research question. Consequently, we should expect that grounded theories are particularly related to the sorts of in-depth data which can be obtained using focus groups, in-depth interviews, diaries, narratives, newspaper stories and the like. So theories about the different ideologies underlying people's thinking, how different sorts of person interact with others, ways children talk about authority figures in their lives and so forth would be examples of middle-range grounded theories. Middle-range theory is not really a mysterious concept – it is just based on a rather ill-defined idea.

There is another way to theory development in grounded theory – this is known as the 'rewrite' technique. According to Glaser:

> One version of rewriting techniques is simply to omit substantive words, phrases, or adjectives; instead of writing 'temporal aspects of dying as a non-scheduled status passage', one would write 'temporal aspects of non-scheduled status passage.' Substantive theory can also be rewritten up a notch: instead of writing about how doctors and nurses give medical attention to a dying patient according to his social loss, one would talk of how professional services are distributed according to the social value of clients . . . In each version of the rewriting technique, the social scientist writes a one-area formal theory on the basis of his substantive theory; he does not generate the former directly from the data. These techniques produce only an adequate *start* towards theory, *not* an adequate formal theory itself. *The researcher has raised the conceptual level of his work mechanically; he has not raised it through comparative understanding.* (Glaser, 1982, p. 226)

In other words, if theory is generated through re-write techniques then its grounding in the data cannot be taken for granted and needs to be assessed against relevant data.

As we will see in detail later, the process of carrying out a proper grounded theory analysis is demanding. The procedures involved are based on constant referral back and forward between the data and the analysis. There are numerous different ways of doing this but none is easy. Not surprisingly, then, some researchers describe their research as being based on grounded theory despite the fact that the work they present shows few indications that the rigorous procedures of grounded theory have been employed. This sort of lip-service to grounded theory is unfortunate since the newcomer to qualitative research may be confused as to what actually grounded theory is in practice. So be wary of the possibility that a study which claims to be based on grounded theory actually is only minimally so. Like all research and especially qualitative research of a high standard, grounded theory methods are exacting, time-consuming and meticulous. They demand close familiarity with the data and such intimacy itself takes a good deal of time and effort to achieve.

The ultimate aim of grounded theory is to develop theory appropriate to the data and justifiable by a close examination of the data. However, much grounded theory research stops short in the development of theory and concentrates on categorisation of aspects of the data. The process of categorisation is fundamental to grounded theory anyway so such descriptive accounts of the data are valuable even though it is difficult sometimes to describe the product as middle-ground theory. Essentially the process involved in grounded theory:

- brings the researcher into close familiarity with their data;
- encourages the researcher to code small elements of the data;
- encourages the researcher to synthesise these various small elements into categories; and
- continually requires the researcher to compare the data with the developing theory (categories) in the analysis.

This process, in the most successful instances, may lead to the development of theory. But it should be noted that the sort of theory that grounded theory generates does not have all of the characteristics which mainstream psychologists, as a whole, regard as the signs of a good theory. In particular, many psychologists assume that a good theory will help them make predictions about what people will do in certain circumstances. This sort of precise prediction is not an aim of grounded theory. The theory developed in a grounded theory analysis may be capable of being applied to new sets of data but it is not usually possible to make causal predictions. According to Charmaz, grounded theory provides the guidelines for the collection and analysis of data which are then used to develop theories which account for and explain that data:

> Throughout the research process, grounded theorists develop analytic interpretations of their data to focus further data collection, which they use in turn to inform and refine their developing theoretical analyses. (Charmaz, 2000, p. 509)

The following are some of the important characteristics of grounded theory:

- *Systematic*   The process by which theory is developed is through the careful application of the general principles and methods of grounded theory.

- *Guidelines*   Grounded theory is essentially a system of guidelines which guide data collection, data analysis and theory building. The emerging research and theory are closely tied to social reality as far as that is represented in the data.

FIGURE 8.1 **Key elements of grounded theory**

- *Inductive processes are more important than deductive processes* This is very different from conventional theory building in psychology in which hypotheses are deduced from theory and these hypotheses are subjected to empirical test. Such an approach to theory building is commonly communicated to psychology students in introductory mainstream psychology textbooks.

- *Theory building is a continuous process* Grounded theory develops theory through a continuous process rather than by critical tests of hypotheses as in conventional theory building. It is impossible to separate grounded theory research into a small number of discrete stages since theory development begins early – even at the data collection stage – and continues to the stage of writing-up.

Some of the main elements of grounded theory are shown in Figure 8.1.

The development of grounded theory

The popularity of grounded theory over the last 50 years is undeniable. But why? According to Thomas and James:

> Grounded theory, and other techniques of analysis in qualitative inquiry are bound to be popular because they meet a need. For while qualitative inquiry is absolutely valid, it is difficult to do . . . it may entail taking part, watching

and listening, in schools and other environments. But when all this is done, what comes next? Such ways of doing research can lead to a floating feeling, a lack of direction. What does one do with one's data? Surely one can't just talk about it. Grounded theory offers a solution: a set of procedures, and a means of generating theory. As such, it has become widely used and its reputation as an accessible and thorough explained method in qualitative inquiry has grown and grown. (Thomas & James, 2006, p. 768)

Barney Glaser (1930–) and Anselm Strauss (1916–1996) published their book *Awareness of Dying* in 1965. Strauss began to work at the medical school of the University of California at San Francisco and gradually realised that hospitals found dying a difficult subject to deal with. He began fieldwork into the topic and hired Glaser to help. The researchers came to the view that the expectation of death both on the part of the patient and the people around him or her had a big impact on interaction between those involved. They distinguished a number of different classifications of this expectation which ranged from open awareness to closed awareness to suspicion and to mutual deception. Nurses had difficulties where the patient did not know that they were dying since they had to avoid revealing it to the patient. The book attracted a lot of attention and, arguably, can be seen as the first occasion when grounded theory was employed in research. Their later book, *The Discovery of Grounded Theory* (Glaser & Strauss, 1967), was essentially an attempt to describe the method of grounded theory and its limitations. It became one of the classics in sociology and beyond.

Glaser and Strauss were intent on closing the 'embarrassing' (Glaser & Strauss, 1967, p. vii) gap between theory and empirical research in sociology. Interestingly, given this intent, Glaser had been a student of both the arch methodologist of sociology, Paul Lazarsfeld, and Robert Merton, the outstanding theorist, at Columbia University. According to Strauss and Corbin (1994), the book had three distinct purposes:

- To provide a rationale for the grounding of theory in data. That is, a method for developing theory in which the development of theory was part of an interplay with research data.
- To provide a logic for and detail of grounded theories.
- To provide a sound basis for thorough qualitative research in sociology given the low status of qualitative sociology at the time.

Probably out of these three, the final purpose has been the book's most startling achievement and its earliest. As we have seen, grounded theory is often described as being in opposition to the dominant and theoretically highly speculative sociology which emerged and enveloped sociology in the first half of the twentieth century and beyond. More specifically, writers tend to specify the reaction of grounded theory as being to the Chicago School of Sociology. The school developed an ecological approach to the sociology of urban areas. It had a big influence of criminology and contributed some of the earliest approaches to quantification to that discipline. It replaced armchair-theorising with an emphasis on the collection of data and its rigorous analysis. But the theory that developed at the University of Chicago tended to think 'big' in terms of very broad processes which were contributing to social and urban change. In the works of some of the earliest members of the Chicago School were elements which linked sociological change to basic natural science models in ecological research. Human communities were treated as if they consisted of subpopulations which operated in response to similar forces to those in ecological populations. So, for example, a subpopulation would begin to invade a territory and eventually achieve dominance only then to fade when another subpopulation began to succeed in the same territory. But the Chicago School was long-lasting and its influence complex – at the time a massive proportion of graduates in sociology were graduates of the school. One of its influences was in terms of the use of standardised measuring instruments for the collection of data.

Of course, it is possible to see in psychology's quantitative dominance many of the characteristics of the Chicago School. Despite the Chicago School's exploitation of the field setting, the focus was on very broad processes rather than the detail of social interaction. Much the same can be seen in much of the psychology of the twentieth century in the sense that the discipline concentrated on what could be quantified. These tended to be fairly gross abstractions. Charmaz (1995) argues that in sociology the theorist and the researcher were largely distinct roles in early twentieth-century sociology. Something of the same can be seen in the divide between the theorist and the empiricist in much psychology during the same period.

According to Thomas and James (2006), 'grounded theory represented a resolution of different epistemological positions and a solution to a broader problem about perceptions of the status of qualitatively based knowledge in the social sciences' (pp. 767–768). They suggest that symbolic interactionism was declining as a force in the social sciences but, more importantly, the 'hard' science approaches of statistics and structural functionalism which squeezed other approaches powerfully was also somewhat in decline. Grounded theory reversed many of the features of the dominant sociology of the time in a number of ways:

- It established qualitative research as a legitimate venture in its own right rather than relegating it to a preliminary or preparatory stage of refining one's research instruments in preparation for the 'scientifically credible' quantitative study.
- The distinction between research and theory was removed by insisting that theory development and data collection were integral. Data collection and data analysis in the sense of theory development were virtually inseparable. Grounded theory provided methods by which theory development could be validated against the empirical data.

Grounded theory can be seen as a general qualitative methodology which enables it to be adapted to a variety of areas of research. Furthermore, grounded theory requires no particular sort of data so it can be employed with diaries, biographies, newspaper and magazine articles, interviews and more. This clearly means that the potential spread of grounded theory is substantial and its penetration into disciplines such as anthropology and psychology as well as fields such as social work and education not surprising.

One of the major developments in grounded theory was the consequence of Glaser and Strauss going somewhat separate ways later in their careers. That is, the version of grounded theory expounded in *The Discovery of Grounded Theory* evolved somewhat differently in the writings of the two men. This resulted in two options of how grounded theory analysis should be carried out. The split became most evident by the 1990s when Glaser criticised

Strauss's then recent ideas and their differences became part of a more general academic debate. Onions (n.d.) provides a comparison of Glaser's approach and Strauss's approach. For example, Onions suggests that in Glaser's approach the good researcher begins with an empty mind (or 'general wonderment') whereas in Strauss's version the good researcher has a general idea of where to begin the research. For Glaser 'the theory is grounded in the data'; for Strauss 'the theory is interpreted by an observer' (p. 8). For Glaser 'The credibility of the theory, or verification, is derived from its grounding in the data'; for Strauss, 'The credibility of the theory comes from the rigour of the method' (pp. 8–9). For Glaser, 'A basic social process should be identified'; for Strauss 'Basic social processes need not be identified' (p. 9). There is more to it than this, of course, but the flavour is captured to a degree by these examples. Perhaps the most telling comparison is that which suggests that for Glaser the characteristics of the researcher are passivity and disciplined restraint whereas for Strauss the researcher is a much more active participant. Furthermore, Glaser's strategy for grounded theory is not exclusively qualitative since anything can be data which the researcher comes across during his or her studies. So quantitative data such as surveys and statistical analyses can be part of the process of theory development in grounded theory from Glaser's perspective. The consequence of all of this is the difficulty in specifying quite what grounded theory procedures are. One solution, of course, is for the researcher to identify which camp they adhere to.

How to do grounded theory

Grounded theory is a means of data analysis directed towards theory development. It is not a specific means of collecting data and a variety of data can be used though textual data are by far the most typical. No particular type of data is required although, as hinted, it does suit some types of data better than others – interview and similar material is well handled by the approach. So grounded theory can be applied to interviews, biographical data, media content, observations, conversations and so forth. It is possible and recommended that the researcher uses a multiplicity of sources in grounded theory. A key characteristic is, of course, that the data should be as richly detailed as possible – that is not simple or simplified. Charmaz (1995, p. 33) suggests that richly detailed data involve 'full' or 'thick' written descriptions. Questionnaires using yes–no and similar response formats do not meet this criterion. As such, data are usually initially transcribed using a notation system – it could be the Jefferson transcription system (Chapter 6) though more typically the transcription is much simpler, such as the orthographic/playscript format.

Grounded theory has been seen as a form of sophisticated filing system (Potter, 1998). In particular, the grounded theory 'filing system' does not simply file items under a range of headings but also provides extensive cross-referencing to other headings or categories in the filing system. So, for example, the grounded theory library catalogue might file the present book under the heading of 'psychology' but it would also be cross-referenced, say, under 'methods' or 'qualitative research'. Potter's analogy is a useful one and serves to remind us that data in grounded theory can be filed under several categories rather than a single one. There are, however, limitations to Potter's analogy:

- The grounded theory 'filing system' may be constantly changed and refined through to the final stages of the research – the theory to be found in the report or publication. Most filing systems remain the same until they cease to be useful – for example, a library cataloguing system might be revised when there are so many books under the heading sociology because it is no longer a useful way of quickly accessing books. At this point, new sub-categories of the category 'sociology' may have to be developed such as sociological theory, industrial sociology, urban sociology and so forth. The system in grounded theory is different – the categorisation process will tend to reduce the number of categories, more clearly describe what each category is, and provide a picture of what is going on in the data.

- The grounded theory 'filing system' is developed through a constant process of comparing the data with the filing categories. That is to say, although some of the filing categories may seem to emerge out of inspection of the data, these categories are constantly subject to adjustment, modification and change in the light of fresh data and whether or not the categories make sense. Indeed, the categories may become more inclusive or less inclusive depending on the researcher's revised understanding of what the categories are about.

- Perhaps a trifle oddly, the grounded theory 'filing system' developed in one study may well be abandoned for other studies and new and different filing systems created. Indeed, the researcher may deliberately choose to ignore other grounded theory 'filing' systems in order to see the extent to which new studies generate grounded theory 'filing systems' which are similar or different from previous 'filing systems'.

There is a huge literature from different disciplines on grounded theory as well as numerous examples of its use. As one might expect, this results in some variation in how grounded theory is carried out. Indeed, any researcher carrying out grounded theory will probably develop their own idiosyncratic working methods within the broad procedures which characterise grounded theory.

It is not possible to divide a grounded theory analysis into discrete, independent steps. Although explanations of grounded theory have to be sequential, a grounded theory analysis involves going backwards and forwards between analytical stages very flexibly. This is not a random process but purposive in that it is based on the constant need to check and test the fit of one's emerging theoretical ideas with the data, the codings, the categories and new data. Memo-writing is an important tool step in this. The memo may be as simple as a notebook in which the researcher records theoretical ideas as they develop in his or her thinking through the process of the grounded theory analysis. These notes do not have to be elaborate theoretical speculation since they may include half-thought-out ideas concerning matters that the researcher needs to think about. At a more conceptual level, they may be suggestions as to how codings, categories and concepts relate or link together. A memo can include diagrams if these are the best way of presenting the ideas. Boxes of text linked by arrows where appropriate (like a flow diagram) might be a typical diagrammatic memo. It is useful to record what aspects of the analysis are interdependent as well as identifying possible relationships. A researcher's categories cannot be understood solely in their own terms – they take their meaning also from what they are not. So to understand a category such as 'male' really needs an understanding of other categories such as 'female' from which it derives part of its meaning. This is known as interdependency.

The memo is not totally independent of the data. The memo needs to include the most important and significant examples of data which are illustrative of the more general run of the data. So the memo should be replete with illustrative instances of data plus problematic aspects of it at the particular stage of the analysis. Of course, the researcher new to grounded theory may struggle to know exactly what to include in the memo. It may be useful to note the following in this regard:

> If you are at a loss about what to write about, look for the codes that you have used repeatedly in your data collection. Then start elaborating on these codes. Keep collecting data, keep coding and keep refining your ideas through writing more and further developed memos. (Charmaz, 1995, p. 43)

Sometimes memo-writing is described as the intermediary step between data and the theory in the final written report or journal article. Sometimes the advice is to start memo-writing as soon as one recognises something of interest in the data, the coding or the categorisation process. This may be a little late in practice. The general consensus is that the researchers should start memo-writing as early as possible – the sooner the better is the dictum to work with. Hence, some researchers prefer to start memo-writing at the stage of developing the research question.

Characteristically, quantitative researchers seek to reduce concepts to a minimum by developing a small number of concepts which explain as much of the features of the data as possible. A famous principle in quantitative research is Occam's razor which states that the researcher should use no more than the least number of concepts needed to account for the phenomenon in question. Conceptual density (Strauss & Corbin, 1999) is a phrase used to describe the richness of concept development and relationship identification in grounded theory. In other words, this is another indication that theory development in grounded theory is quite different from that in quantitative research. The main stages in the development of a grounded theory are shown in Figure 8.2. You may notice that this figure is rather more complex than any of the equivalent ones in Chapters 7 and 9–12. This simply reflects the characteristics of grounded theory. The key components of the grounded theory method include coding/naming, comparison, categorisation, memo-writing, theoretical sampling and the literature review. The following describes each of these and follows Charmaz's (1995, 2000) procedural recommendations and Bryman's (2004) scheme:

Step 1   Developing a research question   Deciding upon a research question is a major step in virtually any research. As any student seeking ideas for a project or dissertation knows, the research question is one of the most difficult aspects of planning research of any sort. The sources of research questions can be many – the opportunity to do research with a particular organisation, personal interest based on experience, matters of public concern, the research literature, and so forth. The research described in Box 8.1 on experiencing symptoms of heart attacks is partially based on (a) the previous research literature and (b) the institutional context in which the authors were working (basically the field of public health). Whether the research was stimulated by personal interest is not revealed by the researchers.

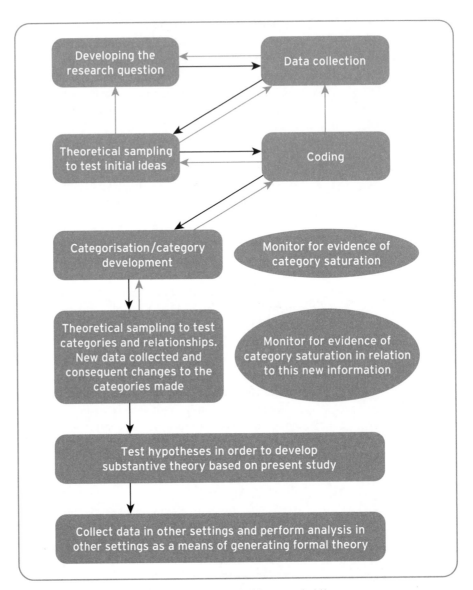

FIGURE 8.2 **The process of theory development in grounded theory**

The role of the literature review in developing research questions in quantitative research is a very clear and important one – quantitative research ideas are almost invariably justified on the basis of the findings of previous research and theory in the field. The literature review is construed as a preliminary stage in any research and is carried out largely in advance of the new research's detailed planning. In other words, quantitative research is viewed as a process of building new research on the foundations of previous research. In distinct contrast, the role of the literature review in grounded theory does not occupy a similar clear-cut position. Sometimes it is argued that the literature review in grounded theory research should be carried out at the end of the research process. So, rather than stimulating the new research, the literature review is primarily to allow the comparison of the new analysis with previous analyses in that field. This helps ensure that the grounded theory analysis is grounded

Box 8.1

ILLUSTRATIVE RESEARCH STUDY

Grounded theory: when a heart attack strikes

Acute myocardial infarction is a heart attack. The blood supply to part of the heart is stopped, causing heart cells to die. Unfortunately, despite the fact that early treatment for heart attacks can be very effective, death can follow. This, of course, depends on whether the victim recognises the symptoms (such as chest pain, nausea and excessive sweating) of the heart attack very quickly – delays of more than two hours are dangerous. Actually, women are less likely to seek medical attention following these symptoms than men. Understanding the meaning of symptoms of a medical condition is a complex process and, naturally, the symptoms of a heart attack may not be properly recognised the first time it happens. All of this and more led Brink, Karlson and Hallberg (2002) to recognise the importance of victim's thoughts, feelings and actions at the time when the symptoms of the heart attack first hit.

The study took place at a Swedish hospital. The participants were a sample of survivors from a consecutive group of victims of acute heart attacks. They were selected to be a fairly varied group in terms of age, education, employment and the severity of their condition. Equal numbers of men and women were chosen. They had agreed to take part in a tape-recorded semi-structured interview which took place in hospital usually between four and six days after entering the hospital. However, no details are provided in the report about the interviews themselves.

The analysis involved the coding of the transcripts of the interviews and began once the first three interviews had been carried out and transcribed. The coding (labelling) process was guided by three questions from Glaser (1978):

- What are these data a study of?
- What category does this incident indicate?
- What is actually happening in the data?

The authors describe how they questioned and compared the phenomena in the data for differences and similarities which helped the researchers to develop concepts. They explain the development of aspects of their analysis as follows:

An example of an initial category from the present data is 'outside imagination', which mirrored one reaction to receiving the diagnosis 'acute myocardial infarction'. Events that were found to be conceptually similar were grouped under more abstract concepts or categories. Using axial coding, categories and subcategories were linked together at the level of properties and dimensions, e.g. the category 'outside imagination' was placed under the larger category 'illusions of invulnerability'. By answering questions of 'who, when, where, why, how and with what consequences', conceptual relationships among categories were developed . . . Finally, in the selective coding procedure, two core categories were developed, labeled *acute reactions* and *health beliefs*. (p. 536)

Acute reactions ranged in extremes from *ready to act* to *delay with seeking care*. Health beliefs ranged from *awareness of risks* to *illusions of invulnerability*.

The researchers then began to understand better what was happening in their data which allowed them to focus. That is, the researchers began to realise that the categories of symptom perceptions had a relationship with the two core categories of *acute reactions* and *health beliefs*. These four different perceptual patterns about the onset of symptoms were labelled as follows (Table 8.1):

- Understanding: this is where the victim understood that the situation was serious and that they needed to do something. Acute reactions = ready to act; health beliefs = aware of the risks involved in the situation.

- Amazement: These individuals felt a sense of amazement that the symptoms were happening to them. Acute reactions = ready to act; health beliefs = illusions of invulnerability.

- Misinterpretation: The victim did not link the symptoms to heart problems – so they thought that the pains, for example, were due to another problem. Acute reactions = tended to delay; health beliefs = aware of the risks.

- Disregard: Some victims just got on with their normal everyday jobs. Acute reactions = tended to delay; health beliefs = illusions of invulnerability.

The grounded theory analysis was validated using 'very short interviews' with different patients who were asked about 'their thoughts, feelings and actions at the onset of the heart attack' (p. 536). However, no details are provided about how this validated the original findings.

So, this is clearly a study based on the principles of grounded theory. That the researchers go beyond the categories that they work up in their analysis to attempt a theoretical understanding can be seen in the typology of symptom perception based on the broad categories of health beliefs and acute reactions. This could be described as a 'model' – or it would be in quantitative research – but equally it constitutes a theory in the sense that it links together different aspects of the analysis.

TABLE 8.1 Brink *et al.*'s typology of reactions to heart attack symptoms

		Acute reactions	
		Ready to act (Forced by others, dramatic symptom onset, pain reaction)	**Delay** (Take medication, wait and see, practical obstacles)
Health beliefs	**Awareness of risks** (Previous experience, knowledge, common-sense, rational thinking)	Understanding of symptoms	Misinterpretation of symptoms
	Illusions of invulnerability (Can't happen to me, outside imagination, never had such problems, unaware of risks)	Amazement at having symptoms	Disregard of symptoms

Based on Tables 1 and 2 of Brink *et al.* (2002).

in the new data rather than in previous theory. At the other side of the debate, the literature review is seen as part of development of the new research. Strauss and Corbin (1999) suggest that the grounded theory methodology may begin in existing grounded theory so long as they 'seem appropriate to the area of investigation'. Then these grounded theories 'may be elaborated and modified as incoming data are meticulously played against them' (pp. 72–73).

Ideally, the decision to use grounded theory should be taken very early in the planning of the new research. This is because grounded theory includes methods for sampling which depend on the feedback of the analysis of the first few interviews, for example. Although it is possible to make the decision to use grounded theory after all of the data have been collected, this is not ideal for the reason just mentioned. Grounded theory is about theory development and hypothesis testing of the sort used in mainstream quantitative psychology is not part of the process. One advantage of grounded theory is that it can be used to research areas for which little or no past research is available or where qualitative methods have not been previously used.

Step 2   **Theoretical sampling**   (This may occur prior to starting data collection but alternatively at various stages in the process of data collection.) There are important differences between sampling in quantitative and qualitative methods:

- Qualitative research tends to use small samples for various reasons but especially because data collection and analysis is so demanding that large samples are impracticable. There is generally no assumption that samples in qualitative research are in some way representative.

- The qualitative researcher seldom knows the characteristics of the population so true random sampling is not feasible.

- Not all participants can be regarded as equal in terms of their contribution to understanding social phenomena. Some people make poor sources of information because of their limited observational, understanding and interpretational skills. The quest for 'rich' data would suggest that certain sources are to be preferred over others. This is not an assumption made by quantitative researchers in their sampling. Marshall (1996) likens this to the situation in which one's car has broken down. Who would you prefer? A passer-by selected at random or a car mechanic?

Grounded theory probably has the most different approach to sampling of all. In grounded theory sampling is usually determined on the basis of the theories one builds up to interpret the data over the period of the grounded theory analysis. This is known as theoretical sampling. Because of the intimate contact of the grounded theorist with their data from the time at which data are first collected, they will be reaching tentative interpretations of their data at various stages before data collection is complete. It is these interpretations which drive the need for further data and further sampling. So the researcher would decide on what further data should be collected on the basis of their evaluation of what additional data would help them in their interpretations. The choices are, of course, between seeking data which might challenge their interpretations but, equally, it might help them elaborate their emerging interpretations (or, in other words, theory).

→ Put another way, theoretical sampling is about how to validate the ideas developed during the memo-writing process which is continuous through the development of a grounded theory. If the ideas that the researcher has noted in the memo are sound and have validity then one should be able to test them by coming up with suggestions about the sort of circumstances in which they apply and the circumstances in which they don't apply. This might involve selecting a participant(s) for inclusion in the research because they might throw up difficulties for one's developing theory. These difficulties might require the researcher to reformulate their ideas or to limit their range of applicability, for example. The task of the researcher is partly to suggest to which samples the theory applies and where it does not apply. It is not simply new sample members who might be recruited; grounded theorists might use theoretical sampling to guide them to other aspects of their data for consideration in the light of the theory. Equally, the researcher may seek new situations to examine whether or not the developing analysis applies there. The point is that such additional sampling of people, situations or data should feed into subsequent memo-writing and theoretical development. In this way, the memos and the ideas therein become ever more closely embedded or grounded in the data.

Although theoretical sampling may apply throughout the range of stages of a grounded theory analysis, it is equally applicable to the initial selection of sources and sites for the initial data collection. Since it is likely that the researcher has some preliminary ideas of what sorts of people or situations will be the most productive in terms of theory development, theoretical sampling applies to the earliest stages of grounded theory research.

Step 3   **Data collection**   Grounded theory takes a very generous perspective on what constitutes data. Typically, in grounded theory analysis, the researcher will begin with a quantity of textual material – the data. This may be in the form of documents; material from the newspapers, magazines or the Internet; or, possibly the most likely, transcripts of in-depth interviews, focus groups, and the like. Indeed, it can be appropriate to incorporate several different forms of data. Of course, probably most grounded theory research would use primary sources such as the above-mentioned interview and focus groups.

Step 4   **Coding/naming**   The data are then subject to a lengthy, complex and demanding close examination by the researcher. In order to achieve this, the researcher undergoes a line-by-line analysis of the text and essentially scrutinises each line for meaning. Each line is numbered sequentially for convenience and reference purposes. Coding is achieved by giving each line of the analysis a descriptive code or codes. (Although the coding usually goes line-by-line, there is no reason why other units of analysis such as sentences, paragraphs, speaking turns, etc. could not be used.) Basically these codes are at a level of abstraction which essentially describes what is in that line of text/data. Sometimes the code is very closely related to the data but, ideally, since the end product is a theory abstracted from the data, codings should aim at a higher level of abstraction than mere description as that is where the theory is going. This is referred to as coding the data. While, in terms of reading about coding, one imagines that this calls for some sort of insightful, meaningful and sophisticated description, in reality the researcher will largely use at least some relatively mundane

→

descriptions. Remember that each of these initial codings is based on just a few words of data and so is likely to be fairly close to the data at this stage. There simply is not enough information to go beyond this. It is also important to understand that these codings are likely to be different for different researchers using exactly the same data. The differences may be simply the words used and essentially the researchers are saying the same thing in different ways. Nevertheless, sometimes the differences may be more fundamental than that. Basically, then, each line's coding describes what is happening in that line or, in other words, what is represented by that line. Coding in grounded theory is therefore the creation of codes and not the application of pre-specified codes as it would be in content analysis. Another way of describing coding, according to Potter (1997), is that it is a process of giving labels to the key concepts or ideas which appear in a particular line (or paragraph, etc.). The main point of coding is to keep the researcher's thinking firmly on the ground of the data. According to Charmaz (1995), line-by-line coding helps the researcher to avoid the temptation of over-interpreting the data such as by attributing motives to the speaker in the text.

The end point of coding in grounded theory will leave the researcher with pages of text and each line coded with a description. It is likely that the researcher will emerge from this stage with broader ideas about what is going on in the data – maybe ideas of how the different codings actually fit together, which codings are much the same as each other despite using different labels, and so forth. The researcher would normally make a record of these ideas in the form of a memo. (See the above section on memo-writing.) There is no reason why the researcher cannot revise any of the codings at any stage during this process.

There are several types of coding that are involved in grounded theory. The most important among these is:

- *Open coding* This is the form of coding described above which works as closely to the original data as possible. It is sometimes known as *in vivo* coding because of this.

The next two forms of coding are more about finding relationships among the open codings.

- *Axial coding* This is the process of relating codings (categories and concepts) together. It is, in a sense, the second major reworking of the data, though the emphasis is on the open codings much more than the data. Both *inductive* and *deductive* reasoning may be involved in the creation of axial coding. Axial coding is about relationships between different aspects of the developing theory. It is about organising the initial codes and identifying key concepts. It is a somewhat controversial feature of grounded theory, with experts disagreeing about its relevance and value. It is key to Strauss and Corbin's (1998) methods but rejected as optional by others (e.g. Charmaz, 2006). Axial coding may be facilitated by any method that helps juxtapose the open codings in a way which helps the analysis. So, for example, writing the open codings on pieces of card or paper may facilitate attempts to form groupings of codings which seem to be similar. Shuffling slips of card and paper on the floor or a desk is much easier than shuffling ideas around in one's mind.

→   ● *Selective coding*   This is the process by which the researcher identifies a category to be at the core of the analysis and relates every other category to that category. It basically involves the development of a major theme or storyline around which all other aspects of the analysis are integrated.

These two latter forms of coding dominate in the next step.

Step 5   **Category development through comparison/constant comparison**   The line-by-line codings obtained earlier represent the starting point of the conceptual analysis of the data and are best seen as a preliminary process in developing grounded theory. These codings need to be organised into categories incorporating several codings. In this way, a conceptual synthesis of the codings begins to develop. The categories need to stay true to the original codings: there is no sense in which the codings should be forced into categories which they do not fit well and there should be no arbitrariness in the categorisation of codings. In other words, although codings are an early step in developing theory, they are too close to the detail of the data to provide, in themselves, a satisfactory synthesis of what is happening in the data. Codings constitute the smallest formal unit in a grounded theory analysis and by combining them appropriately we may move on to a better perspective about how to understand the data. So the process of building codings into categories or inducing categories from the codings is crucial to theory development.

Of course, the combination of data into broader categories is a common feature of analysis in quantitative research as well as qualitative research. For example, in quantitative research statistical procedures such as factor analysis and cluster analysis are used in order to provide the researcher with ways of grouping variables essentially into broader categories. Such statistical techniques are not generally available to qualitative researchers. Furthermore, this sort of statistical/empirical classification process in quantitative methods concentrates on what the data share rather than considering the data in their entirety. That is, it draws up categories based on correlations and ignores anything not based on correlation. Put another way, category development in quantitative research involves neglecting a great deal of the data which do not correlate across variables. In qualitative research, the aim is to synthesise all aspects of the data into an analysis.

In addition, the categories need to be understood as fully as possible by the researcher whose tasks include labelling the categories effectively so it is clear what the category is about. All of this means that the researcher may need to work tirelessly on their categories since this level of analysis moves the analysis towards theory development. Furthermore, the categories need to be compared to ensure that they do not overlap. It is a possibility that categories given different labels are actually much the same thing. So, for example, the researcher might begin to recognise that their category of 'anti-democratic principles' is redolent of existing ideas and theory such as 'authoritarianism'. While grounded theory analysis in one of its versions (Glaser's) should not be influenced by the research literature at this stage, it is inevitable that a researcher's knowledge of research and theory may have some impact on category development.

There are two important principles which are essential to understanding category development in grounded theory. They are *constant comparison* and *category saturation*. Each will be discussed in turn next.

→

To take constant comparison first, this is a process of critically checking any aspect of the analysis against other aspects of the analysis. The object is to critically assess the extent to which these different aspects work in relation to each other. By checking to see how well the elements of the analysis fit, gel and articulate together and making changes and adjustments wherever necessary, the analysis begins to develop coherence, leading to refinement in the analysis. If we take the line-by-line codings, constant comparison would involve the researcher checking things such as:

● Do differently coded lines have different content – or have different codings been used for much the same content?

● Do similarly coded lines have similar content – or are the same codings being used for very different things?

Furthermore, the comparison process can be used more widely in assessing theory development. For example:

● Interviews with people occupying similar roles in an organisation could be compared in terms of their experiences of the workplace – how they account for their actions within the workplace, for example.

● Comparisons between one data set and another – or even one study with a further study.

● Comparisons of categories derived from the codes with the original codings.

● Comparisons of any aspect of the grounded theory analysis with the original data.

Unlike quantitative analysis, grounded theory does not condone forcing ill-fitting categories onto data. Instead the categories, etc. of the analysis are reconsidered and modified to allow a better fit with the data. Glaser wrote:

> Comparative analysis can also be used to compare conceptual units of a theory or theories, as well as data, in terms of categories and their properties and hypotheses. Such conceptual comparisons result . . . in generating, densifying and integrating the substantive theories into a formal theory by discovering a more parsimonious set of concepts with greater scope. (Glaser, 1982, p. 228)

So it should be clear that the term 'comparative' is used somewhat differently in grounded theory from the way it is used in psychology and the social sciences in general (Glaser, 1982). In grounded theory comparison serves the process of theory generation and the comparison processes may include ensuring the accuracy of the evidence, specifying a concept, checking a research hypothesis, etc. Comparative analysis can involve social units of any size ranging from individuals through to nations and world groups.

We can now turn to the other important concept: saturation. The concept of category saturation is used in grounded theory to indicate the point at which the analysis can go no further. This is the point at which doing further comparisons, etc. fails to necessitate further refinements to the theory. The concept of saturation can be used in relation to decisions about whether or not to terminate data gathering – especially helping the researcher decide whether to interview additional participants. When additional interviews cease

→ to generate anything of substance which is different from what has emerged before, then this is likely to be the appropriate moment to stop recruiting new participants. It is somewhat like searching the Internet. Google for 'grounded theory' and thousands of web pages will be listed. However, in a sort of law of diminishing returns, you will find that you learn everything of importance from the first few websites you visit and that eventually new pages turn up nothing but familiar stuff. That is the time when the web search would be over. Much the same happens in grounded theory analysis.

Saturation as applied to the categories being developed (category saturation) occurs when after many comparison steps the researcher finds that the categories do not change and nothing new is being learnt about the categories. The key thing is that grounded theory is about theory development and when one's analyses (comparisons) cease to develop one's theoretical understanding then there is no point in further analysis. It should be stressed that theoretical saturation applies to *all* of one's categories at the same time – not partial sets of categories.

Step 6   **Theoretical sampling, etc. to test categories and relationships**   During this stage of the analysis, there is still work to be done to check the theory against the data. The principles of theoretical sampling are again employed to seek new data to test the adequacy of the relationships which have been identified during the process of the analysis. One is not merely seeking evidence that will confirm what has emerged but also evidence which may bring about a questioning of the theory and its concepts together with a possible revision of that theory or of some of the concepts.

Step 7   **Test hypotheses in order to develop substantive theory based on the present study**   A theory based on categories and relationships between categories is clearly of value. However, such a theory would be more useful if it allowed us to go beyond the basic theory to develop hypotheses about how the theory relates to other aspects of the thing being researched. For example, when Glaser and Strauss's book *Awareness of Dying* was discussed earlier it was pointed out that there were several different categories of awareness possible: open awareness, closed awareness, suspicion and mutual deception. These categories became much more interesting when Glaser and Strauss found that these different categories of awareness of dying affected the ease of interaction between medical staff and patients. The testing of this 'hypothesis' and its confirmation extended the grounded theory towards being a substantive theory.

Step 8   **Collect data and perform analysis in other settings as a means of generating formal theory**   The grounded theory has now been generated in a particular sort of research setting. Does the theory have any potential to be useful in other research settings? Of course, this potential partly depends on the nature of the theory that has developed. But, for example, the theory described in Box 8.1 concerning the perception of symptoms of heart attack might have some relevance to the perception of cancer symptoms, for example, or the way we respond to bad medical news in general. The more that the theory generalises to other situations, the closer it comes towards being a formal theory about a particular phenomenon. Many researchers do not take grounded theory to this stage.

When to use grounded theory

Grounded theory is explicitly a way of developing theory so that it closely fits the data on which it is based. It is not a data collection method as such even though it has a lot to say about what data ought to be collected as the analysis proceeds. Unlike several qualitative analysis methods in this book (e.g. discourse analysis and narrative analysis) it is not associated with a particular sort of content. The grounded theory approach changed the way of carrying out qualitative data analysis forever. It is possible to see elements of grounded theory in most of the methods described in other chapters. What is not so evident is when one would use grounded theory in preference to the other methods described in this book. Grounded theory places considerable intellectual demands on the researcher and proper training in the method is reputed to take quite a number of months. Furthermore, the grounded theory approach of combining data collection with data analysis in a sort of interactive way is not the easiest of things to do either practically or intellectually. It is perhaps unsurprising to find that not every researcher who claims to use a grounded theory approach to data analysis seems to adhere to all aspects of its rather demanding methodology.

What sort of research aims does grounded theory have the most to contribute to? According to Potter (1998), it works best when the issues involved are easily handled from the perspective of 'a relatively common sense actor'. In other words, where the theory developed is pretty close to the 'everyday notions' of the participants in the theory. Perhaps this is inevitable in any research which gives a 'voice' to the participants in the research. Put another way, grounded theory may simply codify the ways in which ordinary people understand and experience the world. But if Potter is correct, this implies that grounded theory does not amount to much of a method of data analysis at all. This, perhaps, belies some of the complexity of the approach. Possibly Potter is referring to cases of grounded theory analysis which fail to achieve more than a basic level of abstraction.

It is probably not unexpected, then, to find that grounded theory is often used in relation to medical illness and interpersonal relationships. These are topics readily amenable to the common-sense inputs of the participants in the research. But, equally, what is amenable to the common-sense interpretations of research participants may well be the sort of research which policy makers find meaningful. That is, the less abstract the theoretical contribution of the researcher is because it is closely tied to common-sense understandings, the easier it is for the policy maker to make use of the theory. The participants, the theory and the policy maker are all 'on the same wavelength'.

This is a slightly depressing view of grounded theory and, perhaps, needs some revision since it implies that grounded theory is rather limited. Grounded theory is not quite so directly tied to particular sorts of data and research as many of the other data analysis methods in this book are. Conversation analysis, discourse analysis, interpretative phenomenological analysis and narrative analysis link analysis with a particular sort of theoretical perspective. This can be seen as a strength but it is also a limitation. Grounded theory is a way of developing theory – it is a theory of data analysis rather than any substantial area of psychology, for example. This makes it very different in scope. So it primarily offers itself to researchers who wish to develop theory without staking a claim as to its pre-eminence in this field. In a sense, its nearest rival for the attentions of the qualitative researchers is thematic analysis which may well generate analyses which can seem very like those of grounded theory. This is not a surprise as they share some of the same procedures. Nevertheless, grounded theory encourages the researcher to go rather further in theory development than does thematic analysis.

Grounded theory offers intellectual stimulation and challenge to researchers rooted in the methodology of mainstream psychology. There is virtually no characteristic of mainstream research in psychology which is not reversed or revised in grounded theory. Not that grounded theory would be antagonistic to using some of the findings of mainstream psychology – relevant information is relevant information in grounded theory – but it would consider that mainstream psychology's approach to theory generation is relatively crude and unproductive.

Evaluation of grounded theory

Grounded theory, implemented in full, is clearly a demanding process. In its fullest form, the resources that it requires may be beyond a student researcher. Nevertheless, the first few steps of grounded theory are reasonably practicable in terms of student research. The impression is that substantial numbers of self-styled grounded theory analyses tend to adopt this 'lite' version of the procedure. That is, the analysis ceases when a 'theory' based on the initial codings has been developed that the researcher finds satisfactory. Grounded theory demands a thoroughness of approach and analytic work which should help students avoid the familiar qualitative research failing 'of trawling a set of transcripts for quotes to illustrate preconceived ideas' (Potter, 1998, p. 127).

When reading some grounded theory analyses, one may not always be convinced that the analysis emerges from the data rather than from such preconceived ideas. However, this risks evaluating a research method in terms of poor examples of the method rather than its better achievements. The more transparent research publications are about the details of the methods employed the better as this will contribute to maintaining high standards.

The case for grounded theory includes the following:

- Grounded theory provided an alternative to the hypothesis-testing approach in research. The hypothesis-testing model of research was dominant in quantitative psychology in the 1960s when grounded theory was first developed. (Of course, hypothesis testing is still very important in mainstream psychology.)
- Grounded theory was influential since it helped base qualitative research on systematic research procedures.
- Because much of the theory generated using grounded theory is closely tied to what research participants say, grounded theory speaks in a voice that is readily understood by people, including policy makers and practitioners in many fields. In other words, grounded theory theories are highly amenable to use in areas of social and public policy.
- Rather than qualitative research being seen as an initial exploratory stage in research, grounded theory showed that qualitative research could be effective in theory development. It encouraged the valuing of detailed qualitative research.

Among the criticisms of grounded theory are the following:

- The potential for collection of data is endless in grounded theory and virtually any textual or spoken material could be subjected to a grounded theory analysis. Because theory development occurs after the data have begun to be collected, theory cannot guide the subject matter for a grounded theory analysis. So there is a sense of any research area will suffice – the theory will emerge.

- Grounded theory almost requires that theory development is delayed until after data collection has begun which makes it difficult to build theoretical depth rather than a multiplicity of theories.

- Vagueness surrounds some of the procedures of grounded theory. Not surprisingly the theory is relatively vague about the mental processes that are involved in theory development compared with the practical steps that the researcher carries out alongside this. It is much easier to describe the process of coding than to explain how to come up with ideas for coding. At another level, grounded theory is far less clear about the processes involved in testing a theory than about those involved in generating theory. The examples in Boxes 8.1 and 8.2 are either silent about the testing process or somewhat vague – perhaps reflecting this criticism.

Box 8.2

ILLUSTRATIVE RESEARCH STUDY

Grounded theory: bullying in the workplace

Workplace bullying has serious effects on its victims. It may seriously affect their ability to maintain social contacts, his or her reputation, professional status, health and so forth. Strandmark and Hallberg (2007) argued that most research on bullying concentrated on issues such as the prevalence of bullying and the relationships between the bully and victim. They suggest that research largely neglected the experience of being bullied.

The researchers employed grounded theory. They recruited their participants from newspaper advertisements and a website. Participants were selected to be heterogeneous in their characteristics. The open-ended interviews were based on an interview guide which included the following themes:

- Thoughts and feelings related to bullying.
- The psychosocial work environment.
- Working group.
- Perceived health.

→

The interviewing process involved probes and clarification questions. The first 15 or so open interviews were carried out alongside simultaneous data analysis. This analysis used coding, memo-writing and fairly standard grounded theory procedures:

> The initial coding process, which started as soon as the first interview was transcribed, was carried out close to the data on a line-by-line basis, while the focused coding took place on a more conceptual level. Constant comparisons were made between different parts of the data, different incidents and experiences, and between different emerging concepts to explore similarities and differences in the data. The preliminary categories were saturated in subsequent data collection. Theoretical sampling was conducted to refine each category and to saturate the categories with information. Thus, saturation meant that additional data did not add new information. During the entire process of analysis, conceptual relationships between categories were hypothesized, sought, and verified in the data. A core category, central to the data, was identified that determined the emerging theoretical framework. (p. 5)

Theoretical sampling was, of course, based on the emerging findings of the data analysis. According to the authors:

> This [theoretical sampling] was carried out either by re-analyzing collected data, going back to informants for additional information, or by interviewing new informants until new data did not add new information. (pp. 4-5)

The analysis of the data led to a core category (central theme) which the researchers labelled 'being rejected and expelled from the workplace'. This basically is the 'story' which emerged from the data – the process by which the victim of the bullying experienced a resolution of the conflict through rejection and expulsion. Of course, other categories were associated with this overriding theme:

- Changing a person's image by means of slander: this refers to the slander and backbiting spread among colleagues in the workplace about the victim of the slander.
- Betraying a person through deceit: this refers to the feeling of being deceived by others in the workplace who appeared to be on their side but who failed to deliver support for them. This included immediate colleagues, union representatives and staff in personnel.
- Devaluing a person through insults: this refers to the negative actions of others which were specifically designed to devalue the victim. The victim felt stigmatised by the bullying and began to feel worthless.
- Legitimising bullying through unjust treatment: this refers to various unfair practices applied against the victim of bullying. For example, one participant complained that she wanted time off to help her prepare her son for a school examination and was refused. On the other hand, another colleague was given ten days' leave for her 60th birthday party!

And there was another category in which the victim could temporarily gain relief from the social support of their family:

- Mobilising power through support: this was the support that the victim sometimes received from their family and, to a lesser extent, managers and others in the workplace.

The authors bring these elements into a conceptual model which ends in the state of being rejected and forced out of the workplace (see Figure 8.3). The authors do not explain the snaking pattern within the diagram.

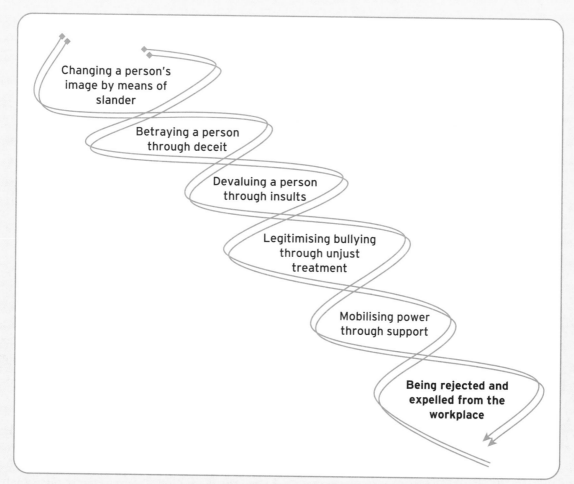

FIGURE 8.3 Strandmark and Hallberg's (2007) model of the process of rejection and expulsion from the workplace. (*Source*: Strandmark and Hallberg (2007))

In many ways, this study presents a relatively complete grounded theory study. Certainly it shows the interplay between data collection and data analysis which characterises grounded theory. Perhaps where it fails is that once the theoretical model has been presented (that which is summarised in Figure 8.3) then the process does not go on to establishing a more formal model which is applicable to workplace bullying in other types of research setting. The authors are aware of the need to do this but fail to go to this final step in grounded theory. In other words, the grounded theory analysis stops early compared with the process described in this chapter and summarised in Figure 8.1. While this is a common occurrence in reports of grounded theory, it is still not the complete process. However, the paper describes a grounded theory analysis which is substantially complete compared to many.

The researchers actually present a literature review both before the study was carried out and to some extent afterwards. This raises an interesting question since the prior literature review simply identifies that the experience of workplace bullying is under researched compared with other aspects of bullying. So in a sense, the prior literature review cannot affect the analysis of the data because the prior literature fails to address this issue. So maybe these are circumstances in which the *a priori* literature would be acceptable to all grounded theorists.

- Many of the aims of grounded theory are to be admired but the method risks providing an excuse for an inadequate qualitative analysis of data. There are no guarantees that grounded theory will produce outcomes which are of any value. Of course, this is true of any of the other methods described in this book. In itself, grounded theory primarily provides a means of processing data in a way which promotes abstract conceptualisations by the researcher – which possibly may result in valuable theory. Grounded theory involves a great deal of hard work which is difficult to abandon no matter the outcome of the process since so much time and effort has been involved. The criteria for deciding the value of a theory are not really apparent in grounded theory.

- Grounded theory might be a 'fail-safe' method of data analysis in circumstances where a researcher has data but has failed to develop appropriate research questions. The lack of other options for analysis may mean that grounded theory is adopted but not for positive reasons.

- Grounded theory concentrates on the development on theory and tends to reject prior consideration of theory in the field because these prior theories may 'sully' the analysis. But there are many circumstances where well-developed theory is available. For example, discourse analysis and conversation analysis both have well-developed theory based on qualitative method. Why not employ this theory? Or should grounded theory be reserved for circumstances in which there is no relevant theory? Both the examples in this chapter (Boxes 8.1 and 8.2) use grounded theory when relevant qualitative theory is unavailable.

- Grounded theory methods encourage the analysis of text on a line-by-line basis. These lines are the result of arbitrary divisions too. So they can be fragments and not even complete sentences. This may encourage the researcher to concentrate on rather small units of analysis. This is rather different from the use of larger units of text which are typically used in discourse analysis (Grbich, 2007; Potter, 1998). This limitation of grounded theory makes it a less comfortable 'bedfellow' for other methods of analysis than would be apparent in the literature. Of course, this is a problem created by the process of line-by-line coding and may not necessarily be a big problem in practice since other levels of analysis (e.g. those in the memo) may be employed. Indeed, when one considers Glaser's lack of enthusiasm for audio-recording and his view of transcription as being time-wasting (Glaser, 1998), this suggests that the researcher's awareness of the content of an interview and their conceptualisation of this can be important aspects of grounded theory – and it is not based on the finicky close analysis usually found in grounded theory studies.

- It may sometimes be difficult to differentiate between the outcomes of a grounded theory analysis and a thematic analysis (Chapter 7). While a thematic analysis is a categorisation process with no great aspirations to theory development, grounded theory analyses may sometimes come up with much the same sorts of data categorisation scheme. Unless the grounded theory analysis goes beyond this by using theoretical sampling and so forth then an opportunity has been lost. But who can guarantee that there is more in one's data than thematic analysis can elucidate?

Of course, our question here is the relevance of grounded theory for psychological research. Howitt and Cramer (2008) pointed out that some grounded theorists write of it as if it is inimical to certain sorts of theory development in psychology. Strauss and Corbin wrote specifically that:

> ... grounded theory researchers are interested in patterns of action and interaction between and among various types of social units (i.e., 'actors'). So they are not especially interested in creating theory about individual actors as such (unless perhaps they are psychologists or psychiatrists). (Strauss & Corbin, 1999, p. 81)

If grounded theory is about the social (interactive) then time will tell the extent to which grounded theory can help in the theoretical development of more purely psychological issues.

CONCLUSION

So important is grounded theory in the development of qualitative research methods that all serious researchers should be familiar with its basic ideas and procedures. Having said that, it is an approach which often seems poorly understood and full-blown examples, from psychology, of its use are hard to come by. In one sense, grounded theory ticks all of the boxes since it promises a theoretical analysis based on qualitative data without theory being reviewed as a prerequisite. This might seem to be a dream scenario to a student with a dissertation or project to write – or even the researcher who has a pile of interview transcripts but no real idea about analysing them. However, it should be clear that grounded theory is personally demanding for the researcher and abstract thinking abilities are at a premium if the analysis is to be anything but mundane.

An important question is whether the sorts of theory that can be derived from grounded theory meets the needs, intellectual or otherwise, of the researcher. Partly the problem lies in the typical sorts of data used in grounded theory studies rather than grounded theory itself. That is, it is difficult to move to a more abstract level from the common-sense explanations provided by participants in the research. Consequently, it is often the case that grounded theory studies generate categories to describe what is going on in the data but things are not taken much further than that. The formal theory promised by grounded theory materialises too infrequently because the range of data available in a study is too limited. Grounded theory needs a rather broader approach to the data available than a typical research study generates.

KEY POINTS

- Grounded theory basically involves a number of techniques which enable researchers to effectively analyse 'rich' (detailed) qualitative data effectively. However, quantitative research findings may also be involved.

- It reverses the classic hypothesis-testing approach to theory development (favoured by some quantitative researchers) by defining data collection as the primary stage and requiring that theory is closely linked to the entirety of the data.

- The researcher keeps close to the data when developing theoretical analyses - in this way the analysis is 'grounded' in the data rather than being based on speculative theory which is then tested using hypotheses derived from the theory.

- Grounded theory does not mean that there are theoretical concepts just waiting in the data to be discovered. It means that the theory is anchored in the data.

- In grounded theory, categories are developed and refined by the researcher in order to analyse (usually textual) data. The analysis should maximise the fit of the developing theory (categories) to the data and any other relevant information source. Since the theory is closely tied to the data, many researchers using grounded theory do not consider previous theory relevant to developing the analysis.

- The theory which emerges in grounded theory research is often described as 'middle range' and is not intended to be far-reaching or to be an all-encompassing 'grand' theory. However, since theories are often based on common-sense ideas from participants they may not be particularly abstract or elaborately synthesised.

- Grounded theory is principally 'inductive' (that is, does not deduce outcomes from theoretical postulates). It is systematic in that an analysis of some sort will almost result from adopting the system. It is a continuous process of development of ideas - it does not depend on a critical test of a hypotheses derived from the theory as is characteristic of mainstream psychological theory development which can be regarded as deductive.

- Comparison is the key process in grounded theory - all elements of the research and the analysis are constantly compared and contrasted.

- Computer programs are available which help the researcher organise the materials for the analysis and effectively alter the codings and categories.

ADDITIONAL RESOURCES

Charmaz, K. (2008). Grounded theory. In J.A. Smith (Ed.), *Qualitative Psychology: A Practical Guide to Research Methods*, 2nd Edition. London: Sage, pp. 81-110.

Dick, B. (n.d.). Grounded Theory: A Thumbnail Sketch. http://www.scu.edu.au/schools/gcm/ar/arp/grounded.html (accessed 2 August 2009).

Hawker, S., and Kerr, C. (2007). Doing grounded theory. In E. Lyons & A. Coyle (Eds.), *Analysing Qualitative Data in Psychology*. London: Sage, pp. 87-97.

Henwood, K., and Pidgeon, N. (2003). Grounded theory in psychological research. In P.M. Camic, J.E. Rhodes & L. Yardley (Eds.), *Qualitative Research in Psychology: Expanding perspectives in methodology and design*. Washington, DC: American Psychological Association, pp. 131-156.

Payne, S. (2007). Grounded theory. In E. Lyons & A. Coyle (Eds.), *Analysing Qualitative Data in Psychology*. London: Sage, pp. 65-86.

CHAPTER 9

Discourse analysis

Overview

- Discourse analysis refers to a variety of ways of studying and understanding talk (or text) as part of social interaction. It sees discourse as being constructed in interaction as well as constructive of interaction.

- Discourse analysis involves the analysis of language at a level beyond individual words.

- The intellectual roots of discourse analysis are largely in linguistic philosophy of the 1950s onwards. Most important is speech act theory in which language is regarded as social action.

- There is an alternative thread of discourse analysis which is based on the ideas of Michel Foucault and is treated separately in this chapter. Briefly, the difference is between a micro-level of analysis concentrating on the constructivist nature of discourse and the macro-level of analysis which concentrates on societal issues and social institutions (see Box 1.2, Chapter 1).

- Discourse analysis may be regarded as a body of ideas about the nature of talk and text. As such it can be applied to much of the data collected by psychologists in the form of language. However, the same data may be used for quite different purposes. For example, in thematic analysis the task of the researcher is to find broad themes in the data.

- A number of theoretical themes are common in discourse analysis. These include rhetoric, voice, footing, discursive repertoires and the dialogical nature of talk. Together with others, such things form the basis of discourse analysis. In other words, analysis in discourse analysis is steered by its theoretical underpinnings.

- The practice of discourse analysis involves a variety of procedures which centre around the processing and reprocessing of the text under consideration. These include transcription and coding/categorisation.

- Discourse analysis is only good for what it was intended. It should not be treated as a 'universal' approach to the analysis of qualitative data. When one's interest is in language as action, it provides both theory and practice to guide the analysis.

What is discourse analysis?

The ways in which language and society interact lie at the heart of discourse analysis. Discourse analysis is centred on social interaction – the way discourse governs individuals' actions. The dialogue of ordinary conversations is its primary focus. Language in discourse analysis is seen as interacting with society – discourse analysis does not assume that language is in its essence communication but that it is social action. Language is not construed as a means of communicating internal cognitive realities to the outside world. Discourse analysis assumes at the most fundamental level that truth and reality are not knowable through language. Stubbs wrote this about discourse analysis:

> The term discourse analysis is very ambiguous. I will use it . . . to refer mainly to the linguistic analysis of naturally occurring connected speech or written discourse. Roughly speaking, it refers to attempts to study the organisation of language above the sentence or above the clause, and therefore to study larger linguistic units, such as conversational exchanges or written texts. It follows that discourse analysis is also concerned with language use in social contexts, and in particular with interaction or dialogue between speakers. (Stubbs, 1983, p. 1)

Twenty years later, a leading exponent of discourse analysis in psychology provided a crisper, less convoluted definition:

> Discourse analysis is the study of how talk and texts are used to perform actions. (Potter, 2003, p. 5)

Nevertheless, Stubbs's insistence that discourse analysis is a very ambiguous term is reflected in more recent comments by psychologists. Thus, Potter suggests that discourse analysis is a somewhat incoherent field:

> . . . in mid 80s it was possible to find different books called Discourse Analysis with almost no overlap in subject matter; the situation at the start of the 00s is, if anything, even more fragmented. (Potter, 2004, p. 607)

Edley supports the idea that discourse analysis risks becoming a catch-all term for all sorts of things:

> . . . there is no simple way of defining discourse analysis. It has become an ever broadening church, an umbrella term for a wide variety of different analytic principles and practices. (Edley, 2001, p. 189)

Part of the problem lies in the fact that discourse analysis features, in various forms, in a wide range of academic disciplines. If we focus primarily on the use of the term 'discourse analysis' in psychology then things are simpler although it remains clear that distinctive approaches are involved. Furthermore, although discourse analysis is often discussed as if it were a radical new approach in psychology, its history in psychology started 30 or so years ago. This is plenty of time, of course, for different schools of thought to develop and the main emphases of research to change. So discourse analysis as it is currently construed by practitioners can be expected to be different from its earlier, tentative beginnings. The interdisciplinary nature of discourse analysis, the process of change which characterises all fields of psychology, personal preference, and differences in intellectual traditions all impinge on the question of exactly what discourse analysis is. Figure 9.1 is a mind-map using ideas from Potter's (2003)

FIGURE 9.1 A mind-map of discourse analysis

synopsis of major features of the development of psychological discourse analysis. All elements of the mind-map should, to some extent, interconnect using arrows. To keep things simple, only the major interconnections are indicated. Several things ought to be stressed:

- Social constructionist thinking is a precursor to discourse analysis and a continuing influence on discourse analytic theory.

- Two major approaches to discourse analysis are to be found in psychology. One is the approach from social psychology beginning with the work of Jonathan Potter (1956–) and Margaret Wetherell (1954–). The other approach is based on the work of Michel Foucault (1926–1984). You will see this referred to as Foucauldian discourse analysis but also Foucaultian discourse analysis – you will also find it without the letter l. It is possible that the Foucaultian version is American. There is no consensus as to why there is this disagreement. The phrase critical discourse analysis is also used for much the same body of work. Ian Parker (1956–) is a well-known advocate of this approach (Burman & Parker, 1993; Parker, 2002). In this chapter we will discuss both approaches and explain how they can be carried out. However, the social constructionist version of Potter and Wetherell is probably the more student-friendly or student-usable of the two and will receive the primary coverage in this chapter but not to the exclusion of the Foucauldian approach.

- Discursive psychology, although having its origins in and being interconnected with social psychological discourse analysis, is a branch of psychology and not, in itself, a form of discourse analysis. It could be described as the body of knowledge resulting from the application of discourse analysis within psychology. It is debatable whether the distinction between discourse analysis and discursive psychology is a necessary one or that it is systematically adhered to. For example, Willig (2008) seems to use the terms discourse analysis and discursive psychology interchangeably. Maintaining the distinction, though, has the important advantage of helping to label more clearly what otherwise goes under the unspecific general label of discourse analysis.

The mind-map gives some credence to Coyle's claim:

> The term 'discourse analysis' has been based on different assumptions and has different aims. This makes it difficult to provide an account of the commonalities of discourse analysis except in the broadest terms and any representation of the field will inevitably satisfy some and irritate others. (Coyle, 2007, p. 99)

However, it would be better to note Taylor's view that discourse analysis is best not regarded as just another method in the methodological armoury of psychologists:

> . . . it is not enough to study what the researcher does (like following a recipe!). We also need to refer back to these epistemological debates and their wider implications. (Taylor, 2001, p. 12)

That is, understanding what discourse analysis is depends more on understanding its intellectual roots than on knowing how to do technical things like Jefferson transcription well or how to perform the mechanics of a discourse analysis. Put this way, the task actually becomes clearer and some of the confusion drops away.

In the discourse analysis tradition, language is regarded as being socially situated. There have been shifts in dominant opinion but, broadly speaking, discourse analysis can be applied to a wide variety of different sort of texts and not just conversation. In a sense, it is largely irrelevant if that text is natural conversation, Internet chatroom talk, newspaper headlines, in-depth but fairly conversational interviews, or what-have-you. All of these have featured in discourse analytic studies. There has been a move away from using interviews as a preferred data source but there is no embargo on such work (see Chapter 3). The key thing is that all of these are clear examples of language use in society. Discourse analysis shifts the conceptualisation of language from what is represented using language to language as social action – what language can do. Quite clearly, then, there is more potential in using naturally occurring language for such studies than, say, instruction manuals for operating household appliances.

At the roots of discourse analysis is what is known as 'speech act theory' (Austin, 1975). In this, language is seen as being part of a social performance. During these language performances all sorts of things happen. People create their own social identities or have them created by others or they are jointly constructed; power relationships are determined, exercised and maintained; and, generally speaking, a lot of social tasks are performed through language. None of this would be possible if a model of language in which it is seen as communicating between internal thought and the external world is adopted. For discourse analysts, language is a practice, not grammatical and other reductionist linguistic principles.

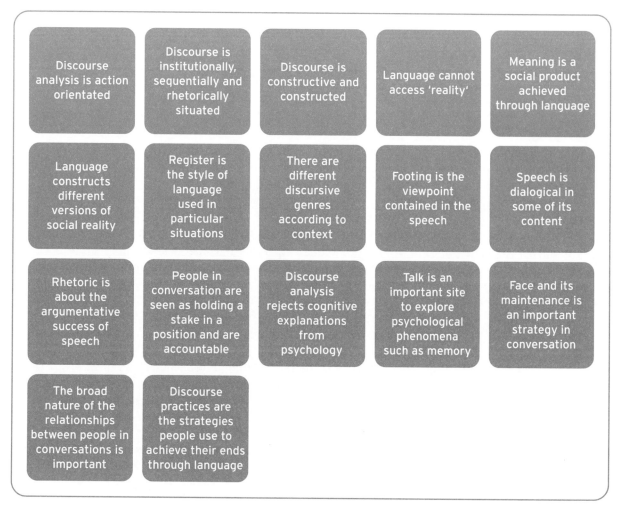

FIGURE 9.2 Some theoretical building blocks of discourse analysis

What are the major theoretical principles of discourse analysis? According to Potter (2003), the following are its core features (see Figure 9.2):

- *Action orientation*   According to Potter, language is the most important context for the actions and interactions of people and they are embedded in social practices such as making invitations.

- *Situation*   According to Potter, discourse is situated in a number of senses: (a) *institutionally situated* – discourse may take place in an institutional setting (for example, a counselling unit) and is spoken by a person occupying a particular identity within that institution (e.g. receptionist) all of which is relevant to what is said; (b) *sequentially situated* – language is situated sequentially in discourse such that what is said at a given time is dependent on but not determined by what went before which, in turn, is relevant to what comes later; and (c) *rhetorically situated* – a segment of discourse may be situated within the context of a rhetorical process and so involve methods of resisting attempts to counter it such as claims that 'you would say that wouldn't you'. See Box 9.1.

Box 9.1
KEY CONCEPTS

Rhetoric

One frequently sees references to the concept of rhetoric in discussions of discourse analysis. Furthermore, the phrase rhetorical psychology is sometimes mentioned. Now the underlying meaning of the concept of rhetoric is simply that of argument or argumentation. Alternatively, it is the practice of using language persuasively and effectively. As a topic of study, rhetoric has a history which goes back to the Greek philosopher Aristotle (384–322 BC) who defined rhetoric in terms of an ability to appreciate what is likely to be convincing in all circumstances. Though for Aristotle, rhetoric was part of speech, its modern usage includes all forms of text. The study of rhetoric was revived to a significant level in the twentieth century in various disciplines though it was not particularly associated with psychology. However, mainstream social psychology from the 1930s onwards developed its own particular version of persuasive communication especially the Yale group led by Carl Hovland (1912–1961), though this partly focused on attitude change – an unpopular concept with many qualitative researchers studying discourse.

It is important not to regard rhetoric as something confined to particularly skilled orators. Rhetoric is intrinsic to all forms of discourse and according to Billig (e.g. 1992, 1996) it is part of the process of giving or expressing views in contexts which do not necessarily appear to be argumental in nature. Billig argues that rhetoric and evaluation are inseparable. However, although discourse analysts subsume rhetoric under their sphere of interest, those psychologists with a special interest in rhetoric do make a case for it being a distinct research field. Rhetoric and discourse analysis are used interchangeably in some publications (e.g. Billig, 1997).

● *Construction*   Discourse, according to Potter, is both constructed and constructive. It is constructed from substantial building blocks including categories, commonplace ideas and broader explanatory systems as well as words, of course. It is constructive in the sense that it can build accounts of the world and also maintain these.

Much as one would like to present discourse analysis as a series of steps from A to Z, it is more than a system of analytic practices (much as grounded theory is). Instead it is built on a theoretical conceptualisation of what language is but also contributes to the development of this theory. Consequently, the would-be discourse analyst should learn as much as possible about its theoretical ideas before much can be gained from learning the seemingly more practical aspects of doing discourse analysis – otherwise it is a bit like writing poetry never having seen a poem. Reading discourse analytic work in books and journal articles is the main route to mastery of the theory. Nevertheless, some of the features of language which inform the work of a discourse analyst can be listed. As such, they constitute a sort of itinerary for discourse analytic work. Understanding the dead-ends in the relevant theory is equally important. So the following list is a theoretical starting point (Wetherell, Taylor & Yates, 2001) – are any of them recognisable in the text (discourse) that you intend to analyse? It constitutes a lightning fast tour around the perspective of the typical discourse analyst:

- Language does not provide a way of accessing some fixed reality.

- Language is constructive or constitutive of social life. Through language things are done such as building social relations, objects and views of the world.

- Meaning is produced in the context of language exchanges between people. There is no cultural storehouse of agreed definitions or meanings which can be applied. In discourse analysis, researchers refer to the co-production of meaning. In other words, the analyst needs to seek to understand the processes by which meaning is created through language. For example, meaning can be regarded as a 'joint production' of two or more individuals in conversation.

- Language is used to construct versions of social reality. It follows then that a researcher should question the text to establish the characteristics of the particular version of reality being constructed in the text. Furthermore, what is accomplished by using this particular version of reality in the text? Discourse analysts use the term interpretative repertoires (often this is interchangeable with the words 'ideology' and 'discourses') to describe the '. . . broadly discernible clusters of terms, descriptions, and figures of speech often assembled around metaphors or vivid images' (Potter & Wetherell, 1995, p. 89).

- 'Discursive practice' is a phrase used to describe the things that happen in language which achieve particular outcomes.

- 'Discursive genres' refers to the type of language which is under analytic consideration. Thus the speech associated with 'The News' may have particular features which are, say, very different from the language used by a priest in church. Thus it may be possible to see contextualisation cues in the type of language used.

- Footing refers to whether the person speaking talks as if they are the author of what is being said, the subject of the words being said, or whether they are using the words of someone else. The footing may change at different stages of any piece of text.

- Speech is dialogical – during talking we incorporate or combine into it things from other conversations. Sometimes this takes the form of reporting what 'Ellie said' or what 'Nick replied'. More frequently, though, the dialogical elements are not presented so directly or indicated to be as such. When a child says 'I mustn't talk to strangers' they are reflecting previous conversations with teachers and parents.

The following are in addition to the above and are taken from Potter and Wetherell (1995):

- Rhetoric refers to the interest that discourse analysis has in how talk can be organised to be argumentatively more successful (persuasive).

- Stake and accountability refer to the way in which people regard others as having a vested interest (stake) in what they do. Consequently, they impute motives to the actions of others which may help to dismiss what the other person has said.

- Discourse analysis actively rejects the use of concepts from cognitive psychology such as personality traits, motives, attitudes and memory stores. Instead, it reformulates these to explain how they are constructed through language. So instead of memory being seen to reside somewhere in the minds of people, discourse analysts have emphasised how memory is socially constructed such as when a family looks together at a family photograph album.

- Talk and the other forms of discourse are regarded as the important sites for understanding typical psychological phenomena. So there is no need for suggesting internal psychological mechanisms to account for what is being said. So racism in talk is seen as the means by which racial discrimination is put into practice. Psychological constructs such as authoritarianism or racist attitudes are also unnecessary and misguided from this perspective. Traditional psychological topics such as the nature of individual and collective identity, the nature of mind, the construction of self and others, and so forth are typical areas of discourse analytic reformulation.

- Discourse analysis does not simply involve the social uses of language. It also focuses on discourse practices in the course of talk and writing. Discourse analysts identify the resources which people use to achieve their ends through language. For example, what are the argumentative strategies used in discourse and what categories are being used. Thus, when newspapers and politicians discuss drugs they use language reflecting war and battle. So they speak of 'the war on drugs' for example.

In addition, the following might be considered important enough for inclusion:

- The concept of face refers to the language strategies which serve to protect the statuses of participants in conversations. The notion of face is drawn from the work of Goffman (1959) to indicate the valued persona of the individual. So we speak of 'saving face', for example. Face saving in a conversation is a collective phenomenon to which more than one member of the conversation may contribute – not just the person at risk.

- Register refers to the language style which is employed in a particular situation. So the language style associated with attending church may differ importantly from that used when returning faulty goods to a shop. Register is dependent on the field of activity (e.g. television interview) and the medium in use (e.g. spoken language versus written language).

- The broad tenor of the relationship in question (e.g. lecturer–student, police officer–suspect).

The development of discourse analysis

One of the traditional ways of understanding language might be termed traditional linguistics. The major concerns of this are matters such as:

- word sounds (phonetics and phonology);
- units which make up words (morphology);
- meaning (semantics);
- word order within sentences (syntax).

This is a largely reductionist view of language which breaks it down into its elements such as sentences, words or even just sounds. Beaugrande (1996) dismisses this as 'language science' since it serves to disconnect language from real life. This sort of atomistic approach to language was rapidly beginning to be replaced in philosophy, history, anthropology, sociology, communications theory and linguistics itself in the mid-twentieth century with a view of language as social performance. According to Willig:

> The assumption that language provides a set of unambiguous signs with which to label internal stages and with which to describe external reality began to be challenged. (Willig, 2008, p. 160)

Language was no longer seen as the means of transmitting internal states to the outside world or describing reality but as doing something in its own right – as constructing any number of versions of reality, for example. The examples of this are many and include Wittgenstein's philosophy and Austin's speech act theory. Psychology, however, was stuck in the 1950s, 1960s and 1970s with a rather moribund understanding of language which focused on how the outside world was represented in language – social representation was the order of the day in terms of psychological research. A chink of light began to shine on psychology when in the 1970s: '. . . social psychologists began to challenge psychology's cognitivism, in the 1980s the "turn to language" gained a serious foothold in psychology' (Willig, 2008, p. 161).

So the roots of discourse analysis were firmly in more fertile soil outside the discipline of psychology. *The Oxford Companion to the English Language* (McArthur, 1992) claims that the origins of discourse analysis were in emerging subfields of linguistics which studied language in units bigger than single sentences:

- Zellig Harris's (1909–1992) work in the 1950s on the relationship between language and the social situation in which it creates it might be the earliest example of this.

- The linguistic anthropologist Dell Hymes (1927–) investigated forms of address between people – in other words, speech related to the social setting.

- It has been suggested by Potter (2001) that the roots of discourse analysis go back to the first few decades of the twentieth century in the work of the Austrian-British philosopher Ludwig Josef Johann Wittgenstein (1889–1951). Wittgenstein's conception of language as a toolkit to do things has clear links with discourse analysis. That is, language does more than merely represent things.

- Speech act theory was developing in the 1950s and 1960s under the influence of two British linguistic philosophers – John Langshaw Austin (1911–1960), especially in the edited book of his work *How to Do Things with Words* (1962) and Herbert Paul Grice (1913–1988), especially his maxims for conversation (Grice, 1975). Speech act theory sees language as social action which is an underlying concept in discourse analysis.

The contribution of speech act theory is to be found in the work of John Austin (e.g. 1975). He used the term performatives for utterances which have a particular social effect. All words perform social acts, according to Austin. There are various aspects to this:

- Locution is simply speaking.
- Illocution is what is done by saying these words such as questioning, commanding, promising, warning and so forth.
- Perlocution is the effect or consequence of these words on the hearer – that is, what the speaker has done.

As stated above, closely associated with speech act theory is the work of Paul Grice, especially in his maxims of cooperative speech. These, above anything else, indicate the way in which exchanges between people are governed by rules which help meet the principle of conversation cooperation. Grice's four maxims are:

- Quality: contributions to conversation should be truthful and sincere.
- Quantity: sufficient information should be provided during conversation.
- Manner: contributions to a conversation should be brief, clear and orderly.
- Relation: contributions should be relevant.

If any of these maxims are violated, so long as the cooperative principle remains operative, the hearer may tend to assume that the maxim is being applied. That is, if the contribution seems irrelevant the hearer will seek to understand it as relevant.

The term discourse analysis was originated by Zellig Harris in a paper published in 1952 – although picked up by PsycINFO at the time, this paper has only been cited five times ever in the psychology literature, indicating the lack of direct influence of Harris's work on psychology. The study of discourse showed rapid growth in the 1960s and 1970s, effectively on a pan-disciplinary basis, but it took until the 1980s before it began making inroads into the discipline of psychology. Its route into psychology was through sociology. Jonathan Potter had carried out research in the sociology department of the University of York in the United Kingdom. In particular, he worked with Michael Mulkay on the sociology of scientists. Mulkay, together with Nigel Gilbert, had published highly influential works on scientific discourse (e.g. Gilbert & Mulkay, 1984). They distinguished between the accounts of work published by scientists in scientific journals and the accounts of work provided by scientists in conversation. Scientific discourse in the two settings was different and used different *interpretative repertoires*. So in the formal setting the empiricist repertoire (formal scientific) was used but in the informal setting a quite different repertoire was used. The latter could be described as a contingent repertoire since it is highly dependent on biographical elements and personalities. The importance of this was that such thinking was best characterised by reference to ideas from discourse analysis. Mulkay ran academic discussion groups on discourse analysis which Potter and other luminaries of the field participated in (University of York, Department of Sociology, n.d.). Jonathan Potter and Margaret Wetherell's *Discourse and Social Psychology: Beyond attitudes and behaviour* was published in 1987. It is regarded as a classic and was a major route for the introduction of discourse analysis into psychology. Potter's initial training was in psychology and sociology. Of course, since this time Jonathan Potter has been associated with Loughborough University and its influential group of researchers in discourse analysis, conversational analysis and rhetoric.

This is to neglect another strand of discourse analysis which originated in the work of the French academic Michel Foucault. This might be considered the major alternative to the Potter and Wetherell version of discourse analysis within psychology. In this context, it is also worth noting that Foucault was trained in psychology which he taught for a while although he is commonly (and more accurately) described as a philosopher or a historian. Foucault's work centred around critical studies of psychiatry, prisons, human sciences and medicine – that is, major social institutions. He worked on the topic of power and the interrelationships between discourse, power and knowledge. His study of psychology is reflected in his 1961 book *The History of Madness in the Classical Age* (English version, Foucault, 2006). In this study, the origins of the concept of 'mental illness' were identified using archival material. Foucault despised modern psychiatry and rejected the dominant view that the treatment of madness by the nineteenth-century medical profession amounted to a form of enlightened liberation which replaced the crudity and brutality of the treatment of the 'mad' in centuries previous. He questioned whether regarding mad people as 'sick' can be seen as advancement. Foucault saw the medical treatment of 'mad' people as basically a means of controlling those who, in some way, challenged the morality of bourgeois society. Mental hospitals, for example, were repositories for paupers in Victorian times. Madness is not historically a fixed category but one which was created through discourse which served a social purpose. Discourses change over time.

Foucauldian discourse analysis made its first significant inroads into Anglo-American psychology in the 1970s but especially in the book *Changing the Subject: Psychology, social regulation, and subjectivity* (1984) by Julian Henriques, Wendy Hollway, Cathy Urwin, Couze Venn and Valerie Walkerdine. In part, the book demonstrated how Foucault's ideas could be applied to a psychological perspective. According to John Shotter (1999): '. . . it can now be seen as one of the earliest outline expressions of the agenda for the sphere of psychological inquiry now coming to be known as *Critical Psychology*' (p. 482). This link between Foucauldian ideas and critical psychology should not be taken to indicate that the Potter and Wetherell version of discourse analysis has no stake to claim on the broad concept of critical psychology. It has (e.g. see Hepburn, 2003). Other examples of the influence of Foucauldian ideas on psychology can be found in the work of Ian Parker, particularly in the field of mental health, in the books *Deconstructing Psychopathology* (Parker, Georgaca, Harper, McLaughlin & Stowell-Smith, 1995) and *Deconstructing Psychotherapy* (Parker, 1999).

The relative impact of the two strands of discourse analysis is difficult to assess. It is notable, though, that the psychological research literature has five times the number of citations for Potter and Wetherell's *Discourse and Social Psychology* than for Henriques *et al.*'s *Changing the Subject*.

Critical discourse analysis is distinguished from other forms of discourse analysis because of its central focus on power and social inequality. So the way in which power is constantly reaffirmed through language is crucial in critical discourse analysis:

> . . . critical discourse analysts want to know what structures, strategies or other properties of text, talk, verbal interaction or communicative events play a role in these modes of reproduction. (van Dijk, 2001, p. 300)

Hepburn (2003) suggests that it also includes issues of politics, morality and social change. Dominance involves the exercise of power by elites, institutions and other social groupings (van Dijk, 2001). This exercise of power is associated with a number of different forms of social inequality – racial, ethnic and gender. Of course, language does not work solely in one direction and so it has potential to serve the interests of disadvantaged peoples such as in the rhetoric of 'black power'.

How to do discourse analysis

Discourse analysis is often presented by practitioners as being a craft or a skill rather than a sequence of things to do from which the analysis emerges. So there are no lists of detailed step-by-step explanations about how to do discourse analysis which, say, the grounded theory literature provides. There is plenty of information about the basic skills involved in data collection (such as interviewing, which is dealt with in detail in this book in Chapter 3) and transcription (which is covered in Chapter 6). The process of analysis in discourse analysis tends to be slightly mystified by practitioners and presented as being difficult. Part of the problem, from the point of view of a newcomer, is that discourse analysis involves disproportionately more theory than most qualitative research methods. Much of what you need to know has been summarised earlier in this chapter, however. Read in depth on these topics and you will progress quickly towards mastering the field. Discourse analysis has a sophisticated conception of language which is highly distinctive and sets the parameters for any new analysis of data. As a consequence, it is extremely important to understand the approach of discourse analysis as well as to study how researchers put together their interpretations by reading the research literature in the field – especially the studies which are closest to your own in content. This takes time and is a continuous process even for the most expert practitioners in the field. Actually, there are different styles of discourse analysis and they do not all show a universal pattern. This makes it doubly important to read the research literature in order to be familiar with the main broad approaches. Such reading will provide the reader with an understanding of the subtlety of the thought behind some discourse analyses. While this is true of all methods, discourse analysis's emphasis on theory is not shared by all other qualitative analysis methods. All of this is to say that the fledgling discourse analyst can learn a lot simply by employing the basic theory as they read through their transcripts – e.g. the register being employed, how awkwardnesses in the conversation are managed, the nature of the rhetorical devices being employed, the discursive repertoires being used and so forth. This is part of all discourse analyses and is the starting point for achieving some originality in one's research.

It is probably obvious, then, that because discourse analysis has this added dimension of theoretical sophistication, the expectations of the newcomer to discourse analysis in terms of theory should not be too high. No one would expect the novice discourse analyst to produce work which is totally original and theoretically innovative. So there will be, initially, a considerable mismatch between what can be seen in the best research reports and what the student is capable of. Typically, a novice researcher closely follows the model of a discourse analysis study which has impressed them and which is close to their research interest. In quantitative research, this is often called a replication study – the sample is varied, maybe aspects of the method and so forth – but, overall, the new study is built closely to the original. Although this may lack in terms of creativity, such replications perform a useful purpose in themselves. Adopting this sort of approach when new to discourse analysis is a good learning exercise and the student can aim much higher once they have built on this experience.

Clear expositions of how to do discourse analysis are somewhat rare. This is partly because the procedure adopted by a researcher may reflect their particular research interests but also because different researchers can have different styles of doing the same thing. In addition, it is generally held that there is no basic set of procedures which guarantees a satisfactory analysis of data. Potter puts things this way:

> There is no single recipe for doing discourse analysis. Different kinds of studies involve different procedures, sometimes working intensively with a single transcript, other times drawing on a large corpus. Analysis is a craft that can be developed with different degrees of skill. It can be thought of as the development of sensitivity to the occasioned and action-oriented, situated, and constructed nature of discourse. Nevertheless, there are a number of ingredients which, when combined together are likely to produce something satisfying. (Potter, 2004, p. 611)

Perhaps more graphic is an earlier description of the process of discourse analysis from Potter:

> . . . doing discourse analysis is a craft skill, more like bike riding or chicken sexing than following the recipe for a mild chicken rogan josh. (Potter, 1997, p. 95)

Discourse analysis is characterised by its practitioners as an 'open-ended' and circular (iterative) process (Taylor, 2001). The discourse analyst has the task of finding patterns though without any clear conception of what these patterns are likely to look like. Taylor suggests that there is 'blind faith' on the part of the researcher that somewhere in the data is something justifying the researcher's investment in the analysis. The analyst will repeatedly go through their data in terms of what fits and what does not fit the tentative patterns formulated by the analyst. This process of examining and re-examining may involve an investment of time which is problematic for researcher's working to conventional timescales and, especially, students working to their own time constraints: 'Data analysis is not accomplished in one or two sessions' (Taylor, 2001, pp. 38–39). Furthermore, it may be difficult to anticipate both the directions in which the analysis will go and the end point of the analysis. With 'rich' qualitative data, new analytic findings may emerge even when the analytic possibilities may appear exhausted.

Despite all of this, there is advice which can be followed. In this section we will present the version of discourse analysis associated with Potter and Wetherell (1987). (For an account of Foucauldian discourse analysis see Box 9.2.) The following is based on Potter's (2003) suggestions about the short sequence of steps to consider when doing a discourse analysis (Figure 9.4). The advice is good but, as with all qualitative research, advice on the analysis only takes seconds to read but putting it into practice is very time consuming indeed:

Box 9.2
KEY CONCEPTS

Foucauldian discourse analysis

According to Parker, Georgaca, Harper, McLaughlin and Stowell-Smith (1995):

> Foucault's work has been invaluable in drawing attention to the way language is organized around different systems of meaning which offer positions of power to certain categories of people and disempower others. These systems of meaning are *discourses*. In recent debates inside psychology, critical writers studying structures of power in discourse have been taking seriously what oppressed people have long known, that the way we talk is bound up with privilege and, sometimes, resistance . . . (p. 10)

These words may seem to be a million miles away from the usual things one reads about in books on research methods – reliability, validity, triangulation and the like. They are not typical of much writing in qualitative research methods for that matter. It is not the usual stuff of psychology, in general, to bring issues of power to the forefront. This means that Foucauldian discourse analysis is somewhat uncomfortable from the typical psychological perspective. But this is the point of Foucauldian discourse analysis – it takes the often benign understandings of phenomena associated with social institutions and reformulates them in terms of power and dominance. This can apply as much to the activities of psychologists and psychiatrists, for example, as other more patently powerful social institutions. Engagement with issues of power distinguishes Foucauldian discourse analysis from the social constructionist discourse analysis of Potter and Wetherell (1987).

These are not happy bedfellows and the academic skirmishes between the two are legion. For example, Parker (2007) writes:

> Discursive psychology . . . wipes away historical analysis and even the social context for the bits of text it analyses. What people say about something is pedantically repeated, and the functions of the talk spelled out to the reader; often the exercise is as pointless as it is mind-numbingly unilluminating. (p. 137)

Or, from the other camp, Potter, Edwards and Ashmore (2002):

> Parker recruits the tortured, oppressed and murdered people of the world to his philosophical position (critical realism), as if their suffering and death bore testimony to his vision, and sided with his (ambivalent and occasioned) dislike of non-Foucauldian discourse analysis, conversation analysis, ethnomethodology . . . (p. 77)

So you have been warned – these things are not just matters of words. Mostly, things are a bit more benign though.

Basically, the typical Foucaldian (critical) discourse analysis treats interviews and similar texts as part of a 'bigger picture' beyond the immediate context in which the words were said. This bigger picture could include, for example, the entire body of psychological writing on mental health. Discourses 'facilitate and limit, enable and constrain what can be said (by whom, where, when)' (Parker, 1992, xiii). Furthermore, discourses also carry descriptions of the *object* of the discourse. So, if the analysis is of marriage, built into the discourses about marriage are 'descriptions' of the nature of marriage. The discourse also identifies

FIGURE 9.3 A summary of Willig's (2008) steps for Foucauldian discourse analysis

the key *subjects* of the discourse – in this case they might be husband and wife but it could also include family, for example. Each of the subjects in the discourse will have their own subjective experiences consequent of the discourse – this is generally referred to as subjectivity or subjectivities.

Foucauldian discourse analysis can be described as macro-textual since it seeks to understand discourse at a broad, societal level. It is about how texts of all sorts relate to major aspects of the organisation of society. The other form of discourse analysis described in this book, based on the interpretation by Potter and Wetherell (1987), could be described as micro-textual since the analysis tends to stay firmly at the level of the social interaction which produced the text.

The materials used in this sort of discourse analysis are any which carry meanings. So Foucauldian discourse analysis can use interviews and other forms of verbal interaction if this meets the purpose of the analysis. However, the method can incorporate books, textbooks, broadcasts, telecasts, films and even pictures. Any of these can be seen as imbued with meanings. Of course, these different types of material can carry very difficult implications and this should be considered as part of the analysis.

The following is a stylised account of how to do Foucauldian discourse analysis (Figure 9.3) (Willig, 2008):

Step 1   Identify how the 'object' is constructed in discourse   The 'object' in Foucauldian discourse analysis is the topic under study which is primarily dependent of the research question being addressed. So it could be marriage, the army, an aspect of psychology, redundancy, or any one of an endless number of topics. The object is treated in the text as having a range of different features and the task of the analyst is to identify the various ways in which the object is construed in the text(s) under consideration. So the analyst needs to identify just where references (direct or indirect) to the object are to be found. There may be circumstances where the object is simply not mentioned by name but it is implied. The object may be referred to euphemistically or in a range of other indirect ways. Simply highlighting them with a highlighter pen may be sufficient to locate such references and associated material relevant to understanding the way in which the object is constructed.

Step 2 **Identify the different discourses involved** So the sections of the text which are relevant to the object of the discourse have been marked up and identified. What is essentially the same discursive object may be constructed in rather different ways. In Box 9.3 we will see that there were two distinctive constructions of marriage: (a) the romantic repertoire and (b) the realist repertoire. So the analytic task at this stage is to review the material very carefully in order to identify the different discourses that are to be found in the data. While the two marriage repertoires mentioned above may appear to be fairly obvious, this overlooks the fact that there might have been expected other discourses such as a religious discourse for marriage which, in fact, did not appear - possibly because of the age group of those interviewed. It is important to remember that discourses are not a characteristic of individuals and that one individual can employ more than one discourse during the course, say, of an interview.

Step 3 **Identify the action orientation - what is gained from using a particular discourse** Just what is the consequence of referring to a particular discourse in relation to its object at a particular point in the text? What is the function of this and how is it related to other constructions which appear at about that point in the text? For example, if the text refers to a romantic conception of marriage then this may allow a divorced man to blame his divorce on his wife for not being romantic. If the text referred to a realist repertoire then it might help the man explain his divorce on the basis that he had become unemployed. In Willig's (2008) words: 'A focus on action orientation allows us to gain a clearer understanding of what the various constructions of the discursive object are capable of achieving within the text' (p. 116).

Step 4 **What are the subject positions of people within a particular discourse?** A subject position refers to where a particular individual is situated within the system of rights, obligations and duties which those who use a particular discourse are buying into. They define 'discursive locations from which to speak and act' (Willig, 2008, p. 116). Suppose that the discourse is a romantic one, then the locations of both partners are essentially defined by this. The romantic discourse's expectations of women are quite different from that of men. Consequently, although they are not rigid in the way roles are, subject positions indicate a lot about what might be said and done from these different subject positions.

Step 5 **What are the implications of the object constructions and subject positions for opening up and shutting down action?** In other words, what is the role of the object construction and subject position in practice?

Keeping with the example of discourses of marriage, a religious discourse might shut-down actions leading to divorce. Just what are the options for action?

Step 6 **What are the consequences of the discourse for the subjective experience of the individual?** What is the relationship between a discourse and subjectivity? Discourses construct social and psychological realities for the individual in terms of (a) seeing the world and (b) being in the world. 'We are now concerned with what can be felt, thought and experienced from within various subject positions' (Willig, 2008, p. 117). So, for example, it might be the case that in terms of the romantic discourse of marriage, a man may experience great confusion if his wife leaves him because he has lost his job.

To anyone who has read Foucault, this account of discourse analysis seems to ignore much of how he understood power. Hook (2001) takes both versions of discourse analysis to task for locating power in the constructive power of language. Hook explains: 'Foucault's conception of discourse is situated far more closely to knowledge, materiality and power than it is to language' (p. 542). But, of course, power changes historically in the discourse of marriage, for example. In the twenty-first century the institutions surrounding marriage can be seen to be much weaker than they were in the nineteenth century when both church and state exercised more power, in part, through language. So perhaps a Foucauldian account of marriage in the nineteenth century would involve discourses which then were more associated with all forms of institutional power. Perhaps, nowadays, the power of marriage lies more in language than in social institutions.

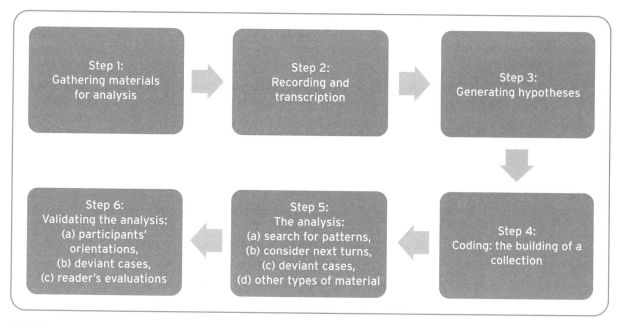

FIGURE 9.4 A Summary of Potter's (2003) Steps in discourse analysis

Step 1

Gathering materials for analysis   Interviews and naturalistic conversation are the main types of data for discourse analysis. However, data from focus groups, the Internet, newspapers, television and a wide range of other sources may, on occasion, be used. The general characteristic of all of these is that they involve interaction. Where, for example, interviews and focus groups are employed, the primary aim of the researcher is to provide what Potter (2003) describes as a 'conversational environment' (p. 80). The purpose is to create a situation in which discursive practices become evident together with the nature of the resources which participants draw upon in these circumstances. If the researcher's preference is to use naturally occurring conversation, then access to this may be substantially more difficult. Just think of such potential resources – police interviews, social services interviews, counselling interviews, television interviews, telephone calls to business, and the like – and it becomes apparent why access to them is difficult. Ethical concerns are clearly important but organisations may have any number of other reasons why they do not wish to share such materials with researchers. There is more discussion on aspects of managing research in the form of interviews and focus groups in Chapters 3 and 4.

Step 2

Recording and transcription   There is no justification for not audio-recording and transcribing the data for discourse analysis. Although some grounded theorists (e.g. Glaser, 1998) have argued that this is time consuming and the researcher would be better off collecting new interview data to inform their analysis, there is little support for this view among the vast majority of qualitative researchers. The function of transcription is to facilitate the analysis and communication with other researchers. In addition, using the Jefferson system allows specific detail to be made available for analysis which traditionally would simply be regarded as inconvenient or a nuisance. Harvey Sacks (1992) realised that such specifics in conversation as hesitations, pauses, coughs and the like were attended to by people engaged in interaction. There is much more information about recording and transcription in Chapters 3 and 6. Generally speaking, the Foucauldian discourse analyst is infinitely less likely to use Jefferson transcription than would a researcher following Potter and Wetherell's constructionist approach to discourse analysis.

Step 3

'Generating hypotheses'   The word 'hypothesis' is not being used in the scientific sense of a testable and refutable relationship. Rather, it indicates that researchers need to develop ideas about what is going on in social interaction in order to stimulate and guide their research ideas. In terms of deciding what topics to address, a number of common possibilities may be relevant to the researcher's work. Researchers often come to collect their data having developed some ideas, questions or a broad set of issues which, hopefully, their research can address:

● The researcher has a general interest in a particular research setting – such as doctor–patient interaction, classroom education, and so forth – and how interaction is carried out in these settings.

● The researcher has substantial amounts of data which they collected for other research purposes but seem under-analysed or even wasted.

● The researcher has received an invitation to carry out research on a particular topic.

→

→ Whatever generated the impetus for the research, there is a need for a focus, perspective, or overview to be applied by the researcher. This may develop at the initial stage of the research although Potter (2003) suggests that it is characteristically the transcription stage since this is the stage at which the researcher begins to really work with their data. For whatever reason, 'the first part of discourse research is often the generation of more specific questions or hypotheses or the noticing of intriguing or troubling phenomena' (Potter, 2003, p. 83).

A discourse analyst may make a log of analytic notes to help with this process of idea generation – much as the memo in grounded theory (see Chapter 8). On the other hand, talking through one's data and analysis with like-minded others in formal or informal discussion sessions may also be productive. For example, a group of researchers may meet to discuss a particular data segment each throwing in his or her own analytic ideas for consideration.

Step 4   'Coding'   Be careful here since in most descriptions of qualitative data analysis, coding is a way of reducing a mass of transcription down into a number of descriptive notes which essentially summarise the original data. The purpose of coding is to encourage line-by-line familiarity with the data but, more importantly, it may be a start to the process of generating analytic ideas. Nevertheless, a closer reading of Potter indicates something rather different about what is done in discourse analysis. He writes:

> The main aim of coding is to make the analysis more straightforward by shifting relevant materials from a larger corpus . . . it is a preliminary that facilitates analysis. Typically it involves searching materials for some phenomena of interest and copying the instances to an archive. This is likely to be a set of extracts from sound files and their associated transcripts. (Potter, 2003, p. 83)

In other words, the process is one in which extracts are selected and put together because, for whatever reason, they seem to have something in common. It is likely that the researcher has developed a description for this – that is a code. This is not a rigid and fixed process since the extracts may be moved to other groupings as the analysis proceeds. There will be rogue extracts which need to be dealt with as best as can be done. The researcher may feel that a particular extract does not fit where it has been grouped or that it is generally problematic. However frustrating such problem cases are initially, in the long run they tend to be productive of new ideas and interpretations.

Step 5   The analysis   The process of analysis involves both inductive and deductive aspects. For example, reading through a particular extract may help instill ideas in the mind of the researcher about the processes going on in the extract. This is inductive and, in everyday terms, relatively speculative because it is based on not a great deal of data. Things do not stop at this since this inductive explanation of what is happening in the data can be evaluated against other related extracts. This is a deductive process which helps to establish whether the explanation is viable or whether it works only in some specific circumstances or that it is a totally blind alley, analytically speaking. Willig gives her account as follows (see Figure 9.5 also):

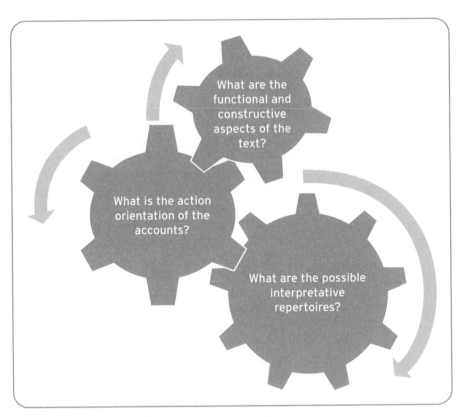

FIGURE 9.5 Willig's (2008) advice to discourse analysts

Analysis of textual data is generated by paying close attention to the constructive and functional dimensions of discourse. To facilitate a systematic and sustained exploration of these dimensions, *context, variability* and *construction* of discursive accounts need to be attended to. The researcher looks at how the text constructs its objects and subjects, how such constructions vary across discursive contexts, and with what consequences they may be deployed. To identify diverse constructions of subjects and objects in the text, we need to pay attention to the terminology, stylistic and grammatical features, preferred metaphors and figures of speech that may be used in their construction [i.e. interpretative repertoires] . . . Different repertoires can be used by one and the same speaker in different discursive contexts in the pursuit of different social objectives. Part of the analysis of discourse is to identify the action orientation of accounts. To be able to do this, the researcher needs to pay careful attention to the discursive contexts within which such accounts are produced and to trace their consequence for the participants in a conversation. This can only be done satisfactorily on the basis of an analysis of *both* the interviewer's and the interviewee's contributions to the conversation. It is important to remember that discourse analysis requires us to examine language *in context*. (Willig, 2008, pp. 100–1)

Potter (2003) discusses four aspects of the analysis (see Figure 9.6):

● *Search for a pattern* The analyst may search through the body of data to establish how regularly a particular pattern occurs. If a pattern is common

FIGURE 9.6 **Things to check during the analysis stage**

then this adds strength to the analysis. Of course, the pattern may be specific to given circumstances which would need to be identified.

● *Consider next turns*   In discourse analysis the sequencing of interaction has important analytic implications. What happens next in interaction is informative about what went before. As a consequence, we will understand better what is under consideration if we understand what comes next. So understanding the next speaker's conversational turn has strong implications for the analyst's understanding of a segment of text.

● *Focus on deviant cases*   Deviant cases are simply parts of the discourse in which very different things seem to be happening compared with the normal pattern that otherwise seems to be emerging in the analysis. Understanding these cases may be analytically much more rewarding than if the usual pattern occurs.

● *Focus on other kinds of material*   There is a range of additional materials which could be brought into any particular analysis. If the study is of telephone calls to emergency organisations then the researcher might find it helpful to compare their findings from this study with studies of other telephone calls to organisations. Equally, the researcher might compare the calls to emergency organisations with telephone calls between friends. This is partly a case of what the study is about and what other types of data are available.

Step 6   **Validating the analysis**   According to Potter (2003), there is no firm distinction between the process of analysis and the process of validating the analysis in discourse analytic work. Hence, some of the procedures used in validating the analysis are similar to those used in the analysis itself:

● *Participants' orientations*   If a particular excerpt is given a particular interpretation by the analyst, it is important to see whether this interpretation is supported by how the next participant in the discourse responds.

● *Deviant cases*   These are used during the analysis but can also be used in the validation stage. Potter (2003) gives the example of news interviews where it has been shown that the interviewer is not held responsible for the views expressed in the interview. But there are deviant cases where the interviewer is blamed or otherwise held responsible. It has been found that these interviews may lead to problematic interaction which has a distracting effect on the interview.

- *Coherence* Do the findings of the new study cohere with those of similar earlier studies? If yes, then this is evidence of validity. However, if the findings of the new study do not fit in with those of earlier studies then the research community may be justified in treating the new study with considerable caution.

- *Readers' evaluations* A range of extracts indicative and illustrative of the researcher's data analysis are included in publications. This leaves the reader in a position to check the researcher's analysis in a way which is impossible with other research methods.

At the end of the analytic process, whenever that comes, the researcher is faced with an important but quite difficult question concerning the worth of the analysis. Indeed, the question may be one of whether the researcher has produced an analysis at all. There is a range of circumstances in which something which looks like an analysis is reported. Nevertheless, does it amount to a serious attempt by the researcher at interpreting the data or even developing new theoretical ideas? Antaki, Billig, Edwards and Potter (2003) suggest a number of ways in which data may be under-analysed:

- *Under-analysis due to summary* Simply summarising, say, the main themes which can be seen in a particular segment of transcript does not constitute an analysis. It may claim to be by the researcher but it adds nothing to the transcript other than brevity. The summary does not move the analysis to a greater stage of abstraction than the original data. Indeed, it takes away the detail on which a discourse analysis could be based.

- *Under-analysis due to taking sides* While qualitative researchers will have a position on many of the topics they research, taking sides with the participant's point of view may lead to a concentration on this point of view which ignores much of the rest of what is going on in the data. As a consequence, the data analysis is incomplete. Antaki *et al.* suggest that by choosing extracts supporting the participant's point of view that the researcher is attempting enlistment rather than analysis.

- *Under-analysis due to over-quotation or isolated quotation* If the researcher resorts to reporting numerous snippets from the text (with little contribution from the analysis themselves) then this does not amount to analysis. For one thing, it separates the text from the context in which it is said. The researcher in this case may contribute brief summaries in his or her own words but these would be descriptive rather than analytic. It is also a problem if the researcher takes a particular extract and leaves it to 'speak for itself', isolated and extracted from context.

- *Analysis failure due to the circular discovery of (a) discourses and (b) mental constructs* For example, the analyst may identify a number of extracts which he or she describes are representing Ideology X or Discourse Y. Then this ideology or discourse is used to 'explain' why a person says particular things. Unfortunately, it is not possible to establish that there is an ideology or discourse underlying language simply on the basis of a series of quotes held to represent that ideology.

→ ● *Under-analysis due to survey*   For example, the analyst may notice that a certain form of discourse is used by some participants and seemingly generalise this to all similar participants. However, without evidence that such a generalisation is possible, such overgeneralised claims essentially boil down to a failure to completely analyse one's data.

● *Under-analysis due to spotting*   Basically this means that the researcher is doing little other than identifying in the data examples of processes which have been identified by discourse analysts as important aspects of language in a social context. It is good that a student does this as part of their development. Nevertheless, such 'spotting' is little different from the activities of a bird-watcher who identifies the 'lesser crested sparrow hawk' or the laboratory technician who identifies someone's DNA. In terms of discourse analysis, this sort of activity does not constitute analysis.

Burman (2004) adds another analytic failing which she feels that Antaki *et al.* may have overlooked because it is so basic that it was taken for granted – 'under-analysis' through not having a question to ask of the data. She suggests that the weakest examples of discourse analysis founder because they do not give the reasons why the particular analysis was carried out and considered worth doing.

A degree of self-reflection about your experiences of your analytic processes will help you assess whether your analysis is worthy of the name.

Box 9.3 presents an example of discourse analysis using the Potter and Wetherell approach.

Box 9.3
ILLUSTRATIVE RESEARCH STUDY

Example of interpretative repertoire research in discourse analysis: For better or worse

Not surprisingly, over the last two or three decades a variety of styles of discourse analysis have emerged. One which is very common is the search for interpretative repertoires (sometimes similar concepts such as different discourses or different ideologies are used instead) which provide the broad structure for talk on a particular topic. Lawes (1999) provides a convincing example of this approach by centring on the way people talk about marriage. She points out some of the issues associated with marriage at the start of the twenty-first century – fewer marriages taking place, more marriages failing, more births to unmarried parents, and the like. She concentrates on the group she identifies as 'Generation X' – that is Western White people born in the 1960s and very early 1970s. The statistical data that Lawes identifies suggests that this entire generation were 'marriage-aversive'.

→

Lawes describes her study as using a form of discourse analysis identifiable as the approach of Potter and Wetherell (1987). Her sample of 20 interviews with 12 male and 8 female 'Generation X' participants is described by Lawes as a 'rather generous sample' for this sort of analysis. There is no attempt to generalise from this sample, in the traditional manner of quantitative research, but, instead, the generalisation would be from the sample of talk she accumulated to show how marriage is understood. Participants' names and potentially identifying information were fictionalised for ethical reasons. A flyer was used to recruit participants though no further details of their location are provided. The interviews generally took place in the interviewee's home and typically lasted for about 90 minutes.

Interviews for the research were open-ended single-respondent interviews. The interaction between the interviewer and the interviewee was included in the analysis. The style of interviewing permitted 'the researcher to participate fully in a relatively informal, conversational exchange' (p. 4). Lawes suggests that because of the nature of the analysis, it is not strictly necessary for the interviewer to remain neutral but may express a point of view. The questions which appeared on the publicity flyer were used to guide the interview. These questions included:

- How is marriage different from other kinds of 'couple' relationships?
- How would you feel about never marrying?
- What is a good enough reason for getting married?
- What is a good enough reason for getting divorced?
- Have you experienced pressure from other people to get married?

The interviews were recorded and eventually transcribed. Just for the record, this amounted to about half a million words! The transcription system adopted is described as being a simplified version of the Jefferson transcription system (Chapter 6) though the precise details are not presented. The illustrative excerpts of transcripts included in the paper contain little indication of Jefferson coding conventions, e.g. such as timings and other symbols. This is a positive feature as such minute detail is not discussed in the paper and the resulting illustrative excerpts are easily read as normal text.

Lawes is very graphic about how she analysed her data and it is worth reproducing what she has to say here:

> Analysing discourse is a lengthy process of 'living with' one's data, reading, re-reading and following up hunches until a pattern of language use emerges. This typically involves looking out for repertoires or discourses which organize the text, signalled by repetitive idioms or metaphors, for instance, one of the most important in this body of talk was the leitmotif of 'success' and 'failure' . . . One simultaneously looks for variability which might signal differences between [interpretive] repertoires; here, agentic talk about success and failure was offset by talk of fatalism and passivity. From these differences, informed hypotheses can be made about the differing functions which [interpretive] repertoires might serve. (p. 5)

Two interpretative repertoires (discourse or ideologies) were identified by Lawes: (a) the romantic repertoire and (b) the realist repertoire. The romantic repertoire deals with 'marriage-in-theory' which 'is presented, without irony, as a true or factual account of what marriage *is*' (p. 7). Finding the 'right' person is a common and effective way of explaining in the romantic repertoire: 'obviously, if you're going to get married then you're with the right person' (p. 7). Commitment is also part of this repertoire and takes the form of events (e.g. engagement) and a process which is ongoing throughout a marriage which works. This interpretative repertoire can be used to discuss both successful and unsuccessful marriages.

The realist interpretative repertoire deals with marriage in the real world. Marriage can wear out and be affected by things such as infidelity, illness and debt. It also can be used in accounts of both successful and unsuccessful marriages. The permanence of marriage is not held to be realistic: 'a gamble you take, isn't it. I think so. I think getting married is probably one of the biggest risks you ever take.' (p. 12)

The two repertoires identified by Lawes can coexist in the talk of a single individual. They are not alternatives in that sense. There are not two groups of people – the romantic and the realist – but they do amount to rather different ways of accounting for different aspects of marriage.

When to use discourse analysis

It is probably correct to suggest that discourse analysis is the most familiar of qualitative data analysis methods among psychologists. Certainly this seems to be the case for countries such as the United Kingdom and Sweden, for example, though it is probably not the case in the United States. This is not to suggest that psychologists in general have a good idea of what discourse analysis is about and how to carry it out. Once it is understood that discourse analysis is primarily a theory-based approach to understanding language in society and the regulative practices of language and their significance for subjectivity then some of the misconceptions that mainstream psychologists have about it as a method of data analysis become apparent. Discourse analysts may have over-stated their claim to being an alternative way of understanding psychological phenomena such as when it is recommended as a soundly based alternative to cognitive approaches to psychology. It is not the answer to every researcher's concerns in psychology. Discourse analysis is not even necessarily an apt choice of research method for addressing qualitative data in general. Discourse analysis is good for what it is good for – that is how language works in social interaction to do things. The nutshell synopsis of all of this is that discourse analysis can, for some research purposes, be counterproductive. Potter put the issue as follows:

> To attempt to ask a question formulated in more traditional terms ('what are the factors that lead to condom use amongst HIV+ gay males') and then use discourse analytic methods to answer it is a recipe for incoherence. (Potter, 2004, p. 607)

So where the researcher is interested in language as social action then discourse analysis has a place. Otherwise, think again. Discourse analysis views things differently from mainstream psychology. Discourse analysis would be a bad choice to use to study the biology of rape but an excellent way to explore how researchers use sociobiological explanations of why men rape or how such sociobiological explanations have been incorporated into everyday under-standings of rape.

So when Potter asks the question 'Is there a discourse analysis answer to any psychological question?' No, is his answer, because:

> One of the mistakes that people sometimes make when they are starting to carry out discourse work is to treat discourse analysis as a method that can simply be plugged into a predefined question: for example, 'I am interested in the factors that cause people to smoke: should I use an observational study, an experimental simulation, or discourse analysis?' What this misses is, first, that discourse analysis is not just a method but a whole perspective on social life and research into it, and, second, that all research methods involve a range of theoretical assumptions. (Potter, 1996, p. 130)

The answer to the questions of whether discourse analysis is the best way to address the analysis of qualitative data is fairly obvious. If the researcher is buying into the theory of discourse analysis then the method is appropriate, otherwise other methods may be more appropriate. Although every qualitative researcher is operating through the medium of language as the core of his or her data, not all qualitative researchers are interested in or need the fine-grained analysis of how language works in social interaction which characterises discourse analysis. So interpretative phenomenological analysis (IPA) (Chapter 11) is dependent on data in the form of language but what it does with the data is quite different. IPA extracts from language people's experiences of phenomena such as pain. Not much of discourse analysis's theory would have any particular relevance to understanding such experiences. Of course, a discourse analyst could take IPA interviews and analyse these as discourse. However, this would probably address none of the issues which IPA is interested in.

Evaluation of discourse analysis

Among the achievements of discourse analysis is that it has brought to psychology theoretically coherent approaches to working with detailed textual material such as in-depth interviews and recordings of conversation. Its limitation is its particular perspectives on how that textual material should be understood and interpreted. Unless one is prepared to buy into this body of theory then the end product will not be recognisably discourse analysis of any sort. For example, for researchers who want to see in their data a way of accessing the realities of their participants' lives, discourse analysis lends little or no support – the reverse is more accurate. Language is not seen as representational in that sense in discourse analysis.

No matter how acceptable the basic principles of discourse analysis may be, it stops well short of providing help for those who want to see in their interview, focus group and other textual data some usable representations of reality. This is a problem which discourse analysis not only critiques other types of research over, but it is a problem for discourse analysis itself in that it begins to marginalise the interview and focus group data that were once at the centre of discourse analysis. The search for natural language to analyse limits the topics which discourse analysis can address – we can only interview victims of sexual abuse about their childhoods, for example. We cannot hope to obtain more naturalistic data. To suggest that we have alternative methods of analysis which are more amenable to a realist perspective on the data merely leaves the problem of how discourse analysis can inform us about reality, if at all.

Langdridge makes an important point in this respect which basically boils down to the issue, 'Is what is appropriate in philosophical debates always good for psychology?':

> Although I have considerable sympathy for the arguments from discursive psychology, simply because there has been a turn to language – or, more accurately, text – in a great deal of continental philosophy does not mean that the equivalent step must necessarily follow in psychology, as if all developments in continental philosophy represent progress (an enlightenment idea itself). Philosophy is a discipline of contestation and, furthermore, if we are to take the claims of the postmodernists seriously, then newer will not always be better or – perhaps more pertinently – what is fashionable will not always be superior to that which is not fashionable. I think that it is ironic indeed that some of the most relativist of psychologists apparently seek to impose a methodological hegemony on the discipline through their unquestioning acceptance of a select group of continental philosophers (and it is a very select group). (Langdridge, 2007, p. 160)

In examination discourse: 'Discuss'!

Of course, Langdridge's point is a fundamental one which reflects a number of themes which arise at various points in this book. But of particular importance is the question of the future direction of qualitative psychology. Just how much freedom do or should psychologists have to develop a distinctly psychological version of qualitative research? To what extent should they be constrained by the philosophical roots of other disciplines? The attention that qualitative psychologists give to philosophy is substantially greater, it would appear, than that which quantitative psychologists devote to the philosophical roots of the quantitative approach. Why is this? How far should quantitative psychologists stray from the philosophical underpinnings of their endeavours?

It is an unfair criticism of discourse analysis to suggest it is an 'anything goes' or subjective approach to research. It is not a means of 'putting words into the mouths' of participants. There is always a risk of this but this can only happen when the 'built-in' checks which should be part of the analytic procedures are rendered ineffective for some reason. Not only is there a substantial variety of ways in which the quality of qualitative research may be assessed (see Chapter 14) but there are inbuilt checking mechanisms which are part-and-parcel of the method as was indicated in the earlier section on 'How to do discourse analysis' (pp. 226–237). Where there is a problem, possibly, it could be the consequence of the limited space available in research publications for the qualitative researcher to provide full support for their analysis. So the reader may not always be in a position to evaluate the analytic claims against the data. Book-length investigations are the most thoroughly presented and argued studies.

Perhaps it is unnecessary to point out that some discourse analytic studies are better than others. Like all areas of research, you will find dismal examples purporting to be discourse analysis. It is not wise to judge the entire field on the basis of the worst examples. Related to this is the warning that the term 'discourse analysis' is not *Appellation d'origine contrôlée* so studies of dubious worth are labelled by their authors as 'discourse analysis' despite their lacking any semblance to what we have discussed in this chapter.

CONCLUSION

Discourse analysis (and qualitative analysis more generally) is a relative newcomer to psychology despite being based on ideas which emerged at about the middle of the twentieth century. Even so, it is more than a quarter of a century since the first psychological discourse analysis studies were published. For comparative purposes, if we take the field of forensic psychology we find that its development as a substantial field of psychology is of much the same vintage. It is probably time, then, that psychology in general came to appreciate that discourse analysis is primarily a way of conceptualising a field of research rather than a method in the sense of operations and procedures leading inexorably to an analytic outcome. For that reason, in this chapter the major features of the theoretical foundations of discourse analysis are emphasised as much as the closely focused procedures which some psychologists would prefer discourse analysis to be.

The discourse analysis literature tends to mystify the analytic processes involved a little. Indeed to talk about discourse analysis as a craft or a skill perhaps indicates that it needs to be learnt 'at the feet' of some Master of Discourse Analysis – an apprenticeship if one prefers. But, as we have seen, there is a lot to be learnt simply by reading and putting what one reads into practice. Take time to learn the basic theory, read some classics in the field and publications closer to your own specific interests, and work with your data in the light of all of this. Although perfection is not guaranteed, you should emerge with a passable analysis.

KEY POINTS

- Discourse analysis is based on early work carried out by linguists and philosophers of language, especially during the 1950s and 1960s, which theorised language to be a working set of resources which gets things done rather than considering language merely to be representational of something. This approach uses larger units of speech and other text than words or sentences. Theory is a major component of discourse analysis and the analytic procedures are not valuable unless combined with an understanding of the accompanying central theory. So discourse analysis is a method in the fullest sense of the word rather than a technique.

- In general, the procedures employed by discourse analysts show more than a passing resemblance to what is done in qualitative psychological research in general. However, there are distinct preferences in terms of the sorts of data used in discourse analysis. Increasingly, in discourse analysis the use of recordings of naturally occurring speech is seen to have advantages over research interviews in most circumstances. The central theme of discourse analysis is the idea of speech as doing things - such as constructing and construing meaning - and this guides the analysis as well as the sorts of data which are appropriate.

- Critical discourse analysis has its roots in both main strands of discourse analysis as covered in this chapter. Its main distinguishing characteristic is its focus on power. It is concerned with such matters as how power is created, reaffirmed and challenged through language.

ADDITIONAL RESOURCES

Arribas-Ayllon, M., and Walkerdine, V. (2008). Foucauldian discourse analysis. In C. Willig and W. Stainton-Rogers (Eds.), *The SAGE Handbook of Qualitative Psychology*. Los Angeles, CA: Sage, pp. 91-108.

Coyle, A. (2007). Discourse analysis. In E. Lyons and A. Coyle (Eds.), *Analysing Qualitative Data in Psychology*. London: Sage, pp. 98-116.

DARG (n.d). Audio Visual Materials. http://www.lboro.ac.uk/departments/ss/centres/darg/audio_video_materials.htm (accessed 20 August 2009).

Potter, J. (2003). Discourse analysis and discursive psychology. In P.M. Camic, J.E. Rhodes and L. Yardley (Eds.), *Qualitative Research in Psychology: Expanding perspectives in methodology and design*. Washington, DC: American Psychological Association, pp. 73-94.

Slembrouck, S. (2006). What is meant by 'discourse analysis'? http://bank.UGent.be/da/da.htm (accessed 13 October 2009).

Walton, C. (2007). Doing discourse analysis. In E. Lyons and A. Coyle (Eds.), *Analysing Qualitative Data in Psychology*. London: Sage, pp. 117-130.

Wiggins, S., and Potter, J. (2008). Discursive psychology. In C. Willig and W. Stainton-Rogers (Eds.), *The SAGE Handbook of Qualitative Psychology*. Los Angeles, CA: Sage, pp. 73-90.

Willig, C. (2008). Discourse analysis. In J.A. Smith (Ed.), *Qualitative Psychology: A practical guide to research methods*, 2nd Edition. London: Sage, pp. 160-185. (Both major types of discourse analysis are covered.)

CHAPTER 10

Conversation analysis

Overview

- Conversation analysis is built on the assumption that the sequence and structure of a conversation are rule-bound and meaningful to participants in the conversation.

- There is a sense in which conversation analysis can be regarded as behaviourist since its analytic practices are based on what can be seen in the transcript of the conversation and are, thus, observable. In other words, a basic methodological principle of conversation analysis is that the analyst concentrates solely on what can be seen to be happening in conversation.

- Conversation analysts focus on natural conversation in the form of recordings of things such as meetings, therapy sessions, telephone calls and the like.

- Conversation analysis was developed in the 1960s by the late Harvey Sacks and Emanuel Schegloff. Jefferson transcription is essential to conversation analysis and was contributed by the late Gail Jefferson.

- Conversation analysis is more to do with a particular approach to the study of language than it is to do with any particular techniques of analysis. A major influence on conversation analysis was the ethnomethodology (originated by Harold Garfinkel) with which it shares many characteristics.

- Among the topics studied by conversation analysis are turn-taking in conversation, the structure of conversational openings and the ways in which mistakes in conversation are corrected (repaired) by the participants in the conversation.

- Conversation analysis requires a close and highly detailed focus of the minute detail of conversation and nothing is ruled out as being irrelevant in a conversation to the analysis of that conversation. So interruptions, pauses and the like are essential information in understanding the conversation from the perspective of the participants.

- Conversation analysis does not draw on psychological explanatory concepts such as motives and feelings. If the members of the conversation refer to them then they are part of the analysis, otherwise they are regarded as unknowable and irrelevant.

What is conversation analysis?

In conversation analysis the conversations of people, irrespective of context, are regarded as being full of both precisely organised and coherent talk. Each word, partial word, utterance and detail about pronunciation has the potential to be meaningful in conversation and consequently has the potential to be analysed. These things are not necessarily planned but if they can be heard in conversation then they may be treated as significant by participants in the conversation (Edwards, 1995). To enter the world of conversation analysis is to enter a world in which detail is regarded as the key to understanding. Conversation analysis was developed by Harvey Sacks and Emanuel Schegloff in the 1960s and its influence began to spread increasingly widely in successive decades. Although conceived as a sociological perspective on language, it has influenced linguists, psychologists and others. Despite Sacks's greater status as the founder of conversation analysis, the first published research paper on conversation analysis was the work of Emanuel Schegloff. Ten Have (1999) suggests that the ethos of conversation analysis has always been '. . . an unconventional but intense, and at the same time respectful, intellectual interest in the details of the actual practices of people in interaction' (p. 6).

According to Loos, Anderson, Day, Jordan and Wingage (2009):

Conversation analysis is an approach to the study of natural conversation, especially with a view to determining the following:

- Participants' methods of
  - turn-taking
  - constructing sequences of utterances across turns
  - identifying and repairing problems, and
  - employing gaze and movement
- How conversation works in different conventional settings.

This definition is not simply about what conversation analysts do but it is also loaded with indications about the way in which they do it. For example, it involves natural conversation, it is about how participants in a conversation do certain things within a conversation, and it is comparative across different settings for conversation. The definition also indicates that conversation analysis is not simply the study of conversation, but that it is the study of conversation carried out in a particular way. Conversation analysis has a special interest in such matters as how participants produce or achieve turn-taking in conversations, how utterances within a given turn in the conversation are constructed, and how difficulties in a conversation flow are identified and rectified. The interpretations of the situation as revealed in the conversation are more salient to conversation analysis than arbitrary, theory-led speculations suggested by previous research (Wooffitt, 2001). So hypothesis testing based on cumulative and all-encompassing theory is not involved.

Conversation analysis has a close ally in discourse analysis of the sort developed by Potter and Wetherell (1987). Indeed, they share a lot in common at the level of conversational detail. However, Foucauldian discourse analysts (Chapter 9) are not, in general, wedded to the ideas involved in conversation analysis.

One of the most difficult but most basic characteristics of conversation analysis is its aversion to considering anything other than that which can be seen or heard in conversation. In our everyday lives, we are used to joking about Freudian slips whenever we hear a slip-of-the-tongue or we try to find other motivations for what people say. Conversation analysis has no truck with such psychologising (or grand sociologising for that matter). So motivations, attitudes and other psychological notions are out but so too are sociologist notions such as culture, social structure, power and gender. What the participants in a conversation see and hear are the basic building blocks of conversation analysis (CA). Antaki makes the point in this way:

> Perhaps the defining mark of CA is its commitment to working with what it sees and hears. Or rather, with what the participants in the scene see and hear. It is wary of explaining what's going on in a scene by appeal to things that are hidden from the participants . . . The most obvious reason why CA doesn't like to appeal to things like a person's inner feelings or motivation is that we usually can't know what those are – and, arguably, it doesn't matter . . . If you and I meet, we work out our business together knowing nothing about our respective inner lives. What we do know about is what each other's *outer* life is like: that is to say, what we say and do. Sometimes we display 'inner' emotions or thoughts; sometimes not; sometimes those displays are meant to be accurate; sometimes not. Nobody hears *pleased to see you* as necessarily accurate (or inaccurate). (Antaki, 2009b).

So, in conversation analysis, the researcher eschews the idea that there are internal psychological processes that explain what is going on in conversation. These are things such as motives, temperaments, personality traits and so forth. Of course, the participants in the conversation, themselves, may well incorporate such psychologising into their understanding of the interaction and, more importantly, mention this psychologising during the conversation. Interaction through talk is not regarded as the external manifestation of inner cognitive processes in conversation analysis. In this sense, whether or not participants in conversations have motives, interests, intentions, personality characteristics and so forth is irrelevant in terms of the researcher's analysis. The domain of interest in conversation analysis is the structure of conversation (Wooffitt, 2001).

A mainstream quantitative psychologist is likely to experience 'culture shock' when reading conversation analysis-based studies for the first time (Howitt & Cramer, 2008). The conversation analysis report often looks like a stripped-down version of the more conventional research report. Of course, conversation analysts from a psychological background accommodate more to psychological traditions in their writings especially where they appear in psychological journals. Nevertheless, often conversation analysis studies have few references to the published literature – that is, the literature review may be sparse. Details of sampling might just be a list or table of the general details of the small number of people that took part in the study. Often there is relatively little detail about the broader social context in which the conversations took place. To expect more is to miss the point of conversation analysis. The intellectual thrust of conversation analysis lies in the belief that the conversation itself and no more is sufficient to understand the principles of what happens when people converse. Consideration of factors beyond the conversation's transcript diverts attention from the important analytic tasks.

Silverman (1998) describes several methodological rules for conversation analysis based on Sacks's writings. The following are some of these basic principles:

- *Methodological rule 1: Gather observational data* Conversation analysis is driven by the data rather than armchair or other forms of grand theory. For Sacks, the data are probably not research interviews.

- *Methodological rule 2: Make a recording* There is no way of remembering the pauses, hesitations, inflections, intakes of breath and so forth which are embedded in and informative about conversations.

- *Methodological rule 3: Concentrate on the conversation as behaviour* This is to emphasise that conversation analysis is not about what is going on in the heads of those involved in the conversation. Group members see what the other people are doing in terms of language – for example, they may be lying, they may be arguing, they may be reporting, and so forth. To understand conversation one needs to concentrate on the conversation.

As we have seen, conversation analysis had its origins in Harvey Sacks's and Emanuel Schegloff's ideas about how a science of conversation could be developed (see also the next section). This means that conversation analysis is 50 or so years old. Not surprisingly, substantial quantities of theory have accumulated along with numerous research studies since the 1960s. As a consequence, the would-be conversation analyst needs to familiarise themselves with this general theory otherwise they risk constantly re-inventing the wheel. Much the same is true for discourse analysis – but it is not true for thematic analysis and grounded theory where the task is to learn the method and not the findings and theory which emerged out of the application of the method. That is, thematic analysis and grounded theory do not refer to any particular sort of content – conversation analysis, on the other hand, focuses on conversation. Thus one cannot regard conversation analysis as a method such as experimental design is – a psychologist learns about experimental design almost as if it is a general resource that can be applied irrespective of circumstance. To use the principles of good experimental design does not involve learning a load of theory derived from experiments. So there is a lot of theory to be learnt on the way to being a good conversation analyst. Fortunately, there are a lot of summaries of conversation analysis theory to help speed up the process (see the recommendations at the end of this chapter). Figure 10.1 summarises some of the main theoretical areas in conversation analysis. Box 10.1 provides a short introduction to some key conversation analysis concepts.

FIGURE 10.1 **Key areas of theory in conversation analysis**

BOX 10.1

KEY CONCEPTS

A short guide to conversation analysis concepts

The following covers some of the major areas of conversation analysis shown in Figure 10.1. It is important to remember that all of the topics dealt with in this box have each been sub-ject to many lengthy studies in books and journal publications. So what can be presented here are just the beginnings of the vast amounts of relevant theory. In other words, the following is to whet your appetite for conversation analysis and not to satisfy it.

Turns, turn-taking and turn construction units (TCUs)

Conversation, in conversation analysis, consists of turns. A turn is essentially 'a turn to speak' or a turn-at-talk. That is, a turn is a person's conversation before a different person takes over the conversation. So a turn can be several hundred words or something much shorter – even just a grunt. Thus the turn is essentially the major unit of analysis for content analysis. The primary focus of conversation analysis is on adjacent turns in order to understand how the second turn is 'designed' to fit with the previous turn. The researcher also examines the nature of the subsequent turns in the conversation. So the strategy is to understand how turns cohere together in patterns. Essentially the researcher is working with the same building blocks of conversation as the participants in the conversation in their task of giving coherence to the conversation. Turns are a creation of the interaction rather than entirely pre-specified. So, for instance, a speaker can signal another speaker that it is a particular second speaker's turn to speak. A speaker who has taken over in the conversation has both the right and obligation to include a 'turn construction unit' (which is basically a complete speaker turn) which includes a 'transition relevance space' at which the next speaker may begin to speak – though it does not have to be the case that the potential next speaker speaks at that point. One question is just how these turns to speak get distributed amongst those party to the conversation. This can happen in very straightforward ways, as in the following. You might wish to check out the Jefferson transcription system in Chapter 6 if you have problems with the following:

```
          (3.2)
   Mom:   (C'n) we have the blessi-ih-buh-Wesley
3          would you ask the blessi[ng¿ please¿
4  Wes:                            [Ahright.
5          (0.2)
6  Wes:    Heavenly fahther give us thankful hearts
7          (fuh) these an' all the blessings °ahmen.
8          (.)
9  Vir:    >°Ahmen.<
(Schegloff, 2007, p. 6)
```

Mom fails to signal the next turn properly in line 2 since the request for the blessing is originally directed generally. She corrects this at the end of line 2 and in line 3 by directly addressing Wesley. The transition relevance space, then, is clear. There is another turn relevance space in line 7, not mentioned by Schegloff, in the 'ahmen' at line 7.

Concerns that turn-taking does not occur in all languages in this way are a potential limitation on conversation analysis theory but also potentially a stimulus to theoretical refinement. 'Italian conversation' or contrapuntal conversation generally is a way of referring to this problem. The basic problem that attention is being drawn to here is that in some cultures speakers may, at times, speak together without this being a mistake or conversational problem. In other words, sometimes in conversation Italians show 'a parallelism of turns or moves by the conversationalist' (Prevignano & Thibault, 2003, p. 166) which means that accounts of conversation based on turn-taking may be inadequate.

Adjacency pairs

This builds on the idea that many turns are essentially pairs – the two turns are by different speakers, they come next to each other in their basic form, and the two turns belong to the same type. Examples of adjacency pairs include question-answer, greeting-greeting, summons-answer, and telling-accept (Liddicoat, 2007, p. 107). An example of a summons-answer adjacency pair is:

```
1 Mom:    hey Becky,
2 Becky:  in a minute
```

Adjacency pairs may seem simple, but they have considerable impact within a conversation because the adjacency pair organises the later turns by setting up expectations about the later interaction. In the above example, the summons-answer adjacency pair signals that Mom has something important or urgent to say. If, instead, she merely talks about something decidedly non-urgent then this expectation is not met by her later turns.

Preference and dispreference organisation

Turn-taking in conversation characteristically suggests that there is a preference for some first turns to be followed by a particular kind of second turn. These are conversational preferences and not psychological ones. The preference is part of the mechanism of conversation or turn-taking. Thus a question like 'are you feeling any better now?' is more likely to be followed by the answer 'yes' rather than a 'no'. Preferred following turns tend to be rather short. Dispreferred second turns tend to be more elaborate and tend to provide an account of why it has been chosen. Preferences in turn-taking are illustrated in the study described in Box 10.2.

Repairs

A key objective in conversation analysis is to find evidence of repeated patterns which arise out of the participants' joint endeavour to produce conversation. An example of such patterns lies in the conversation analysis notion of 'repair'. Things go wrong in conversation and all sorts of problems can occur. Repair describes the process by which the participants in a conversation go about correcting these errors. It is argued that the pattern is for members of a conversation to prefer the repair to be done by the person who made the error in the first place – that is, the preference is for repairs to be self-corrected rather than corrected by another member. There might be a very short gap before the next person to speak actually begins. This gap may be used by the person who caused the problem to correct or repair it. This would be classified as a transition space repair since it essentially took place in the area of transition between the two exchanges. However, it is clear from conversation analysis that 'repair' is a complex matter. For example, simply in terms of where the repair takes place there are several possibilities apart from the transition space repair. So the repair could also be effected (a) in the turn where it occurred (same turn repair), (b) in the turn after it occurred (second position repair), (c) in the turn after the turn in which it occurred (third position repair), and so forth. What this means is that the person making the repair varies with the point in the conversation exchange. This is shown in Figure 10.2.

A simple repair can be seen in the example above – the key turn is this:

> (3.2)
>
> 2 Mom: (C'n) we have the blessi-ih-buh-<u>Wesley</u>
>
> 3   would you ask the blessi[ng¿ please¿

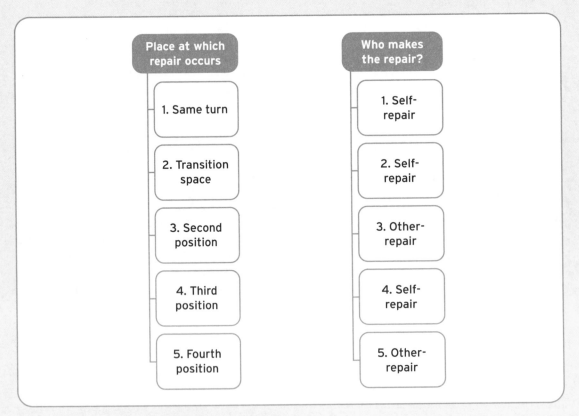

FIGURE 10.2 Positions for self- and other-initiated repairs

This is a simple self-repair. Mom initially made an open request which meant that anyone around her table could have responded. She quickly repairs this error by specifically addressing Wesley. Things get much more complex if we distinguish who initiates the repair from who makes the repair.

Opening conversation

The topic of Schegloff's (1968) paper – the first published conversation analysis paper – was 'Sequencing in conversational openings'. This study was based on 500 or so openings taken from telephone calls involving a disaster centre. In this paper, Schegloff formulated the first rule of telephone conversation (the distribution rule for first utterances). This rule states that whoever answers the call speaks first. Deviant cases in which this rule is broken are used in order to develop the analysis of conversational openings further. So, for example, in the following telephone conversation the police have called the American Red Cross but there is a one second gap at the start of the conversation at which point the rule suggests that the American Red Cross should say something like 'hello'. However, this does not happen and so it is the Police who try to sort out the conversational problem. The following excerpt illustrates this happening in a conversation:

```
. . . one second pause
Police:   Hello
Other:    American Red Cross
Police:   Hello, this is Police Headquarters . . . er, Officer Stratton . . . (Schegloff, 1968, p. 1079).
```

Closing conversation

Conversation does not end it closes. Speakers use a variety of practices to close conversations (Liddicoat, 2007). These are sequences in the conversation which do not necessarily end in closure but are points at which closure may be chosen. Closing sequences are familiar in telephone conversations:

```
Don:   okay?
Phil:  okay
Don:   bye
Phil:  bye
```

In conversation analysis, the exchange of 'bye' in the above is the closing sequence. The 'okay?' and 'okay' are described as pre-closing sequences. The pre-closing sequence in this case is intended to verify the appropriateness of bringing the conversation to an end. It is fairly self-evident that Don's 'okay?' potentially could lead to the end of the conversation. However, this is not necessarily so, as in the following illustration:

```
Don:   okay?
Phil:  just one last thing . . .
```

Of course, there is a problem with this. Don could say okay at many stages in the conversation without it signalling the verification of the end of a conversation. The concept of 'Closing implicative environments' is used to describe the series of actions in a conversations where the ending of the conversation is a possibility. These can take the form, among others, of announcing closure ('I've gotta go now'), making arrangements ('Let's meet outside the lecture on Thursday'), formulating summaries ('So we won't invite Jacqui'), appreciations ('I'm really grateful that you cared enough to call') and back references ('You've got a note of the arrangements for next week?').

Gaps

There are places in a conversation where it is possible that another speaker will take over – this is not a certainty. Such places are known as transition relevance spaces. Usually if there is a transition from one speaker to another it occurs smoothly without either a gap or an overlap of speakers. But, of course, problems do arise. Liddicoat writes:

> The normal value for the transition space, a beat of silence, indicates that nothing special is being done in the transition between speakers. However, it is possible that the transition space may be longer than normal, for example as a gap, or shorter than normal, as in the case of overlap. Both of these possibilities have an interactional importance above and beyond speaker change itself. (Liddicoat, 2008, p. 79)

Some gaps in conversation are attributable to a particular person in the conversation but for others no such responsibility exists. Usually these are distinguished in Jefferson transcription – if the gap is a 'collective responsibility' then it is placed on a separate line but if it is identifiable as 'belonging' to another speaker then it is placed appropriately as part of their turn. However, when in doubt the fallback position is 'attribute the gap collectively' and there is a degree of variability in this aspect of transcription. Gaps can be repaired as in the following, though, in this case, the conversation remains problematic because the gap of 0.6 seconds is followed later by a long one of 2.5 seconds:

D: .hh 'cause that's no fun, is it?

    (0.6)

D: when you are having to struggle like that.

M: huhm

    (2.5)

(simplified from ten Have, 1999, p. 121)

Overlaps

Places where there is no gap between the turns of speakers and no overlap of speaker's words is where *latching* occurs. This is signalled in Jefferson transcription with an = sign. Overlapping is produced by any of the speakers in the conversation. The speaker who is speaking up to the point at which the overlap occurs may be responsible because they signalled the end of their turn but carried on speaking or, on the other hand, the second speaker simply comes into the conversation too soon. Overlaps where a speaker comes into the conversation slightly early can indicate that the second speaker in the turn has understood 'the trajectory' (Liddicoat, 2007, p. 85). Instances of this would include when a student asks a lecturer a question which the lecturer answers or reformulates before the student has completed the question.

Overlaps can be problematic such as when two speakers self-select to take the next turn.

Membership categorisation device

Language is full of numerous membership categories – dad, doctor, student and so forth. The information brought into a conversation by the introduction of a membership category can be highly significant in the conversation. For example, to explain that Gill is Andrea's mother is to introduce a membership category which is laden with information relevant to the contents and structure of communication. Of course, some membership categories tend to go together, such as mother, daughter, son, father, family and so forth. Such a collection of member categories which go together is known as a membership categorisation device. One problem with membership classification analysis is that it is heavily reliant on what the researcher says a particular category brings to the conversation. That is, the information is partly extrinsic to the data being analysed which is not typically the case in conversation analysis.

Membership categorisation is a feature of conversation analysis. Membership categorisation analysis is derived from this but is to some degree established independent of conversation analysis (Butler, 2008).

The development of conversation analysis

Conversation analysis is generally accepted to have originated in the work of the American sociologist Harvey Sacks (1935–1975). However, equally influential on its long-term development was the work of Sacks's friend from postgraduate days, Emanuel Schegloff (1937–), who carried out a great deal of the formative work in the field and Gail Jefferson (1938–2008) who brought the detailed transcription of conversation to the level of a fine art (see Chapter 6). Sacks had published relatively little when he was killed in a car accident and so it was down to Schegloff and Jefferson to take the crucial steps of gathering together Sacks's lectures which had been recorded and then transcribing and organising them into a book.

Sacks had trained as a lawyer which partly stimulated his interest in language and may have encouraged his concern with what, to others, might appear the minutest detail. Probably more important are the direct influences on Sacks in terms of how social scientific research should be done. Two strands of sociological thinking are usually cited as being influential on Sacks and, consequently, constitute the intellectual roots of conversation analysis. These were social interactionism especially as they appeared in the work of the sociologist (Erving Goffman) and the ethnomethodology of Harold Garfinkel.

Erving Goffman (1922–1982) was a Canadian-born sociologist. His major contribution was his dramaturgical account of social interaction (e.g. Goffman, 1959). For Goffman, social interaction should be thought of as a social institution which has its own organisation in terms of norms and moral obligations. This is not reducible to the psychology of any individual involved in the interaction – an assumption of conversation analysis too. Goffman's work involved naturally occurring behaviours in all of their complexity:

> Like Goffman, Sacks had no interest in building data-free grand theories or in research methods, like laboratory studies or even interviews, which abstracted people from everyday contexts. Above all, both men marveled at the everyday skills through which particular appearances are maintained. (Silverman, 1998, p. 33)

> Goffman insisted that social interaction is to be conceived as a social institution in its own right, with its own normative organization and moral obligations, which, in turn, are linked to other aspects of the social world through face, role and identity. (Heritage, 2003, p. 3)

Sacks wanted Goffman to be his PhD supervisor but Goffman withdrew. Basically, Goffman did not like conversation analysis's (relative) neglect of the non-conversational aspects of social interaction (Silverman, 1998).

The other major influence on Sacks's thinking lay in the 1960s ethnomethodology developed by the American sociologist, Harold Garfinkel (1917–). Garfinkel's key concern was to understand the way in which social interaction in real, everyday life is conducted. A particular focus of ethnomethodology was the ordinary conversation. The word 'ethnomethodology' indicates Garfinkel's method of studying the common-sense 'methodology' used by people (ordinary conversationalists) to conduct their social interactions. Interactions between people consist of largely unproblematic sequences and Garfinkel wanted to know how interaction is managed and constructed to be largely problem free.

A key Garfinkelian notion was his belief that interactions between people involve the search for meaning. This is not to suggest at all that everyday interaction is meaningful in itself – the suggestion is that members of a social interaction see it as meaningful and try to understand what is happening as meaningful. Garfinkel relied on a sort of 'experimental' research to demonstrate this. In McHugh (1968), students attended 'counselling' sessions in a university's psychiatric section. This was a set-up since the student did not interact directly with the counsellor and the only feedback from the counsellor was a random reply of 'yes' or 'no'. Thus this was a totally incoherent, chaotic and meaningless social situation. The students, however, did not see the situation in this way and imposed meaningful, organised views. Garfinkel's task was with the fine detail of the sense-making/meaning-finding processes in social interaction. This focus influenced Harvey Sacks.

There was a further type of and more direct influence on the development of conversation analysis. In the 1960s, Sacks became interested in occupational practices of employees working at the Los Angeles Suicide Prevention Center (Heritage, 1984). (Sacks had gone to work alongside Garfinkel at the Center for the Study of Suicide at The University of California, Los Angeles.) The Suicide Prevention Center received telephone calls from suicidal people or people who were involved in some way with a suicidal person. These conversations were routinely recorded and transcribed by a secretary though fairly clumsily and inadequately (Cmerjrkova & Prevignano, 2003). These transcripts allowed the telephone calls to be examined in a new way by Sacks. The staff at the Center were preoccupied with getting the name of the caller because this allowed the unit to document its credentials as an organisation deserving public financial support. According to Schegloff in an interview, Sacks married their problem with:

> . . . a particular call to the suicide center in which someone 'didn't hear' what the answerer at the Suicide Prevention Center had said and by the time the 'repair' was accomplished (we weren't calling it repair at the time, of course; it was just an observation), somehow the caller had managed to avoid identifying himself. (Cmerjrkova & Prevignano, 2003, p. 23).

It appeared to Sacks and Emanuel Schegloff that something interesting was happening. That is, if the person answering the telephone at the Suicide Prevention Center could not get the caller's name at the beginning of the call then they would not get their name at all during the course of the conversation. The usual process in the 'successful' calls was that the Center would answer the phone by saying something like 'Hello, I'm Alan Davies, can I help you?' and the caller would reply something like 'Hello, I'm Sue Collins'. However, if the caller replied saying something like 'Sorry – I did not hear your name' and the Center repeated 'This is Alan Davies' but the caller did not then give their name then there was a problem – the Center never got the caller's name. Schegloff (Cmerjrkova & Prevignano, 2003) identifies this realisation as the moment conversation analysis began. Following this, Sacks began to work in earnest with the data from these telephone calls and, also, with recordings that he managed to acquire from a number of group therapy sessions with adolescents conducted by a psychologist affiliated with the Center. Telephone conversations and psychotherapy sessions have had a rich tradition in conversation analysis since then.

One last notable feature of conversation analysis needs to be mentioned: the contribution of Gail Jefferson to conversation analysis. Her major development was the system of conversation transcription which is virtually, nowadays, universal in conversation analysis work. This is discussed in much greater depth in Chapter 6 on transcription.

How to do conversation analysis

There are three important stages in conversation analysis:

● *Obtaining/making a recording*   This may be audio alone but it increasingly might be a video. Video is a little more tricky than it sounds because of the preference for/insistence of conversation analysts that their data should be natural conversation. The precise parameters of what sorts of talk is acceptable as conversation are unclear – perhaps talk produced in overtly research settings is the main source of contention. Also, conversation analysis would not generally be considered as a way of studying plays and books because they do not contain real-life conversation. It should be noted, then, that the birth of conversation analysis was out of recordings and transcriptions of real-life telephone conversations and psychotherapy sessions. There is no question that these are real-life conversations of sorts. The advent of video-recording has brought to conversation analysis the possibility of incorporating visual aspects of conversation – such as gaze which is indicative of whether a participant is paying attention. The use of video brings its problems, though, including that of the participants being identifiable. According to Heath and

Luff (1993) offering a final veto to the participant often is enough to sway them towards agreeing to being videoed.

- *Transcription*   In conversation analysis, the recordings are always transcribed, nowadays, using the Jefferson transcription system (Chapter 6).

- *Analysis*   This involves the identification of notable features of the transcription (or recording) and then developing ideas about the nature of the conversational devices involved in these significant features. Conversation analysis does not start with theoretical notions to be tested against the conversational data. Instead, the analysis seeks to understand the nature of the rules used by people in everyday life while making conversation. The participant's interpretations of the interaction as revealed by the conversation are the basis of conversation analysis.

The fundamental strategy of the conversation analyst is to work through their fragments of conversation making notes where anything strikes them as being of interest or significant. The number of observations that can be written down as a part of the analysis is unlimited, though the analyst must confine their analysis to what can be observed in the data. So they do not personally speculate about the motives of the speaker or whether the speaker was trying to achieve some unrevealed outcome in the conversation. The mindset of the conversation analyst is on what can be seen in the transcript in possibly what seems at first trivial, irrelevant detail. The transcripts used by conversation analysts are messy in the sense that they contain symbols and notation representing non-linguistic features of the conversational exchanges. The transcript tries to show fidelity to the original recording and so includes false starts to words, gaps between words and gaps between participants' turns, for example. Although sometimes one sees simplified transcripts which are light on symbols, this may not always be seen as good practice since it removes something that the reader might consider important if only it had been included.

According to Drew (1995), the following are the major methodological matters which underlie carrying out a conversation analysis:

- Conversation analysis aims to identify the sequential organisation and patterns of conversation.

- A particular contribution by a participant (i.e. a turn) is regarded as consequent on the sequence of turns which come before it in a conversation. It is an assumption of conversation that each turn should fit appropriately and coherently with the previous turn. In other words, adjacent turns should fit together effectively and meaningfully. Of course, this does not always happen in reality in which case there may be ensuing difficulties in the conversation. But the basic assumption of both the analyst and the participants in the conversation is that turns succeed each other meaningfully.

- Conversation analysts study the design of each turn or the machinery of conversation. That is, how is it possible to understand the activity that the turn is designed to perform in terms of the detail of the verbal construction of the turn?

- Participants are active participants in conversation and develop analyses of the verbal behaviours of others in the conversation. However, the conversation analyst unravels the nature of these analyses from the detail of each participant's utterances. Contributors to a conversation interpret one another's intentions and attribute intention and meaning to each other's turns through their talk. (The researcher finds out about these intentions and meanings through examination of the transcript. The researcher does not provide them and does not seek other evidence of what they might be, e.g. by interviewing participants in the conversation later.)

- The researcher seeks to show the recurrence and systematic nature of patterns in conversation. The patterns are demonstrated and tested by the analyst. This involves referring to collections of instances of the feature of conversation which is being studied. If the researcher is studying how lecturers bring tutorials to an end then the collection would be of transcriptions of the ends of tutorials.

- Conversation analysis presents the evidence in such a way that other researchers can confirm or challenge the ones made by the original researcher. This involves making entire transcripts available to other researchers or the provision of excerpts from the data which demonstrate particular features of the analysis (i.e. they are not selected simply because they support what the researcher claims). The extent to which such data exchange occurs appears not to have been documented as yet.

- The researcher can then move on by attempting to apply their analysis to other domains of conversation. This may involve data gathered from new and different research locations which allows their analysis to be generalised (or otherwise) in new circumstances.

While it is common to read that conversation analysis has no set way of proceeding, there are some fairly strict parameters within which conversation analysis operates. Understanding these should help keep the novice conversation analyst on the 'straight and narrow'. Ten Have (2007) suggested a seven-step model of the research practices involved in a conversation analysis. Ten Have's steps are probably best regarded as an idealised account of the research process. It is unlikely that they precisely describe the procedures of any particular conversation analyst. The steps are summarised in Figure 10.3.

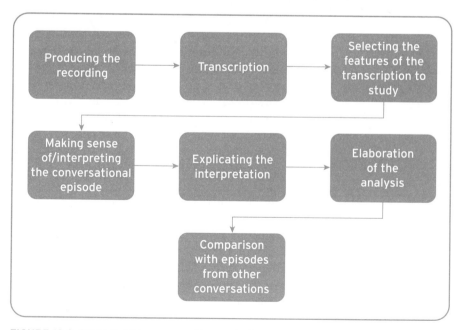

FIGURE 10.3 **Steps in doing conversation analysis**

Step 1   **Producing the recording (i.e. the materials to be analysed)**   The recording is vital in conversation analysis. Indeed, the analyst may prefer not to 'collect data' in the sense of making a recording of conversation themselves. Instead, it is part of the tradition of conversation analysis that the researcher uses extant recordings in the form, say, of telephone conversations routinely recorded by organisations. In terms of data, conversation analysis is less attracted to recordings of conversations that the researcher makes happen such as qualitative interviews and focus groups. Thus the ethos in conversation analysis encourages the choice of naturalistic or naturally occurring conversations whenever it is available. Of course, what is natural conversation is a problematic issue, in itself. The conversation analyst does not need to be present at the conversation, say, making notes and the analyst would see no point in doing so. Of course, the recordings are done by a machine but humans decide what is to be recorded and when it is to be recorded. Apart from this, a recording is basically unselective and what is recorded is not the product of the conversation analyst's questions and it has not undergone a tidying-up process. This original recording remains a point of reference throughout the analysis and later. In this way it can be used for checking purposes (Drew, 1995) but it can also be subjected to a completely new analysis in a way which mostly is not possible in psychology because of the problems of accessing data.

This is, perhaps, a slightly traditional or idealised view of the data for conversation analysis in that it stresses the importance of non-interventionist data collection – that is, the secondary use of recordings already made for non-research purposes. However, there is no embargo on the use of other data and you will find good examples of the use of researcher-initiated data (e.g. focus groups) being used for conversation analysis.

As in most aspects of research, there are choices to be made and, so long as the choices are consistent with what the researcher wishes to achieve, the details of the data are a factor in the analysis and not a stumbling block.

Step 2   **Transcription**   Transcription is dealt with at some length in Chapter 6. Conversation analysis needs detailed transcriptions of conversation. Although some of the transcriptions that are used in this chapter are light on symbols indicating additional features of speech beyond the word itself, it has to be remembered that we have used examples from different periods in the development of conversation analysis – so modern standards do not always apply. Transcription systems cannot, by definition, completely capture what is on the recording any more than the recording is an exact reproduction of the original conversation. The transcription system imposes its own characteristics on the data which, for most purposes, cause no difficulty. However, the transcript is not complete and the analyst may need to check the transcription against the original recording or, perhaps, check parts of the analysis against the original recording where there may be doubts. Even within these limits, the individual transcriber may produce a transcript which is different in some way from the product of other transcribers of the same recording. Partly for this reason, the tradition is that the researcher should transcribe their own data in conversation analysis. This may help generate the familiarity that the analyst needs with their data but it also means that the analyst is familiar with what can be heard on the recording – that is, there is more information available to the analyst than can be found in the transcript. Having the transcript in front of them, nevertheless, means that the researcher is encouraged to focus on the rich but minute detail of conversation.

It is not unusual for a conversation analysis study to be based on just a few minutes of conversation especially where this raises special issues (as in the examples in Boxes 10.2 and 10.3). One consequence of this is that the research reports can contain all of the transcribed data on which the analysis is based. In other words, the data are completely available to other researchers to 'validate' (see Chapter 14 on quality in qualitative research). This is unusual in most forms of qualitative and quantitative research.

Box 10.2
ILLUSTRATIVE RESEARCH STUDY

Conversation analysis: Feeling good and emotional labour in the beauty salon

Emotional labour is relational work that people do as part of their paid job. It is a concept which makes apparent aspects of work which are often unacknowledged such as masking one's own personal feelings in favour of a positive company persona, mending colleagues' egos, intervening to prevent arguments and so forth. There is an idea that such emotional labour is unrewarded which puts women, in particular, at a disadvantage since it is not regarded as a skill or talent – merely something that women do naturally. 'In the highly gendered, low-paid world of beauty therapy' (Toerien & Kitzinger, 2007, p. 163) not only do the workers provide the services formally charged for but they have to do the work of emotionally pampering as well as physically pampering their clients in order to ensure that they will be repeat customers. This involves making the client believe that she is being treated individually and not as part of some production line. Toerien and Kitzinger point out that research has discussed emotional labour generally but that studies of the mechanics of how emotional labour is done had not previously been carried out:

> . . . emotional labour is dependent on subtle interactional competences that beauty therapists must practise routinely; they cannot just turn them on for special, emotionally charged situations, like dealing with an enraged or grieving client. (p. 163–164)

Emotional labour is not a concept from conversation analysis but more broadly from sociology.

The data are a six and a half minute recording of interaction in a beauty salon in which the apparent task is removal of hair from the customer's eyebrows. Usually this would involve discussion of what method of hair removal would be employed – waxing or plucking. But this episode is different – a negative case – as waxing is clearly the method to be employed. Although the recording generated 110 lines of Jefferson transcription, only 22 lines were discussed in the analysis. We learn nothing about the setting of the interview other than it is somewhere in small-town UK, nothing about the beauty therapist (BTh) and nothing about the client (Cli).

```
01 Cli     >>Thing is<<um (.) I nor:mally: (0.4) get
02         them just plu:ck:ed. = 'Cause sometimes when
03         I get 'em wa:xed they sta:y red for a:ges?
04         Like not just a day but (0.4) a
05         [    few da:ys?    ]
06 BTh     [(Are) you quite se:n]sitive
07         [with it.        ]
08 Cli     [Re:ally sensi]tive skin.
09         (.)
10         And I got a [Date tonight so] uhha ha ha ha
11 Bth                 [we'll see how   ]
12         I'll see how yuh- <I mean .hh it's not really
13         really hot the wax so you should be o:ka:y
14         with it. Hhh [  but  ] we- I'll do one little=
15 Cli                  [Yeah?]
16 BTha    bit and if it fee:ls like it is fa:r too hot
17         then we'll lea:ve it <'cause if you're
18         [ going out      ] you don't=
19 Cli     [(°and/can just°)]
20 BTha    [want (to be red #eyes] do: you#.
21 Cli     [eheh heh heh heh .hh ]
22 Cli     Yea:hh. Can just pluck 'em (.) °or something.°
```

If we ignore conversation analysis for a moment, we can see the emotional labour involved in this excerpt. The customer has some concerns about having the wax treatment which she fears might leave a red mark and she has a date that night. The beauty therapist offers a trial with the wax which she tells the customer is not really hot. So here she is doing emotional work dealing with the woman's concerns and also with them in relation to her date that night. But how is all of this to be seen in conversation analysis terms?

The client's turn in lines 1, 2 and 3 is constructed as a statement indicating what she normally has done – her eyebrows are simply plucked. Waxing is presented as potentially problematic and she essentially offers a reason for not using waxing without telling the beauty therapist not to wax but to pluck. Reading on through the transcript to the beauty therapist's turn starting at line 12 and going through to line 17 we can see a repair at line 12 when the beauty therapist corrects herself ('<I mean .hh') from what appears to be indicating that she is going to go ahead with the waxing ('I'll see how yuh') to being rather more reassuring (caring of the client's emotions) by raising the possibility of the trial. But the way that this turn is constructed seems to indicate that everything is ready for the wax treatment and that plucking has not been planned for as an alternative. According to Toerien and Kitzinger (2007), the crucial thing in the beauty therapist's turn between lines 12 to 17 is:

... she tailors all aspects of her response to the client's concerns; her response is hearably 'non rote'. Her immediately responsive turn (lines 6-7) is a good example of this. Note how she avoids leaping to an immediate decision, but instead displays herself to be working toward one that is fitted to the individual client ... This turn is not only built to show that she is taking into account the client's concern about her skin's reaction to waxing, but also that she recognizes that not all clients are the same - that certain skin types may be more prone to redness than others. (p. 166)

In this report, Toerien and Kitzinger (2007) succeed in demonstrating some of the ways in which emotional work (largely to do with making the client feel special by treating her as an individual) is constructed conversationally on this occasion in the beauty salon. It is not intended as a general perspective on emotional work and talk but a demonstration of the utility of conversation analysis in this context. Despite the lack of situational detail not being usual in psychology research reports, the focus of conversation analysis on the participants' utterances is highlighted by their omission. In actuality, it is difficult to imagine what more detail could have added in terms of the analysis. That is not to say that such detail would be irrelevant to other forms of analysis, merely that it does not particularly help conversation analysis. By the way, in line 20 where it reads '[want (to be red #eyes] do: you#? the # sign means that the words in between are spoken in a shaky voice.

Box 10.3

ILLUSTRATIVE RESEARCH STUDY

Conversation analysis: Learning disabilities and categories

Antaki, Finlay and Walton (2007) take a common theme in conversation analysis - identity in conversation - which they investigate in relation to institutional talk between care staff and residents (people with learning difficulties). They argue that, conversationally, disempowerment may be on the agenda despite the stated purpose of the conversation being to solicit the views of the residents. Antaki *et al.* are not arguing that this disempowerment is a regular feature of life in this sort of care institution but that the potential for it is there - despite requirements on staff to recognise that their clients have the ordinary rights of any other citizen. Antaki *et al.* suggest that disempowerment is shown most obviously:

> ... simply in the process of interaction, in the ways in which turns are taken, troubles signalled and so on. What we see is that the staff direct the interaction towards certain statements, signal when a resident's utterance is a source of trouble and lead the residents to producing particular types of statements ... In doing so, the identities of the residents as incompetent and dependent, and the identities of the staff as knowledgeable and as in charge are acted out in the moment-by-moment details of the interaction ... (p. 12)

However, Antaki *et al.* suggest that there is a more subtle and analytically interesting way in which identity is dealt with conversationally. In the conversation studied, the staff involved in the discussion session conversationally linked care-workers in a set of categories which included friends and family members. In this way, the residents were coached about who they should regard as friends, i.e. friends, family members and care-workers. Antaki *et al.* point out that coaching someone about something implies that they need coaching:

> In effect, the staff treated the residents as having an identity impaired in its powers of basic social discrimination. They are treated as being unable to tell who their friends are, and being in need of having to count care staff among them. (p. 13)

The data on which this conclusion is based include the following:

119		Mel	<u>what</u> kind of relationship do you have with her dear
120			(1.9)
121		Nat	<u>al</u>right
122			(1.0)
123		Mel	umm
124			(.3)
125		Tim	(coughs)=
126	→	Nat	= (is) she (.) she's <u>al</u>right
127			(.2)
128		Mel	she's <u>al</u>right =
129		Nat	= yeah =
130	→	Ann	= <u>so</u> she's a <u>friend</u> =

(Antaki *et al.*, 2007, p. 10)

Line 130 is an instance of what is referred to as a formulation which is an example of the more general category of adjacency pair. The formulation may summarise some of what has gone before or, as in this case, it can draw out the implication of what has gone before. The formulation has a preferred response – agreement. In other words, 130 is constructed in a way that the likely (conversationally preferred response) is agreement. According to Antaki *et al.*, such formulations are substantially commoner in institutional talk and ordinary conversation is characteristically egalitarian. The formulation is full of interpretation and does not have to be totally consonant with what has gone before. After all, 'alright' in British vernacular language does not signal that something is good merely that there is no particular problem or issue. So Nat has not indicated a good relationship which might be equated with friendship – a tendentious interpretation by Ann. The conversation went on as follows and Ann's tendentious interpretation is confirmed by Mel:

131	Nat	= yeah (.) °she's a [friend°
132	Ann	[yeah
133		(.5)
134	Nat	Stacey's a friend
135		(.2)
136	Mel	right (.6) so er (.3) . . .

(Antaki *et al.*, 2007, p. 10)

Of course, some might suggest that a single sample of conversation, no matter how interesting, does not replace evidence of the frequency of such conversational disempowerment of people with learning disability. Antaki *et al.* are well aware that their data can only answer questions about how this disempowerment is achieved. Conversation analysts do not refer to personality traits and attitudes as ways of explanation, of course, but some might well describe Ann and Mel as patronising in their interaction with those who live in the care home. Is there no point at which such characteristically patronising aspects of conversation warrant becoming explanatory in their own right? Furthermore, if other workers do not show this pattern then how can we explain conversation solely in terms of conversational structures rather than aspects of personality? Furthermore, has the learning impairment got nothing to do with the structure of the conversation? Would, say, a university student be so ready to categorise a lecturer as their friend simply because another student interprets their comment that lecturer X is 'alright' to mean that lecturer X is the student's friend?

Step 3   **Selecting the features of the transcription to study**   Ten Have (2007) recommends that the researcher concentrates on a feature of the conversation selected for analysis. That is, it is not analytically useful to try to deal with the entirety of the conversation and, consequently, it is necessary to select a feature (or possibly features) to form the starting point for the analysis. Of course, what can be expected from an application of conversation analysis methods depends very much on the level of sophistication of the researcher. A student exploring the basic procedures is obviously operating at a different level from the advanced researcher who is working on an important and novel theoretical issue. The novice conversation analyst does not need to choose an area of research which is startlingly original. Indeed, it is still a useful learning experience for a student to replicate someone else's work. This could take the form of selecting a well-established concept which is pertinent to a particular piece of conversation that the student has selected or, at a more advanced level, essentially replicating someone else's published work in a different conversational context. The examples in Boxes 10.2 and 10.3 are obvious candidates for this but there are many others.

→   Harvey Sacks is presented in the conversation analysis literature as being rapaciously interested in the conversation that surrounded his everyday life. Of course, such a general interest, in itself, is not the certain path towards the development of any field of research. Many people are fascinated by conversations but have no contribution to make in terms of conversation analysis. The preference for ordinary, mundane conversation expressed by Sacks does not instantly help in identifying topics for research. Indeed it is a little daunting to read how out of mundane data can emerge interesting research findings – it sets the bar a little too high, if anything. Of course, there are some principles which can be applied to a conversation in order to identify features for research:

- Parts of the conversation which seem not to be going well are a likely area of focus. These can, in part, be identified from the words but also from where repairs occur.

- Once some basic understanding of conversation analysis theory has been achieved, then this may suggest issues for consideration. For example, it is often suggested in conversation analysis that there is a preference to allow self-repair of errors rather than repairs by others in the group. This may be so but is it the case in all conversations – what about where friends are having a drink together? Is this a situation in which the mistake is repaired or is it one where it is highlighted, say, in the form of a humorous comment or laughter?

- There may be parts of the conversation which the researcher simply does not understand. It is unclear what conversational processes are involved. Such excerpts pose an analytic challenge.

While conversation analysis tends to rely on features intrinsic in the data to suggest areas for development by the researcher, it can underplay factors extrinsic to the data itself as stimuli for research ideas. For example, the applied relevance or applicability of research findings is a common justification for research. Sacks, himself, was somewhat dismissive about the possible applications of conversation analysis. Nevertheless, both the highlighted examples of conversation analysis in this chapter (Boxes 10.2 and 10.3) use extrinsic arguments as justification for their choice of data. For Toerien and Kitzinger (2007) this is achieved by drawing in the concept of emotional work from outside conversation analysis and for Antaki, Finlay and Walton (2007) the external stimulus is the rights of people with learning difficulties.

While as part of a training exercise in conversation analysis it may be appropriate to simply pick out a 'noteworthy' feature of a conversation or several conversations to pursue, this is difficult to maintain as a strategy at more advanced stages. In a sense, it is a common issue in research just how to identify a topic to research. Howitt and Cramer (2008) discuss this in some detail. The short answer is that the sophisticated level of asking conversation analysis research questions requires a sophisticated level of knowledge of the research literature. Now this is fairly typical of most of the qualitative data analysis methods described in this book and reinforces the need to appreciate that qualitative methods should be regarded as areas of research more than as research design, data collection and data analysis techniques. There are few

→

short cuts to achieving this other than careful and detailed reading of research publications. Probably many a time-pressured student studying for their first degree in psychology will wince somewhat at this suggestion. Reading does not guarantee, of course, good ideas but without reading in one's chosen academic field then there is virtually no chance that they will emerge. It is likely that any researcher's early work will be strongly derivative of the work of others but gradually a distinctive approach and style can develop. To be sure, fortune favours any researcher who finds a golden nugget of previously unnoticed detail in conversation but that, in general, is not how developments in the field are likely to unfurl. Of course, gaining access to recordings of a particular sort of conversation might, in itself, provide just the stimulus that the researcher needs. One never knows – out of a researcher's non-research activities may arise an interest in and opportunities for them to investigate a particular sort of natural conversation.

Of course, social change may bring changes relevant to the study of conversation analysis. For example, mobile telephones and regular telephones with caller identification make Sacks's original observations and notions about the initial turns in conversation defunct. Suddenly the telephone tells its user who is calling – or at least whose phone is calling. So what are the new rules of telephone conversation? Or are the old rules applied and problems created as a consequence? Conversation changes – so why not conversation analysis?

No matter how tentatively, it should be possible to wrestle from conversation an issue that conversation analysis can help answer. Take heart, for example, from the following comment by a student:

> I decided to take the Conversation Analysis course in my third year, which was a much more technical introduction to the basic mechanisms of ordinary conversation. Within a few weeks of starting that course, CA became a passion. I found myself listening to people's conversations in a new way in my everyday life. Then in one class [the lecturer] briefly mentioned CA research on people with communication disorders and mental health problems, and I knew right away what I wanted to do for my final year project. I've known a lot of families which include people with Alzheimer's and I worked in a residential home which included Alzheimer's patients for nearly a year. I wanted to work on ordinary conversations with people with Alzheimer's in the hope that Alzheimer's could become less frightening to people. So that's what I did . . . (cited in Kitzinger, 2007, p. 137)

Step 4 **Making sense of/interpreting the conversational episode** Researchers are part of the culture that produced the conversational episode. Hence, they can use their own common-sense knowledge of language to make sense of the episode. This is appropriate since it is essentially what participants in the interaction do when producing and responding in the conversation (in adjacent turns, for example). Typically the analyst may ask what aspects of the conversation do or achieve during such exchanges. The relations between different aspects of conversation can then be assessed. Of course, the process of interpretation will be built on the following and more:

- A detailed reading and re-reading of the conversation to familiarise oneself with what is going on in the conversation.

→   • An attempt to use the content of the conversation to access how the members of the conversation are making sense of each of the turns and other elements of the conversation.

   • The researcher's personal understanding of conversational exchanges as a person generally involved in conversations.

   • The researcher's general knowledge of research and theory in conversation analysis.

Step 5   **Explicating the interpretation**   The conversation analyst is a member of the broad community whose conversations they study. Consequently, as we have seen, the researcher's native or common-sense understanding of what happens in an episode from a conversation is an important resource. Nevertheless, this is insufficient as an explication without bringing the links between this resource and the detail of the conversational episode together. That is, the analyst may feel they know what is happening in the conversation but they need to demonstrate how their understanding links to the detail of the conversation. The analyst needs to be sensitive to the fit of their analysis to the data but prepared for instances where the analysis and the data simply do not work together. It may also involve revising the explication.

Step 6   **Elaboration of the analysis**   Once a particular episode has been analysed, it has to be set in the context of the rest of the conversation transcription. This may allow a fuller understanding on the episode in question though, equally, the entire transcription may raise questions about the adequacy of the analysis so far. Later sequences in the conversation may in some way, directly or indirectly, relate back to the analyst's chosen and key conversational episode. This referral back may help the analyst appreciate how the people in the conversation made sense of the original episode. The consequence of this may be a need to reformulate the analysis or replace it entirely with a new, better fitting analysis.

Step 7   **Comparison with episodes from other conversations**   A conversation analysis need not end with a particular conversation and the researcher's analysis of it. There is the question of whether other instances of conversation, seemingly similar, support or detract from the analysis. This stage is extremely important because individual conversational episodes are not considered in conversation analysis to be unique. The mechanisms and ways in which a conversational episode is both produced by conversationalists and understood by other conversationalists are expected to re-occur across different conversational episodes. Some conversation analysis studies collect together different 'samples' of conversation so that comparisons may be made to find similarities and dissimilarities which may help refine the analysis.

Distinguishing between Steps 4 to 7 above is not so easy in practice as it is in theory. But they can be usefully seen as part of a schematic way of looking at the processes involved in conversation analysis. It is not being suggested that these different steps constitute a necessary and invariant sequence through which every conversation analysis will necessarily progress. It is important to remember that it is only the short-term aim of conversation analysis to interpret a particular episode taken from a conversation. The real aim of conversation analysis is the basic ethnomethodological objective of understanding the methods and structure of everyday social activity.

When to use conversation analysis

Conversation analysis is a particular approach to understanding language in action, so it cannot be regarded as a general approach to qualitative data analysis in the way that, say, thematic analysis and grounded theory are. It is a method of research in a full sense of the term method rather than the modern usage which fails to distinguish techniques for collecting and analysing data from a systematic view of how knowledge should be developed in a particular field. Conversation analysis is a fully fledged approach to how we should study conversation. Understanding what this is depends on understanding the intellectual roots of conversation analysis especially in ethnomethodology. It is hard to write more than a few sentences about conversation analysis's stance on data collection – the substance of the appropriate data is little more or less than that recordings of naturally occurring conversations should be used. This is clear and not very demanding to implement in the sense that data-collecting skills are not at a premium. It is how conversation analysis deals with conversation which distinguishes it. We should not forget that conversation in groups has been studied in various ways by psychologists. For example, group decision making, jury decision making, some attitude and opinion research, and so forth each fundamentally involve conversation. However, none of these approach conversation in a way which would satisfy the principles of conversation analysis. It seems easier to say what conversation analysis is by providing an 'agenda' of the sorts of things that conversation analysts investigate. For example, Butler explains:

> The focus [of conversation analysis] is on investigating the sequential organization of talk-in-interaction, and examines various conversational practices, including the organization of turns-at-talk, actions such as asking, telling, agreeing and assessing, and how things such as coherence, 'trouble', and word selection are relevant and consequential for the production and understanding of conversation, or, talk-in-interaction. (Butler, 2008, p. 19)

So the circumstances in which a researcher should consider conversation analysis are (a) where the data are in the form of conversation but (b) when the analysis of conversation is in terms of how conversation is done, how it is sequenced, and how the participants in the conversation understand what is happening. Quite clearly, conversation analysis should not be used when you have data in the form of conversation but the research questions are of a different order. For example, one would not use conversation analysis to answer questions like 'Do men use more instrumental talk?', 'Does conversation in groups lead to more group cohesion?' and 'Are juries biased against young witnesses?' These are all valid questions to ask about conversation. However, they are not the sorts of question that conversation analysis would answer.

Evaluation of conversation analysis

It is difficult to evaluate conversation analysis as a general method for the qualitative psychologist's toolbox. It was never developed to be a general approach to the analysis of verbal data – instead it is a theoretically embedded approach to understanding the structuring and sequencing of conversation. However, this in no way detracts from the power of the conversation analysis approach when applied to conversational data. The growing interest in conversation analysis over the past 40 or 50 years is testament to the power of its perspective. What is more surprising, perhaps, is the general fidelity of much recent conversation analysis work to Sacks's original vision of conversation analysis. Can this survive conversation analysis's adoption by psychologists? Many essential conversation analysis ideas have made their way into psychology through the often closely related approach of discourse analysis discussed in Chapter 9. One question, then, is the extent to which conversation analysis will begin to absorb psychological ideas and the extent to which the original anti-psychology stance of conversation analysis will or will need to change in psychological conversation analysis. Remember that conversation analysis sets itself expressly against internal psychological mechanisms as explanations of everyday conversation. Now quite a lot of these psychological mechanisms seem relevant to what goes on in some conversations. The long-standing idea of suggestibility is a good example of this. Suggestibility is a sort of generalised tendency to be influenced by attempts at verbal coercion – so, for example, some people more susceptible to falsely confess during police interviews than others. Just why should a psychologist not be prepared to include such factors in explanations of conversation other than that Sacks says that this sort of thing is inappropriate? Why is it any more reasonable to import a sociological concept such as 'emotional labour' (see Box 10.2) into conversation analysis than a psychological concept of suggestibility? In this context, then, it is worth noting the following comment about the work of Emanuel Schegloff, one of the founders of conversation analysis:

> [Emanuel Schegloff] on the other hand, often takes his analyses that extra small step into speculating about conversational participants' motives or intentions (e.g., Phyllis found the topic boring; Shane's stance on etiquette was ironic), but only after a detailed examination of the conversational moves and as it is warranted by the empirical evidence. (Lapadat & Lindsay, 1999, p. 72)

In many ways, conversation analysis is alien to the ways in which much psychological research is carried out. As Silverman suggests:

> Sacks's work presents something of a paradox. On the one hand, it deals with everyday events, like a telephone conversation or a newspaper story, with which we are all familiar. On the other, Sacks's analysis of these events derives from a highly complex way of reasoning, leaning to a level of detail which even his peers can find challenging. (Silverman, 1998, p. 1)

Most qualitative data analysis techniques involve an attention to detail which is different from that involved in quantitative data analysis. Conversation analysis, nevertheless, is somewhat out on a limb when it comes to the extent of the detail that it addresses. In many ways this is refreshing but it can also be frustrating when the analysis is somewhat dull or uninspired. Nevertheless, conversation analysis brings a new perspective which is different from, and consequently refreshing, in qualitative data analysis methods. At its best, conversation analysis is an invigorating discipline.

A useful summary of some of the general features of conversation analysis can be found in ten Have (2009). Among these are the following issues:

- The competence at conversation which is assumed by conversation analysis seems to be a sort of generalised conversational competence rather than a relatively specific one. This is fine when the conversation under study is fairly run-of-the-mill and everyday. In this case, the analyst can employ their own personal everyday conversational competence to help in the analysis of conversations. But what does this say about the conversations which occur in organisations which are highly specialised? What competency can the analyst employ in such contexts? For example, imagine the conversation was between senior managers at an investment bank. What analyst is competent to analyse this?

- There seem to be problems associated with the difference between interpretation and analysis. Interpretation tends to be to do with understanding the individual as an individual episode whereas analysis is a term for a broader activity in which mechanisms and procedures are proposed which apply more generally. A great deal of conversation analysis, as a consequence, may be described as interpretation rather than analysis.

CONCLUSION

In psychology, conversation analysis is beginning to provide a new focus or a new set of analytic tools which may benefit and invigorate a range of applied fields of research together with a relatively new (to psychology) perspective on language. Nevertheless, conversation analysis draws on intellectual traditions which have not gained much ground in psychology since their introduction into sociology in the 1950s and afterwards. Ethnomethodology is the most important influence on the development of conversation analysis but has not been adopted at the core of psychological research. Furthermore, conversation analysis reverses many of the principles which have guided mainstream psychology's research methods. For example, the focus on conversation with little attention to the context of the conversation or the details of those taking part in the conversation seems to overturn good practice in many areas of psychology.

KEY POINTS

- Conversation analysis emerged in the 1960s in the context of developments in sociological theory. Ethnomethodology was developed by Garfinkel and reverses the approaches of the grand-scale sociological theories of that time. Ethnomethodology concerned itself with everyday understandings of ordinary events constructed by ordinary people.

- Conversation analysis is a logically tight and consistent approach to understanding how conversation works. As such, it is best seen as a theory of language rather than a research method. Of course, conversation analysis does have its own specific way of working but this is entirely within the agenda laid down by Sacks and his colleagues. As such, if you wish to buy into the method then you are also buying into the theory. One corollary of this is that theory and method go hand-in-hand. Thus it is not possible to carry out the method without understanding the theory.

- Conversation analysis requires a detailed analysis and comparison of the minutiae of conversation as a process. Little is drawn into the analysis from outside the conversation. So conversation analysis has no interest in many psychological ideas such as personality, attitudes and so forth. In that sense, it is an alternative way of doing research from these familiar psychological approaches.

- Close analysis of the data is an essential characteristic of conversation analysis. In particular, the Jefferson conversation transcription system encourages the researcher to examine the close detail rather than the broad thrust of conversational data. The transcription is interpreted, reinterpreted, checked and compared within itself but also with other transcriptions of similar material in the belief that there is something 'there' for the analyst to find.

ADDITIONAL RESOURCES

Antaki, C. (n.d.) *An Introductory Tutorial on Conversation Analysis.* http://www-staff.lboro.ac.uk/~sscal/sintro1.htm (accessed 13 October 2009).

Drew, P. (2008). Conversation analysis. In J.A. Smith (Ed.), *Qualitative Psychology: A practical guide to research methods*, 2nd Edition. London: Sage, pp. 133–159.

Higher Education Learning Academy, Psychology Network (2009). Conversation Analysis Practical, http://www.psychology.heacademy.ac.uk/php?p=137/ (accessed 13 October 2009). Contains a PowerPoint lecture plus examples of conversation.

Liddicoat, A.J. (2007). *An Introduction to Conversation Analysis.* London: Continuum.

ten Have, P. (2007). *Doing Conversation Analysis: A practical guide.* London: Sage.

Wilkinson, S., and Kitzinger, C. (2008). Conversation analysis. In C. Willig and W. Stainton-Rogers (Eds.), *The SAGE Handbook of Qualitative Psychology.* Los Angeles, CA: Sage, pp. 54–72.

CHAPTER 11

Interpretative phenomenological analysis (IPA)

Overview

- Interpretative phenomenological analysis (IPA) was primarily developed within health psychology in the 1990s as a way of understanding the experience of health issues such as pain. It has also grown in social psychology and clinical psychology.

- The primary concern of IPA is with how individuals experience phenomena and the psychological interpretations of these experiences.

- Like social interactionism and other perspectives, IPA assumes that people attempt to make sense of (give meaning to) their experiences.

- IPA has its roots in phenomenology together with hermeneutics and symbolic interactionism. It emphasises the ideographic as well as the nomothetic. Case studies or small samples characterise the IPA approach.

- Semi-structured interviews tend to be the preferred data for IPA analyses. In these interviews, people are encouraged to freely recall their experiences. The questioning style is designed to encourage richly detailed descriptions of experiences of phenomena. Alternative sources of data may be used if they meet the method's requirements.

- The recording of the interview is usually transcribed using a literal, verbatim approach.

- The account of one participant is usually analysed in depth before the researcher moves on to compare this with accounts from other participants. Themes developed in the initial analysis may be used or added to for the later analyses. Similarities and differences between accounts are important aspects of the analysis.

- Following a period of data familiarisation, the researcher notes impressions and ideas in the left-hand margin of the transcript.

- The researcher looks for themes in the account. Themes should be clearly related to what was said in the interview though they are normally expressed somewhat more abstractly or theoretically than would characterise the words of the participant. Each theme is usually given a short descriptive title. The themes are identified, wherever they occur, by this name in the right-hand margin of the transcription.

- Once the themes have been identified, the analyst groups or clusters them together into broader, more encompassing superordinate themes. These superordinate themes and sub-themes may be listed in a table in order of their assumed importance, starting with the most important. Short verbatim quotations are usually selected to illustrate the theme and the line number from the transcript given as a means of locating the original.

- The major themes are discussed partly in relation to the wide psychological literature on that topic.

- IPA deals with internal psychological processes such as cognition. It is, thus, one of the most clearly psychology-based approaches to qualitative research.

- There is considerable variation in procedures used in IPA.

- Template analysis is different in that it starts with pre-existing psychological concepts, ideas and theory in order to suggest possible themes. These may then be modified or added to in the light of the interviews.

What is interpretative phenomenological analysis?

According to Smith, Larkin and Flowers (2009, p. 1) interpretative phenomenological analysis (IPA) is 'committed to the examination of how people make sense of their major life experiences'. More than most of the qualitative research methods described in this book, IPA has its origins in psychology. It was first discussed by Jonathan Smith (Smith, 1996) and it has grown in popularity since then. Essentially, IPA is about the experiences of individuals working from the basic assumption that the individual who experiences something is the expert about their experiences. The meanings which the individual uses to understand their own experiences and the insights that they supply are central to this approach. Much of the early work on IPA was broadly in the area of health psychology but clinical psychology and social psychology also featured. Reid, Flowers and Larkin (2005) suggest that the following topics are among those where IPA has made an impact: palliative care; people's reproductive decision making, e.g. abortion and adoption; mental health, drugs and addiction, and eating disorders; quality of life assessment following serious illness; new genetics – such as when patients need support following genetic tests; chronic illness such as long term back-pain; and dementia and other degenerative diseases. Examples of titles include:

- 'An exploration of the experience of mothers whose children sustain traumatic brain injury (TBI) and their families' (Clark, Stedmon & Margison, 2008)

- 'Biographical disruption and the experience of loss following a spinal cord injury: an interpretative phenomenological analysis' (Dickson, Allan & O'Carroll, 2008)

- 'What is the mechanism of psychological change? A qualitative analysis of six individuals who experienced personal change and recovery' (Higginson & Mansell, 2008)

Nevertheless, other areas of research away from the field of health psychology are being researched using IPA especially clinical psychology and social psychology. Examples of non-medical topics include:

- 'Opportunities of student influence as a context for the development of engineering students' study motivation' (Jungert, 2008)

- 'The presentation of masculinity in everyday life: contextual variations in the masculine behaviour of young Irish men' (Johnston & Morrison, 2007)

- ' "Getting into trouble": a qualitative analysis of the onset of offending in the accounts of men with learning disabilities' (Isherwood, Burns, Naylor & Read, 2007)

All of these titles reflect fairly open and general research questions. IPA is not about testing hypotheses but about understanding personal experiences of the world. Furthermore, since IPA tends to deal with life-changing events for the most part, it is not the most obvious candidate for casual research on fellow students, for example.

Basically, IPA can be used wherever a person's psychological experiences are being studied through the person's own perspective. The data collection method of preference for IPA researchers is in-depth qualitative interviews, though it is possible that other data might be used – if it deals with an individual's experiences in their own words. However, the surest guarantee that the data will be appropriate for IPA analysis is a carefully constructed, in-depth qualitative interview. As the name IPA implies, the method's primary concern is in the provision and analysis of detailed descriptions and interpretations of conscious experiences (phenomena) in the personal accounts of individuals or a small number of individuals. (Throughout this chapter we use the word phenomenon in this sense which is derived from phenomenology.) Richardson, Ong and Sim (2006) provide a good example of an IPA investigation to chronic pain. Eight people with chronic, widespread pain were interviewed along with a small number of family members. Small samples are typical of interpersonal phenomenological studies because of the amount of labour involved in their analysis. The researchers found, for example, that the experiences of participants could be classified as (a) optimistic about the future, (b) pessimistic about the future and (c) overwhelmed with uncertainty concerning the future. The last category was the dominant one. This provides an example of the basic assumption of IPA that people try to make sense of their experiences and among the aims of IPA is for the researcher to understand the meaning given to these experiences. Hence, in an IPA study, it is important that the researcher:

- provides an accurate and effective description of people's experiences;

- tries to make sense of these experiences.

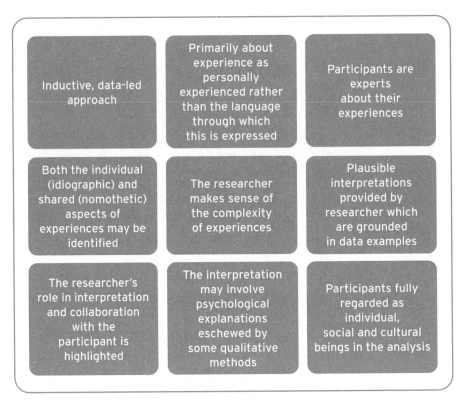

FIGURE 11.1 **The key elements of interpretative phenomenological analysis**

Put another way, the researcher is trying to interpret the interpretations of the people studied in the research. In IPA it is recognised that ultimately it is the researcher's own conceptions of the phenomenological world which form the basis of how the phenomena are understood. This acknowledges that the researcher can never completely know another person's phenomenological world though they can perhaps get usefully close to accessing it.

IPA has links with other forms of qualitative analysis – in particular, thematic analysis and it has similarities to narrative analysis. Figure 11.1 indicates some of the key features of IPA including those identified by Reid *et al.* (2005). Clearly, with its emphasis on the phenomenological interpretation of experiences, IPA has its own particular focus which is not shared by other qualitative research methods. Similarly, because it does not regard participants in the research as mere providers of text or conversation to be interpreted as conversation, IPA incorporates more elements of the person into the analysis than is typical of, say, conversation analysis and discourse analysis. The focus on how things (phenomena) are experienced is probably the clearest defining characteristic of IPA. Box 11.1 presents an IPA analysis which very much illustrates the general style of the method.

Box 11.1
ILLUSTRATIVE RESEARCH STUDY

Phenomenological analysis: the experience following brain injury

Traumatic brain injury may leave the individual with profound distress. Major changes occur in their circumstances due to the physical and intellectual disabilities which can follow. Depression, anxiety, obsessive-compulsive disorder, and post-traumatic stress disorder are some of the outcomes which researchers have noted. Roundhill, Williams and Hughes (2007) discuss the relevance of the concept of 'loss' (as in bereavement) to understanding survival from traumatic brain injury. There are many ways in which the 'loss' of the person that the victim of traumatic brain injury was is a good metaphor for the situation that they face. A growing research literature has developed which has concentrated on questionnaire methods of assessment of bereavement although a small number of studies have explored the experience of such bereavement processes qualitatively. Of course, the experience of bereavement is the sort of phenomenon that phenomenological research would have an interest in. The dual process model of grief suggests that it is an 'oscillating' process between (a) 'loss orientation' and (b) 'recovery orientation'. The study that we will consider (Roundhill et al., 2007) attempts to understand the experience of bereavement over a substantial, two-year period following survival. The criteria for inclusion were (a) surviving severe traumatic brain injury that had occurred at least two years before, (b) having insight, memory, verbal skills and so forth so that they could actively participate in the research, and (c) the person had experienced no important bereavements during that period of time.

The participants in this research were recruited with the help of a charity dealing with survivors of traumatic brain injury. A pilot study was employed which involved a victim who had written and given talks about his experiences. He was also part of the discussion with the researchers about what to include in the interview. The participants in the research were six survivors of road traffic accidents and one survivor of an assault. The report includes an informative table summarising the participants' characteristics, i.e. their fictitious names, their gender, their age, the type of trauma they had experienced, and the number of years since the injury.

The interview itself was the typical semi-structured kind used in IPA and covered the areas of 'loss, coping, awareness, and current self-identity' (Roundhill et al., 2007, p. 244). All of the interviews were recorded and transcribed though no description is given of the transcription method. According to the authors, they analysed the data using the procedures for IPA (Smith, Jarman and Osborn, 1999). They also suggest that the analysis took a 'reflexive stance' in which the analyst's role in the interpretation and construction of themes was attended to. The 'reflexive stance' involved keeping a 'reflective journal' during the data collection and analysis stages. This is rather like memo-writing in grounded theory. In this, the analyst 'endeavored to maintain an awareness of the application of the DPM [Dual Process Model] while remaining open to the development of new themes that were not necessarily congruent with the grief theory' (Roundhill et al., 2007, p. 244).

→

TABLE 11.1 The theme structure from interviews about traumatic brain injury

Superordinate theme: emotion focus	Superordinate theme: progress focus	Superordinate theme: issues of control	Superordinate theme: post-injury growth
• Example: 'The brain is obviously trying to protect the body, the person inside of it . . . it would just be too much to take in. It wouldn't be well enough to handle it.' **Martin**	• Example: 'Well first of all I try to address any particular problem that comes along myself. I always try to do it, as I said to you about helping myself with memory and things like that . . . And "try" is a very wide – although it's three letters it can be very, very long.' **Mark**	• Example: 'If you don't do it, nobody else can do it for you. You've got to do it for yourself. You've got to give yourself something for a goal.' **Don**	• Example: 'I'm completely different, because in my younger days I was a bit of a tearaway. I've quietened down. It's definitely positive, because I would have probably ended up in prison, for a long time, or dead.' **Ken**
• No sub-themes provided	• No sub-themes provided	• No sub-themes provided	• No sub-themes provided

Quotations from Roundhill *et al.* (2007).

So, it is very clear that the analysis was in part led by pre-existing theory although the research was open to ideas emerging from the interviews. The researchers identified four superordinate themes in their analysis but no subordinate themes. The lack of subordinate themes in the analysis is surprising though it may be a consequence of the very limited number of data sources involved in the study. The structure of their analysis is presented in diagrammatic form in Table 11.1.

Traditional views of bereavement have tended to describe it as a number of stages which have to be 'worked through'. However, this is very different from recent research as encapsulated into the dual process model of bereavement. According to Roundhill *et al.*:

> The DPM posits that individuals need to 'dose' their exposure to the pain of loss, suggesting the need for relief from active mourning and to attend to other demands. The model also enables the consideration of the benefits of a degree of denial in the process of adjusting to loss. This orientation away from grief work serves not only as a protective function against overwhelming feelings but also enables other stressors, such as altered role, identity, and the demands of new tasks, to be confronted. The parallel with adjustment following severe TBI [traumatic brain injury] seems clear here, with the individual being required to acknowledge and adjust to circumstances which are often significantly different. (p. 250)

Roundhill *et al.* suggest that the evidence of the sort of oscillation process between 'loss orientation' and 'recovery orientation' in the dual process model was poorly supported by the interviews. That is, grief does not drip away allowing the individual to accommodate to their new situation. Despite what the dual process model suggests, it would seem that the survivors of traumatic brain injury initially swing heavily to dealing with the loss and then move on to the recovery process. These different processes, they say, are in a state of dynamic equilibrium and it is not that the stages are worked through and thus dealt with. The process, according to Roundhill *et al.*'s participants, may be described in terms of stages as shown in Figure 11.2.

FIGURE 11.2 **Stages in the bereavement process in traumatic brain injury survivors**

It is not the purpose here to evaluate Roundhill *et al.*'s contribution to theory. Much more important in this context is how using IPA can lead to theory development. By conceptualising the processes involved in traumatic brain injury survival in terms of bereavement, the researchers offer a way of thinking which makes intuitive sense. However, the dual process model has assumptions which fail to be demonstrated in the experiences of the traumatic brain injury victim. Hence, this is potentially an important theoretical contribution. Not all IPA analyses demonstrate such an impact on theory. But, as an illustration of IPA, Roundhill *et al.*'s paper has a lot to offer, especially for those who suggest that qualitative research merely confirms the obvious. Like many qualitative research reports, there is only limited discussion of the analysis stages and some expansion of these would benefit newcomers to IPA research.

The development of interpretative phenomenological analysis

Every data analysis method has assumptions built into it. This is clearly the case with quantitative data analysis but equally so for qualitative data analysis methods. Quantitative psychology, as we saw in Chapter 1, reflects to a good measure the assumptions of positivism and hypothesis testing. Qualitative data analysis methods, including IPA, grow from philosophical and theoretical roots which need to be understood in order to appreciate the nature of the method in full. It is probably fair to suggest that the melange of influences on IPA is different in some respects from the general influences on qualitative research. One very obvious thing which hardly warrants a mention is that IPA emerged out of the discipline of psychology and is largely confined to that discipline though it appears in nursing studies, for example. This has the consequence that IPA is more amenable to drawing on pertinent research and theory from psychology than some other methods. It is also far less about understanding language than some other forms of qualitative analysis such as discourse analysis and conversation analysis. IPA acknowledges the influence of some major philosophical traditions in psychology and the social sciences. These influences on IPA are illustrated in Figure 11.3.

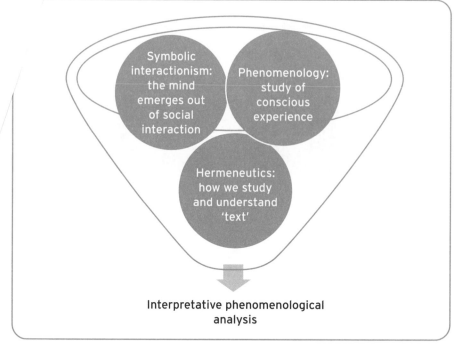

FIGURE 11.3 Some influences on interpretative phenomenological analysis

The origins of IPA are seen as lying in Jonathan Smith's paper published in 1996 – 'Beyond the divide between cognition and discourse: using inter-pretative phenomenological analysis in health psychology' – in which he argued the case for:

> . . . an approach to psychology which was able to capture the experiential and qualitative, and which could still dialogue with mainstream psychology. (Smith *et al.*, 2009, p. 4)

In terms of the origins of IPA, there are very clear claims that it has its roots in key philosophical postions:

> One important theoretical touchstone for IPA is phenomenology, which originated with Husserl's attempts to construct a philosophical science of consciousness. A second important theoretical current for IPA is hermeneutics – the theory of interpretation. A third significant influence is symbolic-interactionism . . . which emerged in the 1930's as an explicit rejection of the positivist paradigm beginning to take hold in the social sciences. For symbolic-interactionism, the meanings which individuals ascribe to events are of central concern, but those meanings are only obtained through a process of social engagement and a process of interpretation. (Taylor, 2008)

Chapman and Smith (2002) also affirm the IPA has its roots in phenomenology and symbolic interactionism and Smith (n.d.), additionally, refers to hermeneutics as being fundamental to the method.

No one should be surprised to find that IPA owes allegiances to phenomeno-logy. The influence of (a) symbolic interactionism and (b) hermeneutics perhaps warrant greater explanation. The following outlines the key features of each of these.

Phenomenology

Phenomenology is the systematic study of conscious experiences. It is a general philosophical movement. The Greek word *phainomenon* means 'that which appears' or 'how things appear'. The founder of phenomenology is claimed to be the Austrian/German philosopher Edmund Husserl (1889–1938). Although some of the basic ideas of phenomenology appear in his *Logische Untersuchungen* (1891), the term phenomenology was first included in *Ideen zu einer reinen Phänomenolgie und phänomenologischen Philosophie* (1913). Whether Husserl should be described as a philosopher or a psychologist is difficult since when he was writing the distinction between philosophy and psychology was not so absolute as it is now. Whatever – Husserl was certainly influenced by major psychologists of the period such as Franz Brentano (1838–1917). Among the basic ideas of phenomenology is that there is no clear independence between human experience and reality. That is, reality is made up from things and events but as perceived within the realm of conscious experience. Thus, it can be suggested that phenomenology, alongside much of qualitative psychology, rejects the idea of an objective reality for experiences. In Husserl's thinking, there is a distinction to be made between what is experienced (which is called the noema) and the nature or manner of the experiencing (noesis). So it is possible to experience something in imagination – such as the day you graduate from university – but this is associated with a complex experience such as the outfit that you have on, what you feel, who is there, and so forth. Another important concept in phenomenological research is *epoché* (or bracketing) which is the way in which the phenomenological researcher tries to avoid preconceptions and presuppositions which play a part in how we understand experiences so that the experiences are experienced as they appear for the very first time.

IPA and other phenomenological approaches are ways of understanding conscious experience from the viewpoint of the person having the experience. Familiar and unfamiliar psychological concepts such as thought, memory, social action, desire and volition are studied in IPA. Experience involves conscious intentionality – particular ideas and images which help constitute the meaning of a particular experience. Phenomenology in a variety of manifestations was a major influence on twentieth-century academic thinking. In particular, the existentialism of Jean-Paul Sartre (1905–1980) and others who were influenced by Husserl. But, in addition, American sociology incorporated a version of phenomenology in the form of ethnomethodology (see Chapter 2, pp. 45–6).

Hermeneutics

Taken literally, albeit in ancient Greek, hermeneutics means the analysis of messages. However, it is more clearly seen as the ways in which we go about studying and understanding texts. Text is not to be seen as merely something that is written down. Following the ideas of the Algerian/French philosopher Jacques Derrida (1930–2004), a text should be regarded as including anything that people interpret during the course of their day-to-day lives. Of course, this definition would include the sort of experiences that IPA focuses on. Meaning is a social and a cultural product in hermeneutics and much of qualitative research. Although hermeneutics was originally applied to biblical texts, it should be clear that the approach can be applied to a multitude of aspects of human activity. In hermeneutic traditions, the meaning and importance of human activity are studied primarily from a first-person perspective. The parts of the text are studied in relation to the entirety in a backwards and forwards, looping process. Such processes are familiar in various forms of qualitative data analysis.

Perhaps the following should be added, though it is a slight detour. The term 'deconstruction' has its origins in hermeneutics. The German philosopher Martin Heidegger (1889–1976) introduced the idea though the emphasis was not the same as the term's modern usage. Heidegger realised that the interpretation of text was influenced by the person doing the interpretation. That is to say, it differs from the text's original meaning. These interpretations have to be deconstructed in order to reveal the contribution of the interpreter to the text's meaning. Such constructions, and hence the necessity of deconstruction, are evident with some religious texts where interpreters essentially alter the original meaning of the texts. So Islam, for example, has various interpretations or constructions despite the original text on which they are based being the same. Under Derrida's influence, deconstruction has come to mean a form of criticism of the interpreter's influence on a text's meaning, whereas it originally meant merely the identification of the different traditions of understanding text. Hepburn provides a summary of how deconstructionism is normally presented in psychological writings:

> Deconstruction is often positioned as the opposite of construction: it is taken simply to refer to 'breaking things down' – the unravelling of a text's assumptions and the overturning of hierarchies. (Hepburn, 1999, p. 651)

In order to gain a more sophisticated understanding of Derrida's concept of deconstruction in psychology, Hepburn (1999) will make a good starting point. But we are beginning to get a long way from IPA with this family tree of philosophy.

Symbolic interactionism

In symbolic interactionism the idea that the mind and self emerge out of social interactions involving significant communications is central. It is a sociological approach to small-scale social phenomena rather than the major structures of society. It has in the past been influential on social psychological thinking, especially what is sometimes termed sociological social psychology. The story of symbolic interactionism begins in the work of the German sociologist, Max Weber (1864–1920) and the work of the American psychologist and philosopher George Herbert Mead (1863–1931). Both of these men brought the issues of subjective meaning and social interaction to the forefront. Although Mead is regarded as one of the most important figures in symbolic interactionism, the term is that of Herbert Blumer (1900–1987) whose account of symbolic interactionism tends to dominate over other variants (Blumer, 1969).

Despite symbolic interactionism being essentially a sociological theory, it is based on a conception of what people are rather than a conception of what the structures of society might be. Unlike the dominant perspective of psychology, for interactionists people are not the passive recipients of socialisation influences. Instead, people are 'out there' in a social world making their own understandings of that world in relation to their understanding of other people and themselves and the interaction between the two. In symbolic interactionism, a person is continually adjusting what they do in response to the actions of other people. This is dependent on the human ability to interpret the actions of others in relation to their own actions. Or, to put it another way, we can treat the actions of others symbolically and treat these actors as symbolic objects. In our imaginations, we are capable of formulating and rehearsing alternative patterns of action in advance of responding. Furthermore, we have the capacity to regard ourselves and the things we do also as being symbolic objects. In the interactionist perspective, humans construct their social world actively and creatively. Significant symbols occur in circumstances where the sender of the communication has the same understanding of the communication as the receiver of the communication. Language consists of communication involving the use of such significant communications. The ordinary, day-to-day interactions between people (and not social structures) are what society is. This means that society is dynamic and changing in response to the (temporary) outcomes of these interactions.

Just how do these processes work? What does it mean to suggest that mind and conceptions of self develop in the social interactions between people? One has to remember that social processes and communications exist prior to the birth of an individual. The child comes into a world in which people are already formed socially and have interacted with each other to create their understandings of the world. The newborn enters this world and, even from a very early stage, can engage in a conversation based on gestures. That is, they are communicating through gestures before they can communicate through language. The early gestures are communication without a conscious intention to communicate but nevertheless have that effect. Communication is not an individual act but one involving two people at a minimum. Communication is the basic social mechanism through which meaning is learnt and established – meaning is dependent on interactions between individuals. The process is one in which there is a sender, a receiver and a consequence of the communication. In this way, the mind and understanding of self arise. Of course, there develops an intentionality in communication because the individual learns to anticipate the responses of other individuals to the communication and can use this to achieve the desired response of others. So the self is purposive. It is in the context of communication or social interaction that meanings come about in the social world.

An excellent example of symbolic interactionist thought can be found in the dramaturgical approach of Erving Goffman (1922–1982), in which human social interaction is regarded as 'scripted'. It is a small step from seeing the importance of interpersonal interaction in the creation of the nature of society and studying the roles which individuals play in interaction. Role-taking is a key mechanism by which we can learn and understand the perspective of others. *Asylums* (1961) is one of Goffman's most influential books. It examines the process of institutionalisation which can be conceived as the inmate's reaction to the structures of such total institutions and the interactions therein. In his book *Frame Analysis* (Goffman, 1974) claims the intellectual influence of phenomenology on his thinking. Ethnomethodology is also steeped in symbolic interactionism.

Finally, it is important to note that IPA is, at its root, basically an *idiographic* approach focused on the individual (as in any case study) as the unit to be understood. IPA accepts single case studies for this reason. Researchers might wish to move from what they have learnt about the individual to make more general statements about individuals. Nevertheless, understanding the individual in their own right is an important feature of IPA. This reflects the classic distinction between idiographic and nomothetic approaches to knowledge which was introduced into psychology by Gordon Allport (1897–1967) in the 1930s although the German philosopher Wilhelm Windelband (1848–1915) was the originator of the distinction:

- Idiographic understanding concerns the individual as an individual in his or her own right.

- Nomothetic understanding is concerned with the study of groups of individuals. This group is considered to represent all individuals in that class of people. As a result, in nomothetic approaches it is appropriate to formulate abstract laws or generalisations about people in general.

How to do interpretative phenomenological analysis

Analysts using IPA do not base their interpretation solely on what the individual in question has to say about their experiences. The analyst adds more to the interpretation. Consequently, IPA involves what Smith and Osborn (2003) call 'a questioning hermeneutics'. They suggest that this involves asking questions of what the participants in their research say such as:

> What is the person trying to achieve here? Is something leaking out here that wasn't intended? Do I have a sense of something going on here that maybe the participants themselves are less aware of? (Smith & Osborn, 2003, p. 51)

Hence, IPA is 'interpretative' and not merely descriptive. The interpretation is not taken literally from the participant's words but is part of a systematic analysis of what is said. One might describe this, then, as a process of critical deconstruction.

Detailed accounts of how to carry out IPA have been provided by Smith and his colleagues (e.g. Smith & Eatough, 2006; Smith et al., 2009; Smith & Osborn, 2003). These accounts of the IPA procedures include acknowledgement of the fact that flexibility is possible and that a researcher may choose to adapt and vary the methods in order to meet the requirements of their own particular study. In other words, IPA methodology is not too prescriptive about how a study should proceed. There are two major aspects of IPA:

- data collection;
- data analysis.

These are dealt with separately in the following sections. Figure 11.4 gives a summary of the main aspects of the analysis.

Prior to attempting your first IPA, it is common sense to read at least a few examples of studies which have used IPA. There are a number of studies which can be drawn on and new ones are being produced all of the time. Examples are provided in Boxes 11.1 and 11.2. Obviously, some will be on topics closer to what you would like to research than others. These, of course, will make the best models to follow.

Data collection: the semi-structured interview

Of course, data collection is dependent, in any study, on the way in which the research question is formulated. This is equally true for IPA. A detailed

FIGURE 11.4 Stages in an interpretative phenomenological analysis

discussion about the formulation of research questions in IPA is provided by Smith and Osborn (2003). Research questions in IPA do not lead to hypotheses since IPA's approach is exploratory and confined mainly by the area of experience that the researcher is concerned with in any particular study. However, it is possible to formulate a general IPA research question: what are the perceptions that an individual (or group of individuals) have concerning a given situation they experience (phenomenon) and how do they make sense of this experience?

Like some other forms of qualitative data analysis, IPA requires much time for data collection, data transcription and data analysis. As a consequence of this, the numbers interviewed in an IPA study are typically small. Just by way of illustration, there are IPA (case) studies with a single participant (Eatough & Smith, 2006) but others with as many as 64 participants (Coleman & Cater, 2005). Sample size depends very much on (a) the aims of the research and (b) the resources of the researcher. In the case of student projects, time and other resources may, perhaps, allow only for a sample of three to six participants

TABLE 11.2 Example of summary of participants' table

Participant	Gender	Age	Type of pain	Years since onset
Debbie	F	48	Traffic accident	10
Chris	M	27	Traffic accident	14
Elle	F	22	Work related	3
Karen	F	39	Medical condition	25
Jay	M	33	Work related	12
Martin	M	27	Medical condition	5

(Howitt & Cramer, 2008). Smith and Osborn (2003) suggest that an IPA sample should consist of relatively similar (homogeneous) cases rather than extremely different examples. One implication of this is that it is better to carry out a study on a specific group such as those with chronic back pain rather than study various types of pain in one study. It is useful to include a table (e.g. Table 11.2) summarising some of the characteristics of each individual participant if the sample size allows this. This allows the reader to contextualise the discussion. Of course, what to include depends very much on the nature and the purpose of the research. It is a useful strategy to adopt where any qualitative study is based on a small number of participants.

Detailed accounts about people's experiences are the foundation of IPA. The quality of the analysis is dependent on the quality of these accounts which lead to the description and understanding that IPA applies. Whatever the textual material used for IPA, it must provide extremely detailed accounts of the experiences. Probably, the level of detail required would be rare, say, in everyday conversations about pain, for example. That is, a great deal of textual material would be ruled out on this basis. The preferred data in IPA, then, is the sort of rich textual material which often can be obtained in open-ended interviewing of the sort discussed in Chapter 3. Of course, the interviewer needs to ensure that the appropriate sorts of description emerge in the interview by using carefully thought-out and relevant questioning. The IPA interview involves a series of open-ended questions intended to help the participant to produce a lengthy and detailed description in their own words. Such interviews will require careful piloting if they are to be maximally effective. So the IPA researcher will normally explore their interview questions and techniques on a small number of people – if the result is that the participants answer freely and extensively then the researcher will probably feel confident that they can move on to the study proper. It should be stressed that other kinds of personal accounts of experiences such as diaries or other autobiographic material could be used subject to the appropriateness of their contents for the purposes of the research.

Nevertheless, to date, IPA uses semi-structured interviews almost exclusively. IPA interviewing techniques are intended to be applied flexibly. So, the questions that have been planned are not read to the participant in a fixed sequence. The interviewer, instead, needs to be free to explore (probe) things of interest as and when they occur during the course of the interview. It is most important that the interview is led by the participant's issues rather than an agenda imposed by the interviewer. Notwithstanding this, a considerable amount of pre-planning is involved. For example, alongside the questions planned it is also possible to pre-plan at least some of the probes which will be needed in addition in order to ensure that fully detailed information is provided. These probes can be included in the interview schedule. But, of course, the interviewer is free to add new questions and probes where necessary during the course of the interview.

Smith and Osborn (2003) make various suggestions about how the interview questions should be written (pp. 61–62). While these are fairly typical of the advice given about in-depth interviewing in general (see Chapter 3), they warrant mentioning here:

- Questions should be neutral rather than value-laden or leading.
- Avoid jargon or assumptions of technical proficiency.
- Use open, not closed, questions.

The style of interview is described by Smith and Osborn (2003) as having the following general features (p. 63):

- Since it takes time for trust and rapport to build up in an interview, it is important to move slowly towards the main areas of interest. The topics studied in IPA tend to be highly personal and sensitive and so they cannot be rushed into.
- There is a distinction to be made between the effective use of probes and using them excessively to the detriment of the quality of the data. The overuse of probes can detract from the quality of the interview by disrupting the participant's account and they can introduce unhelpful diversions.
- It is important to ask a question at a time and provide sufficient time to ensure a proper and full answer. The participant may need to think and it is quite wrong to interrupt this with another question.
- The interviewer needs to be sensitive to the effect that the interview is having. The interviewer may need to change the way in which a particular interviewee is interviewed if there appear to be problems or difficulties. There are many different ways in which these may be coped with according to circumstances. A short break or a new style of questioning would be among the possibilities.

It would hamper the interview if the researcher seems unfamiliar with the questions that are to be answered and so spends much of the time checking the questionnaire. Consequently, it is far better if the researcher commits the interview schedule to memory so as to allow a more natural and smooth flow to the interview. (Of course, it is reasonable to take a short break while you check the interview schedule to see if you omitted anything. The interviewee will understand the need for this. It should be done in their presence.) There is every reason to vary the sequence of the interview in the light of what the participant says during the course of the interview. As a rule of thumb, it is best to let the interviewee say what they want to say at the point at which they choose to say it. So if the interviewee provides information on something which comes later in the interview's agenda then collect the information at that time and try to remember not to ask the participant for the information again. For example, if the participant is asked a general question about pain but, during the course of their answer, they go into detail about when the pain started then the later question about how the pain started should mentally be deleted from the list.

Furthermore, remember that the interview is guided by what the participant has to say. It is impossible for the researcher to anticipate everything that might be of relevance for inclusion in the list of questions. There will be circumstances, especially at the start of a research study, when the interviewee may raise issues which seem of interest and relevant to the topic in question but this material does not fit neatly into the list of topics included in the interview schedule. Whenever these circumstances arise, the interviewer should seek to question the participant about these new matters. Of course, this means that the interviewer needs to have the flexibility to develop the questions 'off the cuff'. The next step, of course, is to consider whether to include questions about this matter in future interviews in the series. In other words, researchers should be sensitive to the material that participants provide and should not necessarily be precisely bound by their interview schedule. This, of course, does not mean that any sections of the interview may be dropped at a whim.

It would be normal in any semi-structured interview to start with the wider picture and then focus on the detail. Thus semi-structured interviews in IPA would normally start with the general question which would be followed by specific questions and probes. For example, if the research is about pain then it would be usual to talk with the interviewee about pain before asking about details such as when the pain is worse or the effects that it has on everyday activities.

A sound-recording is made of the interview so that a full record of what has been said is available to the researcher. The sound recording has the advantage that the researcher is free to pay close attention to what the interviewee is saying rather than trying to make notes. Video-recording is not common though might be considered. However, the advantages of video-recording might not outweigh its disadvantages.

In IPA the sound recordings are transcribed prior to data analysis. It is far more convenient to read and check a transcript than it is to move backwards and forwards through different parts of a recording of an interview. Of course, you may need to go back to the original tape for clarification, etc. A transcript also facilitates the ability of the researcher to see relationships between the data and the analysis being carried out on that data. With interpretative phenomenological analysis, transcription is usually a version of the literal, secretarial-style (playscript) transcription in which the words said and by whom are the only things recorded normally. Generally, the Jefferson-style transcription in which extralinguistic features such as voice inflections, pauses and other aspects are included will have no place in IPA (see Chapter 6 for a discussion of transcription). Nevertheless, there is no embargo on transcribing such additional features as the expression of emotion. Normally, wide margins are left on each side of the transcribed interview to allow comments to be made about any such relevant features. At the time that the transcription is done, the researcher is free to makes notes about any thoughts or impressions they have since they may, otherwise, be forgotten. These notes may be made on the left-hand margin and the right-hand margin reserved for noting themes which emerge in the analysis stage. Transcription might take eight times the length of the interview. Furthermore, it is desirable not to take short cuts when transcribing the data.

Data analysis

The IPA method, as presented in the literature, may be seen as consisting of four to six main steps. The precise number depends somewhat on the number of interviews carried out and, to a lesser extent, on the duration of the interviews. A single case may be appropriate. Not surprisingly, many of these steps can be seen to be highly reminiscent of the steps in other forms of qualitative analysis:

Step 1   **Initial case familiarisation and initial comments**   As in any qualitative research, the researcher needs to have a high level of familiarity with their data. This is achieved in part by collecting the data oneself, if possible, but also through doing the transcription and eventually reading and re-reading through those transcripts a number of times. The transcription has two margins on each side and the researcher may use the left-hand margin to make a note of anything which might occur to them as being of interest in the data. This is a little like memos in grounded theory. There are no particular rules about how this is achieved. For example, there is no reason to break the transcription down into units of any particular size and there is no requirement that comments are provided for all sections of the transcription. The analyst may include attempts to summarise or interpret what was said in the interview. At a later stage, the comments may seek to confirm, change or point out inconsistencies between what is said and the attempts to summarize or interpret what is in the transcript.

Step 2   **Preliminary theme identification**   Following further familiarisation with the data, the researcher begins to make notes of the major themes that can be identified in what is said in the transcript. The themes are summarised in a few words which constitute a brief phrase or title for the theme. As many words as do the job is the limit to this. The themes are written down in the right-hand margin against the text to which they refer. Basically, there should be a relationship between the theme and what it says in the text but the theme should be expressed in more theoretical or abstract terms. Anyone struggling with this stage might look at grounded theory (Chapter 8) for ideas about how to proceed.

Step 3   **Search for theme interconnections**   Of course, many of the themes that are identified may group together to form broader or superordinate themes. That is, the researcher examines their list of themes and looks for connections between them. These interconnections lead to ideas about what these superordinate themes might be. So a superordinate theme is a cluster of similar but partially distinct themes. Themes which seem to be similar may be listed together and given a more inclusive title. The development of superordinate themes may be carried out in the following ways:

- Electronically by 'copying and pasting' the names of the themes into a word processor document and then moving them around to form closely related clusters.
- The analysis could be carried out using a qualitative analysis computer program such as NVivo.
- Write the names of the themes on index cards or slips of paper. They can then be moved around on a large flat surface of a desk or table. The spatial connections between the themes can then be explored.

The researcher needs to ensure that the themes developed truly relate to what has been said in the interviews. So it is important to compare the theme

→

titles with the data which ostensibly belongs with the theme. So short excerpts (including the page and line number where they appear) of what the participant said which led to the themes should be compared with the superordinate theme title. Some themes may be dropped if they do not fit into any of the superordinate theme clusters – or because it turns out that there is generally little in the data which serves as evidence of the worth of the theme.

It is at this stage that a student researcher may become stuck in the analysis and needs to be helped to move their analysis forwards by thinking rather more conceptually than had previously been necessary to identify themes. Categories and themes need to be replaced by more abstract and superordinate levels of analysis – this is the interpretative stage. According to Biggerstaff and Thompson:

> Moving away from a purely descriptive level of analysis often poses a difficulty, probably because . . . students have a prior grounding in positivist approaches . . . and consequently may feel a sense of discomfort in making interpretations . . . Yet this is where some of the challenges faced by students encountering qualitative methodologies (including IPA) have arisen. In our experience, this fear, though still encountered in some students, is groundless at both theoretical and practical levels. (Biggerstaff & Thompson, 2008, p. 220)

Step 4   **Systematic table of themes**   This is a visual way of presenting the structure of superordinate and subordinate themes which have been developed out of the analysis. They are ordered in terms of their overall importance to what the participant was seen to have said, starting off with the most important superordinate theme. The table may include a short phrase from a participant's account to illustrate the theme. It should be noted where the information from the transcript is located. A generic table illustrating this is provided in Table 11.3.

TABLE 11.3 **The structure of the illustrative quotations table for the superordinate Theme A: The phenomenon of paranoia.**

Superordinate Theme A: The phenomenon of paranoia	Superordinate Theme B	Superordinate Theme C
(a) Perception of harm: *'People would sit around talking about me, I thought'* Victor 1	(a) Sub-category 1: Illustrative quote	(a) Sub-category 1: Illustrative quote
(b) Type of harm: *'It felt like people I hardly knew were backstabbing me'.* Janet 1	(b) Sub-category 2: Illustrative quote	(b) Sub-category 2: Illustrative quote
(c) Intention of harm: *'It felt like I was being deliberately persecuted.'* Norman 2	(c) Sub-category 3: Illustrative quote	
(d) Acceptability of the belief: *'It was MIS that was behind all of the plotting and telephone tapping.'* Mary 1		

In their work, Campbell and Morrison (2007) refer to the broadest themes as superordinate themes and the sub-categories (e.g. Perception of harm) as master themes.

Based on Campbell and Morrison (2007) and Howitt and Cramer (2008).

Step 5 Analysis of further cases   Where the study is not a single case study, the analysis proceeds to the other cases in much the same way. Themes from the first case may be used for the ensuing cases but, alternatively, each of the new cases can be examined anew. Given the idiographic–nomothetic distinction used in IPA, the researcher needs to consider where the themes are similar between different participants and where they are different and exclusive to a particular individual. This gives an indication of the nature of the variation across different cases. Once all of the transcripts have been analysed, it is appropriate to produce the final table containing the thematic structure unravelled in the analysis. It will take a similar structure to that in Table 11.3.

Step 6 Writing up the analysis   The write-up – a project report, a dissertation, a journal article – is best conceived as the final stage of the analysis. This is a common assumption in qualitative research. The report needs to include all of the themes which seemed important in the analysis. Each needs to be carefully described and illustrated with exact quotes from the interview transcripts. Each example should be clear and sufficient to illustrate the theme. The report is where the researcher interprets or makes sense of what participants have said. It is important to make it clear what is interpretation and the basis on which the interpretation has been built. There are two ways of presenting the results in a report. One way is to divide the report into a separate 'Results' and 'Discussion' section. This 'Results' section should describe and illustrate the themes but the 'Discussion' section should show the relationship between the themes identified and the existing literature on the research topic in question. The other way is to have a single 'Results and Discussion' section where the presentation of each theme is followed by a discussion of the literature that is relevant to that theme. Either is acceptable. (See Chapter 13 for a fuller discussion of qualitative report writing.)

Box 11.2 illustrates the use of IPA in the context of a case study approach.

Box 11.2

ILLUSTRATIVE RESEARCH STUDY

Interpretive phenomenological analysis: the alcoholic woman and self and identity

Shinebourne and Smith (2009) describe a case study using IPA of an alcoholic woman's experience of addiction and its impact on her sense of self and identity. Adopting a case study approach involving a single individual is an accepted procedure with IPA. So this research represents the nomothetic orientation of some IPA research. IPA researchers argue that where a person's descriptions of their experiences are exceptionally rich or where the case in question is particularly compelling for other reasons, the case study approach becomes particularly appropriate. There are copious amounts of quantitative research available on alcoholism and alcohol use. Although qualitative research is not so common there is a belief that qualitative methods make available to the researcher the lives of alcoholics as they are actually lived. Radley and Chamberlain (2001) make an argument for the unique power of the case study which renders the research impossible to reduce to a few variables.

The 31-year-old single woman in the study is given the name Alison. She was an attendee at a women's day centre concerned with problematic alcohol use. Although the researchers interviewed four women in total, Alison's interview material was exceptionally rich and detailed. The researchers had a prepared interview schedule which they applied flexibly. Three separate interviews were conducted with Alison, producing about three hours' worth of recordings which were transcribed verbatim for the purposes of the analysis. The first interview was carefully reviewed and issues for further discussion were noted and raised at the second interview. Some of the original questions were returned to in each of the three interviews. This interview structure is an interesting one and may have advantages for relatively inexperienced researchers.

The analysis process followed the initial stages which are outlined in the present chapter. Of course, it was a case study so some of the later stages were not included. Radley and Chamberlain's analysis reports not just the superordinate themes but sub-themes too. In addition, very short illustrative quotations were selected for each theme and the line numbers on the transcript from which they were taken also noted. The theme structure is illustrated in Table 11.4 although the original paper simply reports the superordinate and sub-themes as a list. This table of themes is the outcome of the sort of back-and-forth process between stages of the analysis which is a feature of most qualitative data analysis methods – if not all of them.

According to the researchers, the first theme illustrates how Alison sees the experience of drunkenness as one of 'flux, oscillation and instability' (p. 155), the second theme presents the

TABLE 11.4 Shinebourne and Smith's (2009) summary of themes with illustrative quotes and page numbers

Superordinate Theme 1: The experience of the self as drunk	Superordinate Theme 2: I created such a character for myself	Superordinate Theme 3: Perception of the self
Metaphoric expressions of the experience of being drunk. 'Big wave' 449	The self changing through drinking. 'Having to drink so much in order to get to this person' 44-45	Metaphors expressing perception of self. 'Mixture of water and fire' 809
Escalating drinking. 'It would just spiral and spiral' 25	The process of becoming the other self. 'My body was taking over a character' 40	Positive appraisals of self. 'Quiet and contemplative' 66
The harmful experience of being drunk. 'Having blackouts, memory loss' 15	Feeling the other self. 'Feeling totally in my body' 1052	Negative appraisals of self. 'I can't really assert myself' 1015
The high and the low of the drinking experience. 'Creative and energetic and interesting' 498	The porous body. 'When you are drunk you are open to spirits visiting your body' 475	Moral judgements of self. 'Guilt and anxiety you have done something wrong' 504-505
Ambivalence and dilemmas. 'If only I could get to that without so much alcohol' 488	The self as a process of becoming. 'From one day to the next I really do change' 1110	

transformation of Alison into another personality when drunk, and the third theme illustrates how Alison sees herself as many different parts and her ambivalence about drinking. Each of these superordinate themes is discussed at some considerable length in Shinebourne and Smith (2009). It is interesting to note how in the original paper, the authors related this final theme of different parts to the general psychological literature on dissociative experiences. In particular, they draw on the work of Seligman and Kirmayer (2008) who:

> maintain that the association between dissociative experiences and trauma is predominantly a Euro-American conception as understood in the psychiatric perspective. In contrast, dissociative experiences in many socio-cultural contexts 'seem to be associated with the expression of alternative selves or identities that were not created in the context of trauma'. (Shinebourne and Smith, 2009, p. 41)

This, of course, provides a refreshingly different perspective on Alison's experiences.

When to use interpretative phenomenological analysis

IPA is about people's experiences. So if the research is about how people have personally experienced significant phenomena such as pain or serious illness then IPA is a consideration in terms of methodology. IPA is not a general tool to tackle any form of qualitative data in the way that thematic analysis and grounded theory can be. Furthermore, IPA is not a finely tuned analysis of how people talk about their experiences. It is a 'what they say' rather than 'how they say it' method. King *et al.* make the distinction more eloquently:

> There is no question that, as a qualitative methodology, phenomenological psychology contrasts with psychologies of the 'discursive turn.' The work of phenomenologists often rests on language, of course. The interviewee 'expresses' her experience; the researcher reads this expression in terms of socially available constructs. Nothing is clearer. The words and the experience – there is a great distinction here between phenomenological and discursive approaches. For, though there is no resistance at all among phenomenologists to the fundamental experience-shaping function of language and discursive practices, the strongly held position of phenomenology is that it is *of experience that language speaks* . . . (King *et al.*, 2008, p. 82)

Of course, the potential research topics which centre around the theme of 'experience' is enormous. Indeed, it is hard to think of many areas of human activity for which how they are 'experienced' is irrelevant.

It is obvious that most of the topics that IPA researchers have addressed are ones which require sensitivity on the part of researchers which the typical student of psychology will not have achieved. So care needs to be exercised before jumping into IPA research lest you step painfully on the sensibilities of your research participants. This is not to suggest that IPA should be out of bounds to student researchers, merely that it may stretch their interpersonal skills and may need careful handling.

Evaluation of interpretative phenomenological analysis

The good news about IPA for many psychologists is that it is an approach to qualitative analysis which grows out of the traditions of psychology. So when one studies an IPA-based paper the very strong impression emerges that it is rooted firmly in psychology. This is so for both qualitative research and quantitative research in psychology. IPA is not at 'war' with mainstream psychology in the way some other qualitative methods present themselves on occasion. So, for example, it is difficult to find in IPA studies the antipathy to cognitive psychology that can be found in discourse analysis.

At the same time, IPA as a method is nowhere near so highly developed as some other qualitative analysis methods. This may be responsible for the lack of fierce methodological debates in IPA compared with other data analysis methods. Perhaps it is early days for IPA procedures and that schisms have simply not had time to develop. IPA is a broad approach to data collection and analysis which is about the development of a specific area of research – people's experiences of significant life events. As such, IPA does not seem to be as concerned to develop a coherent body of phenomenological theory in the way that other qualitative methods delve deeply into developing their theoretical infrastructure. No doubt this will gradually change and a systematic phenomenological approach will emerge enveloped in new theoretical ideas.

Any researcher new to qualitative research and IPA probably will be less perplexed by its data collection methods than by the process of analysis. Just how does a researcher go about the process of interpreting what is said in an interview in a way which moves beyond the literal meaning of the words to their psychological implications? No matter how close a description is to a full account of the analytic process, there is a stubborn void when it comes to explaining just how to go about an interpretation. Of course, previous theory may be a starting point but it is not a necessary starting point in IPA. Smith discusses this very problem in relation to hermeneutic analysis in general, irrespective of discipline:

> I am left feeling there is still a gap, however: When I try to make sense of this person saying this thing, what is actually happening? Interpretation is a mystery, invokes a sense of wonder and I'm not sure the hermeneutic theory has got near to explaining or saying all there is to say about that mysterious process. Partly because the type of encounter envisaged by hermeneutics was different, when it comes to explaining what is happening when one person tries to make sense of what another person is saying, I would suggest there is still a great deal that remains unknown. (Smith, 2007, p. 11)

Perhaps it is not comforting to know that even the experts have the very problems faced by the rest of us. But at least it is a shared frustration. Again, the more one reads publications on any method the sooner one not only appreciates the difficulties but experiences the various types of analytic solutions that researchers have put forward.

You will find a discussion of template analysis in Box 11.3. This has many similarities to IPA but may be more varied in the ways in which themes are identified. Meier, Boivin and Meier (2008) discuss a procedure called theme-analysis which has many of the characteristics of thematic analysis discussed in Chapter 7. However, like IPA, theme-analysis is built solidly on phenomenological approaches to psychology. They present a detailed account of their method, which has both qualitative and quantitative components. Specifically, it is an approach to the changes which occur during psychotherapy.

Box 11.3

KEY CONCEPTS

Template analysis

IPA is not the only way of analysing qualitative data in a way which generates themes. The point of template analysis is to generate a coding scheme (template) which identifies the themes in the data as developed in the researcher's analysis and organises them in a way which is both meaningful and productive. In template analysis the themes are arranged in a hierarchical manner with the broadest categories at the top of the hierarchy and the narrowest themes at the bottom of the hierarchy. The themes, in part, may be developed *a priori* (in advance) of the data analysis. The sources of ideas may well be pre-existing theories, though, equally, they may be the insight of the researcher or dependent on directly examining the data. No matter the source of the themes, they must be established as worthwhile against the actual data. Themes essentially capture the perceptions and experiences of the participants.

Unlike, say, grounded theory, coding in template analysis merely consists of checking the template themes against the data to indicate places in the data where a particular theme can be identified and placing a label or code next to it. Once an apparently satisfactory template is developed on part of the data, it is applied and evaluated against all of the data and, perhaps, modified in the light of this.

See King (1998) and Crabtree and Miller (1999) for discussions of templates.

CONCLUSION

Compared with discourse analysis (Chapter 9), for example, IPA seems to be much more content orientated. That is, the domain of IPA is phenomena as experienced by the individual – albeit interpreted through the analysis of the researcher. Although its origins are in the fields of social and health psychology, human experience is an important aspect of many fields of psychology. Thus, IPA eventually may have a niche throughout much of the discipline. Since IPA is built on theories of human experience (especially phenomenology and hermeneutics), one would not expect it to compete with qualitative methods primarily concerned with the theory of language (e.g. conversation analysis and discourse analysis). While the potential is there for a researcher to explore the role of language in action in IPA, this is not too easy a task since IPA accepts that at the core of what people say is something of substance which warrants interpretation and analysis in its own right – not quite the subjectivist/relativist position of other qualitative methods.

Cognitive psychology is often very critically addressed by exponents of discourse analysis – perhaps a better phrase is that cognitive psychology is rejected in discourse analysis. This is most certainly not the case with IPA which accommodates to theory about internal psychological states and cognition. IPA is about a psychological phenomenon which theories of language as action simply do not attempt to incorporate – experience. Probably there could be an extensive debate about the extent to which experience is mediated through language but the bottom line is that IPA theorists do not need to take a strong position on this. They simply need appropriate ways of developing theory about experience.

In short, IPA has radically different historical origins from many of the other methods of qualitative data analysis in this book. Its openness to traditional psychological approaches while insisting on the importance of human experience makes it more amenable to researchers firmly committed to mainstream psychology. One does not have to abandon a belief that mainstream psychology has made substantial progress in terms of understanding the person to be attracted to IPA.

KEY POINTS

- Interpretative phenomenological analysis developed out of the work of health psychologists in the 1990s. Its historical roots are primarily in the philosophies of phenomenology and hermeneutics though the influence of sociology (especially symbolic interactionism) and psychology, in general, are also readily apparent.

- IPA, regarded as a derivative of the phenomenological tradition in psychology and philosophy, is clearly distinguishable from traditional phenomenology in that the researcher is not the person whose experiences are studied. Instead people having undergone significant types of life experience provide descriptions of their experiences. The researcher both describes and interprets these experiences using a variety of psychological concepts and theories.

- IPA shares many techniques with other qualitative methods. In particular, the primary aim of the analysis is to identify themes in what participants have to say about their experiences. The main processes of analysis involve the literal transcription of pertinent interview data which is then processed by suggesting themes which draw together aspects of the data. Further to this, the researcher may seek to identify superordinate (or master) themes which embrace a number of themes identified during the analysis process.

- IPA theory tends to be rather more inclusive of general psychological theory of many different sorts than, say, grounded theory which proponents claim is incompatible with certain kinds of psychological theorising. In many ways, IPA is situated relatively close to thematic analysis – its methods are similar. Nevertheless, thematic analysis lacks the content specificity and theoretical underpinnings which characterise IPA.

ADDITIONAL RESOURCES

Birkbeck College, University of London (2009). Interpretative Phenomenological Analysis. http://www.ipa.bbk.ac.uk/references (accessed 20 August 2009).

Eatough, V., and Smith, J.A. (2008). Interpretative phenomenological analysis. In C. Willig and W. Stainton-Rogers (Eds.), *The SAGE Handbook of Qualitative Psychology*. Los Angeles: Sage, pp. 179–195.

Smith, J.A., and Eatough, V. (2006). Interpretative phenomenological analysis. In G.M. Breakwell, S. Hammond, C. Fife-Shaw and J.A. Smith (Eds.), *Research Methods in Psychology*, 3rd Edition. London: Sage, pp. 322–341.

Smith, J.A., and Osborn, M. (2008). Interpretative phenomenological analysis. In J.A. Smith (Ed.), *Qualitative Psychology: A practical guide to research methods*, 2nd Edition. London: Sage, pp. 53–80.

Smith, J.A., Larkin, M., and Flowers, P. (2009). *Interpretative Phenomenological Analysis: Theory, method and research: understanding method and application*. London: Sage.

Storey, L. (2007). Doing interpretative phenomenological analysis. In E. Lyons and A. Coyle (Eds.), *Analysing Qualitative Data in Psychology*. London: Sage, pp. 51–64.

Walton, C. (2007). Doing discourse analysis. In E. Lyons and A. Coyle (Eds.), *Analysing Qualitative Data in Psychology*. London: Sage, pp. 35–50.

CHAPTER 12

Narrative analysis

Overview

- Narrative is a story linking events in a chronological fashion. It involves an interpretation of what we and others do and is produced during social interaction. Narratives are overwritten with moral, evaluative and other themes which are important in understanding how the individual relates to the events.

- Narrative psychology has grown since the 1980s to study the 'storied' self of people. This, basically, is the idea that people think, perceive, imagine and act morally according to narrative structures. Narrative psychology is concerned with the content, structure and function of the stories which we create to account for what is happening to us.

- Narrative analysis is a form of qualitative analysis which is dependent on the ideas developed in narrative psychology. This stresses how narrative is a metaphor for personality. Narrative can be analysed using a wide range of qualitative methods. However, the phrase narrative analysis is best reserved for analyses based on the theory underlying narrative psychology – rather than, say, discursive psychology.

- In a narrative, there are changes that occur over a period of time which involve a number of different characters and some form of action. The term 'emplotment' is used to describe how the narrative is put together, including plots and subplots.

- Narrative may be understood using virtually any qualitative research method. For example, social constructionist approaches to narrative concentrate on the ways in which narrative is produced in social interaction. However, this constructionist point of view is not the focus of narrative analysis based on narrative psychology. This sometimes offers a 'realist' interpretation of narratives which assumes that narrative can help the researcher understand how an individual thinks and feels about substantial and ongoing aspects of their life.

- The roots of narrative psychology can be seen in the writings of Wilhelm Wundt, Sigmund Freud, John Dollard, Charlotte Buhler and Gordon Allport. In particular, the interest of some of these in researching people's life stories or life history was fundamental to the emergence of narrative psychology. However, the work of Theodore Sarbin and Jerome Bruner in the late twentieth century was the immediate stimulus to its development.

- The narrative interview can take a number of forms. Perhaps the most systematic is that of McAdams, which helps the interviewee generate a narrative-based account of important events in their life. These interviews are the commonest material on which narrative analysis is carried out.

- Narrative analysis proceeds in a number of different ways. This chapter discusses Crossley's approach in the main.

What is narrative analysis?

The term 'storied self' appears in discussions of narrative. This refers to the way in which we create our 'self' using narratives and stories to account for what has happened or what is happening to us:

> Narrative psychology is concerned with the structure, content, and function of the stories that we tell each other and ourselves in social interaction. It accepts that we live in a storied world and that we interpret the actions of others and ourselves through the stories we exchange. Through narratives we not only shape the world and ourselves but they are shaped for us through narrative. (Murray, 2003, p. 95)

People who have undergone some sort of trauma provide instances of how they often try to make sense of the events that they are going through by creating stories or narratives. A narrative is essentially a written or spoken account of connected events with an underlying time dimension. It is a story and takes the form of a story. This definition, however, fails to indicate just how much our narratives have to do with social interaction and matters such as identity. A narrative is closer to being a substantial chunk of one's life (a life history) than it is about what happened, say, when we went out last night. To tell a friend on the telephone that you went to the movies last night and had an ice cream does not amount to a meaningful narrative for the purposes of narrative analysis. According to Sarbin:

> The story has a beginning, middle and an ending. The story is held together by recognizable patterns of events called plots. Central to the plot structure are human predicaments and attempted resolutions. (Sarbin, 1986, p. 3)

In this chapter, we will regard narrative analysis as a system of analysing narratives using the basic concepts of narrative psychology. However, researchers from other disciplines (and sometimes within psychology) would have a very different view of what narrative analysis is. We will see something of this range during the course of this chapter.

The difficulty of locating narrative analysis as a field of research

Narrative analysis is a very widely used term which is not always used exclusively for qualitative research (Garson, n.d.). Leaving the quantitative approaches aside, there are several different approaches to understanding narrative, some of which have their origin in linguistics and sociology but the origins of others are the work of psychologists. While it is difficult to draw the boundaries for the topic of narrative since it spreads through several disciplines, one can meaningfully identify the start of narrative psychology as being in the 1970s and especially the 1980s under the influence of psychologists such as Jerome Bruner, Theodore Sarbin, and Kenneth and Mary Gergen. Given this wide disciplinary interest in narrative, it is not surprising to find that the various approaches do not boil down to a single central method. Figure 12.1 gives a brief glimpse of some influences of other disciplines on narrative, important events in the history of narrative psychology, and aspects of narrative analysis. There are also forms of therapy based on narrative (e.g. White & Epston, 1990). Of course, a person's identity which can be studied through narrative is of therapeutic importance. The important thing here is that narrative analysis is just part of the research field 'narrative' and that other disciplines have their own approaches to the topic. Narrative analysis is a multitude of different things,

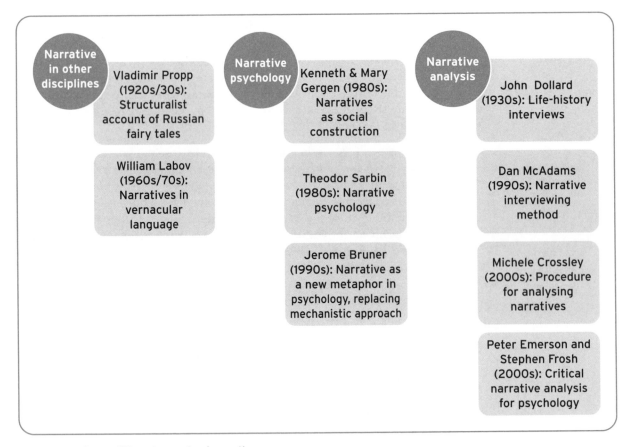

FIGURE 12.1 **Some different aspects of narrative**

as we shall see, and it is difficult to specify just what its boundaries are. Narrative analysis is probably too young a field in psychology for a complete consensus to have emerged about exactly what it is and how it is done.

Narrative analysis does not usually involve the fine-grained, line-by-line analyses which characterise, say, some discourse analysis and all conversation analysis (Chapters 9 and 10). Of course, if the researcher wishes to study just how a person constructs versions of their self, for example, through language and conversation in the form of narrative then discourse analysis and conversation analysis may be the appropriate choice. Such an essentially social constructionist (see Box 1.2 in Chapter 1) position on narrative is advocated by Kenneth and Mary Gergen as a way of understanding narratives. More usually, however, narrative analysis as discussed in this chapter accepts that people construct their selves, their identities, their attitudes and so forth in ways which differ according to the social context of the construction. Nevertheless, it also takes the view that narratives communicate things which are the reality of people's lives as they live them. In other words, one point of view is to treat narratives as the person saying something about the real experiences of their lives (e.g. Crossley, 2000).

What is a narrative?

According to Murray (2003), narrative functions to provide order where there is disorder. In other words, the narrator is attempting to bring organisation to something which is essentially disorganised and, consequently, lacking meaning. Disruptions to life due to personal, financial, health or other problems provide challenges to the everyday routine and narratives help to restore order and meaning. Consequently, narrative psychology has adherents in the fields of clinical and health psychology where such stressors are commonplace among clients. McAdams (2008) suggests that there are six agreed principles which can be drawn from narrative psychology concerning personal narratives (as opposed to, say, the narratives in books). Personal narratives are sometimes referred to as self-narratives in the narrative psychology literature. The putative agreed principles are:

- Principle 1: The self is storied.
- Principle 2: Narratives integrate lives and provide a coherent account of the individual 'scenes' in the narrative.
- Principle 3: Narratives are told in social relationships.
- Principle 4: Narratives change over time.
- Principle 5: Narratives are cultural texts and reflect the culture and the culture's ways of talking narratively.
- Principle 6: Some narratives are better than others in that narratives are intrinsically intertwined with morality and that some personal narratives reflect psychologically more healthy selves.

These principles are largely self-evident, of course, yet big steps in terms of an alternative to aspects of mainstream psychology.

Broadly, narrative psychology is concerned with the stories which we produce to tell about ourselves and the implications of these stories for understanding our lives. This is a natural part of interaction and people speak narratively even when they have not been asked to do so. Narratives have a point to them which may be in the form of some sort of moral message. Narrative analysis is the application of concepts from narrative psychology to understanding the narratives produced by individuals. In narrative analysis the researcher concentrates on specific instances of narrative to understand the ways in which stories are made by people and how these stories are used in order to understand the world. The perspective of narrative analysis is primarily that of the teller of the story, not the hearer of the story. The hearer (the researcher) carries out the analysis and interpretation but the focus is the person supplying the narrative. It is part of the task of the researcher to elicit suitable data for analysis and there are special techniques of qualitative interviewing which encourage the production of suitable narrative information.

Narratives, then, are part of the way in which people represent their self and the social world both publicly to others and privately to themselves. The main characteristics of a narrative are as follows:

- A narrative involves some sort of transformation which occurs over time.
- There is some sort of action.
- There are various characters.

The word 'emplotment' is sometimes used to describe the ways in which the various parts of a narrative are put together to make a story which would include major plots, some subplots, and diversions and digressions from the main story. The plot gives a narrative structure and connects the story's beginning with the story's end. But, more than that, the plot links different episodes in order to tie the story together.

It should be very clear that the following is *not* a narrative account of someone's life:

> I left school when I was sixteen and worked at various jobs for a while. Nevertheless, when I was twenty I went to university. During my time there I became engaged to Chris and we got married three years later. We have three children. I work as a lawyer and my partner is an accountant.

It is not simply that the story is short. The problem is it is little more than a few 'beads on a string' (Dollard, 1935, p. 3). What is clearly lacking is any truly personal information and any use of information in a way which reflects the culture in which the life is lived. Look at the following and the richer narrative style quickly becomes apparent.

> My father died when I was eleven and there wasn't a lot of money in the family though we were well cared for. So I left school when I was sixteen to get some cash. I remember that at one stage I had three jobs at one time and helped Mum in a small way financially. Nevertheless, when I was twenty I went to university because mother had remarried and didn't need me so much. I didn't have much of a sense of direction in my life until I met Chris, my partner since then. When things were more secure, we got married three years later when Emma, our first child, was on the way. I was offered a job by her father in his law firm. She felt it important to have the security of a career and she has worked as an accountant ever since the children got a bit older.

Of course, it is part of the task of the researcher to carry out their research in ways which are conducive to the production of rich narrative. Otherwise it might not happen. Of course, qualitative interviewing is one way of getting rich data but geared to the needs of the research. So, qualitative interviews are typical of the data used in narrative analysis.

Narratives have a range of functions in the context of social interaction including the following:

- Holding the attention of others in conversation – once a story is being told then the chances of being interrupted by another is reduced.

- Narratives can be used to provide a way of looking at problems faced by the individual. The narrative can be used to blame others or life's circumstances for the individual's problems.

- Narratives can be used to evidence things that the individual claims. For example, rather than simply express a dislike or prejudice against a neighbour, putting things in the form of a story from one's own experiences tends to be more accepted and successful.

Social constructionism and narrative

Of course, the way in which a narrative is structured depends on factors such as who is the narrator, who is the audience and what is the social context. But it can also be treated as something more real – something representing the substance of people's lives. Thus narrative is slightly problematic within qualitative psychology since it can be regarded as a form of social product in the context of social constructionism. The consequence of this is that the narrative should be regarded as emerging out of the situation of its production and that it will vary accordingly. This is very evidently the basis of the narrative theory of Gergen and Gergen (1983). In contrast, many narrative theorists tend to view a narrative more as if it were some form of *ethnographic* testimony. William Labov (1927–), a linguist who studied vernacular narratives, regarded narratives as essentially real (Labov, 1972). One of the key characteristics of postmodern, qualitative psychology is the rejection of the idea that there is a 'self' or 'identity' which can be studied as if they were some physical object, unchanging and immutable. Social constructionist views of the self hold that self and identity are intimately and inseparably linked to language and language practices which are part and parcel of our everyday lives and social interaction. As a consequence, the postmodernist view is that there is no archetypal self which can be understood in isolation from the practices of social interaction and interpretation. According to Crossley (2007), 'If there is no "one" essential nature or self to describe, then the concept of "a" self, of "having" or "possessing" a self, must be abandoned' (p. 132).

Typically, social constructionist approaches to psychology have a difficulty. This boils down to the question of what is happening when people are using language – just what is going on inside of the person when they produce conversation, etc. of the sort that discourse analysts and conversation analysts focus upon? Surely people can be reflexive in the production of language, for example, so just how does this work? By concentrating on what can be observed in language and conversation, discourse analysis and conversation analysis simply side-step important psychological issues, the argument goes. This is sometimes referred to as the *loss of the subject*. If narrative psychology is to avoid the social constructionist's loss of the subject then the idea that narratives allow the construction of a variety of subjective positions none of which is the 'real' position has to be replaced. Narrative psychology provides an approach to analysis offering opportunities to include this missing subjective element. The subjective element is regarded as 'essentially personal, coherent and "real"' (Crossley, 2007, p. 131). The way in which a person thinks and feels about what is happening to them is a psychological reality. This is not to deny that people can be contradictory, fragmentary, varied and changeable in terms of how they construct matters in different contexts. It is merely to argue that within this range of possibilities it is usually possible to identify a coherence or relationship between what people say and their experience of self.

So, according to Crossley, narrative psychology adopts what she describes as an underlying realist epistemology (though not all narrative psychologists would agree with this as we have seen). The idea is that there are facts about a person's conscious experiences of self, etc. which are there to be found out and known by the researcher and it is the task of narrative psychology to seek out and know these 'facts'. None of this is to reject the relativist argument but it is to imply that somewhere there is a usable degree of consistency – that there is 'something' there. In contrast, the constructionist discourse analysis would regard this as a fundamental (and fatal) problem and reject the use of language to study an individual's experience of a single self. Instead, the discourse analyst would look at the various ways in which self is constructed in the narrative or the narrative interview. Crossley is essentially putting forward the critical realism viewpoint although she does not identify this as such.

A narrative is usually longer than the 'accounts' which are a feature of discourse analysis. The discourse analyst's task can be achieved with relatively short pieces of text but not so narrative analysis. If we take for granted that psychological narrative analysis has the core task of exploring self and identity, then substantive narratives are needed in order to carry out this work. Furthermore, narrative psychologists concentrate on the actual contents of the narrative rather than its discursive features. The narrative will concern some significant event or trauma in the person's life. These events are the reason why the narrative has been produced in the first place. Examples of topics which could be effectively studied using narrative analysis are the experience of childbirth, pregnancy, stillbirth and abortion. Of course, these are the very sorts of topic which interpretative phenomenological analysis (Chapter 11) could also research.

The development of narrative analysis

Some psychologists in the early twentieth century were adherents of the life history, which is essentially narrative, as a means of studying important aspects of people's real lives. According to Murray (2003) we can trace the study of narratives in psychology at least back to Wilhelm Wundt (1832–1920) who in his *Volkerpsychologie* would stress the importance of myths in human life. Others have suggested that Sigmund Freud (1856–1939) developed his psychoanalytic theories by listening to the narratives of his patients in therapy. The names of John Dollard (1900–1980), who we discussed in Chapter 2, and

Charlotte Bühler (1893–1974), a German-born psychologist who helped develop humanistic psychology and was interested in development over the lifespan (Bühler, 1933), should also be mentioned. She carried out studies, for example, exploring the diaries of adolescents. John Dollard's work was varied and included the famous frustration–aggression hypothesis. When he did his research in 'Southerntown' in the 1930s (Chapter 2), he initially was planning an interview study of the personality of Black people. Dollard explored life-history interviews to try to understand and define their qualities. His definition was:

> We will propose an initial common sense definition of the life history as a deliberate attempt to define the growth of a person in a cultural milieu and to make theoretical sense of it. It might include both biographical and autobiographical documents. It is not just an account of a life with events separately identified like beads on a string . . . ; if this were true, every man would be a psychologist, because every person can give us data of this type. The material must, in addition, be worked up and mastered from some systematic viewpoint. (Dollard, 1935, p. 3)

Although this is not quite the same as narrative (for one thing it is a broader approach), his definition can be seen as close to narrative since it includes a person in a cultural milieu and involved oral narratives among other things. In his book on the *Criteria for the Life History* he included other matters such as the role of the family in cultural transmission, the importance of specifying the social situation, and the importance of treating the individual as part of a culture.

Gordon Allport (1897–1967) is also frequently mentioned in the development of narrative psychology. His lifelong interest was in personality research where he developed a trait-theory to account for the ways in which people differ. However, his early work included a life-history study of refugees from Nazi Germany (Allport, Bruner & Jandorf, 1941). It is notable that Jerome Bruner, one of the authors of this report, was to write some highly influential material on narrative psychology nearly half a century later (e.g. Bruner, 1986).

Linguistic work in the 1920s had also begun to lay down the principles of narrative. Vladimir Propp (1895–1970) was born in Russia and worked in the field of folklore. His famous work was *Morphology of the Russian Folk Tale* which only gained circulation in the West in the second part of the twentieth century although it was published in Russia in 1928. He broke the folk tales into small narrative units which are referred to as 'narratemes' which essentially constitute the underlying structure of these folk tales. He identified 31 in all. These included (a) absentation, which involves a family member leaving the secure home environment, producing tension in the story; (b) interdiction in which the hero is warned not to do something; (c) violation of interdiction, which basically leads to the entry of the villain in the story, and so forth. Quite simply, Propp was suggesting structural elements that went into the various stories.

The study of written language, however, as important as it is, is not the only sort of language of interest to researchers including psychologists. During the 1960s, Labov championed the movement away from written language to studying the actual language spoken by people as members of communities. He also made clear the point that Dollard had been concerned with. That is, that narrative is something social but which is nevertheless accessed through individuals:

We study individuals because they give us the data to describe the community, but the individual is not really a linguistic unit. Many of the people in sociolinguistics disagree with me on this point, and they think that reality lies in the individual speaker, and I take the position that's just the reverse. There are no individuals from a linguistic point of view. (Quoted in Gordon, 2006, p. 341)

Labov established in the 1960s/1970s that the characteristics of conversation in real-life settings can be very different from what emerges in settings where people are being studied by the researcher. One exception to this is where the speaker uses narrative in research settings since this narrative seems to be very similar to the narrative of ordinary everyday conversation:

The effort to observe how speakers talked when they were not being observed created the Observer's Paradox. Among the partial solutions to that paradox within the face-to-face interview, the elicitation of narratives of personal experience proved to be the most effective. (Labov, 1997, p. 395)

For Labov, a narrative structure is based on there being a temporal structure between a minimum of two clauses. If reversing the two clauses changes the interpretation of the order then these become narrative clauses. One of the principal things which Labov did (Labov, 1972; Labov and Waletsky, 1967) was to provide linguists and narrative psychologists with a general structure by which oral narrative can be understood as a sequential process. The structure of an oral narrative consists of:

- an orientation section (e.g. 'I was walking down the street with Sally who had just split up with her boyfriend');
- an optional summary or abstract in Labov's terms (e.g. 'Her ex caused a big row in public');
- a sequence of narrative clauses (e.g. 'We saw him on the other side of the street and tried not to let him know we had seen him');
- a complicating action which makes the events out of the ordinary (e.g. 'He walked over and began threatening me');
- a resolution (e.g. 'I told her to get away down the street and I was left to deal with him but he backed-off quickly');
- an optional coda/closing section (e.g. 'He's got a reputation for being a trouble maker and loosing it at the drop of a hat');
- an evaluation where the view of the narrator is made clear, though it can occur anywhere in the narrative and at more than one point (e.g. 'I suppose I was asking for trouble talking to Sally').

In personality theory, the influence of the narrative perspective was beginning to be felt in the 1970s and 1980s. In particular, Silvan Tomkins (1911–1991) began writing about script theory in personality. In this the individual creates a script of their emotional life, featuring salient scenes from their life. It is these different scripts and emotional scenes which constitute the important individual differences between people since these are unique to them (Tomkins, 1979). McAdams (1985) developed a life-story model of identity in which he contended that:

> . . . people begin, in late adolescence and young adulthood, to construe their lives as evolving stories that integrate the reconstructed past and the imagined future in order to provide life with some semblance of unity and purpose . . . The most important individual differences between people are thematic differences in the stories that comprise their narrative identities . . . apparent in the story's settings, plots, characters, scenes, images, and themes. (McAdams, 2006, p. 13)

The point of narrative theory in personality is that the narrative is internally generated and shows how a person's behaviour and experiences may be influenced by this as much as by the 'vagaries of external situations' (McAdams, 2006, p. 13).

However, it is the work of Theodore Sarbin and Jerome Bruner which tends to be identified as the foundation of modern narrative psychology. Theodore Sarbin (1911–2005) proposed that the tradition of mechanistic metaphor which underlies psychology should be replaced with narrative as the basic (or root) metaphor of the discipline. In dominant psychology, many of the characteristics of behaviourism can be seen still in the way humans are conceived. That is, they are treated as if they were mechanisms in which, for example, a stimulus resulted in a response. Thus, the basic metaphor of psychology is that of a machine. Sarbin proposed what he calls the narrator principle:

> . . . human beings think, perceive, imagine, and make moral choices according to narrative structures. Present two or three pictures, or descriptive phrases, to a person and he or she will connect them to form a story, an account that relates the pictures or the meaning of the phrases in some patterned way. On reflection, we discover that the pictures or meanings are held together by the implicit or explicit use of plot. (Sarbin, 1986, p. 8)

Of course, the shift in the underlying metaphor of psychology from that of a machine to that of a story is a radical and decisive shift. It is one which has important implications for how personality is studied. The change from the concentration on personality traits to personal stories is both a change from the nomothetic to the idiographic and a change to an understanding of the person over time rather than at the moment.

The work of Jerome Bruner (1915–) on narrative is to be found in his books *Actual Minds, Possible Worlds* (Bruner, 1986) and *Acts of Meaning* (Bruner, 1990). Bruner differentiates between two forms of thinking: (a) the paradigmatic mode – essentially the scientific method which involves classification and categorisation and (b) the narrative approach which concerns how we form everyday interpretations of our world which are expressed in the form of stories. For Bruner, the most clearly defining characteristics of narrative are as follows:

- It deals with people as if they were characters or actors in a unique story of things that happen and describes their mental states.

- The narrative need not be 'real' and so it can be imaginary.

- Narratives involve relationships between the exceptional events of the story and what is ordinary. The former can only be understood as extraordinary in terms of the latter.

In social psychology, Kenneth Gergen (1935–) and Mary Gergen (1938–) argued for a view of narrative which is firmly embedded in social constructionist thinking (Gergen & Gergen, 1983, 1986). This was rather different from, say, the conceptualisations of Propp concerning fairy tales and those of Labov concerning vernacular story telling which assume that there is something 'real' to be known from the study of narrative. It is inevitable that personal (or self) narratives are involved with the teller's identity. Gergen and Gergen argue that identity is socially constructed but, additionally, the social construction of self takes place through narrative. Gergen puts it this way:

> It is largely through discourse that we achieve the sense of individuated selves with particular attributes and self referential capacities. To be sure, there is 'something' beyond discourse, but what there is makes its way into the practices of cultural life largely through linguistic interpretation. With the discursive construction of identity foregrounded, there are significant ways in which identity is importantly fashioned through narrative. (Gergen, 1998, p. 10)

We have already indicated a social constructionist version of the nature of narrative leaves the researcher in a difficult position when questions of reality are raised. In social constructionist thinking there is an assumption that narrative is the product of interaction and context. It can also change, and another inter-action or another context will produce a different narrative. For that reason, a partial social constructionist view prevails in narrative analysis which accepts the basic argument but counters with the assertion that despite everything, there remains something of substance – something real – which can be learnt about the individual from narrative. In this respect, the Gergen and Gergen approach is something of a sideline in the field.

How to do narrative analysis

Any data which contains personal narratives might be suitable for analysis. Hiles and Čermák (2008) list the following among types of narrative:

- oral versus written narratives;
- fictional versus historical/personal narratives;
- life-story narratives versus isolated event narratives;
- crafted versus spontaneous narratives;
- public versus private narratives.

Murray (2003) suggests that in the research context, the interview is the most likely way of collecting narrative data. He suggests that the two main forms of interview are life-history interviews and episodic interviews. The life-history interview (biographical interview) might begin with a request that the participant tells the interviewer the story of their life starting as early in life as they wish right up to the present time. Probes may be interspersed as appropriate to facilitate the narrative process. The episodic interview is much more focused on particular topics of the life history and seeks to get an extended account of these. The potential range of topics is substantial, of course, and could include things such as one's first week at university, the death of a close relative, being in hospital and so forth.

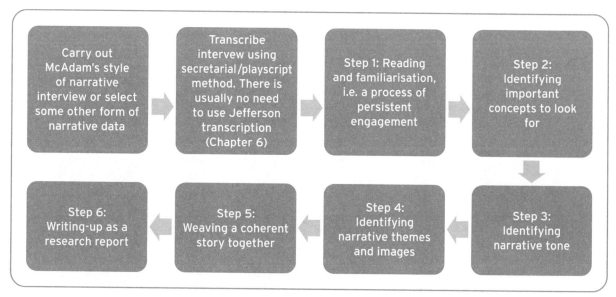

FIGURE 12.2 Crossley's (2007) analytic method for narrative analysis

Michele Crossley's approach to narrative analysis (Crossley, 2000, 2007) typically uses interview data but is not necessarily confined to this. The interviews that she uses are based on McAdams's (1993) procedure when interviewing for narrative analysis. Although much of what appears in Chapter 6 deals with the basics of qualitative interviewing, McAdams's approach is substantially different and has specific rather than generic applications so will be dealt with separately here. Figure 12.2 provides a schematic overview of the stages in Crossley's approach to narrative analysis, including extra considerations about the preliminary data collection phases.

Although a narrative analysis can be carried out on narratives not obtained using McAdams's protocol, *if* you are intending to collect fresh data for a narrative analysis then it may be wise to use McAdams's approach. The important point is to remember that you want your participant's narrative so aim for lengthy contributions from them and relatively short contributions from you. There are other forms of narrative collection (e.g. Mischler, 1986) but, for a novice, the McAdams method is accessible. If you wish to follow McAdams's protocol, you should cover the following areas or use his exact questions (see Figure 12.3):

● *Section 1: Life chapters* The interviewee should think of their life as a book containing a number of different chapters (up to about eight) and identify two or three main chapters. This section of the interview has the potential for being lengthy so it is wise to limit it to half an hour or so. The interviewee is (a) asked to name each chapter, (b) describe the broad contents of the chapter, and (c) explain how one chapter is followed by the next chapter.

● *Section 2: Key events* The interviewee should be asked about eight key events – which McAdams calls nuclear episodes. These could involve a specific occurrence, a critical incident, a peak experience, a low experience, a turning point or an early memory. The eight key events are:

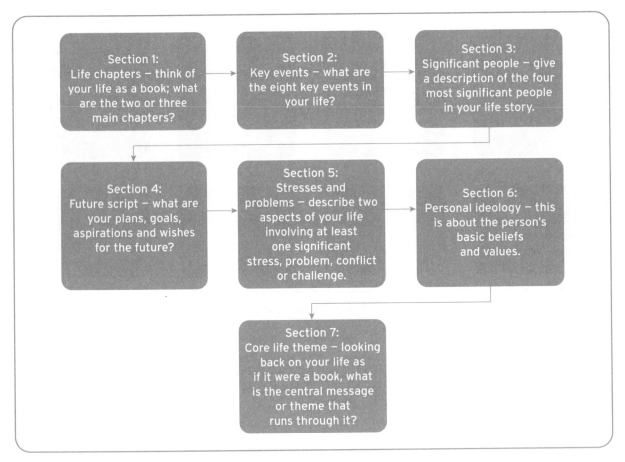

FIGURE 12.3 McAdams's (1993) semi-structured narrative interview protocol

(a) The peak experience/highspot of their life.

(b) The worst or lowest point of their life.

(c) A turning point in their life – this can be one that they only saw as a turning point retrospectively rather than when it happened.

(d) The earliest memory they have in their life with details such as who was present, the situation and feelings/thoughts.

(e) A very important childhood memory – good or bad – that stands out.

(f) An important memory from their adolescence – good or bad.

(g) An important memory from adulthood – after the age of 21 years – which may be good or bad.

(h) One other important memory from any stage of life.

- *Section 3: Significant people*   The interviewee is asked to give the name, relationship with themselves, and impact on their lives of *four* people. The list is limitless and ranges from parents through lovers to teachers, etc.

- *Section 4: Future script*   Up to this point, the interviewee will have talked about their past and their present. They are then asked about their plans and dreams for the future. Just how will the plan help them be creative in the future and contribute to the lives of others?

- *Section 5: Stresses and problems* We all have stresses and problems at some stage in our life histories. The interviewee is asked to describe two areas of life where such conflicts, stresses and problems have affected them.

- *Section 6: Personal ideology* This section of the interview considers the interviewee's basic beliefs and values by questioning them about their religious and political beliefs. The following areas are covered:

  (a) The participant is asked whether they believe in some sort of god or deity or a reigning force.

  (b) The participant is asked for a nutshell account of the religious beliefs.

  (c) The participant is asked to explain how their beliefs are different from those of most people they know, if they have any.

  (d) The participant is asked to describe how their religious beliefs changed during their life. Have they ever changed rapidly?

  (e) The participant is asked to describe their political orientation.

  (f) The participant is asked to explain what is the most important value in life.

  (g) The participant is asked to mention anything else that the interviewee could tell the researcher which would help the researcher understand the interviewee's basic beliefs and values about life and the world.

- *Section 7: Core life theme* At the end of the interview, the interviewee reflects back on their life story and identifies the core/life theme that runs through the narrative of their life.

According to Crossley (2000), interviews for narrative analysis should be sound-recorded to allow the interviewer the freedom to concentrate on what the interviewee is saying. Transcription should generally be the playscript/secretarial type for reasons of speed of transcription and keeping the transcription easy to read without the clutter of unnecessary detail. Of course, if for some reason the research question requires the sort of detail that goes into Jefferson transcription (Chapter 6) then it is appropriate to use it. Crossley suggests that such a basic transcript takes about four hours for every hour of interview. The transcript should have each line numbered and there should be wide margins on each side of the text much as with interpretative phenomenological analysis, for example. It is worth noting, however, that Hiles and Čermák (2008) recommend that the text is broken down into meaningful segments rather than arbitrary lines as in most transcription methods. In this approach, the segments would be numbered rather than the lines.

Step 1 Reading and familiarisation As with many qualitative data analysis methods, the first stage of the analysis is to read carefully through the transcript of the interview (or other narrative materials) repeatedly to achieve familiarity but also to think about the themes that appear to describe the data. Crossley (2007) suggests that six such readings is about the right number.

Step 2 Identifying important concepts to look for This involves trying to grasp the main elements of the narrative that need to be identified. Based on McAdams (1993), there are three areas to explore and get a feeling for in the transcript:

→ ● *Narrative tone*   Broadly speaking the tone of the narrative can be assessed from both the content of the individual's story and the way or form in which it is told. For example, an optimistic story can have that narrative tone because good things happen in the story. Alternatively, there can be an optimistic narrative tone not because of the bad things that happen but simply because the outcome is positive.

● *Imagery*   Each person uses a unique form of imagery in story telling which is characteristic of them. Just what sort of imagery does the individual use when describing the 'chapters' for their life narrative and the key events of their life? This may indicate 'personally meaningful images, symbols and metaphors' (Crossley, 2007, p. 140). The next question to ask is where do these images, symbols, and metaphors come from? Family background or time in the armed forces may have big influences on these, for example. Equally, the source may be a wider one from within the culture.

● *Themes*   What themes dominate in the narrative?

Step 3   **Identifying narrative tone**   Narrative tone should be assessed in terms of (a) the contents of the narrative and (b) the manner and style of reporting the experiences. This is more detailed than in Step 2. This is essentially a matter of judgment though it is not intrinsically difficult.

Step 4   **Identifying narrative themes and images**   Crossley (2007) argues that the researcher should look for both the narrative themes and the images at the same time. This is because there may be considerable overlap in terms of the themes and images. At this stage, you might wish to look at Box 12.1 which discusses six different interpretative perspectives which might be applied to the narrative.

Step 5   **Weaving all of this together into a coherent story**   The images and themes have now been identified but need to be put into a new story form – the story form of a report of a qualitative analysis.

Step 6   **Writing-up as a research report**   Analysis and writing-up are difficult to separate in qualitative research. Separating the two is somewhat arbitrary. This is a common comment on qualitative research practice. See Chapter 13 for details about writing-up qualitative research.

Box 12.2 describes the narrative analysis of the writings of a cancer sufferer.

Box 12.1

PRACTICAL ADVICE

Six interpretative perspectives that might be applied to the narrative analysis

Hiles and Čermák (2008) provide a model for what they call narrative oriented inquiry (NOI) though most of the steps in their approach are similar to those of Crossley (2000, 2007). What is helpful in their approach is that they suggest six different interpretative approaches for narrative analysis (Figure 12.4). It is these that we will concentrate on here.

- *Analytic perspective 1: Sjuzet-fabula*   This refers to the distinction between (a) the fibula which is the events which are being recounted in the narrative and (b) the sjuzet which is the way in which the events are being told in the narrative or the 'spin' of the narrator. The convention is that in the transcript of the data the sjuzet is underlined. The sjuzet is not essential to the narrative but it is essential to how the narrative is being told. So the analyst would go through the transcript underlining words, phrases or even entire segments which involve things such as 'emphasis, reflection, asides, interruptions, remarks, and various expressions representing the sequence/causality/significance of the events being related in the story' (Hiles and Čermák, 2008, p. 156). The separation of sjuzet from fabula is not without its problems, of course. Sometimes it will not be clear which of these two categories parts of the narrative belong to. To help deal with this, try reading the story but missing out the underlined material. What is read out ought to be passable as a story, though perhaps lacking much expressiveness. The underlined material (the sjuzet) is about how the narrator positions themselves in relation to the events.

- *Analytic perspective 2: The holistic-content perspective*   This is primarily about the events recounted in the narrative but not exclusively so. It involves searching for patterns within the story which link the narrative's key aspects with the total picture presented (i.e. the best way of describing the narrative overall). In other words, what are the major parts of the narrative and how do they relate to the entirety of the narrative? By repeatedly reading the narrative, different themes will become apparent, some of which recur at different points. These reoccurring themes are the important ones. At the same time, during the analysis the researcher needs to identify the core narrative – the one which is meaningful, stands out in terms of importance and which goes all the way through the narrative. How do the themes relate this major narrative?

- *Analytic perspective 3: The holistic-form perspective*   This concentrates on the narrative's form as opposed to its content. What is the plot of the narrative? Hiles and Čermák mention the four major categories of narrative: (a) romance, which means the affirmation of the social order rather than something to do with love; (b) comedy, which involves breaking then restoring the social order; (c) tragedy, which involves the loss of social order; and (d) satire, which involves a 'cynical challenge to the social order' (p. 157). Do any of these effectively describe the totality of the plot?

- *Analytic perspective 4: The categorical-content perspective*   This amounts to a sort of content analysis. The researcher, informed by their research question, identifies the themes which run through the narrative. These themes, in a qualitative analysis, are closely grounded in the data rather than imposed by the researcher.

→

- Sjuzet-fabula perspective
- Holistic-content perspective
- Holistic-form perspective
- Categorical-content perspective
- Categorical-form perspective
- Critical narrative analysis perspective

FIGURE 12.4 The main interpretative perspectives in psychological narrative analysis

- *Analytic perspective 5: The categorical-form perspective* This involves choosing some aspect of the narrative which is a particular feature. For example, crying might recur during the narrative. How does this relate to the general form of the narrative? Any feature could be chosen so long as it is about the form of the narrative rather than its content.

- *Analytic perspective 6: The critical narrative analysis perspective* This is the approach to narrative analysis presented in Emerson and Frosh's (2004) *Critical Narrative Analysis in Psychology*. In many ways this approach can be seen as clearly social constructionist since it concentrates on how viewpoints are built up, meanings created, and similar constructionist themes. Furthermore, the proposed methodology is based on a very close reading of the data of the sort which would not be uncommon in discourse analysis and which is a regular feature of conversation analysis. They refer to research on sexually abusive boys which was based on interview material. They suggest that this method provided them with narrative accounts which:

  a) makes more available the kinds of textual material that can contribute to understanding in their own words and from their own points of view how they make sense of themselves and their behaviour, and b) illustrate the social discourses, beliefs and assumption that may be organizing and sustaining these accounts. Thus, it is argued, personal narrative can offer a critical window on processes of social construction of gendered identity that, in relation to sexual abuse, have two apparently contradictory functions. On the one hand, they sustain the 'male monopoly' of abusiveness; but on the other hand, they may also show signs of, or resources for, resistance or alternatives to a boy's apprenticeship to discourses of abusive masculinity. (Emerson & Frosh, 2004, p. 17)

The reference to 'critical' is hinted at in this since what Emerson and Frosh are dealing with is male power, part of the agenda of any critical psychology.

Box 12.2
ILLUSTRATIVE RESEARCH STUDY

Narrative analysis: therapeutic emplotment in a famous cancer sufferer

Crossley (2003) took what she describes as a case study approach to a narrative analysis of the writings of the journalist John Diamond concerning the oral cancer that led to his death in 2001. Oral cancer is treatable if detected early but often it is not and about a quarter of sufferers die. John Diamond was the husband of the famous television chef Nigella Lawson and wrote a regular newspaper diary in which his experiences during the time of his illness were recorded. These were eventually published as a book together with another autobiographical account in a separate book. The diary entries were the basis of Crossley's analysis. According to Crossley, one of the most fundamental consequences of serious illness is the way in which it shatters our perceptions of our life's development and change over time. People see their lives as projecting into the future. Serious illness drastically changes this lived time since projections of life into the future are in some doubt; the start of a serious illness brings a 'halt' to life. Researchers have found that the major problem for people in such circumstances is to find a new or revised meaning to one's life. Narrative and storytelling are an important way of reattaching meaning to life. The term emplotment describes the process of making sense of life through narrative. Of course, other people impinge on these narratives - family, friends and the medical profession. Del Vecchio Good, Munakata, Kobayashi, MaHingley and Good (1994) describe what they call 'therapeutic emplotment' to refer to the interpretative activity which takes place within clinical interviews. In this, the medic and the patient 'create and negotiate a plot structure within clinical time, one which places therapeutic actions within the larger therapeutic story' (Del Vecchio Good et al., 1994, p. 855). Crossley saw in John Diamond's diary entries illustrations of this 'therapeutic emplotment'.

The diaries cover the period 1996-2001. There are six main stages which underlie John Diamond's diaries, according to Crossley. These are illustrated in Figure 12.5. The approximate duration of each stage is given since the slowness of the passage of time is a key feature of the diaries. Crossley explains that these stages come from a position of hindsight (knowing the outcome) and 'provide a fuller and more coherent picture' of the process than can be found in the original diaries. The following discuss some of the main ideas that Crossley mentions at each stage:

- *Pre-cancer: touch wood phase*   At this stage Diamond had thought that he had cancer but then believed this to be incorrect. So he describes how he played with the idea of imagining that he was someone who had just been diagnosed with cancer. He writes about practising the words 'I have cancer' in his head and asks about just how he should say them. Crossley suggests that it is almost as if saying the words and writing them down will, as in a superstition, make them untrue. He believed a 'definitive test' had shown that the lump in his neck was just an unusual sort of cyst. Distressingly, a little later John Diamond's doctor rang to say that he did have cancer. Of course this left him with a dilemma about whether he should deal with this in his column.

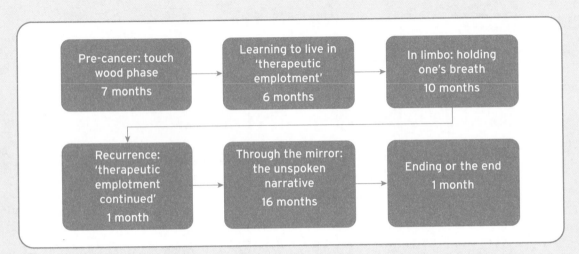

FIGURE 12.5 **The stages of John Diamond's diaries**

- *Learning to live in 'therapeutic emplotment'* In Crossley's paper, this is the longest section. During this period of time, John Diamond's diaries are dominated by descriptions of the various treatments and their effects. Rarely does the horizon of his future rise beyond the treatments; his focus is on the outcome of recovery. It seems that the diary column is being used as a way of coping with the illness and involves attempting to convince himself and his readers that things will turn out alright. He manufactures a sense of optimism in what he writes. Those around him tell him that he will be 'ok', though they probably don't believe what they are saying, he suggests, and the doctor presents the news of his cancer as if it would involve two months of misery followed something akin to bad sunburn due to the radiotherapy. The 'word' from everyone is of a positive prognosis and he goes along with this. He suggests that protracted illness lacks much by way of a plot and there is a sense of tedium about it. The person that he sees in the mirror is not him.

- *In limbo: holding one's breath* John Diamond's surgery and radiotherapy are complete. The 'therapeutic emplotment' had stressed the speed of the treatment process but ending with some sort of 'certainty'. Nevertheless, after all of this John Diamond did not know whether he was cured and he would not know this for weeks or even years. This uncertainty is hard to live with. According to Crossley, others in a similar position have documented this state of affairs.

- *Recurrence: 'therapeutic emplotment continued'* Nearly a year after his treatment had stopped, the cancer is back or, according to Diamond, it had never gone away. It is like 'back to business as usual' as he faces more surgery to restore his tongue. He summons more hope and finds some sort of comfort in the fact that this was the old cancer and not a new one emerging. He hopes to be able to speak better and still writes of there being a chance of a cure.

- *Through the mirror: the unspoken narrative* During this phase Diamond's belief in modern medicine is beginning to erode. He even suggests that part of himself thinks that he has become the victim of a medical confidence trick and his faith in the words of surgeons has failed. During a nine month period he writes about the experience of chemotherapy which he calls a 'stale hell' and he cannot sleep or eat. Diamond has become resigned as he enters a doctor's office to be told just how much longer he has to live. He has heard bad news 20 or more times before during the course of his cancer. However, he is told that he is in remission and that chemotherapy seems to have worked. Though he is in a sceptic phase, a few months later there is a swelling in his neck and the cancer has spread to his lungs.

- *Ending or the end*   About four years after the first appearance of his cancer, he begins to write about how the novelty of cancer has worn off and what he regarded as 'big news'. His cancer has become 'mundane' since cancer goes and comes back – that, for him at that stage, was the nature of cancer. During this phase the doctor tells John Diamond that they would have to start treatment again. His newspaper diary writes jokingly about chemotherapy and how he will have to wear one of those 'jokey' baseball caps like child leukaemia patients. But a week or so later, Diamond is rushed to hospital. The next day he is dead.

The concept of therapeutic emplotment allows one to see how cancer doctors provide a plot structure to patients for their lives in which the treatments are couched within a story of 'hope' – a belief that the patient will be cured. The experience is portrayed as one of immediacy and things being for the moment rather than involving distant horizons. Endings to the therapeutic emplotment are not often made explicit in therapeutic encounters. The focus is the treatment. According to Crossley (2003), John Diamond's diaries illustrate this therapeutic emplotment well in the stage of *Learning to live in 'therapeutic emplotment'*. Of course, there are other narratives which co-exist with that of therapeutic emplotment such as uncertainty and fear which will sometimes surface and, in John Diamond's case, were clearly evident in the stage of *'Through the mirror: the unspoken narrative'*.

In Crossley's (2003) paper some of the elements of her more general methodology can be seen, although some are naturally missing given the nature of the diary data with which she was working. Stripped of the methodology for collecting narratives through narrative interviews and the need to transcribe the interview, the paper is working with the bare bones of her suggested methodology. However, we can see all of the steps of the method described in this chapter in Crossley's paper (see Figure 12.2). Quite clearly, data familiarisation has to be thorough before any substantial analysis can begin. It is the second stage, *Learning to live in 'therapeutic emplotment'*, which is perhaps not quite what one is expecting from Crossley's (2000, 2007) account of her analytic procedures. It would seem that, in Step 2, an additional factor should be mentioned. That is, sometimes the important ideas for an analysis do not come out of the data but from a knowledge of the research literature and its reflection in the data. The concept of 'therapeutic emplotment' is not an idea that Crossley formulated herself. Instead it was something that she was aware of from the research literature. Of course, some forms of qualitative analysis encourage the view that concepts emerge out of the data. This may be true but it is simply not always the case. One could, of course, suggest that Crossley's (2003) paper is best regarded as a illustrative case study rather than an analysis. When one reads her original paper carefully, although it contains many interesting points, it relies very much on the work of Del Vecchio Good *et al.* (1994).

Crossley's (2003) paper employs data somewhat different from those which might emerge from a narrative interview with a cancer sufferer. In particular, it has quite a long timespan and it is not based on data collected at a particular point in time. Thus, it demonstrates quite clearly how the dominant narrative can change markedly during the course of an illness. This sort of data is not normally available to researchers. The study does provide understanding based on compelling data about the lived experience of being a cancer patient. Although this is not normally the stuff of psychology, it is invaluable for those with a clinical or counselling interest in health and illness.

When to use narrative analysis

Narrative analysis, by definition, is applied to data which meet the criteria of narrative. Essentially this means any data with a story-like quality, and may be produced by an individual or in interaction with others including researchers. It will describe a series of life-events but goes beyond merely giving a chronological account of those events. So a narrative will be a rich, detailed account frequently interspersed with a range of comments of a more personal nature. A variety of data sources meet these criteria but the data obtained from narrative interviews are preferred by many psychologists. There are many ways of conducting a narrative interview, though the procedure developed by McAdams (1993) provides a strong structure for a newcomer to narrative analysis and in-depth interviewing. These interviews are not conversational in style since their main objective is to obtain a detailed narrative from the participant. However, if you wish to use other forms of narrative data (diaries, autobiographies, etc.) then that is appropriate too.

The term narrative analysis tends to refer to a wide variety of approaches to the analysis of narrative data. Analysis can concentrate on the structural properties of the narrative, investigations of the conversational or discursive properties of narrative, through to the way in which self or identity are constructed using narrative. In this book we mean by narrative analysis approaches to analysing data based on the principles of narrative psychology. In other words, a distinction is made between narrative analysis (grounded in narrative psychology) and the analysis of narrative – a more generic phrase which covers several different approaches. There are alternative approaches in the analysis of narrative and quite what options are available depend to some extent on the nature of the narrative and the interests of the researcher. Most forms of narrative could be analysed using thematic analysis (Chapter 7), grounded theory (Chapter 8) and discourse analysis (Chapter 9). If the narrative is conversational in origins then conversation analysis (Chapter 10) could be appropriate. Furthermore, it is possible that the data could be analysed using interpretative phenomenological analysis (IPA) (Chapter 11) since people's descriptions of significant experiences may have many of the features of narrative. There are many similarities between narrative analysis and IPA. However, even though narrative analysis is to some extent phenomenological in approach, it is sufficiently different from IPA to require separate consideration. Narrative analysis refers to concepts such as self and identity primarily in relation to the narrative. IPA would concentrate much more on how the events in the narrative are experienced rather than what the narrative has to say about identity.

Remember, though, that all of these are ways of analysing narratives, and whether it is helpful to refer to all of them as narrative analysis is questionable. Put another way, the analysis of a narrative is best not confused with narrative analysis. In this book, the term narrative analysis is used for a form of analysis which depends on concepts from narrative psychology. The potential for confusion is probably self-evident by now. Figure 12.6 details some of the various ways in which narrative may be analysed qualitatively.

The methods of narrative analysis described in detail in this chapter are orientated primarily to understanding personality in a rich and full form, including matters such as self and identity. This does not preclude structural approaches to narrative which investigate the narrative structure and its functions, for example.

FIGURE 12.6 The analysis of narrative versus narrative analysis

Evaluation of narrative analysis

Narrative analysis, as referred to in this book, is based on theory about the role of narrative in the lives of individuals. The metaphor of narrative has been strongly advocated as an alternative to other metaphors which have been used in psychology. So it is proposed as an alternative to the mechanical metaphor which has people regarded as if they were machines. Positivist psychology, especially where it breaks behaviour down into stimulus–response units, is a good example of the machine metaphor. Other metaphors have been provided by psychologists – for example, Kelly's personal construct theory uses the metaphor of people as scientists. With the narrative metaphor, individuals are seen as complex and interpreters of a series of life events. In other words, the narrative metaphor has people who try to understand themselves and their lives in a social and cultural context. There is a sense of unfolding plot in narratives and they do more than simply account for the past. Narratives inevitably portray the individual as a moral being since narrative and morality are intertwined.

It is inevitable, then, that the evaluation of narrative analysis has to involve an evaluation of narrative psychology in general. Unfortunately, and this may appear a little harsh, narrative psychology is relatively recent, disparate in approaches taken, and lacks a strong synthesis as yet. In other words, it appears to the newcomer to be a somewhat chaotic set of ideas. There are clearly some tangible achievements in narrative psychology – there are narrative-based approaches to therapy, for example (e.g. Morgan, 2000). However, the impression as yet is of a field which is clearly expanding but one which is not yet fully focused – that is, it is waiting to find its focus. This impression seems to apply to narrative analysis too. Attempts to describe the process of narrative analysis are not so well developed as for other qualitative methods.

Furthermore, narrative analysis is relatively infrequent compared to other methods of qualitative analysis. There may be a number of reasons for this. One is, of course, that narrative psychology is too young as a field of research to have reached a stage where its methods are fully established. Another is that narrative psychology has not, as yet, developed a body of theory analogous to that which underlie, say, discourse analysis and conversation analysis. In this context, it is noteworthy that some of the proponents of narrative psychology waited until late in their careers to address the topic formally. This is unusual in research where one would normally expect innovations to come from younger people, eager to build their careers.

So, anyone who attempts a narrative analysis will probably feel a little out on a limb compared with users of most of the other qualitative data analysis methods described in previous chapters. Models are harder to come by, theory more difficult to clarify. But, in the end, anyone interested in narrative analysis is interested in interpreting the stories we tell about our lives in our everyday lives. This is much more about self and identity than any of the other approaches in this book although some of the other methods address topics such as identity regularly. Narrative analysis, certainly as described in this chapter, is much more closely associated with the study of personality than it is, say, with the study of language. So it all boils down to the question of what you, as the researcher, are interested in. Among the attractions of narrative psychology is that it is non-reductionist in the sense of seeking to look at the individual as a person in a social environment in totality.

CONCLUSION

By doing narrative analysis you are stepping into the world of narrative psychology which is different from the other approaches in this book while retaining a broadly qualitative ethos. This means, for example, that the researcher familiar with the methods of discourse analysis has quite a lot to learn when it comes to carrying out a narrative analysis. They are not totally compatible approaches. They may not share the same epistemological assumptions in every or even most respects. But it is not surprising that psychologists who have a highly developed understanding of the study of language (i.e. discourse analysts) will have some difficulty with an approach which is more an approach to personality than it is to the theory of language. This applies to some of the other qualitative methods in this book but the contrast seems more real in terms of narrative analysis.

Of course, the usual rule of academic study applies here – the more reading on a topic that one does, the more sophisticated one's ideas become. This is inescapable and it is a point that has been made several times in this book. Of course, some sources of information are better than others and some are better at certain times in one's studies than others. So broad overviews, such as the one in this chapter, are very useful at the start of one's studies whereas looking at how other researchers have carried out their research and reported their findings will be more important when you are a little more actively involved in research.

Finally, the problem of where to locate narrative analysis perhaps needs revisiting. Narrative is not really the province of any particular epistemology of research. We have seen that researchers from a wide range of different epistemological positions can claim some sort of interest in the topic of narrative. However, this begs the question of whether any analysis of narrative can or should be narrative analysis. We can take the example of the views of Benwell and Stokoe (2006) who argue that there are 'many different versions of narrative analysis' (p. 143). This, of course, depends somewhat on what the cake is seen as being and how the slicing is to be done. They include in their list of different 'sources' of narrative analysis the following:

- The structuralist approach (including Labov) which links things such as ethnicity, class and gender to 'different structures and ways of telling directly and unproblematically' (p. 143).

- The phenomenological realm of 'real' experience. They describe Crossley's (2003) approach as 'strange hybrid of constructionist *and* referential understandings of language, in which language is a window on the mind/experience *and* the site of identity construction' (p. 143). Whether this is or is not fair comment on her writings, Crossley's position in terms of practice appears to be largely one of acknowledging the social constructionist position while advocating narrative realism (Schwandt, 2001).

- The psychodynamic realm of the unconscious.

- A social constructionist approach to the data from narrative interviews as being co-constructed by the interviewer and the narrator.

- The interview is regarded as social interaction purely and simply with the stories told and the process of identity construction within the interview being the consequence of the production of the narrative.

- Conversation analysts and discourse analysts regard narrative as being of interest because it is part of their declared aim of analysing everyday language.

This reinforces the earlier point that there are many different ways of analysing narrative. But there are many different ways of analysing conversation and many different ways of analysing discourse but conversation analysis and discourse analysis are not the best ways to describe all of these. Terminology loses its meaning if allowed to drift too widely. For that reason, it is suggested that narrative analysis is a term best reserved for the analysis of narrative using narrative psychology ideas and concepts.

KEY POINTS

- Narrative psychology is a form of psychology which uses the metaphor of 'narrative' in order to understand personality. As such, it is a developing field in psychology and different from other forms of qualitative research because it is embedded in this general approach to personality. Narrative analysis is a term best reserved for analysis of narrative which is founded on the precepts of narrative psychology rather than those of discursive psychology or phenomenology for example. Narrative psychology has self and identity as central themes. Time will tell if this or some other specific meaning will prevail.

- Narrative analysis is typically based on some form of narrative interview. This is any approach to semi-structured interviewing which seeks to maximise the narrative content of the data. Narrative refers to the stories that we tell about our lives which join together events in the context of evaluative material, commentary and so forth which are informative about the development of our lives as we describe them in the story.

- Narrative analysis is the least standardised approach to qualitative data analysis included in this book. There are relatively few accounts of how to carry out a narrative analysis compared to other forms of qualitative analysis such as grounded theory for which there is voluminous 'how-to-do-it' literature.

ADDITIONAL RESOURCES

Crossley, M. (2000). *Introducing Narrative Psychology: Self-trauma and the construction of meaning*. Buckingham: Open University Press.

Garson, D. (n.d.) Narrative Analysis. North Carolina State University. http://faculty.chass.ncsu.edu/garson/PA765/narrativ.htm (accessed 14 July 2009)

Hiles, D., & Čermák, I. (2008). Narrative psychology. In C. Willig and W. Stainton-Rogers (Eds.), *The SAGE Handbook of Qualitative Research in Psychology*. London: Sage, pp. 147–164.

Mishler, E.G. (1986). The analysis of interview-narratives. In T.R. Sarbin (Ed.), *Narrative Psychology: The storied nature of human conduct*. New York: Praeger, pp. 233–255.

Murray, M. (2008). Narrative psychology. In J.A. Smith (Ed.), *Qualitative Psychology: A practical guide to research methods*, 2nd Edition. London: Sage, pp. 111–132.

Riessman, C.K. (n.d.). Narrative Analysis. http://eprints2.hud.ac.uk/4920/2/Chapter_1_-_Catherine_Kohler_Riessman.pdf (accessed 13 October 2009). (Originally published in *Narrative, Memory, Everyday Life* (2005). Huddersfield: University of Huddersfield, pp. 1–7.)

PART 4

Planning and writing up qualitative research

The final part of this book is concerned with some of the practical issues facing anyone planning and writing up qualitative research. Chapters on qualitative report writing, assessing quality in qualitative research, and research ethics follow. These are issues which need to be considered from the time that you first begin to plan your research. In a curious way, the write-up of a study is a sort of blueprint for the study. So it is something of a pity, then, that the report is the last thing to be written! Nevertheless, it is worthwhile thinking of the sorts of thing which need to go into your report early on. This will help you plan your work a little better. Although this may seem impossible – and it is – it is always important to keep the final product in mind from the moment that you begin planning your research.

The final report is what you will be assessed on. It does not matter, say, how good your interviewing skills are if the report of your research is fragmentary or incoherent. Having a constant image of the final product in mind will help you address questions such as 'How big does my literature review have to be?', 'How much time can I devote to fieldwork?' and 'Have I got enough data for my analysis?' Keeping one's mind on the big picture helps pre-empt problems.

So Chapter 13 deals with writing a qualitative research report. Qualitative research reports tend not to follow precisely the standard structure of a quantitative research report. There is no single structure for qualitative reports which will suit all forms of qualitative research. Generally a version of the structure of the quantitative research report is used, modified wherever necessary. This has the big advantage of being familiar to all psychologists irrespective of their chosen style of research. They feel comfortable reading reports which utilise the standard quantitative research report structure. One advantage is that the reader will know just what to expect in the report (abstract, method, analysis, for instance) and, perhaps more importantly, where to find it. It is a reminder of the high standards of clarity, accuracy and argument that psychology, as a discipline, expects. It is an interesting question to ask whether qualitative research in psychology should have its own distinctive style and characteristics. Just what is the point of a psychologist doing qualitative research using the same approach that a linguist or sociologist would? There are signs that distinctive psychological styles of qualitative research are developing but there is a long way to go. Furthermore, from the point of view of this book, it is important that qualitative and quantitative methods in psychology become resources available to all psychologists.

Chapter 14 is about quality in qualitative research. This is an area which can be subject to fierce debate not only between qualitative and quantitative psychologists but between different sorts of qualitative psychologist. Along with a large chunk of statistics and practical classes, all psychology students have the concepts of reliability and validity drummed into them. Unfortunately, reliability and validity do not address all of the quality issues in quantitative psychology but they can be decidedly inappropriate for qualitative research. The arguments are complex but understanding quality criteria are as important for qualitative as for quantitative studies. There is quite a lot for all psychologists to learn in Chapter 14 which will take them well beyond reliability and validity issues. Actually Chapter 14 goes far beyond what is found in general psychology methods textbooks in trying to establish criteria which can be used to evaluate research. The sort of criteria which can be used by students to evaluate their initial efforts at qualitative research are presented. However, the chapter goes beyond this to consider the criteria that could be used to evaluate professional qualitative psychology research – and quantitative research in many respects. Chapter 14 should convince even the most sceptical quantitative researcher that qualitative research is not methodologically unsophisticated. The typical qualitative psychologist probably worries more about issues of research methodology than the typical quantitative researcher. Of course, qualitative and quantitative research vary in quality – not every study is good. But it is a fundamental misunderstanding of qualitative research to equate it with a lack of rigour.

The final chapter of this book deals with ethics and data management in qualitative psychology. It is virtually impossible to carry out any research in psychology without formal ethical approval these days. It is argued in

Chapter 15 that qualitative research is an ethically problematic endeavour. It is not correct to suggest that the typical piece of qualitative research is in some way 'morally' superior to quantitative research. Qualitative researchers have a very different relationship with those who take part in their research from the typical quantitative researcher. Cooperative research activity between researcher and researched characterises qualitative research and much of the data produced in qualitative research is clearly co-constructed. Some qualitative researchers seem to involve themselves more in the lives of those who take part in their research than do quantitative researchers. Chapter 15 takes us through the underlying ethical principles which underpin all psychological research. Some of this is nowadays quite routine – informed consent, freedom to withdraw from the research and confidentiality. But this is only the beginning of ethics in relation to qualitative research. The chapter describes some of the ethical problems which can develop in qualitative research as a consequence, sometimes, of the relationships between researcher and researched but also because data in qualitative research are more transparent. A good example of this is the question of how to deal with data collected from a group of people who are known to each other. A researcher who carries out in-depth interviewing with both partners in a relationship potentially walks in an ethical minefield.

CHAPTER 13

Writing a qualitative report

Overview

- Writing a qualitative practical report, like any other psychological report, is not easy and it needs time and experience to become good.

- It is always useful to follow the model of a published report which is as close as possible in terms of style and content to the research that you have carried out and want to write up. This provides a sound framework for your work and makes the checking of the details of report writing easier.

- Many characteristics of a good practical report are shared by both quantitative and qualitative approaches. In particular, evidence of creativity, diligence and care, and a questioning approach to what is written are universally expected.

- Qualitative research is based on full and rich data often collected by open-ended methods. The analysis which the researcher presents should also be full, rich and transparent in that the researcher carefully and thoroughly considers both congruent and non-congruent aspects of the analysis and tries to resolve any problems rather than ignore them.

- Often the broad structure of a qualitative report can be very similar to that of a quantitative report and the structure of the latter is recommended as a starting point for the write-up.

- Most disparity with the conventional structure probably arises in connection with the reporting of methodological matters in qualitative research. In particular, it is important to devote substantial amounts of space to the method of analysis employed. This is sometimes overlooked in qualitative report writing but not to do so is a fundamental mistake.

- Considerable care is needed to select appropriate data (text) to support the qualitative analysis. Systematic presentations such as tables and even simple statistics, where appropriate, can make a great deal of difference.

- Care and attention to citations and reference lists are as important for the qualitative report as for the quantitative report.

Is a qualitative research report different?

Obviously, the purpose of writing is to communicate your research activities to other people. Equally, during the course of writing a research report, a great deal is learnt concerning whatever one is writing about. Through the writing process it is possible to develop one's ideas in ways that mere thinking alone is unlikely to match. So it is important to consider report-writing as not just communicating one's thoughts but as a way of having one's thoughts. Not surprisingly, then, writing research reports is a difficult task – it is hard to communicate clearly and think at the same time. Writing a good research report is a complicated if not downright exasperating task. It involves skills like juggling lots of different elements into the right order but also a conundrum about what to include and how much. Do not regard report writing as a tedious chore set as a sort of rite-of-passage during your studies. Not surprisingly, for many students, report writing is outside their comfort zone. Good essay-writing skills will help but there is a lot to learn in addition about style, content and structure. Things do get easier with time and experience but report writing never becomes a cinch because the quality bar gets higher as you advance through your studies into professional level research.

Like many things in life, following the example of others can make things more straightforward. So you will almost certainly find it helpful to follow the examples of 'experts'. The more you read published research reports the clearer what is expected becomes. Of course, one has to be a little selective about which publications to use – some are more accessible to beginners than others. University and college libraries (and cyberspace for that matter) are packed with shelf after shelf of psychology journals with titles along the lines of *The Journal of Space Psychology* or *The Journal of Applied Cognition and Cognitive Therapy* or *Applied Behavioural Studies*. Time spent looking through the hefty volumes of pertinent journals on library shelves will repay itself. Much more convenient are the electronic versions of journals some of which most university libraries will subscribe to. Journal articles can be downloaded directly to a computer and printed out which makes life easier, if not exactly fun.

It is worthwhile always having a relevant journal article on your desk in front of you to serve as a model for your own writing. This will help you with relatively simple matters such as what sort of structure a research report should have and what headings and subheadings they use. Additionally, they can help with the complex and all-important matter of style. Any old journal article will not do – you need one which deals with similar things to your research, especially where a similar methodological perspective is employed. There is, naturally, a risk of picking a poor or unhelpful or impossibly difficult article but, generally speaking, the benefits are enormous. The advantages include:

- you have before you a guide to an appropriate structure for your report;
- you can see just how things such as citations and references are done and how they should look;
- the acceptable and effective styles of communication will become more apparent;
- you will form an impression of the appropriate level of detail to include in your report; and
- you might even learn some psychology.

In the end, there is no sure-fire formula guaranteed to produce brilliant research reports; nevertheless emulating good role models gives you better than a standing start in the race.

While journal articles do, of course, vary in quality, the good news is that most journals employ several levels of quality control. The most important of these is what is known as 'peer review'. This means that articles submitted to the journal's editor for possible publication will be read and commented upon by experts in the field in question. Rarely would a journal article be accepted for publication without further work being required. The article will probably need to be revised, corrected or improved in some way. While the system is not infallible and poor work can slip through the net, generally it ensures that published articles meet an acceptable standard of quality in terms of content but also conform to the accepted structure. Some journals are more prestigious than others so one can expect to find higher standards throughout in these. Usually, journals produced by the professional bodies for psychologists such as the British Psychological Society and the American Psychological Association demonstrate the highest standards.

Journal articles tend to be better guides to report writing than books. Although qualitative (and quantitative) research is frequently published in book form or as chapters in books, these often are less formal than the style adopted in journals and so are less useful as models for your own writing. Furthermore, books are produced to the 'house style' of their publishers. So, for example, the referencing system used in this book differs in some ways from the style used by, say, the American Psychological Society in its journals.

Remember that the reports which students write at different stages of their studies serve different functions from journal articles – their purpose is educational development and assessment. This has some relevance to things such as word limits but, less obviously, the contents of the reports. Relatively brief reports are expected from students as part of practical classes in psychology. Often these are as short as 1000–2000 words. Final year dissertations are much more substantial and may vary between 5000 and 20 000 words. For postgraduate work such as doctoral (PhD) dissertations the word length increases markedly and may be 80 000 words or even more in the United Kingdom. The important thing to bear in mind is that the 'rules' about word length vary from institution to institution so it is not possible to be definitive about word limits here. So always check this locally.

As a rule of thumb, it is likely that a qualitative research report requires more words than a quantitative one. The main reason for this is that many qualitative research reports include substantial amount of text to illustrate the analysis – they may also include transcriptions of interviews, for example. It is especially important to check whether these 'extras' are included in the word limit or not. Generally they will not be but it is best to have clarity on this matter from your lecturer or supervisor.

Where to aim: the overall characteristics of a good qualitative report

Any research report needs to aim for a high academic standard in all respects – some of which are more important in qualitative reports than in quantitative ones. While it is hard to define precisely what the ingredients of the perfect qualitative research report are, they include the following:

- The overall structure of the report is consistent throughout and is logically coherent from beginning to end.

- The report demonstrates that the researcher fully understands the nature and assumptions of their chosen methodology and recognises that each methodology has its particular distinctive characteristics not necessarily shared by other methodologies.

- The reader of the report should have sufficient detail at all stages so that they can evaluate for themselves how satisfactory the research is.

- Ideally, the report should demonstrate evidence that its author has been creative (such as in relation to the development of the research ideas or in the analysis). This is not simply being different for its own sake but it is evidence that the work is moving research in the field forward in important directions.

- At the same time, the report should demonstrate that its author has been diligent and exacting in their preparations for the research (e.g. the literature review), the data analysis and in all aspects of writing the report.

- It should be evident that key concepts and the research findings are fully and properly understood by the report's writer. Always use concepts appropriately and with care.

- Reports can have different target readerships and should be geared to communicating well to this readership. A report solely for the academic community will be written differently from one for, say, a government department.

- The aim is clarity and openness in all stages of the report. There should be no attempt to disguise problems or uncertainties by writing vaguely or opaquely. Obfuscation is inappropriate.

- There is probably more variety in the structures of qualitative reports than there is in quantitative reports. Qualitative researchers are more amenable to 'creative' deviations from the norm. Nevertheless, whatever the final structure it should render the report both coherent and comprehensible.

- The qualitative report should resonate with the qualitative research ethos. So the report should be informed by and reflect the qualitative approach in terms of things such as the researcher's perspective, subjectivity, the historical and cultural context of the topic of the research, and the richness of the data.

- Self-questioning of one's own ideas, arguments and data is an important and necessary characteristic of academic work. Similar but balanced questioning of the work of other researchers should be combined with this.

- Attention to detail in terms of general presentation such as basics like grammar, spelling, paragraphing and the like is part of the overall impression created by any report. While word processors such as Microsoft Word can help enormously with spelling especially, paragraphing is down to the individual.

The qualitative ethos

The phrase 'qualitative methods' covers a vast range of different approaches, not all of which are in perfect harmony with each other. There are strong debates between qualitative researchers just as there are between quantitative researchers. Nevertheless, most qualitative researchers share a 'qualitative' culture which ensures that they have more in common with each other academically than they have with quantitative researchers. An understanding of the distinctive characteristics of qualitative research methodology is essential preparation for writing a qualitative research report. Although these characteristics are discussed at various stages throughout this book, some common features of qualitative research can be summarised as follows. It should not be assumed that all qualitative researchers subscribe to each in equal measure:

- Data collection methods are open-ended rather than constrained by highly structured questions that allow little flexibility in terms of responses.
- Data analysis is similarly open-ended in that the analytic task is to fully understand/account for the data rather than use the data to answer very specific research questions or hypotheses.
- Data collection aims at obtaining very full, rich data usually of a verbal/textual nature.
- Data analysis aims to engage with the richness of the data.
- Data analysis is generally exploratory rather than confirmatory.
- Data description and data analysis each have an important role and need to be balanced. Data description without analysis is regarded as unsatisfactory.
- There is a close linking of theory with method. Many qualitative methods are notable for their extensive and distinctive theoretical and epistemological underpinnings.
- The analysis should be transparent, which means that it is clear how the analysis is linked to the total body of data through the use of quotes illustrating the range of data as well as the analytic interpretation.
- The analysis needs to be characterised by plausibility, credibility and meaningfulness to both the researcher and the reader.
- The qualitative researcher incorporates their own personal perspective into their research reports, possibly by providing a reflexive (see Box 13.1) account of the study in which the possibilities for subjectivity and bias are acknowledged and incorporated.
- Qualitative research should acknowledge the context in which the data is collected and its implications for the data analysis.

Of course, many of these characteristics are generally not shared with mainstream psychological research where issues such as hypothesis testing, reliability and validity tend to be pre-eminent. These general characteristics of qualitative research can help guide the researcher and suggest strongly the features of qualitative research reports. Nevertheless, you will need to familiarise yourself with the variety of approaches which can be found in qualitative analysis. Each has its own fairly specific characteristics and expectations as well as features of the general qualitative approach.

Box 13.1

KEY CONCEPTS

What is reflexivity?

The concept of reflexivity has a range of meanings in the social sciences though it is not particularly important in mainstream psychology writing. It is commonly mentioned in some forms of qualitative research. It was a concept introduced in sociology by Talcott Parsons (1902–1979) to refer to the capacity of people in modern society to be conscious of and to give accounts of their actions. If you consider that mainstream psychology was dominated by the behaviourist analysis of behaviour as the product of a stimulus and systems of rewards, the importance of Parsons's concept of reflexivity is self-evident. Similar conceptions can be found in more recent sociology such as in the work of the British sociologist Anthony Giddens (e.g. O'Brien, 1999). But these are not the current ways in which the term reflexivity is used in qualitative psychology. Broadly speaking, reflexivity refers in qualitative psychology to the ways in which the researcher has a variety of influences on the research data and research findings. Reflexivity, although it applies in quantitative research, has tended to be dismissed by quantitative researchers as something of a nuisance which if it can be eliminated results in better research. There are numerous ways in which reflexivity has been squeezed out of quantitative research. For example, the common advice to students writing up a quantitative research study is not to write in the first person (I, me, my, etc.). This is tantamount to suggesting that the researcher's experience of the research is irrelevant to the research. This is essentially a nonsense but one which psychologists have gone along with for decades in droves. One does not have to read too deeply in the field of qualitative psychology to appreciate that such personal references are common. According to Nightingale and Cromby, reflexivity involves:

> . . . an awareness of the researcher's contribution to the construction of meanings throughout the research process, and an acknowledgment of the impossibility of remaining 'outside of' one's subject matter while conducting research. Reflexivity then, urges us 'to explore the ways in which a researcher's involvement with a particular study influences, acts upon and informs such research.' (Nightingale & Cromby, 1999, p. 228)

In other words, reflexivity pushes psychologists towards a radical re-think of how they present their role in research.

There are two major types of reflexivity which are involved in qualitative research according to Willig (2008):

● *Personal reflexivity* This involves considering how we as the researcher influence and guide research. A whole range of factors can be involved including our life experiences, our politics, and our biases, attitudes and beliefs. What role have these played in shaping the research which we carry out? Not only does it involve the influence that our characteristics have on our research but it also includes the influence that our research has on us.

● *Epistemological reflexivity* This involves the researcher reflecting on the assumptions underlying the research which contributed to the way that the researcher thinks about their research and their research findings. The sorts of questions raised might include the research question and its impact on what emerged in the research and just how did the research method employed influence the findings of the research.

Burr also finds two meanings of reflexivity but they do not entirely or significantly equate to those above of Willig. Thus, Burr suggests the following as the first of two meanings of reflexivity:

> . . . it is used to draw attention to the fact that, when someone gives an account of an event, that account is simultaneously a description of the event *and* part of the event because of the constitutive nature of talk. (Burr, 2003, p. 156)

In other words, the status of the researcher as the expert - the authoritative voice - in quantitative research cannot be sustained in qualitative research because it allows a multiplicity of voices and hence no definitive account. Thus, qualitative research is open to debates about power and authority within research. In practice, qualitative researchers are more open to referring the research process back to the participants than is typical in quantitative research. (Of course, this may be to describe bad practice in quantitative research since the stage of 'debriefing' is supposed to accompany all research with human participants. In this, the voice of the participant is supposed to be heard.) Burr's second meaning of reflexivity is:

> . . . reflexivity refers to the fact that constructionism itself is not exempt from the critical stance it brings to bear on other theories. Social constructism, as a body of theory and practice, therefore must recognize itself as just as much a social construction as other ways of accounting. (Burr, 2003, p. 157)

Actually Burr is giving a particular version of a more general reflexivity thesis - the application of theory to the theory itself and the researcher.

Ultimately, these versions of reflexivity boil down to something quite important - that qualitative research reports can differ quite radically in terms of the style of content from those of the typical quantitative report. So a qualitative report may include more references to the actions, thoughts and opinions of the researcher. The trick, of course, is getting this balance right. The student researcher might feel that it is appropriate to keep such contributions on the light side as they can appear frivolous unless carefully thought out. The traditions of report writing in psychology are strong and it is best to keep broadly within the usual parameters though an intelligent reflexive perspective can make a welcome addition to any qualitative report - and quantitative report for that matter.

Although these criteria for qualitative research broadly constitute the underlying requirements of qualitative research, there can be problems in meeting the criteria:

● Sometimes the data collected fail to meet the requirement of 'richness' of content. The main reason for this is that a novice researcher may not have the interviewing skills to elicit extensive and detailed responses from their participants. Clumsily asked or confusing questions, poor rapport and being uncomfortable with silences are interviewer characteristics which may impact the richness of the data negatively and substantially. Without some experience of in-depth interview methods, it is risky to initiate certain sorts of data collection in circumstances in which time is at a premium. In these circumstances, it might be safer to employ, for example, focus group methodologies for data collection which are a little less demanding on the skills of the researcher – but only if this is appropriate. But the important lesson is that qualitative data collection demands a high level of interviewing skills and similar skills which need training and experience. They are not natural gifts bestowed on qualitative researchers.

● A thorough qualitative analysis requires a substantial investment of time and energy. Inevitably, if these are skimped the analytic work is unlikely to extend much beyond being a mundane commentary. A typical example of this is where the putative 'analysis' consists of little other than a few interesting quotations taken from the data which are then strung together with a commentary which does nothing more than point out that different people mentioned different things. This might be described as the 'he-said-this-whereas-she-said-that-but-then-they-said-the-other' approach. This does not constitute a quantitative analysis any more than it is good enough in quantitative data analysis to merely give a table of the data with no further discussion.

The qualitative approach can encourage the inclusion of things which are rare or even unacceptable in quantitative reports. For example, because the general perspective of the researcher and the impact of this on the analysis are important in qualitative research, qualitative reports frequently include material from a personal and reflexive perspective. In contrast, in quantitative research this is almost unheard of because subjectivity runs counter to the quantitative method's search for infallible objectivity. It is perfectly acceptable to refer to 'I' and 'we' in a qualitative report though not simply to report 'I did this and then we did that' which is somewhat clumsy anyway and misses the point. In qualitative research reports, the researcher becomes the subject of the discussion when issues of perspective, bias, subjectivity, and so forth come to the fore.

The structure of a qualitative report

The conventional approach to research report writing in mainstream psychology involves several components as illustrated in Table 13.1. This is well tested and works well for much quantitative research. It is a neat and orderly sequence which deals with the major features of quantitative research well but not always perfectly. It is especially well suited to reporting laboratory experiments. The reason is that laboratory experiments are built on a number of assumptions. The

TABLE 13.1 The basic heading structure of a qualitative report based on traditional psychology report structure

A conventional quantitative report	A qualitative report
Title	Title
Abstract	Abstract
Introduction	Introduction
Method	Method
Results	Results and Discussion (alternatively Findings or Analysis and Discussion)
Discussion	
Conclusions (optional or sometimes merged with the Discussion as Discussion and Conclusions)	Conclusions (optional)
List of references	List of references

most important is that research proceeds through an orderly process of theory building and hypothesis testing. Thus it is essential to understand what research has previously been carried out and what theories have been developed to account for the empirically observable data. From this background, new hypotheses are derived to test the theory. This means that a relatively straightforward hypothesis can be tested by the researcher in some way. This leads to a situation in which the 'results' of the research are separated from the 'discussion' of the research. This is usually quite easy because the results section simply describes the outcome of the test of the hypothesis. The interpretation of the results then follows in the 'discussion' section. In some circumstances, this structure can cause problems even for those committed to quantitative methods. For example, those who conduct surveys involving numerous different questions or measures may find the rigid distinction between results and the interpretation of the results leads to fairly stilted and, consequently, unsatisfactory reports. The structure can cause more profound problems for qualitative researchers.

The difficulty is that the conventional structure is based on the very particular view of how psychological research proceeds that has just been described. It involves assumptions about how progress is achieved in research which are not shared by qualitative researchers. In qualitative research, the analysis of the data and the interpretation of this analysis are intimately related. For example, the 'themes' which are derived in a thematic analysis are not pre-ordained but are developed as the researcher processes the data repeatedly. The argument for the themes, the themes themselves and the meaning of the themes cannot clearly be differentiated as separate sequential stages. Hence, the conventional structure of quantitative reports, for some, profoundly misrepresents the nature of qualitative research.

Similarly, and more particularly, it should be noted that even the idea of a literature review prior to collecting data imposes a particular view on how an investigation should proceed – that is, the literature review is there partly to structure what is thought about, what the relevant data are, and how they are interpreted. What if the researcher shunned this and wanted the analysis really to be led by the data? If this is the assumption, then a literature review prior to data analysis may be seen as undesirable. Pure versions of grounded theory and conversation analysis, for example, would eschew the pre-analysis literature review. In other words, the structure of the conventional research report carries its own baggage concerning the nature of research.

Despite this, it is commonly recommended that the structure of qualitative research reports should adopt a modified version of the conventional laboratory report structure. The change is only modest since it usually involves little more than amalgamating the results and discussions sections together. Sometimes it is suggested that this is called 'Findings' rather than 'Results and Discussion'. There are some obvious advantages to this:

- The skills that have been applied to producing quantitative reports can easily be transferred to writing qualitative reports.
- It is a familiar structure which all psychologists are well used to.
- By using much the same report structure, the differences between qualitative and quantitative report writing are levelled.

While these are advantages, there is a big disadvantage – that is, it makes it too easy to forget that a qualitative report needs to be substantially different in certain aspects of its content. Thus, very different things need to be included in the various sections of a qualitative research report. We can adopt the conventional structure but we need to constantly adapt it to the requirements of qualitative research.

This is illustrated clearly in Table 13.2 which provides more detail about what may go under each heading in a qualitative report. These subsections include ones which would simply be seen as inappropriate in a quantitative

TABLE 13.2 A detailed structure for a qualitative report

The major components of a qualitative report	Some appropriate subsections – including possible sub-headings	Common faults
Title	This should be informative about the general content of the report. Often a title and subtitle are used.	Not sufficiently informative about the contents of the report.
Abstract	(a) Brief summary of reason for the research. (b) Brief summary of method of the research. (c) Brief summary of findings of the research. (d) Brief summary of conclusions.	Failure to summarise *all* major components of the report. Especially common not to summarise findings and conclusions in qualitative reports.
Introduction	(a) Orientating paragraph. (b) Justification and clear statement of the aims of the research. (c) Literature review as appropriate. (d) What has emerged from the literature review which impinges on the research that you carried out? (e) Explanation of why a particular qualitative method was selected as being appropriate. Avoid writing a general justification for choosing qualitative and not quantitative methods. There are many qualitative approaches. (f) Statement of the specific research question you wish to address in your study. Hypotheses are largely inappropriate in qualitative methodology.	Material not sufficiently focused towards the study carried out – that is, too general and wasteful of reader's time. Material does not have a coherent structure especially the literature review. The use of sub-headings may help considerably. Material vague and insufficiently detailed because original sources have not been read.
Method	(a) Rationale for the methodological approach (if not more appropriately placed in the Introduction). (b) Design of the study including interviews/focus groups, etc. (c) Procedures, interviews and other data collection methods used. (d) General information about participants in the research. (e) Ethical considerations. (f) Transcription of data. (g) Strategy for the data analysis. (h) Procedures for assessing the reliability and validity of the analysis.	Failure to present detail of data collection methods used (e.g. focus groups or in-depth interviews) which may be very pertinent to the interpretation of the data. Very common to gloss over the details of the qualitative research analysis, leaving considerable doubt about what was done – or even whether it was truly a qualitative analysis.

TABLE 13.2 (*continued*)

The major components of a qualitative report	Some appropriate subsections – including possible sub-headings	Common faults
Results and Discussion (findings)	(a) The analysis of the textual material. (b) Quotes illustrating aspects of the analysis or for detailed discussion. (c) Possibly simple quantification to indicate the incidence of different features of the analysis. (d) Tables (e.g. several quotes illustrating a theme or perhaps contrasting the quotes from one sample with those of another). (e) Reflections on methodology and analysis. (f) The major features of the analysis. (g) How the research findings relate to those from other studies in this area of research. (h) Describe attempts to validate the analysis such as discussing it with the original participants. (i) Any methodological issues which place limitations on the research findings. (J) Further implications of the research in terms of possible fruitful lines of inquiry.	Failure to carry out a thorough, systematic analysis. Instead, a few themes are identified and illustrated with quotes without any attempt to embrace all of the data or develop better-fitting themes or categories. This amounts to a failure to recognise the rigour of qualitative methods. Inconsistencies in the analysis.
Conclusions (optional)	In modern practice, a conclusions section is relatively uncommon in many fields of research. Where they appear, the conclusions are often incorporated with the Discussion section and do not appear as a separate sub-heading. Qualitative research studies, because of their nature, may not be conducive to being summarised by a few conclusions.	A common fault is for a conclusion to be stated which does not follow from what has been written previously in the report.
List of references	Follow prescribed method. This may be the standards set by the American Psychological Association publications manual, the department in which you are studying, or some other authority. Consistency is probably the most important requirement.	There are numerous errors that can be made. These are largely avoided by being clear what set of rules you are following and use an appropriate model. Failure to do so will result in inconsistency.
Appendices	Transcripts. Any other materials.	The use of appendices is significantly affected by the type of report that you are writing. Where space is at a premium, the use of appendices has to be sparing. In other reports (e.g. the PhD thesis), accuracy and completeness are more important than amount of space used so the use of appendices may be much more generous.

report. Even where they appear to be the same they can be very different. So it is not unusual to include tables in a qualitative report but these are more likely to be tables of themes or quotes than they are to be quantitative in any way. For example, in qualitative research a table may list the participants and describe some of their characteristics. In this way, details about individual members of the group of participants are presented. In quantitative research, such features are more likely to be presented in terms of sample means and standard deviations.

The qualitative report in detail

Without doubt one of the best ways to learn how to write up a qualitative research report is to study the writings of researchers in the field which is of interest to you. Of these, you will find journal articles the best source of good models which to emulate. This is because journal articles are required to adhere to particular standards of content which chapters in books, for example, are not. Do not forget, either, that lecturers have the journal article as an 'ideal' in their heads by virtue of their training in psychology. So adopting the style of a psychology journal which publishes qualitative research (e.g. *Qualitative Research in Psychology*) is probably the best strategy. As you get further into your studies, the more you are likely to read such articles as preparation for your research, e.g. as part of the literature review. As already mentioned, having a relevant article in front of you as a model is a really good idea as few of us can memorise every last intricate detail of how to write a journal article. Qualitative researchers are probably more likely to go beyond the field of psychology in their literature review so be warned that the standards of report writing are different in disciplines other than psychology. Also be aware that for some qualitative researchers, the aim is to reject all aspects of the quantitative research project so substantial departures from the quantitative writing style happen sometimes. This is most likely in journals of lower status.

Importantly, the qualitative ethos more readily accepts the role of the researcher in the production of knowledge than does the ethos of quantitative research which can be caricatured as the objective quest for extracting knowledge from reality – in contrast, qualitative research can be caricatured as the subjective construction of knowledge. These are caricatures but, nevertheless, capture something of the difference between the two approaches. One consequence of these differences, as already explained, is that qualitative research reports tend to include more discussion of the researcher's subjective impressions throughout. In other words, writing about how the researcher experienced carrying out the interviews, how the researcher's previous experiences contributed to the research, how the researcher's attitudes and beliefs were impinged by the research findings, and so forth may be included, though omitting the mundane.

The following sections take you through each of the sections of a qualitative research report. We would highlight the importance of *all* aspects of the report and especially what appear to be simple or even trivial matters such as the title and the abstract. These are the initial point of entry for readers into what your research is about. The clearer these are and the more informative, the better the initial impression that the reader will have. They are there to give the reader a good idea about what the report has to say and, as such, structure the reading of the main body of the text. Similarly, although details such as citing sources correctly and listing your references seem more like chores than contributions to the quality of your report, students who do these properly will find that their work is regarded as better quality than those who are slipshod or haphazard about these.

Writing a good title

Research reports are not a diary or chronology of the things that the researcher does. Rather, they tell a story in a relatively structured and comprehensible fashion. Usually, the reader becomes interested in a report because of its title, first, and its abstract, second. These constitute the information about a research report's contents recorded on publications' databases such as PsycINFO and, as such, influence greatly whether a report will be read or ignored (along with search terms that the author supplies to index the article). Consequently the title of a research report needs to be a compact statement of what the report is about. Titles are short (usually about 20 words is the limit) which means that words should not be wasted. Redundant phrases such as 'a study into . . .', 'an investigation into . . .' and 'an experiment on . . .' are seldom seen as a consequence. Furthermore, fanciful or smart plays on words are generally avoided because they communicate little about the content of the report directly. While the titles of novels may indicate little about the book's content and still be effective, this is not the case with research reports. Here are some titles culled from the PsycINFO database using the search terms conversation analysis (CA), grounded theory (GT), interpretative phenomenological analysis (IPA), discourse analysis (IPA), thematic analysis (TA) and narrative analysis (NA):

- *Discovering communicative competencies in a nonspeaking child with autism* (Stiegler, 2007) CA

- *When May calls home: The opening moments of family telephone conversations with an Alzheimer's patient* (Kitzinger & Jones, 2007) CA

- *Interacting via SMS: Practices of social closeness and reciprocation* (Spagnolli & Gamberini, 2007) CA

- *Never-ending making sense: Towards a substantive theory of the information-seeking behaviour of newly diagnosed cancer patients* (McCaughan & McKenna, 2007) GT

- *Interpretive subgroup analysis extends modified grounded theory research findings in oncologic music therapy* (O'Callaghan & Hiscock, 2007) GT

- *Peer devaluation in British secondary schools: Young people's comparisons of group-based and individual-based bullying* (O'Brien, 2007) GT

- *Women's reflections upon their past abortions: An exploration of how and why emotional reactions change over time* (Goodwin & Ogden, 2007) IPA

- *Investigating the ways that older people cope with dementia: A qualitative study* (Preston, Marshall & Bucks, 2007) IPA

- *Resilience and well-being in palliative care staff: A qualitative study of hospice nurses' experience of work* (Ablett & Jones, 2007) IPA

- *Constructing identities in cyberspace: The case of eating disorders* (Giles, 2006) DA

- *'I haven't even phoned my doctor yet.' The advice-giving role of the pharmacist during consultations for medication review with patients aged 80 or more.* (Salter, Holland, Harvey & Henwood, 2007) DA

- *Constructions of racism in the Australian parliamentary debates on asylum seekers* (Every & Augoustinos, 2007) DA

- *Patient perceptions of factors influencing adherence to medication following kidney transplant* (Orr, Orr, Willis, Holmes & Britton, 2007) TA

- *'Why can't they do anything for a simple back problem?': A qualitative examination of expectations for low back pain treatment and outcome* (Campbell & Guy, 2007) TA

- *Barriers and facilitators of evidence-based practice perceived by behavioural science health professions* (Pagoto et al., 2007) TA

- *Cracking the code of genocide: The moral psychology of rescuers, bystanders, and Nazis during the Holocaust* (Monroe, 2008) NA

- *Exploring young women's understandings of the development of difficulties: A narrative biographical analysis* (Brooks & Dallos, 2009) NA

- *'Do you know what I mean?': The use of pluralistic narrative analysis approach in the interpretation of an interview* (Frost, 2009) NA

All of these have been accepted for publication in professional journals so meet acceptable standards. It is evident from reading them that each tells us quite a bit about the nature of the research being reported though some do so better than others. Nevertheless, some of the titles include eye-catching elements such as 'Why can't they do anything for a simple back problem?' and 'I haven't even phoned the doctor yet' which probably are not very informative in themselves and could be omitted without much or any loss in the information conveyed. In these cases, the eye-catching elements work because they are associated with very lengthy titles – in one case 25 words long, which exceeds the conventional maximum length for a title. Just how typical this selection of titles is of qualitative research papers in general is unknown. Nevertheless, it seems common to use a two-part 'title: subtitle' structure consisting of a title followed by a colon followed by a subtitle. This is also not uncommon in quantitative research reports.

Interestingly, the title alone often also gives enough information for the reader to have a good idea of what sort of qualitative analysis the report employs. This is especially the case with the CA and the IPA examples. Of course, the impression created by the title can be confirmed by checking the associated abstract.

What goes into the Abstract?

The abstract is a short precis or summary of the research *report*. Word limits for the abstract are generally very tight and typically journals will limit them to 100 or 150 words. The task is to cover as much as possible of the report's contents in that space. This provides the reader with an opportunity to judge whether the report is relevant to them or, in the case of a student report, it helps the lecturer understand what is coming next in the main body of the report and gives some preliminary indications of how good that report is likely to be. Of course, writing the perfect abstract is no easy task and no two researchers would write an identical abstract for the same report. In other words, there is an element of judgement in terms of what to include and what to leave out.

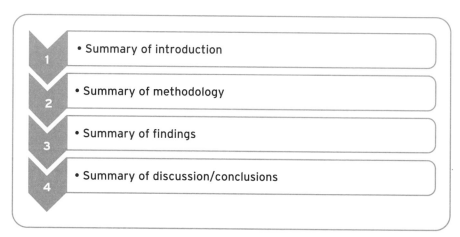

FIGURE 13.1 **What goes in the Abstract?**

The key to writing a satisfactory abstract is to ensure that all of the major sections of the report are summarised. These are (1) the Introduction, (2) Methodology, (3) Findings, and (4) Discussion/Conclusions sections (Figure 13.1). It is unsatisfactory (though a common failing) to leave any out. Probably the commonest error is to concentrate on summarising just the Introduction and Methodology sections, leaving little or no opportunity to summarise the Findings and Conclusions. This is notable in quite a few qualitative reports.

Some journals, but by no means a majority, require a structured abstract in which subheadings corresponding to the major sections of a research report are included. This disciplines the author into dealing with the entirety of the report. *It is a useful tip to write your abstract using the subheadings of the sections of the report given in Figure 13.1.* These may be subsequently deleted if necessary since in this context their purpose is merely to provide a structure to ensure that all necessary sections are covered.

What goes into the Introduction?

The Introduction is the place to set out the purpose, justification and background to the research to be reported later. In other words, it is the rationale for the research that is about to be described. There are certain essential elements, which can be supplemented by others according to circumstances if so desired (see Figure 13.2).

Initial orientating material

This introduces the reader to the broad area of your research using a few brief sentences or paragraphs. The initial paragraph or two of orientating material is extremely important since this begins the process of introducing the background to and the reasons for all that follows. If these paragraphs do not do their job clearly then the reader may fail to appreciate what comes later – they even get a misleading impression of what is to come. The temptation, especially for novices, is to begin with one or two extremely general paragraphs which, in themselves, contribute little or nothing to the substance of the report – which is that defined by the title and abstract. The key to the introductory paragraph(s) is that they should focus the reader's attention immediately on the research to be described. There are any number of ways, of course, for starting

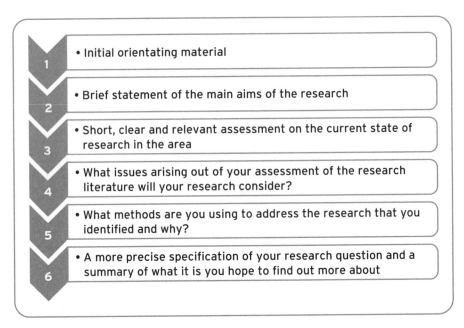

1 • Initial orientating material

2 • Brief statement of the main aims of the research

3 • Short, clear and relevant assessment on the current state of research in the area

4 • What issues arising out of your assessment of the research literature will your research consider?

5 • What methods are you using to address the research that you identified and why?

6 • A more precise specification of your research question and a summary of what it is you hope to find out more about

FIGURE 13.2 What goes in the Introduction?

a report so it is difficult to give rules about what to do – the important thing is to start with a strong and pertinent statement.

Brief statement of the main aims of the research

What is it that the research attempts to achieve? Research is portrayed as a purposeful activity which is directed to achieving some sort of goal. Of course, it is necessary to tailor your research goals to the research in question and it is not possible to provide a simple statement of research aims which can be adapted for all types of qualitative research. Some of the possibilities might include the following but there are many more:

- The aim of the research was to identify the major themes emerging in focus group discussions of the experience of living with cancer.
- The aim of the study was to explore how text messages are used to maintain friendships after people have moved away from home to a university.
- The major focus of the research was to examine how conversational errors are repaired between friends compared with strangers.

Make a short, clear and relevant assessment on the current state of research in the area

In short research reports, you should not attempt to review all of the literature in the field, though in a long report (PhD dissertations, for example) you may spread more widely. How specific the research review which you describe is will depend partly on how extensive the relevant research literature is. The less extensive, the more widely drawn will be the material from the literature. For conversation analysis and grounded theory, especially, remember that one view is that the analysis is ideally 'unsullied' by past research findings so you may wish not to review previous conversation analyses or grounded theory analyses since this may lead your own analysis inappropriately. Nevertheless, it may be appropriate to discuss other aspects of the research literature pertinent to your general theme. Also, a retrospective literature review will allow the researcher to compare their new analysis with those of others.

What issues arising out of your assessment of the research literature will your research consider?

When trying to understand report writing in psychology, it is important to remember that research is regarded as a process which goes through a number of steps before the research yields its findings. One of the steps in this is the literature review. Now the literature review that is included in the research report is not intended to be all-inclusive or exhaustive and it is not intended to consist of everything that the researcher has read. The literature review is an account of the research literature in so far as it helped the researcher to identify some important issues arising out of previous research. Examples of such important issues might be:

- Thus it is clear that research on doctor–patient interaction has failed to explore how the initial greeting by the doctor influences the later interaction with the patient.
- It is apparent, on the basis of this literature review, that the topic of how neighbours end disputes has not been extensively addressed by researchers to date. Therefore, there is a need for studies of the processes involved.
- It seems that public concern about the levels of knife crime among some young people has created a need for research which elucidates the nature of these concerns.

What methods are you using to address the research that you identified and why?

In qualitative research, the major methods are not entirely familiar to many psychologists, in general, as they are for quantitative methods. Partly as a consequence, qualitative research reports tend to include relatively extended discussions of the analytic methods and techniques used. In particular, extended accounts of the theoretical and conceptual background to the analytic method employed are frequently presented. Of course, how much to include of such material is a difficult matter to decide upon since there are so many different factors involved. If the word length you have is particularly short then clearly there is little space to be devoted to this. Typically, word lengths for practical reports tend to be fairly small at around 2000 words. A dissertation is typically much longer than this and may range from around 6000 to 20 000 words for undergraduate dissertations (though they are usually at the shorter end in psychology) to 80 000 words for PhD theses. As a student, it is desirable to give some background to the type of qualitative analysis you have carried out.

A more precise specification of your research question and a summary of what it is you hope to find out more about

Most qualitative research by its nature is exploratory of things such as turn-taking in conversation, people's life histories, themes in how people talk about being victimised by crime and so forth. Specific research hypotheses are rarely tested in qualitative research and, to many qualitative researchers, such attempts seem alien.

What goes into the Method section?

The following components ought to be considered for inclusion in the Method section of your report. It is unlikely that all of them will be appropriate for every qualitative report but it is always helpful to consider their inclusion (Figure 13.3):

Rational for research method and general approach employed

In the Method section, it is appropriate to provide a more detailed rationale and broad description of the research methods used. To some extent the Introduction will have provided some information but the precise techniques employed need some explanation. For example, you may decide to use a focus group methodology rather than interviews or you may get the participants to write a life history rather than use in-depth interviews. So it is important that you explain your choices. Of course, there is rarely a clear best single data collection method so you are explaining what led to your decision and, where appropriate, the drawbacks of this choice.

Study design

You need to explain something about your choice of participants (or available textual material) in your research and why they are appropriate for your research.

1. • Rational for research method and general approach employed
2. • Study design
3. • Procedure/interviews/other data collection methods
4. • General information about the participants in the research
5. • Ethical issues
6. • Transcription of interview data
7. • Data analysis
8. • Reliability and validity issues

FIGURE 13.3 What goes in the Method section?

There may be special reasons why it is appropriate to use a qualitative approach with this particular group of participants or reasons why it might be preferable to use one data collection method rather than another. Furthermore, you may choose, perhaps, to carry out an unstructured interview rather than the more usual open-ended questioning. What were the reasons for doing this? In other words, in the study design section you can provide details of your selected approach for obtaining your participants and obtaining data from them. Often, your choices are less obvious than at first appears and by justifying them everyone will come to understand your research better.

Procedure/interviews/other data collection methods

To indicate, for example, that you used open-ended questioning tells the reader only a limited amount about the style of interview that was conducted. It says nothing about the context (physical, etc.) and nothing about the nature of the interaction between the interviewer and interviewee. For example, what steps were taken to ensure that the interviewee was relaxed and communicative with the interviewer (i.e. rapport)? What is the framework for the interview questioning? None of these things is obvious from a simple statement like 'An open-ended approach to interviewing was employed.' Furthermore, it says nothing about the characteristics, experience or competence of the interviewer, all of which may have a bearing on the way in which the interview proceeds. So there is a range of helpful detail about the data collection methods that could be included. This, of course, is not restricted to interviews and is as relevant to other data collection methods. So, for example, if archival materials were to be used there is a great deal to be explained about how this was done – how materials were obtained, selected, prepared and so forth.

General information about the participants in the research

This section provides the necessary information for the reader to understand the nature and extent of your 'sampling'. In quantitative research the participants are usually described in quantitative terms such as the distribution of age, sex and other salient features to the research. Obviously one has to be selective in how much information is summarised in qualitative research. Basic demographic information of the sort just mentioned would possibly be appropriate. How were the participants recruited? What organisations, for example, were they drawn from?

In a quantitative report the following would be the minimum sort of information that should be provided and there is no reason why many qualitative studies should not emulate this level of detail and beyond:

- The total number of participants.
- The numbers of participants in different categories – for example, the number of counsellors involved and the number of clients involved in a study of counselling.
- The gender characteristics of the participants.
- Some indication of the typical participants in the research and possibly an indication of the spread of their ages.
- Major characteristics of the participants or groups of participants. Often this will be university students but other research may have different participant

characteristics, e.g. pre-school children, visitors to a health farm. These may also be presented in numerical form as frequencies.

- It is good practice, but not common, to give some indication of refusal rates and drop-out rates for the participants. Refusal rates are the numbers who are asked to take part in the research but say no. Drop-out rates are the numbers who initially take part in the research but for some reason fail to complete all of the stages. Sometimes this is known alarmingly as 'the mortality rate' or the 'experimental mortality'.

- Any inducements or rewards given to participants to take part in the study. So, for example, being given monetary rewards or course credits would be mentioned.

In qualitative research, it is possible to say more about the personal backgrounds of the participants than would be usual in quantitative research reports. Remember that where participants are not numerous in qualitative research, it is possible to supply a table summarising some of the characteristics of each participant. In this way, the reader gets a picture of each participant and not average scores for a group of participants as is usual in quantitative research. As an alternative, there are circumstances in which it might be desirable to provide a sort of potted biography of all or some key participants in the research. While this may not be appropriate, say, in the case of a discourse analysis or a conversation analysis where such material may be seen as superfluous, biographical material may flesh out our understanding of what is being said in some forms of qualitative analysis.

Ethical issues (see also Chapter 15)

In this section you should (a) briefly describe the formal institutional arrangements covering the work, (b) describe the ethical arrangements as you have presented them to your participants as part of the recruitment to your research, and (c) identify any particularly interesting or problematic ethical matters related to your research.

Most if not all universities have an Ethics Committee governing research with human participants. So it is probable that you have had to apply for ethical approval in some way or otherwise demonstrated that your work meets the required ethical standards. There may, of course, be arrangements for general ethical approval for research which is of a particular style or there may be a fast track method of obtaining ethical approval for research which lacks potentially problematic aspects.

Whatever the general arrangements, there will be some form of 'contractual' ethical arrangement between you and the participants in your research. Sometimes researchers provide a written statement of the ethical procedures that they will employ which is signed by the participant to acknowledge their understanding of these arrangements. Typical arrangements of this sort might include informed consent (where the participant knows in some detail the nature of the research and the procedures that are to be used), an understanding that the participant may withdraw themselves and their data at any stage, that anonymity and confidentiality will be respected, and so forth.

There may be specific ethical issues related to the research in question which would not be entirely covered by the typical, general ethical arrangements employed by psychological researchers. For example, the writing-up of

case studies may be particularly problematic a
identified in some circumstances – for example
position in an organisation and nobody else h

Chapter 15 deals with general ethical issue:

Transcription of interview data

The transcription process is an important sta;
data. There are several different approaches to transcription (see Chapter 6),
each of which serves its own special purposes for different styles of research.
Simple literal transcription of the interview or focus group needs no expertise
on the part of the transcriber other than listening and word processing skills.
Jefferson coding includes much more information about the social interaction
between the participants in the focus group or between the interviewer and the
interviewee. It is a much more skilled task requiring good understanding of
the underlying strategy of this sort of transcription. You should describe the
transcription method employed in some detail, deviations from the standard
method of doing things, and who did the transcription. In qualitative analysis,
the process of transcription is usually regarded as an important part of the
analysis of the data as the researcher becomes familiarised with the contents of
the interviews, etc. as a result. Each transcription can take several hours. During
this stage, preliminary ideas about the analysis of the data may emerge. So it
is helpful to the reader, for example, to know that the researcher transcribed
their own data or if the task was delegated to an assistant.

Data analysis

The process by which the researcher analyses qualitative data is often missing from qualitative research reports. This is not a good thing as the process
involved is a critical aspect of qualitative report writing. There is a great deal
actually to be said about a qualitative analysis which the reader ought to know
over and above understanding what the broad analytic framework is. Here are
some of the things to include:

- What was the process of familiarising oneself with the data? For example,
  did the analyst transcribe the data/carry out the interviews, etc. themselves?

- What broad methods were used to organise the data analysis? For example,
  were computers involved in some way and, in this case, what programs were
  utilised? Some comments on what the program does may be appropriate as
  this may not be common knowledge. Of course, it is possible to tackle the
  organisation of the data analysis in other ways. For example, what was done
  with the transcripts? Were they separated into sections and put on index
  cards for comparative purposes, for example?

- What data-coding strategies did the researcher use? Was a diary/notebook
  used to jot down ideas? At what level did the initial coding proceed? For
  example, was the initial coding on a line-by-line basis? What methods were
  used to integrate the many initial codings into broader categories? What
  procedures were used to check the fit of the codings to the data? Thus,
  potentially, there is a lot of information to be provided. Given that a good
  qualitative research project devotes copious time to this process, failing to
  include such information risks the suspicion that the appropriate stages have

not been employed or, at the very least, leaves the reader very much in the dark about the care and effort that went into the data analysis.

● It is especially important to indicate any points at which the data analysis method employed departs substantially from the typical approach used by researchers using the same broad method.

Reliability and validity

It should be understood by now that qualitative research takes a wide variety of different forms. Consequently, the objectives of different sorts of qualitative methods should be taken into account when deciding precisely what sort of assessment of 'reliability' and 'validity' is appropriate. To what extent do different researchers involved in the analysis agree on the codings for data categories? There is no necessary assumption in qualitative research that different researchers analysing similar material will necessarily come up with the same qualitative analysis as each other. This is, of course, true of quantitative research where it would not be expected, in general, that every quantitative analyst would generate exactly the same analysis for complex data. The complex issue of reliability and validity in qualitative research together with general issues of quality in qualitative research are dealt with in Chapter 14.

What goes in the Results and Discussion/Findings section?

Typically, in qualitative research, it is not possible to make the rigid distinction between the results of the data analysis and the discussion of the data analysis that applies to quantitative research. Consequently, it is best to combine these two sections into one – either calling it 'Results and Discussion' or 'Findings'. This is because in qualitative research it is often impossible to distinguish between the findings of the analysis and the researcher's interpretation of the data. Just what should go into the 'Findings' section? There are two main components (Figure 13.4):

● The findings from your analysis.

● The data to support your analysis – that is usually quotations from the data which can help the reader both understand your analysis and, to a degree, assess the adequacy of your analysis.

The overriding rule should be that these should be presented as objectively and carefully as possible within the broad parameters of the academic approach:

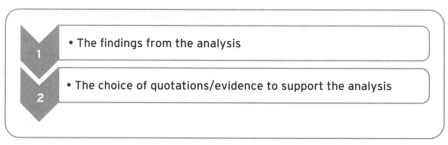

FIGURE 13.4 What goes in the Findings section?

The findings from the analysis

The findings of your qualitative research should be presented as transparently as possible. Details of how you developed your findings should be presented as far as you can. It is also appropriate to discuss ideas that you have rejected. There is nothing wrong with expressing reservations that you have about any aspect of your report.

The choice of quotations/evidence to support the analysis

Qualitative research at its best adheres to the highest possible academic standards. That is, one's arguments are carefully assessed against criteria such as logical consistency and empirical data wherever possible. For this reason, the selection of quotes to illustrate the analysis needs to be carefully done. The idea is *not* simply to pick quotes from the data which seem to illustrate the analysis particularly well but to also indicate the extent to which the analysis actually fits the data. In other words, simply selecting supporting quotes because they neatly fit in with your analysis is not good enough because it disguises problems in your analysis. A number of issues are pertinent to the presentation of quotes:

- At a very basic level, the qualitative researcher should ensure that the quotes that they employ in their reports truly do illustrate or represent what they are claiming in their analysis. Though this is basic, experience suggests that students do not always use quotes which seem to be particularly relevant to the point that is being made in their analysis. There can be any number of reasons for this. The most likely is that they have not formulated what it is they are trying to say in their analysis clearly enough to be able to identify exemplars. The second likely reason is that their analysis was inadequately based on their data in the first place.

- How representative are the quotes? The reader, if given just one quote in support of the analysis, simply cannot assess how well other potential quotes would have fitted the data. This is made more difficult in circumstances in which the reader does not have access to the full transcription of the data. There are ways around this, of course. One is simply to put as many quotes which illustrate a particular aspect of the data as you can into a table or box which the reader can then critically consider (as is recommended in IPA as discussed in Chapter 11). This is particularly useful for small studies and most convincing when all relevant quotations can be included. An alternative is for the researcher to discuss the range of material which is relevant to a particular aspect of the analysis and to highlight potentially problematic aspects of the data. So, for example, if the analysis identifies particular themes in the data, the researcher may choose to mention any data which are problematic in relation to that theme. A further advantage of tables and boxes to present quotes is that it is possible to set up a comparison of different groups of participants. Differences between the sexes could be drawn out using a suitable table – that is, a table in which there are two columns of quotations, one for female participants and the other for male participants. Furthermore, the use of tables and boxes can alleviate some of the pressure on space.

- There is a case for quantifying aspects of a qualitative analysis. It is somewhat disconcerting in a qualitative report to read comments such as 'Most interviewees mentioned "grieving"' since there is nothing wrong with stating the precise percentage. Words such as 'most' can imply just about anything from a small majority to nearly all. Using some simple but precise quantitative statements such as '90 per cent of the e-mails we studied included the theme "friendly greetings"' is not simply more informative but also indicates the extent to which the researcher has been thorough in checking his or her analytical categories against the actual data.

- There have been arguments made about just how distinct quotations should be from the main body of the analysis. Typically, quotes may be typed in italics for emphasis or indented and started on a new line. While this seems quite reasonable, it has been suggested that by making the quotes distinctive, the reader is tempted to skip reading them and so fail to appreciate the nuances of the analysis and monitor the quality of the argument being made by the researcher. There is probably little that can be done about this in many cases. For example, it is impossible to camouflage an extract of Jefferson-transcribed text as it is so characteristically different from most text and exchanges in interviews between interview and interviewee also readily stand out.

- While some qualitative methods value exact precision in the transcripts of data extremely highly, there are qualitative studies in which this degree of precision is not particularly helpful. This raises the question of what is a useful quote for inclusion. For example, how useful is a quote which is full of local regional dialect and language? Similar problems may occur when the speaker is poor at English because it is their second language, for example. Should such a quote be supplemented by indications of the meaning of the dialect words and constructions? This clearly loses fidelity with the original quote but, perhaps, helps the reader get something out of it which otherwise they might not. Similarly, what does one do about quotes which are translated from another language into English prior to the qualitative analysis? Is this appropriate for the purposes of the study? Even if it is, what can be done to assess whether the translation is accurate? One technique which could be used is back-translation in which the translation is further translated back into the original language by a second translator. The two versions could then be compared for similarity. These are important issues but their impact is likely to be different for different theoretical orientations. It seems unlikely that a conversation analyst or a grounded theory methodologist would be willing to analyse translations because these have less than perfect fidelity to the originals and the nuances of the original language may be lost or may even be untranslatable. How could a Jefferson transcription be applied meaningfully to a translation which may well be in a language which is very different in structure, inflections and so forth from English? On the other hand, a researcher who is interested in the experiences of migrant workers in the United Kingdom may find the translations adequate for the purposes of their study. There are qualitative analyses published which employ translations simply because the paper is written in a different language from that of the participants. Typically what happens is that the original text is reproduced in one line and the translation given in the next. In conversation analysis and some forms of discourse analysis, both versions are given the Jefferson symbols.

- Identification coding of each quote to indicate which participant in the research was the source of the quote. Although it would be somewhat unethical to refer to the source of the quote by their actual names fictitious ones could be used. On the other hand, it is probably more useful to use an identification code which provides some information about the participant. For example, F1, etc. could be used for female participants and M1, etc. for male participants. Of course, a more elaborate scheme could be used. Unfortunately, this has to be balanced against the increased risk that the information in the code could reveal the identity of the participant to a reader. This is probably a bigger risk where the sample of participants is small. One of the big advantages of identification coding is that for reports with numerous quotes it is easy to know which quotes come from the same source. If quotes are not numerous and they come from a small number of participants then this might indicate that the researcher has not sampled the data widely for illustrative quotations.

- Most importantly, quotes in qualitative research are not merely there for illustrative purposes. They serve a vital role in the analysis of allowing what might be described as an informal but vital assessment of the 'reliability' and 'validity' of the analysis which some qualitative researchers believe to be important. However, the meaning of these terms in qualitative analysis is not the same as their quantitative analysis meaning (see Chapter 14). They refer to the presentation of adequate evidence for the reader's scrutiny. Without the provision of sufficient exemplars in the form of quotes, the reader cannot realistically and adequately evaluate the value of the analysis for themselves on the basis of the limited excerpts available to them.

- Consider ways in which the entire transcripts can be circulated to whoever has an interest in seeing them. The Internet makes this easy in many cases though more needs to be done to increase this form of circulation.

What goes in the Conclusions section?

Given the exploratory nature of much qualitative research, it is frequently impossible to draw up a short list of conclusions which does not appear clumsy or in some other way awkward. This is true for many areas of quantitative psychology as well and Conclusions sections are commonly omitted as a separate heading from research reports. They are probably best confined to quantitative studies which have tested a small number of hypotheses. This, of course, is not the strategy of most modern qualitative research. So while you may consider the use of a Conclusions section, you may feel that there are no benefits from including one for your qualitative study. Since a qualitative report may be more about developing analytic ideas than confirming them, it may prove difficult to present a list of conclusions from your study without it appearing too terse or too simplistic. In general, include such a section only after considerable thought and then be prepared to abandon it if it appears to undermine or detract from the quality of your report.

Of course, none of this means that you should end your report abruptly. The 'Results and Discussion' (or 'Findings') should end with an effective concluding statement which rounds off the report.

References

The reference list is a major feature of all reports written by academics. Usually the reference list is begun on a separate page at the end of the report (but before any appendices). If space is at a premium, then the reference list may follow immediately after the final section of the main body of the report (e.g. the 'Conclusions' if there is such a section). The reference list is crucial as a source of and documentation of the evidence used in support of all aspects of the argument that you have made in your report. The references provide the starting point for others to check out your claims if they so wish. So, in order for the reader of your report to be able to check the accuracy and detail of your claims, you must indicate to them the sources of information that you have used. Simply suggesting that 'researchers have discovered that' or 'it is obvious that' is poor scholarship. Identify as precisely as you can the source of your claims. Doing this involves two main components:

- The citation: You cite your sources in the text as, say, '(Donovan & Jenkins, 2003)'. 'Donovan & Jenkins' gives the name of the authors and '2003' is the date of publication (dissemination) of the work. There are many systems in use for giving citations, but in psychology it is virtually universal to use this author–date system. It is known as the Harvard system but there are variants of this and we will use the American Psychological Association's version, which is the basis of those employed throughout the world by other psychological associations.

- You provide an alphabetical list of references by the surname of the first author. There is a standard format for the references, though this varies according to whether it is a book, a journal article, an Internet source and so forth. The reference contains sufficient information for a reader to track down and, in most cases, obtain a copy of the original document.

It is not uncommon, in our experience, for references actually not to contain the support for the argument that they might be expected to. This is clearly bad form and should be avoided.

The citation

While citations in the text of your report may seem straightforward enough, a few things need to be remembered:

- The citation should be placed adjacent to the idea which it supports. Sometimes confusion can be caused because the citation is placed at the end of a sentence which contains more than one idea. Thus, think carefully about exactly where you place the citation – there is nothing wrong with having it part way through a sentence if this is the clearest thing to do.

- Cite your actual source of information and not someone else's whose book or report you are using. So if you read the information in Arrowsmith (2009) then you should cite this as the source. Arrowsmith (2009) may be a secondary source containing material about phenomenology which you think is important. Students are short of time and resources to read only original publications from which to draw information no matter how desirable this is seen to be. So although this would not be at all common in professional report writing, student research reports will often contain citations such as (Dominic, 1999, cited in Arrowsmith, 2009). In this way the ultimate source of the idea is acknowledged but the actual source that you used is also given. To attribute to Arrowsmith ideas which the reader might recognise as those of Dominic would cause great confusion and is fundamentally misleading anyway. In your reference list you would list Arrowsmith (2009) and also Dominic (1999). See also Box 13.2.

● According to APA guidelines, citations with two authors are cited as, for example, Abbottsbury and Pilkington (2007) and as (Abbottsbury & Pilkington, 2007) when in parentheses. Citations with several authors involve more complexity. If there are between three and five authors then their names should all be listed the first time the citation appears but subsequently the reference is given as Brownlow et al. (2010), for example (with the

Box 13.2

PRACTICAL ADVICE

Dealing with secondary sources

The rules for making citations are that they should refer to stuff that you have actually read and not things that you have only read about. So you incorporate the author and date of the publication that you have read (Madonna, 2007) into the text and give the citation in full in the reference list. Unfortunately, this causes special problems for students who may only have read about Madonna (2007) in a secondary source such as a textbook. So what should you include by way of a citation in this case? If you simply cite the textbook from which you got the material then there is a problem since the textbook writer (Donague, 2010) appears to be the originator of the idea, which is not the case. Three different solutions are available to students which are probably more or less equally acceptable:

● In the main body of the text give the original source first followed by 'cited in' then the secondary source (Madonna, 2007, cited in Donague 2010). Then in the reference list simply list Donague (2010) in full in the usual way. This has the advantage of keeping the reference list short.

● In the main body of the text give the original source (Madonna, 2007) but in the reference list insert.

> Madonna, S. (2007). Reflexivity in pop lyrics. *Journal of Psychological Music Research*, 5 (3), 361-72. Cited in Donague, M. (2010). *Introduction to Modern Psychology*. Hereford: Quickbuck Press.

This method allows one to note the full source of both the primary information and the secondary information.

● In the main body of the text give the original source (Madonna, 2007). Then in the reference list insert.

> Madonna, S. (2007). Cited in Donahue, M. (2010). *Introduction to Modern Psychology*. Hereford: Quickbuck Press.

The last two versions are similar except that the first includes details of both the original and the secondary source. Different lecturers may prefer different versions so check this just in case. No matter what, choose one method and do not mix it with others in your report. Consistency tends to be seen as a virtue in psychology reports.

'et al.' followed by a full stop to indicate an abbreviation). If there are six or more authors then this is given as Brownlow et al. (2010) for the first and subsequent citations.

● Stylistically it is very easy to fall into the trap of presenting the literature review as a list rather than a summary. The main problem is illustrated in the following fictitious example:

> Thomson (2004) was the first to point out that turn-taking in young children does not follow the same 'rules' as that in adults. Berelson (2005) extended this to include turn-taking in adolescents. Abbottsbury and Pilkington (2007) then found that children's turn-taking when conversing with adults was very different from when they are in conversation with other children . . .

This has a fairly monotonous structure in which every sentence begins with a citation. It tends to give the impression that the person mentioned is more important than the idea or research that they contributed. The sooner that you drop this habit the more smooth and professional your writing will appear. It works far better if your writing concentrates primarily on the ideas and research and the citation is treated as secondary as in the following rewriting:

> Early research on conversational turn-taking suggested that children (Thomson, 2004) and adolescents (Berelson, 2005) do not follow the same rules as adults. It also appears that children adopt different turn-taking strategies when conversing with other children than with adults (Abbottsbury and Pilkington, 2007).

This is better because it focuses on the argument rather than the authorities in the field. The argument will be clearer if it is given prominence.

● When you cite several sources at the same time (Brownlow, 2006; Perkins & Ottaway, 2002; Singh, 2009, 2010) do so in alphabetical order (and then date order if necessary).

● When an author has published several relevant articles in a single year then you need to take special steps to distinguish them. So if Kerry Brownlow published two papers in 2009 then they should be identified by the addition of a letter at the end of the date. So Brownlow (2009a) and Brownlow (2009b) are clearly different publications. They should also be given the extra identifying letter in the reference list. Since the reference list is in alphabetical order, then it is this order which determines which is 'a' and which is 'b'. If both are being cited then to condense things one would put something like (Brownlow, 2009a, b). It is advantageous to distinguish papers by the same author (authors) from each other as soon as possible in your personal documentation/notes since this saves a lot of time later re-reading the articles to identify what is in each of them.

● Try to be honest when listing your citations. There is a preference, of course, for up-to-date citations and thus a temptation to cite sources that you have not used. Avoid this as your lecturers are unlikely to be fooled by citations which, though up to date, are difficult to obtain, for example. Box 13.2 explains how to be honest in making citations. It is important to demonstrate that you have read up-to-date material.

Using a referencing and citation computer program such as *Endnote* or *RefWorks* will pay dividends in the long term though learning to use them takes some time. Your usual word-processing program will be used for your report writing. All of the programs work by allowing you to enter references into a standard template (or several standard templates) and then select them for inclusion in your work in the form of citations and a reference list. You would input details such as the authors, the title of the publication, and so forth into the referencing/citation program. The style of the output can vary greatly according to the user's choice so that the common styles used by academic publications are all covered. These programs are costly, though bona fide students sometimes get heavily discounted purchase prices for the whole program or a student version. But before spending any money it is worth checking whether your university or college has a site licence to use bibliographic software of this sort. Students intending to do a PhD or work in academia should seriously consider the use of these programs. One needs to balance the pros and cons since the time consumed in learning the program may not be offset by the advantages. For more introductory work than a doctoral programme, referencing tends not to be a repetitive process since student essays, etc. are mostly on different topics and so use very different sources. Thus these programs may not be too useful until later stages when references may be used many different times for different reports and publications.

Reference list

References are given under a main heading at the end of your report. Do not confuse a reference list with a bibliography and make sure you use the term bibliography only if that is what you have given. A reference list only contains the sources which you have mentioned in the main body of your report. In contrast, a bibliography is a list containing everything that you have read in the preparation of your report. This may be much longer than the reference list as a consequence because it includes things that you have not cited in the text. Generally a list of references is preferred in academic work. Items in reference lists are *not* numbered in the Harvard system, they are merely given in alphabetical order by surname of the author.

One problem with reference lists is that the structure of individual items varies depending on what sort of source it is. The structure for books is different from the structure for journal articles, for example. Both are different from the structure for Internet sources. Unpublished sources have yet another structure. In the world of professional researchers, this results in the publication of massive style guides for citing and referencing. Fortunately, there are just a few standard patterns. Remember that the house styles of book publishers differ in some respects from other standards. The house style of Pearson for example, as seen in the references at the end of this book differs slightly from that recommended here in this chapter since we are concentrating on the American Psychological Association's style, which is probably the most important available. It is suggested that you obtain examples of reference lists from journal articles which correspond to the approved style. They constitute a compact style guide.

Normally journal names are underlined, as are book titles. This is a printer's convention to indicate that emphasis should be added. In the final printed version, it is likely that what is underlined will appear in italics. If preparing a manuscript for publication, this convention should be followed. If it is a report or thesis then it is appropriate for you to use italics for emphasis instead of the underline. This has the advantage of being less cluttered and has positive advantage for readers with dyslexia as underlining often makes the text harder to read.

The following is indicative of the style that you should adopt for different sorts of source:

- *Books* The structure of the book reference is as follows: Author family name – author initials each followed by a stop/period – (date of publication in brackets) stop/period – title of book with capitals as in example, stop/period – place of publication, colon, publisher name.

  > Silverman, D. (2001). *Interpreting qualitative data: Methods for analysing talk, text and interaction*. London: Sage.

  > Glaser, B., & Strauss, A.L. (1967). *The discovery of grounded theory: strategies for qualitative research*. Chicago: Aldine.

- *An edited book* Author family name – author initials each followed by a stop/period – (Eds. or Ed.) stop/period (date of publication in brackets) stop/period – title of book with capitals as in example, stop/period – place of publication, colon, publisher name.

  > Willig, C., & Stainton-Rogers, W. (Eds.). (2008). *The Sage handbook of qualitative research in psychology*. London: Sage.

- *Chapters in books* Author family name – author initials each followed by a stop/period – (date of publication in brackets) stop/period – title of book chapter with capitals as in example stop/period – initials of editor each followed by stop/period – editor family name – (Ed.) – title of book with capitals as in example (pp. pages of the chapter) stop/period – place of publication, colon, publisher name stop.

  > Charmaz, K. (2008). Grounded theory. In J.A. Smith (Ed.), *Qualitative psychology: A practical guide to research methods* (pp. 81–110). London: Sage.

- *Journal articles* Author family name – author initials – (date of publication in brackets) stop/period – journal article title in lower case except for first word – stop/period – title of journal in italics or underlined, with capitals on first letter of first word – comma – volume number of journal in italics – comma – pages of journal.

  > Potter, J. (2005). Making psychology relevant. *Discourse & Society, 16*, 739–747.

- *Web sources* For any sort of publication on the Web more or less simply follow the appropriate style such as given above and then the http address from which the source was downloaded. So for an article in an online journal the reference would follow this broad style:

  > Burman, E. (2004). Discourse analysis means analysing discourse: some comments on Antaki, Billig, Edwards and Potter's 'Discourse analysis means doing analysis: a critique of six analytic shortcomings.' *Discourse Analysis Online*, 1. Retrieved August 29, 2009, from http://www.shu.ac.uk/daol/articles/closed/2003/003/burman2003003-t.html.

For an Internet article based on a website the style is:

> Garson, D. (n.d.). *Narrative analysis*. Retrieved August 20, 2009, from North Carolina State University. Web site: http://faculty.chass.ncsu.edu/garson/PA765/narrativ.htm.

There are other types of reference but the above cover most of the circumstances. See recommendations at the end of this chapter for sources of more information. Generally the easiest thing is to get a reference list from a recent APA journal and follow this as an example.

CONCLUSION

It should be obvious by now that successful qualitative report writing is a highly demanding task in which a wide range of skills needs to be employed. Equally clearly, one's initial attempts at report writing can be hampered by this complexity and one's lack of skill and knowledge. By taking a systematic approach to report writing based on a standard writing-protocol such as presented in this chapter, some of the initial difficulties can be overcome. Remember, that as a student, by writing a research report you are presenting your achievements for assessment. This means that your report must effectively communicate otherwise you will appear to be muddled in your thinking. As we have seen, although it is hard work, many of the basics are straightforward. Reference lists and citations may be mind-crunchingly boring to do but they are governed by simple rules. The sooner one adopts a systematic approach to them the sooner getting them right will be routine in your work.

Other aspects of a report can be seen as crucial to effective communication. The title and the abstract are vital to effective communication. The title is the first information that the reader has about the nature of your study. The more informative it is then the sooner that the reader begins to understand your report. So choose a title that communicates quickly and clearly some key aspects of your study. Similarly, the abstract lays out before the reader a readily absorbed roadmap through the main body of the report. The better that you do the abstract the easier the reader's task is in relation to the main body of the report. If a reader does not have a very clear understanding of your report having read the abstract, then all sorts of misconceptions may be built up and the general impression created of confusion on your part. A good abstract requires a systematic approach to what is covered, as we have seen.

The headings and subheadings you use in your report provide the structure through which the reader absorbs the material. It is, therefore, important that you as the writer ensure that what appears under each heading and subheading is logical and in its proper place. One of the functions of headings and subheadings is to tell the writer what sorts of things should be placed in those sections. Not being systematic about this can make your writing very difficult for the reader to absorb – which does not make a good impression.

KEY POINTS

- It is helpful if you adapt the quantitative report writing conventions when you write up qualitative research. This provides a structure which is generally familiar to all psychologists. However, it is difficult to separate the results section from the discussion section so they may be combined together as a 'Findings' section or 'Results and Discussion' session. As your skills develop, then it may be appropriate to modify this structure still further.

- Careful attention to every aspect of the report is essential for success. Although using citations correctly can seem like a chore, for example, failure to do so is easily spotted and may undermine what is an otherwise extremely well-presented report. It is in your interest to master these technicalities.

- Do not fail to include significant aspects of the detail of the method that you employed and your process of analysis. It is a common failing in qualitative write-ups not to explain how the analysis was performed in some detail. This is a fundamental error.

ADDITIONAL RESOURCES

American Psychological Association (APA). *The Publication Manual of the American Psychological Association* (2001), 5th Edition. Washington, DC: American Psychological Association.

APA Style Resources. http://www.psychwww.com/resource/apacrib.htm (accessed 22 August 2009).

Bibby, P. (n.d.). How to Write a Laboratory Report. School of Psychology University of Nottingham. http://www.psychology.nottingham.ac.uk/staff/dmr/c81mpr/HOW%20TO%20WRITE%20A%20LABORATORY%20REPORT.pdf (accessed 22 August 2009).

Centre for Writing Studies (2008). Writer Workshop: Writer resources. University of Illinois at Urbana-Champaign. http://www.cws.illinois.edu/workshop/writers/citation/apa/ (accessed 7 August 2009).

Dr Paper Software (n.d.). APA Style Basics. http://www.thewritedirection.net/apaguide.net/apaguide.pdf (accessed 22 August 2009).

Lang, K.M.S. (2009). Practical Tips for Completing your Psychology Dissertation: A Recent Graduate Student's Perspective. http://www.apa.org/apags/edtrain/dissertationtips.html (accessed 22 August 2009).

Liverpool Hope University (n.d.). General Guidelines for Writing Qualitative Research Reports. http://209.85.129.132/search?q=cache:IafE5i7rCjAJ:hopelive.hope.ac.uk/psychology/leveli/rsw/Qualitative_Report.doc+General+guidelines+for+writing+qualitative+research+reports&cd=1&hl=en&ct=clnk&gl=uk&ie=UTF-8 (accessed 13 October 2009).

University of Sussex (n.d.). A Quick Guide to Writing a Psychology Lab-Report. http://www.sussex.ac.uk/Users/grahamh/RM1web/How%20to%20write%20a%20lab%20report.pdf (accessed 22 August 2009).

CHAPTER 14

Ensuring quality in qualitative research

Overview

- The development of generally accepted criteria for evaluating the quality of qualitative research studies is important for a number of reasons. Novice researchers
need to be able to self-monitor their own work as part of their learning process.
Professional researchers' research proposals have to be evaluated before their work
can be commissioned and before their research papers can be published, for example.

- The criteria of qualitative research quality vary, to some extent, in terms of
whether a realist or a relativist position underlies the research. Realists believe
that there is a reality which can be tapped by the researcher; relativists assume
that there are many windows through which researchers try to view reality though
none captures it. The quality criteria for realists tend to be similar to those of
quantitative researchers.

- There are some broad quality criteria which seem to be shared by all types of
researcher: for example, the originality of the research, the importance of the
research question asked, and the extent to which the study is convincing.

- Newcomers to qualitative research ought to consider factors such as the investment of time and effort into data transcription and analysis, why the particular
analytic approach that they are taking is relevant to their research, and the
thoroughness of the fit of their analysis to the data. Qualitative research requires
intense effort and intellectual rigour to achieve satisfactory quality.

- Reliability and validity are treated differently in qualitative research compared
with quantitative research. Since it assumes a multiplicity of perspectives on
the world, reliability is not seen as a crucial feature of much qualitative research.
Similarly, validity is treated by qualitative researchers as built-in because of the
preference for real-life based data such as recordings of natural conversations.
Respondent validation of the findings of qualitative research is another aspect
of validity which rarely occurs in quantitative studies.

→

- Triangulation is seen as a way of increasing the quality of a qualitative study by using two or more data-gathering methods. However, the way in which these are synthesised or brought together in the analysis is crucial to the process.
- The criteria for evaluating professional qualitative research are complex. One scheme for doing this is described in detail.

How should qualitative research be evaluated?

Just what is it that makes a qualitative study a good one? What are the best criteria to distinguish the best qualitative studies from the dross and lacklustre? These are questions of particular importance to novice researchers in any field of research who need the answers to help them develop their research skills. So understanding quality criteria is clearly important to students. Just how will others judge one's work and by which criteria? Researchers need to be able to evaluate their own work's quality while learning to be critically but constructively evaluative of the work of others. There are numerous useful quality criteria in qualitative research but quite when to apply them is not always obvious. Quality guidelines need to be applied cautiously since not all of them apply equally to every qualitative study and some in some contexts may be controversial. Of course, the criteria of excellence for the work of students writing up their earliest qualitative projects are less demanding than those for the work of professional researchers who have submitted their research findings for publication or who are seeking funding to pay for the research they wish to do. Being clear about evaluative criteria helps us steer our qualitative research in the right direction.

Not surprisingly, quality criteria in qualitative research are more extensive for professional research than for student work. The quality criteria, for example, developed by the government and other bodies which commission and/or fund research are very stringent, as we shall see. Funding bodies need criteria to allow them to prioritise applications for funding and, perhaps, they may act as criteria against which draft reports of finished research can be assessed and revisions requested. The sheer variety of different styles of qualitative research means that quality criteria are not always ubiquitous. As a consequence, one needs to understand the epistemological foundations of each qualitative method before quality criteria can be applied with certainty.

Newcomers to qualitative research will quickly become aware of the somewhat confusing array of different qualitative perspectives. Put simply, no single 'qualitative method' exists that all qualitative researchers subscribe to – and so no single set of criteria can be applied to the evaluation of qualitative research. We saw in Chapters 1 and 2 and throughout this text how qualitative research emerged from a variety of historical, philosophical and empirical traditions. These can only be loosely bundled together as 'qualitative research' since they are disparate in nature and, sometimes, they are not entirely compatible. For example, discourse analysis and conversation analysis have relatively little in common with interpretative phenomenological analysis and narrative analysis. They serve very different purposes and have sometimes incompatible epistemological bases. Much the same is true for quantitative research. As anyone who has studied psychological research methods knows, laboratory and field research fundamentally conflict. The methodological requirements which excite an experimentalist probably seem unrealistic and unhelpful to other quantitative researchers who prefer the challenges of research in real-life settings. Characteristically, quantitative researchers are accommodating to the different types of research despite their own particular predilections and preferences. Qualitative researchers seem much more involved in epistemological issues than quantitative researchers, perhaps because their field of research is not so well established. This can result in healthy debates on the relative merits of different epistemologies.

Inevitably, then, given all of this, evaluative criteria for qualitative research have been a matter of some disagreement and no complete consensus exists on what the appropriate criteria are (Seale, 1999). Some qualitative researchers have accepted that concepts such as reliability and validity (as used routinely in quantitative studies) may have a place in qualitative research whereas others believe that similar but distinct criteria should be applied instead. Yet others have questioned the appropriateness of any quality criteria which have their origins in quantitative research to qualitative research for fear of stifling the vigour of qualitative approaches. There are three opposing views about the evaluation of qualitative methods (Mays & Pope, 2000):

- *Extreme relativists* This group rejects all quality criteria for qualitative research on the grounds that the different qualitative methods are unique and present a valid perspective though it is different from that of other methods. Consequently, 'this position means that research cannot derive any unequivocal insights relevant to action' (p. 50).

- *Antirealist position* Adherents to this point of view suggest that qualitative research constitutes a distinctive research paradigm. Thus conventional criteria such as reliability, validity and generalisability simply do not apply. This point of view rejects the realist idea that there is a single social reality and substitutes the idea that there are multiple perspectives on the social world which are constructed as part of the activities of researchers. There are some appropriate criteria of quality in qualitative research (e.g. such as the credibility of the analysis to both readers of the research and the participants who took part in the research) but these are different from conventional approaches.

- *Subtle realist position* This accepts that the process of doing research imposes a subjectivity and that different qualitative methods will produce a different perspective on reality. Nevertheless, the subtle realists fundamentally accept that there is a basic reality that can be studied, albeit problematically. The subtle realist sees the purpose of research as an attempt to represent that reality (rather than precisely identify the truth). Thus, potentially, different sorts of research approaches can be examined comparatively. The subtle realist position allows quality criteria adopted from quantitative research to be used to assess the value of qualitative research.

The outcome of all this is that qualitative researchers have to negotiate a variety of conflicting positions which put methodology '. . . in danger of getting a bad name' (Seale, 1999, p. 166)! Seale, who describes himself as a subtle realist, argues that the credibility of qualitative research, sometimes, appears to be a consequence of its adherence to an underlying philosophy:

> Philosophy is often presented as underpinning the craft of social research, being an arena where various attempts at providing foundations for judging truth claims have come and gone, yet present day opinion seems nowadays, paradoxically, to conclude on antifoundationalism as itself being a philosophical foundation for social research. I think that it is time for social researchers to exploit this paradox, by breaking free from the obligation to fulfill philosophical schemes through research practice, while remaining aware of the value of philosophical and political reflexivity for their craft. (Seale, 1999, p. 466)

Antifoundationalists, to be clear, have a philosophical position which says that there are no particular principles which underlie all forms of valid investigation or inquiry. Seale's point is that antifoundationalism has itself become the basic principle of qualitative investigation! In that sense it is paradoxical – a bit like the suggestion 'The first rule is that there are no rules'. This is important since it questions the extent to which adherence to the philosophical foundations of a particular qualitative method is paramount in determining the value of the research. After all, quantitative researchers rarely bind themselves to the philosophical foundations of their methods. For example, those quantitative researchers whose work takes place exclusively in the psychology laboratory scarcely acknowledge the influence of the logical positivist school of the philosophy of science when evaluating their research and often shun some of the trappings of positivism in their work. Why should qualitative researchers be different from quantitative researchers in this respect? Nevertheless, the incompatibilities between qualitative methods due to their varying philosophical bases cannot be ignored entirely – certainly at the present stage of their development.

One good example of this problem might not appear to be a philosophical problem at all at first glance – but it is. Should a researcher wish to use grounded theory (Chapter 8) procedures in their research then they may find the 'literature review' problematic. A grounded theorist adhering to the original Glaser and Strauss (1967) formulation of grounded theory may initially be intrigued by the argument that there should be no conventional literature review. The reason is that if the analysis is to be closely tied to the data then extraneous influences such as the conclusions of previous research may adversely affect this ideal. That is, an analysis is highly suggested by the previous research in the field. There were good reasons why grounded theory, after all, reversed many of the principles of conventional research in ways that not all qualitative methods do. But what if a researcher employs the methods of grounded theory but also has the temerity to carry out a literature review? Does that invalidate their work? Since numerous grounded theory analyses also involve a literature review then one can only suppose that researchers do not find this too problematic in practice.

Despite the disagreement about how different evaluative criteria for qualitative and quantitative research should be, nevertheless the issues of reliability, validity and replicability dominate in discussions of the topic. It seems to be accepted that although these may be useful, it is possible that other quality criteria may be more sensitive to the particular needs of qualitative researchers. That is to say, a qualitative study that is reliable, valid and replicable in conventional terms may fail to meet other important but largely unspoken criteria of quality in quantitative research.

Some quality criteria for quantitative research

Just what quality criteria are applied to quantitative research? Are they useful for assessing qualitative research? A brief list of some of the possibilities follows:

- Is the study original and innovative in any way?
- Does the study address research questions which are theoretically, practical, or socially important?
- Does the study convincingly establish the claims that the researcher makes?
- Does the study contribute new perspectives on the issues being addressed?
- Does the study resolve important uncertainties that previously dominated the field?

In general, these criteria would seem to be equally applicable to qualitative and quantitative research. It is probably not surprising, then, to find that some researchers have attempted to identify universal quality criteria which apply irrespective of the type of research in question. For example, Denscombe (2002) includes the following criteria, which overlap considerably with the ones just mentioned:

- The contribution of new knowledge.
- The use of precise and valid data.
- The data are collected and used in a justifiable way.
- The production of findings from which generalisations can be made.

Commonsensical as these criteria appear, it is obvious that quality criteria such as these involve interpretation and judgement. For example, just what is the intended meaning of phrases such as 'new knowledge' and 'precise and valid data'? Is not every study a new contribution to knowledge even if that study merely replicates earlier ones? How 'precise and valid' do data have to be to make a study worthwhile and just how do we assess their degree of precision and validity? In the end, this shows that quality criteria are subject to interpretation. You might be wondering at this point just what relevance criteria such as these have to the work of students. Surely it is not the purpose of the research done by students to come up with earth-shatteringly new findings. Box 14.1 gives a brief account of some criteria which students might wish to apply to their own efforts.

Evaluating quality in qualitative research

As discussed throughout this book, there is an important distinction between qualitative data collection methods (such as in-depth interviews, participant observation, focus groups and so forth) and qualitative data analysis methods (such as discourse analysis, grounded theory and conversation analysis). Recognising the distinction can remove some confusions which are relevant to the assessment of quality in qualitative research. Quite simply, there are researchers who prefer to use qualitative data collection methods, perhaps because the research is exploratory or because the richness of the data is attractive to them, but nevertheless prefer to use quantitative methods in order to analyse the data. Of course, the criteria of quality will be different in these

Box 14.1

PRACTICAL ADVICE

Quality criteria for new researchers

This chapter contains a great many ideas about evaluating the quality of qualitative research. But most of these apply to the research rather than the researcher. Just what does the novice researcher need to do to ensure that their early attempts at qualitative research are as effective as possible? Many of the criteria to be found in this chapter are not routinely discussed in reports of qualitative research though they are commonly dealt with in general discussions of qualitative methodology. Such discussions often fail to meet the immediate needs of novice qualitative researchers since the basic requirements of qualitative research are not so well established as those for quantitative research where significance testing, reliability and validity are familiar basic quality indicators.

The following are some ideas which those new to qualitative research might consider as helpful advice and which may help ensure the quality of their qualitative research:

● What preparation have you done? Immersing yourself in the qualitative research literature and undergoing specific training in qualitative research would be important steps. It is difficult to understand where you are going with a qualitative research project unless you have a good idea of all of the stages in such research.

● Are there intellectually valid reasons for deciding to do a qualitative rather than a quantitative analysis? Negative reasons such as a desire to avoid using statistics are not good enough to justify a qualitative approach. Sometimes what is presented as a qualitative analysis would have been much better had a quantitative approach been adopted.

● What is the specific qualitative method that you are using and why is it appropriate for your research? Qualitative research is not a single, generic approach to research but comprises a set of, often, interlinking methods each of which has its own rationale, characteristics and value. So why is it that you intend to carry out a discourse analysis rather than grounded theory?

● What resources can you bring to your qualitative data collection and analysis? Because of the nature of qualitative data collection and data analysis methods, considerable personal skills are needed on the part of the researcher. Qualitative research is *not* a matter of distributing questionnaires, tests or other measuring devices but it requires skills such as good interviewing techniques, good person management and quickness of thought. In-depth interviewing is a skill, as is facilitating a focus group. The qualitative researcher needs to be in a position to devote considerable amounts of time to activities like transcribing their interviews as well as some degree of knowledge about their chosen qualitative method. The point is that qualitative research demands both personal and time resources. If either of these is lacking, there will be a constraint on the quality of your qualitative research.

● How thorough have you been in coding or categorising your data? It is tempting to be selective in the extent to which you analyse your data. There may be good reasons for being selective but just what is your justification for doing so? If, say, you choose to categorise or code just a small part of your data, you risk failing to optimise the categories that you begin to formulate. It is difficult to know how effective your categories or codings are unless you apply them to all of the data (or a systematic selection). Unfortunately, since the reporting of the analysis process is rarely complete, the reader may assume wrongly that your analysis concentrated on the entire set of data when you chose merely part of the data.

- Have you gone through a process of refining your codings or categories? It is an important feature of qualitative research that the initial steps of the analysis process (the codings and categories) are refined by a process of checking and rechecking against the data etc. The aim of this is to both improve the fit of the codings and categories to the data and to combine and redefine the codings and categories.

- Which aspects of your data fit the codings or categories that you have developed? To what extent do the codings or categories apply to participants in your research? So avoid using comments such as 'most participants', 'frequently' and 'rarely' as these fail to indicate with any precision the extent to which your analysis applies throughout your group of research participants. Just why can't you say precisely the number of participants that a particular aspect of your analysis applies to?

- Was your qualitative analysis easy to carry out? Qualitative analysis is not intended to be easy since a good researcher continually challenges what they have achieved at every stage of the analysis in the hope of producing something more superior. Quality in qualitative research does not come easily.

circumstances than if the researcher used the same qualitative data method to collect the data but a qualitative data analysis method in order to analyse the data. 'Rich' data in themselves do not determine the appropriateness of the data analysis method. In other words, judge the value of a qualitative study in relation to what the researcher is trying to achieve and do not simply use the same set of criteria unselectively in all circumstances.

General academic justification and features of the research

There is one school of thought which argues that the criteria for evaluating a qualitative research study are basically the same as those employed generally in academic work of all types. Thus they ought to be applicable to qualitative and quantitative research but, additionally, history, literature, chemistry and so forth. Essentially this view sees intellectual detachment and a questioning stance together with an organised and systematic approach to the issue in question as crucial to quality. This broadly seems to underlie the approach taken by Taylor (2001) to quality in qualitative research. Taylor's criteria are as follows:

- How well the research is located with regard to previous publications on the topic.

- To what extent is the argument employed coherent and intellectually persuasive (rational) as opposed to being based on emotion.

- To what extent does the report contain an analysis based on systematic interpretation of the data rather than leaving the data 'to speak for themselves'.

- How fruitful are the findings of the research?

- How relevant is the research to social issues/political events?
- How useful and applicable are the findings?

Let us look at these criteria a little more carefully.

How well is the research located in regard to previously published research on the topic?

Academic research is conventionally conceived as a cumulative process in which there is a gradual building of research findings, new concepts and new theories. For the individual researcher, this process is often seen as being based on a review of previous research in the research area in question. Not only does the literature review enable the researcher to understand what is known about a field of research but it also allows the researcher to identify aspects which are particularly in need of further consideration and ones which researchers have failed to address. But then the researcher formulates new research, collects new data, analyses that data and attempts to synthesise their analysis in terms of their own research findings and those of other studies. Much qualitative research adopts this model but not all. Some qualitative researchers, as we have seen, eschew the early literature review and begin with the data that they wish to analyse and then proceed to analysing it. They turn to the previous research only after this as a way of assessing the adequacy of their analysis against similar analyses of similar data. Of course, variability in qualitative research is generally regarded more positively than from the quantitative perspective where variability in research outcomes is put down to negative things such as problems in terms of research design and data collection methods. Variability in the qualitative tradition is not only to be expected but is also regarded as a more positive feature. In short, this is not a universal criterion in qualitative research.

To what extent is the argument employed coherent and intellectually persuasive (rational) as opposed to being based on emotion?

Research reports do not simply report research findings. Good research reports involve a well-thought-out and clear argument which leads to a conclusion which follows from the data and the argument. Academic argumentation is a rational and usually cool process dominated by clarity of thought. Academic argument tends to shun arguments which are expressed in terms of emotion rather than rationality. Furthermore, rhetorical argumentation is also avoided. This is not to say that academic writing has to be dispassionate or uninvolved with the topic of the research – but the way in which these are articulated in the research report is important. Much good psychological writing builds from the commitment of the researcher to the outcome of the research. Nevertheless, restraint and balance are the major and overriding expectations of academic arguments. Clearly the data obtained, together with the tightness of the logic of the argument, are crucial in appropriate styles of argumentation. It is important in the academic method that the writer is not seen as merely expressing unfounded personal opinions but is making a case which carries conviction. Thus this criterion could be applied to all qualitative research.

To what extent does the report contain an analysis based on systematic interpretation of the data rather than leaving the data 'to speak for themselves'?

Qualitative data analysis almost invariably involves a great deal of analytic effort if the expectations of researchers are to be fulfilled. There is nothing implicitly in data which equates to analysis. The analysis of data is a complex matter which partly involves the data but goes beyond the data into methodological and theoretical issues. In short, a good qualitative research report includes a significant analysis of the data. The implications of this are difficult to understand in the abstract. Just what does a research report look like if it does not include a significant data analysis? Such a report can happen, for example, when the researcher has in-depth data in the form of interviews but simply selects just a few quotations and strings these together with a linking commentary. This does not amount to a qualitative data analysis. It is the sort of thing that a competent journalist might do but it is not what qualitative research is about. It does not matter how interesting the quotes may be, in themselves they do not provide analysis of the data as a whole. Data analysis is about the synthesis of the material into something representative of but nevertheless different and more abstract than the original data. The analysis gives coherence to the data. It is erroneous to think that data speak for themselves. Stringing large amounts of textual data together may be entertaining but it does nothing to accumulate understanding. After all, novels are entertaining but we do not consider them a qualitative analysis. In qualitative research, researchers develop coding categories which derive from the data and provide, ideally, a close fit with the data in its entirety. In this way the analysis is created or synthesised from the data but it is different from the data itself. The nature of the analysis is partly dependent on the type of qualitative analysis method employed. Data quotations cannot substitute for analysis but they can illustrate and give life to the analysis. So, clearly, an analysis of the data must be regarded as a universal quality criterion for quality research.

How fruitful are the findings of the research?

Fruitful research is productive in terms of new and vigorous ideas, concepts, theories, problems, issues and so forth. It is probably easier to recognise mundane research which is not fruitful than it is to specify just what is fruitful in the best research. Mundane research leaves the reader feeling no wiser and lacking intellectual stimulation because of the lack of new ideas – there is nothing intellectually invigorating to reward the reader. Of course, the fruitfulness of research may be a longer-term matter. For example, crucial studies are those which have a long-term impact by generating and stimulating new investigations and innovative research pathways. The classic studies in any field of research are those that achieve precisely this – this might lead us to the conclusion that fruitfulness is a universal criterion of quality in qualitative research.

How relevant is the research to social issues/political events?

Some qualitative researchers in psychology indicate that they have interests in political and social issues. This is especially the case with those who designate themselves critical psychologists or critical social psychologists. The idea that research should be socially relevant is long established. *The Society for the Psychological Study of Social Issues* was founded in 1936 to help provide 'social and behavioral scientists opportunities to apply their knowledge and insights to the critical problems of today's world' (RadPsyNet, 2009). This society had its origins in psychologists' desire to use their discipline to help solve the social and economic problems of the Great Depression. Interestingly, it was not until 1951 that the similar organisation primarily for sociologists, *The Society for the Study of Social Problems*, was established. Quantitative psychology has contributed a thread of socially relevant research through much of its history which means that social relevance is not a criterion exclusive to qualitative research. It then is notable that some leading qualitative researchers such as Parker (1989) have deplored what they see as the failure of much qualitative research to effectively handle and incorporate social and political concepts – especially the concept of power. On the other hand, there are branches of psychology which are primarily qualitatively orientated to which this criticism cannot be applied. Feminist psychology is primarily qualitative but is primarily built on social and political concepts. Of course, there is also a big difference between research which is based on realistic data (as most qualitative research is) and research with a social and political agenda. Thus, social and political relevance is not a universal criterion of quality in qualitative research and so should be used with caution.

How useful and applicable are the findings?

A purely academic approach to research would stress that the primary function of research is to provide knowledge and understanding of the world. Although some would dismiss this as a sort of 'ivory tower' approach, very little research is designed because of its potential applicability in the short term. For many psychologists, then, understanding the subject matter is the primary objective of research and its application perhaps a bonus rather than a requirement. Historically, in psychology, applied research tended to be dismissed as being of less importance and lacked the esteem granted more purely academic approaches. It was seen as mundane and pedestrian compared with more theory-driven research. But the applied–theoretical dichotomy is a false one and there are excellent examples of applied research which are theoretically fruitful. For example, consider the early research of Harvey Sacks which eventually gave rise to conversation analysis (see Chapter 10). In this he studied how telephone calls to emergency services can 'go wrong', resulting in vital information not being obtained or the call abruptly terminated. Of course, clinical psychology, educational psychology, forensic psychology and organisational psychology, for example, from mainstream psychology are all fields where the useful and applicable can go hand-in-hand with the highest academic and theoretical standards. In short, usefulness and applicability constitute a criterion of quality which does not apply to all qualitative research nor to qualitative research exclusively.

Overall, it cannot be claimed that Taylor's criteria apply solely to qualitative research since they closely echo criteria which have proven useful in evaluating quantitative research. Furthermore, Taylor's criteria do not amount to a quality-control check-list which can be readily applied to all qualitative research. They do help us clarify which criteria are appropriate to different research methods. In this sense, they provide a starting point for evaluating qualitative research.

Validity in qualitative research

The concept of validity in traditional quantitative research is usually defined in terms such as 'validity is the extent that something measures what it is intended to measure'. This is its usage in relation to traditional psychometric measures such as personality tests, intelligence measures and so forth. Typically this is referred to as construct validity. Quite simply, the issue is to establish how well or the extent to which a psychological measure assesses a theoretical concept (construct) which it is supposed to measure. There are, of course, other forms of validity that quantitative researchers refer to. For example, does the research method validly reflect 'real life'? This is a common issue in relation to the question of the value of traditional laboratory experiments which many have regarded as too artificial to have much, if any, bearing on 'real-life' processes. The term 'ecological validity' has been put forward for this. This refers to the extent to which a study captures 'reality' or 'real life'. There is no statistical way of deciding whether a study is ecologically valid, it is a matter of judgement. Quite clearly many laboratory experiments are so divorced from reality that they lack ecological validity. This tends to overlook the experiments which take place in naturalistic settings. There is a further concept of validity – external validity. This is sometimes confused with ecological validity but is different in that external validity is the extent to which research findings from one research setting can be generalised to other settings.

Just what is the relevance of these traditional types of validity to qualitative research? Ecological validity tends to be assumed tacitly by some qualitative researchers but this really depends on the data collection method involved. Much qualitative research centres on naturally occurring text such as conversations. So, for example, an analysis of emergency telephone conversations, such as that by Sacks (1992), would seem to have built-in ecological validity as it is dealing with an everyday real-world happening. These conversations were routinely recorded by the emergency services for their own purposes – but they constitute data which are appropriate for the purposes of qualitative researchers. Equally, it would be reasonable to assume that a study of news broadcasts based on videos of actual newscasts would also be ecologically valid. But one should not assume the same degree of ecological validity for all qualitative data collection methods. For example, the in-depth psychological research interview may be just as beset with problems of ecological validity as other forms of research. The research interview is not normal everyday real-life conversation by any stretch of the imagination. For example, it is governed by very different rules from everyday conversation (e.g. the interviewee does not have an equal reciprocal right to question the interviewer). Ecological validity can also be a problem in terms of data collected from focus groups or through participant observation when the researcher's true identity is known.

Of course, the conventional concept of validity employed in quantitative research is not without its problems especially when applied to qualitative research. A typical definition of validity is 'the extent to which something measures what it purports to measure', the implication being that there is something out there in the real world which is fixed in its nature and which the researcher is attempting to tap into. So the validity of a measure of intelligence is the extent to which it can be shown to relate to something identifiable as intelligence. The last few sentences, of course, would be alien to many qualitative researchers, particularly those who do not hold to a realist position.

Validity is discussed by qualitative researchers in a number of ways different from its use by quantitative researchers. For example:

- In qualitative research, the issue of validity is usually interpreted as the extent to which the analysis fits the data (usually text). So it is the *validity of the analysis* which is the focus not the objective validity of some scale or measure used. A valid analysis fits the data well.

- There is a tendency to assume that qualitative research is intrinsically more valid than quantitative research. More generally, since the qualitative method is seen as a superior way of obtaining understanding of the social and psychological world, then its validity is not really in question. Even if this were to be true of qualitative research in general, it needs to be established for each qualitative study.

- The fidelity of the transcription (e.g. of a conversation) to the original source can be regarded as an indication of the validity of the transcription. Qualitative researchers using transcripts should make stringent efforts to ensure this sort of validity is maximised by checking the transcript against the recording and referring back to the recording whenever appropriate.

The phrase 'justification of analytic claims' is used by Potter (1998) rather than the term validity. This is a useful way of looking at validity in qualitative research since it pinpoints a significant conceptualisation used by qualitative researchers. There is an entire repertoire of ways in which quality in qualitative research can be assessed, according to Potter. Although a little dependent on the type of qualitative research in question, the focus for validity in qualitative research tends to be on the analysis and not the data. Nevertheless, you will find some qualitative researchers who are as concerned with matters such as the validity of the sampling method as much as any quantitative researcher.

Validity in qualitative studies according to Mays and Pope (2000) involves the following criteria though, as we shall see, other researchers have suggested additional ones:

- *Triangulation*   This approach is based on the notion that different methods of data collection should yield comparable results if they are to be considered 'valid'. In qualitative research triangulation would involve several different sources of data possibly gathered from members of different interest groups, for example. There should be convergence in the results arising from different data sources. A fundamental, but essential, assumption of this is that weaknesses in one source of information should be compensated by the other sources of information. For instance, the researcher might wish to compare interviews with therapists, their clients and partners of the clients. If much the same results emerge from the analysis of each of the three groups, then some would regard this as evidence of validity. Mays and Pope (2000), however, suggest that triangulation is best seen as an approach to making sure that the data collection and analysis is comprehensive – and productive of a greater degree of thought and contemplation about the analysis. (See also Box 14.2 for an extended discussion of triangulation.)

Box 14.2
KEY CONCEPTS
Triangulation

Triangulation can be used, for example, when trying to identify the location of an illegal radio station. There are scientific instruments which can indicate the direction from which the radio station is broadcasting by using very directional aerials. However, the radio station could lie anywhere in that direction – it could be ten kilometres or a thousand kilometres away. By setting up the detection apparatus in a different location, a new direction for the radio station can be found. The two direction lines can be plotted on a map and the intersection of the two found. This intersection precisely pinpoints where the radio station is broadcasting from. Unless the transmitter is moving, the authorities know precisely where to go to close the illegal transmitter down.

The concept of triangulation is used in both qualitative and quantitative research but not in precisely the same way. Essentially in quantitative research triangulation refers to measuring a variable using more than one method such as using teacher ratings of pupils' *and* paper-and-pencil tests to measure intelligence, the assumption being that the two distinct measures of intelligence should correlate if the measures have some validity. This is extended in Campbell and Fiske's (1959) multitrait-multimethod matrix approach to include the measurement of more than one concept. For example, the researcher might research creativity and intelligence using several different measures of intelligence and several different measures of creativity. The measures of intelligence ought to correlate together better than they do with the measures of creativity and vice versa. In this way, the value of the measures can be assessed and also the extent to which the concepts being measured are truly different.

None of this translates precisely to qualitative research where the use of triangulation raises a number of important issues because of the varying epistemological assumptions underlying different sorts of qualitative study. As a simple example, take the researcher who is interested in how employees talk about the ethos of their workplace. One could do this by interviewing a sample of employees of all grades combined. But would it not be better to also carry out focus groups with groups of employees from different grades? Few would dispute this, but when it comes to analysing this 'triangulated' data just what are the researcher's assumptions? One could adopt the realist assumption and compare the outcomes of the interview study with the outcome of the focus group study in the expectation that they will reveal much the same analytic outcomes as shown in Figure 14.1.

But is that what we should expect? Would we expect that a focus group involving employees of different grades would be unaffected by the diversity of job statuses in the group? Would you really say certain things in front of the boss, for example? You might be happy to say things to a researcher in the anonymous context of an interview that you would not if your boss was present. In other words, the context of data collection can make a big difference to the data and, consequently, to the analysis. This would be expected from any contextualist position such as the anti-realists and the extreme relativists discussed earlier (p. 358). This is illustrated in Figure 14.2. The two sources of data are unlikely to totally converge and they are unlikely to be entirely divergent. It is obvious that these are the extreme possibilities and that in particular cases some position between the extremes of complete convergence and complete divergence will be found.

FIGURE 14.1 **Triangulation by method**

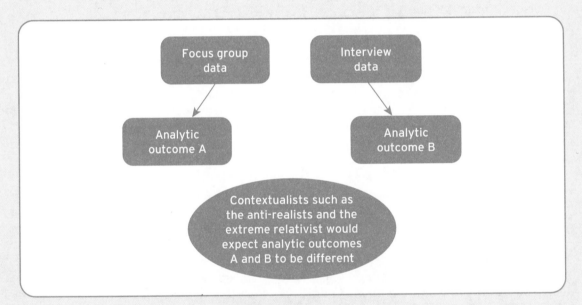

FIGURE 14.2 **Triangulated focus group and interview data**

A distinction must be made between:

- the use of mixed methods; and
- triangulation.

Triangulation does, of necessity, involve mixed methods but the use of mixed methods does not necessarily imply the use of triangulation. Mixed methods refers to the use of more than one research method in a study. Moran-Ellis *et al.* (2006a) stipulate that these different research methods should be based on different meta-theoretical perspectives. They suggest that this can be a mixture of quantitative and qualitative components or a mixture of very different sorts of qualitative data such as positivistic, interpretive, phenomenological and visual. The use of mixed-methods tends to be associated with certain areas of qualitative research especially health and education where the practical policy implications of research are, perhaps, the most evident and where strengthening the research findings by the use of mixed methods has the most obvious advantages. It is less common for theoretical or academically orientated qualitative studies to employ mixed methods – the point is that the different methods can be employed to research very different things and that the comparison between methods required in triangulation is not part of the research:

> 'Triangulation is an epistemological claim concerning what more can be known about a phenomenon when the findings from data generated by two or more methods are brought together' (Moran-Ellis *et al.*, 2006a, p. 47).

In other words, triangulation is conceived as a way of increasing our understanding over and above what the methods achieve in isolation.

What has been claimed in this respect?

● *Increased validity model of triangulation*   Quantitative researchers, especially, have claimed that the use of two measurement methods enable the researcher to know if something has been accurately measured (Campbell & Fiske, 1959). If two measures do not correlate with each other, then one or both of the measuring instruments is inadequate. Nevertheless, even if they both correlate with each other, then one should not forget the possibility that the two measures share the same flaw – for example, what appears to be a correlation between two different measures of intelligence is actually a consequence of a response set shared by the two measures.

● *Different perspectives – complementarity*   This perspective on triangulation takes the view that the use of multiple methods provides the researcher with multiple perspectives on the phenomenon being studied which is in line with the idea that the phenomenon itself is multi-faceted. While this meaning of triangulation diverges widely from the origins of the concept, it effectively takes a demonstrably qualitative stance on the use of multiple methods.

Just how are the different methods employed in a study combined in the analysis? Triangulation is not always the intention of researchers using multiple methods. Sometimes mixed methods are used in a study for quite different purposes:

● One method can be used to inform the second method; for example, if the researcher carries out a focus group study as a way of generating ideas for a later questionnaire study. In this, one method is seen as subservient to another.

● Mixed methods can be used to increase the depth of the data collected on the phenomenon in question. For example, the researcher may find it helpful to study media reports dealing with a particular issue in conjunction with an interview study; for example, in a study of how the public views immigrants.

● Sometimes a researcher may use mixed methods in a study to economise on data collection. So, for example, it may be that the researcher obtains a variety of different types of information from a single sample of participants but the different aspects of the data are reported entirely separately.

So what should happen when a researcher seeks to integrate different methods of data collection within the same analysis? According to Moran-Ellis *et al.*, the researcher needs to generate 'tangible relationship' accounting for the different methods, the different data, and the different perspectives involved. Thus merely highlighting differences is not integration. Analytic statements need to be developed which show how the different methods of data collection relate to each other if integration is to be achieved. For example, how does the data from in-depth interviews with managers relate to the data obtained by participant observation?

If the researcher genuinely wishes to integrate mixed qualitative methods then models of how to do this are scarce. One method is called 'following a thread' by Moran-Ellis, Alexander, Cronin, Fielding and Thomas (2006b). This entails the analysis of each different data set separately. Then each of the different data sets is subject to a relevant analysis to identify key themes and analytic questions for subsequent analysis. So an analytic theme is followed from the initial data set through to the other data sets. Thus while the thread is developed inductively in the primary data set it is explored in a more focused manner in the other data sets. Of course, the analysis will start several times in each of the data sets.

- *Respondent validation or member checking* This is simply a check on the extent to which the researcher's account corresponds to those of participants in the research (or new individuals comparable to the participants). The assumption is that if the participants in the research can accept the researcher's analysis then this constitutes evidence of its validity. The difficulty, of course, lies in the assumption that a researcher's perspective should be shared by the participants. So one question is under what circumstances should such a correspondence be expected. If we remember that substantial parts of qualitative research in psychology owe at least something to ethnomethodology, such a congruence might be regarded as an important criterion. Ethnomethodology seeks to understand the meanings of the social world as seen by ordinary members of that world. An approach which is common in qualitative research of various sorts is to have meetings with research participants in which the researcher presents their research findings. The intention is to promote discussion about the researcher's findings and to allow participants to question the researcher's analysis. Of course, quantitative researchers might regard such 'insider' research as being potentially biased or partisan since it suggests that the researcher is not truly independent but, instead, acts as a conduit for different interest groups.

- *Clear description/explication of the methods of data collection and analysis involved* The procedure for data collection and the processes of data analysis should be crystal clear in a good qualitative report. Information about the way in which the data were collected can have an important bearing on the interpretation of the data. The information can also help address more mundane issues such as the representativeness of the analysis beyond the particular data in question just as it can in quantitative research. Generally speaking, the analytic processes involved in qualitative research are time consuming as well as being meticulous and demanding. This is the only way of producing an analysis which has good fidelity to the data. There is no point in conducting a high quality study without demonstrating this quality to the reader.

- *Reflexivity* This is a big issue in qualitative research. Essentially it refers to the sensitivity or awareness of the researcher to how they may influence the nature of the data collected and the analysis. For example, the prior assumptions and the biases of the researcher may have an unshakable impact.

Consequently, the expectation is that the researcher should explicate their own experiences, attitudes, values and other potentially 'biasing' factors which may have an impact on the analysis or are pertinent for other reasons. For example, the psychological and social distance between the researcher and the participants can be a crucial aspect of methodology. Qualitative researchers tend to be closer to their participants than quantitative researchers. These relationships are openly discussed in much qualitative research.

- *Attention to negative or deviant instances*   The role of negative or deviant cases is very different in qualitative research. In quantitative research, the search for trends in the data includes even the smallest correlation, association or difference – so long as it meets the test of being 'statistically significant'. Perfect relationships are rare in quantitative research. The implication of this is that deviant cases are typical in quantitative data. The smaller the association found in the quantitative study the greater the impact of these deviants, however. This notwithstanding, it would be virtually unknown in quantitative research to give such deviant cases much attention. Instead they are largely ignored because they are conceived as the result of 'randomness' or 'noise', i.e. measurement error. It is almost as if deviant cases are irrelevant. On the other hand, in much qualitative research the deviant case is regarded as an essential part of the analysis. The detail involved in qualitative research often makes it evident that a particular individual or a particular aspect of the data is deviant in the sense that it is incompatible with the overall analysis as it is understood at that time. The researcher is obliged to seek to incorporate deviant cases into the analysis. Deviant cases are not 'swept under the carpet' in qualitative research.

Further criteria are mentioned by Taylor (2001) and Potter (1998). The first two are from Taylor and the final three from Potter:

- *Richness of detail in the data and analysis*   The whole point of qualitative analysis is to develop descriptive categories which fit the data well. So one criterion of the quality of a study is the amount of detail in the treatment of the data and its analysis. Qualitative analysis requires intense processing of the data. Consequently, if the researcher just presents a few broad categories and a few broad indications of what sorts of material fit that category, then this would not appear to be a good quality study. Of course, richness of detail is not readily tallied so it begs the question of how much detail constitutes richness. Should richness of detail be assessed in terms of numbers of words, the range of different sources of text, the verbal complexity of the data, or how? Similar questions apply when it comes to the issue of the richness of detail in the analysis. Just what does this mean? Is this a matter of the complexity of the analysis and why should a complex analysis be regarded as a virtue in its own right? In quantitative research, in contrast, the simplicity of the analysis is regarded as a virtue if it accounts for the detail of the data well. It is the easiest thing in the world to produce coding categories which fit the data well – if one has numerous coding categories then all the data is likely to be fitted into the analysis. Nevertheless, the fact that each of these categories fits only a very small part of the data may imply that the coding scheme is inadequate.

- *Using quantitative techniques where appropriate*   Opinions vary greatly on this but some qualitative researchers are willing, in some circumstances, to incorporate quantitative techniques into their, otherwise, qualitative study. For example, qualitative data collected using systematic sampling techniques may be acceptable to some qualitative researchers despite the fact that some very different approaches to sampling have been proposed for qualitative research.

● *Openness to evaluation* In quantitative research reports, the reader is often very distanced from the data. All that is provided, typically, are some summary statistics such as tables, charts, descriptive statistics such as means, and brief indications of the outcomes of inferential statistical analysis such as *t*-tests. In most quantitative reports, the data are not presented for independent examination. In contrast, in qualitative research reports substantial or key textual data are presented to support the analytic interpretation. As a consequence, it could be argued that a qualitative research analysis is more open to evaluation, challenge and questioning by the reader than with other forms of research. In fairness, many qualitative reports include a minimal amount of the data used in the study – just a few examples which illustrate the point being made. This is rarely sufficient to question the analysis. Of course, where textual data are provided in full in the form of transcripts the openness of the analysis to challenge is beyond doubt. Potter (1998) points out that a great deal of what the researcher claims has to be taken on trust in qualitative research. This could be remedied by making data files more available, e.g. over the Internet. Of course, there is another issue. Just how can the reader of a qualitative research report who disputes a particular analysis truly challenge the analysis? What does it mean to challenge an analysis? Some online qualitative research journals solve this problem by allowing debate to follow the publication of an article.

● *Coherence with previous studies* Notoriously, in quantitative research, very similar studies can produce very different or, even, inconsistent outcomes. Nevertheless, the coherence of a qualitative study with previous studies has been offered as a criterion of how convincing a study is. Qualitative analyses which are at variance with previous research are more likely to be questioned. This can be regarded as a replicability issue since not only may the coherence of the new study with earlier studies strengthen the new study but, similarly, it may add strength to the older analyses (just as it would for quantitative studies). There are problems with this criterion. For example, if the new qualitative study uses analytic ideas from older studies then, almost inevitably, the analyses will appear to cohere.

● *Participant's own understandings within the data* A rather different aspect of the 'validity' of a qualitative analysis is inherent in the tendency for speakers to interpret what previous speakers have said, for example. In this way, the new speaker's understanding of what went before is incorporated into the data. For example, if the new speaker quickly changes the subject of the conversation then this may give indications of their understanding of what went before. It might be indicative of the belief that the previous speaker has made some sort of *faux pas* which may need to be hidden. In other words, the data have self-checking features for the careful analyst which confirm or disconfirm the analyst's earlier analysis.

Box 14.3 describes an advanced scheme for the quality evaluation of, specifically, qualitative research.

Box 14.3

PRACTICAL ADVICE

An advanced quality evaluation scheme for qualitative research

Governments spend large amounts of money on all sorts of social research. Increasingly this involves qualitative research from many different spheres of research – health, welfare, probation and so forth. Inevitably, the question arises of how this research can be systematically evaluated. Clearly consistency in the criteria and the way in which they are applied is important for public organisations if not researchers. Given the lack of agreed standards for quality in qualitative social research, Spencer, Ritchie, Lewis and Dillon (2003) were invited to formulate criteria relevant to the research commissioned by the government. They engaged in a process in which they:

- reviewed the available criteria in the published literature;
- interviewed key individuals involved in conducting and managing research.

It was important to Spencer *et al.* that the quality criteria that they developed were appropriate to qualitative research and were not ones which could be applied to research in general. They identified various areas of focus in the quality appraisal (Figure 14.3). For each aspect of the qualitative study under consideration, Spencer *et al.* provide a minimum of one 'appraisal question' but sometimes as many as five. The appraisal questions are essentially evaluative criteria. A number of quality indicators were suggested for each of these though the scheme allowed for additional criteria to be introduced in specific instances.

   The following gives a good indication of the substantial nature of the appraisal questions for each aspect of the research together with illustrative examples of possible quality indicators. The complete assessment document can be downloaded – see Additional Resources at the end

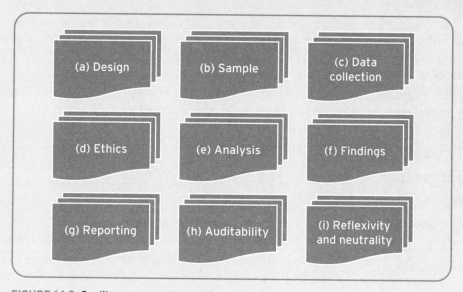

FIGURE 14.3 Quality assessment areas for evaluation

of this chapter. It is important to note that their quality criteria conflict with the viewpoints of some qualitative researchers in some instances. Spencer *et al.*'s evaluation questions are given and illustrative quality indicators for each of these then provided.

(a) Design

Appraisal question 1 'How defensible is the research design?'

Illustrative quality indicators:

1a) How well does the report discuss the relationship between the overall research strategy and the aims of the study?

1b) How effectively does the report discuss the limitations of the research design especially in terms of the value of the evidence used in the study?

(b) Sample

Appraisal question 2 'How well defended is the sample design/target selection of cases/documents?'

Illustrative quality indicators:

2a) Does the study describe carefully the population involved and demonstrate how the sample selected is related to the population? For example, is the sample typical of the population or does it represent diversity in the population?

2b) Does the study explain the rationale for the selection of the sample or the research settings or the documents involved in the analysis?

Appraisal question 3 'Sample composition/case inclusion – how well is the eventual coverage described?'

Illustrative quality indicators:

3a) Does the study provide the reasons why some of those approached to take part in the study did not participate and what sort of cases were not included as a consequence of the procedures adopted? (For example, would people without transport be unable to participate in the study?)

3b) Does the report explain how the sample members could be accessed and the methods by which they were approached? These may affect participation in the research.

(c) Data collection

Appraisal question 4 'How well was the data collection carried out?'

Illustrative quality indicators:

4a) Does the report describe who collected the data, the procedures and materials used to collect data, and supply information about the origins and authorship of documents used?

4b) Does the report describe crucial features of fieldwork such as the conventions used when taking field notes and discuss how the circumstances and methods of fieldwork might have an influence on the data collected?

(d) Ethics

Appraisal question 5 'What evidence is there of attention to ethical issues?'

Illustrative quality indicators:

5a) Does the report describe consent procedures, the information given participants, the confidentiality and anonymity arrangements for data and the participants' identities, the nature of the information about services available following the study, and the consent procedures?

5b) Does the study contain a discussion of the possible adverse consequences of taking part in the study and how these were avoided?

(e) Analysis

Appraisal question 6 'How well has the approach to, and formulation of, the analysis been conveyed?'

Illustrative quality indicators:

6a) Does the report clearly indicate how analytic categories, etc. have been created and deployed?

6b) Is the form of the raw data described (e.g. transcripts, interview notes, documents)?

Appraisal question 7 'How well has diversity of perspective and content been explored?'

Illustrative quality indicators:

7a) Does the report discuss the relevance of negative cases or unusual cases?

7b) Does the report systematically try to categorise or explain the variation found within the data?

Appraisal question 8 'How well have detail, depth and complexity (i.e. richness) of the data been conveyed?'

Illustrative quality indicators:

8a) Has the report used quotations or observations from the data which contribute to the understanding of the data?

8b) Does the report identify and discuss patterns, linkages and associations in the data?

Appraisal question 9 'Contexts of data sources – how well are they retained and portrayed?'

Illustrative quality indicators:

9a) Does the research describe in detail relevant details of the setting of the study such as the history, background and characteristics of the research setting?

9b) Are the data managed in a way which retains contextual material which is relevant to individual cases?

(f) Findings

Appraisal question 10 'How credible are the findings?'

Illustrative quality indicators:

10a) Do the findings 'make sense' and exhibit a 'coherent logic'?

10b) Do the findings cohere with what is known from other sources?

Appraisal question 11 'How has knowledge/understanding been extended by the research?'

Illustrative quality indicators:

11a) Does the report clearly and credibly discuss what contribution to knowledge and understanding is made by the research?

11b) Are the aims and design of the study contextualised by what is currently known and understood?

Appraisal question 12 'How well does the evaluation address its original aims and purposes?'

Illustrative quality indicators:

12a) Are there clear relationships between the purposes of the study and the findings as set out?

12b) Does the report explain and discuss the nature of the limitations of the study in terms of the study's aims?

Appraisal question 13 'Scope for drawing wider inference - how well is this explained?'

Illustrative quality indicators:

13a) Does the report include a discussion of the extent to which the findings of the study can be generalised more widely than the sample selected for research?

13b) Does the report contain detailed description of the study's context so that the applicability of the findings to other settings may be assessed?

Appraisal question 14 'How clear is the basis of evaluative appraisal?' (This would apply primarily to qualitative research which is designed to evaluate a social, policy, or institutional initiative.)

Illustrative quality indicators:

14a) Does the report indicate the nature of the source of any evaluative judgements included, such as whose judgement was involved and how the judgement has been reached?

14b) Does the report discuss the unintended consequences of the intervention and what caused them?

(g) Reporting

Appraisal question 15 'How clear are the links between data, interpretation and conclusions, i.e. how well can the route to any conclusions be seen?'

Illustrative quality indicators:

15a) Does the reporting demonstrate links between the analysis and the original data presented which are conceptual in nature and do not merely reiterate the data in similar descriptive terms?

15b) Does the report describe negative instances which do not fit with the analysis because, for example, they lie outside the scope of the analysis? Alternatively, the report attempts to show how negative instances could be brought within the main analytic framework.

Appraisal question 16 'How clear and coherent is the reporting?'

Illustrative quality indicators:

16a) Does the report make clear by highlighting or summarising the key points in a way appropriate for the target audience of the report?

16b) Is the report's structure clear enough to help the reader through the material and does it include signposting such as subheadings to help the reader further?

(h) Auditability

Appraisal question 17 'How adequately has the research process been documented?'

Illustrative quality indicators:

17a) Are the main documents used in the study included in the report? This would include letters to organisations and individuals, questionnaires, instructions for data management, etc.

17b) Are the strengths and otherwise of the methods used and the data sources employed discussed?

(i) Reflexivity and neutrality

Appraisal question 18 'How clear are the assumptions/theoretical perspectives/values that have shaped the form and output of the evaluation?'

Illustrative quality indicators:

18a) Does the report indicate or discuss the perspectives and values of the researchers which may impact the methodology or substance of the report?

18b) Is there evidence in the report that the researchers are open to revising the conceptualisations, theories and assumptions in the light of their experience of the research process?

Reliability in qualitative research

Reliability and validity have emerged as basic quality control issues in quantitative research. This chapter has discussed the various ways in which validity has been raised in relation to qualitative research. What about reliability in qualitative research? This is much less frequently discussed by qualitative researchers than the concept of validity. There are a number of reasons for this – most importantly is that various qualitative methods have different epistemological positions relevant to the issue of reliability.

In quantitative research, the concept of reliability is applied to the measures (of variables) which the researcher is using. There are two main usages of the concept reliability:

- The term test–retest reliability is used to indicate an assessment of how stable or consistent 'scores' on a measure are at different points in time. The belief is that, in general, a measure which correlates with itself over time is a reliable measure – and, hence, a good one. This is the case only to the extent that what is being measured can be expected to be stable over time. So, if we are measuring something which by its very nature is chronologically unstable, good test–retest reliability should not be expected. People's moods are transitory so a good measure of mood might be expected to be unreliable over time. Of course, in quantitative psychology things are usually measured because they are believed to be enduring and unchanging characteristics, such as intelligence, reaction times and so forth.

- The other meaning of reliability in quantitative research is the internal consistency of a measure. In quantitative research, measurements often consist of a set of items (questions, frequently) which are summed in some way to get the measure. These are the ubiquitous scales found in quantitative research. The internal consistency of the scale (the extent to which all of the items are measuring the same thing) is regarded as an indicator of the quality of the measure.

Neither of these has much bearing on most qualitative research. Qualitative researchers eschew the use of scales for various reasons – especially because they violate the requirement of richness of data which underlies most qualitative research. Furthermore, many qualitative researchers would reject the notion that there are fixed, measurable characteristics of individuals. As a consequence, reliability of the sorts just discussed is irrelevant. Qualitative researchers are more likely to regard their data as *situationally bounded*, that is, they do not necessarily expect to find the data they obtain from individuals to be consistent across research situations. For example, they are aware that different researchers may obtain different perspectives from interviewees.

The notion of reliability may be relevant to just a few aspects of qualitative research. For example, the transcription of interviews and other data is regarded as part of the discipline of qualitative research. Consistency of transcriptions between transcribers using the same method would be an ideal. This equates to the reliability of the transcription across different raters. This is rarely, if ever, formally assessed.

CONCLUSION

Very few of the traditional criteria which psychologists use in quantitative research apply to qualitative research directly. Qualitative and quantitative research simply do not have the same intellectual roots and, in various ways, they are in conflict. Indeed, it may well be the case that if traditional evaluative criteria can be applied to qualitative research then that research may well be based on the ethos of positivism. There are a number of criteria for evaluating qualitative research but these largely concentrate on evaluating the quality of the coding or categorisation process (the qualitative analysis). They are best regarded as indicators of quality rather than proof of quality in qualitative research. This contrasts markedly with quantitative and statistical research where there are procedures which may be applied to decide the worth of the research. Significance testing is one obvious example of this when we apply a test of whether the data are likely to have been obtained simply by sampling fluctuations. Internal consistency measures of reliability such as Cronbach's alpha also have such cut-off rules. This leaves it a little uncertain how inexperienced qualitative researchers can best evaluate their research.

In ending, to emphasise how difficult the evaluation and appraisal of qualitative research can be, it is worth mentioning Dixon-Woods *et al.* (2007) who studied three different ways of assessing qualitative research studies. One was the scheme described in Box 14.3, the second was another systematic system, and the third was expert opinion using no particular scheme. The study design involved having a set of 12 research reports evaluated using the various evaluation methods. Dixon-Woods *et al.* point out:

> Our qualitative and quantitative data suggest that using a structured approach appears to sensitize reviewers to aspects of research practice. However, a structured approach does not appear more likely to produce higher levels of agreement between or within reviewers: in fact, the highest level of agreement is (arguably) achieved without using a structured approach. It could also be argued that the judgements produced using structured approaches are over-elaborated, and biased towards procedural aspects of research practice. (Dixon-Woods *et al.*, 2007, p. 46)

KEY POINTS

- Qualitative research, characteristically, has different goals and assumptions from those of quantitative research. As a consequence, it is important that evaluative criteria which are applied to qualitative research reflect this. It cannot be claimed that there are universal criteria of quality in qualitative research. But this is also true in quantitative research. The criteria for evaluating a survey, for example, are different in many respects from those for evaluating a laboratory experiment.

- Nevertheless, there is a degree of overlap in the applicability of quality criteria across qualitative and quantitative research. That is, some criteria may be of value to evaluating both types of research. Criteria such as the quality, persuasiveness and coherence of the researcher's argument, how well the research is related to previously published research, the potential of the findings for generalisation and so forth would be largely common to both qualitative and quantitative research.

- Other criteria are more exclusively applicable to qualitative research (or quantitative research for that matter). These criteria include in qualitative research such matters as how well the analysis fits with the understandings of the research participants and the richness of detail in the data.

- The criteria for the evaluation of professionally produced qualitative research may be somewhat different and more demanding than what could be expected of newcomers to qualitative research. This is partly because the requirements of a purely academic research exercise may be very different from those for research commissioned at considerable expense by, say, the government. This is not to suggest that newcomers cannot benefit from the more demanding criteria but merely that initially these criteria would be hard to implement fully in terms of the work of novice researchers.

- Qualitative research includes a wide variety of different approaches which may or may not share philosophical and pragmatic assumptions. Thus sensitivity to the differences in perspectives which demand different evaluative criteria is essential. There is no sense in which the evaluative criteria discussed in this chapter fit all qualitative research equally.

ADDITIONAL RESOURCES

Seale, C. (1999). Quality in qualitative research. *Qualitative Inquiry*, 5 (4), 465–478.

Spencer, L., Ritchie, J., Lewis, J., and Dillon, L. (2003). *Quality in Qualitative Evaluation: A framework for assessing research evidence. A Quality Framework*. Cabinet Office: Government Chief Social Researcher's Office. Strategy Unit. http://www.gsr.gov.uk/downloads/evaluating_policy/a_quality_framework.pdf (accessed 12 August 2009).

Willig, C. (2008). *Introducing Qualitative Research in Psychology*, 2nd Edition. Maidenhead: Open University Press. (Chapter 9, 'Quality in qualitative research').

Yardley, L. (2008). Demonstrating validity in qualitative psychology. In J.A. Smith (Ed.), *Qualitative Psychology: A practical guide to research methods*, 2nd Edition. London: Sage, pp. 235–251.

CHAPTER 15

Ethics and data management in qualitative research

Overview

- Psychological ethics are the essentially moral principles which have been developed to govern all aspects of psychologists' work including research.

- The historical origins of modern research ethics were in disturbing medical experimentation that took place in Nazi Germany. In addition, concerns about the use of deception in psychological research itself also played their part.

- Psychology's professional bodies (e.g. the American Psychological Association and the British Psychological Society) have published detailed ethical guidelines. While they are substantially similar, this chapter is based on the more comprehensive American Psychological Association's ethics. So, for example, American Psychological Association ethical principles cover issues to do with the publication of research findings such as plagiarism and fabricating data.

- Deception, informed consent and confidentiality have emerged as being among the most important concepts in ethics, though the range of issues is much wider. A researcher needs to be aware of the processes involved in seeking ethical approval from both the organisation they work for and the organisation within which they propose to carry out their study.

- It should not be assumed that qualitative research is ethically unproblematic. While qualitative research avoids some of the worst ethical violations which have sometimes characterised quantitative research, qualitative research generates its own ethical problems not all of which are effectively covered by present guidelines. This is partly a consequence of the ways in which qualitative researchers collect data. For example, the chapter examines some of the ethical problems of studies in which a single interviewer interviews couples in an interactive context.

- There are legal and ethical requirements about the management of personally identifiable data. Once data have been anonymised then these requirements do not apply. It is recommended that the researcher provides written information to participants about important features of the study and obtains their written agreement to participation.

Does qualitative research need ethics?

Research ethics in qualitative research overlap considerably with those governing quantitative research. However, qualitative psychologists often orientate themselves very differently to their subject matter, people, which brings about extra demands in terms of ethics for qualitative research. Among the most obvious difference between qualitative and quantitative research is the way in which participants in research are viewed and treated. Laboratory experimentation, for instance, ignores everything but a few fairly restricted features of their research participant's behaviour (no rich data collection here). Importantly, the laboratory researcher carefully manipulates the behaviours of those participating in the study. It is no coincidence that these participants were once known as subjects since the term is indicative of the power relationship between researcher and participant – it is that of a powerful person (the researcher) versus a subordinate one (the subject). Such participants in this sort of research are effectively disregarded as persons – by reducing them to just a few variables. Or, in the typical field research, questionnaires are distributed to participants whose function is to tick boxes rather than to express the richness of their thinking. These may be caricatures but they contain an essence of truth. The impression is of a somewhat alienated relationship between the quantitative researcher and their research participants. The quantitative researcher, it could be argued, tends to demean the participants in their research by refusing to regard them as whole human beings.

Not surprisingly, some qualitative researchers are tempted to regard their research as ethically or morally superior to that of the quantitative psychologist. Some of the reasons for this are obvious – the qualitative researcher, in general, seems more interested in their research participants as people and seeks to maintain their human dignity. As Brinkman and Kvale (2005, p. 162) put it: 'The qualitative boom has been accompanied by a tendency among qualitative researchers to portray qualitative inquiry as inherently ethical, or at least more ethical than quantitative research.' They are describing what has been referred to as *qualitative ethicism* (Hammersley, 1999). This is the tendency of qualitative researchers to regard their research in overwhelmingly ethical terms almost as if achieving ethical goals was the purpose of research.

Psychologists, like many other professions, conduct themselves through the use of a set of moral principles known as 'ethics'. The American Psychological Association probably has the most extensive ethical code but others, such as the British Psychological Society, have their own similar codes. The ethical issues facing qualitative researchers can be very different from those facing the quantitative researcher despite some obvious areas of overlap. The relationship between the qualitative researcher and their participants is distinctive perhaps largely as a consequence of the qualitative researcher's search for rich data. This demands a very different approach to data collection compared with the much more restricted data typical of archetypal quantitative research. Despite this, in practice, the ethical issues facing qualitative researchers tend to be covered by identical ethical codes which govern quantitative research. This clearly may not be completely satisfactory where qualitative research has particular ethical poblems.

While it is tempting to regard ethics as a set of rules or regulations which govern the activities of psychological practitioners and researchers, reality is somewhat different. Ethical principles, for example, can be described as procedural matters in practice but this way of looking at ethics faces difficulties. No system of rules is self-interpreting and so even where we think that we have a good rule then 'we still need to know when and how to apply the rule' (Brinkmann & Kvale, 2005, p. 159). Ethical principles require interpretation in relation to the detail of a situation facing a researcher. Put another way, using an old chestnut, it is an moral principle that one shouldn't kill but what if by killing a extreme dictator one could save many thousands of lives? What then? Does the principle about not killing still apply or does some other principle begin to take precedence? Much the same is true for research ethics – that is, whether an ethical principle should prevail in a particular situation may depend as much on details about the situation as the nature of the ethical principle itself. For example, the confidentiality of information supplied to a researcher by a participant is generally required in most ethical guidelines for researchers. But what if during the course of an interview the participant makes threats to kill a neighbour with whom he has a dispute? Should this information be confidential? And suppose the man goes on to kill his neighbour: is the researcher blameless and beyond reproach because they maintained confidentiality?

Psychological researchers sometimes identify such dilemmas in their work. Just how should they go about resolving them? Well, the ethical principles of psychologists by and large give the responsibility for monitoring ethical standards to the researcher(s) carrying out the research and the psychological community in general. This might include (a) the researcher(s) seeking the advice and assistance of other psychologists when there are potentially any ethical issues and (b) the entire psychology community monitoring at an informal level the ethical standards employed in the different fields of psychology.

Ethical guidelines sometimes make exceptions where the law or a specific organisation allows certain sorts of research activity which otherwise would seem to be ethically dubious. This clearly is a situation in which there is a conflict between the ethics and the law which some might see as a reason to question the law rather than a reason to disregard the ethics. Ethics are not simply organisational matters but individual matters too. One's personal ethics may mean that one does not do what is otherwise permissible. Researchers did not have to include deceit in their research if they found it objectionable even if when it was ethically permitted. There are areas, of course, where the law is less restrictive than ethical principles. For example, the law generally does not punish psychologists who have sex with their adult clients even though it is against ethical principles.

It is important to remember that qualitative research has gained entry to a number of professional areas of psychological research including health psychology, clinical psychology, counselling and psychotherapy, educational psychology, work and organisational psychology, and community psychology (Willig & Stainton-Rogers, 2008). This increases the ethical demands in qualitative research.

The development of ethics in psychology

Ethics are an important aspect of modern psychological and social scientific research. The modern ethical codes can be traced back to what was known as the Nuremberg Code which was essentially developed to govern medical research. The medical profession in Nazi Germany had an appalling record of unnecessary and inhumane medical experimentation on human beings. The most notorious was Dr Josef Mengele who, for example, gave intense voltages of electrical shock to women concentration camp inmates in a study of their endurance levels. At the trial of some of these Nazi doctors in 1947, the judges did not merely deliver a verdict but considered principles for the appropriate conduct of medical research. Six of these principles were adopted from elsewhere but another four were contributed by the court. Collectively these are referred to as the Nuremberg Code. The impetus for the code came from these extreme medical experiments. Many of these principles will be familiar to anyone with a basic knowledge of psychological ethics. For example:

- Consent to take part in research should be entirely voluntary and given only by people with a legal capacity to give consent. The person should have enough knowledge of the research to give consent in an informed manner.

- The participant in the research has the right to bring the research to an end – but unlike the modern versions of this only if they are mentally or physically unable to continue to the end of the research.

Other aspects of the code do not seem to have exact modern equivalents in ethical codes. For example, the Nuremberg Code indicates that an experiment should provide findings which are for society's good and that unnecessary studies should not be carried out. Following the Nuremberg Code, the American Psychological Association developed its set of ethical principles in 1953 which influenced and guided ethical thinking beyond just psychology and throughout social scientific research (Blodgett, Boyer & Turk, 2005).

Concern grew about the ethics of psychological research from this time onwards and became especially focused on the laboratory experimentation which characterised social psychology in the 1950s to 1970s. While much of this experimentation was of a high intellectual standard and creative and inventive, to be successful it frequently required that participants were misled or misinformed about the true nature of the research (Korn, 1997). Deception dates back to 1897 in psychology when Leon Solomons told participants, some of the time untruthfully, that either one point or two points were touching them in a study of sensory discrimination. What they were told influenced what they perceived. Korn (1997) found that the use of deception in social psychological research substantially increased in the three decades following the Second World War. Much of the classic research of social psychologists used deceit in some form and sometimes the deception was extreme. Deception studies began to attract considerable criticism, especially from the late 1960s onwards. The work of Stanley Milgram (1933–1984) was a particular focus (e.g. Milgram, 1974). In his famous studies he led participants to believe that they were delivering intense electric shocks to another person as part of a study of learning. In truth, the research was about the influence of the experimenter in encouraging obedience to the researcher's instructions.

In recent years, considerable ethical scrutiny has been applied to researchers studying humans (and animals for that matter, though this is not an issue for qualitative researchers and hence not covered in this chapter). Institutions such as universities, health services and the prison service have introduced ethical committees to overview research conducted within their ambit. This is usually two-fold:

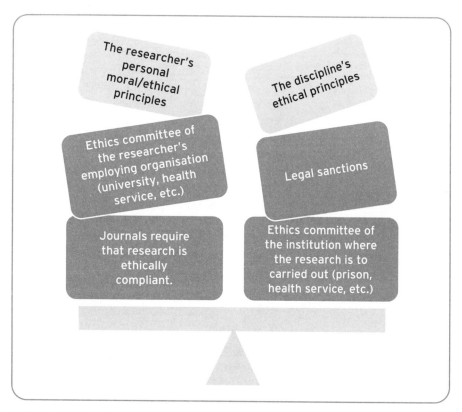

FIGURE 15.1 The ethical environment of qualitative and other research

● institutions monitor research by researchers who work for the institution;

● institutions monitor research in their institutions by researchers from outside of the institutions.

In addition to this are the ethical principles of the researcher's discipline. The complexity of ethical control is illustrated in Figure 15.1. While the aim is to pre-empt possible ethical problems, sanctions can be applied against those who violate ethical requirements. These may be instigated by the professional body to which the researcher belongs but also by their home institution. Finally, there is the risk that participants may sue researchers and their employers when research oversteps the mark.

Ethical guidelines are important because of the protection that they offer researchers as well as the broad moral principles enunciated. Gross ethical violations by researchers risk bringing psychology as a profession, and not just the offending individuals, into disrepute. The negative consequences of this for all members of the discipline are potentially serious. Organisations and individuals gain autonomy by the application of clear and accepted ethical principles. Self-regulation is generally seen as beneficial given the possible excesses of government legislation concerning the conduct of research. Autonomy is a characteristic of many successful professions such as medicine and the law. They are not entirely free from government legislation but they operate somewhat independently of it. Professions such as medicine emerged as powerful independent bodies during the nineteenth century (Howitt, 1992). Their autonomy left them largely in control of most of the major aspects of their professional activities. Ethical standards are one way in which a profession regulates itself and avoids outside intervention.

Qualitative research in psychology is very different from the medical research which brought about the earliest ethical codes for researchers. Ethical codes have become increasingly sophisticated over the years and entered areas which those who framed the Nuremberg Code could not have foreseen. Clearly, modern research demands high ethical standards. For that reason, in this chapter the American Psychological Association's ethical code is adopted. This is the most demanding and comprehensive available. The most recent version of the American Psychological Association's manual on ethics was first made available in 2002 and came into effect on 1 June 2003 (American Psychological Association, 2002). The American Psychological Association's code covers the gamut of the professional work of psychologists, including their roles as educators and practitioners as well as research roles. So, for example, you will find that the code requires that psychology teaching should exhibit fidelity to the current state of knowledge in the discipline.

There are two important points which should be borne in mind by qualitative and other researchers:

- The American Psychological Association guidelines do not simply apply to professionals in the field of psychology but also students affiliated to the organisation.

- There is an assumption that psychologists should know the relevant ethical standards which apply to their work and the American Psychological Association rejects ignorance of these standards as an excuse.

General ethical principles for qualitative research

The APA argues that ethics should be based on five different integrating principles (Figure 15.2). These apply just as much to qualitative as to quantitative research.

FIGURE 15.2 **The basic principles of APA ethics**

Principle A: Beneficence and nonmaleficence

The work of psychologists should be seen as being to the benefit of people with who the psychologist engages with professionally. That is, their work should be of benefit to their clients, widely defined. Equally, there is a requirement that psychologists should seek to avoid harm to those with who they interact as clients and participants in research. While this seems a reasonable principle, there are circumstances where there may be some doubt about its applicability. For example, what if the research involves interviews with prisoners and they reveal to the researcher that they have committed crimes which are not known to the authorities? Should the principle of beneficence apply and the researcher not pass on the new information to the authorities? What if the prison makes such revelation a requirement for cooperation in the research?

Principle B: Fidelity and responsibility

Essentially the work of a professional psychologist involves relationships of trust with other people. Consequently, they are expected to:

- take responsibility for what they do;
- conduct themselves in accordance with established professional standards;
- make it clear that ethics have a role in all aspects of their professional activities and inform clients and others of this. They have a responsibility to monitor the ethical conduct of other members of the psychological community including their colleagues.

Principle C: Integrity including accuracy, honesty and truthfulness

Integrity should be manifested throughout every part of a psychologist's professional work. So, for example, it is generally accepted that in some circumstances deception may be appropriate when there are clear benefits from the research which substantially outweigh the risks. Nevertheless, even then, the psychologist should correct any harmful consequences.

Principle D: Justice – equality of access to psychology's benefits

Psychologists, for example, should be aware of their actual and potential personal biases in order that all people experience fair and just practices in the context of the work of psychologists. For qualitative researchers, this is another way of expressing the reflexivity of the research process. Furthermore, psychologists should neither condone nor engage in unjust practices and should be aware of means by which injustice may be manifest.

Principle E: Respect for people's rights and dignity

It is held that people have the following rights: privacy, confidentiality and self-determination. One consequence of this is that psychologists need to understand why some people may be vulnerable and not able to make autonomous decisions. Children, those who have intellectual limitations and some elderly people are obvious examples of this category. This principle also means that psychologists need to respect (and be able to recognise) differences between groups of people in terms of culture and roles. So characteristics such as disability, culture, age, ethnicity, gender, gender identity, language, nationality, race, religion and socio-economic status are all matters for consideration and respect. This involves an expectation that psychologists not only try to avoid biases against such groupings but also hold a critical stance towards others who fail to reach the expected standard.

Box 15.1 indicates some of the complexity of ethics in a characteristic qualitative study.

Box 15.1

ILLUSTRATIVE RESEARCH STUDY

Micro-ethics in qualitative research: stuck between research participants

Research ethics tends to dwell on the researcher-participant relationship but the models of research in qualitative research methods can be somewhat more demanding. What about research situations in which a researcher studies both partners in a couple? What problems does this create? Forbat and Henderson (2003) report how one of them interviewed a 'fictionalised' couple, Andy and Bella, about their relationship. Bella has health issues and Andy is her carer. While one partner was being interviewed, the other would keep out of the way and vice versa. This care relationship was undergoing problems and the interviewer feared that violence might be involved. Andy told the interviewer about a particularly 'tense' episode in their relationship. One dilemma for the interviewer was whether to raise this incident with Bella. The ethics of this are somewhat uncertain since just what is the meaning of confidentiality in the context. For example, would it be right to publish Andy's version of the truth alongside Bella's version?

Forbat and Henderson (2003) describe a number of ethically based dilemmas which are inherent in the situation just described:

- *Conflict of interest*   Andy and Bella may have different expectations of what the research was about. For Andy, it may be to communicate the difficulties of the caring relationship whereas for Bella it may be to communicate the loving nature of their relationship. Similarly, the interest of the researcher in the research might be to fulfil quite a different purpose.

- *Imbalance*   The researcher may have a preference for one particular viewpoint in the situation. Given that Bella represents a group of people who have rarely had a 'voice' in society then the researcher might prefer to present things from the point of view of the most disempowered person in the relationship. Forbat and Henderson argue that partiality is likely in these situations and needs to be acknowledged in the write-up. Not to do so is to employ the sort of power relationship which characterises a great deal of quantitative research. If qualitative researchers wish to employ more egalitarian approaches in which participants in research are 'partners' with the researcher in the research process then it is important to acknowledge this partiality.

- *Taking sides*   The researcher might be expected to take sides in the situation by Andy and Bella. While it is important to avoid doing so, what this means is that information from interviews with one of the partners must not spill over into the interviews with the other partner. Will there be a process of sharing the transcripts, for example? This clearly entails some discussion between the researcher and the couple being interviewed about how this issue is to be managed and contained.

- *Intrusion*   Research on two participants can be much more intrusive into their relationship than research involving just one partner. A reasonable policy would be one of 'non-disclosure' but this would have to be agreed by all involved. This might be dealt with simply by one of the partners withdrawing from the study if things got uncomfortable. However, in a relationship situation then this may not be quite so easy as it might at first appear. What was it about the situation which led the other partner to withdraw? Had they something to hide? Just how would it be explained to their partner? So the freedom to withdraw in this case is constrained in these circumstances.

- *Influence*   In the dyadic research, the first partner to raise a particular issue is having a disproportionate influence on the way that things proceed. There is a possibility that the particular subject matter was introduced by one of the partners with the expectation that it would be raised with the other partner or even in the hope that the researcher will take sides on the issue. So, there are problems about whether to raise the issue with the other partner.

- *Disseminating results*   Ethical problems arise in a number of ways in respect of publication. First of all, confidentiality becomes more problematic when more than one partner is interviewed since there is extra information which may make it easier for the partners to be identified by others. But there is another problem – if quotes are given from both partners in a publication then each partner would find it far easier to identify what the other partner had said during the interview.

Ethical procedures in qualitative research

The basic ethical requirements for qualitative research are the same as for any other form of psychological research with human participants. There are some special problems for qualitative researchers, as we shall see, but the following are key matters which may be an issue for researchers.

Institutional clearance

A large proportion of psychological research is carried out within organisations such as schools, hospitals and prisons – and, of course, universities. Many institutions require formal approval before they allow research to take place within the institution and before they allow members of their staff to carry out research there or elsewhere. Generally, but not always, the responsibility for granting approval lies with an ethical committee. (Sometimes the authority for approving the research may rest with a single individual such as the head of a school.) The procedures can appear to be cumbersome (for example, lengthy forms to fill) though sometimes the committee has a fast-track procedure which can be used where the research is not at all ethically problematic. Qualitative researchers have the same obligations as any other researcher to obtain ethical clearance from the organisation that they are affiliated to and any organisation where they wish to conduct their research. For example, a university researcher wishing to carry out research in a prison might need to follow the procedures of both organisations. Although it may appear that qualitative research involves relatively benign methods of data collection, this is something that the qualitative researcher cannot take for granted. It is as necessary to make a detailed assessment of the ethical implications of one's qualitative research proposals as it is for any other type of research. Of course, some of the materials with which qualitative researchers work may not require ethical clearance – especially where it involves archival material and other data not collected directly from human participants such as where media contents are analysed. However, in almost all other cases it is incumbent on the researcher to obtain the necessary ethical approval.

Such an application should:

- exhibit transparency in that it accurately and patently represents the true nature of the research;
- be accurate in terms of the information provided;
- be clear in terms of what it communicates about the proposed research;
- avoid misleading in any way such as through lies, partial truths or by omission;
- act as a template or protocol for the research that is actually carried out – if there are changes then it will probably be necessary to seek further approval.

Since most research by students will take place in a university setting, the ethics vetting procedures universities have are of interest to those planning qualitative research studies. The ethics committee is likely to be a generic committee dealing with *all* research involving human participants irrespective of the disciplinary background of the research. So it would deal with research from disciplines such as sociology, business studies, biology and so forth. One approach involves a two-tiered process of ethics clearance:

- The first stage involves unproblematic research which meets basic ethical standards and raises no ethical difficulties. Such research can be identified using a basic screening questionnaire.
- The second stage is for research which cannot meet these basic standards to be reviewed in detail by the ethics committee. The research may then be approved, approved with provisos or refused ethical clearance, which means that the research cannot take place.

There may be provision for blanket approval of broad or generic styles of research which meet certain criteria and which meet basic ethical requirements. This speeds up the clearance process research.

Screening questions can be used to identify unproblematic research proposals fairly effectively. The following is a list of the sorts of issue the screening questionnaire might address. Because of their apparent irrelevance to qualitative research, matters to do with invasive physiological or biological techniques have been left out of consideration. If you are planning a research study, decide between true and false for each of the following statements which are based on an ethics screening questionnaire used at one British university. Respond to each of the statements honestly:

- The researcher(s) involved in the study has prior experience of and/or adequate training in the methods to be employed.   TRUE/FALSE

- An experienced member of staff will supervise student researchers and junior researchers directly.   TRUE/FALSE

- The researcher(s) is not in a position of direct authority over participants in the study (such as when students are recruited by teaching staff at a university to be participants in the research).   TRUE/FALSE

- The participants will not be members of vulnerable groups (i.e. children less than 18 years old, elderly people above the age of 65 years, women during pregnancy, individuals with a mental illness, prisoners or otherwise detained people or any other vulnerable group).   TRUE/FALSE

- The research procedures are not likely to cause distress of a physical, social, emotional or psychological nature.   TRUE/FALSE

- The research procedures are not physically or psychologically demanding on the participants.   TRUE/FALSE

- The study does not expose participants to risks or distress greater than the risks and distress of their normal lifestyle.   TRUE/FALSE

- If the study includes observations or recording of participants, they will be informed in advance that this will be involved.   TRUE/FALSE

- Participants can choose whether to take part free from any pressures and based on informed consent.   TRUE/FALSE

- Participants will be fully informed about the study's objectives and details of the procedure before the research commences or at the end if the information would risk invalidating the study.   TRUE/FALSE

- Deception is not used in the research either by withholding information from participants or by misleading them in ways which could harm or lead to their exploitation.   TRUE/FALSE

- Where the use of deception is proposed, it is unavoidable given the purposes of the study.   TRUE/FALSE

- Where deception is used, participants will be debriefed about the true purpose of the study soon after its completion.   TRUE/FALSE

- Consideration has been given to how participants will react on being told that information has been withheld or that there has been deliberate deception.   TRUE/FALSE

- Participants will be told that they may withdraw from the study at any stage and require that their data (e.g. tapes, notes) are destroyed.   TRUE/FALSE

- Information about participants in the research will be confidential and not identifiable except with prior agreement.   TRUE/FALSE

- Videos and audio-recordings will be kept in a secure place and not allowed to be used by third parties.   TRUE/FALSE

- Video and audio-recordings of participants will be destroyed within six years of the completion of the investigation.   TRUE/FALSE

- The researcher has not been offered inducements to do the research by a third party (except for their contractually agreed salaries or for expenses). TRUE/FALSE

- Participants will not be offered inducements other than basic expenses to take part in the study. TRUE/FALSE

How do you decide whether your research is free of ethical problems based on the above? Well unless you answered TRUE to all of the statements which are relevant to your research then there may be ethical problems with your work. This means that you would have to submit a detailed proposal for approval by the committee. Of course, ethical requirements can vary from institution to institution so you need to check what procedures are in place where you are working or studying. Nevertheless, the above will give you a flavour of what might be involved. The following sections provide more information about the ethical basis of these screening items.

As you are probably beginning to realise, obtaining ethical clearance can involve a whole lot of form filling.

Informed consent in the recruitment of research participants

It is one of the basic ethical principles that participants agree to take part in research freely and in the light of knowledge concerning the nature of the research. This means that participants:

- should not be put under any pressure to participate in the research (such as being coerced or because they fear the consequences of not taking part in the research); and

- should understand just what participating in the research will involve.

The point is that unless the conditions are met then a person may agree to take part in the research but might have refused had the true nature of the research been clear to them. Informed consent applies to a full range of psychological activities such as assessment, therapy and counselling but its role in research is crucial. It basically means that participants should understand what they are agreeing to before they should be allowed to agree to it. Those who lack the capacity to understand what they are being asked to agree to (e.g. children) require special protection. It is obvious that the principle of informed consent means that the researcher should not bamboozle the potential participant into taking part but should explain clearly and in appropriate language just what the research is about. Equally obviously, the way in which things are explained to a university student may need to be different from that given to an elderly person. Informed consent is not absolutely required and sometimes ethical codes permit exceptions. For example, the law might permit studies without informed consent, say, in military contexts. In these circumstances, the researcher's personal ethics may be more important in ensuring that potential participants are fully aware of the nature of the research.

The following provisions would generally suffice to justify the claim of informed consent:

- Potential participants are given accurate information about the purpose, procedures and approximate duration of their commitment.

- Participants need to understand that they have the right not to take part in the research and that they may withdraw from the research at any stage. It is usually accepted by researchers that this freedom to withdraw includes the withdrawal of any data provided up to this point. Tapes might be given to the participant who withdraws or the transcripts may be shredded and so forth.

- Participants need to know what consequences might ensue from not taking part in the research. Most often there will be no consequence but this is not always the case. For example, I have conducted research in a therapeutic organisation working with sexually abusive men which required, contractually, that the men had to take part in research. Thus a man who refused had failed to fulfil the contract and might be regarded as uncooperative and further treatment refused.

- Potential research participants should be told about features of the research which might have a bearing on their decision whether or not to participate. So the potential risks, discomforts and negative outcomes should be considered by the researcher and communicated to the participant. One instance of things which might need to be communicated might be the identity of the body funding the research if there is one. Some participants, for example, might be willing to take part in research if it was supported by a charity but not if it were funded by big business.

- If the research has particular potential benefits then the participant may consent to take part in procedures which they otherwise wouldn't. These benefits may be for the community in general, the academic community or for the individual participant. This fuller picture may not be apparent to potential participants unless it is explained to them.

- The extent of confidentiality should be explained to the potential participant. Anonymity is usually guaranteed in research. Nevertheless, this cannot be the case for every piece of research. There may be, for example, legal constraints or a contractual agreement between the authorities and the researcher that some sorts of information have to be disclosed such as unknown crimes. Confidentiality issues can be complex in qualitative research as indicated in Box 15.2.

- Incentives or rewards for taking part in the research need to be made clear to the potential participant prior to the research. Although the general view is that payments or other rewards for participating are best avoided, if they are to be given then this should be made clear in advance. There are several potential reasons for this, including the possibility that the participant may feel offended by a cash payment or some other form of reward. Their motives for participation may be to them much more altruistic and payments may compromise their goodwill.

- It would be usual to provide the name and contact details of a third party who may be approached about the bona fides of the researcher as well as further details about the research and their rights as participants. Students doing research would, for example, give details about the person supervising their research. If this person works at a university then this in itself would help confirm that the researcher can probably be trusted.

- There are additional issues when considering videoing interaction as discussed in Box 15.3.

Box 15.2
PRACTICAL ADVICE
Confidentiality problems in qualitative research

Unlike a great deal of quantitative research in which participants are put through the research procedures on an individual basis, as we have seen, sometimes in qualitative research data are collected from a group of individuals. This is particularly the case with focus groups. The researcher cannot guarantee the confidentiality of things said in a focus group as the other group members have access to this information. Where the focus group is made up of strangers then this may reduce the salience of the problem. However, what about circumstances in which members of the focus group know each other? Things which are said in the group may 'leak' out later, perhaps to the embarrassment of the participants. One way of dealing with this would be to warn potential participants of the possibility that they may know other members of the group, thus giving them the opportunity of withdrawing when the problems become clear to them. This sort of problem, of course, may be to the detriment of the quality of the data if the members find these circumstances inhibiting and, possibly, avoid mentioning certain things.

Another confidentiality issue arises from the detailed information which qualitative researchers obtain as part of their research. The more idiosyncratic the detail in a qualitative report, the greater the possibility that a particular individual can be identified. Of course, the vast majority of readers of a qualitative research report may have no idea of the actual individuals involved but that does not apply universally. Research carried out in a particular organisational setting may not be transparent about identities to the research community but it may be obvious to those in that particular work setting just who is who. For that reason, organisations sometimes require a right of veto on the publication of research carried out in that organisation to prevent what might appear to be critical material becoming public.

There are circumstances in which it is not necessary to obtain informed consent. Nevertheless, the requirement that the research is not likely to cause the individual involved stress or harm applies – damage to an individual's reputation is an obvious risk which should be monitored. The main circumstances in which it is permissible to carry out research with no prior consent being sought are as follows:

- The research is based on the use of anonymous questionnaires or observations in natural settings. It is important to maintain confidentiality, nevertheless.
- The study involves the use of archival materials rather than new data collection. The requirement of confidentiality applies here too.
- The study involves jobs or similar organisational matters but the research puts the participants in no jeopardy related to their employment. Again confidentiality is assumed.
- The research is about 'normal educational practices, curricula or classroom management methods' in an educational establishment.
- If the law or institutional regulations allow research without informed consent then it is ethical to carry out research in these circumstances.

Box 15.3
PRACTICAL ADVICE
Obtaining informed consent for voice recordings and photographic images

Qualitative researchers frequently record interviews and, increasingly, video interactions. So they, especially, need to be aware that such recordings come under the requirement of informed consent. The APA ethical code does, however, allow that there are exceptions in certain circumstances to this requirement.

Recording or photography which occurs in naturalistic public settings does not require informed consent normally. Of course, if the setting is not actually a natural one because, for example, the researcher has dropped a coin to see whether passers-by attempt to return it to its owner or simply keep it for themselves, then this does pose a risk that unsuspecting participants might be identified personally or even harmed by the recording or photography. Part of the problem is that it is the researcher in these cases who puts the inadvertent participant at risk. In completely natural settings, if the person being filmed or recorded does or says something which is illegal or improper then the researcher has not encouraged this.

The APA code indicates that where research requires deception and this deception is itself ethical, then it is appropriate to obtain consent to use the recording at a debriefing session following the research. In the debriefing session, relevant information should be provided to the participant and questions answered by the researcher.

Several of the above are particularly pertinent to qualitative research. It should be noted that the above is based on the American Psychological Association's ethics, which may not be guiding the ethical committee at your university, for example.

It is generally accepted, nowadays, that a researcher will formally obtain the agreement of participants to taking part in the research in the light of information about appropriate detailed knowledge of what the research entails and other information such as the freedom of the participant to withdraw from the study unproblematically. There are a number of advantages to this. The overriding one is, of course, that the researcher has evidence of agreement to participate. Generally speaking, the *consent form* is used to do this but verbal agreement in the course of an interview is an obvious, viable, method in some circumstances. Another important advantage of the consent form is that they generally require the researcher to stipulate details about the ethics-related features of the research which otherwise the researcher may not have considered. Typically a consent form consists of two parts:

- A one page or so description of the study. This is the information sheet or study description.

- A one page form giving details of the 'ethical contract' between the participant and the researcher. This is the consent form itself.

So what should go into each of these? There is no universal consent form though you can track down a lot of them on the Web easily. However, your particular university or other institutional location may have its own procedure for consent, including a template for the consent form. Your own department may have its own preferred procedure which you should follow. Each consent form, however, has to be tailored to the particular research study in question. Remember that there are circumstances where consent may have to be obtained from a third party, e.g. where the research involves children. Copies of the information sheet and the consent form should be given to each participant for them to retain. Nevertheless, the following should be helpful in general.

The information sheet/study description

The information sheet or study description must be written in everyday language commensurate with the individuals being recruited to take part in the research. The information should provide details of the involvement of the participants in the research and the nature of any potential risks stemming from participation. The study description sheet should include the following:

- What the project is about – that is, what the study aims to achieve.
- What the participant is required to do in the study together with details of the time commitments that the research places on its participants.
- What the arrangements for confidentiality of the data are.
- What the arrangements concerning the privacy of personal data are.
- What the arrangements for the security of the data are.
- Who will have access to the data.
- The purposes for which the data shall be used.
- The extent to which participants will be identifiable in publications.
- The voluntary nature of participation in the study.
- The participant has a total right to withdraw from the study (including withdrawing their data) without having to give a reason or explanation for this. If appropriate, a statement indicating that withdrawal from the study has no contingent consequences such as the withdrawal of medical services.
- What benefits might the research bring the participant.
- What risks or potential harm does the research pose for participants.
- If you are intending to do further research (e.g. follow-up interviews) at another time or if there is a possibility of doing so, you need to obtain permission from the participant to contact them in future at this stage. The flexibility to do so is an important feature of qualitative interviewing so avoid the possible situation that this cannot be done by building this permission into your information sheet. The Data Protection Act, in the United Kingdom, prevents such unagreed follow-ups. See the later section on the Data Protection Act.
- Contact details for the research team or the supervisor in the case of student research which can be used to obtain further information.
- Contact details for the institution's Ethics Committee in case issues arise which cannot be appropriately dealt with by the researchers or the supervisor.

The consent form

The typical consent form includes various statements about the project and the ethical arrangements which the participant signs to indicate their consent to the study. So the consent form should include things such as the following suitably modified for the particular research project being planned:

- The title of the research project
- Statements indicating things such as the following:
  - I have been informed about and understand the nature of the study.
  - Any questions that I may have had have been answered to my satisfaction.
  - I understand that I am free to withdraw myself and my data from the research at any time and that there would be no adverse consequences to me for doing so.
  - No information about me will be published in a form which could potentially identify me.
  - My data, in an anonymous form, may be used by other researchers.
  - I consent to participate in the study as outlined in the information sheet.
- Space for the signature of the participant, their full name, and the date of the agreement.

It is suggested that you use the above to guide yourself when writing your own information sheet and consent form. This is not to make life harder for you unnecessarily but to encourage active consideration of the ethical status of your qualitative research. The different methods used by qualitative researchers to collect data have radically different ethical requirements. For example, it is relatively easy to ensure data confidentiality by using anonymity, etc. when conducting an in-depth interview but highly problematic in relation to focus group data where the researcher simply cannot guarantee privacy and confidentiality given the numbers of participants who cannot be bound effectively by the ethical principles which apply to researchers. Furthermore, if a researcher conducts a participant observation, then many of these considerations may not always apply. For example, it is generally accepted that observational research in public places may not require the agreement of those observed if they are going about their usual activities in public places. Yet this is a complex area so it is important to check with your local Research Ethics Committee which may have a rather different viewpoint. The point is that a 'one-size-fits-all' approach to obtaining consent is probably inappropriate.

It is important to give consideration about what can be done with the data obtained in qualitative studies. You need the permission of your participants to make it available to other researchers. Not to do so can be a problem because (a) qualitative research has an ethos which stresses the importance of making one's data available to other researchers for verification, etc. but also (b) it may be a requirement of the research's funding body that the data are archived and made available to other researchers. The UK Data Archive (n.d.) has details of the ethical and practical necessities of sharing data.

Legal and ethical management of data

The management of the data collected by the qualitative psychologist is not merely a matter for the Research Ethics Committee of the institution where the researcher works, but it may become a matter for data protection legislation. Thus many of the things included on the information sheet and consent form discussed in the previous section are as much about data protection legislation as they are about research ethics. The concept of 'transparency' is used in data protection to refer to the openness of the research to the data givers. Such legislation is common in Western countries but, of course, the detail of the legislation will vary from country to country. In the United Kingdom the relevant legislation is the Data Protection Act (1998). The legislation strikes a balance between the privacy of participants in research and the value of research in modern society though it applies to all forms of personal data – not just that obtained through research. Universities will have institutional and departmental data protection officers whose task, essentially, is to ensure that procedures for data handling comply with national legislation. They should be consulted if you are in any doubt as to how the legislation should be implemented for your particular research.

Anyone who carries out research which involves the collection or use of personal information about individuals who can be identified from that data has to comply with the data protection legislation. The sort of data (qualitative or quantitative) and whether or not it is stored in a digital, electronic form or in hard copy, manual form are immaterial. These basic requirements should indicate that the rich, detailed data that qualitative researchers collect fall very firmly and decisively into the domain of data protection legislation. The only exceptions to this are data which already are publicly available such as electoral registers and so forth.

Personal information is just about any information which can be identified as being about a particular individual. It may come as some relief to know that once any personal identifiers are removed from data then the data protection legislation no longer applies. By employing such procedures as not using participant's real names or those of anyone else mentioned in the research and removing identifying material about locations and so forth the legislation ceases to apply. However, there are arguments that this is, in some cases, an unsatisfactory way of dealing with qualitative material. For example, Nespor (2000) raises issues to do with the anonymisation of identifying features for the place that the research was carried out. If the researcher removes such contextual information then the consequence is that useful features of the data are made unavailable to the reader. It makes a big difference to how data are understood if the full context is provided. Remove this context and something important is lost. Just a final point on this – remember that the digital recording stored on your computer counts as data under the Data Protection Act so you must ensure that the anonymisation procedure has been carried out on this just as much as it applies to any transcriptions of the data. (Some practical issues in relation to anonymisation are discussed in Box 15.4.)

This brings us to the question of what happens if the data from the research are not turned into an anonymous form and so the Data Protection Act applies. Quite a number of things follow. One is that the Data Protection Act actually requires that the data are only kept as long as they are needed for the purposes explained to those who provided the data. Consequently, the researcher is left to destroy the data at an appropriate stage *if* the data are not anonymised once the research is completed.

If the data come under the data protection legislation then you must also give consideration to their safe keeping. So where are the hard copies to be stored – who has access to the data in this form? Equally, where the data are

Box 15.4

PRACTICAL ADVICE

How to anonymise your data

Antaki (2009a) lists ten different guidelines for anonymising data. Although some of them make most sense for conversation analysis, they do constitute some sound advice about selecting replacement names for the participants in your research. Before doing this you really need to identify every name used in a transcript as well as any contracted names (e.g. Sam for Samantha). If you don't do this then you will waste time since you may, for example, initially choose a name which has no appropriate shortened version:

- Try to use names which have the same number of syllables as the real name and involve accents placed in the same place. This will allow them to be fitted into a Jefferson transcription better.
- Keep the new name the same gender as the original name.
- Ensure that the new name has appropriate shortened or diminutive versions if the transcript requires this.
- It is usually best to maintain the ethnicity of a person when choosing a new name in circumstances in which ethnicity is important in the transcript or if it is important to the analysis you are developing.
- Use new names which are similar to the original in terms of how common it is. For example, John for Peter seems fine but John for Peregrin obviously violates this suggestion.
- Maintain age, class and locality conventions represented in the original name as effectively as possible.
- Usually country names should be left in except in those circumstances in which they will help to identify the person in the transcript.
- Leaving in the actual name of a city is all right if doing so does not identify the person in the transcript. Changing the names can cause all sorts of difficulty as a city such as London cannot be effectively replaced by Bath or Aldershot, for example.
- Town and village names can be replaced by something similar in length, etc. if they risk identifying the participant.
- Institutional names (e.g. names of a particular university) need to be replaced if they risk disclosing a participant's identity.

Wiggins and Potter (2008) make some suggestions about using computer software such as Adobe Audition and Adobe Premier to anonymise participants in a digitally recorded sound recording or a video. For example, Adobe Premier can be used to blur the faces of members of a focus group, etc. and Adobe Audition can distort voices to make the speaker unrecognisable in a sound recording. It is possible to replace identifying names with the name digitally reversed in sound recordings using Adobe Audition. The advantages of this is that the word length and intonation remain unchanged. While this does allow actual recordings and videos to be presented in public, the question remains whether this is sufficient anonymisation – for example, the same program could be used to reverse the name back so that the name would be identifiable. The issue raised by Wiggins and Potter is an important one but the adequacy of their solution needs to be debated.

stored on computer, the question is one of who can gain access to the computer. In other words, procedures have to be decided on to ensure that the personal data are available only to the persons stipulated in the 'contract' with the participant.

When deception may be used

The deception of research participants is regarded as being unacceptable in psychological research in most circumstances. Some psychologists have gone so far as to recommend that deception should be prohibited (e.g. Baumrind, 1985). There are various reasons for this. Systematic research evidence has been summarised as follows:

> the available evidence suggests that the direct experience of deception and the suspicion of deception carry with them the potential of provoking significant cognitive-emotional as well as behavioral responses. To the extent that these responses are bound to introduce systematic error variance in the data, they impair, and possibly destroy, experimental control. In light of this danger . . . we conclude that the prohibition of deception is a sensible convention . . . (Ortmann & Hertwig, 2002, p. 125)

This has implications for the work of qualitative researchers. A more trusting relationship needs to be built up in qualitative research between the researcher and participants. Only in this way can the need for rich, in-depth interview data or participant observation data be met. Bowen summed this up in the following way:

> From an ethical standpoint, risks and concerns are greater in qualitative research than in quantitative research. This is mainly because of the close involvement of the researcher with the research process and with the participants. Qualitative researchers often become immersed in the life of respondents. Ethical concerns arise also because qualitative research offers considerable interpretative latitude to the researcher and the data are, on a whole, rife with personal opinions and feelings. (Bowen, 2005, p. 214)

To the extent that it could be reasonably expected that physical pain or emotional distress will be caused then deception should *not* be used. So what are the circumstances in which deception may be legitimate? The ethical guidelines suggest that where the research potentially has 'scientific, educational or applied value' then there is a case for considering the use of deception. What this means is that the researcher should establish the credibility of other ways of carrying out the research. Only where there seems to be no effective alternative to the use of deception should deception be considered. A risk assessment should be carried out to establish the pain and distress the study is likely to produce. But there is more to it than this. It is unlikely that the researcher who proposes a study involving deception can dispassionately evaluate the viability of alternative methods and, perhaps, the amount of pain or distress that the research may arouse. Consequently, it is important to consult with other members of the psychology community about the issue as they may well be in a better position to provide a balanced assessment in this situation.

The use of deception brings its own responsibilities. Most importantly, the researcher has a responsibility to reveal and explain the deception as soon as possible. The recommended stage for doing this is immediately after the data have been collected from the participant. Sometimes there may be a reason to delay the revelation of the deception until the data have been collected from all of the participants. Irrespective of the stage at which the deception is revealed, there should be ample provision for giving the participant the right to withdraw his or her data from the study. In addition, it should be noted that the ethics of the British Psychological Society (2006) make a distinction between deliberate lies and omitting to mention important details about the research's nature. Lying by omission may be as unacceptable as lying by commission. The British Psychological Society indicates that the test of whether omitting information is undesirable may be found in the reaction of participants when they are told that they have been deceived (i.e. at the debriefing). If their response is negative (such as anger, evidence of discomfort) then this clearly indicates that the procedure is unacceptable in this case and consequently should be reviewed. What should happen next is not indicated by the British Psychological Society, though the choices of abandoning or modifying the research are obvious ones.

Research with subordinates and those relatively less powerful

Researchers frequently occupy a relatively powerful position compared with the participants in their research. This may be inevitable since in order to have access to participants, the researcher often has the trust of important members of organisations such as schools, hospitals and charities. Furthermore, one has only to remember the frequent suggestion that psychological research is largely carried out on university students to see that here is a relationship based on power – the university academic researcher over the student research participant. Refusing to participate is more often than not the only power that such potential participants have. Given these power-based relationships which have their basis outside of the research setting, there is the possibility that adverse consequences may follow if they declined to take part in the research. Similarly, they may feel under pressure not to withdraw from a study that they feel unhappy about in these circumstances. Of course, the impact of the superior–subordinate differential can be different when the researcher is also the participant's lecturer and there are inducements to take part in the research or if there are requirements that students take part in a number of research studies as part of their degree programmes. One way around this ethical problem, for example, is to offer other ways for students to obtain course credits which do not involve taking part in the research. Power is an especially important issue in the qualitative interview as discussed in Box 15.5.

Inducements to encourage participation

There are a number of ethical considerations which result from offering money or other incentives to potential participants as an inducement to and a reward for becoming a participant in a research study. These include the following:

● Rewards in terms of money or gifts to research participants should be small. Payments can be more than inducements to give up a little time; if they are too large they consequently may be coercive. Large rewards may make it virtually impossible for an impecunious participant to say no. Research

Box 15.5

KEY CONCEPTS

Power relationships in qualitative interviews

While these would not be regarded as an ethical issue by most psychologists, there is a sense in which qualitative researchers, especially, should be aware of the power relationships which exist within their interviews. These are relevant to how the qualitative researcher construes their relationship with the participants in the research and are relevant to the way in which the qualitative researcher carries out their research. They undermine the common claims of some qualitative researchers that they have a more democratic or egalitarian relationship with their research participants than is typical of quantitative researchers. The power differentials in qualitative research are a little more subtle, admittedly, but the fact that they are there should make us question the extent to which ethics are effectively dealt with by qualitative researchers.

According to Brinkmann and Kvale (2005), qualitative researchers tend to neglect the following power characteristics of the qualitative interview:

- *Interview power relations are asymmetrical*   It is the researcher who defines the nature of the interview by initiating it, by deciding what topics will be covered, by asking the questions and also by terminating the interview process. The researcher is dominant in the relationship.

- *Interviews are largely a one-direction dialogue*   Question asking takes place in one direction only – from the researcher to the participant. Participants don't ask questions and to do so would be disruptive and failing to play the interview by the rules. They are there to answer them.

- *The instrumentality of the interview*   While normal conversation is frequently an end in itself with no other purpose or a joint activity, the research interview is there to serve the needs of the researcher. Out of the interview, the qualitative researcher gains text, narratives and so forth which are used by the researcher in fulfilment of their research interests primarily. It is generally less clear what participants in research gain from participation.

- *The manipulative dialogue contained in interviews*   According to Brinkmann and Kvale (2005), the researcher follows a largely hidden agenda during the interview. They suggest that the interviewer seeks to obtain information without making it clear to the participant just what it is they are seeking.

- *The researcher monopolises interpretation*   Ultimately, it is the researcher who is responsible for the interpretation of the data which the interview provides. The interviewee supplies the material for the analysis or interpretation but contributes nothing else to the process unless the study involves respondent validation.

guidelines do not stipulate what would be a reasonable reward though some institutions may set limits. One formula for rewarding modestly might be to pay out-of-pocket expenses for items such as bus or train fares to get to the research site plus a small amount of money, paid on an hourly basis, to recompense a little for lost time. Generally, researchers tend to prefer not to pay research participants but sometimes there may be a case for doing so.

Box 15.6

PRACTICAL ADVICE

Inducement issues in qualitative research

While conventionally the issue of inducements in research is put forward as if it were one of the researchers paying to encourage people to participate in their research, there is another aspect which can be overlooked. Participants in research may have expectations of the research in terms of pay-offs for them which were not intended by and cannot be met by the researcher. For example, in Howitt (1992) the participants sometimes agreed to be interviewed because of an expectation that the researcher might be able to do something to help them with the false accusations of child abuse that the research was about. Some participants were under the impression that the researcher was in a position of some power with regard to this. He was not. Of course, it would be wrong to let participants in such research volunteer in the expectation that there would be such a pay-off. A different version of this problem, from his case studies, is exemplified by the parents who clearly admitted sexual abuse of their child but expected, from taking part in the research, some vindication of what they did. Again this is a motive coming from the participant which was not encouraged by the researcher and with which the researcher could not collude.

There is the negative consequence that paying participants might set up an expectation that they always should be paid. Where a researcher cannot afford to pay because they have no relevant funding, this ethos would make for difficulties. Student researchers, of course, probably do not have the financial resources to make any payments to participants in research.

● While this is probably uncommon, from time to time the inducement of professional psychological services are offered as a way of encouraging research participation. Of course, it is assumed that the service provider should be competent to deliver these services. So this would not apply to student researchers because they lack the competence to offer such services. An example of such services offered as an inducement would be counselling. If services are offered, the ethical guidelines advise that the exact nature of the services and the limitations on the provision of these services (e.g. the number of counselling sessions offered) should be given to the potential participants. Furthermore, any risks associated with the psychological service should be clarified.

Box 15.6 discusses some of the practical details associated with the use of inducements in qualitative research.

Debriefing as ethics and methodology

Irrespective of the nature of research, during the final stages debriefing of the participants should take place. Debriefing ideally should involve both the researcher and the research participant in a 'mutual' discussion of the nature of the research, the results of the research, and the conclusions from the research as far as possible. Obviously the debriefing may take place long before any research conclusions are available. One strategy to overcome this is to prepare a summary of the research and its findings for circulation to the participants at a later stage. During the debriefing session itself, the researcher should seek to identify and correct any misconceptions that the participant may have developed about various aspects of the research. There are sometimes good scientific, academic or humane reasons for withholding certain information – or alternatively postponing the main debriefing for a more suitable occasion.

There may be other reasons for a two-stage debriefing process – for example, the research may involve two or more data-gathering stages separated by a considerable period of time. Too much information at the end of the first stage may risk unduly influencing the data which the participant contributes at the later stages of the research.

If one regards debriefing as a method of dealing with ethical issues then this is to ignore its other important functions. Debriefing is the stage at which the researcher learns about the research from the viewpoint of the participant. Properly, the debriefing phase should involve the taking of careful notes since there is a sense in which it is data – and this is especially so for qualitative research with its emphasis on rich data. The debriefing may enrich the interpretation of the main data in any sort of research and should be considered an essential component of research studies.

Of course, issues may be raised during the debriefing which suggest that there was harm done to the participant in the research as a consequence of deception (or other features of the study for that matter). Reasonable efforts should made to deal with any such harm which is identified during the course of the debriefing. Researchers, and especially student researchers, do not have the appropriate counselling skills to deal with significant distress. So the researcher should have appropriate courses of action for the participant so that they may contact a relevant professional who should be able to deal with this matter. Helplines and other facilities may be appropriate when the distress is caused by things such as interviewing about intrinsically distressing matters such as abortion, drugs and mental health issues. Similar helpline details are often given by the media when emotive topics are featured on television, for example. There has been research on the effectiveness of debriefing (e.g. Epley & Huff, 1998; Smith & Richardson, 1983) and it seems clear that debriefing may be insufficient to deal with the effects of deception.

The ethics of report writing and publication

The ethical concerns of research do not end with the debriefing of participants following data collection. There are a number of ethical issues which arise in relation to publishing the data which should be noted.

Ethical standards in reporting research

The fabrication of data is ethically wrong and this applies to students as well as professional researchers. There will be circumstances in which a researcher realises that there are errors in the data analysis which they have published journal articles about. These are most likely to be computational or statistical errors and where they occur then it is important to make reasonable efforts to correct the errors. This can be achieved by printing corrections or retractions in the journal where the research was first published. Occasionally more malicious circumstances arise. Many years ago, I was part of a team which employed a particular interviewer. Sometime later, a friend of this interviewer told me that some of the interviews had been fabricated. Fortunately, the research team had already identified that this interviewer's data were systematically different from those of the other interviewers and excluded it from the analysis, though, of course, we were not able to show that it had been fabricated. Thus falsification may occur at different stages in the research process.

Plagiarism

Plagiarism occurs when someone takes the work of another person without properly acknowledging its source and gives the impression that it is their own work. Psychologists should not plagiarise and the same should be true of psychology students. Merely citing the source of the material is not sufficient to avoid the charge of plagiarism in circumstances where a large chunk of someone else's work is reproduced. Material that you have quoted directly should be identified using quotation marks and, of course, the pages from which the quotation was taken given in the citation.

In student work, plagiarism may result in firm disciplinary action by their university which, if it is extreme or persistent, may cost a student their degree. Similarly, at the professional level, there may be profound consequences in cases of plagiarism. A famous TV psychiatrist in the UK, Raj Persaud, was suspended by the medical profession for undermining public confidence in his profession through dishonest conduct after he was found guilty of plagiarising the work of others in his publications (MailonLine, 2008).

Making data available for verification

Once your analysis of your data has been published then the data themselves should be available for checking by those competent to do so. This is not for the purpose of giving other people the opportunity to take your data and publish it in some other form. To do this would require your agreement. Making the data available is a way of allowing the claims of the original researcher to be validated. The person wishing to check the data may be required to meet the cost of supplying the data in a verifiable form. Of course, the data should not be made available if by doing so the confidentiality of the source (i.e. their anonymity) might be compromised. Also, and this may happen with funded research, the data may not be made available to other researchers if a third party has proprietorial rights over the data.

It is worth noting that the typical qualitative research paper gives more access to the data than does the typical quantitative research paper which supplies only summary tables and other output. Remember that one should get the signed permission of the participant to distribute the data to the wider research community.

Appropriate credit for authorship of publications

A psychologist should not stake a claim for authorship of a publication to which they have not contributed substantially. The authorship of a publication should start with the individual who has contributed most to the publication and end with the person who has contributed least but nevertheless substantially enough. Senior membership of a research organisation in itself does not warrant inclusion in the list of authors – this is determined by the responsibility that the individual carries for doing the research and writing it up. Those who made a minor contribution may be acknowledged in a footnote. It does not merit a position in the list of authors. Publications which originated out of student dissertations usually ought to give credit to the student as the first (principal) author.

Repeated publication of the same data

It is not proper to publish the same data in several publications. If, for some reason it is done, then the fact that this was originally published elsewhere should be acknowledged in later publications.

The Internet raises special issues which are dealt with in Box 15.7.

Box 15.7

PRACTICAL ADVICE

Ethics and qualitative research on the Internet

Qualitative researchers are attracted to the Internet partly because it is a rich source of text of all sorts in a readily accessible digital form. For example, e-mail not only is a rich source of modern communications but is governed by its own stylistic rules. This interest brings with it ethical issues which are different from those of mainstream research. There are available research ethics for conducting research on the Internet. The British Psychological Society has guidelines for conducting research on the internet:

> www.bps.org.uk/document-download-area/document-download$.cfm?file_uuid= E6917759-9799-434A-F313-9C35698E1864&ext.pdf

While these are not specific to qualitative research, Shaw (2008) sees some vital ethical issues in them from the point of view of qualitative researchers.

Verification of participant's identity

There are clearly problems verifying the identity of people on the Internet. For example, chatrooms and discussion forums do not identify contributors other than with what is likely to be an alias. What, for example, if an identity on the Internet appears to be that of a child but, in reality, it is a paedophile pretending to be a child either for purposes of enacting fantasy or to groom a child? What legitimate use could the researcher put the data to? The Internet could be used to contact individuals in order, say, to obtain some demographic information but, of course, that information itself cannot be further verified. Other forms of data collected from the Internet – such as online research questionnaires – may have exactly the same limitations. The culture of masking one's identity on the Internet may increase the likelihood that bogus identities are used even though they may be presented as genuine. This is, naturally, a possibility in other forms of research but face-to-face contact reduces the risk of misleading information. However, as identity is increasingly seen as not a fixed matter but situation specific (e.g. one's identity at work may be very different from one's identity at home) then because a virtual identity is different from a day-to-day identity then there is a sense in which this issue does not matter. There is no reason why a qualitative researcher should not be interested in Internet behaviour in its own right without its reflecting some other aspect of a person's identity although the interplay between the two is of interest.

The Internet – is it a public or a private space?

Although it is clear that in many instances, the Internet is treated as a public space by Internet users and they expect their contributions to be disseminated with few limitations, there may be some circumstances in which the Internet user may believe that their communications are private and will not be published. Shaw argues that such users are few in number as most are well aware of the possibility that their contributions will be distributed.

Confidentiality

There may be limitations on a researcher's ability to keep Internet and e-mail information confidential. One reason for this is that the source website may store information about its members and link this to unsecured e-mail content. Similarly, care is needed not to link material used in research to the person's log-in ID which may then, inadvertently on the researcher's part, allow tracking using search engines, etc.

Informed consent

Shaw points out that it is possible for an Internet researcher to set up a special chatroom for the purposes of research which is password protected and the participants indicate their willingness for their material to be included in the research. They could even ask questions about the research before committing themselves to it as in regular informed consent. Unfortunately, this is not the sort of naturalistic data favoured by most qualitative researchers. So is it acceptable for researchers to use material routinely published on the Internet for their research? For Shaw, this is largely not a problem since she says that such individuals have already consented for their contributions to be published. However, would it be correct to suggest that such individuals were happy to have their words subjected to psychological interpretations which then are also published, albeit in a research journal?

Debriefing procedures and the Internet

Of course, debriefing individuals contributing freely to the Internet but essentially anonymously is as difficult as raising issues of their identity with them. However, it is a different matter when a researcher is using an online questionnaire. It can be argued that in these circumstances an automatic debriefing should be incorporated in the researcher's questionnaire design. This debriefing could appear on the screen once the participant has submitted their completed questionnaire and also if they terminate their involvement before the questionnaire has been fully completed. The debriefing information could include standard debriefing information such as how the data may be withdrawn, contact information should this be necessary, an explanation of what will be done with the data, a fuller account of what the research was about, and so forth.

CONCLUSIONS

Ethical principles should be applied at every stage of a research study. The requirement for fidelity would cover the literature review just as much as the treatment of the data. Ethical principles are broad-brush tools which could never cover every little detail of all types of research. They are principles to be used with care and with sensitivity. Ethics go beyond methodology in the sense that they link with the wider context of research and impose duties on the research community which need to be undertaken seriously, thoroughly and thoughtfully. Research ethics are not for the individual researcher alone – they involve all of the psychological community and colleagues of active researchers, in particular. Except in the simplest of cases, there is every reason to go to colleagues, lecturers and professors for ethical advice. The overwhelming majority of research which is planned by students presents few ethical challenges but that does not mean that problems never arise. Relatively routine issues such as confidentiality and the secure storage of data would be characteristic of the main areas where the student researcher needs to pay care and attention. Their lecturers and supervisors should take an active interest in the ethical aspects of their research. Not all ethical problems are apparent before the start of a research study and some vigilance is required in order to identify any which emerge in the course of the research.

Ethical principles involve an element of judgement in day-to-day research situations. Any student who wants hard-and-fast rules does not fully understand the nature of ethics. Take a situation which may arise quite commonly in qualitative research where participants may answer a wide variety of questions asked by the researcher or may choose to mention things which might not have been mentioned outside the research context. Although causing distress in research is largely to be avoided, according to ethical principles, there will be occasions when participants agree to take part in research knowing the nature of the research but then talk about things which upset them. For example, paedophiles interviewed about their offending behaviour may freely agree to take part in research fully understanding the sorts of issues that the researcher will ask about. The offender may weep because he cannot cope with the nature of his offence. Simply because the offender is upset does not make the research unethical. The offender's distress would be acceptable to most psychologists if the research has potential social benefits or is important for some other reason.

Of course, there are circumstances where factors such as the triviality of the research's purpose would make the creation of similar levels of distress unacceptable. For example, it would be wrong to interview people about their sexual abuse as a child simply as part of a study of the influence of interviewing style on the amount of information generated. The means are not justified by the ends, in this case.

Ethics in relation to qualitative psychological research have yet to be fully charted. The complex relationships between qualitative researchers and their research participants may mean that new ethical issues emerge which are uncharacteristic of those which apply to quantitative studies. Group interviews and group observation methods present ethical challenges for research which have no exact parallels in quantitative work.

KEY POINTS

- Qualitative research differs from quantitative research in its orientation to those who participate in a research study. Qualitative research values the person as an entirety. The ethical problems which arise in qualitative research can, therefore, be very different from those which arise in quantitative research. Some of these issues are not obvious from standard research ethics and require the active vigilance of the researcher.

- The ethical environment in which research takes place is complex and includes bureaucratic elements. It is no longer the case that researchers simply have to be aware of the ethical standards expected from them as members of an academic discipline. Generally, the formal seeking of ethical approval is a key part of any research project. Ethics are not an afterthought but integral to effective planning of research.

- Psychological ethics are based on broad principles rather than prescribed behaviours. As a consequence, the consideration of the ethical aspects of research is an active part of its planning. Ethical issues may have to be revisited in the light of what happens in the course of the research. Because qualitative methods are extremely variable in nature, the qualitative researcher needs to be extra-vigilant and avoid complacency.

ADDITIONAL RESOURCES

Brinkmann, S., and Kvale, S. (2008). Ethics in qualitative psychological research. In C. Willig and W. Stainton-Rogers (Eds.), *The SAGE Handbook of Qualitative Research in Psychology*. London: Sage, pp. 263–279.

Brown, L.S. (1997). Ethics in psychology: cui bono? In D. Fox and I. Preilleltensky (Eds.), *Critical Psychology: An introduction*. London: Sage, pp. 51–67.

Economic and Social Research Council (n.d.). Research Ethics Framework. http://www.esrcsocietytoday.ac.uk/ESRCInfoCentre/Images/ESRC_Re_Ethics_Frame_tcm6-11291.pdf (accessed 23 August 2009). (This contains a number of case studies useful for qualitative researchers as well as an ethical checklist. It may be of greatest interest to PhD students since their work may well be supported by the ESRC.)

Mauthner, M., and Birch, M. (2002). *Ethics in Qualitative Research*. London: Sage.

Roth, W.-M. (2004). Qualitative research and ethics. *Forum: Qualitative Social Research*, 5 (2), Article 7. http://www.qualitative-research.net/index.php/fqs/article/view/614/1331 (accessed 23 August 2009).

(This discusses ethical problems stemming from the close relationship between researcher and participants in qualitative research.)

GLOSSARY

This is a glossary both of terms in this book and also a general glossary of key concepts in qualitative research to support general reading in the field.

Abstract: A short summary of the overall contents of a research report.

Account: An attempt to explain, justify or legitimate some action.

Accountability: In conversation analysis, ethnomethodology and some forms of discourse analysis, this refers to the expectation that the actions of individuals are, in principle, to be accounted for.

Action: Differs from behaviour because the latter can be simply reflexive or reactive and there is no requirement that behaviour has to be meaningful. Action then refers to actions which are meaningfully orientated to other people. It is a term largely originating in George Herbert Mead's symbolic interactionism.

Action orientated: In qualitative research, a term used to describe the major characteristic of language viewed from a discourse analysis perspective – that is, the idea that language does things.

Action research: This is a term for research which involves experimentation, etc. in an attempt to address a particular social problem. The social problem guides research, not the interests of the researcher. It involves research studies which investigate a social intervention in order to assess its degree of effectiveness. It was first introduced into psychology by Kurt Lewin.

Adjacency pairs: Two turns in conversation which follow a standard and expected pattern for those involved, e.g. one person says 'good morning' and the other person replies 'good morning'. From conversation analysis.

Advocacy: Combining the normal role of researcher with political action which attempts to change a situation, etc. in the interest of the group being studied.

Agency: This is a concept somewhat like that of free will but sociological in nature rather than psychological as in the case of free will. Agency or human agency indicates the ability of individuals to plan and assess their own actions, develop hopes and wishes, and reason about their situation. The opposite to agency would be the idea that what people do is determined by matters external to themselves – that is determinism.

Aide-memoire: A list of things such as questions or issues to cover used as a memory aid in, for example, qualitative interviewing.

Allo-ethnology: The ethnology of others (other cultural groups).

Analysis of variance: The statistical technique which allows a researcher to analyse complex experimental designs such as two-way and three-way factorial experiments.

Analytic generalisation: The process by which the analysis of a particular case is linked to a more general theory.

Analytic induction: Part of the process of analysing qualitative data. Having become intimately familiar with their research data (usually the transcripts), the researcher attempts to develop working ideas or hypotheses to explain what is going on in the data. The idea is then tested against other instances or parts of the data. It is essentially the opposite of the deductive processes used to generate hypotheses from theory which are then tested as demonstrated in the positivist approaches to research.

Analytic rigour: The stance in analysis which encourages the analyst to check the various stages of the analysis one against the other and apply the quality criteria appropriate to that type of qualitative analysis.

Androcentric: Giving precedent to 'men's' viewpoint and thereby neglecting women's experiences

Anonymisation: The process of changing names, locations, etc. in recordings, transcriptions and reports which otherwise might prejudice the anonymity of participants in research.

Anti-essentialism: The belief that there is no predetermined or 'natural' nature of the world and people. In particular, there are no predetermined essential characteristics of people.

Antifoundationalism: The philosophical view that there are no principles which underpin all types of valid research investigation or inquiry.

Antinaturalism: This is the view that social phenomena cannot be effectively studied using the methods of the natural sciences. It is associated with the idea that social sciences should attempt to understand rather than seek causal explanations.

Antirealist: Rejects the realist position that there is a single reality to be studied.

Applied research: Research which focuses on seeking solutions to problems.

Archival research: Research based on archived documents of any sort.

Archive: A collection of any sort of documents.

Artefact: Any sort of artefact of cultures including photographs and diaries.

Attribute: A general property of anything which may have more than one category (e.g. gender). Used much as the quantitative concept of variable is.

Attrition: The loss of participants from a research study due to things such as failure to turn up for an interview.

Audit trail: Documentation of the research process and data collection in order that others can verify the researcher's activities and thoughts about their data.

Authenticity: The idea that qualitative research by its very nature and approach creates a genuine understanding of the experiences of those whom it studies.

Autobiographical account: A life-history account in the words of the person in question rather than the researcher.

Autobiography: A lengthy, self-produced account of one's life.

Auto-ethnology: This is the ethnology of ourselves (our culture) either carried out by ourselves or by others. More recently it has come to mean attempts to combine ethnographic together with autobiographical (inwardly looking) approaches.

Axial coding: In grounded theory, it is the process of linking together (relating) the analytic codes and concepts to one another. It is only important in certain variants of grounded theory.

Behaviourism: The school of psychology which regarded what is measurable and observable as the basis of good scientific knowledge. So behaviour was typically broken down in stimulus–response units and the conditions under which a stimulus produces a particular response studied. So it is deterministic in nature and essentially reductionist.

Bias: When research is subject to the pre-existing judgements, etc. of the researcher which affect the outcomes of the research.

Biographic method: This refers to procedures used to both generate an individual's life-stories and also to interpret those life-stories.

Biographic writing: Forms of writing which are biographical in character.

Biography: A lengthy account of someone's life produced by another person.

Body: In the body–mind dichotomy, the body is the physical part which deals with emotions, etc.

Bracketing (in ethnomethodology): This is the setting aside of common-sense assumptions about the world so that the researcher can study how these assumptions are made to work in everyday social interaction.

Bracketing (in phenomenology): This is a term from phenomenology (especially Edmund Husserl) which indicates the stance of the researcher when attempting to suspend normal judgement based on their everyday understanding of the natural world. Consequently, if fully achieved, the phenomenon (phenomenological object) can be perceived more directly without the assumption that the phenomenon refers to something that is 'real' in the 'real' world (i.e. without the assumption of realism). In this way, the phenomenological nature of perceiving and remembering can be studied.

Breaching: A deliberate violation of social conventions for research purposes – especially in ethnomethodology. It allows the study of how individuals cope with and negotiate the new situation and make it meaningful.

Bricolage: Refers to the multiple methodologies used in qualitative research.

Bricoleur: Because of the multiple aspects of the field of qualitative research (bricolage), some use the term bricoleur to describe the qualitative researcher. This is because of the sheer diversity of the tasks involved in qualitative research.

CAQDAS: *See* Computer-Aided Qualitative Data Analysis Software.

Career: The process of progression through a social setting.

Case: In qualitative research this is a specific instance of the thing chosen for study. In quantitative research, a case refers to an individual participant usually but can be any single instance of the unit of analysis (a family, an organisation, etc.).

Case study: A research investigation based on a single unit of analysis – study of one individual, one factory, one episode of news, etc.

Categories: Classes or divisions of things.

Causation: Where changes in something are responsible for changes in something else.

Chronology: An account of events, etc. in the order in which they happened.

Closed questions: A closed question is one which supplies the interviewee or respondent with a limited range of answers from which to choose to answer the question. It is associated with quantitative approaches in psychology. Most psychological scales, tests and measures adopt this approach as it eases quantification and analysis of data.

Code: A named category used to break data down into its components.

Code book: *See* Coding frame.

Coding: This is the procedure of categorising similar aspects of one's data under the same verbal label (e.g. 'anxiety about the future', 'money worries' and 'stress-free period of life' – or whatever is appropriate). Coding is a flexible process and the categories may change in the light of experience with the data. In quantitative research the categories would be pre-specified by the researcher whereas in qualitative research the categories generally are based on the researcher's involvement with the data.

Coding frame: A listing of the codes to be applied in a data analysis setting which defines the codes and provides guidelines for their use.

Coding manual: In quantitative analysis, this is a set of instructions containing all of the categories that can be used to categorise each aspect of the data.

Coding paradigm: In grounded theory it is another term for 'theoretical codes'.

Cognition: Internal processes of thought.

Cognitive psychology: That branch of psychology which studies mental thought processes involved in language, memory, problem solving, etc. Cognitive psychology is largely quantitative in nature and frequently criticised by qualitative psychologists such as those involved in discursive psychology.

Cognitivism: This is the belief in the ability of internal mental states postulated by the researcher to contribute to understanding of psychological phenomena.

Collective narratives: Narratives produced/shared by a number of people.

Computer-Aided Qualitative Data Analysis Software: Usually referred to as CAQDAS. This refers to computer programs such as NVivo which can help the qualitative researcher organise, code and recode qualitative data. Many researchers do not regard its use as essential since cutting and pasting, etc. on a good word processing program will allow much the same flexibility. Popular with grounded theory analysts.

Concept: This is a general, abstract idea which develops from specific instances.

Confidentiality: The protection of the anonymity of participants in research.

Constant comparison: The process of checking an aspect of the data and analysis against all other aspects of these.

Constructive alternativism: This is George Kelly's name for his theory which accepts that there is one true reality but that it is experienced from one of numerous perspectives – called alternative constructions.

Constructivism: The idea that people have a role in creating their knowledge and experiences.

Constructivist grounded theory: An approach to grounded theory identified by Kathy Charmaz but dismissed as qualitative data analysis by Barney Glaser rather than being grounded theory.

Content analysis: A very general term to refer to ways of categorising textual data to allow comparisons to be made between aspects of the data and to describe the contents of the data.

Contextualism: This is the idea that different conversational contexts have different standards to determine what is accepted as knowledge. So different social contexts have different epistemological criteria and standards.

Contrast questions: These help individuals make sense of their social worlds by asking them in what way two things are different or asking them to compare two things.

Convenience sampling: The recruitment of an easily accessible group of people to provide data for a study. For example, university students may choose to study other university students because of the ease of doing so.

Conversation analysis: An approach to studying language built on the assumption that conversation is governed by 'rules' which are understood by members of that conversation.

Cooperation: Grice's idea that conversation is a cooperative activity.

Cooperative inquiry: Involves research activity in which researchers work with non-researchers on topics where they share interests.

Core category: From grounded theory, this is an analytic category which is central, occurs frequently, and generates connections readily with other categories in the analysis.

Counter-discourses: The idea from Michel Foucault that for every political discourse which claims to be the truth there is another discourse which challenges its legitimacy.

Covert research: A form of participant observation or ethnographic research in which the observer is not identified as a researcher to those studied.

Creation myth: Accounts of the creation of a culture which are widely accepted by members of that culture but, nevertheless, are essentially myths. By extension, the idea of creation myths has been used to cover accounts of the origins of academic disciplines, etc.

Crisis: The point at which an earlier paradigm of research becomes untenable in the light of current research findings and a new way of seeing things is likely to develop. Often used by qualitative researchers to suggest that present quantitative methods are failing.

Crisis of legitimation: The authority of the interpretative texts which characterise postmodern psychology is open to question and cannot be addressed using the conventional criteria of positivism such as reliability and validity since these are not accepted in postmodernism. There is, then, the question of how to discriminate between good and bad interpretations. That is, the crisis of legitimation is the problem of who can legitimately claim the best interpretations of text and the criteria on which such legitimacy can be based.

Critical discourse analysis: A form of discourse analysis in which the production, maintenance and removal of social power is a major analytic concern.

Critical narrative analysis: A form of narrative analysis which claims to take a critical social perspective.

Critical psychology: Approaches to psychology which assume that power is an important influence on people and how the discipline contributes to social inequalities.

Critical realism: A doctrine which combines an acceptance of an objective, external world (i.e. the realist perspective) with the view that we can know the world only through the medium of our thought and perception. The central problem then becomes accounting for the relationship between the two.

Cultural anthropology: A branch of anthropology which uses ethnographic, linguistic and other methods and data to study human cultures.

Debriefing: Discussing with participants the purposes of one's research and their reactions to that research after their participation in the research is complete.

Deception: Essentially misleading the participants in a study about the real purpose of the study.

Deconstruction: The analysis of text to identify or expose the underlying contradictions and ideological assumptions below the superficial meaning. It is based on the work of Jacques Derrida.

Deductive: A way of conducting research in which hypotheses drawn from theory guide the research. Typical of quantitative research.

Deductive coding: The production of codes on the basis of prior knowledge, theory and assumptions. The codes are not developed in interaction with the data.

Delphi group: A group of experts brought together in a forecasting study. It uses a facilitator to summarise what the experts have said. The experts are encouraged to revise their forecasts on the basis of what the others in the group say in one or more further rounds of forecasting.

Depth interview: An extensive and detailed interview. In this book the term qualitative interview is preferred.

Descriptive: Concentrating on identifying the features and characteristics of things rather than influences or effects or explanations.

Descriptive phenomenology: This is another name for Edmund Husserl's transcendental phenomenology.

Determinism: This is the philosophical idea that everything in human and social life is causally determined by a sequence of things which went before. Hence, behaviourist stimulus–response theory can be seen as deterministic.

Deviant cases: In analysis, cases which do not fit with the thrust of the analysis. In qualitative research, deviant cases are regarded not as a nuisance but as a stimulus towards a more refined analysis.

Dialogical: Taking the form of a dialogue or including dialogue.

Diary: A personal chronicle of events either requested by a researcher or instigated by oneself. It provides appropriate text for some forms of qualitative analysis.

Disconfirming case analysis: *See* deviant cases.

Discourse: Can simply mean the verbal exchanges between people but can also mean a system of ideas, images, metaphors and so forth which are used to construct things in particular ways.

Discourse analysis: Various approaches to the study of language which either identify types of discourse within it or the means by which the discourse is constructed.

Discursive construction: The process by which people socially construct phenomena through the use of talk, language and conversation.

Discursive practice: This is the talk/conversational activities of people which involves the way in which meanings are created and understood.

Discursive psychology: A variety of psychology which is based on the principles of social constructionist discourse analysis. It identifies mental and social concepts as being a construction of social interaction. For example, rather than memory being something residing somewhere in the human mind, memory can be socially constructed in interaction such as over a family photograph album.

Discursive resources: Things which can be used in creating discourse such as narrative, rhetoric and so forth.

Discursive turn (also the turn to discourse): The trend especially in social psychology for researchers to study discourse rather than more traditional psychological issues. It is analogous to the 'turn to language'.

Documentation: Any form of record which belongs to a participant which did not involve the researcher's intervention. So photographs, newspaper cuttings, official documents and so forth may all be useful in some forms of qualitative research (especially ethnography/participant observation).

Double hermeneutic: Used by some interpretative phenomenological analysis researchers to describe the situation in which researchers engage in the process of making sense of a person's own making-sense processes.

Dramaturgical: *See* Dramaturgy.

Dramaturgy: Erving Goffman's sociological view that context, time and the audience are related to the actions of people. It is drama in the sense that one person is presenting themselves to another in a performance which is built on values, expectations and so forth.

Emergent data: Data which emerge as the data collection proceeds.

Emergent theory: A rather dubious concept which implies that theory is in some sense inherent in the data and emerges under analytic scrutiny.

Emic: An analysis of cultures involving the perspective of members of that culture.

Empirical evidence: Evidence based on experience or observation.

Empiricism: The belief that the validity of knowledge comes from it being based on observation.

Emplotment: The process by which a sequence of events is transformed into a chronological narrative or story form with an identifiable plot.

Empowerment: This refers to processes by which personal and community strength can be achieved such as in terms of the development of the self and the social and spiritual. Often refers to the inclusion into decision making processes of people previously excluded. It is a concept used in feminist psychology and by Foucauldian discourse analysis, for example.

Epiphany: Something which happens in a person's life story which changed them or provided a significant turning point.

Epistemological assumptions: The particular assumptions underlying a particular epistemological position.

Epistemology: A central area of philosophy which focuses on various aspects of knowledge such as its nature and its sources. So it is possible to speak of qualitative and quantitative psychology having different epistemological foundations or assumptions.

Epoché: *See* Bracketing (in phenomenology).

Essentialism: The idea that things have an essential nature which is capable of being identified.

Ethics: The principles of proper conduct including in research.

Ethnographic: To do with ethnography.

Ethnographic methods: Methods of close study of a natural group such as participant observation, in-depth interviewing and documentary evidence.

Ethnography: Research in which the researcher immerses themselves in a social setting to observe events directly. Ethnography also can refer to the product of ethnographic research.

Ethnology: The branch of research which studies cultures and their social structures. It is the equivalent of social (cultural) anthropology.

Ethnomethodology: A subfield of sociology which seeks to explain how social order is achieved through interaction.

Etic: The analysis of cultures from the perspective of a non-member of that culture (a stranger).

Existant: Something that exists.

Existential phenomenology: A version of phenomenology based on the writings of the philosopher Martin Heidegger.

Externalisation: In the social construction of reality the stage at which a way of thinking about the world is incorporated into social practices.

Extreme case formulation: The use of extreme case formulations in discourse is to build up or exaggerate things. The outcome can be that the account seems more plausible.

Extreme relativist: One who assumes that different methods of qualitative inquiry provide a unique but valid perspective on the world.

Face: From Erving Goffman, it refers to an image of the self expressed in terms of socially approved attributes.

Facilitator: The person responsible for running a focus group. The facilitator may be an expert in this activity employed by the researchers for that purpose.

Feasibility study: A precursor to the main study which attempts to indicate the financial viability or general practicality of the major research.

Feminism: A form of discourse aimed at equality for women. Issues to do with gender differences and women's rights are central.

Feminist research: A form of qualitative research drawing on feminism for its focus and viewpoint.

Field notes: These are the records made by a participant observer or ethnographer of all aspects of what has been observed together with any comments that the researcher has to make on these notes.

Fieldwork: The stage of data collection in the actual research site.

Fit: The degree of match between such things as the categories and data.

Focus group: A form of group interview conducted by a researcher (facilitator or moderator) designed to stimulate group interaction rather than individual comments.

Focused coding: This follows initial coding and it is a process of reviewing the initial codes to possibly combine codes into more general ones or to reject ones which are not useful.

Footing: From Erving Goffman's theory but common in discourse analysis. This refers to the frame that is being using in interaction. A change of footing is a change in that framework.

Formal theory: The analytic outcome at the end point of theory development in grounded theory.

Formulation: In conversation analysis, a summary of the main thrust of what has gone before.

Foucauldian discourse analysis: A form of discourse analysis deriving from the work of Michel Foucault which seeks to identify the discourses within textual material of all sorts.

Frame: From Erving Goffman's theory but occurs in discourse analysis. This refers to mental structures which determine the way that we act, what are good and bad outcomes of our actions, etc. A frame determines the way we see the world. The interpretation of talk is determined by the frame that the listener understands is applicable at the moment.

Funnelling: Structuring question order from the most general question down to the most specific question.

Gatekeeper: Persons who 'open the doors' in a social setting thus enabling the research to be carried out.

Genealogy: Michel Foucault's concept which describes his method of identifying the history of important ideas.

Gestalt psychology: The term Gestalt means a shape or figure. It is a theory that holds the mind to operate in a holistic way and that it operates in a manner of self-organisation. Gestalt psychology was influential on social psychology.

Goodness of fit: *See* Fit.

Grand theory: Any sort of theory so long as it involves a very broad and general explanation of a social or psychological phenomenon. Usually used in the context of grounded theory to indicate sociological theory before the 1960s.

Grounded theory: A form of analysis (and to a lesser extent data collection) which includes a multitude of methods to generate theory/analysis which is a close fit to the data.

Group discussion: A procedure for data collection in which a group of participants debate some issue among themselves for the benefit of the researcher. There is no assumption that the discussion will be led by a facilitator as in focus groups.

Hard data: Data based on a natural science approach to research – putatively 'objective' data. Similar to quantitative data.

Hawthorne studies: A major industrial study involving interviews, participant observation and so forth. The Hawthorne effect denotes the tendency for industrial production to improve following research and other interventions irrespective of the nature of that intervention.

Hegemony: The dominance of any group over others.

Hermeneutics: Generally this is the study of the interpretation of texts, though its modern usage extends to anything subject to interpretation.

Holistic: The idea that the whole is more than the sum of its parts. So things cannot be effectively studied by breaking them down into their component parts.

Holistic view: The viewpoint of the holistic approach.

Homogeneous sampling: Sampling or recruiting people to ensure that they are relatively similar rather than very different. Some experts on focus groups recommend homogeneous sampling to ensure that participants interact freely together.

Humanism: A general term to philosophies, methods and beliefs which have human beings at their centre as opposed to, say, divinity. A very loosely defined idea.

Humanistic psychology: Psychology based on humanism.

Hypothesis: A proposed explanation which may be subject to further test or something accepted as true for purposes of developing an argument.

Hypothetical realism: A form of realism which assumes that the cognitive abilities of people have evolved through a process of engagement with the external (real) world.

Hypothetico-deductive: The idea in quantitative research that a researcher develops hypotheses from theory and tests these hypotheses empirically as part of the process of theory building. It is the antithesis of the qualitative approach.

Idealism: The philosophical view that accepts only minds and ideas – physical objects only exist in perception.

Identity: Individuality or sense of a personal or social self.

Ideology: A broad set of beliefs which form a relatively coherent perspective on the world and the way things should be. It is a doctrine.

Idiographic: Concentrating on the explanation of the individual (person) rather than the characteristics of groups.

Illocation: What is done by speaking words such as threatening, instructing and demanding.

Imagery: Mental pictures/images.

In vivo coding: Using the words or concepts employed by participants in the research to name the codes developed while analysing data. It is a grounded theory idea.

In-depth interview: A lengthy interview intended to obtain extensive rich and detailed information from an individual. Referred to as qualitative interviewing in this book.

Induction: The development of theory out of data. Deductive is the development of hypotheses to test theory.

Information sheet: See Participant information sheet.

Informed consent: Where individuals agree to take part in research on the basis of full knowledge of the important features of the data collection process.

Inter-coder reliability: The extent to which two coders agree on how to categorise or code each aspect of the data.

Internalisation: In the social construction of reality this occurs when shared conceptions of the world have become incorporated into social practices which are then internalised into the thinking of individuals.

Interpretative phenomenological analysis: A form of qualitative research which concentrates on the experiences of people with health issues and so forth.

Interpretative repertoire: Culturally provided systems of linguistic devices which are used to build accounts. Often difficult to distinguish from ideologies and discourses.

Interpretivism: A view of social research which requires the researcher to understand the subjective meaning of interaction.

Intersubjectivity: Basically this is to do with things which occur between two people or two minds. It is a descriptive term of the nature of the self and human activity. The experiences, meanings, actions and so forth of the individual are created intersubjectively through the interaction of two or more people. They are constructed through these interactions which involve both agreements and disagreements which lead to shared, co-produced states.

Intertextuality: The way in which features of one text (widely defined) are represented in some way in another text.

Interview: A formal conversation between a minimum of two people. In the research setting, this consists of an interviewer who largely asks the questions and an interviewee who largely answers them.

Interview guide: A list of areas to cover in a semi-structured interview.

Interview schedule: A list of questions to be asked in a structured interview. Similar to an interview guide but more formal and systematic than an interview guide.

Iterative process: A process characterised by repetition and recurrence. Usually, the process leads to a small but worthwhile improvement which can be built on by further reiterations.

Jefferson transcription: This is a way of turning recordings into written text which includes additional, non-lexical, features such as pauses, overlaps, loudness and so forth. It is a requirement for conversation analysis data.

Joint action: Interaction and the outcomes of interaction are regarded as being jointly produced by those who are interacting rather than interaction being seen as a succession of contributions from individuals.

Key informant: Members of the community who are crucial or important in the process of planning and executing participant observation or ethnographic research.

Latent code: Codes which go to a level of analysis deeper than the superficial features of the data.

Life-history interview: A semi-structured interview designed to collect long-term biographical information and description from individuals.

Life-story interview: *See* Life-history interview.

Linguistic repertoire: Or discursive repertoire. It refers to the clusters of ideas or other things which tend to co-occur when people construct accounts.

Literature review: Usually the written evaluation of the main arguments and research findings in the research literature on a particular topic included in the research report. Often used to refer to the entire process including the literature search.

Literature search: The procedures by which a researcher identifies and locates the pertinent previous publications on a particular research topic. It largely consists of searching databases such as PsycINFO.

Locution: Speaking.

Locutionary act: Performing an act of speech.

Logical positivism: A school of the philosophy of science which holds that the task of science is to develop theory which leads to general laws. This is particularly associated with behaviourist psychology. It is based on logical inferences based on observable facts.

Loss of the subject: The criticism of social constructionist approaches which argues that constructionism, because of its concentration on social interaction, disregards and can say nothing about the individuality of the actors in such exchanges.

Manifest codes: Codes developed in qualitative analysis which are closely related to the superficial content of the data.

Manner: One of Grice's maxims which suggests that brevity, clarity and orderliness characterise appropriate contributions to conversations.

Maximum variation sampling: Choosing participants not to be representative but to provide the greatest variety in relation to the topic of the research.

Meaning making: The process of making something meaningful.

Memo: A detailed 'diary' or record of a researcher's thoughts and ideas relevant to the analysis of their research. This has its origins in grounded theory.

Memo writing: The process of creating a memo.

Metaphor: The imagery incorporated into speech or any other form of text.

Methodolatry: The idolatory of method – valuing method above knowledge.

Methodology: The study of the rules, procedures and practices by which research in a particular field of research obtains knowledge. Thus, conversation analysis has its own distinct methodology. However, it tends to be used in psychology to refer to the techniques by which data are gathered – questionnaires, focus groups, etc.

Microanalysis: An analysis concentrating on the smaller detail of the data.

Mixed method: A mixture of qualitative and quantitative approaches to research (or any other broad categories of method).

Moderator: The same as a facilitator.

Modern psychology: Psychology is a very ancient area of intellectual interest. In this book, modern psychology refers to the psychology developing after the 1870s when the first psychology laboratories were set up in Germany and the United States.

Multiple case studies: Using several case studies but keeping them distinct analytically.

Multi-strategy research: Research combining qualitative and quantitative methods.

Naive realism: The unquestioning belief that there is a reality for researchers to identify. Critical realists and others may share this basic belief but accept that research taps a variety of realities or perspectives on reality.

Narrative: This can be used to refer to any spoken or written material. However, it is generally taken to refer to material which takes the form of a story.

Narrative analysis: This can be any form of analysis of narrative although, in psychology, it is probably best reserved for the analysis of narrative based on concepts, etc. from narrative psychology.

Narrative explanation: This is an explanation of events which takes the form of a story about past events. The story gives an account of and an explanation for the events.

Narrative identity: An individual identity as constructed through narrative.

Narrative inquiry: The broad field of interdisciplinary study of narrative.

Narrative psychology: The investigation of the nature of human experience and story-based accounts of these experiences. An approach to psychology which sees in stories and narratives a way of understanding the progression of personality through life.

Narrative realism: This is the idea that personal stories are the lived nature of human existence. It reflects the told character of existence.

Narrative tone: This is a term from McAdams. It refers to the broad tone of the story under study. For example, some narratives are replete with optimism and hope whereas others indicate mistrust or resignation.

Naturalism: Basically the idea that social and human sciences should adopt the scientific (natural science) approach.

Naturalistic: Research taking place in a real-life setting which involves little or no researcher-imposed control.

Naturalistic inquiry: Forms of research which stress the importance of studying social action from the viewpoint of social actors. That is, first-hand accounts from participants in social interaction are the basis of understanding.

Naturalistic paradigm: The assumption that there is no single true interpretation of reality. The focus of research is on how individuals create their own understanding of reality within the context of their social existence.

Negative case: A case or an instance in the data which goes against the hypothesis/analysis as it has developed up to that point.

Negotiated reality: Reality as created between two or more people interactively.

Noema: This is a concept from Edmund Husserl to describe the phenomenological idea of the object, i.e. the content of a phenomenon such as a thought or perception.

Noesis: The nature or manner of experiencing rather than what is experienced. From phenomenology.

Nominal group: A decision making group in which group members present a solution to a problem, the different solutions are listed, and finally the group members rank these different solutions in terms of preference.

Nomothetic: Law-like generalisations based on a number of cases. Usually based on measures taken by the researcher.

Normative: Based on generally accepted standards of evaluation.

Null hypothesis testing: The approach in inferential statistics in which the aim of the researcher is to accept or reject the null hypothesis. This is the basic approach to significance testing that all psychology students learn.

NVivo: A common commercial form of computer-aided qualitative data analysis software.

Objective: Unaffected by personal characteristics including motivations and values.

Objectivism: A philosophical viewpoint that social phenomena and their meaning exist independently of social actors. The idea that there is a reality which can be known independently of the person involved in knowing this reality.

Ontology: An aspect of metaphysics in which the nature of being and existence is the focus of study.

Open coding: In grounded theory this is the process of data category development closely based on the data under consideration. It involves assigning codes to the lines of transcript, etc. It is the first analytic stage in coding development which then becomes increasingly conceptual.

Open interview: Another name for unstructured interviews.

Open-ended observation: Observation with no pre-conceived observation categories in mind. The observation categories are generated from the data.

Open-ended question: A question which the interviewee answers freely without the constraints of fixed alternative answers from which to choose.

Open-question: *See* Open-ended question.

Operational definition: When a concept is defined in terms of the procedures used to measure it.

Oral history interview: A qualitative or semi-structured interview which involves the participant describing past events, etc. and reflecting on them.

Origin myth: An account of the origins of something (e.g. psychology) which is symbolic rather than factual in nature.

Other: Any other individual apart from the self though it carries the implication of stranger in some contexts.

Overall theme: The major topic in the data.

Overt research: Research in which it is evident to the participants that they are being researched.

Paradigm: A concept from Thomas Kuhn's *Structure of Scientific Revolutions*. A paradigm is a broad way of conceiving and understanding a particular area of research. Sometimes this can be put into crisis because of its failure to deal with new knowledge from research. This can result in a paradigm shift in which the crisis results in a radically different way of looking at the previous paradigm. However, paradigm is a very loosely used concept and is often used to denote a particular and distinctive way of looking at a branch of study. Qualitative psychology is sometimes referred to as a different paradigm from that of mainstream psychology.

Participant feedback: Comments, etc. from a participant in a research study to the researchers on their experience of being in the research or on the analysis of the data formulated by the researcher.

Participant information sheet: Information detailing aspects of the research particularly pertinent to the issue of informed consent. It is usually accompanied by an ethics consent form.

Participant observation: A form of fieldwork in which the researcher is actually in a particular research situation witnessing personally what is happening. It has its origins in cultural anthropology.

Performative: An utterance of language which has a particular social effect.

Perlocution: The consequence of speech on the hearer – that is, the act that the speaker has carried out.

Personal documents: Any form of documentary material written for personal rather than official reasons, e.g. diaries, letters, autobiographies, photographs.

Perspectivism: Essentially the idea that there are different perspectives which guide ideas. Closely related to relativism.

Phenomenological psychology: Forms of psychology built on phenomenological ideas.

Phenomenology: The careful description of everyday conscious experiences as they are experienced. Associated with many different types of philosophy including Edmund Husserl's transcendental phenomenology and the existentialism of Jean-Paul Sartre.

Pilot interview: An interview carried out with the purpose of evaluating critical aspects of an interview in order to deal with unanticipated problems in its implementation.

Pilot study: A preliminary study which is designed to evaluate the feasibility and value of a larger-scale study.

Piloting: The process of trying out a research study or an interview, etc. in order to identify problems or to evaluate a methodology or procedure.

Polysemy: The idea that a word or text can have a number of different meanings.

Positioning: Establishing one's personal position within or in relation to a particular discourse. It is also possible to position another person within a particular discourse.

Positivism: A philosophy attributed primarily to Auguste Comte which holds that valid knowledge is that based on what can be observed through the senses – or empirically to put it another way. More generally it is the use of the methods of natural science to study psychological or social scientific issues.

Postmodern: After the modern period, which was the historical period when science dominated thinking and science was seen as the solution to all problems. The postmodern period is associated with philosophical ideas different from those of positivist science in which ideas of an accessible 'reality' have been replaced by ideas of multiple 'realities'. There is little precise agreement as to the meaning of the term other than it represents a rejection against the 'modern' thinking which followed the Enlightenment.

Postmodernism: The ideas and philosophies associated with the postmodern period. The precise nature of these is difficult to specify but qualitative researchers express a range of postmodern principles.

Post-structuralism: This would be embraced by the term postmodernism but it is not quite the same. It largely refers to the intellectual attack on structuralism that emerged in 1970s France with the work of influential figures such as Michel Foucault, Jacques Derrida, Jean Baudrillard and Roland Barthes. In particular, amongst the structuralist notions attacked by the post-structuralist, the idea that meanings are stable is rejected in favour of the view that they constantly change and shift. This applies to the categories underlying explanations by academics.

Post-structuralist theory: Theory based within the post-structuralist perspective.

Practice: The everyday activity of practitioners – but is often extended to refer to the everyday activities engaged in by people such as how they go about doing conversation.

Pragmatism: A philosophical position which accepts the value of knowledge solely in terms of its usefulness to humanity's goals and needs. It assumes that knowledge is relative.

Prescriptive coding: Coding which is decided upon prior to examination of the data. It is not an approach to coding which fits readily with the ethos of qualitative research.

Primary research: Research for which the data are collected by the researcher who subsequently carries out the analysis. Secondary research can refer to data re-analysed by another researcher later but it can also refer to a subsequent, unanticipated analysis by the researcher who collected the data.

Prompts: Additional questions or queries which an interviewer incorporates into an interview to clarify answers or encourage the elaboration of what has been said.

Purposive sampling: The selection of members of a sample with a particular purpose in mind – for example, recruiting participants because they have experienced chronic illness.

Q methodology: This is a method with its antecedents firmly in early research on the statistical technique, factor analysis. It can be used to explore subjective experiences. Q methodology has appeared in recent discussions of qualitative research but has little in common with the approaches used in this book. The Q sort is a method of data collection.

QDAS: Qualitative Data Analysis Software – same as CAQDAS.

QSR NVivo: The full name of NVivo.

Qualitative: To do with the qualities of things rather than quantities.

Qualitative content analysis: The analysis of text using categories which arise out of the data. Very little if at all different from thematic analysis.

Qualitative research: Research which is based on rich textual rather than numerical data.

Quality: One of Grice's maxims which suggests that what is said in conversation should be truthful and sincere.

Quantification: Turning into numbers.

Quantitative research: Research which either collects data in a numerical or quasi numerical form or otherwise seeks to impose quantities on the analysis. Typically mainstream psychology.

Quantity: One of Grice's maxims which suggests that sufficient information should be provided in conversation to make what is said understandable.

Queer theory: This is a form of post-structuralist theory which provides a critique of issues to do with sexual identity and is critical of non-gay ways of thinking and heterosexism. Queer theory is strongly influenced by Michel Foucault.

Radical behaviourism: The behaviourist philosophy formulated by B.F. Skinner. Among its characteristics is the proposal that all behaviour is determined rather than subject to free will. In this way, among many others, radical behaviourism is the antithesis of the assumptions of qualitative psychology.

Reactivity: The tendency of the process of being studied to affect the activities of those being studied.

Reading: A particular perspective on a text.

Realism: The theory that there is an external world which is independent of thought and our perceptions of that world.

Realist epistemology: The assumption that there is a real, physical world which can be directly studied. Often held to be a fundamental of science and positivism.

Received view: A passed-on view of the nature of things or the world which is adopted uncritically by the receiver of that world view.

Reductionism: The belief that the whole is a sum of its parts. Thus, complex aspects of human activity can best be studied by breaking them down into their component parts. The antithesis of holistic.

Reductionist: To do with reductionism.

Reflexivity: The stance in research in which the researcher considers the implications of the knowledge they create in terms of the procedures of data collection, the biases of the researcher, and their presence in the situations they investigate.

Relation: One of Grice's maxims which suggests that good contributions to conversation should be relevant to the conversation.

Reliability: The idea from quantitative research that measures should exhibit consistency over time and internally over the various sub-sections of the measure.

Repair: Attempts to remedy or otherwise deal with 'embarrassing' errors in conversation.

Research question: In academic research of all sorts, the research question is the question which the research seeks to address.

Respondent validation: This is a fairly common term in qualitative research by which the opinions of the participants in the research (or similar groups of people) are approached about the findings of a research study in which they took part for their comments and evaluation.

Rewrite techniques: *See* Rewriting.

Rewriting: This is an approach to creating general theory in grounded theory analysis. It literally involves rewriting a grounded theory analysis in an attempt to generate a more widely applicable theory; for example, by simply writing a theory in less specific terms as an aid to aid generalisation.

Rhetoric: The methods by which arguments are made persuasive and convincing.

Rhetorical psychology: The psychological study of rhetoric.

Root metaphor: Different ways of studying a particular discipline adopt different metaphors to suggest the broad nature of that which is being studied. Behaviourism had the root metaphor of people as machines. The term root metaphor then refers to the basic way in which people are conceived in research. The term comes from narrative psychology which has the basic metaphor of people as story tellers.

Sampling: Although this means the process of selecting a representative group of participants to represent the population in quantitative research, it has a very different meaning in qualitative research. The commonest use is in theoretical sampling which means the selection of further cases or instances by selecting those which will contribute most to theory development.

Saturation: When additional participants or data no longer bring new information which encourages the refinement of the analysis. That is, nothing new is being learnt by doing more data collection. It can serve as a means of deciding when no further participants will be recruited but, equally, it can be indicative of when a particular stage of analysis is complete.

Science: Natural sciences such as physics, chemistry and the like.

Scientific method: Usually used as a synonym for positivism.

Scientism: The belief that the natural sciences have primacy and authority compared with other approaches to knowledge, e.g. religious and philosophical knowledge.

Secondary analysis: The analysis of data by researchers who were not involved in the original study of that data. Alternatively, it is the further analysis of data in ways which were not anticipated originally by the researcher.

Selective coding: In grounded theory this is the process by which one of the categories in the analysis is identified to be the core category. All other categories are then related to this. It is a late stage in the building of theory.

Semiology: The discipline involved with the study of signs.

Semiotics: The study of signs and the processes by which they produce meaning. It involves the search for the deeper meaning of documents and other material.

Semi-structured interview: Alternatively in-depth or qualitative interviews in which the interviewee is encouraged to talk in depth and at some length about a topic(s). The interviewee is free to answer in whatever way he or she wishes. The interviewer often has only a skeletal version of the questions they intend to ask. In other words, a semi-structured interview has a loose structure compared with that of a structured interview and a relatively tight structure compared with an unstructured interview which has no prepared structure at all. Semi-structured interviews are generally the choice of qualitative researchers.

Sense making: The process of giving meaning to events.

Sensitivity: *See* Theoretical sensitivity.

Sign: A term in semiotics referring to the signifier or manifestation of a sign and the signified (the meaning of the sign).

Situationally bounded: The idea that qualities are not fixed in research but change with the situation in which they are assessed.

Social construction: Some aspect of knowledge created by people through interaction or the process of doing this.

Social constructionism: The idea that knowledge is constructed by people during interaction.

Social constructionist: To do with social constructionism.

Social constructionist discourse analysis: The form of discourse analysis particularly associated with Jonathan Potter and Margaret Wetherell. It contrasts with Foulcaudian discourse analysis.

Social representation: A concept from Serge Moscovici. It refers to the way that members of a culture collectively share a constructed understanding of the nature of a social object. Once a highly influential theory in social psychology but essentially replaced by not dissimilar ideas from social constructionism.

Sociolinguistics: The study of language in terms of its social and cultural aspects.

Soft data: Data collected not using 'objective' natural science methods. Possibly similar to qualitative.

Software package: Computer program or set of program such as NVivo in qualitative research.

Speech act theory: The theory of language particularly associated with J.L. Austin which draws to the forefront of analysis how things are done with words or language as social action.

Stake: The assumption of members of a conversation that speakers have a vested interest in the positions they put forward in conversation.

Story: A set of meaningful events presented with a chronological structure.

Structuralism: Ways of theorising about the world which are concerned with the unobservable structures which underlie the world. Since these structures cannot be observed, they have to be inferred. Mental structures are often proposed in psychology. However, structuralism was the first major school of psychology in the modern period. Piaget adopted a form of structuralism in his theories of child development. Most likely, however, in qualitative psychology structuralism refers to sociological thinking immediately prior to the current postmodern (poststructuralist) period.

Structured interviews: Interviews in which all of the questions are standardised in advance of data collection. Almost invariably, this involves offering a limited range of response alternatives for the interviewee to choose from.

Subject position: In discourse analysis, this is the location of the individual within a discourse that they employ. So it is the rights, obligations and duties which, for example, the citizen has in a law-and-order discourse.

Subjectivism: The idea that everything including interpretations, etc. reflect nothing but reports of the views of individuals. Another closely related word for this is relativism. An alternative use of the term indicates that subjectivity is essentially what we refer to as reality. The latter usage comes from phenomenology.

Subjectivities: The idea that different individuals have different lived experiences of the world. Hence, it is the plural of subjectivity.

Subjectivity: Most usually in qualitative psychology this refers to the lived experiences of people such as their experience of self. Alternative meanings are concerned with epistemology and refer to personal viewpoints, unwarranted arguments, or biased accounts. It is, therefore, just the personal view of an individual.

Substantive theory: This, in grounded theory, is the stage of theory which is developed prior to the formal theory which is the outcome of grounded theory.

Subtle realist position: The acceptance that different research methods impose different subjectivities and, consequently, different perspectives on reality. The idea of a basic reality is accepted though it is problematic to study it. The task of researchers is to represent what is possible of that reality.

Superordinate theme: A cluster or group of themes (sub-themes) which are related in some way and given a descriptive label.

Symbolic interactionism: This is a major approach to social psychology originating in the work of George Herbert Mead and Herbert Blumer. Basically it is the idea that a person develops meanings for the world through social interaction with the world. These meanings then determine the individual's interaction with the world.

Talk-in interaction: A phrase used in conversation analysis which essentially describes the nature of conversation as construed in that field.

Template analysis: A form of analysis which pre-specifies many of the categories used in the analysis.

Text: Any data which are imbued with meaning. They do not have to be words or other forms of verbal data but usually are.

Thematic analysis: This is a form of qualitative analysis which seeks to 'work up' or identify the major areas (themes) in the textual data studied.

Theme: A 'topic' identified within some text.

Theoretical coding: In grounded theory, this is a higher level of coding which applies a set of codes which developed out of the data at an earlier stage of the analysis. The researcher has essentially derived a theoretical model which is being applied to the data.

Theoretical sampling: A term originally from grounded theory which describes the process of choosing new cases or even research locations on the basis of their capacity to inform the analysis that has been achieved thus far.

Theoretical sensitivity: In grounded theory this refers to the personal qualities of researchers which equips them to develop good quality grounded theory. It is dependent on factors such as previous experience, reading in the field of interest, the ability to understand data, and insight.

Thick description: There is a lack of clarity about the meaning of this. Although it implies the collection of a lot of detail about something that is being studied, it also involves a degree of initial interpretation in its intentions, meanings, circumstances and so forth.

Three-part list: The idea in conversation analysis that in ordinary conversation the use of lists of three 'items' are common and conversationally effective. For example, I came, I saw, I conquered.

Transcendental phenomenology: This term describes the sort of phenomenology associated with Edmund Husserl. It is the study of what is left when consciousness is stripped of hypotheses about the phenomenon being studied. It is the consciousness following bracketing or epoché.

Transcription: The process of putting into the written word data which are in spoken form such as interviews, conversations, telephone calls and focus group interaction. It almost always involves audio (and sometimes video) recording in modern qualitative research.

Transparency: The openness of a researcher's procedures (including analysis) to inspection and criticism.

Triangulation: The use of three (or more) different sources of information to help establish how sound a researcher's inference is. The triangulation may include different data sources, researchers, methods and so forth. Essentially more than one vantage point is being used to assess one's conclusions. Generally, this implies that there should be convergence of the conclusions from, say, different methods which may not be a warranted implication for qualitative methods.

Turn: In conversation analysis the bounded contribution of an individual in a conversation separated by other speakers (or the beginning or end of the conversation).

Turn-taking: The notion from conversation analysis that during conversations individuals take turns in being the speaker.

Unit of analysis: The major unit which is under consideration in a research study. In psychology, this is the individual but the concept could be used to refer to neurons, groups, institutions, cultures and so forth. In qualitative research, the unit of analysis can be a particular aspect of text, for example.

Unstructured interview: An interview which has no pre-planned structure. Sometimes used synonymously with semi-structured interview. However, a semi-structured interview has an interview guide to pre-structure the interview to a degree.

Validity: A quality criterion in the quantitative epistemology. Of dubious value in qualitative research.

Variable: Something that can be named and measured. It is an endemic common term in quantitative psychology but a rarity in qualitative writing.

Verstehen: From German. The word means 'understanding'. It is a difficult concept because of its many related meanings in social sciences. Wilhelm Dilthey, a German philosopher, first used the word in distinguishing the natural sciences from other sciences. The former seeks general laws whereas the human sciences seek to understand meaning. Max Weber used it to mean where a researcher approaches another culture or subculture using the perspective/point of view of that culture or subculture rather than the researcher's own.

Written discourse: Language in its written form.

Written language: Language as it is written down as opposed to spoken.

REFERENCES

Ablett, J.R., and Jones, R.S. (2007) Resilience and well-being in palliative care staff: a qualitative study of hospice nurses' experience of work. *Psycho-Oncology*, *16* (8), 733–740.

Adams, W.A. (2000). Introspectionism reconsidered. Presented at 'Towards a Science of Consciousness'. http://www.waadams.net/published%20documents/Introspectionism%20Reconsidered.pdf (accessed 13 August 2009).

Allport, G.W. (1940). The psychologist's frame of reference. *Psychological Bulletin*, *37*, 1–28.

Allport, G.W., Bruner, J., and Jandorf, E. (1941). Personality under social catastrophe: an analysis of 90 German refugee life histories. *Character and Personality*, *10*, 1–22.

Altheide, D.L. (1996). *Qualitative Media Analysis*. Qualitative Research Methods Vol. 38. Thousand Oaks, CA: Sage.

American Psychological Association (2002). Ethical Principles of Psychologists and Code of Conduct. http://www.apa.org/ethics/code2002.html (accessed 23 August 2009).

American Psychological Association (2009). PsycINFO: Your Source for Psychological Abstracts. http://www.apa.org/psycinfo/ (accessed 5 July 2009).

Antaki, C. (2007). Mental-health practitioners' use of idiomatic expressions in summarising clients' accounts. *Journal of Pragmatics*, *39*, 527–541.

Antaki, C. (2009a). Anonymising Data: Ten Guidelines for Changing Names in Transcripts. http://www-staff.lboro.ac.uk/~ssca1/pseudos2.htm (accessed 26 August 2009).

Antaki, C. (2009b). What Counts as Conversation Analysis – And What Doesn't. http://www-staff.lboro.ac.uk/~ssca1/analysisintro.htm (accessed 26 June 2009).

Antaki, C., Billig, M., Edwards, D., and Potter, J. (2003). Discourse analysis means doing analysis: a critique of six analytic shortcomings. *Discourse Analysis Online*, *1* (1). http://www.shu.ac.uk/daol/previous/v1_n1/index.htm (accessed 26 June 2009).

Antaki, C., Finlay, W.M.L., and Walton, C. (2007). The staff are your friends: intellectually disabled identities in official discourse and interactional practice. *British Journal of Social Psychology*, *46*, 1–18.

Ashmore, M., and Reed, D. (2000). Innocence and nostalgia in conversation analysis: the dynamic relations of tape and transcript. *Forum: Qualitative Social Research*, *1* (3). http://qualitative-research.net/fqs-texte/3-00/3-00ashmorereed-e.htm (accessed 21 August 2009).

Ashworth, P. (2008). Conceptual foundations of qualitative psychology. In J.A. Smith (Ed.), *Qualitative Psychology: A practical guide to research methods*, 2nd Edition. London: Sage, pp. 4–25.

Atkinson, M. (2008). Max Atkinson Blog. Gordon Brown's Gaffe Shows what Gail Jefferson Meant by a 'Sound Formed Error'. http://maxatkinson.blogspot.com/2008/12/gordon-browns-gaffe-shows-what-gail.html (retrieved 25 February 2009).

Atkinson, J.M., and Heritage, J. (1984). Transcript notation. In J.M. Atkinson and J. Heritage (Eds.), *Structures of Social Action: Studies in conversation analysis*. Cambridge: Cambridge University Press, pp. iv–xvi.

Austin, J.L. (1962). *How To Do Things With Words: The William James Lectures delivered at Harvard University in 1955*. J.O. Urmson (Ed.). Oxford: Clarendon.

Austin, J.L. (1975). *How To Do Things with Words*. Cambridge, MA: Harvard University Press.

Baars, B.J. (1986). *The Cognitive Revolution in Psychology*. New York: The Guilford Press.

Barbour, R. (2007). *Doing Focus Groups*. Los Angeles, CA: Sage.

Barker, R.G. (1968). *Ecological Psychology*. Stanford, CA: Stanford University Press.

Barker, R., and Wright, H. (1951). *One Boy's Day. A specimen record of behaviour*. New York: Harper and Brothers.

Barlow, D.H., and Hersen, M. (1984). *Single Case Experimental Designs: Strategies for studying behavior change*, 2nd Edition. New York: Pergamon Press.

Baumrind, D. (1985). Research using intentional deception: ethical issues revisited. *American Psychologist, 40*, 165–174.

Beaugrande, R. de (1996). The story of discourse analysis. In T. van Dijk (Ed.), *Introduction to Discourse Analysis*. London: Sage, pp. 35–62.

Becker, H.S., and Geer, B. (1982). Participant observation: the analysis of qualitative field data. In R.G. Burgess (Ed.), *Field Research: A sourcebook and field manual*. London: George Allen and Unwin, pp. 239–250.

Benneworth, K. (2006) Repertoires of paedophilia: conflicting descriptions of adult–child sexual relationships in the investigative interview. *The International Journal of Speech, Language and the Law, 13* (2), 190–211.

Benwell, B.M., and Stokoe, E. (2006). *Discourse and Identity*. Edinburgh: Edinburgh University Press.

Berelson, B. (1952). *Content Analysis in Communication Research*. Glencoe: Free Press.

Berger, P.L., and Luckmann, T. (1966). *The Social Construction of Reality: A treatise in the sociology of knowledge*. Garden City, NY: Anchor.

Bevis, J.C. (1949). Interviewing with tape recorders. *Public Opinion Quarterly, 13*, 629–634.

Biggerstaff, D., and Thompson, A.R. (2008). Interpretative phenomenological analysis (IPA): a qualitative methodology of choice in healthcare research. *Qualitative Research in Psychology, 5* (3), 214–224.

Billig, M. (1992). *Talking of the Royal Family*. London: Routledge.

Billig, M. (1996). *Arguing and Thinking: A rhetorical approach to social psychology*, 2nd Edition. Cambridge: Cambridge University Press.

Billig, M. (1997). Rhetorical and discursive analysis: how families talk about the royal family. In N. Hayes (Ed.), *Doing Qualitative Analysis in Psychology*. Hove: Psychology Press, pp. 39–54.

Billig, M. (2008). *The Hidden Roots of Critical Psychology: Understanding the impact of Locke, Shaftesbury and Reid*. London: Sage.

Blodgett, L.J., Boyer, W., and Turk, E. (2005). 'No thank you, not today': supporting ethical and professional relationships in large qualitative studies. *Forum: Qualitative Social Research, 6* (3), available on the web http://www.qualitative-research.net/index.php/fqs/article/viewArticle/31 (accessed 7 August, 2009).

Blumer, H. (1969). *Symbolic Interactionism: Perspective and method*. Englewood Cliffs, NJ: Prentice Hall.

Bogardus, E.S. (1926). The groups interview. *Journal of Applied Sociology*, *10*, 372–382.

Bowen, G.A. (2005). Preparing a qualitative research-based dissertation: lessons learned. *The Qualitative Report*, *10* (2), 208–222.

Braun, V., and Clarke, V. (2006). Using thematic analysis in psychology. *Qualitative Research in Psychology*, *3*, 77–101.

Brink, E., Karlson, B.W., and Hallberg, L.R.-M. (2002). To be stricken with acute myocardian infarction: a grounded theory study of symptom perception and care-seeking behavior. *Journal of Health Psychology*, *7* (5), 533–543.

Brinkmann, S., and Kvaale, S. (2005). Confronting the ethics of qualitative research. *Journal of Constructivist Psychology*, *18* (2), 157–181.

British Psychological Society (2006). Ethical Principles for Conducting Research with Human Participants. http://www.bps.org.uk/the-society/code-of-conduct/ethical-principles-for-conducting-research-with-human-participants.cfm (accessed 23 August 2009).

Brooks, E., and Dallos, R. (2009). Exploring young women's understandings of the development of difficulties: a narrative biographical analysis. *Clinical Child Psychology and Psychiatry*, *14* (1), 101–115.

Brower, D. (1949). The problem of quantification in psychological science. *Psychological Review*, *56* (6), 325–333.

Bruner, J. (1986). *Actual Minds, Possible Worlds*. Cambridge, MA: Harvard University Press.

Bruner, J. (1990). *Acts of Meaning*. Cambridge, MA: Harvard University Press.

Bryman, A. (1988). *Quantity and Quality in Social Research*. London: Routledge.

Bryman, A. (2004). *Social Research Methods*, 2nd Edition. Oxford University Press.

Bryman, A., and Bell, E. (2003). *Business Research Methods*. Oxford: Oxford University Press.

Bühler, C. (1933). *Der Menschliche Lebenslauf als Psychologisches Problem*. [The Human Course of Life as a Psychological Problem.] Leipzig: Hirzel.

Bulmer, M. (1984). *The Chicago School of Sociology*. Chicago, IL: University of Chicago Press.

Burgess, R.G. (1982). Styles of data analysis: approaches and implications. In R.G. Burgess (Ed.), *Field Research: A sourcebook and field manual*. London: George Allen and Unwin, pp. 235–238.

Burgess, R.G. (1984). *In the Field: An introduction to field research*. London: Allen and Unwin.

Burman, E. (2004). Discourse analysis means analysing discourse: some comments on Antaki, Billig, Edwards and Potter's 'Discourse analysis means doing analysis: a critique of six analytic shortcomings'. *Discourse Analysis Online* http://www.shu.ac.uk/daol/articles/closed/2003/003/burman2003003-t.html (accessed 6 August 2009).

Burman, E., and Parker, I. (Eds.) (1993). *Discourse Analytic Research: Repertoires and readings of texts in action*. London: Routledge.

Burr, V. (2003). *Social Constructionism*, 2nd Edition. London: Routledge.

Butler, C.W. (2008). *Talk and Social Interaction in the Playground*. Aldershot: Ashgate.

Calder, B. (1977). Focus groups and the nature of qualitative marketing research. *Journal of Marketing Research*, *14* (3), 353–364.

Campbell, C., and Guy, A. (2007). 'Why can't they do anything for a simple back problem?': a qualitative examination of expectations for low back pain treatment and outcome. *Journal of Health Psychology*, *12* (4), 641–652.

Campbell, D.T., and Fiske, D.W. (1959). Convergent and discriminant validation by the multitrait–multimethod matrix. *Psychological Bulletin*, *56*, 81–105.

Canter, D. (1983). The potential of facet theory for applied social psychology. *Quality and Quantity*, *17*, 35–67.

Chapman, E., and Smith, J.A. (2002). Interpretative phenomenological analysis and the new genetics. *Journal of Health Psychology*, *7* (2), 125–130.

Charmaz, K. (1995). Grounded theory. In J.A. Smith, R. Harré and L.V. Langenhove (Eds.), *Rethinking Methods in Psychology*. London: Sage, pp. 27–49.

Charmaz, K. (2000). Grounded theory: objectivist and constructivist methods. In N.K. Denzin and Y.S.E. Lincoln (Eds.), *Handbook of Qualitative Research*, 2nd Edition. Thousand Oaks, CA: Sage, pp. 503–535.

Charmaz, K. (2006). *Constructing Grounded Theory: A practical guide through qualitative analysis*. Thousand Oaks, CA: Sage.

Chomsky, N. (1973). Psychology and ideology. *Cognition*, *1*, 11–46.

Clark, A., Stedmon, J., and Margison, S. (2008). An exploration of the experience of mothers whose children sustain traumatic brain injury (TBI) and their families. *Clinical Child Psychology and Psychiatry*, *13* (4), 565–583.

Clarke, V., Burns, M., and Burgoyne, C. (2008). Who would take whose name? *Journal of Community and Applied Social Psychology*, *18* (5), 420–439.

Clay, R. (2005). Too few in quantitative psychology. *APA Monitor on Psychology*, *36* (8). http://www.apa.org/monitor/sep05/quantitative.html (accessed 18 July 2008).

Cmerjrkova, S., and Prevignano, C.L. (2003). On conversation analysis: an interview with Emanuel Schegloff. In C.L. Prevignano and P.J. Thibault (Eds.), *Discussing Conversation Analysis: The work of Emanuel Schegloff*. Amsterdam: John Benjamins, pp. 11–55.

Coates, J., and Thornborrow, J. (1999). Myths, lies and audiotapes: some thoughts on data transcripts. *Discourse and Society*, *10* (4), 594–597.

Cohen, D. (1977). On Psychology: Noam Chomsky interviewed by David Cohen. Excerpted from *Psychologists on Psychology: Modern Innovators Talk About Their Work*, Taplinger, 1977. http://www.chomsky.info/interviews/1977----.htm

Coleman, L.M., and Cater, S.M. (2005). A qualitative study of the relationship between alcohol consumption and risky sex in adolescents. *Archives of Sexual Behavior*, *34*, 649–661.

Comte, A. (1975). *Auguste Comte and Positivism: The essential writings*. G. Lenzzer (Ed.). Chicago, IL: University of Illinois Press.

Cowles, E. (1888). Insistent and fixed ideas. *American Journal of Psychology*, *1* (2), 222–270.

Coyle, A. (2007). Discourse analysis. In E. Lyons and A. Coyle (Eds.), *Analysing Qualitative Data in Psychology*. London: Sage, pp. 98–116.

Crabtree, B.F., and Miller, W.L. (1999). Using codes and code manuals: a template organizing style of interpretation. In B.F. Crabtree and W.L. Miller (Eds.), *Doing Qualitative Research*, 2nd Edition. Newbury Park, CA: Sage.

Crossley, M. (2000). *Introducing Narrative Psychology: Self-trauma and the construction of meaning*. Buckingham: Open University Press.

Crossley, M.L. (2003). Let me 'explain': narrative emplotment and one patient's experience of oral cancer. *Social Science and Medicine*, *56*, 439–448.

Crossley, M.L. (2007). Narrative analysis. In E. Lyons and A. Coyle (Eds.), *Analysing Qualitative Data in Psychology*. London: Sage, pp. 131–144.

Danziger, K. (1997). The varieties of social construction. *Theory and Psychology*, 7 (3), 399–416.

Danziger, K., and Dzinas, K. (1997). How psychology got its variables. *Canadian Psychology*, 38, 43–48.

Davidson, J. (1984). Subsequent versions of invitations, offers, requests, and proposals dealing with potential or actual rejection. In J.M. Atkinson and J. Heritage (Eds.), *Structures of Social Action: Studies in conversation analysis.* Cambridge: Cambridge University Press, pp. 102–128.

Dearborn, G.V.N. (1920). Review of the Lia-speaking peoples of Northern Rhodesia. *Journal of Abnormal Psychology*, 15 (4), 283–288.

Del Vecchio Good, M., Munakata, T., Kobayashi, Y., Mattingly, C., and Good, B. (1994). Oncology and narrative time. *Social Science and Medicine*, 38, 855–862.

Denscombe, M. (2002). *Ground Rules for Good Research: A 10 point guide for social researchers.* Buckingham: Open University Press.

Denzin, N.K., and Lincoln, Y.S.E. (2000). Introduction: the discipline and practice of qualitative research. In N.K. Denzin and Y.S.E. Lincoln (Eds.), *Handbook of Qualitative Research*, 2nd Edition. Thousand Oaks, CA: Sage, pp. 1–28.

Dereshiwsky, M. (1999). The Five Dimensions of Participant Observations. http://jan.ucc.nau.edu/~mid/edr725/class/observation/fivedimensions/reading3-2-1.html.

Dickson, A., Allan, D., and O'Carroll, R. (2008). Biographical disruption and the experience of loss following a spinal cord injury: an interpretative phenomenological analysis. *Psychology and Health*, 23 (4), 407–425.

Dixon-Woods, M., Sutton, A., Shaw, R., Miller, T., Smith, J., Young, B., Bonas, S., Booth, A., and Jones, D. (2007). Appraising qualitative research for inclusion in systematic reviews: a quantitative and qualitative comparison of three methods. *Journal of Health Service Research Policy*, 12 (1), 42–47.

Dollard, J. (1935). *Criteria for the Life History.* New Haven, CT: Yale University Press.

Dollard, J. (1937). *Caste and Class in a Southern Town.* Garden City, NY: Doubleday.

Drew, P. (1995). Conversation analysis. In J.A. Smith, R. Harre and L.V. Langenhove (Eds.), *Rethinking Methods in Psychology.* London: Sage, pp. 64–79.

Du Bois, J.W., Schuetze-Coburn, S., Cumming, S., and Paolino, D. (1993). Outline of discourse transcription. In J.A. Edwards and M.D. Lampert (Eds.), *Talking Data: Transcription and coding in discourse research.* Hillsdale, NJ: Erlbaum, pp. 45–89.

Eatough, V., and Smith, J.A. (2006). 'I feel like a scrambled egg in my head': an idiographic case study of meaning, making and anger using interpretative phenomenological analysis. *Psychology and Psychotherapy: Theory, Research and Practice*, 79, 115–135.

Edley, N. (2001). Analysing masculinity: Interpretative repertoires, ideological dilemmas and subject positions. In M. Wetherell, S. Taylor and S.J.E. Yates (Eds.), *Discourse as Data: A guide for analysis.* London: Sage, pp. 189–228.

Edwards, D. (1995). Sacks and psychology. *Theory and Psychology*, 5 (3), 579–597.

Ehlich, K. (1993). HIAT: a transcription system for discourse data. In J.A. Edwards and M.D. Lampert (Eds.), *Talking Data: Transcription and coding in discourse research.* Hillsdale, NJ: Erlbaum, pp. 123–148.

Emerson, P., and Frosh, S. (2004). *Critical Narrative Analysis in Psychology: A guide to practice.* Basingstoke: Palgrave MacMillan.

Epley, N., and Huff, C. (1998). Suspicion, affective response, and educational benefit as a result of deception in psychology research. *Personality and Social Psychology Bulletin*, 24, 759–768.

Every, D., and Augoustinos, M. (2007). Constructions of racism in the Australian parliamentary debates on asylum seekers. *Discourse and Society*, *18* (4), 411–436.

Festervand, T.A. (1984–85). An introduction and application of focus group research to the health care industry. *Health Marketing Quarterly*. Special Issue: Marketing ambulatory care services, *2* (2–3), 199–209.

Festinger, L., Riecken, H.W., and Schachter, S. (1956). *When Prophecy Fails: A social and psychological study of a modern group that predicted the destruction of the world*. New York: Harper Torchbooks.

Finkelhor, D., Mitchell, K.J., and Wolak, J. (2000). *Online Victimization: A report on the nation's youth*. Alexandria, VA: National Center for Missing and Exploited Children.

Fish, S. (1989). *Doing What Comes Naturally: Change, rhetoric and the practice of theory in literary and legal studies*. Oxford: Oxford University Press.

Flick, U. (2002). *An Introduction to Qualitative Research*, 2nd Edition. London: Sage.

Flyvbjerg, B. (2006). Five misunderstandings about case-study research. *Qualitative Inquiry*, *12* (2), 219–245.

Fontana, A., and Frey, J.H. (2000). The interview: from structured questions to negotiated text. In N.K. Denzin and Y.S. Lincoln (Eds.), *Handbook of Qualitative Research*, 2nd Edition. Thousand Oaks, CA: Sage Publications, pp. 645–672.

Forbat, L., and Henderson, J. (2003). 'Stuck in the middle with you': the ethics and process of qualitative research with two people in an intimate relationship. *Qualitatative Health Research*, *13*, 1453–1462.

Foucault, M. (2006). *History of Madness*. Abingdon: Routledge.

Freud, S. (1909). *Analysis of a phobia of a five-year old boy*. London: Pelican Freud Library, Vol. 8 Case Histories.

Freud, S. (1918). *Totem and Taboo*. Translated by A.A. Brill. New York: Moffat, Yard Co.

Frost, N. (2009). 'Do you know what I mean?': the use of a pluralistic narrative analysis approach in the interpretation of an interview. *Qualitative Research*, *9* (1), 9–29.

Garson, D. (n.d.). Narrative Analysis. North Carolina State University. http:// faculty.chass.ncsu.edu/garson/PA765/narrativ.htm (accessed 14 July 2009)

Gee, D., Ward, T., and Eccleston, L. (2003). The function of sexual fantasies for sexual offenders: a preliminary model. *Behaviour Change*, *20*, 44–60.

Gergen, K.J. (1973). Social psychology as history. *Journal of Personality and Social Psychology*, *26* (2), 309–320.

Gergen, K.J. (1985a). The social constructionist movement in modern psychology. *American Psychologist*, *40*, 266–275.

Gergen, K.J. (1985b). Social constructionist inquiry: context and implications. In K.J. Gergen and K.E. Davie (Eds.), *The Social Construction of the Person*. New York: Springer-Verlag, pp. 3–18.

Gergen, K.J. (1998). Narrative, moral identity and historical consciousness: a social constructionist account. Draft copy appearing as 'Erzahlung, moralische Identiat und historisches Bewusstsein. Eine sozialkonstructionistische Darstelung.' In J. Straub (Ed.) (1998) *Identitat und historishces Bewusstsein*. Frankfurt: Suhrkamp. http://www.swarthmore.edu/Documents/faculty/gergen/Narrative_Moral_Identity_and_Historical_Consciousness.pdf (accessed 12 August 2009).

Gergen, K.J. (1999). *An Invitation to Social Construction*. London: Sage.

Gergen, K.J., and Gergen, M. (1983). Narratives of the self. In T.R. Sarbin and K. Scheibe (Eds.), *Studies in Social Identity*. New York: Praeger, 54–74.

Gergen, K.J., and Gergen, M.M. (1986). Narrative form and the construction of psychological science. In T.R. Sarbin (Ed.), *Narrative Psychology: The storied nature of human conduct*. New York: Praeger, pp. 22–44.

Gergen, K.J., and Graumann, C.F. (1996). *Psychological Discourse in Historical Perspective*. New York: Cambridge University Press.

Gergen, M. (2008). Qualitative methods in feminist psychology. In C. Willig and W. Stainton-Rogers (Eds.), *The SAGE Handbook of Qualitative Research in Psychology*. London: Sage, pp. 280–295.

Gibbs, A. (1997). Focus groups. *Social Research Update*, 19 http://sru.soc.surrey.ac.uk/SRU19.html (accessed 12 February 2009).

Gilbert, G.N., and Mulkay, M. (1984). *Opening Pandora's Box: A sociological analysis of scientists' discourse*. Cambridge: Cambridge University Press.

Giles, D. (2006). Constructing identities in cyberspace: The case of eating disorders. *British Journal of Social Psychology*, 45 (3), 463–477.

Glaser, B.G. (1978). *Theoretical Sensitivity: Advances in the methodology of grounded theory*. Mill Valley, CA: Sociology Press.

Glaser, B.G. (1982). Generating formal theory. In R.G. Burgess (Ed.), *Field Research: A sourcebook and field manual*. London: George Allen and Unwin, pp. 225–232.

Glaser, B.G. (1992). *Basics of Grounded Theory Analysis. Emergence vs forcing*. Mill Valley, CA: Sociology Press.

Glaser, B.G. (1998). *Doing Grounded Theory: Issues and discussions*. Mill Valley, CA: Sociology Press.

Glaser, B.G., and Strauss, A.L. (1965). *Awareness of Dying*. Chicago, IL: Aldine.

Glaser, B.G., and Strauss, A.L. (1967). *The Discovery of Grounded Theory: Strategies for qualitative research*. New York: Aldine de Gruyter.

Goffman, E. (1959). *The Presentation of Self in Everyday Life*. Garden City, NY: Doubleday.

Goffman, E. (1961). *Asylums: Essays on the social situation of mental patients and other inmates*. Garden City, New York: Anchor.

Goffman, E. (1974). *Frame Analysis: An essay on the organization of experience*. London: Harper and Row.

Goodwin, P., and Ogden, J. (2007). Women's reflections upon their past abortions: An exploration of how and why emotional reactions change over time. *Psychology and Health*, 22 (2), 231–248.

Gordon, M.J. (2006). Interview with William Labov. *Journal of English Linguistics*, 34, 332–351.

Grbich, C. (2007). *Qualitative Data Analysis*. London: Sage.

Grice, H.P. (1975). Logic and conversation. In P. Cole and J. Morgan (Eds.), *Syntax and Semantics 3: Speech acts*. New York: Academic Press, pp. 41–58.

Gumperz, J.J., and Berenz, N. (1993). Transcribing conversational exchange. In J.A. Edwards and M.D. Lampert (Eds.), *Talking Data: Transcription and coding in discourse research*. Hillsdale, NJ: Erlbaum.

Hammersley, M. (1996). The relationship between qualitative and quantitative research: paradigm loyalty versus methodological eclecticism. In J.T.E. Richardson (Ed.), *Handbook of Qualitative Research Methods for Psychology and the Social Sciences*. Leicester: BPS Books, pp. 159–174.

Hammersley, M. (1999). Some reflections on the current state of qualitative research. *Research Intelligence*, 70, 16–18.

Harris, Z. (1952). Discourse analysis. *Language, 29* (1), 1–30.

Heath, C., and Luff, P. (1993). Explicating face-to-face interaction. In N. Gilbert (Ed.), *Researching Social Life*. London: Sage, pp. 306–327.

Henriques, J., Hollway, W., Urwin, C., Venn, C., and Walkerdine, V. (1984). *Changing the Subject: Psychology, social regulation and subjectivity*. London: Methuen.

Henwood, K., and Pidgeon, M. (1994). Beyond the qualitative paradigm: A framework for introducing diversity within qualitative psychology. *Journal of Community and Applied Social Psychology, 4,* 225–238.

Hepburn, A. (1999). Derrida and psychology. *Theory and Psychology, 9* (5), 639–667.

Hepburn, A. (2003). *An Introduction to Critical Social Psychology*. London: Sage.

Hepburn, A. (2004). Crying: notes on description, transcription, and interaction. *Research on Language and Social Interaction, 3* (3), 251–290.

Heritage, J. (1984). *Garfinkel and Ethnomethodology*. London: Polity.

Heritage, J. (2003). Presenting Emanuel A. Schegloff. In C.L. Prevignano and P.J. Thibault (Eds.), *Discussing Conversation Analysis: The work of Emanuel A. Schegloff*. Amsterdam: John Benjamins, pp. 1–10.

Higginson, S., and Mansell, W. (2008). What is the mechanism of psychological change? A qualitative analysis of six individuals who experienced personal change and recovery. *Psychology and Psychotherapy: Theory, Research and Practice, 81* (3), 309–328.

Hiles, D., and Čermák, I. (2008). Narrative psychology. In C. Willig and W. Stainton-Rogers (Eds.), *The SAGE Handbook of Qualitative Research in Psychology*. London: Sage, pp. 147–164.

Hook, D. (2001). Discourse, knowledge, materiality, history: Foucault and discourse analysis. *Theory and Psychology, 11,* 521–547.

Howitt, D. (1992). *Child Abuse Errors*. London: Harvester Wheatsheaf.

Howitt, D. (1995). *Paedophiles and Sexual Offences Against Children*. Chichester: John Wiley.

Howitt, D., and Cramer, D. (2008). *Introduction to Research Methods in Psychology*. Harlow: Pearson.

Howitt, D., and Cumberbatch, G. (1990). *Pornography: Impacts and Influences*. London: Home Office Research Unit.

Howitt, D., and Owusu-Bempah, J. (1994). *The Racism of Psychology*. London: Harvester Wheatsheaf.

Hutchby, I., and Wooffitt, R. (1998). *Conversation Analysis: Principles, practices and applications*. Cambridge: Polity Press.

Isherwood, T., Burns, M., Naylor, M., and Read, S. (2007). 'Getting into trouble': a qualitative analysis of the onset of offending in the accounts of men with learning disabilities. *Journal of Forensic Psychiatry and Psychology, 18* (2), 221–234.

Itzin, C. (Ed.) (1993). *Pornography: Women, violence and civil liberties*. Oxford: Oxford University Press.

Jahoda, M., Lazarsfeld, P.F., and Zeisel, H. (1933). *Die Arbeitslosen von Marienthal*. Leipzig: S. Hirzel.

Jahoda, M., Lazarsfeld, P.F., and Zeisel, H. (2002). *Marienthal: The sociography of an unemployed community*. Edison, NJ: Transaction Books.

Jefferson, G. (1996). On the poetics of ordinary talk. *Text and Performance Quarterly, 16* (1), 1–61.

Jefferson, G. (2004). Glossary of transcript symbols with an introduction. In G.H. Lerner (Ed.), *Conversation Analysis: Studies from the first generation*. Philadelphia: John Benjamins, pp. 13–23.

Johnston, C.A.B., and Morrison, T.G. (2007). The presentation of masculinity in everyday life: contextual variations in the masculine behavior of young Irish men. *Sex Roles, 57,* 661–674.

Jones, D., and Elcock, J. (2001). *History and Theories of Psychology: A critical perspective*. London: Arnold.

Jungert, T. (2008). Opportunities of student influence as a context for the development of engineering students' study motivation. *Social Psychology of Education, 11* (1), 79–94.

Kelly, G.A. (1955a). *The Psychology of Personal Constructs. Volume 1: A theory of personality*. New York: Norton.

Kelly, G.A. (1955b). *The Psychology of Personal Constructs. Volume 2: Clinical diagnosis and psychotherapy*. New York: Norton.

Kidder, L.H., and Fine, M. (1997). Qualitative inquiry in psychology: a radical tradition. In D. Fox and I. Prilleltensky (Eds.), *Critical Psychology: An introduction*. London: Sage, pp. 34–50.

King, N. (1998). Template analysis. In G. Symon and C. Cassell (Eds.), *Qualitative Methods and Analysis in Organizational Research*. London: Sage.

King, N., Finlay, L., Ashworth, P., Smith, J.A., Langdridge, D., and Butt, T. (2008). 'Can't really trust that, so what can I trust?': a polyvocal, qualitative analysis of the psychology of mistrust. *Qualitative Research in Psychology, 5,* 80–102.

Kitzinger, C. (2007). Editor's Introduction: the promise of conversation analysis for feminist research. *Feminism and Psychology, 17* (2), 133–148.

Kitzinger, C., and Willmott, J. (2002). 'The thief of womanhood': women's experience of polycystic ovarian syndrome. *Social Science and Medicine, 54* (3), 349–361.

Kitzinger, C., and Jones, D. (2007). When May calls home: the opening moments of family telephone conversations with an Alzheimer's patient. *Feminism and Psychology, 17* (2), 184–202.

Klein, L. (2001). Orbituary: Professor Marie Jahoda *The Independent*, 8 May http://www.independent.co.uk/news/obituaries/professor-marie-jahoda-729096.html.

Kohlbacher, F. (2006). The use of qualitative content analysis in case study research. *Qualitative Social Research, 7* (1). http://www.qualitative-research.net/index.php/fqs/article/view/75/154 (accessed 25 June 2009).

Korn, J.H. (1997). *Illusions of Reality: A history of deception in social psychology*. New York: State University of New York Press.

Kracauer, S. (1952). The challenge of qualitative content analysis. *Public Opinion Quarterly, 16,* 631–642.

Krueger, R.A., and Casey, M.A. (2000). *Focus Groups. A practical guide for applied research*, 3rd Edition. Thousand Oaks, CA: Sage.

Kuhn, T. (1962). *The Structure of Scientific Revolutions*. Chicago, IL: University of Chicago Press.

Kvale, S. (1996). *Interviews*. Thousand Oaks, CA: Sage.

Kvale, S. (2007). *Doing Interviews*. Los Angeles, CA: Sage.

Labov, W. (1972). *Sociolinguistic Patterns*. Philadelphia: University of Pennsylvania Press.

Labov, W. (1997). Some further steps in narrative analysis. *The Journal of Narrative and Life History, 7,* 395–415.

Labov, W., and Waletzky, J. (1967). Narrative analysis. In J. Helm (Ed.), *Essays on the Verbal and Visual Arts*. Seattle: University of Washington Press, pp. 12–44.

Lambert, S., and O'Halloran (2008). Deductive thematic analysis of a female paedophilia website. *Psychiatry, Psychology and Law, 15* (2), 284–300.

Langdridge, D. (2007). *Phenomenological Psychology: Theory, research and method*. Harlow: Pearson Education.

Langford, D. (1994). *Analysing Talk*. London: MacMillan.

Lapadat, J.C., and Lindsay, A.C. (1999). Transcription in research and practice: from standardization of technique to interpretive positionings. *Qualitative Inquiry, 5*, 64. http://qix.sagepub.com/cgi/content/abstract/5/1/64 (accessed 27 August 2009).

Lawes, R. (1999). Marriage: an analysis of discourse. *British Journal of Social Psychology, 38*, 1–20.

Liddicoat, A. (2007). *Introduction to Conversation Analysis*. London: Continuum.

Locke, A., and Edwards, D. (2003). Bill and Monica: memory, emotion and normativity in Clinton's Grand Jury testimony. *British Journal of Social Psychology, 42* (2), 239–256.

Loos, E.E., Anderson, S., Day, D.H., Jordan, P.C., and Wingate, J.D. (2009). Glossary of Linguistic Terms. http://www.sil.org/LINGUISTICS/GlossaryOfLinguisticTerms/WhatIsConversationAnalysis.htm (accessed 25 June 2009).

Lunt, P., and Livingstone, S. (1996). Rethinking the focus group in media and communications research. *Journal of Communication, 46* (2), 79–98.

Luria, A.R., and Bruner, J. (1987). *The Mind of a Mnemonist: A little book about a vast memory*. Cambridge, MA: Harvard University Press.

Lynd, R.S., and Lynd, H.M. (1929). *Middletown: A study in contemporary American culture*. New York: Harcourt, Brace, and Company.

Lynd, R.S., and Lynd, H.M. (1937). *Middletown in Transition: A study in cultural conflicts*. New York: Harcourt, Brace, and Company.

MacMillan, K., and Edwards, D. (1999). Who killed the princess? Description and blame in the British press. *Discourse Studies, 1* (2), 151–174.

MacWhinney, B. (1995). *The CHILDES Project: Tools for analyzing talk*, 2nd Edition. Hillsdale, NJ: Erlbaum.

MailonLine (2008). 'Dishonest' TV psychiatrist Dr Raj Persaud suspended after admitting plagiarism. http://www.dailymail.co.uk/news/article-1027762/Dishonest-TV-psychiatrist-Dr-Raj-Persaud-suspended-admitting-plagiarism.html (accessed 3 July 2009).

Marchel, C., and Owens, S. (2007). Qualitative research in psychology: could William James get a job? *History of Psychology, 10* (4), 301–324.

Marsh, P., Rosser, E., and Harré, R. (1978). *The Rules of Disorder*. London: Routledge & Kegan Paul.

Marshall, M.N. (1996). Sampling for qualitative research. *Family Practice, 13*, 522–525.

Matheson, J.L. (2008). The voice transcription technique: use of voice recognition software to transcribe digital interview data in qualitative research. *The Qualitative Report, 12* (4), 547–560.

Mayo, E. (1949). *Hawthorne and the Western Electric Company: The social problems of an industrial civilisation*. London: Routledge.

Mays, N., and Pope, C. (2000). Assessing quality in qualitative research. *BMJ, 320*, 50–52.

McAdams, D.P. (1985). *Power, Intimacy, and the Life Story: Personological inquiries into identity*. New York: Guilford Press.

McAdams, D.P. (1993). *The Stories We Live By: Personal myths and the making of the self*. New York: William C. Morrow and Co.

McAdams, D.P. (2006). The role of narrative in personality psychology today. *Narrative Inquiry*, *16* (1), 11–18.

McAdams, D.P. (2008). Personal narratives and the life story. In O. John, R. Robins and L.A. Pervin, *Handbook of Personality: Theory and research*. New York: Guilford Press, pp. 241–261.

McArthur, T. (1992). *The Oxford Companion to the English Language*. Oxford: Oxford University Press.

McBain, W.N. (1956). The use of magnetized tape recording in psychological laboratories. *American Psychologist*, *11* (4), 202–203.

McCaughan, E., and McKenna, H. (2007). Never-ending making sense: Towards a substantive theory of the information-seeking behaviour of newly diagnosed cancer patients. *Journal of Clinical Nursing*, *16* (11), 2096–2104.

McHugh, P. (1968). *Defining the Situation: The organization of meaning*. Evanston, IL: Bobbs-Merrill.

Meier, A., Boivin, M., and Meier, M. (2008). Theme-analysis: procedures and application for psychotherapy research. *Qualitative Research in Psychology*, *5*, 289–310.

Merton, R.K. (1949). *Social Theory and Social Structure*. New York: Free Press.

Merton, R.K. (1987). The focussed interview and focus groups: continuities and discontinuities. *Public Opinion Quarterly*, *51* (4), 550–566.

Merton, R.K., and Kendall, P.L. (1946). The focused interview. *American Journal of Sociology*, *51*, 541–547.

Merton, R.K., Fiske, M., and Kendall, P.L. (1956). *The Focused Interview: A manual of problems and procedures*. Glencoe, IL: The Free Press.

Michell, J. (2003). The quantitative imperative: positivism, naïve realism and the place of qualitative methods in psychology. *Theory and Psychology*, *13* (1), 5–31.

Milgram, S. (1974). *Obedience to Authority: An experimental view*. New York: Harper and Row.

Miller, P.J., Hengst, J.A., and Wang, S-H. (2003). Ethnographic methods: applications from developmental cultural psychology. In P.M. Camic, J. Rhodes and L. Yardley (Eds.), *Qualitative Research in Psychology: Expanding perspectives in methodology and design*. Washington, DC: American Psychological Association, pp. 219–242.

Mishler, E.G. (1986). The analysis of interview-narratives. In T.R. Sarbin (Ed.), *Narrative Psychology: The storied nature of human conduct*. New York: Praeger, pp. 233–255.

Monroe, K.R. (2008). Cracking the code of genocide: the moral psychology of rescuers, bystanders, and Nazis during the Holocaust. *Political Psychology*, *29* (5), 699–736.

Moran-Ellis, J., Alexander, V.D., Cronin, A., Dickinson, M., Fielding, J., Sleny, J., and Thomas, H. (2006a). Triangulation and integration: process, claims and implications. *Qualitative Research*, *6* (45), 49–55.

Moran-Ellis, J., Alexander, V.D., Cronin, A., Fielding, J., and Thomas, H. (2006b). Analytic integration and multiple qualitative data sets. *Qualitative Researcher*, *2*, 2–4.

Morgan, A. (2000). What is Narrative Therapy? http://www.dulwichcentre.com.au/alicearticle.html (accessed 2 September 2009).

Morrison, D.E. (1998). *The Search for a Method: Focus groups and the development of mass communication research*. Luton: University of Luton Press.

Muehlenhard, C.L., and Kimes, L.A. (1999). The social construction of violence: the case of sexual and domestic violence. *Personality and Social Psychology Review*, 3, 234–245.

Murray, M. (2003). Narrative psychology. In J.A. Smith (Ed.), *Qualitative psychology: A practical guide to research methods*. London: Sage, pp. 111–131.

Natason, M. (1973). *Edmund Husserl: Philosopher of infinite tasks*. Evanston, IL: Northwestern University Press.

Nespor, J. (2000). Anonymity and place in qualitative inquiry. *Qualitative Inquiry*, 6, 546. http://qix.sagepub.com/cgi/content/abstract/6/4/546 (accessed 26 August 2009).

Nightingale, D., and Cromby, J. (Eds.) (1999). *Social Constructionist Psychology*. Buckingham: Open University Press.

Nikander, P. (2008). Working with transcripts and translated data. *Qualitative Research in Psychology*, 5, 225–231.

O'Brien, C. (2007). Peer devaluation in British secondary schools: young people's comparisons of group-based and individual-based bullying. *Educational Research*, 49, 297–324.

O'Brien, M. (1999). Theorising modernity: reflexity, environment and identity in Giddens' social theory. In M. O'Brien, S. Penna and C. Hay (Eds.), *Theorising Modernity: Reflexity, environment and identity in Giddens' social theory*. London: Longman, pp. 17–38.

O'Callaghan, C., and Hiscock, R. (2007). Interpretive subgroup analysis extends modified grounded theory research findings in oncologic music therapy. *Journal of Music Therapy*, 44 (3), 256–281.

O'Connell, D.C., and Kowal, S. (1995). Basic principles of transcription. In J.A. Smith, R. Harré and L. Van Langenhove (Eds.), *Rethinking Methods in Psychology*. London: Sage, pp. 93–105.

O'Connell, D.C., and Kowal, S. (1999). Transcription and the issue of standardization. *Journal of Psycholinguistic Research*, 28 (2), 103–120.

Onions, P.E.W. (n.d.). Grounded Theory Applications in Reviewing Knowledge Management Literature. http://www.bmu.ac.uk/research/postgradconf/papers/patrick_Onions_paper.pdf (retrieved 10 October 2009).

Orr, A., Orr, D., Willis, S., Holmes, M., and Britton, P. (2007). Patient perceptions of factors influencing adherence to medication following kidney transplant. *Psychology, Health and Medicine*, 12 (4), 509–517.

Ortmann, A., and Hertwig, R. (2002). The costs of deception: evidence from psychology. *Experimental Economics*, 5 (23), 111–131.

Owusu-Bempah, J., and Howitt, D. (2000). *Psychology Beyond Western Perspectives*. Leicester: BPS Books.

Pagoto, S.L., Spring, B., Coups, E.J., Mulvaney, S., Coutu, M.-F., and Ozakinci, G. (2007). Barriers and facilitators of evidence-based practice perceived by behavioral science health professionals. *Journal of Clinical Psychology*, 63 (7), 695–705.

Parker, I. (1989). *The Crisis in Modern Social Psychology*. London: Routledge.

Parker, I. (1992). *Discourse Dynamics: Critical analysis for social and individual psychology*. London: Routledge.

Parker, I. (Ed.) (1999). *Deconstructing Psychotherapy*. London: Sage.

Parker, I. (2002). *Critical Discursive Psychology*. London: Palgrave.

Parker, I. (2005). *Qualitative Psychology: Introducing radical research*. Maidenhead: Open University Press.

Parker, I. (2007). *Revolution in Psychology: Alienation to emancipation*. London: Pluto.

Parker, I., Georgaca, E., Harper, D., McLaughlin, T., and Stowell-Smith, M. (1995). *Deconstructing Psychopathology*. London: Sage.

Passmore, J. (1967). Logical positivism. In P. Edwards (Ed.), *The Encyclopedia of Philosophy*, Vol. 5. New York: Macmillan, pp. 52–57.

Patton, M.Q. (1986). *How to Use Qualitative Methods in Evaluation*. Newbury Park, CA: Sage.

Pole, C., and Lampard, R. (2002). *Practical Social Investigation: Qualitative and quantitative methods in social research*. Harlow: Pearson Education.

Potter, J. (1996). Discourse analysis and constructionist approaches: theoretical background. In J.E. Richardson (Ed.), *Handbook of Qualitative Research Methods for Psychology and the Social Sciences*. Leicester: British Psychological Society, pp. 125–140.

Potter, J. (1997). 'Discourse analysis as a way of analysing naturally occurring talk', in D. Silverman (Ed.), *Qualitative Research: Theory, methods and practice*. London: Sage, 144–160.

Potter, J. (1998). Qualitative and discourse analysis. In A.S. Bellack and M. Hersen (Eds.), *Comprehensive Clinical Psychology, Vol. 3*. Oxford: Pergamon, pp. 117–144.

Potter, J. (2001). 'Wittgenstein and Austin', in M. Wetherell, S. Taylor and S.J. Yates, *Discourse Theory and Practice: A Reader*. London: Sage, pp. 39–56.

Potter, J. (2003). Discourse analysis and discursive psychology. In P.M. Camic, J.E.D. Rhodes and L. Yardley (Eds.), *Qualitative Research in Psychology: Expanding perspectives in methodology and design*. Washington, DC: American Psychological Association, pp. 73–94.

Potter, J. (2004). Discourse analysis. In M. Hardy and A. Bryman (Eds.), *Handbook of Data Analysis*. London: Sage, pp. 607–624.

Potter, J., and Edwards, D. (1990). Nigel Lawson's tent: Discourse analysis, attribution theory and the social psychology of fact. *European Journal of Social Psychology*, 20, 405–424.

Potter, J., and Hepburn, A. (2009). Transcription. http://www-staff.lboro.ac.uk/~ssjap/transcription/transcription.htm (17 June 2009).

Potter, J., and Wetherell, M. (1987). *Discourse and Social Psychology: Beyond attitudes and behaviour*. London: Sage.

Potter, J., and Wetherell, M. (1995). Discourse analysis. In J.A. Smith, R. Harré and L.V. Langenhove (Eds.), *Rethinking Methods in Psychology*. London: Sage, 80–92.

Potter, J., Edwards, D., and Ashmore, M. (2002). Regulating criticism: some comments on an argumentative complex. In I. Parker (Ed.), *Critical Discursive Psychology*. Basingstoke: Palgrave MacMillan, pp. 73–81.

Preston, L., Marshall, A., and Bucks, R. (2007). Investigating the ways that older people cope with dementia: a qualitative study. *Aging and Mental Health*, 11 (2), 131–143.

Prevignano, C.L., and Thibault, E.A. (2003). Continuing the interview with Emanuel Schegloff. In C.L. Prevignano and P.J. Thibault (Eds.), *Discussing Conversation Analysis: The work of Emanuel Schegloff*. Amsterdam: John Benjamins, pp. 165–172.

Prus, R.C. (1996). *Symbolic Interaction and Ethnographic Research: Inter-subjecitivity and the study of human lived experience.* Albany, NY: State University of New York Press.

Psathas, G., and Anderson, T. (1990). The 'practices' of transcription in conversation analysis. *Semiotica, 78*, 75–99.

Puchta, C., and Potter., J. (2004). *Focus Group Practice.* London: Sage.

Radley, A., and Chamberlain, K. (2001). Health psychology and the study of the case: from method to analytic concern. *Social Science and Medicine, 53*, 321–332.

RadPsyNet (2009). Society for the Psychological Study of Social Issues (SPSSI). http://www.radpsynet.org/notices/orgs.html#spssi (accessed 8 August 2009).

Rapley, T.J. (2001). The art(fullness) of open-ended interviewing: some considerations on analyzing interviews. *Qualitative Research, 1* (3), 303–323.

Reid, K., Flowers, P., and Larkin, M. (2005). Exploring lived experience. *The Psychologist, 18* (1), 20–23.

Richardson, J.C., Ong, B.N., and Sim, J. (2006). Remaking the future: contemplating a life with chronic widespread pain. *Chronic Illness, 2* (3), 209–218.

Rennie, D.L., Watson, K.D., and Monteiro, A.M. (2002). The rise of qualitative psychology. *Canadian Psychology, 43*, 179–189.

Roberts, C. (2007). Qualitative Research Methods and Transcription. http://www.kcl.ac.uk/schools/sspp/education/research/projects/dataqual.html (accessed 14 October 2009).

Roundhill, S.J., Williams, W.H., and Hughes, J.M. (2007). The experience of loss following traumatic brain injury: applying a bereavement model to the process of adjustment. *Qualitative Research in Psychology, 4*, 241–257.

Sacks, H. (1992). Lecture 1: Rules of conversational sequence. In E. Jefferson (Ed.), *H.Y. Sacks Lectures on Conversation; Vol. 1*, 3rd Edition. Oxford: Blackwell.

Sacks, O. (1985). *The Man Who Mistook his Wife for a Hat.* London: Picador.

Salter, C., Holland, R., Harvey, I., and Henwood, K. (2007). 'I haven't even phoned my doctor yet.' The advice giving role of the pharmacist during consultations for medication review with patients aged 80 or more: qualitative discourse analysis. *BMJ, 334*, 1101.

Sarbin, T.R. (1986). The narrative as a root metaphor for psychology. In T.R. Sarbin (Ed.), *Narrative Psychology: The storied nature of human conduct.* New York: Praeger, pp. 3–21.

Schegloff, E.A. (1968). Sequencing in conversational openings. *American Anthropologist, 70*, 1075–1095.

Schegloff, E.A. (2007). *Sequence Organization in Interaction: A primer in conversation analysis*, Volume 1. Cambridge: Cambridge University Press.

Schwandt, T.A. (2001). *Dictionary of Qualitative Inquiry*, 2nd Edition. Thousand Oaks, CA: Sage.

Scott, M.M. (2005). A powerful theory and a paradox: ecological psychologists after Barker. *Environment and Behavior, 37*, 295–329.

Seale, C. (Ed.) (1998). *Researching Society and Culture.* London: Sage.

Seale, C. (1999). Quality in qualitative research. *Qualitative Inquiry, 5* (4), 465–478.

Seligman, R., and Kirmayer, L. (2008). Dissociative experience and cultural neuroscience: narrative, metaphor and mechanism. *Culture, Medicine and Psychiatry, 32*, 31–64.

Settles, I.H., Pratt-Hyatt, J.S., and Buchanan, N.T. (2008). Through the lens of race: black and white women's perceptions of womanhood. *Psychology of Women Quarterly, 32,* 454–468.

Shaw, R.L. (2008). The Society's Guidelines for Ethical Practice in Psychological Research on the Internet: what do we make of them? *Qualitative Methods in Psychology Newsletter, 5* May, 7–9.

Sheldon, K., and Howitt, D. (2007). *Sex Offenders and the Internet.* Chichester: Wiley.

Shinebourne, P., and Smith, J.A. (2009). Alcohol and the self: an interpretative phenomenological analysis of the experience of addiction and its impact on the sense of self and identity. *Addiction Research and Theory, 17* (2), 152–167.

Shotter, J. (1995). Dialogical psychology. In J.A. Smith, R. Harré and L. Van Langenhove (Eds.), *Rethinking Psychology.* London: Sage, pp. 160–178.

Shotter, J. (1999). The social construction of subjectivity: can it be theorized? Review of Julian Henriques, Wendy Holloway, Cathy Urwin, Couze Venn, and Valerie Walkerdine: changing the subject: psychology, social regulation and subjectivity. *Contemporary Psychology, 44,* 482–483. http://pubpages.unh.edu/~jds/CP_99.htm (accessed 7 August 2008).

Shye, S., and Elizur, D. (1994). *Introduction to Facet Theory: Content design and intrinsic data analysis in behavioural research.* Thousand Oaks, CA: Sage.

Silverman, D. (1997). The logics of qualitative research. In G. Miller and R. Dingwall (Eds.), *Context and Method in Qualitative Research.* London: Sage, 12–25.

Silverman, D. (1998). *Harvey Sacks: Social Science and Conversation Analysis.* Cambridge: Polity Press.

Smith, J.A. (1996). Beyond the divide between cognition and discourse: using interpretative phenomenological analysis in health psychology. *Psychology & Health, 11* (2), 261–271.

Smith, J.A. (2007). Hermeneutics, human sciences and health: linking theory and practice. *International Journal of Qualitative Studies on Health and Well-being, 2,* 3–11.

Smith, J.A. (2008). Introduction. In J. Smith (Ed.) *Qualitative Psychology: A practical guide to research methods,* 2nd edition. London: Sage, pp. 1–3.

Smith, J.A. (n.d.). Interpretative Phenomenological Analysis (IPA): What Is It? http://209.85.135.132/search?q=cache:tHPcBzfHLNQJ:www.ccsr.ac.uk/methods/festival/programme/wiwa/smith.doc+hermeneutics+IPAandcd=1andhl=enandct=clnkandgl=ukandie=UTF-8 (accessed 29 August 2009).

Smith, J.A., and Eatough, V. (2006). Interpretative phenomenological analysis. In G.M. Breakwell, S. Hammond, C. Fife-Schaw and J.A. Smith (Eds.), *Research Methods in Psychology,* 3rd Edition. London: Sage, pp. 322–341.

Smith, J.A., and Osborn, M. (2003). Interpretative phenomenological analysis. In J.A. Smith (Ed.), *Qualitative Psychology: A practical guide to research methods,* 2nd Edition. London: Sage, pp. 57–80.

Smith, J.A., Jarman, M., and Osborn, M. (1999). Doing interpretative phenomenological analysis. In M. Murray and K. Chamberlain (Eds.), *Qualitative Health Psychology: Theories and methods.* London: Sage, pp. 218–241.

Smith, J.A., Larkin, M., and Flowers, P. (2009). *Interpretative Phenomenological Analysis: Theory, method and research: understanding method and application.* London: Sage.

Smith, S.S., and Richardson, D. (1983). Amelioration of deception and harm in psychological research: the important role of debriefing. *Journal of Personality and Social Psychology, 44,* 1075–1082.

Spagnolli, A., and Gamberini, L. (2007). Interacting via SMS: practices of social closeness and reciprocation. *British Journal of Social Psychology*, *46* (2), 343–364.

Spencer, L., Ritchie, J., Lewis, J., and Dillon, L. (2003). *Quality in Qualitative Evaluation: A framework for assessing research evidence. A Quality Framework*. Cabinet Office: Government Chief Social Researcher's Office. Strategy Unit. http://www.gsr.gov.uk/downloads/evaluating_policy/a_quality_framework.pdf (accessed 12 August 2009).

Spradley, J.P. (1980). *Participant Observation*. New York: Rinehart and Winston.

Ssasz, T. (1986). The case against suicide prevention. *American Psychologist*, *41* (7), 806–812.

St Louis University, Qualitative Research Committee (2009). Qualitative Research Journals. http://www.slu.edu/organizations/qrc/QRjournals.html (accessed 5 July 2009).

Stiegler, L.N. (2007). Discovering communicative competencies in a nonspeaking child with autism. *Language, Speech, and Hearing Services in Schools*, *38* (4), 400–413.

Stokoe, E.H. (2003). Mothers, single women and sluts: gender, morality and membership categorization in neighbour disputes. *Feminism and Psychology*, *13* (3), 317–344.

Strandmark, M., and Hallberg, LR-M. (2007). Being rejected and expelled from the workplace: experiences of bullying in the public service sector. *Qualitative Research in Psychology*, *4*, 1–14.

Strauss, A., and Corbin, J. (1990). *Basics of Qualitative Research: Grounded theory, procedures and techniques*. Newbury Park, CA: Sage.

Strauss, A., and Corbin, J. (1994). Grounded theory methodology: an overview. In N.K. Denzin and Y. Lincoln (Eds.), *Handbook of Qualitative Research*. Thousand Oaks, CA: Sage, pp. 273–285.

Strauss, A., and Corbin, J. (1998). *Basics of Qualitative Research: Grounded theory, procedures and techniques*, 2nd edition. Newbury Park, CA: Sage.

Strauss, A., and Corbin, J. (1999). Grounded theory methodology: an overview. In A. Bryman and R.G. Burgess (Eds.), *Qualitative Research*, Vol. 3. Thousand Oaks, CA: Sage, pp. 73–93.

Stubbs, M. (1983). *Discourse Analysis: The sociolinguistic analysis of natural language*. Oxford: Blackwell.

Taylor, C. (2008). Online QDA. http://onlineqda.hud.ac.uk/methodologies.php (accessed 29 August 2009).

Taylor, S. (2001). Locating and conducting discourse analytic research. In M. Wetherell, S. Taylor, and S.J. Yates (Eds.), *Discourse as Data: A guide for analysis*. London: Sage, pp. 5–48.

ten Have, P. (1999). *Doing Conversation Analysis: A practical guide*. London: Sage.

ten Have, P. (2007). *Doing Conversation Analysis: A practical guide*, 2nd Edition. London: Sage.

ten Have, P. (2009). Methodological Issues in Conversation Analysis. http://www2.fmg.uva.nl/emca/mica.htm#N_1_ (accessed 1 July 2009).

Thomas, G., and James, D. (2006). Reinventing grounded theory: some questions about theory, ground and discovery. *British Educational Research Journal*, *32* (6), 767–795.

Titchener, E.B. (1898). The postulates of a structural psychology. *Philosophical Review*, *7*, 449–465.

Tolman, E.C. (1948). Cognitive maps in rats and men. *Psychological Review*, 55 (4), 189–208.

Tomkins, S.S. (1979). Script theory. In H.E. Howe, Jr, and R.A. Doemstbeoer (Eds.), *Nebraska Symposium on Motivation* Vol. 26. Lincoln, NE: University of Nebraska Press, pp. 201–236.

Toerien, M., and Kitzinger, C. (2007). Emotional labour in the beauty salon: turn design of task-directed talk. *Feminism and Psychology*, 17 (2), 162–172.

University of York, Department of Sociology (n.d.). Culture, Interaction and Knowledge: Sociology at York – Past, Present and Future. http://www.york.ac.uk/depts/soci/about/45yearpersreflect2.htm (accessed 20 June 2009).

UK Data Archive (n.d.). Manage and Share Data: Consent, confidentiality and ethics in data sharing. http://www.data-archive.ac.uk/sharing/confidential.asp (accessed 26 August 2009).

van Dijk, T. (2001). Principles of critical discourse analysis. In M. Wetherell, S. Taylor and S.J.E. Yates (Eds.), *Discourse Theory and Practice: A Reader*. London: Sage, pp. 300–317.

Vidich, A.J., and Lyman, S.M. (2000). Qualitative methods: their history in sociology and anthropology. In N.L. Denzin and Y.S. Lincoln (Eds.), *Handbook of Qualitative Research*, 2nd Edition. Thousand Oaks, CA: Sage, pp. 37–84.

Watson, J.B. (1913). Psychology as the behaviorist views it. *Psychological Review*, 20, 158–177.

Wetherell, M., and Potter, J. (1988). Discourse analysis and the identification of interpretive repertoires. In C. Antaki (Ed.), *Analysing Everyday Explanation: A casebook of methods*. Newbury Park, CA: Sage, pp. 168–183.

Wetherell, M., Taylor, S., and Yates, S.J. (2001) (Eds.). *Discourse as Data: A guide for analysis*. London: Sage.

White, M. and Epston, D. (1990). *Narrative Means to Therapeutic Ends*. New York: Norton.

Whyte, W.F. (1984). *Learning from the Field: A guide from experience*. Beverly Hills: Sage.

Whyte, W.F. (1943). *Street Corner Society. The social structure of an Italian slum*. Chicago: University of Chicago Press.

Wiggins, S., and Potter, J. (2008). Discursive psychology. In C. Willig and W. Stainton-Rogers (Eds.), *The SAGE Handbook of Qualitative Research in Psychology*. London: Sage, pp. 73–93.

Wilkinson, S. (1997). Feminist psychology. In D. Fox and I. Prilleltensky (Eds.), *Critical Psychology: An introduction*. London: Sage, pp. 247–264.

Willig, C. (2008). Discourse analysis. In J. Smith (Ed.), *Qualitative Psychology: A practical guide to research methods*, 2nd edition. London: Sage, pp. 160–185.

Willig, C., and Stainton-Rogers, W. (2008). Introduction. In C. Willig and W. Stainton-Rogers (Eds.), *The SAGE Handbook of Qualitative Research in Psychology*. London: Sage, pp. 1–12.

Witzel, A., and Mey, G. (2004). I am NOT opposed to quantification or formalization or modeling, but do not want to pursue quantitative methods that are not commensurate with the research phenomena addressed. *Forum: Qualitative Social Research*, 5 (3), Article 41. http://www.qualitative-research.net/fqs-texte/3-04/04-3-41-e.htm (accessed 15 August 2009).

Wooffitt, R. (2001). Researching psychic practitioners: conversation analysis. In M. Wetherell, S. Taylor and S.J. Yates (Eds.), *Discourse as Data: A guide for analysis*. London: Sage, pp. 49–92.

Woolgar, S. (1996). Psychology, qualitative methods and the ideas of science. In J.T.E. Richarson (Ed.), *Handbook of Qualitative Research Methods for Psychology and the Social Sciences*. Leicester: BPS Books, pp. 11–24.

Wundt, W. (1912/1973). *An Introduction to Psychology*. New York: Arno Press.

Yin, R.K. (2003). *Case Study Research: Design and methods*, 3rd Edition. Thousand Oaks, CA: Sage.

NAME INDEX

Cumming, S.   149
Cushing, Frank Hamilton   116

Dallos, R.   338
Danziger, K.   21, 24
Davidson, J.   147
Day, D.H.   245
Dearborn, G.V.N.   39, 40
Del Vecchio Good, M.   313, 315
Denscombe, M.   361
Denzin, N.K.   7, 9
Dereshiwsky, M.   112
Derrida, Jacques   279, 280
Diamond, John   313–15
Dichter, Ernest   57, 63
Dickson, A.   273
Dillon, L.   375–6
Dilthey, Wilhelm   26
Dixon, William J.   63
Dixon-Woods, M.   381
Dollard, John   41, 52, 297, 298, 300, 302, 303
Dominic   350, 351
Donague (2010)   351
Drew, P.   256, 258
Du Bois, John   149
Du Bois, W.E.B.   38
Dyson, Freeman   53
Dzinas, K.   24

Eatough, V.   282, 283
Eccleston, L.   168
Edley, N.   216
Edwards, D.   35, 228, 236, 245
Ehlich, K.   149
Elcock, J.   13
Elford, J.   55
Elizur, D.   24
Emerson, Peter   298, 312
Epley, N.   406
Epston, D.   298
Evans, A.   55
Every, D.   338

Fechner, Gustav   18, 22
Feigl, Herbert   16
Festervand, T.A.   93
Festinger, Leon   41, 51
Fielding, J.   372
Fine, M.   41
Finkelhor, D.   180
Finlay, W.M.L.   261–2, 263, 264
Fish, S.   189
Fisher, Ronald   22, 24
Fiske, D.W.   369, 371
Fiske, M.   92
Flowers, P.   272, 274
Flyvbjerg, B.   38
Fontana, A.   62
Forbat, L.   390
Foucault, Michel   xix, 21, 137, 215, 217, 224, 225, 231

Freud, Sigmund   xvii, xix, 18, 36–7, 39, 40, 47, 57, 63, 190, 297, 302
Frey, J.H.   62
Frosh, Stephen   298, 312
Frost, N.   338

Galton, Francis   24
Gamberini, L.   337
Garfinkel, Harold   xviii, 45, 48, 244, 253, 254, 270
Garson, D.   298
Gee, D.   168
Geer, B.   132
Georgaca, E.   225, 228
Gergen, Kenneth J.   xix, 20, 21, 44, 51, 189, 298, 299, 301, 305, 306
Gergen, Mary   298, 299, 301, 305, 306
Gibbs, A.   90, 97, 99, 101
Gilbert, G.N.   48, 53
Gilbert, Nigel   224
Giles, D.   337
Glaser, Barney G.   44, 45, 48, 187, 188–9, 190, 193, 194–5, 199, 205, 206, 212, 232, 360
Goffman, Erving   xviii, 222, 253–4, 281
Good, B.   313, 315
Goodwin, P.   337
Gordon, M.J.   304
Graumann, C.F.   189
Grbich, C.   212
Greeley, Horace   62
Grice, Herbert Paul   46, 223, 224
Gumperz, J.J.   149, 152
Guttman, Louis   23, 24
Guy, A.   338

Hallberg, L.R.-M.   199, 209
Hammersley, M.   11, 12, 384
Harper, D.   225, 228
Harré, R.   119–20, 121
Harris, Zellig   223, 224
Harvey, I.   338
Heath, C.   255
Heidegger, Martin   17, 280
Henderson, J.   390
Hengst, J.A.   117
Henriques, Julian   48, 225
Henwood, K.   26, 338
Hepburn, A.   140, 141, 154, 225, 280
Heritage, J.   152, 254
Hersen, M.   35
Hertwig, R.   402
Higginson, S.   273
Hiles, D.   306, 309, 311
Hiscock, R.   337
Holland, R.   338
Hollway, Wendy   48, 225
Holmes, M.   338
Hook, D.   231
Hovland, Carl   220
Howitt, D.   39, 49, 60, 72–3, 165, 166, 168, 171, 180, 213, 246, 264, 284, 288, 387, 405

SUBJECT INDEX